Putin's Russia and the Falsification of History

Putin's Russia and the Falsification of History

Reasserting Control over the Past

Anton Weiss-Wendt

BLOOMSBURY ACADEMIC
LONDON • NEW YORK • OXFORD • NEW DELHI • SYDNEY

BLOOMSBURY ACADEMIC
Bloomsbury Publishing Plc
50 Bedford Square, London, WC1B 3DP, UK
1385 Broadway, New York, NY 10018, USA
29 Earlsfort Terrace, Dublin 2, Ireland

BLOOMSBURY, BLOOMSBURY ACADEMIC and the Diana logo are trademarks of Bloomsbury Publishing Plc

First published in Great Britain 2021
This paperback edition published 2022

Copyright © Anton Weiss-Wendt, 2021

Anton Weiss-Wendt has asserted his right under the Copyright, Designs and Patents Act, 1988, to be identified as Author of this work.

Cover design by: Tjaša Krivec

Cover image: A mud-caked bust of Joseph Stalin emerged when a lake in Kusa, Russia, was being partially drained for repairs to a dike (© Oksana Yushko).
For details see page 153 of the book

All rights reserved. No part of this publication may be reproduced or transmitted in any form or by any means, electronic or mechanical, including photocopying, recording, or any information storage or retrieval system, without prior permission in writing from the publishers.

Bloomsbury Publishing Plc does not have any control over, or responsibility for, any third-party websites referred to or in this book. All internet addresses given in this book were correct at the time of going to press. The author and publisher regret any inconvenience caused if addresses have changed or sites have ceased to exist, but can accept no responsibility for any such changes.

Every effort has been made to trace copyright holders and to obtain their permissions for the use of copyright material. The publisher apologizes for any errors or omissions and would be grateful if notified of any corrections that should be incorporated in future reprints or editions of this book.

A catalogue record for this book is available from the British Library.

A catalogue record for this book is available from the Library of Congress.

Library of Congress Cataloging-in-Publication Data:

Names: Weiss-Wendt, Anton, 1973- author.
Title: Putin's Russia and the falsification of history: reasserting control over the past / Anton Weiss-Wendt.
Description: New York; London: Bloomsbury Academic, 2020. | Includes bibliographical references and index. |
Identifiers: LCCN 2020019758 (print) | LCCN 2020019759 (ebook) | ISBN 9781350130531 (hardback) | ISBN 9781350130548 (ebook) | ISBN 9781350130555 (epub)
Subjects: LCSH: Russia (Federation)–Politics and government–1991- | Putin, Vladimir Vladimirovich, 1952—Influence. | Propaganda–Russia (Federation) | Disinformation–Russia (Federation) | Political culture–Russia (Federation) | Historiography–Political aspects–Russia (Federation)
Classification: LCC DK510.763.W45 2020 (print) | LCC DK510.763 (ebook) | DDC 947.0072–dc23
LC record available at https://lccn.loc.gov/2020019758
LC ebook record available at https://lccn.loc.gov/2020019759

ISBN: HB: 978-1-3501-3053-1
PB: 978-1-3502-0315-0
ePDF: 978-1-3501-3054-8
eBook: 978-1-3501-3055-5

Typeset by Deanta Global Publishing Services, Chennai, India

To find out more about our authors and books visit www.bloomsbury.com and sign up for our newsletters.

To Vlad Kolesnikov (1997–2015)

Anton Weiss-Wendt is Research Professor at the Norwegian Center for Holocaust and Minority Studies. His recent publications include *A Rhetorical Crime: Genocide in the Geopolitical Discourse of the Cold War* (2018) and *The Soviet Union and the Gutting of the UN Genocide Convention* (2017).

Contents

List of Figures	viii
Acknowledgments	ix
List of Acronyms	x
Introduction	1
1 A Geopolitical Meaning of History	7
2 State Affiliates Manufacturing the "Historical Truth"	43
3 For Victory, For Stalin, For Putin!	83
4 Militant Patriotism	121
5 Monumental Mediocrity	149
6 Hijacking the Holocaust	185
7 Injustice of Historic Proportion	223
Conclusion	251
Notes	263
Bibliography	293
Index	300

Figures

1	Russian foreign ministry hosts a reception to mark the 75th anniversary of victory in the Battle of Stalingrad. Moscow, February 2, 2018. Viacheslav Prokofiev/TASS	28
2	Press conference on the question of authenticity of Romanovs' remains. Moscow, November 13, 2015. Alexander Scherbak/TASS	70
3	International biker show in Crimea. Sevastopol, August 18, 2017. Alexei Pavlishak/TASS	78
4	Immortal Regiment parade. Narian-Mar, May 9, 2018. Anton Taibarei/Nenets Autonomous Region Administration	91
5–8	Immortal Regiment parade. Barnaul, May 9, 2019. Nina Tatarnikova	99–107
9	President Vladimir Putin attending the unveiling ceremony of a monument to the victims of political repression. Moscow, October 30, 2017. Alexei Nikolskii/Russian Presidential Information and Press Office/TASS	115
10	Historical reconstruction of the Battle of Berlin. Moscow region, April 23, 2017. Sergei Bobylev/Russian Defense Ministry Press Office/TASS	131
11	Alley of Rulers unveiled in Moscow. Moscow, May 26, 2017. Artem Geodakian/TASS	157
12	Ivan the Terrible monument unveiled in the city of Orel. Orel, October 3, 2016. Alexander Riumin/TASS	171
13	Sculptor Salavat Scherbakov and his statue of Mikhail Kalashnikov in the works. Moscow, January 20, 2017. Valerii Sharifulin/TASS	175
14	President Vladimir Putin and Prime Minister Benjamin Netanyahu visit Moscow's Jewish Museum and Tolerance Center. Moscow, January 29, 2018. Alexei Nikolskii/Russian Presidential Information and Press Office/TASS	207
15	Karelia Memorial head, Yuri Dmitriev, found not guilty of producing child pornography, Petrozavodsk, June 28, 2018. Igor Podgornyi/TASS	226

Acknowledgments

It has become a tradition for me to start the acknowledgment list by thanking my home institution, the Norwegian Center for Holocaust and Minority Studies, and its director, Guri Hjeltnes. Although Oslo is a distance away from Moscow, Norway is a neighboring country to Russia after all. I can hardly imagine a better working place to contemplate the purpose of history in general and its political application by "Putin's regime" in particular. Among other colleagues at Oslo, I want to single out chief librarian Ewa M. Mork, who was indispensable—as she has always been—in procuring certain books and articles I needed for my research.

It is my intention to put a human face on history politics, which may otherwise remain an abstract matter. I am grateful to Nina Tatarnikova, who aptly captured in her photographs the spirit of Immortal Regiment, by far the most popular annual public event in Russia. Another gifted Russian documentary photographer, Oksana Yushko, takes credit for the book's front cover image. Several scholars took their time to read through and comment on certain chapters in the book: Ivan Kurilla, Nikolay Koposov, Nanci Adler, Vassili Schedrin, and Victoria Kheterer. To all of them, I am thankful.

My collaboration with Bloomsbury Academic goes back to 2012. Rhodri Mogford was my very first contact in the editorial office. Currently a Publisher at Bloomsbury, Rhodri is also the person who has enthusiastically embraced the present book project. In addition to Rhodri, I have had the pleasure of working with several of his colleagues at Bloomsbury over the years: Beatriz Lopez, Claire Lipscomb, Laura Reeves, and Emma Goode.

The book is dedicated to Vlad Kolesnikov, a teenager from Podolsk who died for his beliefs. In the wake of the Russian annexation of Crimea, Vlad publicly expressed his opposition to the Kremlin's aggressive policy vis-à-vis Ukraine. Consequently, he was harassed by school authorities, abused by his peers, and ostracized by his own grandfather, a former KGB officer. Feeling isolated, he succumbed to pressure and on Christmas Day, 2015, took his own life. Vlad Kolesnikov has written the modern history of Russia in his own blood.

Acronyms

BRIC	Brazil, Russia, India, and China
CIS	Commonwealth of Independent States
EISR	Expert Institute of Social Research
KGB	Soviet Security Police (1954–1991)
MGIMO	Moscow State University of International Relations of the Russian Foreign Ministry
MID	Ministry of Foreign Affairs of the Russian Federation
NKVD	Soviet Security Police (1934–1946)
NOD	National Liberation Movement
NTS	National Alliance of Russian Solidarists
RAN	Russian Academy of Sciences
RIO	Russian Historical Society
RT	Russia Today
RVIO	Russian Military Historical Society
SERB	Russian Liberation Movement
USHMM	United States Holocaust Memorial Museum
VAK	Supreme Attestation Board
VIO	Free Historical Society

Introduction

On January 21, 1948, the US Department of State released a document collection, *Nazi–Soviet Relations from 1939 to 1941*. Selected records of the German Foreign Office dealt specifically with the Molotov–Ribbentrop Pact and the secret protocol attached to it. The document collection served to pinpoint the origins of the Second World War and to simultaneously warn of the Soviet designs for postwar Europe. While some American commentators hailed the State Department publication as a perfect way of getting at the Soviets, others saw no particular gain in the adversaries in the nascent Cold War hitting each other "over the head with the stick of 'history.'" The Soviet response was quick to arrive. On February 9 the Soviet Information Bureau issued a six-thousand-word statement, "Falsifiers of History," which put the onus for the outbreak of the war on the United States and Britain. The formal statement did not directly engage with the documents in the US publication, pressing home that American business had financed Hitler's war industries while the British negotiated the disastrous 1938 Munich Agreement.[1] Stalin personally edited the draft statement and insisted that the original title be changed to "Falsifiers of History." It was subsequently translated into English and distributed worldwide in a pamphlet format.[2]

It is not just the selective facts and their interpretation that make "Falsifiers of History" so special. Rather, it is the odium attached to all those who do not buy into it and a general sense of ownership of history. The pamphlet nails generic opponents as "enemies of democracy, people who have lost their senses." They slander the Soviet Union because "they are mortally afraid of the historical truth." Instead of engaging with an argument, the Soviet publication served circular logic: "Of course, the falsifiers of history and slanderers have no respect for facts—that is why they are dubbed falsifiers and slanderers." It is a dichotomy inbuilt in a historical record: the progressive, peace-loving Soviet Union versus the reactionary, aggressive United States and Britain; the objective and honest approach to historical truth versus distortion and hoax; irrefutable facts versus concealed facts. Providing affirmative answers to the rhetorical questions, "Falsifiers of History" left no space for debate. It can be summed up in a single proposition: "The indubitable fact that the policy of the Soviet Union was and is the correct policy."[3]

Another inference in the pamphlet is absolute state control over historical evidence and its instrumentalization. The Soviet Union did not object on principle to a British initiative to publish selected German documents among those captured by the Allies. It regarded it inadmissible, without "joint consent and . . . careful and objective verification." In effect, that proposition amounted to censorship. According to Moscow, *The Nazi–Soviet Relations from 1939 to 1941* was a tendentious, treacherous publication that aimed to undermine USSR's international influence and undercut the support of the "progressive elements" within the United States who sought better relations with Russia.[4] The documents that appeared in "Falsifiers of History" thus took issue not so much with specific historical events as with their consequences.

For those versed in early Soviet history, and rhetoric, the 1948 pamphlet is no particular revelation. What distinguishes this particular publication from many others is that it furnished a prime example of historymaking, that it represented the personal opinion of Stalin, that it was aimed specifically at the West, and that it was part and parcel of the emerging Cold War discourse. Fast forward seventy years, and the "falsification of history" is among the catchphrases used by the Putin regime. Russian nationalists today refer back to the 1948 Soviet publication as an original list of all the contentious issues currently used to distort the history of the Second World War. In 2015, an extended edition of "Falsifiers of History" was reprinted in a book format by Nikolai Starikov.[5] "Falsifiers of History" serves as a powerful refrain to a story I am telling in the present book, and hence the title.

* * *

The Russian literature is rich in aphorisms about the idea of history. The celebrated Soviet poet Alexander Tvardovsky had expressed it in the late 1960s as follows: "Those who eagerly conceal the past are unlikely to be in harmony with the future" (*kto priachet proshloe revnivo, tot vriad li s budushchim v ladu*). Of the many Russian intellectuals who had contemplated on the meaning of history, two in my view were right on target. The nineteenth-century thinker and writer Alexander Herzen once quipped that the "Russian government, as providence in reverse, is taking care of the past not the future." Satirist Mikhail Zadornov, in the waning days of the Soviet Union, put it yet differently: "Russia is the great country with an unpredictable past." All these maxims directly apply to Putin's Russia.

The future is history, poignantly chose Masha Gessen as a title for her latest book.[6] The Russian state began speaking in the language of history beginning in the mid-2000s, and fully embraced the (archaic) new lingua in the wake of the political crisis of 2011–12.[7] In Putin's Russia, obsession with the past comes in lieu of plans for the future. As a core memory, the Second World War is getting sanitized of all the blood and gore associated with a military conflict. What is left is an element of triumph, which in itself becomes a constituent of an ideology. Hence, there emerges a generic historical picture framed by bravery and sacrifice. This quasi-religious interpretation fits well with the so-called traditional values superimposed by the Orthodox Church. The result is as alarming as it is fascinating: the current generation of Russians is less afraid of war than were the Soviet citizens during the Cold War.[8]

The Russian language has rendered quite a few neologisms in recent years. One of them is *political technology*. It stands for political manipulation, tested for the first time on a large scale during Boris Yeltsin's reelection campaign in 1996 and perfected during Putin's two decades in power. The closest association would be that of *spin doctors*, though at a considerably larger scale. One may effectively argue that political technology has been guiding both the domestic and foreign policy of Russia under Putin. Alongside other segments of applied knowledge, it has steered historymaking as well. In fact, the core principle of political technology, namely utilizing elements of seemingly incompatible ideologies to win popular support, translates directly into a syncretic type of history promoted by the Kremlin.[9] Two sides of the coin, it ultimately ensures the regime's survival.

Such term as "geopolitics," which was labeled pseudoscience during the Soviet times, have not only been embraced by the Putin regime but also been made into a cornerstone of its ideology.[10] That ideology, of course, is nothing more than the Bolshevik "means justify the end." Even less clear is the end result sought. So far, Putin has clearly demonstrated just two things: his desire to stay indefinitely in power and to continue confrontation with the West. Translated into history politics, it promotes the composite image of a good, strong tsar and the autarkic, pre-Petrine Russia. The kind of syncretic history promoted by the Putin regime is possible to achieve only through the unscrupulous recycling of and juggling with facts. In other words, the Russian state is practicing what it has attributed to others, namely the falsification of history.

This book should be read as a chronicle, not as an attempt at cultural analysis. I proceed on the assumption that the discourse developed by scholars such as Catherine Merridale, Svetlana Boym, Dina Chapaeva, and Alexander Etkind, among others, accurately reflects on Russian memory politics.[11] I seek to demonstrate how a proliferation of history-related practices in post-Crimea Russia has been effectively used by Putin to cement his power. My perspective makes me reject the conventional understanding of history politics as the collective attempt to rationalize the past.[12] I put the emphasis on the word *politics*, devised and steered from the top. History is of strategic importance for the regime, the way economy, defense, sports, and so on are.

The book is overflowing with names. It is my intention to demonstrate the intricate links between various individuals and agencies engaged in historymaking. I seek to lay bare the internal workings of the top-down system that is using history as a political tool. For that matter, I am interested in the practical application of memory laws rather than in their genesis, to give just one example.

I approached this project with a certain trepidation. As an empirical historian, I work primarily with archival sources, anything from the mid-nineteenth-century Russian municipal records to the recently declassified US diplomatic cables from the early 1990s. Given that historymaking is a work in progress, in this book I am extensively using the Russian electronic media—one of the key battlegrounds where matters of history are being fought over. With the focus on the past eight years, and given the traditional Soviet/Russian penchant for secrecy, I did not expect to get hold of any documents of state provenance pertaining to the subject of the present study. I was amazed, indeed flabbergasted, to discover numerous policy documents related to Russian history politics readily available on the internet. Particularly striking are minutes of the meetings where various governmental agencies and academic entities get together to discuss the status and way forward on matters of history. That fact alone makes us move past the debate on whether such a thing as an official Russian policy on history exists. It would be as if the Russian government decided to publicize the internal discussions underlying a massive doping scheme during the Sochi Winter Olympics or the decision-making process leading up to the annexation of Crimea. Thus, I had to restate my original question from the substance and goals of Russian history politics to why the Russian government wants everyone to know about it. Reformulated yet again: Why does the Putin regime not bother to conceal the systematic manipulation of all things history in which it has been implicated? Is that, too, part of the devious tactics Putin is known for?

Another problem embedded in writing a history of the present is that it does not have a closing date.[13] There is always a temptation to include yet another anecdote, follow up on yet another recent development. At the same time, there is also a chance of missing on an element otherwise important to the story. Things are moving so fast in Russia nowadays, and also in the field of history, that I have developed almost a phobia not to miss anything of substance. To give just one example: some of the state officials discussed at length in the book—Minister of Culture Vladimir Medinskii and Minister of Education Olga Vasilieva—were let go after a cabinet reshuffle in January 2020. The phrase *as of this writing*, which I am using throughout the book, means winter 2020. In other words, my intellectual endeavor is by default incomplete.

The book features an abridged scholarly apparatus. A complete endnote list can be downloaded at Bloomsbury.com/Weiss-Wendt-Putins-Russia-and-the-Falsification-of-History.

* * *

I begin the book by outlining how geopolitics informs the government conception of history. The strategic use of history by the Putin regime became evident by the mid-2000s, when the Russian foreign ministry clashed with its Baltic counterparts over the issue of wartime collaboration with the Nazis. While the establishment of a state commission against the falsification of history in 2009 attracted considerable public and academic attention, practical efforts to devise a state policy on history three years later did not. A watershed event, the 2011–12 pro-democracy protests reinforced the Kremlin's idea of history as a political battlefield. Increasingly, the regime justified its legitimacy by evoking historical destiny. International repercussions of Russia's aggression against Ukraine in 2014 entrenched that belief. One crucial area where it was immediately felt is primary research. Given that archives have no means of control over possible interpretations of historical evidence derived from their holdings, the authorities have consistently restricted access to researchers, foreign and local alike. Meanwhile, state agencies such as the Ministry of Culture and presumably independent bodies such as the Academy of Sciences began looking for ways to engage Western scholars sympathetic to Russia, and its history. Inside Russia, ominously, historical research gets increasingly censored. Stalin's crimes and the Second World War are the two subjects most difficult for Russian historians to safely navigate. As a sign of things to come, in late 2016 authorities unveiled plans for an institute of history politics, to be steered by political scientists. Academic freedom as such may eventually expire in Russia.

Chapter 2 sketches the major actors in Russian history politics. Tightly linked to the government, most of them operate as nongovernmental organizations. First out was Natalia Narochnitskaia's Historical Perspective Foundation (2004), followed by Alexander Diukov's Historical Memory Foundation (2008), and Boris Shpigel's World without Nazism (2010). One individual who contributed the most to historical mythmaking in Russia is the former minister of culture Vladimir Medinskii. Medinskii supervised the 2012 institutional expansion, which saw the establishment of two historical societies. Although the Russian Orthodox Church falls into a different category, it has positioned itself as a major player insofar as historymaking is concerned. Bishop Tikhon, arguably the most influential cleric, stood behind the creation of a hugely successful "Russia: My History" theme park. While the influence of the Orthodox Church on Russian history politics, due to its cozy relationship with the Kremlin, is still comprehensible, the same cannot be said about the Night Wolves biker club. The club leader, Alexander Zaldostanov, has carved a niche for himself by serving grotesque in lieu of contemporary Russian history. His annual biker festival in Russian-occupied Crimea has become the most anticipated event of the year. Targeting different audiences, these and similar entities are collectively advancing a state agenda on history.

Of all historical events, the government is keen on sustaining popular memory of just one—the Great Patriotic War—which is the subject of Chapter 3. Victory Day celebration is a massive government operation with strong political overtones. Popular participation is being ensured by means of Immortal Regime—a grassroots initiative misappropriated by the state. The Soviet victory over Nazi Germany has assumed elements of a cult, essentially becoming a civil religion. President Putin takes much credit for that. He is also an exponent of the relativist view on Stalin, according to which the Soviet dictator should be judged on account of both his failures and his achievements. Often digging in the past for a usable commentary on current politics, Putin had learned his history lesson in the Soviet school.

Derived from the Soviet model, patriotic education in Putin's Russia has a salient militaristic element to it, which I discuss at length in Chapter 4. Since 2001, the state has been running comprehensive five-year patriotic education programs. The latest edition considers patriotic education within the framework of geopolitical confrontation with the West and puts emphasis on military duty. Unsurprisingly, then, the Ministry of Defense has been playing an increasingly important role in youth education. The ministry is supervising the newest and by far the largest military children's organization in Russia—the Youth Army. Defense Minister Sergei Shoigu projected his vision of Russian military history onto a giant new Orthodox cathedral, to be opened in 2020 in Patriot, a military theme park near Moscow. To assist Shoigu and other state bureaucrats in their endeavor is a so-called unified textbook on history, proposed by Putin back in 2013. The new type of textbook effectively substitutes select facts for analysis, making contested issues in history appear uncontroversial. Deliberate simplification is also a hallmark of historical reconstructions, which have become immensely popular in recent years. Militarism colored the anniversary of lifting the siege of Leningrad while relativism dictated that the anniversary of the Bolshevik Revolution remained a nonevent in Russia. A purview of memorial days in the Russian calendar projects a doctored history that serves to legitimize the present regime.

Commemoration takes different forms, the most common of which is monumental art. Chapter 5 examines the kinds of monuments that have been erected in Russia in the past decade and speculates why. Low cost of production is conducive to replication, the trend actively promoted by Medinskii's Russian Military Historical Society. Mass-produced saints, tsars, and war heroes that now dominate the Russian memorial landscape help reinforce the government perspective on history. In those few instances where and when the authorities approved of a Stalin monument, in Yalta and Moscow, state officials invariably resort to relativism in justifying their decision. Otherwise, Stalin is typically worshipped by few but vocal communists. Public indignation that accompanied earlier attempts to elevate Stalin (outside of North Caucasus) gave way to resignation. Monuments honoring Felix Dzerzhinsky, however, provoke little or no controversy. Putin's earlier career and the positive image of the security services cultivated in today's Russia did, no doubt, help remove a stigma attached to the name of the original leader of what is now called FSB. As to Putin himself, the presidential administration is opposed on principle to displaying his statues. Several such homages to the Russian leader—universally of dubious artistic quality—did appear since the annexation of Crimea, nevertheless.

Among particular war heroes who have been celebrated in Russia in recent years is Alexander Pechersky. Chapter 6 asks how come that Pechersky became a public face of the Holocaust commemoration in Putin's Russia. The story of a Jewish revolt in Nazi death camp Sobibor, led by the Red Army officer Pechersky, alongside the Soviet liberation of Auschwitz constitutes the core of the official Russian narrative of the Holocaust. This discourse has been formalized and given full government support in the wake of the Russian aggression against Ukraine in 2014. Evoking the Nazi murder of the Jews constitutes yet another propaganda front for the Putin regime, however. While Moscow has been successful in courting Russian-speaking Jews in Israel, it hardly managed to insert itself into an international discourse on the Holocaust. Once the 2018 Russian blockbuster *Sobibor* failed to be nominated for the Oscars, the Holocaust appears to have slid off the foreign political agenda.

Chapter 7 examines the direct impact of the state policy on history on nonconformist individuals, memorial projects, and independent institutions. The government is using the letter of the law in its determination to crush political dissent. Several new and/or amended articles of the criminal code enable prosecution based on certain interpretations of history. Most often, alleged offenders—who tend to be opposition supporters—are hit with Article 354.1 ("glorification of Nazism") and Article 282 ("incitement of ethnic hatred"). Since the crackdown began in earnest in 2012, memorial sites commemorating victims of Stalin have also come under attack. Thus, the authorities effectively took over Perm 36 Gulag Museum, closed down another museum at Yoshkar-Ola, and attempted to relativize Stalin's crimes at Sandarmokh in Karelia. Opposed to the regime's efforts to normalize Stalinism are a handful of nongovernmental organizations such as Memorial and the Sakharov Center. Harassed by means of the so-called Foreign Agent law, there is little they can do to rescue the youth from under the barrage of militant patriotism promoted by the government. Among the bright spots is the emergence of independent, innovative initiatives in the field of history, and the establishment of a professional historical association.

1

A Geopolitical Meaning of History

In February of 2019, *Nezavisimaia Gazeta* carried an opinion piece by Vladislav Surkov, one of the architects of Putinism. Surkov is the right person to turn to in the discussion on whether Putin's Russia possesses an ideology. He is the mastermind behind Putin's 2000 election campaign, the creator of a pro-Kremlin youth group Nashi, and the author of the key concept *sovereign democracy*. A professed opponent of a civil society, Surkov claims the honor of shaping the "new Russian system."[1]

Surkov is brutally honest in justifying the authoritarian form of rule superimposed on Russia, and he does it in the language of history. Indirectly comparing Putin to de Gaulle in France, Atatürk in Turkey, and the founding fathers in the United States, Surkov predicts a long life for the rejuvenated Russia. In his interpretation, the present period is the logical succession and extension of Moscovite Rus, the Russian Empire, and the Soviet Union. He sees "historical rationale" in reversing the "unnatural and ahistorical" collapse of the Soviet Union by means of rebuilding a strong Russia under Putin. Assuming the existence of the so-called deep state—a neologism that denotes a conspiratorial belief in the existence of dark forces that effectively run the country—Surkov proclaims it an uncomfortable reality. In rejecting the failed promise of democracy, Russia has no need for strong institutions, which is just a façade anyway, Surkov admits. To come on top in geopolitical battles of today, Russia unashamedly displays attributes of a police state. Here Surkov turns to his main thesis. The present form of governance, he insists, is inevitable as it is unique to Russia. That uniqueness manifests itself in boundless trust between President Putin and the Russians, whom Surkov has come to call "deep people." If not the "good" tsar, the people of Russia have acquired the right ruler (*pravilnyi pravitel*) in the face of Putin. The idea of Putinism will outlive Putin—not unlike Marxism did Marx—and reign supreme for decades if not a century. Furthermore, Putinism has proven an attractive model also outside Russia, pinpoints Surkov.[2] Political observers agree that without the go-ahead from Putin, the Surkov manifesto would not have been made public.[3]

Many an analyst has tried to explain the fundamentals of Putin's rule in Russia. One of the concepts often aired is "mafia state." US senator John Kennedy, who visited Moscow in July 2018 as part of the six-member delegation of the Republican lawmakers, evoked it too. Talking to reporters, Kennedy stated: "There is no political philosophy in Russia. It's sort of like saying what's the political philosophy of the mafia. Their philosophy is money and power. That's the philosophy of Putin. He rules with an iron hand. He's a dictator. You cannot trust Putin." Political scientist Alexander

Morozov, who provided a commentary on the senator's visit, described Kremlin's policy vis-à-vis the West as "total trolling." That policy includes hacker attacks, a propaganda outlet Russia Today, courting far-left and far-right European politicians, and so on. However, policymaking elite as such is never homogenous, which translates into a power struggle between different agencies and individuals who vie for Putin's attention. That explains numerous contradictions, though not momentous perhaps, that had underlined certain Russian policies.[4] To the conduits of the key concepts inferred earlier—paternalism and kleptocracy, quasi-decentralization and post-ideology—I am adding one more, historymaking.

As far as history politics in Russia are concerned, one may identify two major upturns: as a reaction to the so-called color revolutions in the mid-2000s and a response to the pro-democracy protests of 2011–12. The latter period is characterized by institutionalization and a dramatic increase in state financing. The past six years have also seen a tendency toward standardization of historical interpretations by means of restrictive legislation. Since the history of Russia is typically taught as political history, anything that falls outside of the established dogma automatically becomes a "falsification." Such a Manichean approach interprets history (i.e., alleged attempts at falsification) from the perspective of national security, as manifested in the 2015 redaction of the Russian national security program. Ultimately, the reading of history in Russia has assumed a utilitarian function of framing the current political setup.[5]

The politicization of history in contemporary Russia is one of the core themes in a comprehensive report, "What Kind of History Does the Future of Russia Need," prepared in 2016 by Free Historical Society (VIO).[6] VIO proceeds from the assumption that history in Russia has become a substitute arena for airing one's ideological and political beliefs. References to "glorious past," in the absence of any current, tangible achievements, aim to rally the population behind the present regime. Building upon the nineteenth-century historiographical tradition, the history of Russia appears as a sequence of empires—with Gorbachev's Perestroika and Yeltsin's "raunchy 1990s" (*likhie devianostye*) as an unfortunate interruption. Many an element in the present Russian historymaking takes from the Soviet model, including veneration of particular events and individuals, a top-down perspective, and militarization of history. Other conceptual borrowings include a linear interpretation of history and the centrality of (Soviet) Russia in world affairs. VIO traces the emergence of the cult of the past in Russia to 2011, and compares it with the inculcation of historical themes into Stalinist ideology in the 1930s. In both cases, one may draw a connection between the revival of state interest in history and the foreboding of cataclysm. There are also marked differences between how history was taught in the Soviet Union and in present-day Russia. Such notions as rebellious people and freedom fighters, present in the Soviet historiography, have been replaced with that of obedience to authority. Anything related to a revolutionary liberation movement, including Vladimir Lenin and the Bolshevik takeover, gets automatically associated with "color revolutions" of the past decades. Extolling each and every ruler in Russian history, on the other hand, serves the singular goal of legitimizing the Putin regime. The social contract between the state and its subjects may be framed as political loyalty versus pride in the thousand-year history of Russia. The image of a paternalistic state by default cannot incorporate mass violence that was perpetrated in the name of that state. Even though the glorification of Soviet victory in the Second World War per se does not cancel out Stalin's terror, it superimposes a dichotomy. Insofar as the regime poses as the guardian of Great Victory, criticizing the former amounts to questioning the latter. Showing the dark side of Russian history invites the accusation of "deforming historical memory." It may even fall into the category of "falsification of history," allegedly pursued as part of the hybrid warfare against Russia.[7]

One of the report's coauthors, Nikita Sokolov, volunteered an allegory of Russian history as promoted by the state:

> One gets the idea that Russia from time immemorial has been a besieged fortress, and that all of its limited resources should be entrusted to the chief commander, who will make decisions singlehandedly. Democracy is impossible, indeed harmful, due to a war situation. . . . All those who disagree become the "fifth column" and "national traitors."[8]

A Declaration of War

This type of philosophy of history began crystallizing during Putin's second presidential term. The first documented attempt to conceptualize the "falsification of history" occurred in 2005. Following the 2004 spat between the Russian and Latvian Foreign Ministries over the Latvian Waffen SS Division, and a subsequent Russian-sponsored resolution in the UN Commission on Human Rights on a related subject, the Duma, on May 27, 2005, issued a statement, "On Attempts at Falsification of History" (for details see Chapter 6). Aiming at domestic audiences, the Russian parliamentarians used street language to nail their counterparts in the Baltic States and Poland. They insisted that holding the Soviet Union co-responsible for the outbreak of the Second World War was immoral and asking present-day Russia to repent for military occupation cynical. By raising compensation claims, the East Europeans sought to paint themselves as an afflicted and humiliated side in the eyes of the Big (West European) Brother. Duma deputies semi-acknowledged that the "smaller nations" had suffered at the hands of both Stalin's Russia and Hitler's Germany, but at that very instant inserted a disclaimer: the fact of incorporation into the Soviet Union safeguarded the Baltic States against obliteration by the Nazis. Hence, the path to Baltic independence in 1991 began on May 9, 1945. The statement ended with a warning against the resurgence of fascism and racial discrimination, and a strong advice to European politicians to avoid "burdening with history a difficult path to the future of the entire European continent." In the opposite case, the Russian lawmakers issued a dark prophecy: the emerging barriers would breed mistrust, fear, and eventually an urge to rearm.[9]

After a few years' hiatus, the issue of history falsification was picked up by Sergei Shoigu, then head of the Ministry of Emergency Situations. In February 2009 Shoigu weighed in by proposing to criminalize the denial of the Soviet victory in the Second World War. In his view, that would bar leaders of certain (read: East European) countries from entering Russia and make mayors of certain (read: Baltic) cities pause before dismantling monuments to the Soviet soldier. Taking cues from the laws against Holocaust denial passed in a number of European countries, Shoigu thought of his proposal as a means of "defending history and the heroism of our fathers and forefathers."[10] Endorsed by Prosecutor General Yuri Chaika, Shoigu's idea was expanded upon by his fellow parliamentarians for the United Russia Party. In the spring of 2009 the ruling party proposed an amendment to the Russian penal code that would make punishable deliberate misinterpretation of the 1946 Nuremberg judgment undertaken for the purpose of whitewashing Nazism. All those who identified members of the anti-German coalition as offenders (i.e., territorial acquisitions by the Soviet Union in accordance with the Secret Protocol to the 1939 Molotov–Ribbentrop Pact) would face a hefty fine and imprisonment for up to three years. This legislative initiative did enjoy popular support, as reported by a state pollster, VTsIOM. Back then, some 60 percent of the respondents—especially people over sixty—backed the proposal to criminalize the said offenses in one form or another. Legal experts, however, remained cold: no one was denying the Soviet contribution to victory over Nazi Germany and/or the Nuremberg verdict per se.[11] In May 2009 Duma's Legal Committee approved of the draft law, but then the process stalled.[12]

The first comprehensive effort by the Russian state to corral history came in the shape of a Commission to Counteract Attempts to Harm Russia's Interests by Falsifying History, established by President Dmitry Medvedev on May 15, 2009. Although state officials had explicitly denied a link to the proposed draft law, the establishment of the commission does appear as a stopgap measure. Presidential decree no. 549—which was not immediately made public—spoke of the deliberate falsification of historical facts and events for the purpose of belittling Russia's international prestige. The commission was expected to analyze alleged attempts at falsification and come up with counterproposals. Coordination would proceed mainly on the federal and regional levels, which reflected in the commission's makeup. Chaired by Sergei Naryshkin, head of the Presidential Administration and a former KGB operative, the commission was comprised primarily of high-level state bureaucrats. The few professional historians among its twenty-eight members—Natalia Narochnitskaia, president of the Historical Perspective Foundation; Vladimir Kozlov, head of the Federal Archival Agency; Andrei Sakharov, head of the Institute of Russian History of the Academy of Sciences; and Alexander Chubarian, head of the Institute of World History within the same institution—took part in the proceedings mainly pro forma.[13]

Shortly after the commission came into existence, academic Valery Tishkov sent a circular letter to the heads of history sections within the Academy of Sciences. The letter requested an annotated list of historical falsifications, and the names of the scholars in each respective institute dealing with this issue. When asked point-blank what a falsification of history entails and if certain falsifications may actually work in Russia's favor, Tishkov became fidgety.[14] Naryshkin meanwhile explained that the commission would only have supervisory functions, nothing like forcing historians to draw politically correct conclusions in their research. Rather, it was supposed to bring together historians capable of systematizing the evidence of the falsification of Russian/Soviet history. In his view, Russia was merely replicating a trend he had observed in the case of the political elites of neighboring states. Instead of building a dialog with

Russia, he argued, the latter were advancing all sorts of claims against it.[15] Particularly unnerving proved the financial compensation claims (e.g., by Lithuania to the tune of up to USD 834 billion).[16] Naryshkin primarily had in mind the three Baltic States, each of which in the fall of 1998 set up a historical commission tasked with establishing the facts and determining the legal status of both Nazi and Soviet occupation. This was interpreted as belittling the role of the Soviet Union, and by extension Russia, in the Second World War.

As Medvedev was clearing his office in anticipation of Putin's resuming his duties as president, the work of the commission also came under review. Besides expediting retrieval of archival records, as deemed necessary by the participating agencies, the commission had achieved precious little in the three years it had existed. Organization and financing were found wanting; the commission met irregularly and did not efficiently publicize its work. Most important, no viable strategy on how to counter the purported falsification of history had emerged.[17] The hope that a mere list of historical falsifications and their adepts would prove valuable reference material for scholars and state agencies alike did not come to fruition. A largely bureaucratic mode of operation, insufficient PR campaigning, and a rather symbolic contribution by professional historians and academic institutions—these factors contributed to the February 2012 decision to disband the commission.

Meanwhile, the 2009 legislative initiative to criminalize the "falsification of history" had fallen through, too. In January 2010, the government killed it by citing legal difficulties. Signed by Vice Prime Minister Sergei Sobianin, the document identified three major problems with the proposal. First, it was unclear what specific acts and which particular periods were meant by "allegations of crimes committed by member countries of the anti-Hitler coalition." Second, it wondered how anyone could possibly twist the meaning of the Nuremberg judgment, since it had already acquired legal force. Third, it failed to identify the authorities that would deal with prospective criminal offenses, especially those that might have "undesirable foreign political consequences." The "Shoigu Draft Law" received criticism even from pro-government historians such as Alexander Diukov, who regarded it as raw and difficult to implement.[18]

In short, during Medvedev's interregnum, the "falsification of history" still remained on the level of a discourse. Coincidentally, the then Russian president, prime minister, and vice prime minister—all had law degrees and hence comprehended the difficulties involved in interpreting history through the prism of criminal law. A carefully choreographed castling in late 2011—as Putin and Medvedev exchanging positions had been dubbed in Russia—and the wave of public indignation that this news had caused made authorities go into extremes in hamstringing history, also by legal means. Putin and his new-old regime wanted history on their side.

Government Agencies Join Forces in the Fight against the Alleged Conspiracy

One of the central documents that expose the workings of Russian history politics is a transcript of a roundtable held in the Federation Council on November 19, 2012. The roundtable, "Countering Attempts to Falsify the History of Nations to the Detriment of Russia's Interests," brought together major stakeholders such as the Federation Council, Foreign Ministry, Prosecutor General's Office, Academy of Sciences, Moscow State University, Federal Archival Agency, and others. Held at the highest governmental level, the roundtable assessed the status of discussions on the falsification of history thus far and mapped the future course of action. A Federation Council committee stated the following four purposes for convening the meeting: (1) consolidation of historical memory for the sake of strengthening collective identity and national security of Russia; (2) making young generations respect their common history; (3) countering the intensified efforts by foreign states to falsify the history of Russia; and (4) designing countermeasures in order to bolster national unity within Russia. Originally printed in one hundred copies, the document eventually made its way on the internet. As an additional justification, the meeting chair said the Federation Council had received a number of requests from ordinary citizens who demanded that the government and the academic community do more to counter the systematic falsification of facts of history. As of late 2012, the Federation Council had concluded that a definitive policy on history and an organizational framework were still missing.[19] The most explicit such document to emerge from within the Russian government, it warrants a close look.

As a basis for the discussion, the Federation Council distributed among the participants three white papers that addressed the problem of falsification of history from the legal, political, and educational points of view, respectively. Not unlike Moscow's reading of international politics, the analysis proceeded from the assumption that Russia was reacting to hostile acts by foreign countries, mainly former Soviet vassals. Russia had to defend itself in the face of deliberate attempts to use historical falsifications in lieu of arguments in the geopolitical confrontation. Both Poland and Ukraine had established an Institute of National Remembrance largely in order to shape a negative perception of the Soviet Union (and, by extension, of Russia as the successor state). The willing misinterpretation of Soviet history created a foundation for political, territorial, and financial claims to Russia. In consequence, Russia would come out weakened. Up until now Russia had failed to come up with effective countermeasures. The 2009 commission did not live up to its expectations, while the Year of Russian History, proclaimed by President Medvedev on January 9, 2012, and a coordinating committee established for that matter were only ad hoc measures.[20]

The legal analysis prepared by the Federation Council impaired its own credibility by volunteering a self-serving interpretation of what actually constitutes "falsification of history."

> There is a need to clearly define the notion of *falsification of history*. We believe that it can be rendered, for example, as a preconceived, unsubstantiated public interpretation (twisting), the denial of historical facts and events, which can be corroborated through a mass of evidence accepted by the historical community. It can also be rendered as referring to non-existing historical facts and events as actually existing for the purpose of forming a negative perception of the history of the Russian state, its people, society, single institutions, and persons thus harming the interests of the society and the state.

The Federation Council's Legal Department distinguished between moral and legal harm. As an example of the latter, it referred to prosecution of wartime Soviet partisans in the Baltic States and the resulting financial claims. Internationally, the revision of the results of the Second World War would threaten Russia with a plethora of claims.[21]

Next, the council's legal experts posed the question whether acts qualified as "falsification of history" may be liable for prosecution. For precedents, they looked at laws against denial of the Holocaust and/or the Armenian genocide. The existing legal practices at both international and national levels defied a uniform conclusion. The internal initiative to prosecute the denial of the Nuremberg judgment debated in 2009 in the Duma proved equally inconclusive. The experts believed that each suspected case of falsification of history required individual expertise anyway. Along with a number of rather predictable suggestions as to how state and quasi-independent organizations might cooperate for the purpose of countering the alleged falsification of history, the Legal Department had one radical proposition: it recommended subsuming this matter under anti-extremist legislation, with the involvement of the FSB.[22]

The Analytical Department of the Federation Council advanced a very different perspective, firmly situating history within the realm of ideology. Radically different from a traditional notion of the role of history, its interpretation warrants a longer quotation:

> We should note the importance of history and historical manipulations in legitimizing "historically founded claims" against the state, in justifying and cultivating support for a particular kind of politics advanced in any given country.
>
> In the modern information world, "soft power" plays an increasingly important role. The falsification or tendentious interpretation of key historical events constitutes the most important trend within the ongoing ideological struggle both internally and internationally. It helps form a positive or negative image of any given country or nationality—depends on specific political goals pursued by certain authorities at any given moment—by increasing or decreasing the capital [earned though its] reputation and image.
>
> We should admit a close link between historical consciousness on the one hand and politics, political struggle, and political competition on the other. The responsible state cannot afford to ignore that link by letting the process of formation of historical memory and the teaching of national history run its own course, for the consequences of so doing prove just too significant. At the same time, these and similar issues should not be blended in historical disputes, academic discussions around specific historical problems—even though that is exactly what sometimes happens in real life when knowledge of history becomes inseparable from political struggle.[23]

First off was Alexander Chubarian, head of the Institute of World History of the Russian Academy of Sciences. The roundtable befitted the Year of Russian History, as proclaimed by President Medvedev, said Chubarian. Correspondingly, the Academy of Sciences was planning, for the first time ever, to devote its entire annual meeting to issues of history. The Russian Historical Society (RIO) reestablished earlier that year had a job carved out for it: countering negative resolutions on issues of history passed ostensibly against Russia by the Council of Europe and certain East European countries. As the chairman of the Association of the Institutes of History of CIS Countries—going into its twelve years—Chubarian rallied against the concept of *colonialism* as applied to Russia. He actually preferred a Stalinist thesis of lesser evil that justified Russia's territorial expansion. Another aspect worth emphasizing, according to Chubarian, is that the industry in the former Soviet republics, including the Baltic States, was built only when they were a part of the Soviet Union. The recurring theme of Soviet occupation goes hand in hand with the ongoing glorification of Nazism in the Baltic. Here Chubarian volunteered an anecdote:

> I want to confidentially share with you once inquiring with the Germans: "Why don't you bring Latvia to heel so that they stop glorifying Nazi accomplices?" The answer I got was this: "Why us? What about you? Business in Latvia is half Russian-owned! The entire economy is in the hands of the Russian business. Let them put pressure [on Latvia]!" That's a complex problem.

As examples of the falsification of history, Chubarian cited equating Soviet and Nazi crimes and questioning Soviet motivation behind driving the Germans out of Eastern Europe. He suggested drawing a parallel between Russia liberating Europe from Napoleon in 1813–14 and from Hitler in 1944–45. Within Russia, Chubarian deemed most important the popularizing of the history of the Great Patriotic War.[24]

Mikhail Ponomarev of the Federation Council spoke of a new world order and a new "morale" that the victory over Nazi Germany had ushered. Belittling the role of Russia (as the successor to the Soviet Union) in winning the Second World War might even result in political, financial, and territorial claims, he warned. Ponomarev, the politician, proposed a series of measures that would constitute a state policy on history, to be coordinated on the federal level. That policy would include passing laws against the whitewashing of war criminals and the revival of Nazism; lobbying with the Council of Europe for a joint curriculum on the history of the Second World War and, specifically, the Holocaust; promoting organizations that monitor manifestations of neo-Nazism and racism; arguing for international sanctions against individuals complicit in razing monuments to the Soviet soldier and/or erecting monuments to known war criminals; increasing state support for literary works celebrating the heroism of the Soviet "liberators"; and sponsoring scholarship on Nazi mass crimes and, especially, the mass murder of Jews. Ponomarev further suggested pressuring the media to give only official interpretations of history. In the narrative he construed, those who stood up to neo-Nazism became the persecuted human rights activists [*pravozashchitniki*]. He finished his statement by proclaiming Russia a great state, quoting President Putin on historical revisionism, and reminding the audience of a forthcoming roundtable on "methodology of state and public anti-Nazi expertise."[25]

Another member of the Federation Council, Alexander Savenkov, indirectly answered to the vexed question why the commission on falsification of history ceased to exist in 2012, just three years after it had been established. The commission reportedly did not set its priorities right. The state was now reestablishing control over the central issue, namely safeguarding the accepted the Second World War narrative. Of all governmental agencies, he thought history, as a subject, belonged most naturally under the purview of Valentina Matvienko in her capacity as speaker of the Federation Council and head of the Scientific Expertise Committee. Trained as a lawyer, Savenkov spent the rest of his short presentation advocating for a systematic publication of documents related to the Nuremberg trial.[26]

The deputy director of the Federal Archival Agency, for his part, identified the newly established Russian Historical Society as the entity that should coordinate the work against the falsification of history. Vladimir Tarasov described document publications as a means of "restoring historical truth," which he immediately contradicted on the example of the 1932–33 famine. "Of course it was a reaction to what was happening in Ukraine," he admitted. His agency published selected documents in order to "neutralize . . ., convincingly refute the stereotype established in Ukraine concerning the exceptional nature of the famine in the former Ukrainian SSR." Other document publications tackled such contested issues as the mass execution of Polish officers at Katyn, Russian–Georgian relations, OUN/UPA, General Vlasov's Russian Liberation Army, and so on.[27] The head of Oriental Studies at the Academy of Sciences also identified Holodomor—the preferred term for the 1932–33 famine used in Ukraine—as one of the subjects that serve "anti-Russian purposes." In this context he mentioned a monument to the victims of the famine erected earlier that year in Kazakhstan's capital city Astana.[28]

Yevgeny Yamburg of the Russian Academy of Education attempted to steer the discussion away from geopolitics and counterpropaganda, which he acknowledged as a framework for the present roundtable. He was concerned about the contradictory views expressed in various history textbooks, for example, with respect to ethnic deportations under Stalin and armed resistance against the colonial policy of the Russian tsars in the Caucasus. Blaming it on the victims does not help the cause of interethnic relations in today's Russia, and specifically in Chechnya, he argued.[29] Alexander Zhuravsky, a government official in charge of interethnic relations, brought the conversation back into an ideological fold. Russian authorities have something to learn from foreign universities, which regularly organize summer schools for scholars from different countries. If anything like this had ever been attempted in our country— he developed his thought—then mainly by foreign foundations which, thanks to God, no longer can legally operate in Russia. Why would the Foreign Ministry, the Ministry of Education (since 2018 the Ministry of Enlightenment), the Academy of Sciences, and other government agencies jointly not fill in the void by engaging scholars abroad? The established Western historians who made a successful transition from Sovietologists to "forgers of Russian history" is a lost cause, he speculated, but "younger guys" could perhaps be influenced as far as their perspective on Russian history is concerned.[30]

Alexei Vlasov, deputy head of the History Department at Moscow State University, situated history teaching within an ideological context. He lamented that historical discipline had been missing from comprehensive study programs offered by branches of Russian universities that had opened in recent years in CIS countries, especially Central Asia. That does not help advancing the dominant conception of history that links together the Imperial Russian and Soviet periods. He proposed arresting this negative development by establishing Russian historical, humanitarian, and information centers abroad.[31]

The most revealing as well as far-fetched perspective on history was offered by Konstantin Dolgov, the Foreign Ministry's official in charge of human rights. He told the gathering that the Foreign Ministry had been monitoring attempts at falsification of history in countries of Western and Eastern Europe. He claimed an existence of a systematic state policy to discredit Russian history and politics in the effort to harm Russia's geopolitical interests. Furthermore, countries such as Poland were using the venue of the European Court of Human Rights to get financial compensation from Russia. Poland built its case around Katyn and Lithuania around the issue of ecological damage inflicted through Soviet occupation. That was a Pandora's Box and, if opened, it would end up costing Russia billions in reparations, warned Dolgov. He argued that Russia should learn from the West to successfully use history as an instrument of soft power. The Foreign Ministry took history politics into account when conducting bilateral relations with countries such as Poland and the Baltic, and also when they sought entry into international and regional organizations that Russia was already a member of. Dolgov allowed for Russian scholars to take a lead on issues of history, yet invited them to assume an "active, offensive position." Having spent a few years in the United States, he said he appreciated the policy of spending huge amounts on promoting works of history there. It could also be done in Russia—namely, carrying out effective PR campaigns in support of specific historical studies targeting both academics and the general public. If such publications appeared only in a select few Russian journals, speculated Dolgov, international audiences were unlikely to take notice, or, worse, take it as yet another aspect of Russian state propaganda. The Foreign Ministry could not produce historical treaties or historical rebuttals of its own, but was ready to lend its hand in promoting them abroad. This whole issue was of strategic importance, and had to be tackled at the state level, with cooperation from the Russian academic community. "The President has set a goal to advance a more offensive position not only on human rights but also on humanities generally," Dolgov stated, concluding his presentation "I believe this can become one of the most important avenues to . . . counter attempts to falsify history."[32]

Alexander Zaliuzhnyi, ex-military and law professor with expertise in national security, had two practical suggestions. First, not only did he approve of a law against glorification of Nazism—the idea of which had circulated for some time—but he also wanted to turn it into a framework law for the entire Commonwealth of Independent States. Second, he proposed incorporating the falsification of history under "extremist materials" as defined in the 2002 law on Countering Extremist Activity.[33]

The meeting chairman gave the last word to Viacheslav Shtyrev, deputy speaker of the Federation Council. In his concluding remarks, Shtyrev effectively confessed that the Russian government was about to put history in a straitjacket. There was no other choice, given the fundamental problem of defining what actually constitutes "falsification of history." Shtyrev admitted to the existence of different schools of thought presenting various perspectives, which cannot be outlawed by default. In the absence of set criteria to determine the correct viewpoint, the Ministry of Education was in no position to work out a formal document that would ensure that textbooks and other publications were free of falsifications of historical events and facts. Deciding which of the two history books that gave opposing views on the same event was an exercise in falsification. Shtyrev was blunt in his proposed solution:

> We know that there are no definite criteria. We talk about it often but hesitate to find a solution. I think we can no longer "remain virgin" on this issue so to speak. I guess we should make up our mind and establish a standard in evaluation of certain historical events. All textbooks, teaching aids, and so on for the use in school should be evaluated against that standard. Only then we can actually establish whether or not historical events and facts have been falsified in certain textbook, whether the assessment is correct or if it's tendentious—based on misrepresentation and hushing up facts.[34]

On the basis of the roundtable, the Federation Council that same day issued a series of recommendation. The document proceeded from the premise that Russia was a great state and constituted a unique civilization. Among its many achievements, Russia had played a major role in saving the world from fascism and positively contributing to the social and economic development of a number of countries. Like other great powers in history, Russia had experienced great victories but also "tragic events and political mistakes." The well-being of the Russian society and the state depended, among other things, on respect for its own history in its entirety. Building on traditional spiritual and moral values, all elements of the Russian society, including state institutions, scholars, and history instructors, had to come together in preserving the historical memory and strengthening patriotism. This had to be in opposition to the falsification of Russian history that had been attempted abroad, including in former Soviet republics [*blizhnee zarubezhie*], during the previous two decades. Among particular faults were the "tendentious description of the Soviet period of Russian history as an uninterrupted sequence of mistakes and crimes committed by the state against its people," belittling the decisive contribution of the Soviet Union to the defeat of Nazi Germany, equipoising Nazism and Stalinism, and questioning the positive impact that the incorporation into the Russian state had had on numerous nationalities. As the falsification of history had become an ever bigger problem, the function of countering it was unanimously delegated to RIO, which had emerged from the ruins of the Commission to Counteract Attempts to Harm Russia's Interests by Falsifying History.[35]

Each participating agency received specific instructions. The Federation Council was tasked with drawing up a law that would criminalize the glorification of Nazism, Nazi war criminals, and their accessories. The Russian government was proposed to variously popularize the idea of a common Russian historical memory, to publish all available materials related to the Nuremberg trial, to help implement a comprehensive expertise of history textbooks and history curricula, to support the RIO and the Russian Association of History Teachers, and to help promote abroad Russian scholarship and popular books on history of Russia.[36]

The Ministry of Education and Science had the longest to-do list. History had to be more extensively taught in school, with the view of fostering patriotism among the students. A new standard on history teaching had to include a clause against the use of materials that falsified Russian history. Such materials had also to be weeded out from history textbooks and teaching aids produced locally and thus not included on the federal register. History had now to be a required subject for all Russian qualifying school exams. It had to be necessarily taught at Russian branch universities in CIS states, with priority given to those prospective students from the former Soviet republics who expressed the desire to study history. The Ministry of Education was expected to reach further targets in cooperation with the Academy of Sciences and RIO. Specifically, the three entities had to work out guidelines for textbook and teaching aid authors. The core guidelines, on the one hand, emphasized the unifying role of the Russian people in providing support and assistance to other constituent nationalities, and, on the other, the contribution made by those nationalities to the Russian state and culture. Only those textbooks that adhered to those particular "recommendations" would be approved by the ministry. The three institutions had to cooperate in advancing the type of historical research that furthered Russia's national interests. The use of new primary sources was particularly welcome with respect to the interwar period. The Foreign Ministry was expected to assist in organizing international summer schools for PhD students and junior scholars, and in establishing Russian history centers at universities in CIS countries. The work of supplying such centers with relevant historical publications was also delegated to Mr. Lavrov's agency.[37]

In addition, the Foreign Ministry had to lobby with the European Council toward establishing a standard school curriculum on the history of the Second World War delineated by the 1946 Nuremberg judgment. The Ministry of Culture was tasked with popularization of Russian history, in particular the "heroism of Soviet soldiers-liberators" in the Second World War as the antithesis of the resurgence of Nazism. Henceforth, only those historical movies that sought expert advice by professional historians would receive state funding. The Ministry of Defense, too, was to contribute toward popularization of historical scholarship, including by means of archival research—exclusively for the purpose of "countering attempts at falsification of history to the detriment of Russia's interests." The institution entrusted with working out an anti-falsification methodology was the Academy of Sciences. A comprehensive program of action devised by the academy had to be communicated with the help of modern technologies, including the internet. Specific proposals on presenting the history of Russia's many ethnic groups would have to aim at reducing interethnic tensions and building nationwide solidarity. Aiming at raising levels of Russian patriotism, all of the initiatives mentioned above—first and foremost, telling the story of Soviet heroism during the Second World War—would have to be backed locally by legislative and executive organs.[38]

Anecdotally, it is quite interesting who the present authorities regard as the original sinner, the quintessential "falsifier of history"—Victor Suvorov. A former military intelligence operative, Suvorov had defected to the United Kingdom, and since 1990 written ten history books, which effectively put the onus for the outbreak of the Second World War on the Soviet Union. His books were wildly successful in the 1990s, and even made it to a recommended literature list for a history textbook for secondary schools.[39]

The Archival Counterrevolution

As attested in the 2012 document, the Federal Archival Agency (Rosarkhiv) has been an important actor in advancing the state history politics. On June 1, 2018, Minister of Culture Vladimir Medinskii congratulated the staff of the agency on its centennial. The agency safeguards Russia's state interests, stated Medinskii. According to him, by helping write an "uninterrupted chronicle of Russia's great history" while "fighting for the purity of the historical truth," the archivists are truly the defenders of the motherland.[40]

It is unlikely that President Putin ever personally ordered the rollback of the liberal policy on archives in place during the 1990s. Rather, argues historian Pavel Polian, functionaries have interpreted Putin's consolidation of power as a signal to halt the process of document declassification and to limit access to archives.[41] One way or another, we are in the presence of an "archival counterrevolution," to quote Nikolay Koposov.[42]

For confirmation, one may turn to top Russian archival officials. Igor Permiakov, director of the Central Archives of the Russian Defense Ministry (i.e., military archives in Podolsk), formulated it as follows: "Archival documents should have an effect [*dolzhny rabotat*]."[43] What he effectively means is that a consciously made selection of documents for publication should project an intended meaning. By the same token, only those documents can be made publicly available that convey a certain point of view. For example, in 2016 the Defense Ministry declassified and published a series of documents on the crimes committed by OUN/UPA. Had it been done more promptly, speculated a certain General Staff member, the Ukrainian population might have been less supportive of the Maidan.[44] Otherwise, the Defense Ministry Archives, in the face of its director, never reveal a principle by which it declassifies select records, except that some of them appear "interesting" or "unique" to him. Instead, he suggests that prospective visitors no longer have to cut through red tape and merely see all the documents that the archives have put online for their convenience. In addition, he argues that whatever documents the archives release work against the "falsification of history . . . by pseudo-historians."[45]

Irina Garkusha, Permiakov's counterpart at the Russian State Military Historical Archives, does not hide her disdain for the general principle that keeps archives open to the public. User requirements are so democratic, she claims, that anyone who has a passport on her and just wants to kill time while waiting out bad weather can get access to the archival collections. Beginning in the mid-2000s, Garkusha said she noticed an increase in the number of historians among the visitors from the former Soviet republics. She complained of "landing forces" comprising some ten to fifteen foreign historians who paid money to copy, en masse, documents on a particular subject.

> We, Russian archives, are opened. There is nothing we can do about it. The only hindrance there is for not providing the files or for refusing to make copies is the poor physical condition of the documents. That's an international practice, so that's that. But how do they then interpret those documents? No need to explain

to the audience here [intergovernmental meeting on countering the "falsification of history"] the role of the army in the Russian Empire. We have everything. Unfortunately, we have no control over how those documents are being used and interpreted.[46]

Authorities urge historians to use documents from Russian and foreign archives, insofar as they serve the purpose of countering the alleged falsification of history as viewed by the government. That is falsification par excellence!

The strategic use of archives by Russian authorities is relatively easy to attest. In the wake of the 2004–2005 Orange Revolution, the Parliament of Ukraine passed the law proclaiming the famine of 1932–33 as an act of genocide.[47] Three years later the Federal Archival Agency published a document collection, *Famine in the USSR, 1930–1934*. The editors did not explain the principle of document selection, which nonetheless becomes obvious from the preface written by the head of the agency, Vladimir Kozlov. "Not a single document supporting the concept of 'Holodomor-genocide' in Ukraine or even a hint to ethnic motivation of what had happened, including in Ukraine, has been discovered," stated Kozlov.[48] The Russian Ministry of Justice had gone one step further by placing, in the summer of 2015, Raphael Lemkin's article "Soviet Genocide in Ukraine" from 1953 on the "Extremist Materials list." Translated into twenty-eight different languages, the annotated article appeared in a book format in Kiev in 2009.[49]

Obviously, the 1932–33 famine in Ukraine is just one of many such examples. On June 22, 2017 (the choice of the date was not coincidental), the Polish Parliament adopted an amendment to the law banning propaganda of totalitarianism. The amendment prescribes the removal of all Soviet-related monuments, including those to the Red Army. Russian politicians instantly labeled that legislative initiative as defiling the memory of the fallen Soviet soldiers who liberated Poland from fascism.[50] Within weeks, the Russian Defense Ministry declassified a cache of documents that "reveal numerous facts of benevolent attitude of the Polish population and the clergy toward the Red Army, of Poles assisting in burials of the Soviet servicemen who had died while liberating Poland, of their promise to commemorate the heroic deeds of the Red Army soldiers by means of monuments—the commitment to be passed from generation to generation."[51] Releasing selected archival records to score political points is a time-honored Soviet tradition, of course.

Doing research in Russian archives has become increasingly more difficult for local and foreign scholars alike. While expulsion of diplomats belongs to the annals of international relations, expulsion of historians does not, until now, that is. Alarms started ringing, not coincidentally, around the time of Russia's aggression against Ukraine in early 2014. Within a year "at least four Western scholars had been fined, deported, or threatened with these penalties while conducting archival research in Russia due to alleged visa violations." In several cases, Russian immigration authorities pulled out researchers straight from the reading room. The authorities—one afflicted scholar speculated—were likely alerted by archivists. For all that, the historians in question were doing research on certain aspects of nineteenth-century Russian and early twentieth-century Soviet history that could hardly be classified as politically sensitive.[52]

Control over access to archives also functions as yet another warning issued to the West. To give just one example, US Holocaust Memorial Museum (USHMM) in Washington, DC in 1993 signed a comprehensive agreement with the Federal Archival Agency on procuring copies of the documents related to the Nazi mass murder of Jews. In 2011 the hitherto seamless cooperation hit a bump on the road and in 2014 came to a complete halt. Since then, USHMM has had only one project going, with the Russian State Archives.[53] Unwittingly, the restrictions on the use of archives could breed complicity, this time among the Western academic community: no institution or individual would dare to challenge Russian authorities for fear of losing the few existing privileges.

Nominally, documents originally labeled as secret should be declassified thirty years after their creation. At least that is what President Yeltsin's 1993 decree on state secrecy and 1992 decree on declassification of records related to mass repression and violations of human rights provide for. However, state authorities have been constantly defying those acts. According to Rudolf Pikhoia, Russia's chief archivist in 1992–96, the FSB had already then prevented a transfer of records related to Stalin's terror to state archives.[54] The situation worsened considerably after Putin came to power. Historians of Stalinism such as Nikita Petrov and Sergei Prudovskii have tried but failed to challenge the FSB in court. As a counter argument, an FSB lawyer has contended that, by calling members of the NKVD troikas "executioners," the plaintiff may harm their relatives as well as the "objective assessment of the 1937–38 historical period."[55] To the opposite effect, the Intergovernmental Commission on the Protection of State Secrecy in March 2014 extended the classification term for NKVD-KGB records for another thirty years. In practical terms, historians can no longer access documents concerning specific perpetrators of Stalin's terror. Two dozen categories enumerated by the commission ensure that essentially any pertinent document produced between 1917 and 1991 will remain off-limits to researchers till 2044. The same concerns the declassification of foreign intelligence records. Director of the intelligence service and head of RIO, Naryshkin, has stated that this will be done only where and when it can be ascertained that no intelligence officials and/or their foreign contacts could potentially be exposed.[56]

In an effort to limit access to archives, the authorities also invoke specific legal acts. One such act is the 2006 law on Protection of Personal Data, even though it explicitly excludes archival documents. Another one is the 2004 law on Archival Matters. Paragraph 25 of that law censors documents that contain information on the private and family life of individuals. Here, too, the prerequisite that the said information may not endanger the security of an individual appears just pro forma. Thus, extrajudicial organs' minutes get whimsically rendered as "sensitive personal information" and Moscow NKVD troika minutes as "confidential information containing signatures of the executioners." According to Alexander Arakcheev, founder of the now closed Gulag history museum in Yoshkar-Ola, some 80 percent of all documents related to Stalin's terror remain off-limits to researchers. As lawyers emphasize, what is important in Russia is not the laws but their (expansive) interpretation and (malicious) implementation. Significantly, 32 percent of the Russians agree that the documents pertaining to Stalin's terror may only be accessible by relatives of the victims, and only insofar as it does not harm state interests. Another 52 percent, according to a Levada opinion poll, seek full declassification.[57]

In addition to the archival collections that remain off-limits to researchers, there are several others that did at some point become available but were recently reclassified. A case in point is the Novosibirsk Regional Archives, which in the spring of 2019 closed access to certain records of the local NKVD. Allegedly, those documents may contain state secrets. More likely, however, it has to do with the ongoing research by Denis Karagodin. For many years, Karagodin has been working to establish the names of the NKVD officials complicit in the judicial death of his great-grandfather back in 1938[58] (for details see Chapter 7). There exists yet another disingenuous practice whereby an investigation file of a certain individual, for instance Admiral Alexander Kolchak, gets eventually declassified and still cannot be consulted by researchers. As a pretext, the FSB refers to the clause that blocks the perusal of legal papers of the victims of political repression who had not been formally exonerated.[59]

Recently, there was a breakthrough on this issue. In the summer of 2019 the Supreme Court ruled that researchers have the right to consult archival records also of those individuals who had not been pardoned. That applies specifically to the archives under the FSB and the Ministry of the Interior.[60] However, even the Supreme Court decision could not make the FSB change its practice. The FSB act in the belief that theirs is not a state archives and, therefore, can do as they please. In fact, it got worse: researchers currently get access to an ever-smaller number of records from individual files and cannot make photocopies.[61]

More alarming still is the purposeful destruction of certain types of documents related to Stalin's terror. In the summer of 2018 the academic community learned about the existence of a secret administrative act from February 2014 that prescribes the physical destruction of personal cards of Gulag prisoners.[62] That was the information historian Prudovskii had received from the police authorities in Magadan while doing research on his deceased relative. The 2014 act was certified by eleven different agencies, including the FSB, the Prosecutor General's Office, and the Ministries of the Interior, Defense, and Justice. Notably, the archival agency's signature is missing. Although the rationale for maculating this particular kind of records is utilitarian—difficulties with storing and cataloging—the potential damage to the study of history is immense. Ironically, it militates against the official mantra of preserving the "historical truth" in the face of alleged falsifications.[63] The Ministry of the Interior denied that personal cards had been destroyed, insisting that they are being digitalized.[64]

The tighter the social control, the more limitations on access to Soviet security police records get superimposed. Perhaps more than any other agency, the FSB practices self-censorship. Local FSB officials in charge of archives innately follow the trope "no good deed goes unpunished" (Soviet proverb: *initsiativa nakazuema*). Provincial FSB archives routinely decline requests from researchers to consult case files of the individuals who were sentenced during the Great Terror, on the grounds that they may contain sensitive secret police information from the 1950s and 1960s. One can occasionally get access to the police investigation files belonging to those who had been formally pardoned (*reabilitirovannye*), sans declassified operational records. What sounds like a burden, actually has been good business for the FSB. Those FSB officials who work with the classified information typically receive a 20 to 25 percent bonus with their salary. The higher the rank, the higher gets the pay, which obviously does not apply to ordinary archivists. Overall, FSB rarely has issues with professional historians per se. Historian Dmitry Volchek has speculated that FSB, when in doubt, considers it more than enough to just sever access to primary sources.[65]

This "leniency" is also becoming a thing of the past, however. In June 2018 military historian Andrei Zhukov was detained in Moscow on charges of publicizing sensitive information related to his research on Soviet military organization in Afghanistan in the 1980s. During the 1990s and 2000s many a document produced by the Soviet Defense Ministry, including classified records (i.e., any post-1947 document), circulated on the internet. Online history forum regulars like Zhukov freely exchanged and commented on those records. Around 2013 history enthusiasts began seeing the writing on the wall: the authorities were about to "clear things up." Their apprehension proved well founded. Zhukov was tried in closed session on the basis of Article 275 of the penal code (high treason). If found guilty, he risks a twelve- to twenty-year prison sentence. As in the case of Yuri Dmitriev (see Chapter 7), authorities are keen on making an example out of Zhukov. The latter's situation may, in fact, be more precarious as it involves FSB while the court documents remain classified. Doing academic research on recent military conflicts such as Afghanistan or Chechnya has never been an easy task for Russian historians—an effective way for the FSB to demonstrate how well it safeguards state secrets. As for historical forum participants, in the wake of Zhukov's arrest they effectively went underground by establishing an intranet of sorts.[66]

It is not just individuals but also cultural institutions that may suddenly find themselves divulging state secrets. One can hardly believe such an iconic institution as the Hermitage in St. Petersburg would engage in illicit activities, but apparently it did. The world-famous museum got an unexpected visit, formally from the Ministry of Culture but actually the FSB. The control commission declared that the Hermitage had in the course of years published a series of documents labeled secret. Those documents related to the state-sponsored sale of museum artefacts in the 1920s and early 1930s. The story of the Soviet Union selling masterpieces abroad to finance the industrialization is actually well known. Now, the control commission sealed and removed the original archival files documenting the financial transactions. A lawyer representing the museum contended that what had just happened is symptomatic of the growing attack on academic freedoms in Russia. At the same time, he speculated that the Hermitage proved an easy target for those in the security agencies who wanted to show their mettle. It could also be a kind of warning issued to the long-term director of the Hermitage, Mikhail Piotrovsky, who had publicly opposed the transfer of St. Isaak's Cathedral to the Orthodox Church. Reportedly, similar raids had been carried out earlier in Pushkin State Art Museum and Historical Museum, both in Moscow.[67]

Despite the significance attached by authorities to the publication of primary sources, Russian archives remain in a pitiful state. Even central repositories in and around Moscow have not seen an upgrade since the Soviet times. To get to the Central Archives of the Defense Ministry, one has to navigate potholes and huge puddles that make up its enormous, neglected territory.[68] The Foreign Policy Archives, a stone's throw from the Foreign Ministry's high-rise, features a smallish reading room on the basement level. CCTV cameras in the ceiling may or may not work while a security guard at the entrance is busy watching crime reality shows on an ancient TV. The Russian State Archives of Social and Political History, a few steps from the Red Square, appear to be frozen in time. On the way to the reading room, one cannot fail to notice (as of 2012) busts of Lenin, Marx, and Engels tacked under the staircase sometime in the early 1990s. Archival personnel would not entertain a personal request for extra light in the dimly lit reading room on the pretext of saving electricity. An academic history bookstore on the main floor—easily the best such in the whole of Russia—takes up a room no larger than 50 square meters. The element of secrecy is superimposed through, among other things, a ban on the use of portable electronic devices in select archives. In the Defense Ministry Archives, researchers are allowed to use only pens, and in the Foreign Policy Archives pencils. In addition, prospective visitors have to account for limited opening hours, deficient or nonexistent finding aids, off-limits subjects, and restrictions on the use of specific records. Fires in provincial archives are so frequent that they no longer attract public attention. The fire that broke out in January 2015 at the Academy of Sciences Social Science Library in Moscow was truly catastrophic: 5.7 million books were lost. In July of 2019 a fire gutted an estimated fifty thousand files at the Russian State Archives of Literature and Arts (RGALI), also in Moscow.[69] The Archives of the Academy of Sciences—the oldest such academic institution in Russia—was, as of spring 2019, under the threat of imminent closure, as a result of mismanagement.[70]

The Soviet participation in the Second World War is the only episode in Russian history that has seen the influx of new source material, unsurprisingly. A case in point is the People's Memory online project launched by the Defense Ministry in late 2015. The project was proposed in July 2013 by the Victory organizing committee and sanctioned the following year by the president. It enables one to trace the service path of Soviet participants in the war, and includes essential information on those killed and/or missing in action. As of spring 2018, the Defense Ministry had digitalized 92 percent, or 106 million pages, of all records concerning Soviet combatants. That makes the People's Memory database one of the largest such in the world.[71]

Going beyond figures, an invitation to explore personal history merely offsets what is virtually a ban on serious historical research on the Second World War in Russia. Tellingly, the number of documents related to specific Red Army units available online through the People's Memory project is significantly smaller at 425,000. Despite year 1947 as a cutoff date for the purpose of classification, only a half of all documents for 1941 and none above the army level have been declassified. This pattern can be traced back to November 2009, when the Defense Military Archives had confidentially instructed its employees to keep even the declassified records off-limits to researchers insofar as they contained "negative information" about servicemen. President Putin's grand promise—delivered during his address to the Federation Council on January 15, 2020—to make available the largest ever collection of wartime records would likely amount to a select cache of documents supporting the official Russian interpretation of history. He proved just that three days later when meeting with war veterans and representatives of "patriotic" organizations in St. Petersburg. According to Putin, the new resource will "shut the foul mouths" of those foreign (read: Polish) officials who have been distorting history by belittling the role of the Soviet Army in liberating Europe from Nazism.[72]

A professional historian, as private individual, cannot receive clearance to work with the classified records. Those who can are military men or FSB officers. As a particular example, consider Yuri Alexeev, former security official-cum-amateur historian. Typically presented in the local press as a researcher and journalist (occasionally, veteran of the First Chechen War), Alexeev actually made his career in the KGB/FSB. Thanks to his credentials—as he told me in private—he received access to the former KGB archives in his native Pskov.[73] His research resulted in a thin book on a specific Nazi concentration camp administered by the Estonian Security Police. From an academic point of view, his study is an abomination. Alexeev, who speaks no other languages besides his native Russian, used in his largely descriptive study exclusively the Soviet war crimes trials records, which he takes at face value. The following quotation attests to Alexeev's skewed, utilitarian idea of history: "Documents and facts once again speak for themselves. This book is my small 'tank,' though not an invitation to raise the barricades. It's just odd that our country is still facing financial claims with respect to Soviet occupation. It's not yet sure who should be a target of such demands."[74] The book was published in 2011 by the Historical Memory Foundation in Moscow, with which he had been affiliated. Subsequently Alexeev came to found a similar foundation, True History, in Pskov. In 2016, the Alexeev-headed entity won a presidential grant to create a series of video lectures on the history of Lithuania in 1938–9. The lectures were based on the research by the head of the Historical Memory Foundation; Alexeev expressed full confidence in Alexander Diukov's expertise.[75]

The Russo-Ukrainian conflict has had one positive, unintended consequence of direct relevance to history-writing. While the Russian archives are once again bolting their doors, the former Ukrainian KGB archives in Kiev did the exact opposite. In the recent years, the Ukrainian Secret Service Archives have become a veritable Mecca for historians of Soviet political mass violence. Unaccustomed to such a degree of openness (since 2014), researchers cannot praise enough the efforts by Ukrainian authorities to accommodate their requests.[76] Russian historian Dmitry Tepliakov has called it a "revolution." Denied access to certain records in Moscow, one may often freely consult them in Kiev (sometimes discovering that previously classified files contain little information that warrants an extra layer of secrecy). The first major studies based on the findings from the Ukrainian archives shed new light on mechanisms of Stalin's terror, for example.[77]

In April 2016 Putin announced that the Federal Archival Agency would henceforth be directly subordinated to the president. This news caught many by surprise, prompting speculations. Critics have raised concern that the president may potentially stall the process of declassification and further restrict access to archives. Putin may constrain the work of the agency or even directly order a destruction of certain types of documents regarded as sensitive to the regime. Historians such as Memorial's Nikita Petrov and the former head of the Russian State Archives, Sergei Mironenko, however, brush off such fears as unfounded. For one, the government could have done all those things, and is actually doing them, with or without Putin taking over the reins. Mironenko even claimed that direct, formal supervision by the president would enhance the status of archives as an institution. Both historians also tend to agree that one of the reasons for this structural change may be the personality of Vladimir Medinskii. Back in 2004 the hitherto independent archival agency was incorporated into the Ministry of Culture, despite the lack of relevant expertise. The aggressive incompetence of the then minister Medinskii, who clashed with Mironenko over the myth of Panfilov's twenty-eight, has caused anguish in the archivist community.[78] When compared to Medinskii, horribile dictu, even Putin appears a better choice.

Of Friends and Foes

Another aspect of the 2012 roundtable on history politics is global outreach. The regime seeks to promote its perspective on history internationally. This is, of course, easier said than done. In their conception of historical discipline, Russian authorities are firmly stuck in the Soviet past. The Russian government approaches history in exactly the same way it approaches international politics. The intention is to support and/ or create centralized supranational organizations to counter international academic associations. Simultaneously, Moscow continues pursuing bilateral relations, whether in foreign policy or in history. Hence, the Kremlin, in the face of RIO, in September 2017 played host to the International Committee of Historical Sciences. This organization was founded back in 1928 on the wave of enthusiasm for international cooperation sparked by the creation of the League of Nations. Comprised of fifty-six national committees, its main, and pretty much only, activity has been holding world congresses every five years. The latest congress was organized in China in 2015 and the next one will take place in Poland. The Soviet Union has participated in the committee's quinquennial congresses since 1955. The Russian national committee is headed by academic Chubarian.[79] The committee's Moscow meeting—first ever in Russia—was organized with the support of the Russian Ministry of Education and, personally, of minister Olga Vasilieva. Vasilieva, who holds a PhD in history (*Kandidat nauk*), said her ministry was willing to engage in joint projects with the committee and expressed the desire to see more young Russian historians participating in the latter's congresses.

Taken out of context, Vasilieva's eagerness to promote Russian scholarship by means of the International Committee for Historical Sciences may strike one as uninformed. Young Russian scholars have been participating in annual conventions of major international academic associations such as the Association for Slavic, East European, and Eurasian Studies (est. 1948) and the Association for the Study of Nationalities (est. 1972/1987) ever since it became possible. The problem is—from the vantage point of the Russian state—that those are individual membership, North American–based associations that trace their origin to American Sovietology.[80] The Kremlin cannot exercise influence over these and similar independent academic associations and therefore chooses to ignore them.

Chubarian had earlier revealed that "we have received a request from the president to intensify and broaden contacts with foreign scholars for the purpose of promoting the historical truth and countering the attempts to distort Russia's role."[81] The list of explicitly pro-Russian Western scholars is rather thin. Among the most odious names are Michael Jabara Carley, professor of history at Montreal University, and Grover Furr, professor of English at Montclair State University in New Jersey. Carley in particular has been courted by the Russian Military Historical Society (RVIO) while university students have even been forced to attend his recent academic lecture at Moscow. Typically, both scholars play down the extent of Stalin's terror on account of the perennial Western hostility toward Russia.[82] Their arguments, methods, and style call forth parallels with Holocaust deniers. There are also a handful of old-school leftists with solid academic credentials such as Stephen F. Cohen. Professor Emeritus at Princeton University, Cohen had been one of the most vocal critics of Putin "demonization" by the West. This and similar views on contemporary Russian–American politics, however, did not make Cohen a frequent guest in Moscow.[83]

Chubarian's revelations appeared in connection with an Orwellian-sounding new entity, International Commission for the Advancement of Objective Approaches to Evaluation of Historical Facts, over whose foundational conference in early June 2016 he presided. The conference brought together scholars from sixteen different countries. In their presence, Chubarian announced the creation of a joint project, Historical Memory, to counter the spread of what he called historical speculations and dilettantism. As it turns out, the commission will deal exclusively with Russian history, more precisely the Western bias toward Russia from the Middle Ages onward. As an Austrian delegate reportedly put it: "We have to fight back the distorted image of Russia."[84]

Chubarian is explicit on the political underpinning of the new commission. For once, its objective is different from that of the Commission to Counteract Attempts to Harm Russia's Interests by Falsifying History (2009–2012). The idea now is to project Russia's viewpoint abroad. In this context, he mentions Moscow's displeasure with NATO's decision to place, on a rotating basis, a military contingent in the Baltic States. Chubarian argues that the West has been targeting Russia in an information war more extreme than that fought during the Cold War. Like Vasilieva does in the case of higher education, he wants Russian historians to contribute as part of the country's soft power. In view of economic and political sanctions, humanities remain a sphere where individual Western scholars and institutions are willing to do business with Russia. As a positive example he brings up bilateral historical commissions with Germany, Austria, and Poland. Some of these commissions, particularly with East European countries, have continued from the Soviet period. Historians, as part of the intellectual elite, are less prone to Russophobia, Chubarian reasons. The work of the newly established commission is being coordinated by RIO, in which he serves as co-chairman. Ostensibly, the international gathering was convened to mark 150 years of the Russian Historical Society.[85] For whatever reason, the grand plans announced for the commission did not materialize and the commission itself has faded from view.

Chubarian is not the only professional historian who has grasped that history is politics in today's Russia. Hence, to make a case for their particular subfield, some historians occasionally find no better way than situate it within current politics. Consider, for example, director of the Institute of Archeology of the Russian Academy of Sciences, Nikolai Makarov. To advance his discipline, he has mentioned a partial destruction of the ancient Palmyra site in Syria by the so-called Islamic State. The

Figure 1 Power play. Sergei Lavrov (b. 1950), long-serving Russian foreign minister, has advanced an aggressive foreign policy, which frequently invokes Soviet victory in the Second World War. Taking his nickname after Vyacheslav Molotov, "Mister No" works closely with court historians such as Alexander Chubarian (b. 1931), head of the Institute of World History of the Russian Academy of Sciences. In spite of occasionally expressing dissenting views, Chubarian dutifully treads the government line on history, in particular the alleged falsification of history. Here, the top diplomat and the top historian attending an event in Moscow in commemoration of the Battle of Stalingrad, February 2, 2018.

present political context requires a new cohort of professional archaeologists educated in a spirit of patriotism, he stated during a joint conversation with President Putin in the summer of 2016.[86]

The government perspective on the past presupposes the existence of so-called historical truth. Any interpretation that does not comply with the officially stated one automatically becomes a "falsification." Declared potently false, it is then dealt with on the level of rebuttal rather than informed discussion. And so RVIO's research director, Mikhail Miagkov, sits in front of the camera and refutes what he claims to be myths about the 1943 Battle of Kursk promoted by German historians and publicized by *Die Welt*.[87] Prior to that, participants in a "scientific and practical" conference under the aegis of RVIO issued a formal declaration. The declaration framed the alleged assault on the memory of this particular battle as part of Western geopolitics targeting Russia.[88]

Cognitive dissonance, which is a defining feature of the Russian society right now, had also reached the history discipline. History professor from St. Petersburg Iulia Kantor, who had supervised the transformation of Perm 36 Gulag Museum after the state takeover in 2014–15, argues against the politicization of history. Yet, she does not put the onus on the state, blaming misconceived historical debates on individual parties instead. As she puts it in reference to the siege of Leningrad: "Incompetent pronouncements on one side provoke equally incompetent pronouncements on the other, so we come full circle."[89]

The drive for uniformity and coordination (German: *Gleichschaltung*) necessarily calls for systematization. The Manichean division of the world into two camps prompts patriotic indexes and blacklists. Thus, in 2015 the Ministry of Culture announced the creation of a patriotic music register, which would include up to ten thousand compositions from the eighteenth century onward. Simultaneously, Goskonsert (a federal agency in charge of organizing major musical events) decided to put together a database of "patriotically inclined" artists to be promoted on the radio.[90]

In January 2016 news broke out that books were burning. The previous month local authorities in Komi Republic received a letter from the presidential administration that ordered a review of books and educational programs that had been developed in the 1990s with support from the Soros Foundation. According to the letter, those books exposed the youth "to alien to the Russian ideology positions and enforce a twisted perception of Russian history." Librarians at three technical colleges in Vorkuta identified and deleted from the catalog close to five hundred such books; fifty-three of them were subsequently destroyed by burning. Among the destroyed books were textbooks in economics, sociology, psychology, philosophy, and political history. Half a year earlier, head of education in Sverdlovsk region ordered history books by John Keegan and Antony Beevor, also published by the Soros Foundation, removed from school libraries.[91] The Soros Foundation has been a subject of relentless pressure since it wound up on the "foreign agent" list in 2015. The war against the (Soros-sponsored) books is ongoing. In the summer of 2019 a history professor at the Russian State University for the Humanities found out that the Foreign Literature Library in Moscow moved the 1998 edition of his monograph to "special storage."[92]

In the summer of 2018 the Cossack band in Ryazan proposed creating an all-Russian register of "enemies of the people" (for a lump sum of sixty million rubles). According to a Cossack leader, "enemy of the people" is a judicial term and part of international law (*sic*). He places in the category of *enemy* those who plot against the ruling regime, commit treason, or spread disinformation. According to him, just any criticism of authorities will be enough to blacklist the individual in question. As to the *people* component, vice versa, it denotes all those who blindly trust the president and his good intentions. The first step toward the register would be establishing an "Institute of Ideological Science" at a local Cossack-run university.[93] As of now, the government has not expressed itself on the merit of the Cossacks' initiative.

The Future Institute of History Politics and an All-Out Attack on the History Front

The year 2020 may yet see the biggest, coordinated attack against Russia's neighbors on the history front. First on the agenda is the creation of a Russian Institute of History

Politics. The idea of establishing such an institution was aired for the first time in late 2016 by the Scientific Council of the Russian Security Council (which came into existence by a 2011 presidential decree). The immediate reason was devising a policy on commemoration of the centennial of the Bolshevik Revolution the following year. Referring to the void left by the dissolution of the commission against falsification of history in 2012, the Scientific Council spoke of foreign states and international organizations driving anti-Russian geopolitics by means of history. The experts singled out six historical problems that Russia should shield against falsification: the colonial aspect of the Russian Imperial nationalities policy; Soviet nationalities policy; the Soviet victory over Nazi Germany; the Molotov–Ribbentrop Pact; the anticommunist uprisings in East Germany, Hungary, and Czechoslovakia; and the Bolshevik Revolution. Remarkably, the keynote address on the falsification of history as a state security threat was prepared by the Ministry of Defense.[94] Quite unexpected it is, of course, not: in 2016 the Ministry of Defense launched a special taskforce dealing with the "falsification of military history" and, more specifically, the history of the Second World War. The research unit is based at the Defense Ministry Archives and employs a number of young historians and sociologists.[95] Three years later, the deputy minister of Defense declared the "shift in the battle for the Russians' historical common sense from defensive to offensive."[96] According to *Kommersant*, an institute of history politics was also conceived by the reconstituted Knowledge Foundation (*obshchestvo "Znanie"*), entrusted with the implementation of the state ideology.

Political scientists affiliated with the Moscow State University recognize "falsification of history" as an element of hybrid warfare. Presupposing the existence of such a comprehensive campaign in the West, the university professors call for the creation of a separate agency, which would "combine the function of coordination with that of planning, organizing, and implementing strategic information operations capable of inculcating Russian positions on [certain] historical events in the Western audience." Such a federal agency would be directly subordinated to the president or his deputies, thus ensuring instant reaction to information attacks aiming at Russia. An unexpected voice of dissent came from academic Chubarian, who objected to putting a political straitjacket on history, preferring, instead to go through the established channels of history departments and, since recently, RIO.[97]

The discussion was picked up in early 2018 by a pro-Kremlin think tank, Expert Institute of Social Research (EISR) and the Russian Political Scientists Society (not to be confused with the Russian Political Science Association). The joint meeting took place in Volgograd, a mere two weeks after the city celebrated the seventy-fifth anniversary of liberation. Putin, who participated in the commemorative events on February 2, swore before war veterans "to stick up [*ne dat v obidu*]" to the memory of the Great Patriotic War and the Battle of Stalingrad. Andrei Shutov, head of the Political Science Department at Moscow State University, emerged as the main proponent of an institute of history politics. In advancing the thesis of continuity of Russian history, he called for a symbiosis of "spiritual values" and the quest for social justice purportedly characteristic of Russians with new technologies. One other guest from Moscow spoke of Russian history as a "positive process marked by victories." Shutov expressly denies building on the example of institutes of national memory that had been established earlier in Poland, Ukraine, and Estonia, yet reserves the right of the Russian state to project its own interpretation of history.[98]

Two months later the EISR decamped in Kaliningrad. The seminar "Memory Wars as a Means to Revise the Present World Order: Recent Challenges to the History of the Second World War" was held at the Baltic Federal University. The newly proposed institute of history politics would bring together the Kaliningrad, Moscow, and St. Petersburg State universities in the effort to back up the Russian state policy and thwart national security threats within the field of history. The institute would also work preemptively, sharing with the public "objective facts on wartime events."[99]

Almost simultaneously, another roundtable, "Responsibility of the Historian: Knowledge, Morality, and Truth," was held in the Duma. One may sense a competition, for the initiative came from a different set of institutions of higher learning: Moscow Pedagogical State University, Moscow Region State University, and the Knowledge Foundation. RVIO also sent a representative. The roundtable proposed a new federal law that would protect historical memory. The law would provide legal safeguards against statements that "undermine historical consciousness of the peoples of Russia, discredit historical symbols, offend the Russian collective memory of the past, as well as ban the glorification of historical adversaries of Russia and traitors to the Motherland." Among the specific proposals aired at the roundtable were instituting mandatory historical expertise of computer games, creating a series of research centers for the study of "mechanisms of manipulating social and historical processes," removing the requirement urging Russian historians to publish scholarly articles that subsequently get registered in Scopus and Web of Science (as "destructive for the Russian history research and education"), and drafting a charter of the Russian historian.[100]

The proposed codex of the historian is in and of itself a fascinating document. At first glance, the draft text projects common sense: historians should maintain their professional integrity, be unbiased and respectful of other interpretations, corroborate their findings and use credible sources. Next comes an odd warning against falsifying one's conclusions and committing professional fraud. The reason for the need to emphasize it is explicated in the document's final provision: "Avoid spreading the information meant to promote wars, instigate national, racial, and/or religious hatred, and undermine the constitutional order, sovereignty, and territorial integrity of the Russian Federation." The ensuing discussion was basically all about that. The red light started blinking as soon as the RVIO began outlining the concept: the future codex is expected to be signed by historians *and* political scientists (read: political spin doctors). Those invited to the roundtable, who have been teaching both history and politics at the university level, tended to think along the same lines. History is a science and yet historians are bound by the social contract. According to Alexei Ananchenko of Moscow Pedagogical State University, the history profession is governed by the same ethical rules as nuclear physics or medicine. Historians should ground their work in a value system that would enable them to distinguish between good and evil. A historian should be aware of the potential consequences of his research. Hence the history guild needs a Hippocratic Oath of its own, committing not to harm the society. As an example of such harm, Vardan Bagdasarian of Moscow Region State University highlighted the study of Stalinism that began in earnest during Perestroika. A disproportionate attention to Stalin's terror (the proverbial year 1937) had degenerated into a general critique of all things Soviet and Russian. In effect, it proved a tool in corrupting the great history of the great country. To put it differently, the deconstruction of history helps make states fall.[101]

The whole discourse essentially boils down to this: by signing the prospective charter, Russian historians would be obliged to sing the glory of the Russian state and simultaneously avoid examining its dark pages. The definition of "falsification," like before, remains hazy. The bigger question is, however, who has the authority to speak in the name of professional historians: the Duma, the Academy of Sciences, or the RVIO. RVIO admits that their initiative would not be supported by all. The emerging consensus is that the charter of the Russian historian would bind together the patriotic scholars who love Russia. As Vladimir Shapovalov, Ananchenko's college at Moscow Pedagogical State University, puts it (with no hint of irony): "We don't want to twist history and create a non-existent bright past; we want to create a really existing bright past, and that's what we mean by positive history." Other countries are welcome to adopt similar documents, which would make it easier to negotiate around contested issues of history internationally.[102]

Working in parallel, in October 2018 Shutov was back in Moscow, chairing the very first meeting of a working group on history politics under the aegis of the Civic Chamber (a consultative organ by the Russian president). This time around he suggested that the institute of history politics would also extend its activities abroad. As if coincidentally, he mentioned a roundtable discussion on the 1943 uprising in Sobibor death camp happening simultaneously with the working group's meeting.[103] The announcement about the establishment of an institute of history politics may come at any time.

President Putin, known for his fixation on the lessons and legacy of the Second World War, went into overdrive in December of 2019. He appears to be raising this issue at every opportunity. That month alone he lectured CIS leaders and top Russian generals on history, touched upon it at his annual press conference and in a meeting with Russian tycoons. Putin's response was a delayed reaction to the European Parliament resolution of September 18, 2019, that, among other things, identified the 1939 Molotov–Ribbentrop Pact as the immediate cause of the Second World War, accused the Russian leadership of whitewashing Stalin's crimes, and called on Russian society to come to terms with the Soviet past.[104] In particular, Putin lashed out against Poland. He blamed Poland for interwar antisemitism, linking it to the demolition of monuments to the Soviet Army that "liberated the European countries from Nazism." Putin's (dubious) argument is that Stalin had not tainted himself by directly communicating with Hitler, unlike the leaders of France and Great Britain. The Polish government subsequently issued a rebuttal.[105]

Russia in Global Affairs, a foreign policy journal with strong Kremlin links, promptly backed Putin by coming up with particular recommendations in the field of history politics. A roundtable discussion on the political implications of historymaking hosted by the journal featured members of its academic board and invited speakers. The frankness with which the participants spoke of the manipulation of history in today's Russia is nothing short of stunning. When it came to interpretation of history, they divided the world into friends and foes. The only international ally on the battlefields of history Russia has is Israel, due to the Holocaust. The monument to the victims of the German siege of Leningrad—to be opened by President Putin in early 2020 in Jerusalem—would put the victims of the siege of Leningrad on the same level with the victims of the Holocaust, Alexei Miller of the European University at St. Petersburg believes. In parallel, Russia should be reaching out to the "Jewish lobby" in the United States, suggests Dmitry Efremenko of the Academy of Sciences. Perhaps to Jews generally, adds Alexander Philippov, professor at the Higher School of Economics in St. Petersburg. As the main adversary, the discussants identify Poland. Currently under the press from Brussels (on account of a controversial reform of the judiciary), Poland is one country and historical narrative Russia could join the EU in attacking, argues Feodor Gaida of the Moscow State University. Some of the propositions sounded far-fetched, say, seeking potential allies in the countries of South Europe with a historically strong left, such as Spain and Greece. The most fascinating, however, appears the perspective of aligning the official Russian and Chinese discourses on the origins of the Second World War. In 2015 Chinese leader Xi Jinping suggested starting the war chronology from the Japanese annexation of Manchuria in 1931. That narrative fits Russia just fine, says senior expert on Russian–Chinese relations at the Academy of Sciences, Alexander Lomanov. If the "world antifascist war" began not in 1939 and not in Europe, then the contention that the Soviet Union bears responsibility for the outbreak of the Second World War is groundless. It was Japanese militarists and not Stalin who had unleashed the war. Russia should be willing to endorse the view that China was the focal point of warfare in the Far East insofar as China would concede that the Soviet Union had played a major role in the defeat of fascism in the West.[106]

From the realm of geopolitics, the discussion then swiftly moved into that of legislature. The key message of Viacheslav Volodin, when he opened the spring session of the State Duma on January 14, 2020, was the "defense of the historical truth" internationally. By "defense" the speaker primarily meant offense against a particular country—Poland. Volodin slammed the resolution adopted by the Polish Parliament five days earlier. The resolution accused Russia of falsifying history and reaffirmed the 1939 Molotov–Ribbentrop Pact as the ultimate cause of the Second World War, which, among other things, enabled the Holocaust. Volodin insinuated that Poland was not an accidental site for "hundreds of concentration camps where Jews, Slavs, and prisoners of war were systematically destroyed," due in part to the antisemitic policy of the interwar Polish government, which "created the ground for future genocide and the Holocaust." He demanded an apology from the Polish government for both its interwar and current policies. That would be the right thing to do vis-à-vis both the Jewish and Slavic nations, Volodin insisted. Like Putin had done earlier, Volodin drew a contrast between the "sacrifice of the Russian people who had saved mankind" and cunning foreign politicians who cannot accept the "role of the Soviet Union in the victory over 'brown plague.'" Volodin declared the "defense of the historical truth" a political priority, to be advanced through various Duma committees, Russian delegations to OSCE, and the Council of Europe. Toward the end, the speaker urged Duma deputies to tune in to President Putin's annual address to the Federation Council the next day.[107]

In his January 15, 2020, address Putin announced a sweeping overhaul of power in Russia. Policy experts agree that, by proposing to amend the Constitution, Putin is preparing the ground for indefinitely remaining on top of the power pyramid. Few commentators paid attention to that segment of Putin's speech in which he spoke of V-Day and the falsification of history. May 9 is the greatest and holiest day in Russia, he said, for the collective memory of the Soviet victory in the Second World War brings the country together. The "impertinent lies and attempts to distort history we're going to counter with facts," he declared.[108] In a matter of days, a hastily assembled working group rubber-stamped Putin's amendments. Overzealous members of the group proposed including in the preamble to the constitution a statement "on the preservation of historical memory as a means to counter the falsification of history." It may read as follows, "pride over our history, the great victories, and the heroism of our forefathers."[109] The trend is unmistakable: history politics in Russia is becoming an element of political technology.

Taking Away Academic Freedom

Policymaking implies practical implementation. It was only a matter of time before patriotic indexes and blacklists assembled by government agencies and/or state affiliates were put to good use. The academia and the very tradition of academic research in Russia is currently under immense pressure. VIO described it as unprecedented as early as 2016.[110] There are some forty thousand professional historians in Russia today. About five thousand are affiliated with one of the seventeen research institutes in existence, and the rest teach at the university level.[111]

Apparently taking cues from Viktor Orbán and his successful efforts to put the Central European University in Budapest out of business, the Putin regime ganged up against the few remaining independent institutions of higher learning in Russia. First in the line was the European University at St. Petersburg, which local authorities had been harassing for years on account of minor, made-up irregularities. Accreditation of the European University was repeatedly withdrawn, restored, and then again withdrawn, preventing it from offering advanced degrees. For a while, in 2017–18, the European University existed only as a research institute. Notably, Putin distanced himself from the bureaucratic process threatening the university's existence.[112] According to a different version, Putin tried to preserve the university but was effectively overridden by political and business interest groups.[113]

In June 2018 authorities struck against another venerable institution, the Moscow School of Social and Economic Sciences. Accreditation of the school was withdrawn on the grounds of substandard curricula. The person who carried out the expert evaluation had been caught plagiarizing his own thesis—an increasingly common event in Russia.[114] The Academy of Sciences—by definition a guarantor of high academic standards—had been gradually hollowed out, especially after the government in 2009 put it in charge of systematizing the alleged efforts to falsify Russia's history and developing a counter methodology. From then onward, insofar as history is concerned, its function and modus operandi has been indistinguishable from that of power ministries.[115] This is just the tip of the iceberg, of course: no one has ever taken into account the colleges and universities in provinces that had been stripped of academic independence.

The current political and administrative setup encourages complicity on the part of the Russian scholarly community. The 2012 Foreign Agent law is targeting, first and foremost, independent NGOs that receive at least part of their funding from abroad. However, it also indirectly affects academic freedom. The stigma attached to the status of a foreign agent, and the financial and legal consequences that follow, make university entities and individual staff jittery about applying for and receiving foreign research grants. The increasingly repressive environment dictates that they err on the side of caution.[116] Scholars are also forced to exercise caution when deciding whether to accept an invitation to present their research abroad. Those who openly support the political opposition, or otherwise promote fair and transparent elections, risk losing their job. That is what happened to Alexei Petrov of Irkutsk State University, who was sacked after being accused of reneging on his teaching duties. The local prosecutor's office received two letters of complaint, one of which claimed that Petrov's history lectures were not patriotic enough, while the other stated that he was spending too much time traveling abroad on business. The actual cause for the dismissal, however, was his role as regional head of Golos, an organization protecting voter rights.[117] The dean of Saratov State University simply proscribed students and the teaching staff communicating with foreigners under the pretext of safeguarding national security.[118] This and similar private initiatives, by 2019, became law. In February of that year the Ministry of Education issued an internal document that regulated contacts between the Russian and foreign scholars. The push apparently came from FSB, which sought to exercise tighter control over hard sciences. From then onward, any bilateral meeting had to be approved by higher-ups five days in advance; at the conclusion of the meeting the participating scholars are due to submit a report. For that matter, Russian citizens working at overseas universities are also regarded as foreigners. If interpreted literally, it would also apply to correspondence with colleagues abroad and any international conferences on Russian soil. Although implementing this draconian ordinance, presented as mere recommendations, is nearly impossible, it will, no doubt, further increase self-censorship.[119] Examples are plentiful. A certain social scientist from the Higher School of Economics at St. Petersburg had to eventually withdraw from an edited book project I have coordinated. The university administration had expressed in no uncertain terms that her teaching career might be affected if she went ahead with the publication. Historian Andrei Zubov, who was infamously sacked from the Moscow State University of International Relations (MGIMO) over his objections to Russia's annexation of Crimea in 2014, has observed a troublesome sign. In 2018, his publishers, one by one, had hinted that his forthcoming books may contain too strong a criticism of the Soviet era.[120]

I could never imagine stating this, but being a historian is a dangerous profession in Russia today. When asked if the detention of Andrei Zhukov had changed the ways he goes about doing his own research, Vitaly Semenov, a fellow military historian, replied in the negative:

> No, it didn't, because in my opinion risks facing the historian in Russia is a constant quantity. It surely won't get any better. If you signed up to deal with history, prepare

to drive at 120 km per hour. There is no point braking, or otherwise you may skid. It didn't increase the extent of danger involved in my work. It's potentially dangerous, like the work of all historians in Russia but also in the CIS states.[121]

The first professional historian in Russia to ever face criminal prosecution on account of his research was Mikhail Suprun. Back in 2007 the German Red Cross signed a cooperation agreement with the Arkhangelsk Pomor University and the Ministry of the Interior to prepare a memory book. The book would list the names of ethnic Germans who were collectively deported in 1941 and German prisoners of war who wound up in the Russian North. In the midst of composing a database, on September 13, 2009, the university professor was apprehended by the FSB. The basis for the detention was a complaint by an individual who did not want the information about his relatives entered in the memory book. The FSB carried out a search, confiscating all the documents and computers. The project was subsequently terminated and the historian himself indicted for "illicitly collecting private data" (Article 25 of the 2004 law "On Archival Matters in the Russian Federation"). The prosecutor's office ran into problems, though, since it had to prove that the published data constituted "sensitive personal and family information." Carried out by the state, extrajudicial sentencing or deportation is something else, however. In the opposite case, no memory book—a well-established international practice—could ever be published.[122] The criminal case against Suprun was dropped in 2011 due to the statute of limitations. That was before Putin returned to power and rallied the population against "enemies within."

One particular scholar who experienced it firsthand is Kirill Alexandrov. An unprecedented smear campaign in 2016–17 that had led to a revocation of Alexandrov's doctorate creates a dangerous precedent. A historian from St. Petersburg, Alexandrov is a recognized expert on Russian collaborationist forces in the Second World War. On March 1, 2016, Alexandrov defended his second dissertation (equivalent to German *Habilitation*) that examined the social background and motivations of a segment of the Soviet officer corps in joining General Andrei Vlasov's army. The defense took place at St. Petersburg Institute of History of the Russian Academy of Sciences. Out of eighteen members of the dissertation committee all but one voted in favor of awarding the candidate a doctoral degree. Outside scholarship, Alexandrov has been outspoken on his political views: in 1991 he defended the Lithuanian parliament; along with Andrei Zubov he belongs to a quintessential anticommunist organization, the National Alliance of Russian Solidarists (NTS); his collected works appeared in 2003 under the title *Against Stalin*.

Alexandrov's PhD thesis, "General Staff and Officer Corps of Military Units of the Committee for the Liberation of the Peoples of Russia, 1943–1946," is a major achievement for just any scholar. Running into over 1,100 pages (i.e., about three times the legal requirement), the study is based on painstaking research in eighteen different archives, half of them in Germany and the United States. Alexandrov's command of primary and secondary sources is impressive. As part of his analysis, he undertakes a biographical study of 185 high-ranking officers in the Vlasov Army. Having spent over twenty years on this project, Alexandrov is rather judicious in his conclusions, emphasizing a variety of reasons that made a relatively large number of Soviet officers change sides. Still, as the larger factor he identifies collective discontent with the communist regime and its repressive policies from the mid-1920s onward. There is little, if any, evidence pointing to low instincts—as has traditionally been ascribed to Vlasov's men in the Soviet/Russian historiography. In addition, Alexandrov explicitly states that those Soviet prisoners of war who joined the Vlasov Army did commit high treason. From a methodological point of view, perhaps the only problem is a certain practical value Alexandrov ascribes to his research. Namely, he believes that his conclusions may be used in formulating a state policy toward preventing the political exploitation of prisoners of war in the enemy's custody (cf. an agenda set before the historians of Russia enlisted by the US Army in the early years of the Cold War).[123] By any standard, Alexandrov's dissertation is by far the most comprehensive piece of research that has been produced on this subject in Russia.

A dissertation abstract published prior to the defense greatly irritated "patriots" of various kinds. The People's Assembly (Narodnyi sobor), which styles itself as a nationalist, patriotic, and religious movement, concluded that Alexandrov was trying to whitewash Vlasov. Consequently, it requested the prosecutor's office to check if the dissertation violated Article 354 of the penal code ("public calls to launch aggressive war"). As the leader of the People's Assembly and aide to the notorious Duma deputy Vitaly Milonov explained: "I don't want him executed or imprisoned. I simply want that such dissertations were no more. I want that individual to change his subject." The St. Petersburg war veterans' organization took it one step further: "The dissertation serves those who seek to conquer Russia. The thesis effectively tests the mechanisms of treason, of which there are many examples: Serbia, Iraq, Libya, Ukraine, Yemen, and Syria. In all those countries the US and NATO made use of the fifth column to create Vlasov-style opposition, and subsequently depose the legitimate governments, dismember them, and install the regimes of their liking."[124] A certain cleric and student of theology said that Alexandrov's research soiled the memory of the fallen in war, defied decency and common sense. The country we live in needs heroes, not traitors, he argued.[125]

Going beyond rhetoric, patriotic organizations found among their ranks "experts" to engage with Alexandrov's argumentation (read: to tear it apart). One such self-styled expert was Alexander Subetto of the Russian People's Line (Russkaia narodnaia liniia), a retired army colonel with a PhD in philosophy and economics. Alexandrov's study is an example of falsification of war history, he stated from the get-go. Even Alexandrov's consistently referring to the Second World War in lieu of the Great Patriotic War and calling the Nazi fascist aggressors as adversaries was, according to the reviewer, an attempt to hush up the fact of high treason by Vlasov and his men. The author's contention that joining the collaborationist forces may be regarded as a form of social protest against Stalinism, was described by the former Soviet military officer as "ideological warfare." While failing to explain Stalin's "economic miracle," Alexandrov allegedly exaggerated the numbers of Stalin's victims. Twenty-seven years after the collapse of the Soviet Union, one Russian citizen accused another, much younger than himself, of "slandering the Soviet order, the Communist Party, and the Soviet people." Alexandrov was guilty of preaching the "ideology of anti-Sovietism and anticommunism." He committed "ideological sabotage" not unlike that by "Bandera fascists" in Ukraine. The reviewer concluded that Alexandrov's dissertation did not meet the criteria of an academic study and urged St. Petersburg Institute of History to vote it down. In the opposite case, it would "inflict a blow to the reputation of history discipline in contemporary Russia."[126]

The street protestors included such dissimilar entities as the Communist Party and the Russian Way movement (Russkii lad). Slogans carried by elderly protestors read: "No dissertation without praising Vlasov"; "Whitewashing Vlasov today—denying the Holocaust tomorrow"; and "Bandera in Ukraine—Vlasov in Russia."[127] The director of the Institute of History had been subjected to unprecedented pressure prior to and after Alexandrov's defense. He did not (dare to) specify who in particular had intimated that the future of the institute was hanging in the balance. Andrei Artizov, Putin's crony who had replaced Sergei Mironenko in the position of director of the Russian State Archives, requested the Supreme Attestation Board (VAK) to carry out an academic evaluation of the just defended dissertation. Artizov did not think it was right that the Vlasov Army was the subject of a doctoral thesis to begin with. The reaction of certain online readers—none of whom had read Alexandrov's study, naturally—was vicious. The author was obviously a Russophobe and forger, while the institute of history was a nest for Lithuanian and Georgian agents (i.e., ethnicity of certain staff at the institute); the seventeen members of the dissertation committee who voted in favor should be sent to the Gulag.[128]

Subjected to a barrage of accusations, Alexandrov's dissertation was eventually sent for academic evaluation. Meanwhile, the scholar claimed that some of his archival notes had been stolen—in order to discredit his research. Shortly thereafter, St. Petersburg city court, taking cues from St. Petersburg State University, opened an investigation into a newspaper article Alexandrov had published back in 2014 in *Novaia Gazeta*.[129] Alexandrov's piece on Ukrainian nationalist Stepan Bandera allegedly contravened Article 354.1 of the penal code ("denial of facts established by the Judgment of the International Military Tribunal at Nuremberg"). Notwithstanding the apparent incompetence and bias shown by the reviewers, the Russian Ministry of Education and Science in October 2017 rescinded Alexandrov's degree.[130] To make matters worse, two months later St. Petersburg court ruled that Alexandrov's article from 2014 constituted "extremist material."[131]

Alexandrov has been doing research for over thirty years and has several hundred academic publications to his name.[132] Remarkably, his earlier publications on Vlasov's army from the early-mid 2000s prompted no public outcry. Obviously, it is not the tenet of his analysis, but the political climate in the country, that has changed so dramatically.

Conclusion

Policymaking on history in Putin's Russia has three important elements: commitment to the cause by the state, failure to find receptive foreign audiences to a Russian perspective on history, and a stranglehold on academia at home. Since 2012 the Russian government has been making extra efforts to strengthen its control over history. Putin began his third presidential term in the wake of unprecedented pro-democracy protests, in what was officially pronounced the Year of History in Russia. A top-level meeting convened by the Federation Council at the end of 2012 aimed to develop a uniform policy on historymaking. As earlier, the objective was formulated as a countermeasure to the perceived threat of "history falsification." Instead of delegating this issue to a special commission, this time around different government agencies pledged to act in concert toward a common goal. Among the participating agencies are the Foreign Ministry, the Defense Ministry, and the prosecutor general's office. Also different is the focus on history per se, even though the Second World War has remained its main component.

Marrying state bureaucracy with academia was expected to yield good results as far as an official Russian position on issues of history is concerned. Yet it did not, for that same reason. The very antidemocratic logic of the present system of governance dictates an unrealistic goal-setting and a deficient methodology. Bureaucrats who owe their career personally to Putin lack the imagination that would enable them to penetrate the Western public opinion, let alone the pluralistic world of academia. Then and again, they display a mixture of naiveté and ignorance in their assessments. Consider individual proposals aired in November 2012 at the intergovernmental roundtable on history falsification. A certain member of the Federation Council believed that by massively releasing documents pertinent to the Nuremberg trial, Russia may superimpose its view on the Second World War. He obviously did not realize that any such comprehensive document publication would also include those records that attest to the Soviet manipulation of the trial in 1945–46.[133] Besides, it is a fairly Euro-centric perspective that does not ring the bell with the countries of Asia to which Moscow has been building bridges. In the West, meanwhile, the Nuremberg trial has been long regarded as an example of victor's justice. Even though a series of academic publications in the 1990s and 2000s (coinciding with the trial's anniversary) had tried to revisit the significance of Nuremberg, they barely succeeded at that. In short, from Russia's perspective, the focus on the Nuremberg trial is ill chosen, also strategically. Take another proposition—influencing young Western historians to put a positive spin on Russian history. A reference to "Sovietology" suggests the governmental official in question had in mind the United States. Given the fiercely independent agenda pursued by American colleges and universities, one has difficulties seeing how the Russian state could possibly interject itself. The only viable option would be establishing fellowships and/or endowed chairs. However, it would cost a great deal of money, which the Russian government does not have to spare, and it still would not guarantee the desired outcome. The system of higher education works just differently in the United States, a fact to which Russian bureaucrats are oblivious.

Due to the freedom of opinion, the US book market has a share of historical works of dubious quality. However, those publications never receive more than a fraction of attention and next to nothing in academia. The mere thought of English translations of heavy-handed Russian-produced historical treatises with a tinge of moralism trying to capture a share of the market in America elicits a smile. By rejecting democratic principles, Russian bureaucrats maneuver themselves in a dead circle: without participating in open forums such as professional conventions, government historians have little chance of convincing their fellow academics about the validity of their thesis. No matter how extensive, no support from the Foreign Ministry can convince anyone outside of Russia to pick up a certain book or attend a particular talk.

The Kremlin sees history as a stick to beat an opponent with. There is no other way of explaining unconventional historical demarches by the Russian foreign ministry. For example, in the spring of 2018 the ministry's charismatic spokesperson, Maria Zakharova, indicted the British Secret Service for the assassination of Grigorii Rasputin back in 1916. She also said London was complicit in the death of Tsar Pavel I, while Great Britain holds a world record in genocide, having decimated the aboriginal population of Australia. Zakharova explained why she made such a statement and why then: it was in response to the accusations by British authorities that Russia stood behind the attempted assassination of Sergei Skripal and his daughter the previous month.[134] A few months later, the Russian embassy in Washington was marking the centennial of the American intervention in Russia's Far East. The Embassy, on its Facebook account, cited examples of alleged American atrocities, counting them in the language of Soviet-type propaganda. The tenet of the "commemoration" makes it clear what sort of a message the Putin regime is giving: external forces are to blame for Russia's internal problems.[135]

Those are random anecdotes that do not necessarily denote a consistent policy. Where the Russian policymaking on history does succeed is in destroying academic freedom. This is a tragedy—not yet acutely felt—of monumental proportions. Starved of foreign research funds and restricted in terms of academic travel (financing archival trips abroad has always been a challenge), Russian historians find themselves pushed in the corner. The precedent of the revoking of Kirill Alexandrov's doctorate cannot but send shockwaves across the academic community. In effect, it makes the subject of a PhD thesis a political choice that tests the levels of patriotism of any given historian. All these happen under the watchful eyes of top-level state bureaucrats who have defended their dissertations on "politically correct" subjects and who actively promote polemical history or directly engage in historical mythmaking. Here I mean, specifically, Medinskii and Vasilieva (see Chapter 2). By stifling academic freedom at the university level, the Putin regime pursues exactly the same goal, namely, segregating the Russian segment of the internet to cement its hold on power.

The other side to the coin is the explicit support by the state for a particular kind of research that may advance its official position on certain historical issues. It bears on professional integrity, which becomes increasingly difficult to maintain in Putin's Russia. High-ranking, old-school academics like Alexander Chubarian or Efim Pivovar have long been part of the academic establishment. They are the bureaucrats among historians, who are incapable of devising new approaches to research and teaching due to their Soviet-time schooling anyway. More complex is the case of middle-level historians who do sincerely want to advance research within their respective fields of study, who do possess professional expertise and have an international network, but who find it difficult to proceed without a state cover (alternatively, find it easier to do so). Ilya Altman, a leading Holocaust scholar in Russia, may serve as a representative example of this type of historians (see Chapter 6).

The idea of history currently promoted by the government is nothing but a variation on the zero-sum game played by Putin politically. Insofar as the survival of the regime depends on elimination of dissent, any interpretation of history different from that advanced by the Kremlin becomes "falsification." Thus, by questioning the established Soviet/Russian thesis on the origins and consequences of the Second World War one fails the symbolic loyalty test. However, while Moscow has by and large succeeded in imposing its black-and-white political model domestically, it simply does not work that way with regard to history globally. There is no need to lay out the basic principles of historical inquiry here. Suffice it is to say that history is not a linear, monolithic, bipolar progression that the Russian leadership with their experience from law and order imagines it to be. While Putin and his acolytes proved successful at meddling in foreign elections, carrying out cyberattacks, and staging armed invasions, they do not possess God's power to change the ways one thinks of history. Like democracy, it can be messy, and so it will remain despite their best efforts to streamline it. Still they can, and do, inflict great damage by eviscerating the historical profession in Russia.

It is not just the perversion of the idea of history and obstruction of independent research: the Russian government is afraid of the revenge of history. Here I mean the deliberate efforts to forestall paying out financial compensation for historical wrongdoings. The Foreign Ministry explicitly refers to this particular aspect of Russian history politics when giving its expert opinion on how to go about countering the "falsification of history." It amounts to the exact opposite: shaping a historical narrative that would invalidate claims for reparations by countries such as Poland or Lithuania. In that respect, Russia is following in the footsteps of Turkey vis-à-vis the Armenians, though without the intensity and consistency displayed by the latter government.

2

State Affiliates Manufacturing the "Historical Truth"

In December 2018 the state-run pollster VTsIOM conducted a poll to find which Russian institutions the citizens trust the most. A total of 86 percent put their trust in the military, 67 percent in the Orthodox Church, and 57 percent in the law enforcement agencies. On the other end of the spectrum is the political opposition, mistrusted by 41 percent of the respondents, and the court system by 36 percent.[1] Popular trust invested in the army, church, and security agencies appears to justify the latter's foray into historymaking.

Like in any other hierarchical political system, the concept of history elaborated in the Kremlin gets passed down to various state agencies, which further advance it via innumerable affiliated organizations. All those entities invariably pose as nongovernmental or volunteer organizations, which is *contradictio in adjecto*. Whether they are seasoned state bureaucrats, professional historians, or just odd personalities—the individuals heading the "NGOs" are interlinked. What may appear an exercise in pluralism is actually a massive operation rigidly coordinated from the top. Next, I sketch the major players in the field of history politics and the ways they interrelate.

Humble Beginnings: Building the Foundation

Some of the organizations dealing with history are constantly in the limelight while others never. When it comes to the long-term impact of any given entity, however, media attention may not necessarily be the right measuring stick. Take, for example, the obscure Historical Perspective Foundation, which stood at the beginning of Russian history politics. The foundation is associated with the name of Natalia Narochnitskaia (b. 1948), a political scientist and historian who spent seven years in the 1980s working in the UN Secretariat in New York. In 2002 she defended a second dissertation at Moscow State Pedagogical University, with the long-winded title, "Russia in Intellectual and Geopolitical World History Projects of the Late Nineteenth and Twentieth Century in the Light of Religious and Philosophical Foundations of History." During her tenure as a member of the Duma between 2003 and 2007, Narochnitskaia served as deputy head of the Foreign Relations Committee. Narochnitskaia was among the few historians who participated in the work of the Commission to Counteract Attempts to Harm Russia's Interests by Falsifying History.

An adept of the idea of Russian World (*Russkii mir*), Narochnitskaia has in various capacities worked to support Russian compatriots abroad. A Putin confidant, Narochnitskaia also enjoys close contacts with the Russian Orthodox Church and, specifically, Bishop Tikhon. Like the Kremlin, Narochnitskaia has no use for democracy and fundamental freedoms. Similarly, she maintains the idea of the conservative, traditionalist Russia battling it out with the postmodernist, liberal Europe. As a pillar of international law, Russia has an edge, she contends. That makes the enemy within a larger threat to Russia. Narochnitskaia regards as the enemy all those who do not appreciate Russia's long history and thus "forsake their mother." Generally, she believes that Russia, and its manifest destiny, has throughout history been under geopolitical siege. Yet, she remains a "historical optimist" in her belief that the status quo will persist.[2]

This worldview translates into an agenda of the foundation she chairs. Established as far back as 2004, the foundation brings together students of geopolitics, history, and media with the purpose of examining the "strategic questions of the past and present of our country in connection with the restoration of historical memory of Russian civilization and the strengthening of national consciousness." The foundation's mission is to counter the falsification of Russian history, on the one hand, and to form a positive image of Russia in the world, on the other. More specifically, it seeks to "devise fundamentally novel solutions for Russian foreign and domestic politics based on the conservative foundation of Russian values and Russia's historical experience." Many books published by the foundation so far has come from Narochnitskaia's pen and all bear characteristic titles: *Russia and Russians in World History*, *The Russian World*, *The Second World War Score: Who and Why Launched the War, For What Cause and With Whom We Fought*.[3] In 2008 the Historical Perspective Foundation went international. That year President Putin installed Narochnitskaia as director of a newly established think tank, European Institute for Democracy and Cooperation. Like the foundation in Moscow—through which the funds have been channeled—the institute in Paris deals, among other things, with the "use of history in current politics," focusing specifically on the "great wars of the nineteenth and twentieth century."[4]

The precedent set by Narochnitskaia and her foundation actually shows that Russia arrived relatively late at the idea of institutionalizing historymaking, following the East European lead. The first such institution to be established was the Polish Institute of National Remembrance, in Warsaw in 1998. The institute's operations are unprecedented in scale: over two thousand salaried staff (five hundred of them in the Warsaw headquarters), the biggest archives in all of Poland, over six hundred publications, several conferences each month, and twelve temporary exhibitions over the years. Meant to be an "apolitical and independent from the government" institution, it hardly fits the bill. The institute's initial role of supervising and processing communist security service archives has expanded to include vetting and prosecution. The function of patriotic education is enshrined through the Office for Commemorating the Struggle and Martyrdom (of the Polish nation). Historians affiliated with the institute have the status of civil servants and receive a higher pay than their colleagues in the Polish Academy of Sciences or state universities.[5] The institute's sleek premises in downtown Warsaw features conference and exhibition facilities; visitors can purchase pens and memory sticks with the institute's insignia.

While the Polish Institute has been perceived from outside as a conservative institution backing up the policies of the state in the field of history, its Ukrainian equivalent has been marred by controversy. Established in 2006, the Ukrainian Institute of National Remembrance has a long list of objectives, including commemoration of the victims of Soviet terror, highlighting the contribution of the Ukrainian people in the fight against totalitarianism, debasing historical myths, helping sustain Ukrainian patriotism, and, most recently, supervising the removal of symbols of Soviet power in Ukraine. The institute is located in a tired early twentieth-century mansion with dimly lit corridors and creaking floors that it shares with several other institutions. Unlike its Polish counterpart, the institute has fewer than twenty officers on staff, with its website featuring information exclusively in Ukrainian.[6] The institute works closely with the Ukrainian Museum of National History, where it periodically organizes temporary exhibitions. Controversy is usually associated with the institute's former director, Volodymyr Viatrovych. Viatrovych has been accused, among other things, of downplaying the role of the Ukrainian Insurgence Army (UPA) in massacring Jews and Poles during the Second World War. The Ukrainian Institute of National Remembrance is likely to pursue a more liberal, inclusive policy following the appointment of a new director in December of 2019.[7]

When compared with these and similar institutions across Eastern Europe, the work of the Historical Memory Foundation in Moscow does not appear as overbearing. For starters, its status is much lower than that of an institute of national remembrance, which was also under consideration for a while in Russia.[8] The foundation came into existence in 2008 as a "nonprofit public organization" for the purpose of "assisting in the unbiased study of essential problems in twentieth century Russian and East European history."[9] The foundation does not disclose the source of its funding—channeled through "sympathetic [former] members of the Russian Duma such as Boris Shpigel."[10] Indeed, Shpigel's World without Nazism (see Chapter 6) had been affiliated with it from the very beginning. Formally, the foundation exists thanks to private contributions and federal grants.

The foundation originally had three people on staff and rented a space in a decrepit building in downtown Moscow. Most of the foundation's work is carried out by director Alexander Diukov (b. 1978) and head of research Vladimir Simindei (b. 1975). Both men are professionally trained historians who had earlier tried their hand at state service. Simindei originally comes from Latvia, where he returned in 2001 as the third secretary of the Russian embassy. Among the other appointments, Simindei sits in the expert group of the Duma dealing with Russian compatriots in the Soviet successor states (as Shpigel did earlier). Diukov, prior to joining the foundation, served as the journal editor in charge of military-related news within the Russian Telegraph Agency (ARMS-TASS). The ultimate litmus test, Diukov's loyalty to the regime, can be ascertained through his position on Stalin. Treading a government line, Diukov calls for a "balanced" view on Stalin that accounts for both his crimes and his achievements.[11] Otherwise, he sees no problem in new monuments to Stalin going up.[12] Like President Putin, Diukov regards the Holocaust and the German siege of Leningrad—commemorated on the same day in Russia—as two sides to the same crime.[13]

Within a rather broadly defined research agenda, Historical Memory deals almost exclusively with the Second World War, more specifically, mass crimes committed by ethnic Ukrainians and Baltic nationals. Diukov and one other staff member of the foundation play a leading part in the Information Group on Crimes against the Person (IGSP), which is styled as an "international human rights organization." As it transpires from the organization's website, its main goal is to disseminate information about mass crimes allegedly committed by Ukraine in Donbass since February 2014.[14]

Despite the salient political agenda of the organization he heads, Diukov periodically asserts his independence on issues of history. Thus, he acknowledges that the mass execution of Polish officers at Katyn in 1940 was carried out by the NKVD (but refuses to speculate on the Soviet decision-making leading up to the crime). He rejects the Soviet treatment of certain ethnic minorities as genocide, but neither does he endorse a similar thesis advanced with regard to Soviet prisoners of war in German captivity. Diukov publicly expressed himself against the harassment of historians Andei Zubov in 2014 and Kirill Alexandrov in 2016–17. He also criticized RVIO (while holding membership in RIO) for their lack of professionalism, and lamented the demise of the Alexander Yakovlev Foundation.

Vladimir Medinskii, the Minister of Truth and Historian in Chief

Before proceeding with the institutionalization of history politics in Russia, I want to profile its chief exponent, former minister of culture, Vladimir Medinskii (b. 1970). Historians make bad politicians and vice versa. It is all the more alarming when a historian drives a politically correct agenda while working in the profession. Still worse is when professional skills acquired from both occupations are combined in pursuit of that agenda. Remarkably, the former ministers of culture and education are both educated as historians—the first such instance since Putin came to power in 1999. Diligent, proactive, loyal, and dull, Medinskii is an asset to the regime.

Medinskii's career path makes him a perfect spokesperson for the kind of historical ideology advanced by the Kremlin. An active Komsomol member and, later, member of the Communist Party, Medinskii in the late 1980s studied international journalism at MGIMO in Moscow. His dissertation (*kandidatskaia*) from 1999 was on Russian foreign policy in the context of a globalized media. In 2004, Medinskii entered Duma on the United Russia ticket. Despite the lack of formal training, in 2011 he defended a PhD thesis in history (*doktorskaia*), "Problems of Objectivity in the Fifteenth–Seventeenth Century Writings on Russian History" at the Russian State Social University in Moscow. Not untypical for hard-core Russian patriots, one of Medinskii's great-grandmothers was a Baltic German and two of his great-uncles were victims of Stalin's terror.

In many respects, Medinskii is a quintessential historian turned government official who promotes historical fiction. Deep at heart, he likely sees himself as an artist, someone who brings history to the masses. In a mirror-image worldview adopted in Russia under Putin, Medinskii, the myth-maker, poses as the myth-buster. That is what essentially led him being noticed in the first place. Known as a history buff, Medinskii in his years as Duma member ran a series of televised lectures and radio programs. The programs addressed traditional stereotypes about the Russian people such as heavy drinking and docility. "The Myths about Russia" has since 2007 been serialized as popular books. With flashy titles and bigger-than-usual scripts, 200-odd page editions with the same title bring to mind big print run pocketbooks published by Lenin's government to help eradicate illiteracy. His polemics take on such stereotypes as corruption and graft, backwardness and laziness, submissiveness and excessive drinking, brutality and authoritarianism. Looking at Russian history, Medinskii declares all of these to be false. He specifically lashes out against the notion that Russia had traditionally posed a threat to its neighbors. The latest in the series, *Russia Never Surrendered: Myths of War and Peace*, appeared in 2016. One can get a good idea of Medinskii's conception of history by just surveying his chapter titles: "Is patriotism in demand right now?"; "We have reconciled to drinking poison about our history and our country"; "a unified perspective on history is set up by the state, or then by just anyone else"; "there was no-one beyond Smolensk in 1611: the state as such no longer existed." He sets the tone in the introductory chapter:

> The reality of today's world is such that any sovereign power in one way or another conducts its own history politics, that is to say, "uses history in their own interests." The state whose elites refuse to systematically influence public consciousness (historical memory) inevitably surrenders a part of its sovereignty. Sure, the state may decide not to do so, but then someone else will be dealing with history, just anyone and from any angle. People meanwhile will have either vacuum or garbage in their heads. A sixth-grader may have difficulties making rational conclusion when someone is telling him that Alexander Nevsky was a hero, and someone else—collaborator. As regards [the question of whether or not there is] a "need" for patriotism and heroic past, this is a fundamental requirement for every viable society and every viable state in conjunction with the necessity to ascertain its historical presence.[15]

To capitalize on the commercial success of the first three books in the series—which reportedly sold in excess of a quarter of a million copies—Medinskii reworked them into one, *Skeletons from the Russian History Closet* (2017). With his usual swagger, Medinskii states from the get-go that "I am not discovering Atlantis (or Troy). I am just selecting facts in a certain order and molding [*prelomliaiu*] them from a particular vantage point." Medinskii further stresses that his is popular history: "For me, historical background is just a picture frame. What I write in my books take place not in the past but in the present, in our own heads, and more broadly—in the collective mind of the contemporary Russia." While the United States essentially has no history, claims Medinskii, "we do have one—great, wise, and rich." The art of historical interpretation is a one-way road, according to Medinskii: "We have no right to think ill of ourselves. We have no right to think ill of our people. . . . We have to remember the good."[16] For lack of space, I cannot go quoting Medinskii indefinitely. Rather than enumerating his statements unsupported by evidence, I looked up what the readers get out of his books.

Those who liked what they read praise the book as a perfect entry in the field of "patriotic education." Irina K. learned from Medinskii that the Russians are a highly cultured and hygiene-conscious people. Even Ivan's the Terrible brutality does not look as bad when compared to the brutality of the wine-drinking Europeans. A certain Tatiana appreciated the author demonstrating the "greatness of Russia's national spirit." Nadezhda A. was in agreement that the book is making Russia and Russians proud, an excellent source for preparing talks on history of Russia and beyond. Dina T. said Medinskii's book lifted her spirits as she was getting tired of hearing what a miserable country Russia is.[17]

According to a quote from *Kommersant* featured on the back cover of yet another book by Medinskii, the Myths about Russia is currently the most popular book series in Russia. The book in question is *Peculiarities of the National PR: The Truthful History of Russia from Rurik to Peter* (2011). As the title suggests, the author makes good of the fallacies of presentism and presumptive continuity, essentially reading the present into the past. To emphasize his disdain for the notion of *truth*, Medinskii peppered his text with *lols* and smileys. Behind the innocent mischief is the ideology that Medinskii feeds to his audience:

> Right before our eyes [history] is being once more used as an instrument. It happens that people rape history. It also happens that history rapes people. In the present case, people are being raped with history. And everyone knows what it is all about: it has nothing to do with discipline [*nauka*] or restoring the truth, but with current politics.[18]

Some of the readers regard it as nothing short of a revelation, for Medinskii applies known PR tricks of today to specific historical events and figures. The message is indeed hard to miss: what Russian authorities are doing today has always been done by states to claim legitimacy. That inference made Vladimir K. declare the book a must for those who love Russia and want to better understand its collective mentality.[19] According to his publisher, Olma Media Group (controlled by one of Putin's cronies, Arkady Rotenberg), the total print run of Medinskii's books reached one million by 2015. He is a member of the Russian Writers Union.

If historical research can advance national interests—as Medinskii has insisted—then substituting a work of fiction for history makes perfect sense. The minister of culture was elated after attending the premiere of the play, "Sedition, 1609–1611," at the State Academic Malyi Theater in Moscow on May 10, 2018. Medinskii came on the stage to receive a huge bouquet of flowers as the author of the original novel that provided the storyline. Published in 2012 and listed as historical adventure novel, *The Wall* marked Medinskii's debut as a fiction writer. The book tells the story of the siege of Smolensk during the Polish–Moscovite War of 1609–1618. According to him, the defense of Smolensk is "cooler than Stalingrad, the siege of Leningrad, and the Brest fortress rolled into one." The theme of high-spirited Russians battling morally corrupt Europeans is strikingly close to the dominant political discourse. Take, for example, one of the characters, the venerable old man Savvatii, who has incorporated some of Putin's neologisms in his speech: "We'll relentlessly pursue the bastards, be it on the road or elsewhere. If we caught them in outhouse, so we'll put an end to them in the outhouse all the same." The heroic pathos of *The Wall* brings to mind the Soviet-era theater pieces lambasting German fascists. Ironically, one spectator audibly reacted to a scene of betrayal in the play as follows: "Aren't they fascists!" One of the play's central ideas is that all troubles and foreign invasions in Russia are due to sedition and unrest. The dialogues are replete with jokes about the Europeans seeing the Russians as barbarians.[20] If further proof is necessary for the political use of history—in this particular case the Polish–Moscovite War—one may want to look at NOD (National Liberation Movement), as it came out in force during the 2015 Unity Day walk in Moscow. One of the banners on display evoked the liberation of Moscow from Polish invaders in 1612 as a rallying cry to "join Putin in liberating [Russia] of American invaders." A quotation from Putin that followed superimposed the ultimate conclusion: "The people liberated Moscow and the country of invaders and those who had betrayed Russia. Subsequently, by their own free will, the people established strong, viable rule." Other NOD activists carried slogans calling for the "cleansing of the fifth column."[21]

The director of the theater said he aimed to create an "outstanding play" on the subject of sedition, topical for Russia. Medinskii magnanimously refused the honorarium, donating it toward the restoration of the Smolensk fortification.[22] A three-hour play involving over fifty actors, two dogs, a rotating stage (newly acquired for the occasion), and video projections: finally, Medinskii got to fully realize himself as an artist and historian, and Putin's loyalist.

It is symbolic that another famous piece of performance art with the same title, Pink Floyd's *The Wall*, projects the exact opposite sentiments to those evoked by Medinskii. Forty years apart, the British rock classics tell the story of isolation and abandonment embodied by the wall, while for Medinskii it symbolizes strength and resilience. The protagonist on Pink Floyd's conceptual album seeks to tear down the wall (as put to action at the band's 1990 legendary live show at the Berlin Wall), whereas Medinskii associates this urge with the enemy. Instead of breaking out, Medinskii invites his audience to safely remain inside the walls: a quintessential illustration of the siege mentality associated with the Soviet Union and currently Russia.

To be fair, Medinskii's is not the only artistic meditation on the subject of walls or, specifically, the Polish siege of Smolensk in the seventeenth century. To coincide with Unity Day (November 4), a St. Petersburg studio released in 2015 an animated feature, *The Fortress: Shield & Sword*. Aimed at 8–10-year-olds, the animation film situates the fictional character of a boy in the middle of a battle, delineated by heroism on the one hand, and treason, on the other. Notably, offense in the children's film follows defense (i.e., first "shield" and only then "sword") and not the other way around. The script was reportedly written already in 2005 and the work on the feature film commenced five years later.[23]

Medinskii outlined his philosophy of history in a 2016 interview to *Novaia Gazeta*. Medinskii sees his mission as the minister of culture to make history accessible to the average person: "Sometimes people want to have it simple." He regards history as both an academic discipline and a tool. Anyone operating with facts does it exclusively in support of one's own subjective position. "History is politics projected into the future," he quipped, "because the contours of the future are drawn from historical myths."[24]

Medinskii is the champion of an idiosyncratic view on history par excellence. Medinskii has consistently defined the odious characters in Russian and Soviet history, such as Ivan the Terrible and Stalin, as "complex historical figures." For example, Medinskii formulates his attitude toward Felix Dzerzhinsky as an open-ended question: Did the demolition of the Dzerzhinsky monument on Lubyanka Square immediately restore order in the country? Preaching relativism, Medinskii insists that one and the same historical figure may be judged differently within a hundred-year span—good and/or bad, a hero and/or a monster. The very word *monument* (Russian: *pamiatnik*) comes from "memory" and thus, according to a top Russian official, is by default non-judgmental. When asked about new monuments to Stalin, Medinskii has this to say:

> Here's another divisive issue. My attitude toward Stalin has changed ten times over the past thirty years. A new aspect necessarily emerges every time I read a new book, new documents, or just memoirs . . . . I would not make any unequivocal statements about Stalin right now. But neither would I ever endorse a state-sponsored monument to Stalin. I believe it would split the nation, which is always a bad thing, especially since 2014, since Crimea. . . . I mean erecting monuments to Stalin is undesirable not because it's in and of itself bad, or very bad, but because it divides the nation.[25]

In short, Medinskii preaches an instrumental use of history. Whatever works to keep the population united in the face of an adversary (read: keep it docile) defines the chosen perspective on history. Historical viewpoints may change along with political circumstances. Those among professional historians who reject this algorithm automatically fall in the category of an adversary, the kind of people who "swim against the tide of history." Although Medinskii defines himself as a "latent monarchist" and identifies with a "liberal wing" of the United Russia Party—if any such ever existed—with respect to history he essentially practices "creative Marxism" of Stalin and Vyshinsky. The latter creed, in its turn, was nothing more than the principle of means justifying the end.[26]

The emerging (composite) image of Medinskii is that of a well-placed individual who invests as much time in busting myths as he does in sustaining them. Medinskii got particularly worked up about one particular battle in the Second World War. Generations of Soviet people grew up with the story of the sacrifice by the twenty-eight soldiers under the command of Ivan Panfilov who perished on November 16, 1941, defending Moscow against the overwhelming German force. Monuments to Panfilov's soldiers dot the Russian landscape, including the ginormous one outside Moscow. In his interpretation of the battle, Medinskii crossed swords with then director of the Russian State Archives, Sergei Mironenko. In July of 2015 Mironenko published an official report from 1948—which had become public knowledge during Perestroika—that painted an accurate picture of what happened on that particular November day. He referred to the original newspaper story from 1942, which had since then been incorporated into the Soviet/Russian myth of the war, as falsification.[27] Mironenko had made similar statements already earlier, publicly. Medinskii was indignant. Mironenko, as an archivist, should mind his business systematizing and preserving records—the kind of work for which the government had been paying him a salary. Interpreting those records, let alone debasing historical falsification, however, lay outside his remit, snapped the minister of culture.[28] One month later Medinskii went one step further, declaring "epic Soviet heroes" such as Panfilov's twenty-eight or Zoia Kosmodemianskaia to be saints and any attempts to question their deeds taboo. All those who disagreed, according to Medinskii, betrayed what was sacred—the memory of the forefathers. They would burn in hell! As a positive example, Medinskii volunteered a story of his friend and opposition supporter. Once, she followed his, Medinskii's, advice and sent her son to one of the summer camps run by RVIO, instead of the French Riviera. The experience of searching for the remains of the Soviet soldiers made the teenager want to "scratch out the eyes" of anyone who spoke ill of Panfilov's men.[29]

To counter the attempts at sacrilege, Medinskii has variously promoted a "people's movie" about Panfilov's twenty-eight. The script was written as early as 2009, and after a teaser trailer was released in 2013, private donations began pouring in. Medinskii appealed to emotions: those thirty thousand ordinary Russians who collected a total of 35 million rubles toward the production of the movie allegedly wanted to protect the memory of the dead at Volokolamsk from "Mironenko & Co." Mironenko only reveals part of the whole truth, according to Medinskii.[30] Cryptically, Medinskii declared he would understand if Mironenko decided to change jobs. He made good on his veiled threat: in March 2016 Mironenko was demoted to head of research at the Russian State Archives. Later that fall, *Panfilov's 28*, the movie, hit the big screen. President Putin was among the first to see it, in a private screening. Although all 35,000-odd private individuals who had donated money were listed by name in the film credits, a bigger financial injection still came from the ministry of culture. Predictably, the movie has little to no artistic value, but much pathos. It is essentially a battle reconstruction whereby combatants identified by their ethnicity rather than nationality. The creators did on the screen what Medinskii has been doing by various other means, namely reinforcing the myth.[31]

In his staunch defense of the legend of Panfilov's twenty-eight, Medinskii is not alone. When facing up to the issue of falsification, though, pro-government historians are treading a fine line. The heroic deed of Panfilov's twenty-eight was not a falsification but, rather, a historical myth, argued Nikolai Svanidze. According to him, debasing this and similar myths is useless, for "they have already entered in circulation, they don't annoy anyone, do harm to no-one. Alright, there is this belief those people were heroes. What should we do now, perhaps remove flowers from their grave? That wouldn't be pretty."[32]

A PhD in History Politics

Ilya Shablinskii, a lawyer and former member of the presidential commission on human rights, has described Medinskii as "Stalin's advocate."[33] Professional (independent) historians are also appalled at Medinskii and his bogus methodology. Some of them have decided to confront the minister. Medinskii's controversial statements on history were thrown into sharp relief in 2016. In April of that year the Supreme Attestation Board (VAK) received a request from three scholars, two of them professional historians, to revoke Medinskii's doctoral dissertation from 2011 as inadequate. The claimants pointed out numerous factual mistakes, faulty logic, instances of plagiarism, and outright fraud, and described Medinskii's work as "absurd." For example, Medinskii appears oblivious to the existence of Church Slavonic language, does not count Denmark as part of Scandinavia, and yet speaks of Yugoslavia and Ukraine in the context of fifteenth-century history.[34]

Indeed, Medinskii's dissertation makes for a curious read. Essentially, it is his popular book series writ large but with a scholarly apparatus. According to Medinskii, an analysis of the stereotypes about the Russian state as advanced by the foreigners may help draw "necessary historical lessons" and thus develop new approaches to the "objective" study of Russian history. In the introduction, Medinskii lists a good dozen methods of inquiry, which he never ends up applying in the body of the text. In fact, he has no methodology at all: Medinskii dismisses critical views on certain aspects of Russian life as biased and praises positive views as historically accurate. Foreign visitors had arrived in what is now Russia with a set of preconceived notions, which in the course of centuries had been magnified and serialized to form a twisted perception of contemporary Russia in the West. Certain Western travelers and diplomats deliberately promoted negative views of Russia with the purpose of slandering the country, he claims. Western historiography, however, has taken travel notes by foreign visitors at face value. The future minister of culture had a particular issue with the label "tyrant," as applied to Russian tsars. By portraying the Russian people as obedient barbarians, he further speculates, the foreigners sought to exploit them for nefarious goals. The ultimate objective was to incite the local population against their rules, prompting a Western intervention. Medinskii assumes a wholly different tone when a certain foreign observer came to appreciate the strong state or called Russia a protector of Christians. That falls in the category of "accurate information."[35]

The formal step-by-step process in cases such as Medinskii's involves three different institutions: a university dissertation council, VAK's expert group, and, ultimately, VAK's presidium. The Ministry of Education typically signs whatever decision the VAK makes. In October 2016 the dissertation council of the Urals Federal University was about to render a negative verdict on Medinskii's dissertation, when the latter asked to postpone the meeting, and VAK hastily forwarded his PhD thesis for review to a different institution of higher learning. The dissertation council of the Moscow State University, under various pretexts, declined to comment, in February of 2017. Later that summer, Medinskii's magnum opus ended up at the Belgorod State University.[36]

Medinskii, who until then had kept a low profile, for the first time responded to his critics in early July. In his interview to *Rossiiskaia Gazeta* he came across as a devoted practitioner of pragmatic fallacy. Also known as presentism, that fallacy essentially denotes using history to prove a point about the present. Medinskii condemns "liberal" historians for bulling him, and rhetorically asks, "Why right now?" His answer is as speculative as his question: it may have something to do with foreign grants or the external pressure to which Russia has been subjected, more generally. While comparing so-called liberal historians to the inquisition, Medinskii defends his right, indeed his mission, as a patriotic scholar to look at the history of his own country from the perspective of Russian national interests. Undermining his own quest for objectivity as a PhD candidate, Medinskii claims that such a thing as objectivity simply does not exist. Quotes from Medinskii are like those coming from George Orwell's pen: "The past is always a reconstruction of the present"; "Who controls history also controls the future" (this is, indeed, a variation on Orwell's line); "Frankly, any history is a history of today"; "History can never be unbiased"; "The true historian ... is analyzing the present through the prism of past experiences"; "One cannot call himself a historian without counting myths among facts"; "Historian is a hostage of own beliefs"; "What's bad is the lack of ideology." As an example, he volunteered the proverbial Panfilov's twenty-eight. That particular legend is better that any fact of an actual battle for, according to Medinskii, it "embodies the suffering and dreams of the Soviet man."[37]

Free Historical Society (VIO), which has been monitoring the process, declared Medinskii's article to be self-incriminating and called upon the Belgorod University dissertation council to strip the outspoken minister of his decree or else disband. VIO's statement is significant because it drew attention to a political underpinning of Medinskii's proclamation in his double role as a historian and functionary. It goes beyond academic research, stated VIO, for the author is a state official who has been actively involved in history politics. It is particularly alarming in a country like Russia where authorities have traditionally interfered with history-writing. As an adept of relativism, Medinskii personifies the current Russian state ideology, which can be reduced to a single sentence: we are lying alright, but who does not? Even the subject of falsification of history, so dear to Medinskii, stops making any sense insofar as the latter makes no difference between facts and their interpretation.[38]

Members of the Belgorod dissertation council came out strongly in support of Medinskii and his research. However, they examined not his dissertation but the argumentation calling for its revocation. What Medinskii's opponents regarded as unscientific, they described as "certain elements of ideological tendentiousness that can occasionally be found in the dissertation." Medinskii is making an important contribution by popularizing history, one of them contended: "No denying he's doing it as a politician, for history is a constituent of politics. . . . He's just a Russophile, and that's what some cannot stand." One other council member plainly declined to critique Medinskii's research, for he regarded the latter a "great man." Mikhail Miagkov, head of research at RVIO who represented Medinskii's interests at the council's meeting, suggested "hatred of Russia and the intrigues by its foes" as the actual motives behind the attack on his boss. Insofar as Medinskii has identified the roots of a campaign of disinformation against Russia already in the fifteenth to seventeenth centuries— Miagkov went on to argue—it is no surprise that certain forces are disputing it now when Russia is under Western sanctions. It is a political hack job, he claimed. The Belgorod University dissertation council passed Medinskii, finding no trace of ideology in his writings while rejecting the original critique as "obscene."[39]

VAK's expert council, however, chose to ignore the above recommendation on October 2 and proposed stripping Medinskii of his doctorate in history. The expert group had ten major objections, including the lack of novelty, the abstract subject matter, deficient historiography, and scholarly misappropriation. Still the biggest problem with the dissertation is the principle that Medinskii has adopted in establishing both accuracy and credibility of any given source: Russia's national interests.⁴⁰ Meanwhile *Novaia Gazeta* has dug up evidence that set in question the very validity of Medinskii's 2011 defense. It turned out that the academic opponents listed in the dissertation's abstract did not participate in the actual defense. Like in a crime flick, the exact moment the critics attempted to get hold of a copy of the abstract from the Russian State Library, the building was evacuated due to rumors of a bomb being planted there. Several members of the VAK expert council have testified that they were expected to, but never got a chance, to read through and comment on the draft dissertation. The decision to award Medinskii a degree was thus taken in camera, pro forma. To the question why, one of those who let Medinskii slip answered back in 2011 to the effect that the train had already gone.⁴¹ Despite all of that, on October 20, the VAK's presidium decided in favor of Medinskii, by fourteen votes against six (including by the only two historians on the board), with three abstaining. In the opposite case, argued Miagkov, it would have opened a Pandora's Box so that just any university student might "denounce" the instructor he or she came to dislike. Fortunately, the discussion was all about scholarship, he concluded. One of those who voted against, Sergei Mironenko of the Russian State Archives, strongly disagreed. He called VAK's decision a "blow to scholarship [*udar po nauke*]."⁴²

Minister of education and fellow historian Olga Vasilieva, took an ambiguous position on Medinskii's dissertation. For one, she put the onus on VAK, which she held responsible for weeding out "bad studies." She did not believe Medinskii's is one of those deficient dissertations anyway. Most important, the two expert commissions found no evidence of plagiarism. As to his methodology, Vasilieva contends that this is the kind of polemical history "we need."⁴³ Notably, academic plagiarism was one of the first issues she tackled in her new job. In September 2016, Vasilieva sacked an official within her ministry who was preparing a document that demanded a court ruling before claims of plagiarism in dissertations could be made.⁴⁴

One final shot at Medinskii's dissertation was fired on March 21, 2018, in the Federation Council. That day Medinskii reported on his achievements as minister of culture during his seven years on the job. He did so by means of statistics, tabulated in a pamphlet that he had distributed among the deputies. One of them, Lyudmila Narusova, questioned the logic behind quantifying culture and said it should be based on morality instead. As for the latter, she argued on behest of a group of professional historians like herself, Medinskii's effort to influence a final decision on the academic quality of his dissertation was immoral. Narusova's tirade was eventually cut short by the Federation Council speaker, Valentina Matvienko. It did not stop there, however. In his program on Rossiia 24, "BesogonTV" (which can be translated as "catharsis"), on May 19 Nikita Mikhalkov offered a fierce defense of Medinskii that has morphed into a scathing attack on Narusova. Notably, the program was initially taken off the air for unspecified reasons. Mikhalkov, a celebrity film director and Putin loyalist, claimed a conspiracy (Narusova was allegedly taking an order from someone) and implied a double moral standard. By analogy, Mikhalkov had Narusova's PhD thesis from 1980 reviewed by an unidentified expert, who, unsurprisingly, found it wanting academically. Among her other alleged sins, Mikhalkov enumerated proposing a bill that would equate celebration of Stalinism to that of Nazism, representing an administrative entity where she does not physically reside, and giving birth to Ksenia Sobchak—a celebrity TV presenter turned opposition politician. All that, Mikhalkov described as a "Harry Potter syndrome," which also served as the segment title.[45]

It is worth keeping in mind that Medinskii defended his dissertation a few months prior to the 2011 pro-democracy protests. What Medinskii's critics failed to notice is the programmatic nature of his thesis. Toward the very end, Medinskii gives a series of practical recommendations, many of which he also implemented after having assumed the position of minister of culture a year later. The author is eager to draw a link between the past and present. Medinskii wants his conclusions to be taken into consideration by government agencies in order to counter a negative portrayal of Russian history. He is concerned that the media has contributed to rewriting history and creating myths. As a result, he argues that the numbers of university students who feel proud of Russia's history are going down. To arrest that development, Medinskii proposes raising "historical consciousness" among undergraduate and graduate students and thus bringing them up as "patriots of Russia." Educational projects, teacher aids, the history curriculum, academic publications—all of these could benefit from his dissertation, insists Medinskii. Furthermore, he seeks a state policy on history. To that end, he proposes creating a historical association that would work closely with, and be supported by, the Duma and the ministry of education. More than just an academic association, it ought to be a "state historical and propaganda organization" that would deal with historical memory and, well, "historical propaganda." Medinskii seeks an active role of the state in historymaking as a means of changing the negative perception of Russia in the West.[46] Medinskii has achieved his stated goal through the establishment of a state-sponsored professional historical association, of which he became the chairman.

The 2012 Institutional Expansion

The institutionalization of history politics accelerated in 2012 with the creation of the Russian Historical Society (RIO) and the Russian Military Historical Society (RVIO). Both regard themselves as the successors of the societies with the same name that existed in Tsarist Russia. The immediate reason for the establishment of RIO and RVIO was the pro-democracy protests, which sounded an alarm within the regime.

The idea to create a professional, state-sponsored historical association occurred simultaneously to several individuals. While few got a chance to read Medinskii's dissertation from 2011—in which he built an ideological foundation for such an entity—the proposal of academic Valery Tishkov (b. 1941) during a joint meeting with President Medvedev in the summer of that year had more interested ears. History was perhaps the only discipline in humanities that did not have a professional association, stated Tishkov. That was an unfortunate omission, given that history, as a "part of culture, is a crucial component of our national consciousness." Another of Tishkov's suggestions was proclaiming 2012 as the Year of Russian History. He justified state support for the history discipline as a safeguard against "all sorts of external barbarians."[47] Both proposals have been implemented.

President Putin sent greetings to the inaugural congress of the RIO in the summer of 2012. In his address Putin emphasized that the original society (established in 1866) brought together not only professional historians but also politicians, diplomats, and military men. The reestablished RIO should fight against the falsification of history on the one hand, and promote the idea of historical congruence—which according to Putin serves as the foundation of statehood—on the other. Putin promised his full support to the new entity.[48]

Influential power brokers among RIO's members and the leadership make it into a political heavy weight. The agenda of the RIO is illustrated by the credentials of its leader, Sergei Naryshkin (b. 1954). Naryshkin wears several hats as Putin's fellow student at a KGB school, former head of the Presidential Administration, high-ranking United Russia Party official, chairman of the now defunct Commission to Counteract Attempts at Falsification of History to the Detriment of Russia's Interests, former chairman of the State Duma, and, recently, member of the Security Council and head of the Intelligence. A historian by appointment, Naryshkin formulated his statement of purpose the best in an article that he penned in October of 2019 for the Serbian newspaper *Novosti*. In his article, which appeared on the twentieth anniversary of the NATO bombing campaign against Serbia, Naryshkin treats history as an element of geopolitics. Naryshkin advances a conspiracy theory, according to which Western political elites manipulate their citizens by falsifying the historical memory of the Second World War. Naryshkin regards any critical perspective on Soviet history as slander against today's Russia. À la his boss, Naryshkin declares the collapse of the Soviet Union (and the Socialist Federal Republic of Yugoslavia) as a "geopolitical tragedy of the twentieth century." Those countries that pursue an independent policy from that dictated by NATO (read: Russia) have their role in the defeat of German fascism willingly belittled. Meanwhile the Soviet victory over Nazi Germany projects the historical mission of Russia to save Europe for Christianity. Naryshkin hails Russia's resolute foreign policy and insists on a multipolar world, the beginning of which he refers back to the 1945 Yalta and Potsdam conferences.[49]

Unlike its geopolitical agenda, RIO's financial fundamentals were less reassuring, until the History of Motherland Foundation came into existence in April of 2016, that is. RIO has positioned itself as a more traditional, academic institution. *Academic* is hardly the adjective that describes the activities of RIO's affiliate, RVIO, which came into existence a mere half-year later. RVIO assumes a different role from that of RIO. It works by volume, inundating Russia with exhibitions and monuments, historical reenactments and plays, and, well, history propaganda.

For all intents and purposes, RVIO is a state-run organization. A presidential decree of December 29, 2012, established RVIO for the purpose of "consolidating state and public efforts" in the study of Russian history and "countering attempts at its falsification," "promoting patriotism and raising the prestige of military service."[50] In 2014, RVIO received 285 million rubles from the state budget, and the following year, another 325 million. In addition, the organization draws support from "private" donors, including giants like Russian Railways and Transneft.[51] As of 2019, RVIO had twelve thousand paying members, and branch offices in all of Russia's eighty-five regions.[52] Judging by its membership, RVIO is, indeed, a continuation of the state. For example, the head of the Crimea chapter is none other than Sergei Aksenov, who has been steering the peninsula ever since the Russian annexation in 2014. It also works the other way around: RVIO's former executive director Vladislav Kononov since 2018 is heading the Museum Department within the ministry of culture. Besides, Kononov's boss has remained the same—the head of RVIO and Minister of Culture Medinskii. Like the Russian state generally, RVIO is quick to dissociate itself from those of its members who have been caught red-handed in criminal offenses. Oleg Sokolov, professor of history at St. Petersburg State University, in November 2019 brutally killed and dismembered his young lover. RVIO subsequently denied that Sokolov had ever held membership in the organization, despite the fact that he had been a member of RVIO's academic board.[53]

RVIO's status as a nongovernmental organization occasionally makes it engage in role-play by seeking formal agreements on cooperation. For instance, in June 2018 a Voronezh chapter signed such an agreement with the local office of United Russia. RVIO proposed to coordinate its activities with the party, while the latter agreed to represent former's interests at central and regional levels.[54] Office space for RVIO local chapters is typically procured through the ministry of culture, while the minister himself supervises all aspects of RVIO's work. When RVIO initiated a collection drive for a monument dedicated to "heroes of the First World War"—bound to be the organization's biggest such project—the ministry of culture backed it up by instructing theaters to support the initiative and do one performance for the benefit of RVIO.[55]

RVIO has been brazenly mixing history and current politics. That is evident, for example, in the kinds of temporary exhibitions it puts together. One such exhibition, *The Soviet Nuremberg*, opened in the fall of 2015 at the State Museum of Contemporary Russian History in Moscow. The display ostensibly centered on the prosecution of Axis war criminals between 1943 and 1949, yet it drew direct parallels to the popular uprising in Ukraine in 2013–14. A "symbolic" panel showing the public hanging of Nazi criminals in Independence Square in Kiev (*Maidan nezalezhnosti*) served as the exhibition's centerpiece. During the opening, Medinskii spoke of the danger of fascism and of the reckoning that would inevitably follow, while Naryshkin accused unspecified Western politicians of courting neo-Nazis.[56]

One other exhibition, *War and Myths*, opened in late 2016 at Moscow's Manezh and since then has traversed the country.[57] The exhibition is the quintessential Medinskii, not least because it is based on his "famous" book with the same title. Short on artefacts, the exhibition is essentially a collection of quotations, photographs, and random facts. The visitors have a chance to meet the impersonators of Panfilov's twenty-eight, be part of a revenge bombing raid on Berlin, and see the holograms of Stalin and major Soviet military commanders. With the soundtrack from the RVIO/Medinskii-produced movie *Panfilov-28* playing in the background, the guests can get the answers to the essential questions, as formulated by Medinskii. In his characteristic folksy language, the historian in chief relates that Stalin should have been executed for his failures in 1941 but was bestowed the highest possible award in 1945; the disproportionate Soviet losses in 1941 were due to the strength of the German Army;

the myth of Panfilov's twenty-eight is a certified history of heroism; the total Soviet military losses were no higher than the German ones; the Sovietization of Eastern Europe was "peaceful"; and so on. Along the way, the exhibition informs the visitors that the Soviet Union was the first country in the world to send man into space and to perform a cardiac surgery, and debases the common myths of the Russian people as lazy and prone to alcoholism. Having "No Retreat" for the subtitle, the exhibition claims to "inflict a blow against the falsifiers of history." By playing down the Soviet contribution to the defeat of Hitler's Germany, the unidentified hostile forces seek to tarnish Russia's international reputation, fuel anti-Russian sentiments, and eventually kick out the country from the UN Security Council. Among the agencies standing up against the falsification of history the exhibition singles out the ministry of foreign affairs and Narochnitskaia's Historical Perspective Foundation.[58]

RVIO's research director, Mikhail Miagkov, summed it up as follows: "Our main objective is to show that the victory of the Soviet people over Nazism in 1945 was the most important event in mankind's twenty-century history. Countering the falsification of the history of the Second World War is a must for all the adequate [*normalnye*] people who want peaceful sky above their heads."[59] Inexplicably, the way the exhibition is organized, the names of Adolf Hitler and Joseph Goebbels stand side by side with those of Leonid Gozman, Mark Solonin, Andrei Zubov, and Gavriil Popov. Miagkov explains away the shocking discovery by pointing to the dissenting views on the Second World War expressed at different times by those Russian historians and public figures. He disputes certain violent episodes, for example, the burning alive 750 Chechens in the village of Khaibakh by the NKVD on February 24, 1944. Hence, presenting it as a fact damages the reputation of Russia, corrupts historical memory, offends war veterans, and confuses the youth at the same time. Otherwise, Miagkov insists, the exhibition superimposes no conclusions but lets visitors decide for themselves.[60]

Cognitive dissonance prevents RVIO from acknowledging that the definition of history politics with which it operates accurately describes its mission. As worded by Yuri Nikiforov, head of RVIO's research department, history politics is an intervention by the state or state affiliates for the purpose of forming a specific collective perception of the past. Next thing, Nikiforov is calling verbatim for a history propaganda assault to counter the imaginary challenge by the West. For a reason, Miagkov is describing RVIO, the NGO, as a "think tank."[61] In other words, RVIO practices what it claims other countries preach.

It is truly fascinating how personalities such as Medinskii manage to contradict themselves within a single sentence, here describing RVIO's objectives. A *Rossiiskaia Gazeta* journalist asked Medinskii what sort of defenses RVIO was holding in the ongoing history war. "Not so much a propaganda outlet," said the minister of culture, "RVIO serves to . . . promote [*propagandirovat*] our military and historical achievements." Raising the levels of patriotism was not their goal either, continued Medinskii. Yet the 2012 decree by President Putin establishing RVIO enumerates "patriotic education" among its goals.[62]

Unlike Naryshkin, Medinskii is not a KGB/FSB man. In today's Russia, however, association with the security agencies goes a long way; in March 2019 RVIO extended the invitation to become a new head of the board of trustees to Sergei Ivanov—former leader of the presidential administration, former deputy prime minister, former minister of defense, former head of the Security Council, and former KGB/FSB operative. Medinskii praised Ivanov as a "person passionate for history, one who knows it well." A major concern for Ivanov, as he has stated, was the alleged falsification of history.[63] The ministry of defense constitutes another pillar. RVIO's Miagkov and the deputy defense minister Andrei Kartopolov cannot praise their respective agencies enough for their contribution to historymaking. According to the latter, both entities closed ranks in the battle over the historical memory of the Russian people.[64] On February 14, 2018, RVIO signed a cooperation agreement with the foreign ministry, aptly identified by the Russian propaganda outlet RT as an agreement "on joint struggle against the attempts to falsify history." Although the document focuses mainly on fostering military historical tourism, Lavrov specifically mentioned the continuous joint efforts to prevent rewriting the history of the Second World War reportedly ongoing in Europe.[65]

Vladislav Kononov, RVIO's former executive director, argued in April 2018 that the Russian state should use all possible means at its disposal to promote the narrative of Soviet wartime heroism. A comprehensive campaign should target people of all ages, say, by crafting a message for children through animation and movies à la Disney and Hollywood. We should learn from the West, he suggested, but shape the contents from the perspective of Russian history, civilization, and state interests.[66]

It was just a matter of time before an entity laying claim on national memory would appear in Russia. The Institute of National Remembrance emerged sometime in late 2015 in the already crowded field of Russian history politics. Of all the comparable institutions, the institute has the shortest and vaguest statement of purpose, something to the effect of utilizing history to help consolidate the Russian society behind the state power. Registered as a noncommercial organization, the institute appears to have the backing of the ministry of education. Unable to compete with the likes of RIO or RVIO, and evidently short of ideas, the Institute of National Remembrance quietly slipped into oblivion.[67]

That certainly is not going to happen to the History of Motherland Foundation, which came into existence in April 2016 by decree of the president. Conspicuously, the news was announced a mere two days after Russian archives had been placed directly under President Putin, as opposed to the ministry of culture. The foundation is supposed to promote national history, disseminate research by Russian historians, help secure access to Russian archives, formulate principles conducive to writing history textbooks, and conduct educational work—all of these with the aim of countering dilettantism and attempts to falsify historical facts. The individuals appointed by the president to serve on the steering committee are all known quantities. The foundation is headed by Naryshkin and the board of trustees by Minister of Education Vasilieva. Among the trustees are Bishop Tikhon, academics Chubarian and Tishkov, top politicians and diplomats Sergei Stepashin and Vladimir Titov.[68] Within a year of its establishment, the foundation had signed a cooperation agreement with RIO.

According to its executive director, Konstantin Mogilevskii (b. 1982), the foundation's main objective is promoting "quality historical knowledge." To do so, the foundation supports exhibitions, conferences, film productions, and book publications. As an important criterion, all of these should be "media-friendly." Simultaneously, the foundation is working to weed out not only historical forgeries—as per definition—but also amateur works. As an affiliated member emphasized, however small the foundation's budget (one hundred million rubles in 2017), it shows that the state is willing to invest in history.[69]

What sets History of Motherland apart from similar entities is its international outlook. The government wants the foundation to "popularize Russian history in Russia and abroad." Although it is not entirely clear how the foundation is expected to fulfill its mandate, certain history-related events may provide a cue. Among recent projects in which it has been involved is the production and worldwide promotion of a feature film *Sobibor* and an exponential growth in foreign editions of the Immortal Regiment.

Unique to Russia is the participation of state security and police agencies in historymaking. The ministry of the interior is one of those agencies that run a memorial project of their own. In December 2011 the ministry launched a "Chronicle of Heroism in Bronze and Granite," which lists the monuments and memorial plaques honoring the slain rank and file, as well as the streets named after them.[70] It maintains a list of museums that tell the history of the police service in Russia. There are currently eighty-two such museums, of which just a few have a dedicated, rudimentary webpage. The depiction of the police work, as well as the Cheka-OGPU-NKVD-KGB-FSB succession, is a throwback to the Soviet times. The archaic exhibition layout cannot but reinforce this conclusion. Otherwise, the narrative that can only be described as heroic features not a single reference to the political mass violence carried out by the Soviet security agencies. In their mission statements, the museums typically emphasize patriotic education and professional pride.[71] Thus, the Central Border-Guard Museum of the FSB in Moscow received the following praise from the RVIO executive director: "While the preservation of the historical truth is the task of each and every one of us today, the museum remains the spiritual fortress safeguarding the country's security."[72] Around the same time, that is, in February of 2019, RVIO unveiled a Museum of History of the Military Commandant's Office in Moscow. The new museum—which among other things displays police anti-riot gear, handcuffs, and electroshock weapons—is apparently also about culture (*sic*). According to the curator and RVIO adviser (who happens to be Medinskii's father), culture is the foundation of national security.[73] Nothing was said about culture during the museum's opening ceremony, though. Rather, the dignitaries spoke of advancing Russian state interests, for example in Syria.[74]

The very term *chekist* is being used once again as an honorary designation for the security police personnel. This serves as a further illustration of the disproportionate power wielded by law enforcement agencies and the military (Russian: *silovye struktury*; *siloviki*) in Russia today. Head of the FSB, Alexander Bortnikov, exhibits pride in the continuity of the Cheka-OGPU-NKVD-KGB-FSB. That was the tenet of his interview to *Rossiiskaia Gazeta* on December 19, 2017, marking the annual Day of the Security Service Official. Desperate times require desperate measures, he said in reference to the Red Terror of 1918–22. The "excesses," commonly known as the Great Terror, he attributes to the incompetence and careerism of the lower-rank NKVD officials. Furthermore, he claims that a significant proportion of the criminal cases from the 1930s, including show trials, had been substantiated. Besides, the bad apples among the NKVD cadres had been duly punished after Lavrenty Beria took over the reins. Bortnikov reinforces the FSB's self-image as a select group of people devoted to protecting the interests of the state.[75]

In view of this and similar pronouncements, it is no longer shocking to see certain members of the police posing (as part of the Descendants of the Heroes initiative) in NKVD uniforms.[76] One can even buy an NKVD uniform for children, suitable for "military reconstructions, role-play, May 9 celebrations, theater plays, and/or photo sessions." As the institutional pride grows, the willingness to acknowledge past crimes diminishes. Sometimes semantics proves the best defense. For instance, the police headquarters in Cheliabinsk got installed in 1985 a memorial plaque, which informed of mass executions carried out in that very building in the 1930s and 1940s. By the early 2000s the plaque had disappeared and, in its place, there appeared another one, which speaks in the abstract of "victims of political repression." The city government is unwilling to restore the original text on the grounds that the historical building has been partially rebuilt. Besides, it might cause "unwarranted associations" and thus undermine the police's reputation.[77]

Besides organizing exhibitions and public events, state affiliates have also tapped into the academic publishing business. The field advanced in the 2000s through independent, internationally recognized history journals such as *Ab Imperio* is now awash with state-sponsored periodicals. First out was the Historical Memory Foundation with its *Zhurnal rossiiskikh i vostochno-evropeiskikh istoricheskikh issledovanii* (journal of Russian and East European historical studies, 2010), followed by the pro-Kremlin Institute of Social, Economic, and Political Studies and *Istorik* (historian, 2015), and the State Museum of Contemporary Russian History and *Zhivaia istoriia* (living history, 2015). *Istorik*, for example, targets individuals "who seek out conservative knowledge about the past and present."

The Orthodox Church Cashing the Check

Not everyone would agree with placing the Russian Orthodox Church in the same category as RVIO. Yet the intricate links leading all the way to the top bind religious and secular authorities in Russia firmly together. The mutually beneficial partnership between the church and the state extends to all aspects of life, including a choreographed perspective on history. Like elsewhere in Europe, in Russia the church is formally separated from the state. The Russian Orthodox Church had been decimated under Lenin and Stalin and continued to be persecuted throughout the Soviet period. In independent Russia, however, the church has steadily reclaimed its influence, especially since Vladimir Putin came to power. In return for loyalty, the Orthodox Church has been given the opportunity to impress so-called traditional values upon the Russian society. Those values include a particular understanding of Russian history.

The growing influence of the Orthodox Church under Putin can be gauged through simple statistics. Back in 1989, 75 percent of the population declared themselves areligious; two decades later 77 percent professed Orthodoxy. There are currently some sixty thousand Orthodox churches in Russia (1,200 in Moscow alone), one-half of them built in the past ten years. Patriarch Kirill (Vladimir Gundiaev) boasted that under his leadership three new houses of worship had gone up every 24 hours.[78] Sainthood is yet another subject for comparison. The Russian Orthodox Church proclaimed as saints a mere seven individuals during the two hundred years of the Russian Empire, as compared to the 1,776 between 1989 and 2017. For the average person, the Orthodox Church stands for a national idea that marries the Russian people and the greatness of Russia. Buttressed by the power of the state, the Russian Orthodox Church has also become a substitute for civic and cultural identity. The push for "traditional values" fits in the general pattern of collective nostalgia.[79]

Emboldened by its endowed status, the Orthodox Church has been siphoning state resources to no end. Since the passing of the 2010 federal law that enables religious organizations to reclaim property, the respective state agency has received over one thousand such requests, 90 percent of them from the Orthodox Church. In 2017, for example, the church got back ninety pieces of real estate. According to Dozhd TV channel, the patriarchate lays claim to some one thousand properties in Moscow alone.[80] A number of buildings confiscated from the church since 1918 had been repurposed to house cultural and historical institutions. One in Orenburg, for example, functions as the Yuri Gagarin Memorial Museum. Despite the fact that patriots of just any ideological tinge swear by the name of Gagarin, the Orthodox Church now wants to kick the museum out. "Gagarin should not have said that he had been up in space but saw no God," as someone put it in lieu of an argument.[81] Next on the list is the Andrei Rublev Museum of Ancient Russian Culture and Art in Moscow. The museum is part of the architectural complex of the Spaso-Andronnikov Monastery, which the church now wants for itself. The museum director fears for the future of his institution, though tactically agrees to work together with the church in search of a mutually acceptable solution.[82] In 2018, at least forty-seven organizations affiliated with the Russian Orthodox Church had received presidential grants, and that was just in the second round of applications.[83]

The Russian Orthodox Church has variously expressed its full support for the Putin regime and its policies. The symbiosis has flourished since the Pussy Riot affair of 2012, which may be regarded as a symbolic turning point in Russian cultural policymaking (on par with the mass political protests of December 2011). Members of the punk group were sentenced on charges of hooliganism, which neither the church nor state authorities found adequate. Consequently, the Duma in the summer of 2013 amended Article 148 of the penal code, "Violation of the Freedom of Faith and Conscience." The new amendment effectively introduced a new offense—public acts committed with the purpose of offending the religious sentiments of believers. The penalty also became more severe: up to three years of imprisonment.[84] As of the fall of 2017 a total of sixteen sentences under Article 148 had been meted out, none of them resulting in an acquittal.

According to Valery Otstavnykh, liberal-minded cleric who until 2013 worked in the Tula diocese, the Moscow patriarchate covertly assisted Russian intelligence operations in Ukraine in 2013–14. Church officials facilitated activities of the notorious leader of pro-Russian separatists and former security service operative, Igor Strelkov (Girkin), first in Kiev and later in Slaviansk. Girkin subsequently fell out with Putin, for which he was berated by Bishop Tikhon, then head of Sretensky Monastery and member of the Presidential Cultural Council. Bishop Tikhon has long acquired the unofficial status of Putin's spiritual confidant and mediator between the latter and Patriarch Kirill.[85] In public, however, Patriarch Kirill initially treaded with caution on Russia's policy on Crimea and Donbass, likely out of fear of losing control over the Moscow patriarchate parishes in Ukraine.[86]

Recently declassified documents of the former Latvian KGB reveal the names of several prominent church officials who had been recruited as agents. For example, the dean of the largest convent in Russia, Mother Sergia (Alexandra Konkova), goes by the name "Veronica" in the KGB documents.[87] An affinity between the Orthodox Church and the FSB was on display on December 20, 2018, celebrated in Russia as the Security Service Official Day. Head of the Novosibirsk diocese, Bishop Tikhon (not to be confused with his more famous namesake, currently the head of the Pskov diocese), stated in his address that teaching morality to the youth is within FSB's competence.[88]

Obscurantism associated with the church in the bygone centuries has made a comeback in contemporary Russia. Among its recent targets is German philosopher Immanuel Kant, who had maintained an uneasy presence in the Russian Kaliningrad enclave. On November 27, 2018, vandals doused Kant's grave, the monument, and the memorial plaque in his native Königsberg/Kaliningrad with pink paint. Anonymous leaflets strewn around the desecrated monument sent an unambiguous message:

> Students of the Baltic Federal University!
> Enough betraying the Motherland! You're studying between the walls that bear the name of an enemy! Use the Orthodox cross to erase the name of the German enemy, the nation that brought so much of misfortune upon us!
> Kant betrayed the Russian Soil, which had embraced him. Get rid of his vile name, demand that the administration denounce it!
> Tear down plaques, erase the alien name from documents!
> Show you're Russian and not some sorts of degenerates who have forsaken their Motherland!!!
> Shame on traitors! Shame on Kant! Long live Russia!

At first glance, the tenet of the message appears clear: compelling the university to strike off "Kant" from its official name. Still, the brazenness of the act is extraordinary given that Kant has been accepted as a sort of local hero (e.g., newlyweds in Kaliningrad traditionally bring flowers to the Kant grave, the honor earlier reserved for Lenin). That indicates that the perpetrators, self-styled as Orthodox patriots, possibly come from elsewhere. What is important here is the timing. The act of vandalism took place in the wake of a state-sponsored campaign to identify worthy individuals whose names would grace Russian airports. For Kaliningrad, Kant was in the lead in an online poll. Reflecting on the preliminary poll results, a certain Duma deputy for Tatarstan argued that bestowing the name of Kant might offend the war veterans. As if coincidentally, a few days after the incident, Russian Empress Elizabeth overtook Kant in the poll.[89] It happened not without the interference of the Baltic Navy leadership, which appealed to the sailors and their relatives to vote against Kant. For the occasion, the German philosopher was labeled a "foreigner and traitor to the Motherland . . . whose books no one bothers to read." Instead of Kant, a vice admiral suggested the rank-and-file vote for a Soviet military commander who had led the East Prussian Operation in 1945.[90] Meanwhile a university student who intended to organize a picket in support of Kant's monument received summons from the local antiterrorism office.[91]

And yet there is more to it. A few days prior to the act of vandalism, Patriarch Kirill delivered a sermon at Kaliningrad. The sermon questioned how one could distinguish those dear to us. Subsequently, Kirill also called on his flock to strengthen public solidarity, like in the times of the Great Patriotic War. Lashing out against Kant and his name was one of the ways the faithful carried through the patriarch's message.[92] After the incident with Kant, just any historical figure runs the risk of being labeled a "traitor" in Russia.

The recent trend is to emphasize the role of the Russian Orthodox Church in boosting the morale of the Soviet troops during the Second World War. RVIO's exhibition, *War and Myths*, in 2016, featured a relevant section.[93] Three years later, the Central Museum of the Great Patriotic War in Moscow held a semi-academic conference, "The Russian Orthodox Church in the Great Patriotic War: The Experience of Patriotic Work Then and Now." The conference was co-organized by the ministry of defense.[94] The clergy get involved in all major state-sponsored projects, for example, the search movement (that works to identify and bury the remains of the Soviet soldiers killed in combat). Their contribution is superfluous: a Sretensky Monastery monk was in June of 2019 telling the volunteers about family values and the moral foundation of the search movement.[95] RVIO's Miagkov often reminds people of cross necklaces belonging to soldiers killed and subsequently unearthed from the former battlefields. He takes it as a proof that the Christian faith had helped the Soviet Union to victory. The Orthodox Church is all too happy to endorse this thesis. The head of the Belgorod diocese went the furthest when in June 2019 he stated that the victory was secured by the believers, while the rest perished. Death in combat was the price they paid for being atheist, he insinuated.[96]

Recently, the Russian Orthodox Church has acquired yet another powerful ally in the government. Olga Vasilieva, minister of education and science between August 2016 and January 2020, shares Medinskii's conception of history. She also happens to be a historian. In 1990 the future minister defended a dissertation "The Soviet State and Patriotic Activities of the Russian Orthodox Church during the Great Patriotic War" at the Institute of History of the USSR. Eight years later, she produced a second doctoral dissertation on a related subject, "The Russian Orthodox Church in Politics of the Soviet State, 1943–1948." While working as a historian of religion, Vasilieva also studied international relations at the Diplomatic Academy of the Russian foreign ministry. In 2012 she joined the government as deputy director in the department of culture and in 2014 served on the committee under the auspices of the ministry of education that prepared a curriculum in Russian history.

Vasilieva's appointment was facilitated through her long-term association with Bishop Tikhon. Back in 2001, the cleric invited her to teach a class at Sretensky theological seminary he was heading; Vasilieva regards Tikhon as an embodiment of the Orthodox priesthood. As a member of the United Russia Party, she gave internal seminars on conservatism.[97] She is also credited for her work on patriotic education.[98] The Orthodox Church predicted that Vasilieva's promotion would make the interaction between the state and the church smoother.[99] Vasilieva met the expectations invested in her by expanding religious education in school. She believes the study of theology—which she regards a scientific discipline—strengthens moral foundations.

Bishop Tikhon, the Future Patriarch and His History Theme Park

Bishop Tikhon (Georgy Shevkunov) has positioned himself as the chief religious ideologist, and in return was effectively given the monopoly on the interpretation of history by the church.[100] Born in 1958 in Moscow, Tikhon made a quick ascent in the church hierarchy in independent Russia. Casting away his degree in screenwriting, Shevkunov entered the Pskov-Pechory Monastery of the Caves as a novice in the 1980s. Not only is Pskov diocese one of the richest, but it is also regarded as the birthplace of the critical concept of Moscow as the Third Rome, in the seventeenth century. In 1995, Father Tikhon was appointed head of the Sretensky Monastery in Moscow. A year later, Vladimir Putin, who had just moved to Moscow as part of the Yeltsin administration, was introduced to Tikhon. Since then the cleric has regularly visited Putin's dacha, including on religious holidays. Putin meanwhile developed a liking for the Sretensky choir. The monastery, it should be noted, is situated not far from the FSB headquarters on Lubyanka Square, and hence boasts a number of former and current high-ranking FSB officers among its flock. As Tikhon once explained to a certain intelligence general and member of the Communist Party for fifty years, by embracing Orthodoxy all his sins would be forgiven. Although Tikhon has denied the consistent rumor of serving as Putin's spiritual leader, his influence on the president is unmistakable. Whether it is the preference for Alexander III in the pantheon of Russian tsars or the philosophy of Ivan Ilyin who had sketched a historical mission for Russia, Tikhon found ways to bond with Putin. He also subscribes to the latter's 2005 dictum of the "collapse of the Soviet Union as the greatest geopolitical catastrophe of the twentieth century" when arguing that "all the Russian people know doing is building empires." Thereby Father Tikhon blessed the syncretic view on Russian history that reconciles Orthodoxy and Bolshevism.[101]

Tikhon is widely credited with creating a multimedia exhibition, "Russia: My History," which from its humble beginning in 2013 is on the verge of becoming a compulsory means of education. The original series of exhibitions, dedicated to the Russian ruling dynasties, and later the 1914–45 period, had gone on display in the Manezh exhibition hall in Moscow. President Putin thought highly of the display and suggested it find a permanent home. The permanent version, which covers all of Russian history, opened in December 2015 in the VDNKh exhibition grounds, also in Moscow. The opening ceremony was attended by Patriarch Kirill, Bishop Tikhon, Moscow mayor Sergei Sobianin, and Minister of Culture Vladimir Medinskii. In his address, Kirill spoke of history as the cornerstone of the national idea.[102] Kirill stated that the state cannot exist outside of the national idea built around a heroic past, which he believes cannot be formulated in the quiet of an office.[103]

The following year a decision was made to build eighteen replicas of the theme park across Russia. In a record two years, fifteen enormous exhibitions—typically in purpose-built hangar-type buildings—were in place, from Yakutsk in Siberia to Makhachkala in the North Caucasus.[104] Some governors decided to wait it out while others, in anticipation of potential dividends, rushed to implement the project locally. It did not go without a scandal. In Tiumen, for example, a local art museum was hastily ordered to vacate its premises to give way for Bishop Tikhon's creation. As a result, the precious collection of Russian religious art was moved when the temperature in that Siberian city had dipped to minus 30 degrees Celsius. If only the patriarchate in Moscow could have seen the appalling conditions in which ancient Orthodox icons were temporarily stored at Tiumen![105]

The sheer size of the exhibition, which contains over three hundred pieces of electronic equipment and takes up forty-plus rooms, dwarfs anything that has previously been seen in Russia in terms of museums. The standard format is occasionally augmented to reflect local specificity. The theme park in Kazan, for example, features additional displays on the history of the Golden Horde, the Kazan Khanate, and subsequently the Republic of Tatarstan. The theme parks are bankrolled by Gazprom, which spent a chunk of its 26-billion-ruble charity fund on "Russia: My History."[106] The work on the exhibition was coordinated by the Patriarchate Cultural Council and Humanitarian Project Foundation headed by Tikhon. A total of one thousand people prepared the flagship exhibition in Moscow that features the latest in technology: video projections, holograms, touchscreens, 3D computer graphics, top light and sound equipment.

According to the official information, scholars from the Academy of Sciences, Moscow State University, and Russian State University for the Humanities participated in writing the exhibition texts. In fact, the texts were mainly composed by two individuals, Alexander Miasnikov and Pavel Kuzenkov. Miasnikov is a philologist, journalist, and book editor from St. Petersburg and Kuzenkov, a historian with a degree from the Russian Orthodox University in Moscow. In the early 2010s Kuzenkov taught at the Sretensky theological seminary where Bishop Tikhon was serving as dean. Since then he has dissociated himself from the "Russia: My History" project, calling it a "striking example of history used in lieu of political propaganda." Facing a backlash from the Russian academic community, back in 2015 Bishop Tikhon ran draft texts with professional historians from the Academy of Sciences. The latter concluded that the texts had been written by dilettantes and had a strong ideological tilt. Consequently, nearly all entries had to be redone. In spite of a tentative agreement to swap texts, eventually Tikhon decided to retain the originals. Miasnikov denies any bias in the exhibition, claiming the authors had only provided facts, which the audience is free to interpret.[107]

A survey of social media indicates an exceptionally high satisfaction rate among visitors. Some state they leave the exhibition as proud citizens of their country—exactly as intended by the organizers. Many visitors say the exhibition helped them brush up on Russian history, while a few claim they also learned new things such as the Europeans having deliberately tainted the image of Ivan the Terrible. Patrons get with them the idea that Russia had experienced spiritual destruction twice in the short twentieth century, at the hands of the Bolsheviks and the liberals. Visitors do not spare superlatives when describing the exhibition: "beautiful history," "uplifting patriotism," "a great visit for whole family," "cool format," a "breath of fresh air," "overwhelmed with emotions," "perhaps the best history museum in Europe." However, the curators of the exhibition may be most pleased with the kind of response shared by a high school history teacher: "I bow to the organizers in the name of Russian educators. You help us bring up the future generations!"[108]

Popular criticism is typically limited to technicalities: the sheer amount of material to process, tedious presentation, lack of artefacts, cacophony, bright lighting, ticket price, and overcrowding (maximum capacity: five thousand). A more pointed, and therefore rare, criticism concerns the explicit Orthodox Church perspective on Russian history (e.g., the scorn reserved for pagan Slavs; as much exhibition space dedicated to the clergy victimized in the 1920s and 1930s as to the Second World War). The enormous resources poured into the exhibition do not balance out the obvious lack of historical and museological expertise on the part of the organizers. Visitors find the presentation level most suitable for secondary school students. Yet, modern, gadget-obsessed kids easily get overwhelmed by the extent of information on display. On average, visitors spend between two and four hours in a single gallery, which means they barely manage to cover one-third of the exhibition.[109] The exhibition's creative team, under the auspices of Bishop Tikhon, literally hung a book on the wall (i.e., a textbook on the touchscreen). In spite of its outward appearance, the exhibition is predictably conservative, indeed archaic. Some visitors remark that, after all, the information presented in "Russia: My History" is widely available on the internet, or else in a school history curriculum. As far as the Orthodox Church is concerned, "Russia: My History" theme park has been a triumph: in 2017 the ministry of education recommended incorporating it into both extracurricular activities for college students and a training program for history school teachers.

Flooded with information, only the most erudite and inquisitive among visitors are able to pick up on the exhibition's agenda, skewed interpretations, and stupendous factual mistakes. Having examined the exhibition's contents, the VIO in December 2017 filed a compalint with the ministry of education and science, with a copy sent to Bishop Tikhon. VIO maintains that the proposal to use the exhibition in the school curriculum violates the principle of separation between state and church, and thus may negatively affect the collective perception of history. Among specific problems, professional historians identified falsely attributed, or even forged, quotations (e.g., Otto von Bismarck, Margaret Thatcher, Bill Clinton); superimposing contemporary political discourse on historical events (e.g., "information war" waged against Ivan the Terrible in the sixteenth century, Dekabrists working for foreign intelligence services); outright falsifications (e.g., masonic conspiracy as one of the causes of the Bolshevik Revolution); selective use of sources (e.g., quoting the head of the KGB in relating the story of political repression in the Soviet Union); notable lacunae (e.g., the so-called Pale of Jewish Settlement); misspelled names; wrong dates; and so on. As members of VIO were able to establish, one of the major sources used in the creation of the exhibition was Wikipedia. More generally, VIO argued that the exhibition celebrated each and every tsar, without ever approaching history from bottom up. VIO called upon the ministry to subject the exhibition to a professional expertise, not unlike that routinely carried out in the case of textbooks.[110]

Bishop Tikhon acknowledged a few mistakes regarding quotations but otherwise found the complaint "odd," on the grounds that the history park is extremely popular wherever in Russia its replica is being built.[111] Tikhon received support, among others, from the director of the Institute of Russian History of the Academy of Sciences Yuri Petrov, the president of the Russian State University for the Humanities Alexander Bezborodov, and the president of the Moscow Pedagogical State University Alexei Lubkov. Bezborodov and Lubkov deemed the exhibition a "serious civilizational project" and an "innovative opportunity for the creation of a transnational historical narrative."[112] Ekaterina Klimenko, who is writing her doctoral thesis on "Russia: My History," has identified the purpose of the exhibition differently: political expedience. The exhibition paints Russian history as an organic bond between the state and its subjects. The state is strong when the people rally behind it, but gets weakened and is consequently attacked by the enemy as a result of internal discord. The Russians are presented as wise people who stand by their leader. Such strongmen as Ivan the Terrible and Stalin come across as complex personalities, whereas state consolidation trumps the policy of mass repression they had instituted.[113] Indeed, Tikhon's pet project keeps spewing historical revisionism. In January 2019 some visitors to the flagship exhibition in Moscow noticed that a few key dates in recent Russian history had been plastered over on the banners. Those dates include the Kursk submarine disaster (2000), the Moscow theater hostage crisis (2002), the Beslan school siege (2004), and the Russo–Georgian military conflict (2008).[114]

The tenet of Kirill's speech at the opening of the latest in the series of exhibitions at Manezh, "The Orthodox Russia, 1914–1945: From Great Upheavals to the Great Victory," in November 2015 can be formulated in a single sentence: "The achievements of any state leader who stood behind the revival and modernization of the country cannot be questioned even if he occasionally committed evil deeds [*otmechen zlodeistviiami*]."[115] Although Kirill was referring to Stalin, unequivocal legitimization of state power also extended to Putin, who shared the podium with the patriarch. This and the more ambitious "Russia: My History" exhibition effectively serve a single purpose—to sanctify state authorities (and by default the cozy relationship between the latter and the church).[116] According to St. Petersburg historian Daniil Kotsiubinskii, the entire project gives validity to an anti-humanist, ideocratic, conspiratorial view on history and historical memory (e.g., pro-democracy protests in Russia in 2011–12 placed in the category of "color revolutions"). In effect, it is a means of propaganda grounded in the "organic" link between monarchy, Orthodox Church, and populism, as had been elaborated in nineteenth-century Russia. Adrian Selin of Higher School of Economics at St. Petersburg is concerned about the popular use of the word *museum* with regard to Bishop Tikhon's project—as it was advertised on a fixed-route cab in downtown St. Petersburg, for example—which effectively boosts its legitimacy.[117]

The publicity that Bishop Tikhon received on account of the "Russia: My History" theme park helped him eventually emerge from the shadows. Posing as the champion of historical justice, he made a series of high-profile statements in 2017. Not all of Tikhon's statements may be considered successful PR. Neither does he always get his way when interacting with other Putin vassals. Although Medinskii had heaped praise on Bishop Tikhon as the "minister of culture of the Russian Orthodox Church and one of the most profound and best-educated people," the latter had effectively failed to convince the former to ban the feature film *Matilda*, which he described as "vulgar." It was Tikhon's sermon a day earlier that motivated a fanatic to drive a minivan loaded with gas cylinders into a movie theater in Ekaterinburg that was set to show *Matilda* (for details see Chapter 4). To *Matilda* Tikhon prefers *Viking*—a brutal biopic of questionable quality telling the story of Prince Vladimir who had brought Christianity to Russia. According to Tikhon, *Matilda* does not do justice to historical facts, while the *Viking* shows the "bitter truth of history."[118]

Catering to the fundamentalist fringe within the Orthodox Church, Tikhon, in November 2017, reopened the discussion on whether the execution of the last Russian tsar and his family at Ekaterinburg in July 1918 qualifies as ritual murder. Remarkably, these kinds of speculations had been put to rest already in the 1990s, when both the state and a synodic commission rendered a negative verdict. Nevertheless, Tikhon's evocations found a receptive ear in the Russian Investigative Committee, which set out to establish a psychologic-historical expertise (whatever that is supposed to mean).[119] As to the reason why, some commentators point out to the latent antisemitism of the committee's director, Alexander Bastyrkin.[120] Naturally, the revival of blood libel—and that is what it essentially amounts to—did not bode well with Jews. The head of the Federation of Jewish Communities of Russia, Alexander Boroda, expressed his disappointment with the decision to go ahead with the investigation of ritual murder. Good at rhetoric, Bishop Tikhon interjected that he never used the word *Jewish* and that he is merely interested in establishing the symbolism of regicide.[121]

Though, by other accounts, resuscitating allegations of ritual murder was a calculated move on the part of Tikhon and the patriarchate, which thus sought to reassert its influence. Still, it remained unclear what sort of lesson the state would draw from this entire affair. The fact that President Putin decided to attend, for the first time ever, the Bishops' Council, had no bearing on a ruling on the tsar's remains that it was expected to issue. Putin's announcement was likely just a political stunt in the run-up to the 2018 presidential elections.[122] It could actually be counterproductive, given Putin's overtures to the Jews in both Russia and Israel (see Chapter 6).

So much was Bishop Tikhon in the news in 2017 that it earned him the informal status of "person of the year." As compared with other recognizable, and thus humdrum, personalities in the church hierarchy, Bishop Tikhon began to eclipse even Patriarch Kirill.[123] In May 2018 Tikhon was appointed chief of the Pskov diocese, which was interpreted as either a form of exile or a path to the top. Within the context of church history, the trajectory from bishop to metropolitan in a mere two and a half years is in and of itself remarkable. Formally, after five years of service, Tikhon would be eligible to assume the position of patriarch of the Russian Orthodox Church, had Kirill decided to vacate it for whatever reason. Tikhon, who had not publicly denied his ambition to eventually become the leader of the church, is now less rigidly subordinated to Kirill,

Figure 2 Obscurantism on the march. Bishop Tikhon (Georgy Shevkunov, b. 1958) has an ambition to become a new head of the Russian Orthodox Church. The influential cleric has contributed, perhaps more than anyone else, to popularization of a syncretic version of Russian history by means of his "Russia: My History" theme park. In 2018 he resuscitated a classic antisemitic trope of blood libel in connection with the murder of the tsarist family one hundred years earlier.

and thus can more freely express himself on the "historical tradition of the state" promoted by Putin.[124]

Much like Putin's statements on issues of history, the Orthodox Church appears ambivalent on rendering judgment on tyrants in Russian/Soviet history. One of the calendars for 2014 produced by the publishing house of the Moscow Patriarchate was devoted to Stalin. Featuring pictures and excerpts from Stalin's biography, the calendar was described as an "excellent gift for war veterans and history buffs."[125] The patriarchate's production line at Sofrino near Moscow features Stalin's portraits, thanks to the factory's director, who believes that the Great Leader had liberated Russia from the Jewish yoke.[126] The Imperial Orthodox Palestine Society, a quasi-nongovernmental organization that works hand in glove with the Orthodox Church in advancing Russia's geopolitical goals, is also marred by neo-Stalinism. The head of the organization is Sergei Stepashin—former director of the FSB, former minister of justice, and former minister of the interior. His deputy, church historian Nikolai Lisovoi, has argued that Stalin's industrialization, pushing back Nazi Germany, and building nuclear deterrence could not have happened in Russia "without God's grace." As to the organization itself, it strives to defend Russia's interests in the Middle East by boasting its "historical presence in the region." The society was recently involved in a scandal that led to the expulsion of two Russian diplomats from Greece.[127] The ambivalence toward Stalin is altogether on the wane. Otherwise, the Orthodox Church would not have built a chapel next to the restored busts of Lenin and Stalin in Amga, Republic of Sakha (Yakutia).

While the Orthodox Church appears to have no problem with public utterances or commercial publications dedicated to Stalin, calls for his canonization is an entirely different matter. Back in 2008, a priest in one of St. Petersburg's suburban churches who claimed that Stalin was a deeply religious person, displayed an icon that featured the dictator standing alongside the recently canonized Matrona of Moscow. The reaction was swift: the St. Petersburg diocese condemned the icon and dismissed the offending priest. In May 2015, news channels reported on yet another icon depicting Stalin, proudly displayed at a former battlefield in Belgorod district. The painting was carried, and subsequently commented on, by prominent nationalist writer and publicist, Alexander Prokhanov. Surrounded by senior military staff, Stalin appears in the picture right under the image of Mother Mary. According to Prokhanov, the icon symbolizes state authorities and the victory of light over darkness. More explicitly than Patriarch Kirill, Prokhanov relieves Stalin of accountability for mass terror on account of the dictator winning the war and saving the nation. The painting was commissioned by the ultraconservative Izborsk Club, where Prokhanov rubs shoulders with the likes of ideologist Alexander Dugin and chairman of the Anti-Maidan movement Nikolai Starikov. The local diocese distanced itself from the event on the grounds that Stalin had not been canonized and that he persecuted the church.[128] An even stronger rebuttal was issued the following month by yet another diocese, which condemned the attempt at de-Stalinization as a deliberate provocation.[129]

The opposite of Stalin's glorification is the commemoration of millions of his victims. As compared with the early 1990s, when the Orthodox clergy played a prominent role in the reburial ceremonies of the executed during the Great Terror at places like Butovo, in the recent decade the church's presence at commemorative events has become noticeably less visible. As a rule, churchmen formally attend such events when representatives of the state do. For instance, the "Restoring the Names" ceremony at the Solovetsky Stone memorial in Moscow on October 29, 2017—held annually under the aegis of Memorial since 2007—has never seen one. Yet, at the opening ceremony of the Wall of Grief monument the very next day, Patriarch Kirill appeared alongside President Putin.[130]

Besides public statements and appearances, the Orthodox Church has indirectly expressed its position on the commemoration of Stalin's victims in the way it approaches former sites of terror. Nowhere has this been most visible than on Solovetsky Islands (also known as Solovki) in the White Sea. Founded in the fifteenth century, the Solovetsky Monastery is one of the finest examples of church architecture in Russia. Besides its illustrious history as a house of God, the monastery has also achieved dubious fame in a pioneer project that came to be known as Gulag. The first ever permanent forced labor camp in the Soviet Union was established under Lenin in 1920 on the monastery's premises. The camp initially hosted political prisoners but gradually was turned into a self-sufficient economic enterprise—the model subsequently expanded to the entire Soviet forced labor camp system. Many a well-known Russian intellectual, politician, and churchman ended up prisoner at Solovetsky camp.[131]

After the Orthodox Church took over the functions that had until then belonged to the museum, it began to consistently purge physical references to the history of the Solovetsky Islands as a site of terror. All wall inscriptions made by prisoners had been chiseled off, cell grates and peepholes removed, and a former execution site was turned into a fun stop for newlyweds. Simultaneously, the new-old owners have been trying to limit access to the Solovetsky Islands to all but believers.[132] In 2017 a group of Solovetsky dwellers formally denounced a recent book by historian Yuri Brodsky as potentially damaging to the "religious sentiments of the believers." Brodsky has acquired a unique expertise in the history of the Solovetsky Islands that he has been studying for some forty years. Allegedly, Brodsky in his study presented a pejorative collective image of Solovetsky monks and thus tainted the reputation of the Solovetsky Monastery and of the Orthodox Church as a whole.[133] Worse still, the claimants urged that Brodsky's book be checked for extremism. Brodsky believes that the wrath of the Orthodox Church was primarily caused by his revelation that in the early days of the Solovetsky camp, authorities coopted over a hundred former monks into the camp administration, as well as by his claim that the late Patriarch Alexy II was a KGB informant.[134]

Just as President Putin had expanded Russia's influence abroad, so had the Orthodox Church its views on the past. In his traditional televised Christmas address, on January 7, 2018, Patriarch Kirill endorsed the Russian bombing campaign in Syria. Russia, said the top cleric, helped to prevent the genocide of Christians in the Middle East.[135] In early March 2018, the leader of the Russian Orthodox Church took part in the commemoration of the liberation of Bulgaria from the Ottoman rule 140 years ago. In his speech, President Rumen Radev of Bulgaria paid respect to the Russian army and to all of the many ethnicities serving within its ranks that helped liberate the country from the Turks. Patriarch Kirill lashed out at the host, stating that Russia alone has the honors, not Poland or Lithuania (which were constituent parts of the empire at the time). "We [stand] for the historical truth, which we had won by our own blood," continued Kirill, "the truth cannot be silenced or misinterpreted for whatever political or pragmatic reasons." That outburst is even more remarkable, given that Radev spoke in front of the monument to Russian tsar Alexander II in Sofia, while the presidents of Finland and Poland were not among the invited guests.[136] The patriarch's history lesson did not sit well with the Bulgarians, unsurprisingly. The vice prime minister went on the national television to berate Kirill for his luxurious lifestyle and the fortunes that he had earned for the church in the 1990s from a duty-free import of cigarettes, while working part-time for the KGB.[137] Condemned by the host nation, Patriarch Kirill received support from different quarters at home, including the Night Wolves biker club. In fact, members of the club were a part of the official Russian delegation to the festivities.

Patriotic Bikers Making History

When biologist Igor Dorogoi was indicted under Article 354.1 in February 2018, among the evidence allegedly attesting to his "glorification of Nazism" was a caustic caption he had added to a photo taken at the Immortal Regiment march. He called it the "march of the junk," in reference to Night Wolves carrying a portrait of Lavrenty Beria, the dreaded head of the NKVD.[138] Night Wolves is formally registered as an "autonomous youth NGO," even though its core is composed of men in their forties. Like all other "patriotic" entities in Russia, the Night Wolves and their leader, Alexander Zaldostanov, who goes by the nickname "The Surgeon," cannot claim a stellar reputation. Artemy Troitsky has recalled Zaldostanov (b. 1964) and his fellow bikers in the late 1980s and early 1990s sporting American and Confederate flags and engaging in petty crime. A particular source of pride for Zaldostanov, according to Troitsky, was his West German wife. An adoration of all things Western at some point turned into hatred.[139]

Bikers have traditionally been outlaws with a pronounced anarchist ethos (the most famous and biggest of them is Hells Angels). The Night Wolves, on the other hand, is primarily known for its close links to the Russian government and, personally, to Vladimir Putin. The Night Wolves first shot to fame in 2010, when the then prime minister Putin was filmed riding along with the bikers in Ukrainian Crimea, a feat he repeated in subsequent years. Why an alliance between Putin, a former KGB officer, and Zaldostanov, a representative of what in the heyday of Perestroika was deemed a counterculture? Outwardly, posing alongside bikers seems like yet another of Putin's photo ops—an opportunity to advance his macho image of a strongman. There is more to this, however, as Mark Galeotti has explained. Putin first met Zaldostanov in 2009, while the latter was organizing a biker festival in Sevastopol. Before Putin openly did so, Zaldostanov advocated the "reunification" of Crimea with Russia. The neo-Orthodox, anti-Western, militant type of nationalism professed by Zaldostanov and his men fit the Russian government's agenda perfectly. Besides, as Galeotti points out, the Night Wolves is an asset in keeping in check groups that are similar, yet genuinely independent and thus potentially hostile to the regime.[140] Back in 2011, Putin made an appearance at a biker festival in Novorossiysk, just across from Crimea. In his speech, Putin praised the Night Wolves for helping promote patriotism and "historical memory." By historical memory he meant the heroic deeds of the Soviet soldiers who fought against Nazi Germany—the backbone of Great Russia.[141] Putin was the one who proposed this theme for the biker festival to Zaldostanov.[142] Putin and Zaldostanov share the same opinion of the role of Stalin in Soviet history: the Soviet victory over Nazi Germany eclipses the mass deportations and the Gulag.[143]

The Night Wolves exercise a particular function by inserting an element of entertainment into Russian historymaking. They position themselves in the heroic template of the Great Patriotic War as a new generation of the defenders of the motherland. The projected generational continuity, however, is typically expressed as a threat: "Banderite, I'll chop your head off for granddad" (*Banderovets, za deda, zagryzu!*).[144] In 2013, Putin personally decorated the Surgeon with a state honor after the group helped restore a Stalin-era fountain in Volgograd. In the midst of the Russian takeover of Crimea, Zaldostanov showed up in the regional capital Simferopol where he spoke of a "fascist" danger and the resolve to defend the rights of the Russian speakers. Wherever the Night Wolves tread is Russia, he declared. Subsequently the Night Wolves joined the notorious "green men" in patrolling the streets of Crimea.[145] It was also Zaldostanov's men who erected the very first barricade in Luhansk in Donbass a while later.[146] The leader of the Night Wolves then proposed resuscitating Kievan

Rus with the capital in either Sevastopol or Kiev.[147] Consequently, the United States, Canada, and a number of EU states put Zaldostanov on the sanction list for his role in "destabilizing the situation in Ukraine and the annexation of Crimea." Taking the news as a badge of honor, in January 2015 he cofounded a pro-Kremlin Anti-Maidan movement. The next month, Zaldostanov, in his trademark custom-made bear-leather jacket, joined the Crimean administration and the speaker of the Russian Duma in unveiling a monument commemorating the 1945 Yalta Conference. Often referred to as the "Yalta betrayal" during the Cold War but enunciated by Putin at the United Nations General Assembly as the "cornerstone of the postwar world order," the tripartite summit effectively sanctioned Soviet expansion in Eastern Europe. Until recently, the two-meter tall figure of Stalin (sitting alongside Roosevelt and Churchill) was the only monument to the Soviet dictator sponsored by the Russian state (see Chapter 5).

Since then, the Night Wolves have firmly established their presence in Russian history politics. The biker club of some five thousand, including Chechen strongman Ramzan Kadyrov and his sidekick Magomed Daudov (the wolf is regarded as the symbol of the Chechen nation), resorts to performance art to fashion an eclectic version of the Soviet past. Not surprisingly, their main means of expression is the motorcycle— the American Harley Davidson, for those who can afford it, that is. As if to address this contradiction, the club's division, Wolf Engineering, built its own bike model based on the Soviet Ural, which they christened *Stalinets* (Stalinite is just a prototype, though, not slated for mass production).[148]

The flags emblazoned with Stalin, and the wartime chant "For victory, for Stalin!" accompany the Night Wolves' provocative stunt that generated extensive foreign coverage. In April–May 2015, and every consecutive year, the club organized a bike ride to Berlin. According to the organizers, they pay tribute to the Second World War dead by visiting Soviet war cemeteries along their route. The Polish and German authorities were caught flatfooted in trying to negotiate between their instinctive desire to bar entry to nationalist bikers and the international norms regulating border crossing. From the perspective of Russian propaganda, however, this was secondary: the Night Wolves were mainly playing to the domestic audiences. In fact, the majority of the fifty-odd bikers that annually make it to Treptower Park in Berlin in 2015 come from countries other than Russia; some of them retain their Russian citizenship while others do not.[149] Unveiled in 1949 and featuring quotations from Stalin, the Soviet War Memorial in Treptower Park and the annual ceremony that takes place there is remarkable in its own right. It is, indeed, a unique example of a victory celebration by the winning country in the territory of the defeated country (imagine Hells Angels converging on Tokyo for a similar celebration!). The Night Wolves' ride to Berlin in 2018 was cosponsored by RVIO. As far as RVIO is concerned, the biker ride alerts the people of Russia and Europe to the attempted falsification of the history of the Great Patriotic War and simultaneously forms a positive image of Russian history.[150] In 2019, the sponsor list got expanded on account of the Central Museum of the Great Patriotic War in Moscow and the ministry of foreign affairs.

A Night Wolves Kaliningrad chapter has modified the concept of a ride onto Berlin to fit the local context. Each biker is joined by a Russian Orthodox priest holding a banner. The biker-priest duos then crisscross the Russian enclave to visit all the international border crossings, accompanied by a religious ceremony.[151] The idea of patriotic, observant bikers has permutated into one of patriotic Orthodox priests who also happened to be bikers. Such a group apparently exists in St. Petersburg, and it also contributes to patriotic education. Group members regularly receive invitations from local schools to be part of the major celebrations and so-called lessons in courage. According to a schoolteacher, kids find it cool seeing the priests arriving on their bikes and even help the latter prepare for their bike rides. Even better, many a priest is a former serviceman. As regards patriotism, the priests perform religious ceremonies on the graves of the fallen Soviet soldiers and promote the Day of St. Peter and Fevronia (July 8)—introduced in 2008 as the Day of Family, Love, and Faithfulness—an antidote to the Western Valentine's Day.[152]

These and similar anecdotes attest to a cozy relationship with the Russian Orthodox Church that the bikers, and personally Zaldostanov, have enjoyed. The first ever Night Wolves biker festival at Sevastopol received a blessing from Patriarch Kirill, to whom Zaldostanov sends birthday wishes each year. The club's twenty-eighth anniversary was celebrated in Moscow on May 31, 2018, with fireworks, drumbeats, and motorcycle stunts. The cherry on the cake, at midnight a group of some five hundred riders were allowed into the Cathedral of Christ the Savior, where they paid respect to St. Nicholas's relics on loan from Bari, Italy.[153] (Imagine Hells Angels getting an exclusive midnight audience at St. Peter's Basilica in the Vatican!)

The Night Wolves, in the face of their leader, regularly sing accolades to the leaders of Chechnya, Abkhazia, South Ossetia, Transnistria, Crimea, Donetsk People's Republic, and Republika Srpska, and occasionally receive decorations from Putin's hands.[154] Zaldostanov often gets, and proudly advertises, invitations to attend formal gatherings under the patronage of the FSB and the ministry of defense. He was also among the invited guests at Putin's (fourth) inauguration as Russia's president in May 2018. Among the Night Wolves' well-wishers are Duma members Vladimir Zhirinovsky and Irina Yarovaia; among the places travelled a Russian air base in Syria. When asked about a Russian opposition leader Alexei Navalny and his corruption investigation, Zaldostanov replied that he thinks it is a smokescreen and that he otherwise associates Navalny with the kind of people who brought the Soviet Union to ruin.[155]

Quid pro quo, since 2013 the Night Wolves have received over 80 million rubles in presidential grants, more recently 3 million for the project "Slavic World" and 9 million for organizing Christmas tree fests for children. According to the grant application, bike and car rides and pilgrimages have the purpose of "uniting brotherly Slavic peoples through popular diplomacy." As for the Christmas tree fest, it would "explain to children the historical and spiritual heritage of Russia and Russia's challenges in a clear, fairytale manner." The fairytale, as understood and executed by the Night Wolves, is populated by grotesque characters loosely painted after Nazis who fight it out with the forces of good—all on wheels—presided over by St. George and the Soviet-style Grandfather Frost. According to Zaldostanov, the show blends history and myth in order to "save the country."[156] Even the adults in the audience find the evil entourage frightening: "We'll pay in bucks to get your strength—to conquer the Russian lands and populate it with bastards."[157] The "infernal Christmas tree"—as it was once advertised on the club's webpage—is typically sold out.

What in 1989 began as the Soviet Union's first ever biker club has by now become a highly centralized quasi-paramilitary force with substantial business interests. Zaldostanov has since long rewritten the Night Wolves charter, installing himself as the club's permanent president. The club has chapters in nearly all the bigger Russian cities while its business entity has offices in over one hundred of them. Several thousand among its members have a firearms license. Care to organize a fest in Moscow?—call the Night Wolves, who also supply fuel to the federal construction agency (Spetsstroi) and provide security services for the defense ministry.[158]

Even today, the major arena for the Night Wolves remains the annual biker festival, which they have been organizing since 1995. Zaldostanov endows Sevastopol—the site of the show since 2009—with the same meaning that Stalingrad had back in 1943. The enormous coverage that the state media gives to the biker festival in Crimea has turned it into one of the major and most anticipated cultural events in Russia.

The 2014 biker show, "The Return," projected a Russian propaganda narrative of the events in Ukraine, albeit in a grotesque, theatrical form.[159] The 2015 edition, "Forging Victory," served another dose of maddening eclectics, portraying the Soviet military triumph over Nazi Germany as God's will. According to a Night Wolves press release, the show proves that "Victory is Christ." Playing himself, Zaldostanov appeared on the stage and shared with the audience that the "great Stalin and the Soviet people emerged victorious in that terrible, religious war and thus barred hell from earth." He described the Soviet Union as a "giant red monastery" and the major urban centers as the twelve cities-apostles blessed by "God's mother Moscow" (one of the apostles, Kiev, proved to be Judas).[160] At a press conference, Zaldostanov spoke of a psychological warfare allegedly waged by the West against Russia. He regards himself a soldier, and "Forging Victory" his counteroffensive in that war.[161] The 2016 edition, "The Fifth Empire," pitched a "morally corrupt" West against a "strong-in spirit" Russia in a dystopian setting worthy of a *Mad Max* movie. As the name of the show suggests, the Night Wolves and their leader celebrate the ascent of Putin's Russia, which they regard as the heir to the fourth and mightiest reincarnation of the holy empire, that is, Stalin's Soviet Union.[162] One episode in the biker show, accompanied by Georgy Sviridov's suite "Time, Forward!" was lifted from the closing ceremony of the Winter Olympic Games at Sochi the previous year. Indeed, with one thousand participants, Zaldostanov compared the scale of the biker show to that of the Olympics.[163]

Zaldostanov has explained the concept of the show as follows:

> I give people what they want, I share the idea that I've run through myself. This is a rebuttal to the enemies of Russia and the humiliation to which they subject our country by discrediting our victory.... This is an extension of our ride onto Berlin. Consider all the hatred toward those who don't want to forget the Great Patriotic War, our victory, our heroes, our traditions.... Not a play or a reconstruction, this is the history of the war as I and the Night Wolves see it.

Zaldostanov believes that all those who have seen the show, including a handful of foreigners, will take back with them a sense of Russian "affability [*radusheie*], a part of the Russian soul."[164]

The Night Wolves' vision of Russian history is conspicuously close to that advocated by the Putin regime. The similarity does not end there. Zaldostanov borrowed the name of the 2017 biker show and now feature film, "Russian Reactor," from Alexander Prokhanov. As if it were coordinated, President Putin, in a televised address to school children on September 1, 2017, spoke of an "inner nuclear reactor of the Russian people that enables it to move forward." That statement, Zaldastanov explained, made him decide to produce a film on the theme of the latest festival.[165] Zaldostanov advertised his show as a "people's miracle-play [*narodnaia misteria*]" and his short film as a "chronicle of a hundred years of Russia's history." To promote their cinematic creation, Night Wolves drove around a replica steam locomotive built on a track chassis and a crude scaled-down copy of the monument to the Soviet soldier in Berlin's Treptower Park.

After years of experience, Zaldostanov feels comfortable in his role of a stage director, and messianic storyteller. As the narrator and main character, Zaldostanov apparently takes cues from a Soviet cinematic portrayal of Grigory Rasputin. The film is essentially one long shot of Zaldostanov wandering zombie-like along the railway tracks and narrating, in a menacing voice, his version of Russian history from February 1917 until today. From an elevated rostrum decorated with composite state symbols of Russia, Zaldostanov ruminates about "mixed-up facts of history" and a mythical "Russian Reactor that has been set in motion to advance the truth and save the world." What follows is the history of an apocalypse, staved off first by Stalin and now by Putin: the February Revolution that brought about destruction; the abdication of Tsar Nikolai II that threw Russia into anarchy; plotted by the "West," the Bolshevik Revolution that pushed Russia into a civil war; the conspiring forces that dismembered the empire by triggering the independence of borderland regions. The segment on Stalin's period of rule that followed is worth citing in full:

> By means of repression and terror, Stalin halted the burning magma of destructive popular energy and channeled it into modernization. He restored justice, revived the people's precious dream of ideal existence. That energy, in the iron grip of Stalin, turned into thousands of factories, smashed Hitler's fascist empire, and painted the entire world the Soviet color red.[166]

After listing postwar Soviet achievements, with emphasis on the space program, Zaldostanov arrived at another rock bottom in Russian history—August 1991 and the dissolution of the Soviet Union. As a result of the persistent efforts of the cunning enemies, he tells the audience, the Soviet empire had collapsed to never rise again: "The great red kingdom, which was the center of the world, was no more." Yet, in the end, the Russian people have embraced God's ways, professes the alpha wolf. It will continue on the straight road to victory, as the entire historical experience has demonstrated, and will no longer stray off the "May 9 path." Russia killed the fascist dragon, and put its sword to rest, that is, until the next enemy attack—Zaldostanov ends his 40-odd-minute invocation, with the Soviet/Russian anthem playing in the background.[167]

As far as storytelling is concerned, it has been a downward spiral for Zaldostanov & Co. The 2018 showpiece was essentially comprised of two uninterrupted sequences, one apocalyptic (Russia surrounded by forces of evil), and another uplifting (Russia breaking through the encirclement). In terms of historical references, all that was left was a copy of the 1930s fountain the Night Wolves helped to restore in Volgograd.[168] Called "Russian Dream," the spectacle—at least its first part—might give one nightmares. The 2019 phantasmagoria, "The Shadow of Babylon," brought to mind a sermon by a cult leader—as always impersonated by Zaldostanov. The latter's creative genius placed Satan and Rockefeller, the Golden calf and the ideology of liberalism, in the ginormous Tower of Babylon, subsequently vanquished by St. George and the "Russian World." As the apotheosis, the Night Wolves rolled out a mock nuclear-powered ship, presented as "Russia, Noah's Ark of Salvation," while their boss ruminated on the enigma of Putin, chosen to implement the "Russian dream."[169] Just how much Russian taxpayers' money had gone into the making of a "Anti-Russophobic Disneyland"—as a pro-Russian Slovak politician and Zaldostanov's personal friend has designated the bike show—is anyone's guess.[170]

The rumors that Zaldostanov has fallen out with Putin have been exaggerated. In August of 2017 the president was seen chatting with the biker in chief in Sevastopol. In 2019, Putin (with Crimean Premier Aksenov in tow) joined in a Night Wolves bike ride, hours before the tenth edition of the show kicked in. Addressing the bikers

Figure 3 The Soviet Union, powerful and cool. Elderly Russians as well as the generations born after 1991 tend to look at the Soviet Union through rose-colored glasses. A peculiar pride in the country that was simultaneously respected and feared is on display again. Among the most dedicated, as well as visible, adepts of the Soviet Union is Alexander "The Surgeon" Zaldostanov. The annual biker festival at Sevastopol in Russian-occupied Crimea organized by his Night Wolves club makes the country of Stalin and Brezhnev look cool. Here is a scene from the eighth edition of the festival, held on August 18, 2017.

and Zaldostanov personally, Putin had this to say: "You have established a wonderful tradition, which brings out the best in the heart of the Russian person, endorses our glorious, heroic history. I'm very pleased that such manly, cool guys set an example to the young people in our country by demonstrating how one should relate to Russia."[171]

While dodging the question if governmental grants for his children's Christmas fest have dried out, Zaldostanov insists he is driven solely by the desire to promote "Russian traditional values and patriotism." Meanwhile the Night Wolves have been aggressively advancing their business interests. Not only did they manage to retain the site currently occupied by Sexton biker club but they also acquired yet another piece of real estate on the outskirts of Moscow. Reportedly, Zaldostanov and company would have no problem securing a building permit from the chief architect's office.[172] In early 2018 the club's name emerged in connection with a construction scandal. The address of a company behind a future building bloc—opposed by the local population—not far from Sheremetyevo airport, coincides with that of a Night Wolves chapter. The cofounder of the chapter is an associate of the local mayor who was sent packing.[173]

The Night Wolves cash in on patriotism every time they feel undercut by rival groups. They do so by resorting to the tested Soviet method of denunciation. In particular, they had a bone to pick with the Bandidos biker club, portrayed on the occasion as a Satanist narco-syndicate. The story goes back to a gang-related murder of a Night Wolves member in Sevastopol in 2012. Three years later, under the aegis of Anti-Maidan, Zaldostanov proposed to ban Hells Angels and Bandidos on the territory of Russia. Those "foreign agents with the headquarter in the USA" allegedly took part in a popular uprising in Ukraine and might as well one day stir up unrest in Russia. The same year in Saratov, Zaldostanov backed up a local businessman cum deputy for United Russia Party in the latter's conflict with a journalist. In his "amicus curiae," Zaldostanov pulled out all the stops by evoking the fifth column, fascism, mockery of Orthodox values, and so on. For all that, the journalist in question, not unlike Zaldostanov, had endorsed Russia's intervention in Ukraine and routinely praised Putin.[174]

Conclusion

The year 2012 saw an entrance of mass-membership government-funded bodies in the field of historymaking. First to arrive on the scene was the RIO, which claims the mantle of the Russian Imperial Historical Society. Nominally a nongovernmental organization, this was obviously not the first such entity to come into existence in Russia. The Historical Memory Foundation and World without Nazism were established in 2008 and 2010, respectively, to back up the work of the Commission to Counteract Attempts to Harm Russia's Interests by Falsifying History. Once the commission ceased to exist, the raison d'être for those organizations also vanished. Besides, those were one-man shows run by Boris Shpigel and Alexandrov Diukov, respectively. While both organizations still hang on (World without Nazism, through 2015), their usefulness for the regime has become markedly less. Although Natalia Narochnitskaia's Historical Perspective Foundation also had rather limited operations, it keeps the honor as Russia's very first think tank with a focus on history.

A sleek website and local chapters are not what primarily set RIO apart from its predecessors. The government unambiguously ascertained its influence over RIO by determining its structure and leadership. The organization's presidium, advisory board, and board of trustees read like a who's who in the Russian academia, interpolated by select top politicians. Presiding over academics and bureaucrats is Sergei Naryshkin, arguably one of the mightiest individuals in Putin's administration. History is not what Naryshkin, a KGB school graduate with a recent PhD in economics, knows best. He takes care of national security, not history.

RVIO encapsulates the idea of history as elaborated by its chairman, Vladimir Medinskii. There is hardly a (self-styled) historian in Russia today who would have violated his/her professional integrity as systematically as Medinskii has done. Medinskii ticks all entries on the historian's fallacies list.[175] His opportunistic, politicized take on history sullies the good name of historian. Still worse, he brags about it. This makes the attempt to expose Medinskii's inaptitude as a historian even more significant.

Although Medinskii held on to his doctoral degree, his opponents such as Ivan Babitskii of Dissernet and Ivan Kurilla of VIO have claimed a moral victory. The ultimate goal was not to strip Medinskii of his academic credentials but to prove that his dissertation was a sham, they argue. However much one can celebrate the effort per se, the truth remains that Medinskii has remained at the helm and in his capacity as minister of culture continued advancing self-defined historical propaganda unabated. Besides, the state control over media ensured that the Medinskii affair did not make a splash as it might, and should, have done otherwise. In real time, in realpolitik driven by the Putin regime, his lieutenants once again came out on top.

With Putin securing his fourth presidential term, Medinskii, Vasilieva, and pretty much all other government ministers remained in their positions. Medinskii has been using all possible means, including fraud, to keep afloat. Consider one of the many letters of support posted on the RVIO's social media account. A typed letter by a group of war veterans pleaded with President Putin to retain Medinskii in the government. Curiously, the letter is dated February 23, 2018, but refers to Putin's successful reelection as president of Russia on March 18. The letter projects the eclectic version of Russian history as promoted by Medinskii. The people want to see concrete changes (in the wake of Putin's presumed victory), began their letter the war veterans. While looking forward to a leadership shift initiated by Putin, the authors of the letter sought assurances from the latter that the "talented patriots who had proved their loyalty to Motherland and to your vision of restoring the Russian Power" would stay on. They surely meant Medinskii, whose appointment as minister of culture put an end to the decadence allegedly celebrated by liberals. Medinskii, the patriot and loyalist, has truthfully served the cause of reforms by saving culture from turning into an "instrument of destruction of traditional Russian values." "Vladimir Vladimirovich, people like Medinskii should be taken care of and protected," concluded the letter, "stop outrage [*bezpredel*] and give Vladimir Medinskii freedom of action for the benefit of Russian culture."[176] The tenor of the letter suggests it has been written at Medinskii's behest. Rather than reforms, however, the new-old minister of culture first had to deal with a scandal. In May of 2018, Medinskii's former deputy was arrested on corruption charges. Under his aegis the bell tower at Novodevichii Convent in

Moscow mysteriously caught fire and hundreds of millions of rubles allocated for the construction of a depository at Hermitage Museum in St. Petersburg vanished.[177]

With Medinskii back in the saddle, RVIO got a backup in the face of Sergei Ivanov, whose status in the FSB and the government is on par with Naryshkin's. The present head of the Russian Orthodox Church, Patriarch Kirill, has experience working for the security service. Although the charismatic leader of Night Wolves, Alexander Zaldostanov, cannot claim that, he is proud of the direct access he has to the highest ranking officials within power agencies, not to mention his near friendship with the patriarch and the president. If one adds to the mix top administrators in charge of their respective units—Medinskii and the ministry of culture, Vasilieva and the ministry of education, Lavrov and the ministry of foreign affairs, Shoigu and the ministry of defense, Chubarian and the Academy of Sciences—then the conclusion is unavoidable: history in Putin's Russia is made by Soviet-style bureaucrats under the supervision of the FSB. By virtue of being incorporated into the Russian governmental structure, history becomes corrupted like all other elements in the power pyramid. If any further proof is necessary, one is invited to check the RVIO website, which features a thank-you section listing various accolades received by the society and often by Medinskii himself. RVIO posts daily news items about its contribution to the study of Russian history. Literally, not a single post reflects on the history of Soviet terror; theirs is one uninterrupted story of heroism and sacrifice—as commanded by the Kremlin.[178]

The Russian Orthodox Church advances the dominant historical discourse as religiously. The claim by historian Alexei Miller that the Russian Orthodox Church under Kirill had taken a "resolute anti-Stalinist and anti-Communist position" simply cannot be substantiated.[179] Minor disagreements aside, Bishop Tikhon sees eye to eye with Medinskii on the course of Russian history. The former's theme park, "Russia: My History," is the epitome of the syncretic history promoted by the latter. Zaldostanov and the Night Wolves take the same perspective on history, turning it into a peculiar kind of entertainment that caters to certain population groups.

The Night Wolves is neither a battle-hardened hit squad nor a traveling freak show. They cannot, and will not, take on Azov Battalion on the Ukrainian front but neither are they out there to merely entertain. The bikers have a certain function in Putin's game plan. After the president, Zaldostanov is easily the most recognized personality in Russia, way ahead of Patriarch Kirill, former prime minister Medvedev or any other, no doubt loyal yet faceless bureaucrat. The government may at some point get tired financing Zaldostanov's antics. On the other hand, his annual biker festival and Christmas fest cost a mere fraction of what the state spends on "patriotic education." When it comes to cost-effectiveness, the returns are relatively high. What really matters is all those young people who pull out their cell phones in order to snap a picture of the Surgeon. While they are admiring his American bike, they may as well listen to his sermon on the Soviet Union's greatness. Zaldostanov and his bikers capture the segment of the population which has not yet a fully formed worldview, particularly in the wake of a rather successful attempt by Alexei Navalny to mobilize youth for opposition cause. In that sense, for Putin, the Night Wolves is indeed an "autonomous youth NGO."

3

For Victory, For Stalin, For Putin!

In March of 2018, two weeks prior to the presidential elections, Putin was asked what in modern Russian history he would have changed if he could. He reaffirmed that it was the collapse of the Soviet Union. The opinion poll by the independent Levada Center in Moscow half a year later posed the question differently: What are you most ashamed of when you think of twentieth-century Russian history? As many as 45 percent of the respondents gave exactly same answer as their president. This marks the highest figure in ten years. As to the opposite sentiment—what events in the twentieth century make Russians feel proud—the top 3 in the list may well have been drawn by Putin himself: victory in the Great Patriotic War (87 percent), space exploration (50 percent), and the "reunification" of Crimea (45 percent).[1] This sequence has logic to it: from one victory, over German Nazism, the native country sailed to another, over Ukrainian "fascism," and that is what cements Russia's status as a superpower.

Vladimir Putin on History and Historymaking

As confirmed by his entourage and himself, President Putin has a keen interest in history. Putin speaks about history often and publicly, as documented by the Kremlin. Insofar as Russia remains a hierarchical political system, what Putin has to say about the past reverberates throughout the country. According to political scientist Stanislav Belkovskii, Putin belongs to a psychological type of people who never admit their own mistakes. To do so, in Putin's eyes, means deligitimization and ultimately self-destruction. The opposite of denial is self-righteousness. Hence Putin genuinely believes that Russia's aggressive posture makes the West appreciate his country more. Therefore, striking a mutually beneficial political agreement with Putin is simply impossible: He expects the United States to soon begin negotiating with Russia for a new division of spheres of influence.[2] Putin builds his political vocabulary on historical precedents, to the same extent as his worldview affects his view on history.

It has now become commonplace to treat Putin's experience as a KGB operative in East Germany on the eve of the reunification as crucial to his worldview. On December 5, 1989, Putin barely managed to prevent a crowd from storming the KGB headquarters in Dresden. When calling a local Soviet Army tank unit for support, he received a devastating answer: "There is nothing we can do without orders from Moscow, and Moscow is silent." That experience, according to several Putin's biographers, has installed in him a fear of popular uprising on the one hand, and an acute sense of betrayal by elites, on the other.[3]

What is important is that Putin genuinely believes that the West has been trying to overthrow him, as confirmed by his former advisor Gleb Pavlovskii, for example. Putin is equally sincere in promoting the ethos of the Soviet victory in the Second World War.[4] These two personal convictions reflect on Russian history politics since Putin's coming to power, and increasingly so since 2011-12. As applied to Russian foreign policy, former US ambassador to Moscow Michael McFaul described it as the strategy of "linkage," namely tying unrelated issues together.

During his first two terms as president of Russia, Putin rarely referred to history beyond 1917. As early as 2001, Putin inscribed "stability" in the long history of Russia and promised no further revolutions, or counterrevolutions. In his annual speech before the parliament on April 25, 2005, Putin called the dissolution of the Soviet Union a "major geopolitical disaster of the twentieth century" and proposed a new conception for the Soviet victory over Nazi Germany. He described it as a civilizational mission and denoted the Red Army as the "soldiers of freedom." Unsurprisingly, the Second World War is the most frequently mentioned historical event in Putin's speeches. The theme of a strong state made Putin eventually embrace other periods of Russian history, too. Perhaps most potently, he broached this subject in 2003, calling the continuum of the Russian state a "historical fit [*podvig*]." The recurrent reference to "one thousand years of Russian history" is obviously self-serving, justifying Putin's building what is essentially an autocracy. The concurrent theme of maintaining national unity in adverse times meanwhile sets a limit on political pluralism in contemporary Russia. Notably, when citing positive examples, the sitting president does not go beyond generalities in the context of older Russian history, yet brings up specific events from the recent past to illustrate negative tendencies.[5] Rhetorically, pre-1917 Russian history came to play an increasingly important role during Putin's third presidential term. The annexation of Crimea in 2014—the highlight of his presidency—has been framed as a corrective to a historical injustice.

To render a more nuanced portrait of Putin as a historical figure, his informal discussions with target audiences may be more useful than his formal addresses. By conversing with members of such entities as RIO, RVIO, and Victory Volunteers, Putin poses as the quintessential "keeper of history" and simultaneously raises the status of those organizations. In November of 2014, for example, Putin met with a group of history instructors and PhD students from a number of universities and institutes of the Russian Academy of Sciences. In the course of the discussion, Putin now and again demonstrated that he was having difficulties accepting the principles of academic history-writing. He ascribes history more power than it actually possesses. Hence, the (imaginary) malignant efforts to falsify Russian history, according to him, have the capacity to rewire the entire Russian society. In the same breath, Putin considers history a science—which cannot be challenged or rewritten—and a means to an end—in which case it can. He admits his incompetence in historical methodology and right after that identifies important history lessons for his country. When advancing his own interpretation of history, Putin invites his audience to be creative and showy: "The outward impression [*obertka*, literally 'wrapper'] should be flashy and captivating [*proizvodiashchei vpechatlenie na umy*]." The goal once again justifies the means: convincing the Russian population that the official interpretation of history is the only accurate one. Putin believes that as long as the government succeeds in demonstrating that its position is correct and just and that this position benefits both the state and its subjects, it will instantly attract millions of supporters.[6]

The way he talks about it, Putin does not read scholarship, though he says he enjoys history novels by the likes of Maurice Druon popular in the Soviet Union.[7] Whenever he is preparing a speech, Putin says, he tries to recall what he has learned, and then double checks on the internet or in books. Due to lack of time, he is "being guided by the sense of justice and utility for the country in the present situation." To translate it into the layman's language: Putin is strategically using the type of history he learned in Soviet school to advance Russia's national interests, which typically coincide with his own. Putin conceives of Russian history, and history-writing, in isolation from the rest of the world. He does not believe academia may be truly independent. He expresses incredulity that, in order to get academic points historians have to publish in internationally recognized journals. Even though those may, indeed, be solid periodicals, he argues, they can also be politicized to a degree, for the money eventually comes from the respective national budgets. In a direct reference to current foreign politics, he proposes that the Russian Academy of Sciences devise their own citation index. This proposal is effectively an extension of the policy of so-called *importzameshchenie*, that is, replacing foreign goods under Western sanctions with one's own products.[8]

Putin is known for being stubborn as a politician. This trait is also carried over on his views on history. For instance, Putin resists the so-called Norman theory on the origins of Kievan Rus, to which even his closest associates such as former prime minister Medvedev, Bishop Tikhon, and RIO adhere. Putin insists the Scandinavians did not arrive in the ninth century to form new elites but were hired by the self-sufficient Russian tribes as a security detail of sorts. Otherwise, he explains his position, it follows that the Russian statehood has its roots somewhere else. Putin regards archaeology an important auxiliary science, insofar as it may help disprove the Norman theory he detests.[9] By the same token, Putin contradicts the mainstream historians who date the emergence of Russian collective identity by second half of the nineteenth century. The president wants to believe the sense of national belonging had emerged simultaneously with the arrival of Christianity in 988 in what later became Russia.[10] Putin also has an issue with Yaroslav the Wise. In the wake of his eleventh-century rule, Prince Yaroslav had failed to outline clear guidelines for succession, which had led to the fragmentation and weakening of the Russian state. In this, Putin sees a negative lesson for today's Russia and urges national unity instead (read: stick with me as the leader of the country). In his indignant incomprehension of Russia's defeat in the First World War Putin comes close to, horribile dictu, Hitler, and his view on Germany's loss in that very war, namely, a stab in the back. Without mentioning Stalin by name, Putin gives the Soviet dictator his due (and directly transfers it onto himself) by attributing the victory in the Second World War to a brutal (*zhestokaia*) form of rule. Unlike science, Putin thinks history can be taught in the subjunctive. Would the Soviet Union have been able to win the war with someone like Nikolai II at the helm? Imagine what would have become of the Russian people if Nazi Germany had come out on top? Yet, at the core of Putin's understanding of the logic of history is simple geopolitics. Consider the attention (and the money that follows) Putin has been paying to ancient Chersonesus within the city limits of today's Sevastopol in Crimea. Putin endorses the historical myth, according to which Prince Vladimir was baptized at Chersonesus and subsequently converted Kievan Rus to Christianity. Hence, by annexing the peninsula in 2014 the Russian people have simply reclaimed their sacral home, not to mention the many Russian literati who spent time in Crimea and the many battles fought on its territory.[11]

Moving into the twentieth century and the great upheaval of 1917, Putin shows preference to the White side in the ensuing civil war, and specifically Anton Denikin. The reason is obvious: General Denikin was an adept of the Russian Empire within its old borders. From among the divergent political views expressed by Denikin at various times, Putin picks and chooses what he likes, for example, the general's desire to recoup Russia's westernmost provinces.[12] Putin is fixated on the Soviet postulate, which dates the beginning of the Second World War back to the 1938 Munich Agreement rather than the 1939 Molotov–Ribbentrop Pact. Along the way, Putin finds a way to kick Poland: while playing victim, Poland had grabbed a piece of Czechoslovakia first. Drawing from the 1970s Soviet textbooks, he contends that Stalin's Russia had no choice but to buy time by striking a deal with Hitler. Classical stories of Soviet military heroism recalled by Putin (e.g., the defense of Brest in the first months of the Russo–German War) come from the very same source. Putin acknowledges the Allies' contribution to the defeat of Nazi Germany, yet immediately starts calculating the casualties, which brings him to the foretold conclusion as to which country should dictate the Second World War narrative. Working backward, he reminds everyone that the Russian grand offensive in the First World War forestalled a German takeover of Paris.[13]

The discussion has been ongoing as to whether Putin is a cunning schemer or a committed ideologist—however ill-defined his ideological message might be—or both. There is enough evidence to suggest that Putin is a true believer, in the mental picture of the world he has created for himself, or rather inherited from the Soviet past. As the Thomas theorem dictates: "If men define situations as real, they are real in their consequence." Hillary Clinton recounts in her otherwise predictable political memoirs one striking anecdote about Putin from the time when she was the US Secretary of State. During her unscripted conversation with the then prime minister Putin in September 2012, Clinton mentioned to the latter about her recent visit to a memorial of the victims of the Nazi siege of Leningrad. In response, Putin told Clinton the story of how his father had only just managed to save his wife from being left for dead in the besieged city. Putin became emotional while reliving this particular episode of his biography set in the Second World War.[14] There and then, he was genuine.

At this point, it may be instructive to compare, if only perfunctorily, views on history as expressed by Putin and his sidekick, Medvedev. During his tenure as president of Russia, Medvedev, too, had conversations with historians, for example in June of 2011 in Vladimir. The angles from which both the former and the current president look at history are rather different. For sure, like Putin, Medvedev always invokes the "falsification of history." After all, the 2009 commission against the falsification of history came together during his tenure. Like his boss, he emphasizes the intrinsic link between history and politics. He appears more nuanced, however, by presenting it as a double-edged sword. From the perspective of the state, keeping history and politics too far apart can be as dangerous as keeping them too close together. The manipulation of history for political purposes has always been the case, argues Medvedev, and not only during the Soviet period. The Russian population should internalize the fact that an event may have different historical interpretations. Simultaneously, they "should not be in the iron grip of the state, which tells them why something happened and why it could not have been otherwise à la those are the good guys and those are the bastards who deserve our silence." As of 2011, Medvedev could not imagine the president or any other state authority "dictating canonical versions for [inclusion in history] textbooks, and telling what should be told where." Furthermore, Medvedev doubted the effectiveness of the anti-falsification commission, in no small part due to the inherent freedom of the internet. The historians who participated in the roundtable at Vladimir took with them the idea that, in the relationship between the state and the history discipline the former cannot dominate while the latter should have an advisory function. Yet, the change was in the air, as expressed in Medvedev's caution: "Still, the way we're having it right now, in my view we are not in a situation where and when the authorities pass down orders to historians, and the historians fulfill their respective wishes." Medvedev also spoke of the importance of maintaining consensus on central issues of history, and specifically the Second World War.[15] In conclusion, when compared to Putin, the lawyer in Medvedev makes him speak of history in a more abstract way.

Putin's perspective on history has remained unchanged. As he reiterated in his address at the Victory Museum in Moscow in April 2019, the historical continuity serves as a consolidating factor, the Russian people should remember and cherish the fact that they are descendants of the victors and heroes, and the memory of the Great Patriotic War is sacred.[16] Putin entertains the notion of *objective history*, which explains his intention to suppress any contested issues and embrace all periods in Russian history. Putin regards servicing the state and the nation as the higher virtue. As the cornerstone of Russian history, the contract between the state and its subjects makes the present regime, by default, a key historical actor. Insofar as the dark pages of history such as Stalin's terror are concerned, Putin does not deny them. Rather, he keeps it at a safe distance, in the belief that "negative history lessons" could be used in lieu of criticism of the current form of rule. That reinforces the relativist claim, according to which everybody suffered, without singling out any particular victim groups. In the final analysis, Putin has endowed the country with the idea of a heroic past in order to (a) beef up the military and national security, (b) conduct Russia's foreign policy from a high moral ground, and (c) make the Russian population more patriotic (i.e., more docile).[17]

Occasionally, Putin speaks commonsense. However, each of his statements that can be so recognized has a caveat or is disavowed by reality. History teaching does not imply ideological uniformity, pontificates Putin, yet it should organically link all the periods of Russian history. Learning about the past should foster critical thinking and simultaneously boost patriotism. Schoolchildren should be exposed to different historical interpretations, insofar as they are objective and undistorted. As far as the Second World War is concerned, Putin regards certain interpretations that have entered school textbooks as "ideological garbage."[18] No country should be stuck in a heroic past, which is harmful to its future. In the very next sentence, however, Putin recommends raising the Russian youth on the best examples from the past centuries. Banning any alternative views on history is counterproductive, Putin admits.[19] Yet the political system that he has created is based on coercion, increasingly by legal means.

Putin's perspective on Russian history revolves around the issue of statehood. Insofar as one can speak of the cult of the Great Patriotic War in Russia, Putin has spearheaded the cult of the (strong) state. One of the Kremlin's top ideologists, Vladislav Surkov, recently expanded this theme into a broader notion of Putin's state as the final development stage (cf. the Marxist doctrine of imperialism as the highest stage of capitalism). The task of relating history to foreign policy has been delegated, unsurprisingly, to Minister of Foreign Affairs Sergei Lavrov. In the spring of 2016 Lavrov published a lengthy treatise, "Russia's Foreign Policy in a Historical Perspective," which took Putin's views on history one step further.[20]

In his speech at Munich in 2007 Putin drew a long list of grievances against the West, the United States and NATO in particular, and lamented the inconclusive end to the Cold War. Russia had conducted an independent and sensible foreign policy throughout its one-thousand-year history, argued the president.[21] That is where Lavrov picked up nine years later, following the military interventions in Georgia, Ukraine, and Syria. The foreign minister states from the get-go that Russia occupies a special place in European and world history. Echoing Medinskii, Lavrov claims that the medieval Rus on occasion demonstrated higher levels of cultural and spiritual development than the rest of Europe. By ingeniously surviving the Golden Horde ordeal, Russia had emerged as the successor to the Byzantine Empire and an important player insofar as a pan-European political configuration is concerned. The important mission of linking Occident and Orient made the Russian Empire possibly the greatest such entity to ever exist. Furthermore, Russia often performed the role of a "savior of the international system." According to Lavrov, historically, peace ensued as an outcome of the negotiations by the rulers of major states. The attempts to unite Europe without Russia, however, inevitably ended up in a disaster such as the end of the Concert of Europe or a world war. Apprehensive of the strong Russia, European powers made consistent efforts to bar it from world affairs.[22]

Notably, while referring to quite a few Russian tsars, Lavrov did not mention a single Soviet leader by name. Soviet mass violence—referred to as "vice" in a single sentence—also fell by the wayside. Equally remarkable is what Lavrov regards as the Soviet contribution to a better world: decolonization and a welfare state. The West did not win the Cold War, which ended due to the collective will of the Soviet people and certain "unfavorable circumstances." Lavrov believes that the Russia of today had inherited the political genius of its predecessor states. The concept of a continuity of Russian history thus translates into the "righteous role of our country as one of the world's major centers that promotes [*postavshchik*] the virtues of development, security, and stability." Taking a shot at Francis Fukuyama's belief in the "end of history" (1992), Lavrov hails a multipolar world order with Russia as one of the pivots.[23]

Drawing a line under the three programmatic documents spanning twelve years, the conclusion is hard to miss: the Russian history validates the Putin regime and its aggressive foreign policy. Keeping aside the historical aspect for a moment, I would declare Putin's 2007 Munich speech, Lavrov's 2016 opinion piece, and Surkov's 2019 theory of Putinism as the three most important policy documents produced by the regime in the course of its twenty years.

Claiming a high moral ground with respect to history makes the Russian leadership speak of the past in the subjunctive. It starts with Putin, who has recently quipped, "Why do we need a world without Russia?" Politics does not take the subjunctive while humanities (*nauka*, in reference to history) do, claims Putin. "As far as history is concerned," he reasons, "all aspects count, both what had happened and what could have happened if we had failed to attain the result we did attain." Mikhail Miagkov, history professor and RVIO's research director, supplements a long list of longue durée historical events that he believes would have turned differently if it had not been for Russia's (positive) role: American independence, the post-Napoleonic world order, the outcome of the Second World War, and so on.[24]

Putin's self-image of a wise leader staying above the fray does not translate into his underlings exercising autonomy on issues related to history. The history that the Russian populace learns is ultimately the history according to Putin. Putin conceptualizes history as a battleground that lets passions fly and hence should be regulated. As expressed by the very same Miagkov in 2016: "First of all, we want to thank you for the tangible changes with respect to history politics in the country in the recent years. As of now, we are enjoying the state support from the very top, and that is very important."[25] If there is one particular episode in modern history with which Russian history politics has been obsessed, it is the Second World War or, rather, the Soviet contribution to the defeat of Nazi Germany.

The Great Patriotic War as Civil Religion

Sociologist Lev Gudkov has followed the evolution of the cult of the Great Patriotic War over the past twenty-five years or so. That cult did begin with Brezhnev, not Putin. The formal celebration of the end of hostilities, May 9, 1945, comes as a substitute for a contextual analysis of the war. Collective suffering remains part of the narrative while state accountability never entered the conversation. As the ultimate triumph, the Soviet victory effectively erases the memory of Stalin's failures and crimes. By extension, it also legitimizes the Putin regime. By confronting fascism, (Soviet) Russia became once and for all a "democracy." Hence, the Kremlin feels no need to disprove the accusations of authoritarianism. What is important right now is less the fact of victory and more the status of a superpower that it had bestowed on the Soviet Union (read: Russia). The Great Victory makes the Great Russia of today. It gives Putin a moral carte blanche in both domestic and foreign affairs. The populace by and large buys into this discourse. The militaristic message that underlies the May 9 celebration does not translate into a collective wish for war. What it does, however, is making the majority of the population acquiesce to a daily ordeal on the one hand, and endorsing limited military interventions like the ones in Ukraine and Syria on the other. Ordinary Russians appear ready to endure, just to avoid a new world war of which the Russian state propaganda has been warning them.[26] The cult of the war works magic for the regime, echoes Nikolay Koposov, for it has the capacity to accommodate both Stalinists ("we won the war thanks to Stalin") and anti-Stalinists ("we won the war in spite of Stalin"). Endorsing the cult implies acknowledging both Russia's superpower status and the lasting validity of the Yalta system. Since the latter proposition had been rejected by the West, the Great Patriotic War becomes a stick to beat it with.[27]

Being witness to the Second World War hysteria in today's Russia, one may be forgiven for thinking it had always been like this. In fact, in 2001, fresh in the president's office, Putin cherished establishing closer ties with America. His foreign minister at the time even compared the emerging cooperation to the wartime alliance. Both President George W. Bush, in 2002, and President Barack Obama, in 2009, paid their respect to the Soviet war efforts by laying wreaths at the Tomb of the Unknown Soldier in Moscow during their respective state visits to Russia. During his tenure as US ambassador to Moscow, Michael McFaul went out of his way to show his appreciation for the Soviet sacrifice in the defeat of Nazi Germany.[28] None of it had had any visible effect, for the simple reason that the May 9 victory is a political construct in Russia. History is part and parcel of the zero-sum game played by the Kremlin, on its own terms.

There is no doubt that the victory cult works well in rallying the Russian population behind the Putin regime. The single event that the Russians feel most proud about is, indeed, the Soviet victory over Nazi Germany.[29] More opaque sounds the claim by top-ranking state officials that the preservation of the memory of the Second World War may help "effectively solve the fundamental problems facing our country." The battle against the falsification of history—in the midst of which the Russian government believes it finding itself—cannot by default improve living standards or contribute to better health care, ease the dependence on export of raw materials or help uproot corruption. The only way it can help the regime, not the country, is politically, by justifying the confrontation with the outside world and thus entrenching the ruling elites.

The present Russian discourse on the Second World War is based on the premise that certain malignant forces have been trying to erase the memory of the Soviet contribution to victory.[30] Needless to say, such a global conspiracy never existed. It makes it all the more difficult for the Kremlin to modify the historical narrative without losing face. Like on the diplomatic front, the Putin regime has maneuvered itself into a corner, forced to pursue the chosen policy until the bitter end.

There are many signs that the cult of the Great Patriotic War is increasingly taking on the character of a civil religion. In 2015, one of the members of the Victory organizing committee suggested introducing a ritual not unlike the Olympic torch ceremony. His idea was to carry a spark from the eternal fire by the Kremlin wall all over Russia. Locally, that would be used to light up oil lamps and candles in churches, thus commemorating the souls of the departed. This particular idea, it should be added, did not take off, over Putin's objections. While the president did not disapprove of the concept itself, he expressed concern that it might unwittingly exclude people of other confessions such as Jews, Buddhists, and/or Muslims—to the detriment of national unity. Putin does see a religious aspect in the May 9 celebration—anyone who put his life at risk was praying to God, he says—but wants it to be inclusive.[31] Still, insofar as the Great Patriotic War carries a religious connotation, that religion is Russian Orthodoxy. That is what a local priest in Khanty-Mansi region said nearly verbatim during a May 9, 2017, celebration. According to the priest, some 85 percent of those who fought against Nazi Germany were Orthodox Christians. Baptists, Adventists, and Jehovah's Witnesses, however, put obstacles on the way to victory.[32]

Insofar as the war has been proclaimed as sacred, questioning it becomes in and of itself a heresy. Sacred symbols should be safeguarded against formalism and banality, says Putin.[33] The head of the 2017 Victory organizing committee put it yet differently: "We will not tolerate the desecration of the historical foundations that our people regard as sacred." This, he added, is important also in the context of world public opinion.[34] Speaking at the opening of an exhibition in 2015, Prime Minister Medvedev referred to the Soviet military contribution as the "holy Victory."[35] In May of 2016 an economics professor affiliated with the Russian Academy of Sciences proposed giving voting rights to an estimated twenty-seven million Soviet citizens who perished during the war. In that way, he explained, the fallen might influence the course of events in the country for which they sacrificed their lives. Perhaps the voting privilege should be extended several generations down, for that same reason. In practical terms, the

Figure 4 May 9 as a ritual. The Russian Orthodox Church and the Ministry of Defense have found a common ground in furthering the official narrative of the Soviet victory over Nazi Germany. Here, a priest is giving a speech at the Immortal Regiment parade in the polar city of Narian-Mar, May 9, 2018.

participants in the Immortal Regiment march should be able to vote on behalf of their relatives whose portraits they are bearing. This initiative ultimately seeks to boost popular consolidation, he admits.[36]

To ignore for a second the absurdity of the proposal: if those millions died in the name of Stalin then, they may as well give their lives for Putin today. Indeed, while fundamentally rejecting the culture of victimhood—which has been embraced in the West—the Russian state has effectively endorsed the cult of martyrdom. Marginal examples attest that the Soviet victory over Nazi Germany is becoming a sacred ritual to the extent that it requires human sacrifice. Images taken in Ekaterinburg on April 24, 2018, show a city blanketed in thick snow. Other images capture a group of schoolgirls and schoolboys in summer uniforms marching in the snow. Observing them is a group of adults, including two military men, all dressed for the weather. As the organizers explained, the children were rehearsing for a marching contest as part of the Sons and Daughters of the Motherland project; they claim that they could not find an alternative, indoor space for the rehearsal.[37] Two months earlier, a certain kindergarten in Volgograd region had paid a tribute to the Battle of Stalingrad. The caretakers made some thirty small children kneel in the snow to form the number 75. Local bureaucrats loved what they saw: "Cool, guys, a beautiful and patriotic flash mob indeed!"[38]

Propaganda by means of history, in the words of RVIO's former executive director, Vladislav Kononov, is engrained in the story of personal sacrifice on the battlefields of the Second World War. According to him, that is what local lore is all about, with the Immortal Regiment as a perfect example. The act of sacrifice further links up to the issue of national security. As Kononov's colleague at RVIO, Sergei Machinskii, has stated, those young men and women who have personally uncovered the remains of a Red Army soldier would never "betray." (By betrayal, he apparently means loyalty to the regime.) Furthermore, he argues that Russia under Putin has reached such a high standard of living that it can now afford to take care of its dead, and not only the living.[39] The reality is, of course, the exact opposite, namely a disproportionate attention being paid in Putin's Russia to the war dead, to the detriment of the present generations.

Emphasized ad nauseam by the leader who positions himself as the only possible one, the Soviet victory over Nazi Germany did, indeed, become a civil religion, even if it may lack certain attributes associated with that phenomenon. By extension, May 9 is now the major religious holiday in Russia. Each religion has its martyrs, which prepares the foundation for further sacrifice. Whether we choose to call it a religion or a quasi-religion, May 9 does in its present form serve as a justification for the current (aggressive) Russian policy at home and abroad.[40] The narrative of the Great Patriotic War is built in opposition to abstract adversaries who allegedly seek to defile the sacred memory of the Russian people. Speaks Vladimir Medinskii:

Without the sacrificial heroism of our soldiers and officers, of the entire Soviet people, the entire history of mankind might have turned differently. It's important to remember that the contemporary world and its wellbeing is conditioned by the Great Victory of our people. . . . Infamous pseudo-historians [*gore-istoriki*] from within the fifth column and influential individuals in our country and abroad are trying to prove the unprovable. They can't stand the truth about the Great Patriotic War and its Heroes. They seek to denigrate, to negate the role of the Soviet Union, which bore the brunt in that horrendous war. The 30 million people that the Soviet Union lost are of no interest to them. First and foremost, they're keen on falsifying the history, the truth about the war.[41]

Consider, for example, the ubiquitous symbol of May 9, St. George's ribbon. The symbol of the Victory Day celebration and by extension of resurgent Russian nationalism, the St. George's is simultaneously the subject of misinterpretation, misappropriation, and rigid application. The black-and-orange ribbon has nothing to do with the Second World War, or with Soviet Russia for that matter. The individuals to last receive St. George's Cross in Russia were those who fought against the Bolsheviks in the Civil War; during the Second World War this decoration was awarded in Nazi-occupied Serbia to soldiers of the Russian Defense Corps.[42] The recent history of the St. George's ribbon began in the spring of 2005. The initiative to publicly display it on May 9 belonged to a Moscow youth support association, Student Society, which started handing over ribbons to passersby. Within weeks, however, the state-owned Novosti news agency claimed it as its own.

The newly acquired tradition of wearing the St. George's ribbon may resemble that of remembrance poppy on Armistice Day in select British Commonwealth countries. Yet consequences of publicly disallowing this tradition are markedly different. Even though St. George's ribbon does not have a juridical status, Russian Railways in May 2017 threatened a disciplinary action against those train conductors who did not wear it. Liberal member of St. Petersburg's city government, Boris Vishnevskii, got formally reprimanded by the speaker for having refused to display the ribbon.[43] Simultaneously, one of the state-sponsored organizations, Victory Volunteers, proposed tightening the St. George's ribbon code; the ribbons distributed by the initiative group are now accompanied by guidelines on how to appropriately wear one. A similar initiative coming out of Moscow City Government called for ad hoc raids for the purpose of identifying the offenders. From now on, wearing St. George's ribbon on a car antenna or a purse is no longer recommended. Misconduct is punishable by fine.[44]

The Making of May 9

In order to comprehend the enormity of the May 9 celebration, one may choose to consult the proceedings of the Victory organizing committee. Putin's decree that established the committee in 2000 was among the president's first major initiatives in the field of history. The Victory committee began as a coordinating body for the annual May 9 festivities but has since then expanded its mandate to patriotic education more broadly. Putin's chairing the committee brings home its significance. Nowhere does Putin outline his conception of falsification of history as explicitly as in the committee's sessions. The very venue superimposes the connection between the latter and May 9. According to Putin, the enemies of today's Russia are trying to undermine its strength and moral authority by stripping it of the status of a victorious nation, with all the international legal consequences that follow. Hence, in his eyes, history is a constituent of geopolitics. The way Putin frames the Soviet role in the defeat of Nazi Germany is well known: a unifying symbol of sacrifice and heroism that creates the foundation of Russian patriotism. That informs his claim that the "falsification of history," among other things, is an insult to the two million veterans of war still alive in Russia.[45] Supporting war veterans is and of itself a geopolitical issue, according to Putin.[46] Recently Putin began attributing the Soviet victory over Nazi Germany to the miracle of a "thousand-year historical Russia."[47]

On March 17, 2015, the Victory organizing committee met in the Kremlin for the thirty-sixth time to discuss the status of preparations for the forthcoming commemoration of V-Day. Putin had this to say when opening the meeting:

> Unfortunately, today we are witnessing [not only] the attempts to revise and misinterpret the events of the war, but also cynical, uninhibited lies, callous slandering of an entire generation who had given their utmost to victory, who had preserved peace on earth. I believe you are all aware of that, so no need to repeat. Sometimes, however, I don't even dare to convey all those shameless conclusions, so-called observations, which have nothing to do with the truth.
>
> Their aims are clear: to undermine the power and moral authority of modern Russia, to deprive it of its status of a victorious country, with all the international legal consequences that follow, to divide and set at loggerheads nations, to use historical speculations in geopolitical games. Sometimes it's pure delirium; hard to believe anyone ever gets to that. Indeed, it's not as harmless [as it may seem], because we're seeing an attempt to put into the heads of millions, especially the youth, absolutely dangerous tendencies and perverted conceptions of history.
>
> Hence, preparations for the anniversary celebration go beyond organizing festivities. It's also a huge educational and media [*informatsionnaia*] work at both national and international level. We're bound to constantly, with the help of arguments, steadfastly, and consistently defend the truth about the war, about the colossal contribution of the Soviet people to Victory, about the unifying and decisive role of the Soviet Union in the defeat of Nazism.[48]

The annual event has come to increasingly resemble a mix between a military operation and the Olympics. That is how the participants in the committee's meetings themselves see it. The sense of confrontation, past and present, was at its highest in the run-on to the seventieth anniversary of V-Day. The leader of the 2015 organizing committee, head of the presidential administration Sergei Ivanov, painted a picture of the ongoing preparations in the face of an unprecedented foreign pressure. That campaign, according to Ivanov, included deliberate efforts to rewrite the history of the Second World War. The Russian people, however, took the defense of the historical truth to heart, assisting state institutions at every step. Displays of the original wartime hardware would work particularly well with children, Ivanov believes.[49] In 2016, Dmitry Rogozin became the head of the organizing committee. Among his other proposals was incorporating the reorganization of the Soviet military industry in 1941–42 into the May 9 celebration.

Putin liked the idea, not least as a useful example from the past that can come in handy today.⁵⁰

The most revealing, perhaps, is how the Soviet victory in the Second World War fits in the Russian foreign policy agenda. According to Lavrov, his ministry has been working hard to preserve the historical memory by means of UN Resolution 67/154 ("glorification of Nazism") and similar initiatives launched in the OSCE and the Council of Europe (see Chapter 6). In pursuit of that goal, Lavrov identifies Israel and the BRIC countries among its international partners. The ministry's dedicated webpage on the wartime Allies and the Nuremberg trial, framed as the Manichean struggle between good and evil, has an international element built in. It also works closely with Russian expats in organizing an annual Immortal Regiment march. The Foreign Ministry keeps a dissident list of its own: those individuals who are being persecuted for the "activities related to important dates in the [history of the] Great Patriotic War."⁵¹ Lavrov's deputy the following year emphasized the falsification of history as a priority. The Foreign Ministry has gone about it in accordance with the foreign political agenda approved by Putin. Those foreign leaders who pay tribute to the Soviet sacrifice by observing the May 9 military parade on Red Square next to President Putin are by default political allies. Lavrov was particularly concerned whether the German chancellor Angela Merkel would, in 2015, travel to Moscow (which Merkel eventually did, though she conspicuously skipped the military parade).⁵²

May 9 also showcases the most recent Russian innovations in the field of military and information technology. While the Russian army is eager to demonstrate its most advanced hardware, the media bosses are not far behind in trying to reach out to the widest possible audiences. Margarita Simonian, head of the preeminent foreign propaganda outlet, Russian Today (RT), has good reasons to be proud. For one, RT captures an audience of seventy million weekly in thirty-eight different countries (out of the 700 million worldwide who can watch RT programs). The channel runs ten multimedia projects on Second World War. Simonian's team is successfully using the new 360-degree video format; from a dedicated webpage one can download anything from documents to screen wallpaper. RT doles out gratis photographs of the Second World War, which even newspapers "traditionally unfriendly to Russia" such as the *New York Times* occasionally reprint, Simonian says. A Russia beyond the "Headlines" project seeks out foreign individuals who, in their respective languages, have something to say about "our war." Another propaganda outfit, Sputnik—which targets mainly Russian expats—serves as a distribution channel for the St. George's ribbon.⁵³

Geopolitics cuts through the memory of the Second World War in Russia. For example, in 2015 the search movement got expanded on account of a Russian–Chinese expedition trying to identify Soviet soldiers' remains on the territory of China. A September 2016 meeting of the Victory organizing committee saw new faces—a Chinese Communist Party delegation.⁵⁴ In March 2019 an RVIO delegation traveled to one of China's borderland prefectures. According to a joint communique, both countries will cooperate in the study of history of the Far East and "confront the attempts . . . to diminish the role of Victory of the Russian and Chinese nations over Japanese militarism."⁵⁵ Three months later, head of RIO Naryshkin spoke of a forthcoming Russian–Chinese history conference and of plans to produce a joint textbook on the history of the Second World War.⁵⁶ In the wake of the Brexit referendum and the election of Donald Trump as the US president, the committee's focus shifted to finding partners abroad. In April 2017, President Putin spoke of international cooperation among "like-minded people" in the defense of the "historical truth of the Second World War." As successful examples he mentioned the worldwide expansion of Immortal Regiment and maintaining Soviet war memorials in foreign countries. These and similar projects have been carried out under the aegis of the foreign ministry. Without being proactive, declared Putin, the entire world order that emerged in the aftermath of the war might collapse.⁵⁷

Among the entities explicitly identified as the medium of Russian history propaganda in foreign countries is Rossotrudnichestvo (the federal agency supporting Russian compatriots abroad and fostering bilateral cooperation in the fields of science, culture, and education) and the Central Museum of the Great Patriotic War in Moscow (colloquially known as the Victory Museum). The former operates via the centers of Russian science and culture abroad and the latter via international inter-museum exchanges. Bilateral relations with foreign universities and the city twinning movement have been recognized as the next prospective arena for expansion.⁵⁸ As yet another venue to "advance the objective historical and current information about the Russian Federation and its role in the victory over Nazism," the government chose the obsolete World Youth and Student Festival, held in October of 2017 at Sochi.⁵⁹

As the heroic portrayal of the Great Patriotic War had acquired the quality of a scripture, tellingly, a new temporary exhibition on the history of the Second World War that opened at the Victory Museum in May 2018 was called *The Historical Truth*. From a museological point of view, the exhibition is indeed a step forward, featuring rare artefacts, interesting charts, innovative placement, lighting, and so on. When it comes to substance, however, the story of the Second World War as told in the new exhibition does not deviate from the officially accepted one. The museum director, Alexander Shkolnik, described the exhibition as a "place where the truth speaks for itself."

The exhibition was opened in conjunction with an international gathering convened at the Victory Museum's initiative. The meeting on May 8 brought together museum representatives from eight countries: the United States, Canada, Brazil, the Netherlands, Hungary, Slovakia, Slovenia, and Luxemburg. Director Shkolnik said those countries had contributed to the defeat of fascism—contrary to the common knowledge that Hungary and Slovakia allied with Nazi Germany, while Slovenia, Luxembourg, and the Netherlands were under German occupation. The participants signed a document establishing an International Committee for the History of the Second World War. According to Shkolnik, the new entity will rally world public opinion against the "glorification of Nazism and the attempts to falsify history."⁶⁰

An association of museums dealing with the history of the Second World War is not a new idea. Curiously, there exists at least two other associations with exactly the same, or similar, name. The original committee, in existence since 1967, has thirteen national affiliates and lists several well-known historians as its members. During the past four years or so, it had not reported any new academic activities.⁶¹ In 2015, an International Association of World War II Museums was also established in Beijing, China.⁶² Hence, the Moscow committee appears to be a ruse, an attempt to misappropriate an idea by filling it with a different content. The choice of the venue is not coincidental either. The memorial complex on Poklonnaia Hill was originally designed to project Russian military glory, while pushing the story of suffering and loss to the background. The museum, in the face of its director, sees its mission in promoting patriotism and defending the "historical truth." By all means, the Victory Museum counts among the select few institutions that set a framework for the Russian history politics.[63]

When it comes to particular countries, Russian influence has traditionally been strong in Serbia. The history of the Second World War also brought Slovenia into Russia's fold. At least that is what Russian state officials believe. In the summer of 2014 Foreign Minister Lavrov opened a museum at the former prisoner-of-war campsite in Slovenia. From the Russian perspective, the importance lies in the fact that Slovenia is an EU and NATO member state, accentuated by heightened geopolitical tensions that particular year. Moscow capitalized on that perceived opening by unveiling two years later a monument in the capital Ljubljana to Russian/Soviet soldiers who perished in Slovenia during both world wars. The monument was commissioned by RVIO. By 2017, RVIO had installed thirteen such monuments abroad, from Serbia to France.[64]

By 2019 the Russian historical establishment decided to change the focus from the Soviet victory in the Second World War to the liberation of Eastern Europe from Nazism. As a matter of precaution, the organizing committee suggested limiting the scope to the actual combat operations to the exclusion of postwar political order (read: enforced Sovietization). This heavy-handed approach has little chance to gain traction in the former satellites. Say, no one would buy Naryshkin's claim that the arrival of Soviet troops in 1944–45 had created the foundation of a new Europe, or that the Soviet spies helped to preserve the cultural treasures of East European countries. More likely, the Europeans would just laugh at the ignorance of the likes of Medinskii, who declared an Anglo-American Air Force responsible for the bombing of Rotterdam (it was, in fact, the Germans who reduced the city to rubble). Neither would the Poles appreciate the resolve to send a Russian parliamentary delegation to the annual Holocaust Commemoration ceremony at Auschwitz, despite not being formally invited. As Konstantin Kosachev, head of the Federation Council Foreign Affairs Committee, declared, "We'll certainly be there, because we're going not to Poland or to the Poles, but to the place which is of significance [*znakovoe, pamiatnoe*] to us." Such manifest arrogance is a prescript for a failure insofar as the ultimate goal is broadening support for the official Russian interpretation of history.[65] Just consider a recent statement by the Bulgarian foreign ministry, which chided its Russian counterpart for advancing a "dubious thesis," according to which the Soviet Union had brought freedom to Europe by defeating Nazi Germany.[66]

In the run-up to the seventy-fifth anniversary of V-Day, President Putin proclaimed 2020 the Year of Memory and Glory in Russia. As a slogan, the presidential decree evoked the preservation of historical memory. The Victory organizing committee—this time headed by the chief of staff Anton Vaino—will retain the coordination function.[67] As star guests, Putin has invited the US president Donald Trump and Chinese leader Xi Jinping (the former has declined the invitation). The coronavirus crisis somewhat dampened history propaganda leading up to May 9, 2020.

The May 9 statistics is truly impressive, here for 2015: military parades in sixty-eight different Russian cities, and navy and air force displays in five; fifteen thousand troops (a 50 percent increase from 2010) marching on Red Square alone; a youth volunteer corps of eighty thousand; a journalist press center rivaling that "at the Winter Olympics in Sochi"; TV coverage on an "unprecedented scale."[68] To show their appreciation, the Victory organizing committee minted a few thousand medals, to be given to the most dedicated among the support staff.[69]

War veterans take center stage in May 9 festivities. When it comes to official figures, however, there is a significant discrepancy. A 2015 figure put the number at 217,515. If one counts in prisoners of Nazi camps, persons who endured the siege of Leningrad, and so-called toilers of the rear, then the number increases to 2.7 million. Government officials, including Putin, typically cite the latter figure.[70] If one considers the individuals who actually fought at the front and who currently receive government pensions, however, the number goes down to 10,000 (2019 figures).[71] Even that estimate appears too high, given that the youngest person who had fought in the war must be ninety years old in 2020. This means that state officials exaggerate the number of Soviet war veterans still alive by a factor of 270.

The fewer the war veterans, the more the initiatives that appear to celebrate their heroism. As a corollary to the ongoing sacralization of the Soviet victory over Nazi Germany, an idea was aired in early 2020 to start capitalizing the word *veteran*. An offense against both common sense and linguistic tradition, this proposition was endorsed by outgoing Minister of Education Vasilieva.[72] An invitation to be creative brought about innumerable "patriotic" projects with names like "Memory Watch," "Remember Each and Every One . . .," "People's Victory," "Volunteers of Victory," "Heirs of Victory," "Ambassadors of Victory," "Faces of Victory," "Fanfares of Victory," "Victory Roads," "Letters of Victory," "Victory Fireworks," "Stars of Victory," "Under the Banner of Victory," "The Light of the Great Victory," "Raising Patriots of Russia," "Strong in Spirit," "True to Heroes' Command," "People's Memory," "Moscow, Belorussian Station, June 22, 1941," "Propaganda Train: The Victory Army," "The Great Victory Achieved through Unity," "With No Statute of Limitations," "The World of Tanks: We Remember It All," "We Don't Abandon Our Own," and so on.

The word *pobeda* (victory) is, indeed, the most popular word in Russia today. There is a low-cost air carrier, Aeroflot's subsidiary, with that name (since December 2014) as also a TV channel (since January 2019). The latter has been launched by Channel One and beams 24/7 Second World War content, including extensive coverage of the Immortal Regiment march. The exploitation of the cult of the Soviet victory in the Second World War has generated a unique term in Russian, *pobedobesie*, which can be rendered as victory bacchanalia or victory hysteria. It goes beyond commercialization. What about a "pleasant to touch" soft toy styled as a Soviet war veteran, or a bottle holder shaped as a puppy wearing the St. George's ribbon? A full Soviet military uniform circa 1943 is available in all sizes, fitting children from 2 to 16. In addition, parents can purchase a medical nurse bag, a mess tin, or an imitation automatic gun. The ubiquitous forage cups are now being sold around May 9 even in bakeries. Erotic underwear, advertised as "costume for a military babe," comes in all sizes and price categories.[73] The 1945 Battle of Berlin, like other elements of the Great Patriotic War, has been appropriated by popular culture. Consider fans of the TsSKA football club who witnessed their team's victory in the Euro League finals in Berlin in May of 2016, receiving a commemorative medal from the club. Modeled after wartime decorations, the medal features a Soviet star and the inscription, "In Honor of the Conquest of Berlin."[74]

Victory kitsch is a manifestation of ignorance, naturally. May 9 celebration keeps generating curiosa. A group of Russian war veterans once received a thank-you card that featured a monument to the American soldiers who fought against the Japanese

Figures 5–6 Victory kitsch. Russian citizens taking part in the annual Immortal Regiment parade, here on May 9, 2019, in Barnaul, to pay respect to the sacrifice borne by their forefathers in the Second World War. Some of the participants show their appreciation by dressing up. In the bottom picture, Youth Army members march in desert camouflage uniform.

in the Pacific. Another time, the May 9 card had a German Tiger tank emblazoned on it.[75] In Ulan-Ude, a banner "thanking granddad for victory" in the Second World War depicted Tsar Nikolai II and his generals during the First World War.[76] A college in Saratov hailed Victory Day by putting up a banner featuring photographs of Wehrmacht soldiers.[77] A billboard in Orel turned veterans into "veterinarians."[78] In St. Petersburg in 2019, a women's band paraded in black uniforms with red-and-white armbands that smacked of Nazi aesthetics.

While no expenses are spared on the annual May 9 celebration, the situation on the ground, particularly outside of Moscow, during the rest of the year is rather different. The city of Omsk in 2017 decided to extinguish the eternal flame for the lack of funds; from then onward it would only be working seventeen days a year.[79] Despite their verbal support for the volunteer movement that searches for the remains of still unburied Soviet soldiers, local authorities, for example in Leningrad region, actively sabotage it, in the pursuit of commercial interests.[80]

The Putin regime rightfully takes credit for a record-high sense of pride in the Soviet victory over Nazi Germany in today's Russia. Simultaneously, the percentage of Russians who take no interest in the Russian history whatsoever has doubled in recent years. In effect, the myth has sucked the life out of what sometimes is described as living history. This is particularly true for young Russians.[81] The sole emphasis on the Second World War has had several side effects, including disregard for family history and local lore. According to a 2011 opinion poll, 80 percent of Russians do not know the first names of their great-grandparents, while 40 percent fail to date the foundation of the city where they reside.[82]

Tank as Historical Weapon of Choice

Russian military history, which occupies a preeminent role in patriotic education, naturally needs a symbol, a representative type of hardware. The problem with small arms, for example, is that they are usually associated with a particular time period: the Mosin-Nagant rifle with the First World War and the Russian Civil War; the PPSh submachine gun with the Second World War, and the Kalashnikov assault rifle with the Cold War. With the ongoing modernization of its military, choosing one particular type of weapon that would stand for Russia's military glory throughout history is not an easy task. Should it be a ballistic missile, nuclear submarine, or perhaps the veteran TU-95 "Bear" strategic bomber? Indeed, a short-range mobile ballistic system, Iskander, briefly became the face of Russian military.[83] Capable of carrying nuclear warheads, in 2014 Iskander missiles were deployed in Kaliningrad region and the newly annexed Crimea, while the image of a launcher with the inscription "Laughing Iskanders" appeared on T-shirts as a rebuke to Western sanctions. Still, the bulky Iskander—which entered into service in the mid-2000s and is currently deployed by Russia in Syria, hardly gives a sense of history. But a tank does.

Although no longer as important in modern warfare as it used to be, the tank bears potent historical references. The Soviet T-34 tank proved one of the best of its kind during the Second World War. From the Battle of Kursk to the Battle of Berlin, the image of a T-34 emblazoned with patriotic graffiti came to symbolize the Soviet military might and purity of purpose. T-34 tanks had been in production between the early 1940s and the late 1950s. The Soviet (and later Russian) army used modified versions of T-34 all the way through 1993. Soviet-era monuments featuring original tanks still dot the Russian landscape. The iconic T-34 made a formal comeback during the 2010 Victory Day military parade on Red Square. The following year, it became the centerpiece of a military parade commemorating a similar event in November 1941. Since 2015, T-34 tanks on parade feature the St. George's ribbon. Minor military parades organized in other cities feature, whenever possible, one or several T-34 tanks—that treasured hardware.

The legendary T-34 is being celebrated by various means. Colloquial references to the tank convey the dual sense of force and grace. The explicit warning, "*kuda priosh kak tank*" (don't you dare push like a tank), does incorporate an element of aggression. One of the best-known computer military strategy games, *The World of Tanks*, was released in 2010 in the Russian language (though it was developed by a Belorussian company). A synchronized tank show at the newly opened Patriot military theme park near Moscow in May 2015 was announced by a commentator as "polite machines"—an allusion to Putin's "polite people" in Crimea, typically referred to in the West as the "green men."[84] Who could have ever thought that a tank would become a part of popular culture, as is the case in contemporary Russia? The 2015 edition of the Night Wolves biker festival at Sevastopol featured, among other militaristic paraphernalia, an actual T-34. The tank was on loan from the Battle of Stalingrad museum in Volgograd.[85]

In a short timespan, the border between national pride and patriotic kitsch has become thinner. For instance, on May 1, 2018, the Museum of the Great Patriotic War in Moscow, in collaboration with REN TV channel, posted a music video recorded as part of the event called Musical Marathon of Victory. The video featured three 6-year-old boys performing a famous Soviet song "Three Tank Drivers, Three Jolly Friends" on top of a T-34 tank displayed on the museum's grounds. Dressed in the cheerful red pants and white blazers, the young performers from a children's musical theater Domisolka diligently sang about the brave tank crew in the Soviet Far East crushing Samurais and "finishing off all the enemies . . . in fierce attack."[86] The video (which saw the boys in between running around playing war) is supposed to remind the viewers of Soviet heroism in the Second World War, never mind that the actual song was composed in 1938.[87] Some parents—certainly those of the little boys—may find it cute, others appalling. Around the same time, a family of three in St. Petersburg, including two children aged nine and fifteen, fell off a moving tank. Pay tank rides were part of the Battle of Steel festival. The children ended up with bruises while their father got literally rolled over by the tank (thanks to the sandy ground, he survived, but with a broken leg). Following the incident, the rides continued like nothing had happened, while the injured man blamed only himself. In fact, he returned to the festival grounds after a brief hospitalization, and received a discount on firing antiaircraft cannons and gratis target shooting.[88] In an interview, the injured man presented himself as a history buff who dreams of serving his country in some "hot spot" one day.[89]

One can buy home slippers in the shape of a T-34, complete with red star and a barrel (priced at the equivalent of USD 14–38). The slippers are recommended as a gift to a friend, or a man, or, specifically, a military man on the Day of the Defender of Motherland (February 23) or Victory Day (May 9). According to a tongue-in-cheek descript of the product, "The T-34 slippers give 100 percent confidence, calm, comfort, and coziness, in short—make you feel like the 'inside of a tank.'" "This gift won't leave your man indifferent," invokes another online retailer, "and an unusual military design will prompt surprise and admiration." Yet another seller suggests using the T-34 slippers beyond special occasions also, on a chilly balcony or during warm summer nights on one's dacha.[90] There are just so many things one can make in the shape of the famous tank. An engineer in Novosibirsk, for example, built a cat house with a moving turret and barrel.[91]

As an apotheosis of the tank-mania, if you will, in 2018 not one but two blockbusters, appropriately titled *Tanks* and *T-34*, hit movie theaters. *Tanks* was screened, among other venues, at the Russian embassy in Washington D.C. For the foreign audiences, the film title was changed to *Tanks to Stalin* (the movie is distributed by 20th Century Fox). *Tanks* tells the story of the T-34 prototype, sabotaged by Nazi German agents and aided by the Soviet NKVD. Set in 1940, the movie ends with Comrade Stalin welcoming the new armory on Red Square. As one film critique has observed, *Tanks* portrays the present ministry of culture better than it does Stalin's era. *Tanks* and *Panfilov-28* have one and the same patron, Medinskii.[92] The second feature film did avoid patriotic propaganda; the word *Stalin* is mentioned only once in the dialogues, even there in a humorous context. Otherwise, the fictional plot of an escape from a Nazi concentration camp on a tank overflows with clichés. In essence, it is a war epic populated with brave Russians and callous Germans and stripped of any subtleties.[93] *T-34* became a box-office hit—the only movie to do so among those financed by the state in 2019—thanks in no small part to the promotion campaign facilitated by Medinskii.[94] Medinskii compared all those who dared to criticize the movie to defeatists who deserted from the battlefield in 1941. Historians and laymen should all rally around the flag (figuratively raised by *T-34*), he stated.[95] Medinskii's passion for war movies has received a boost: a Christmas gift of sorts, in January of 2019 Laos returned to Russia thirty fully operational T-34 tanks, which until then had been part of its military. The agreement was reached a year earlier during Defense Minister Shoigu's visit to Laos. The newly acquired hardware shall be used for military parades, museum displays, and film shooting.[96]

The ultimate link between the past and present of the T-34 tank, as a historical reference and a manifestation of current geopolitics, can be traced to a certain military encounter between pro-Russian separatists and Ukrainian forces in Donbass in 2014. The former got hold of a tank that had until then been part of a Second World War monument. Seventy years after the end of the war, Russian proxies managed not only to start off the tank's engine but also to fire at and destroy a Ukrainian dugout.[97] From a Russian perspective, that may symbolize the revenge of history.

Immortal Regiment: The State Repurposes People's Memory of the War

The story of the Immortal Regiment project vividly demonstrates how the Russian state has been able to claim monopoly on the representation of the Second World War. The original initiative belonged to a group of journalists working for the independent TV2 channel in Tomsk. Sergei Lapenkov, Igor Dmitriev, and Sergei Kolotovkin did not fail to notice that the official celebration of May 9 increasingly featured state officials, with a handful of war veterans typically concluding the parade. To reverse this trend, they proposed bringing in relatives of those who took part in the Great Patriotic War. In so doing, the journalists were thinking of their own grandfathers who had participated in the war. The municipality gave the green light and the announcements were carried on the local radio and TV. Carrying portraits of their family members who had fought against the Nazis, on May 9, 2012, ordinary citizens took to the streets of Tomsk. Some six thousand people gathered that day in Tomsk, which was more than the number of people who usually showed up for formal May 9 gatherings. Personal involvement made the parade an emotional affair. Still, state TV channels did not cover the Tomsk march, except for a local crew of Channel One (who apparently did not receive clear instructions on whether or not they should film the event). That was enough, however, for other local broadcasters to spread the news across the country. Thus, Immortal Regiment was born.[98]

The founding group conceived of Immortal Regiment as a noncommercial and apolitical project, which was affixed in a statute. A handful of communists who attempted to join the march were chased away and so were the individuals who intended to carry a group portrait of Soviet leaders, including Stalin. Lapenkov and his team thought big, anticipating some fifty cities across Russia holding similar marches the following year. Most of their associates who staffed local organizing committees were fellow journalists. With the benefit of hindsight, they made the strategic mistake of not seeking a juridical status for Immortal Regiment. In Moscow, the Tomsk trio was approached by Nikolai Zemtsov, then local parliamentarian for the Communist Party and later Duma deputy for United Russia. Zemtsov promised to take up their cause with the mayor's office but sought extensive media coverage. The journalists insisted on the noncommercial nature of Immortal Regiment while continuing negotiations. The first installment of Immortal Regiment in Moscow took place in 2013 on Poklonnaia Hill. The Moscow organizing committee subsequently decided they no longer required Zemtsov's services. The latter, meanwhile, had registered Immortal Regiment Russia as a trademark, eventually becoming its co-chairman. A promotion campaign followed, complete with red banners and award ceremonies. The former Soviet movie star and presently President Putin's confidant, Vasilii Lanovoi, joined the organization's board of trustees and went on a concert tour titled "Immortal Regiment." In the wake of a very public spat with the "patriotic" actor, the Tomsk journalists threw in the towel.[99]

In the run-up to the seventieth anniversary of V-Day, Lapenkov and his close associates took part in a meeting under the auspices of the Victory organizing committee. Even then, cooperation with state authorities still appeared possible. The then head of the presidential administration, Sergei Ivanov, just said that there was such a thing as Immortal Regiment and that this initiative should be supported in the provinces.[100] Simultaneously, Ivanov informed Putin that Immortal Regiment had got an official logo, a design code, and standard uniforms for volunteers.[101] A few years down the road, the Federal Agency for Youth Affairs was "providing a volunteer escort to the victory parade and the Immortal Regiment people's walk."[102]

Since September 2015, Immortal Regiment Russia has existed as a "public patriotic movement." According to the official website, the movement's history began in 2007 in another Siberian city, Tiumen. The 2012 gathering at Tomsk is mentioned only in passing, as the place and year where and when the Immortal Regiment got its name. The movement's symbol is St. George slaying the dragon, placed within a red star.[103] Next to nothing has been left of the Immortal Regiment's original concept, described by Igor Dmitriev as the "story of peace of love." He and his Tomsk colleagues feel mortified seeing overzealous mothers bringing to the parade their little ones in buggies shaped like tanks, airplanes, submarines, and so on. They have no clue as to what war entails, Dmitriev agonizes, and yet they want to send their sons into a new military conflict. Equally incomprehensible is the association of Immortal Regiment with "war heroes" of the separatist Donbass and Luhansk Republics (e.g., T-shirts inscribed with "Donbass Youth" and "Donbass Speaks Russian" worn by certain participants).[104]

Conspicuously, independent Immortal Regiment uses a stork, also set inside a red star, as its symbol. The most cherished aspect of the original project is over 406,000 personal stories available through its website. The geographical and numerical growth of Immortal Regiment has been proportionate to a number of violations of its 2012 statute. Among the most common infringements is self-promotion by political parties, the use of advertisement, displaying portraits of Soviet politicians, and the use of coercion in recruiting participants among school and university students.[105]

The Immortal Regiment initiative highlights the ever-present tension between the state and private citizens in Russia. From the outset, authorities in some cities did cooperate with Lapenkov and his contacts while in others, they did not. In Kemerovo, for example, the organizers were given the following proposition: the march would get the green light only if it displayed the United Russia paraphernalia. A year later, however—once bureaucrats got an order to that effect from the Victory organizing committee—they quickly assembled an Immoral Regiment composed of school children. Similarly, occasional disparaging references to the Immortal Regiment as "slandering the traditional way of celebrating May 9" ceased once President Putin walked in the march's front row in Moscow in 2015.[106]

The state takeover of the Immortal Regiment initiative has both imbued it with an unintended meaning and turned it into a formality. Immortal Regiment, Moscow, for example, has organized pickets in support of United Russia Party. Despite the calls to keep politics apart, many a local march in suburban Moscow in 2019 featured organized groups by United Russia. In 2017 in Crimea, the organizing group was forced to submit an application for the march on behalf of Immortal Regiment Russia. This has, no doubt, to do with the situation in Sevastopol the previous year where two rival marches—one popular and another state-sponsored—took place simultaneously. The conflict escalated further in 2019 when the state branch office of

Immortal Regiment in Sevastopol literally stole some five hundred portraits from its competitor.[107] The Tomsk group wrote a letter to President Putin decrying the popular initiative being turned into yet another bureaucratic venture open to corruption. They received no reply. Meanwhile, online trolls have begun discrediting the original leaders of Immortal Regiment as paid agents of the US State Department and/or of Mikhail Khodorkovskii.[108] Putin, it should be told, describes the overhauled Immortal Regiment as an "absolutely honest, sincere project that should stay that way and evolve freely."[109] Furthermore, he disavows the sentiment that the annual walk has increasingly become a militaristic event.[110]

In its present form, Immortal Regiment functions as a cross between an Orthodox Easter procession and the Soviet November 7 parade. When it comes to displaying icons and/or images of Stalin—the comparison is indeed uncanny.[111] This is, of course, not how millions of Russians who participate annually in Immortal Regiment see it. Participants stress how friendly the crowd is. A positive comparison of the May 9 march to a pilgrimage translates back into an idealized image of Russia. Taking no note of the superabundant military paraphernalia, ordinary Russians emphasize the lack of "anger and aggression." No one makes a big deal about a portrait of Stalin here and there, drawn in the sea of people ostensibly united for a common purpose. That purpose, however, is typically being identified in negative terms. As one participant has stated: "Our people stand as united as ever and, if necessary, will rise as one in order to tear into pieces anyone who dares to encroach on our land."[112] Among other organized groups marching on May 9, 2018 in Moscow were Wagner mercenaries and members of the disbanded Ukrainian security detachment Berkut, Cossacks, and supporters of Novorossia (i.e., carved-up Donbass). No less conspicuous were the sheer number of children dressed up in military uniform. Immortal Regiment increasingly resembles a pro-Putin election rally, argues blogger Ilya Varlamov.[113] The regime has successfully manipulated public opinion by linking military losses to imperial grandeur, says Lev Gudkov.[114]

Another emerging aspect that makes Immortal Regiment similar to Soviet-era mass events, say, May Day parade, is the use of coercion in ensuring public participation. Consistently denied by authorities, this is particularly true in the provinces.[115] Since 2015 schools began receiving quotas on participation in the now annual march (e.g., in Samara). Reports abound about rehearsals, sometimes several in a row, held ahead of the Immortal Regiment march in select cities. Thus an organized group in Obnisk was instructed on how to carry banners and veterans' portraits properly, to keep pace, and march in columns.[116] A group of students in yet another city in Moscow region, Korolev, formally complained about being forced to participate in the May 9 march. The school administration failed to reasonably respond why the obligatory military training was scheduled to take place at the exact time and place Immortal Regiment was supposed to go off, particularly since May 9 is an official holiday. Bound by the decree issued by the city government to "ensure [*obespechit*] the participation of school students," the school leadership had held several meetings with students and their parents. As a compromise solution, the school column would take part in Immortal Regiment as planned, but without the six students who had filed an objection.[117] A state-sponsored Immortal Regiment typically features city fathers walking in the front row, followed by

Figures 7–8 Immortal Regiment as a statement of loyalty to the new Russia and the old Soviet Union. Some of the participants in the annual Immortal Regiment parade proudly display their colors, whether it is the FSB or the former USSR, here on May 9, 2019, in Barnaul.

organized groups of school and kindergarten children, postal and sanitation workers, and so on. Anthropologist Alexandra Arkhipova, who has studied patterns of May 9 celebration throughout Russia, thinks of Immortal Regiment as a kind of ideal social order. The majority of participants join the annual parade voluntarily. According to Arkhipova, they are motivated by phobia: the apprehension that the memory of their loved ones may otherwise vanish and the fear of being overwhelmed by a hostile world, unless they close ranks with the Immortal Regiment, that is. Counterintuitively, Immortal Regiment may also function as a means to vent individual frustration about the daily hardships à la "my grandfather fought for my future, and look what we've got now."[118]

The debate on whether Immortal Regiment has become a genuinely popular event is ongoing. The numbers are, indeed, staggering. In 2014 half a million people in 450 different places in five countries participated in the march. The following year

Figures 7–8 (Continued)

Immortal Regiment expanded onto twenty countries.¹¹⁹ According to Levada, in 2017 some 26 percent of Russians intended to take part in the march. Official figures for 2018 were one million participants in Moscow and 10.4 million for the entire country. The headcount, however, especially in the provinces, renders a different picture. Out of 300,000 people who live in Liubertsy, Moscow region, anywhere between three and four thousand reportedly showed up for the event in 2017. Even then, half of them were organized in groups (i.e., students, sportsmen, workers, state employees, and so on), as attested by the placards some of them were carrying. In yet another city not far from Moscow, schools and veterans' organizations lined up much like they did at the annual May Day parade during the Soviet times. A certain student has confided that ten of them from the same grade were expected to report, but only a half bothered to do so.¹²⁰

A photographer captured portraits of anonymous veterans "for hire" in Moscow lying in a dump after the event; one person on a portrait turned out to be an NKVD official who "helped expose anti-Soviet activities of the enemy" (as per a contemporaneous newspaper article).¹²¹ In Mordovia, top officials, including a bishop, posed with a portrait of one and the same war veteran, though differently inscribed.¹²² At the same time, when navy cadets in Arkhangelsk came up with the idea of carrying the portraits of British and French sailors who died as part of the Allies' sea convoys during the Second World War, they were advised by local authorities against it, due to a "complicated international situation."¹²³

When gauging the success of Immortal Regiment, state officials typically emphasize its international aspect. Thus, the head of the 2017 Victory organizing committee boasted that the event—which he described as an "international public endeavor"—was held in fifty different countries the previous year. He expressed satisfaction that citizens of host countries have joined the Immortal Regiment in increasing numbers. In the former Soviet republics, it is the students from Russian schools and Russian branch colleges, alongside war veterans, who keep up the momentum.[124] The worldwide expansion of the Immortal Regiment has been coordinated by Zemtsov, the mastermind behind the hostile takeover.

In 2017 Russian compatriots marched for victory in such unlikely locations as Ulaanbaatar in Mongolia and Ottawa in Canada. In 2018, portrait bearers passed through central Lisbon, Beirut, London, Manchester, Rome, Calgary, Barcelona, Madrid, Zurich, Geneva, Skopje, Ankara, Vienna, Liege, Belgrade, Sofia, Berlin, and Seoul, among other world cities. Sixteen cities in Israel and twenty in the United States hosted the march. In Montreal, Russian expats collected money to fly a giant St. George's ribbon behind a light aircraft. Lapenkov has written to the organizing committee in Canada, wondering if they could think of a better way to use their money, say, by helping the elderly.[125] Some 1,200 people marched in 2018 in Lisbon. The column was headed by Yulia Samoilova, a Russian singer who represented her country in the Eurovision song contest held in the Portuguese capital around that time. The delegation received an "invitation" to join Immortal Regiment from the Russian embassy in Portugal, which in turn got a signal from the foreign ministry in Moscow.[126] Eventually, Immortal Regiment reached as far as the Antarctic (i.e., the Russian research station).

A foreign edition of Immortal Regiment is sometimes billed as "WWII veterans' remembrance walk." The claim of representing *all* Second World War veterans is bogus; Russian authorities made no known efforts to reach out to British or American war veterans. The geographic—quite prodigious as a matter of fact—expansion in the past few years has brought about no rethinking of the original (post-Tomsk) concept that marries national pride and militarism. Characteristically, Immortal Regiment Russia began squeezing out Immortal Regiment Tomsk as the organizing body abroad as well. Though, according to Lapenkov, it is not always easy to do due to a larger freedom of choice exercised by Russian compatriots.

In Estonia, Immortal Regiment takes place in Tallinn, Narva, and Sillamäe—the three cities with the largest proportion of Russian speakers, some of them Russian citizens. The number of participants in Tallinn tripled from ca 700 in 2016.[127] A smallish march has been attempted even in Kiev. Although the former president of Ukraine, Petro Poroshenko, cannot claim partiality with respect to Russia, he was on target when defining Immortal Regiment as a part of Russian hybrid warfare.[128] I agree with sociologist Igor Eidman, who has argued that the state mobilization of ethnic Russians abroad by means of Immortal Regiment is nothing but an effort to sustain the fifth column, ready to defend Kremlin's interests in a potential confrontation.[129]

Participants in the 2016 edition of the march in London were bussed from all over the Great Britain. Among the portraits they carried, observers spotted Stalin and the following year Arsen "Motorola" Pavlov (a Russian guerilla commander assassinated in October of 2016 in Donetsk).[130] By 2019 Stalin made it to the seat of the American government. Passersby experienced mixed emotions on observing a few hundred current and former Russian citizens with the Russian ambassador to the United States at the helm marching along Pennsylvania Avenue.[131]

Images of Stalin, which emerge with increasing frequency at the march, eventually gave life to something bigger. In 2019 Immortal Regiment split once again, except that now the initiative passed from the state back to the (conservative) grassroots. On May 9 that year the Communist Party organized in Moscow and several other Russian cities a march of its own. Immortal Stalin Regiment, as the name suggests, attributes the Soviet victory over Nazi Germany exclusively to Stalin's genius. Replicating the Immortal Regiment design code, Stalin is flanked by Lenin, Beria, Soviet military commanders, and, occasionally, portraits of the fallen relatives. Besides the communists, the newest edition of Immortal Regiment brought together a motley group consisting of war veterans, Stalinist youth, schoolkids in khakis, and unidentified men in NKVD uniforms. The most popular slogan at Moscow hailed Stalin as the father of the nation.[132]

Stalin is Dead, Long Live Stalin!

Stalin began regaining popularity in Russia around 1993–94, buoyed by the general nostalgia for the Soviet past. Since then, Stalin has consistently been ranked as the third or fourth most popular historical figure ever. Counterintuitively, the relative prosperity during Putin's first two presidential terms made the population even less critical of all things Soviet. Still, as Nikolay Koposov has argued, during his earlier years as the country's president, Putin did not want to jeopardize the relations with the West while rebuilding a strong Russia. Hence, in the first half of the 2000s Stalin has been reclaiming public space only gradually.[133]

Along with tolerance toward Stalin grew the proportion of Russians who see the need for a strong leader, two out of five in 2017.[134] Hence, Stalin came at no. 1 when Levada asked that same year whom the Russians considered the ten most outstanding figures in world history.[135] Despite the clear tendency, the most recent figures by Levada caused a minor earthquake. By April 2019 a record 51 percent of Russians felt positive about Stalin. If one also takes into account those who say they are indifferent, less than a quarter of Russian citizens have anything bad to say about the dictator. The sense of respect toward Stalin grew by 12 percent within one year. Those are the highest levels of approval ever registered in Russia.

The question is how to interpret these figures. Ksenia Kirillova of Radio Liberty has come up with a convincing explanation. According to Kirillova, Stalin has mutated from a historical figure to a composite embodiment of the features expected of present rulers. Stalin is a winner, a commoner, and a relentless fighter against corruption. In addition, Stalin stands for a socialist utopia that nostalgia for the Soviet past entails. In a way, the Putin regime shot itself in the foot by allowing a positive image of Stalin (e.g., in September 2019 Putin jokingly referred to Stalin as "daddy" and "father of the nation"). While Putin is still getting credit for a tough stance against the West, his inability to reign in the bureaucracy compares negatively with Stalin's in the popular mind. In the eyes of many—as the opinion polls confirm—Putin is not resolute enough in his action. As for the question of Stalin's terror, the standard mechanism of denial kicks in, namely diminishing the scope of repression and the role of Stalin as its ultimate architect.[136] The opinion polls attest to a shift in the popular perception of Stalin's terror, increasingly believed to have affected only the ruling elites.[137] Tellingly, mass protests against establishing a monster landfill in Shies in Arkhangelsk region—which dominated online discussions in Russia in 2019—drew inspiration from various sources; the protestors' makeshift camp featured, among other imagery, a giant portrait of Stalin.[138]

As Free Historical Society (VIO) poignantly observed, during the past decade the fragile consensus regarding Stalin's crimes that had existed since Perestroika has corroded. In the wake of the annexation of Crimea the "immune system of the nation has been compromised, gone is the antidote that might have been used in case of a poisoning by the deadly venom of Stalinism."[139] Yet the popular embrace of Stalin goes beyond the negation of collective suffering set in motion by the tyrant. Insofar as Stalin personifies ultimate authority, a positive attitude toward the dictator entails willingness to sacrifice one's own life in the name of the state.[140]

VIO's Kurilla has speculated about the possible reasons that make the Kremlin embrace Stalin. First, it may be a way of probing whether the general public is ready for a radical reassessment of national history. Second, it may be a means to assert control, for the regime can at any time weigh in against the resurgent cult of Stalin and thus pose as a voice of moderation. Third, the Kremlin might have zoomed in on the Stalin era when searching for an appropriate political language to justify the annexation of Crimea. Finally, it may revere Stalin for the maximum expansion of the Soviet empire and the tough stand against the West.[141] Like Kurilla, I regard this last hypothesis as the most compelling.

Unlike Medvedev, Putin has been circumspect when speaking about Stalin's crimes.[142] The furthest he went in condemning Stalinism was at a meeting of the Presidential Human Rights Council on October 1, 2015. When discussing the future monument to the victims of Stalin's terror, he designated it "one of the most bitter and difficult pages in Russia's history, as instructive as victories and triumphs." Even there and then, however, he qualified it by admonishing his audience to "objectively and responsibly" approach this subject.[143] No surprise, then, that a Putin doll is selling next to Stalin, for example in post-Olympic Sochi.[144] Who would win a competition, Stalin or Putin, for a larger number of private cars emblazoned with their portrait is hard to say.[145] Still, how ordinary Russians evaluate Putin's governing style vis-à-vis Stalin's may render a skewed picture. Putin, as liberal journalist Anton Orekh has remarked, does have some shades of gray. Consider, for example, the respect with which Putin had treated one of his critics, human rights activist Liudmila Alexeieva. Beside an element of political correctness befitting the president of the country, Orekh speculates, Putin appreciates both his trusted friends and sworn opponents.[146]

The Putin regime is post-ideological, Memorial's Alexandra Polivanova has argued. Neither Stalinist nor anti-Stalinist in his world outlook, Putin is interested exclusively in the preservation of power.[147] In that sense, what observers picked up from Putin's exclusive interview with Oliver Stone is off the mark. Many news outlets have cited Putin on Stalin. "Stalin was a product of his era," stated Putin and warned against "demonizing" the dictator. "We are trying to talk about his merits in achieving victory over fascism," he said.[148] What Putin intended to convey, however, is the ideal of a strong state (*derzhavnost*), which he attributes to the Russian people.[149] Ruthless tsars, victorious military commanders, or assertive Communist Party first secretaries for that matter—all share a singular positive trait in the eyes of Putin, namely, the ability to hold on to power, the art of survival.

Russia watchers have learned to read between the lines, but even they were confused by a monologue on Putin and Stalin that Kremlin's arch propagandist, Dmitry Kisilev, delivered on March 24, 2019 on Rossiia One. Kisilev provided a rather unusual commentary on Putin's recent message to the prosecutor general's office to mete out sentences appropriate to the gravity of the crime, in other words, to jail fewer people. Kiselev interpreted it as the president's attempt to squeeze out the "little Stalin" sitting in each and every Russian. In his interpretation, the Little Stalin seeks blood and approves of repression while the Great Stalin carried out industrialization and won the war (which deserves praise).[150] Like everything else in Russia, Kisilev's take on Stalin must have been preapproved from above. What he was effectively saying is that Putin, the magnanimous leader, has been helping his people overcome their proclivity for violence. It may be seen as a corrective, a disclaimer of sorts, to Surkov's designating Russians as "deep people." Hence, it turns out that it is Putin himself who has been carrying out the de-Stalinization of Russia the right way.

One of the problems is that the very notion of Stalinization is vague. Indeed, how expansive a public presence should Stalin reclaim before we start speaking of the "creeping de-Stalinization" in Russia? Aware of this dilemma, those who feel nostalgic for all the right things they believe had happened under Stalin just keep pressing forward in their adulation of the past. Can Stalinist-era art be segregated from the personality of Stalin, for example? Sure thing, says RVIO, which organized three exhibitions dedicated to so-called Socialist Realism within a span of six months in 2015–16. The biggest of the three, displaying works of Alexander Gerasimov, opened at Moscow's State Historical Museum in February of 2016. More than anyone else in visual arts, Gerasimov had advanced the cult of Stalin from the mid-1930s through the death of the dictator. The director of the museum insists, however, that the exhibition has nothing to do with Stalin, save for a few paintings on display featuring the Soviet leader. It can be that Gerasimov found his calling under Stalin's patronage rather than that he served the tyrant, he argues. To the question of why then to even display portraits of Stalin, the director answered along the familiar lines that we "need to show everything." The exhibition curator, at the same time, is unambiguous in his assertion that, yes, Gerasimov merely carried through Stalin's vision. Many a visitor comes to see the exhibition precisely because of Gerasimov's prominence in shaping Stalinist culture, he observes. Minister of Culture Medinskii, who attended the opening ceremony, was his usual self when advancing the principle of historical relativism. This time around, Medinskii could not hold back his enthusiasm for the bygone era:

> When you look at these paintings, you understand that we're not just talking about Communist propaganda, but about people who truly believed in what they were depicting—they were trying to make the world better, to perfect it. Perhaps not everything worked out for them, but they had faith, multiplied by a lot of talent, which led to the creation of remarkable works that need to be studied and displayed.[151]

Stalin and his era have been gradually appropriated by mass culture. Matreshka dolls with the image of Stalin have been a permanent feature of tourist bazaars. Now one can dine at restaurants named after Stalin (Novosibirsk, Nizhnii Novgorod), hire security services from Chekist (Tiumen), get pipelines repaired by Stalinism (Sochi), consume a fizzy drink "Leader [*vozhd*]" (Krasnodar region), buy a bottle of Soviet Champagne that marks 1937 as the year when it was first created, and pay Beria (Volgograd) to carry out soil works. In December 2016 a new meat restaurant called NKVD opened in downtown Moscow. The menu, featuring an appetizer "à la Stalin," announced tongue-in-cheek that, if you have not yet been seated/incarcerated (Russian: *sidet*), it is not your good but the restaurant's bad.[152]

What we are witnessing is the process of normalization of Stalin, which in and of itself is a radical step from what only recently was taboo. Say, the head of the Russian space program, Dmitry Rogozin, invited to test a new spaceship by using "Stalin's methods."[153] A Kaliningrad businessman running for office on the Civil Platform ticket (a political party founded in 2012 by Mikhail Prokhorov) demanded restoring not only a monument to Stalin but also the Gulag punitive system.[154] The chief executive of the state-run VTB bank showed up at an investors' party in Moscow dressed up as Stalin.[155] The Central Election Commission, responding to a formal challenge, in 2016 sanctioned the use of images of Stalin (though not photographs) in the election campaign. The Communist Party called the decision a "breath of fresh air" and promised to further popularize Stalin.[156] A high school in Perm displayed a banner that featured Stalin, alongside other notable individuals.[157] In the aggregate, all these disconnected episodes make Stalin a neutral household name. Simultaneously, it sustains a more ominous popular sentiment, "Stalin would have taken care of you [*Stalina na vas net*]." That sentiment was perhaps reflected best in a banner that appeared in Balakhna, Nizhegorod region, in December 2019, on the occasion of Stalin's anniversary. Stalin, brandishing an AK-47, appeared as Arnold Schwarzenegger's character in *Terminator*. The inscription, in Russian, read "75 Years of the Great Victory" while another, in English, "I'll be back."[158]

While the general acceptance of Stalin is growing, resistance beats retreat. It has got to the point that a public expression of disagreement with the adulation of Stalin may cause a violent reaction. One such incident took place in 2015 in Tobolsk. A youngster physically assaulted an elderly man who dared to tear off a portrait of Stalin displayed in a bus. No less shocking was a rather pedestrian reaction of the bystanders. As one of them was quoted saying, the only possible explanation for the elderly man's rash behavior is that he must have suffered under Stalin.[159] Poet Sergei Gandlevskii did the same a year later in a Moscow subway and was reported to the police by a passerby.[160] In Vladivostok, a self-confessed Stalinist lashed out against the newly erected monument to Alexander Solzhenitsyn. He placed a sign "Judas" on the statue, labeling Solzhenitsyn a traitor and Russophobe. He also lamented that the city authorities did not endorse the result of an opinion poll that called for the erection of a monument to Stalin in Vladivostok.[161] In Arkhangelsk, however, such a monument has been erected. A local historian considers it the indirect cause of a fine that he had got for having installed a memorial plaque as part of the "Restoring the Names" project under the aegis of Memorial.[162] In Magadan, in late 2016, vandals defaced the famous monument by Ernst Neizvestnyi by tagging "Stalin lives" on it.¹⁶³ The extent of repression has reached the point that ordinary people are once again afraid of the consequences if they share with Memorial information about Stalin's victims among their relatives.¹⁶⁴

Critical, or even satirical, views on Stalin also sometimes get censored. A case in point is a British–French feature film, *The Death of Stalin*. Two days prior to its scheduled release in Russia in January of 2018, the ministry of culture suspended its license. What made it problematic in the eyes of Russian bureaucrats was not the subject but the genre: it is a comedy. Had it not been for such a strong reaction, the film would have likely passed unnoticed—a B movie of limited artistic and historical value. The reasoning given by top Russian officials as to the decision to ban the movie made even seasoned observers raise their eyebrows. Radio Liberty ran a headline: "Stalin's Death Cancelled." A group of lawyers employed by the ministry of culture petitioned Medinskii to postpone the release until summer 2018. The lawyers found the movie extremist for "aiming to arouse hatred and hostility, to humiliate the dignity of the Russian (Soviet) people, and to promote human inferiority." They further insinuated that the film creators intended to "falsify our country's past, so that the life of the Soviet people during the 1950s would only invoke dread and aversion." What they essentially were objecting to is the comical, unfaltering portrayal of Stalin's entourage engaged in a life-saving operation in the wake of their boss's death. Medinskii proved himself a master casuist by arguing that *The Death of Stalin* ridicules all things Soviet, including victims of Stalinism.¹⁶⁵ He called the movie a "mockery of history."¹⁶⁶ Everyone had a (negative) opinion of the movie, whether they saw it or not. The Russian Communist Party urged to ban it as an "instrument of information war waged against Russia."¹⁶⁷ Duma deputy Natalia Poklonskaia approved of Medinskii's judgment, yet regretted he did not act as resolutely earlier in the case of *Matilda* (see Chapter 4).¹⁶⁸ Both movies were on occasion labeled a provocation. A *Komsomolskaia Pravda* journalist insinuated that the kind of comedy might as well have been produced by Hitler.¹⁶⁹ A former deputy minister of culture implied that showing a movie about the death of a dictator in the run-up to the presidential elections may give a wrong signal.¹⁷⁰ The Kremlin was among the last to weigh in. Putin's press secretary Dmitry Peskov said withdrawing the license was the right thing to do.¹⁷¹ Eventually, the prosecutor general's office checked the movie for extremism but found none.¹⁷² This statement of fact, however, still did not let ordinary Russians appreciate *The Death of Stalin*. A court of arbitration in Moscow in June of 2018 rejected a challenge to the decision to block the screening of the movie in Russia.¹⁷³ All in all, whenever the name of Stalin pops up in popular (Western) culture, Russian authorities prefer it changed to Hitler. That is what happened with a Hollywood action movie, *Hellboy*. In the Russian edition, Hellboy refers to the ghost of Hitler in conversation with Baba Yaga.¹⁷⁴

Any positive mention of Stalin and/or the NKVD inevitably stumbles against the fact of mass terror, carried out by the latter on the former's order. The most common reference point as to the regime's efforts to commit the victims of Stalin's terror to memory is the state policy framework on Memorialization of the Victims of Soviet Political Repression signed by Prime Minister Medvedev on August 15, 2015. Upon a close reading, the document strikes one as vague and convoluted. Building on other policy documents such as the national security strategy, the new framework is expected to contribute to patriotic education. Contradictions like these dot the program. One may hardly disagree that Russia may only become a genuine Rechstaat if it pays respect to the victims of the Soviet regime. The policy framework describes as unacceptable the "continuous attempts to justify repression . . . or deny it altogether as a fact of our history." These affirmations, however, work against yet another objective of "strengthening the country's positive image abroad." One of the program's underlining principles is to "condemn the ideology of political terror," while another is to "objectively analyze both the achievements of the Soviet period and its tragic pages, including mass political repression." The list of victim groups subject to commemoration is also instructive: the clergy, the elites who were forced to immigrate, the peasants who fell victim to so-called dekulakization and the subsequent famine, and all those who wound up in the Gulag. Not a single ethnic group is mentioned by name, especially those seven peoples that were deported in their entirety in 1941–44. Neither does it address the issue of accountability. These omissions may be explained on account of the program's expected outcome, namely strengthening ethnic unity as a prerequisite for a strong Russian state. The covert objective of the new state policy comes forth toward the end of the document. In effect, the program seeks to extend state control onto the interpretation and commemoration of Stalin's terror; all references are to federal outlets to the exclusion of the likes of Memorial. Last but not least, one does not fail to notice that this is a *policy framework* rather than a federal program (e.g., on patriotic education). In other words, it serves only as a recommendation. The program was supposed to be implemented in two phases, 2015–16 and 2017–19.[175]

Now that the program has been officially completed, it is obvious that it failed to deliver on all counts: expanding access to archives, setting up monuments at mass burial sites, conducting research and archaeological excavations, creating relevant museum exhibits and educational programs. The reality on the ground cannot be farther from the stated goal of boosting the society's moral health by means of learning of/from its tragic past. In fact, the situation has got worse (see Chapter 7). In retrospect, according to Ivan Kurilla, the intention behind the 2015 policy framework might be to merely counterbalance the growing popularity of Stalin.[176] That it failed to achieve as well. I would go further than Kurilla in proposing that this and similar initiatives constitute an attempt to superimpose an official discourse on Stalin's crimes and their commemoration. This is just one of many examples of *Gleichschaltung* in Putin's Russia.

The ambivalence surrounding the 2015 policy framework carries over to a central monument to the victims of Stalin's terror. Aired for the first time in 2010, the idea for the memorial was in late 2014 endorsed by Putin. "It's surely strange that here in Moscow we still haven't got around the question of committing those victims to memory. That should be done," said the president who has conveniently forgotten about the existence of a so-called Solevetsky stone in downtown Moscow and the annual commemoration ceremony that takes place there. Taken as a positive sign by many, the monument in the works did not receive universal support, notably from Memorial. Some critics wanted the memorial to replace/augment the Solevtsky stone in the symbolic center of Soviet terror, Lubianka Square. Still others did not want Putin to take credit for such a monument. Some state officials believed the memorial should be truly a "people's monument" and therefore suggested financing it through individual donations. That proposition angered certain victims, who pointed out that the terror was perpetrated by the state and the cost of the monument should be paid for by the state. The most controversial, however, proved to be the very concept of the monument, which called forth for such a design that would offend no one and yet serve as a starting point for a meaningful discussion about Stalin's legacy. The general public had no say on the final design, to be selected on the basis of an open competition.[177]

The outcome is, no doubt, a powerful, yet abstract Wall of Grief, which opened on the busy Sadovy Ring Road on September 30, 2017, in the presence of President Putin and Patriarch Kirill. Putin, without mentioning Stalin by name, spoke vaguely of "tragedy," "terrible past," "cruel blow," and "dark events." It should never be forgotten or justified, invoked the president of Russia. In the same breath, Putin warned against settling scores, which according to him could prompt dangerous confrontation within the society.[178] The monument not just passes in silence the issue of responsibility but, indirectly, also excuses the perpetrators. The memorial complex features four stone stelae with the words *know, remember, condemn,* and *forgive* inscribed on them. Yuri Samodurov, former director of the Sakharov Center, has rhetorically asked who

Figure 9 Ambivalent about Stalin. President Putin and Patriarch Kirill share more than just their KGB past. Inconvenient history appears the only thing that can put a dent on a present, mutually beneficial alliance between the church and the state. Both leaders refuse to unequivocally condemn Stalin while referring to his role in winning the war. Neither of them is willing to confront the question of agency—the millions of perpetrators who had got away with their crimes. This came to bear also during the opening ceremony of the Wall of Grief, formally known as the "monument to the victims of political repression," in Moscow on October 30, 2017.

exactly millions of Gulag victims and their descendants are expected to "forgive." An online petition to remove that particular word as inappropriate generated a mere few thousand signatures.[179]

One way of approaching the Russian state policy on commemoration is to determine how much support individual victims of Stalin's terror actually get in today's Russia. According to official figures, in the period 1991–2014 a total of 3,510,818 victims have been formally exonerated, including 264,085 children of the falsely accused. As of 2012, some 800,000 victims of Stalinism were still alive. In Moscow, the Gulag survivors get an extra monthly allowance of Rbl. 865 (USD 13), plus Rbl. 554 (USD 8.5) to compensate for medicines. On top of that comes a Rbl. 3,330 annual payment. Outside of Moscow, monthly allowances are significantly lower.[180] To compare, war veterans in Russia receive on average a monthly allowance of Rbl. 4,052 (USD 62).

Nikolai Arakcheev of the now closed Gulag history museum in Yoshkar-Ola observes a drop in public interest in the history of Stalin's repression in recent years. At the moment, it is mainly the relatives of the victims who are continually working on this subject, not least because everyone else is effectively denied access to archives. The number of professional historians doing research on this central aspect of Stalinism is also growing thinner. According to Arakcheev, researchers do not want to attract the attention of the security agencies or have difficulties publishing their findings.[181]

Opinion polls (here from 2017) tend to confirm this tendency. While 75 percent of the Russians are aware of Stalin's terror, that figure drops to 46 percent among the 18–24-year-olds. Slightly over one-third of the respondents put the blame on the state, and over one-half consider the victims innocent. The most common answer to the question of how many people fell victim to political repression is "hundreds of thousands." The percentage of people who do want *not* to disturb the past and therefore speak less of Stalin's terror grew within five years from 37 to 47.[182] Konstantin Andreev, who runs educational programs at the Gulag History State Museum in Moscow, supplies yet another example: among the high school students visiting the museum, only a quarter can give a coherent answer to what Gulag is.[183] These figures can be safely attributed to the impact of patriotic propaganda pursued by the regime.

As the Immortal Regiment initiative took off at Tomsk, some liberal commentators suggested holding an alternative annual march, Immortal Barracks, in memory of the victims of Stalin. That idea, however, did not lift off. Samodurov invited the supporters to be realistic: such an initiative would barely bring together 5,000–7,000 people, and that in Moscow. It is not just that the authorities would be unlikely to sanction the prospective march. The dominant memory culture in Russia does not account for mass victimization at the hands of the state.[184] Here one may be reminded that the official Day of Remembrance and Grief in Russia falls on June 22—the beginning of Hitler's attack against the Soviet Union in 1941. Thus, grief comes to expression only as a part of the foundational myth of the Great Patriotic War.

Formally condemning Stalin and Stalinism has been on the agenda ever since Perestoika. However, passing a judgment on a particular individual and his role in history is a tricky business generally. The regime has beaten the civil society into submission, so that any public anti-Stalin initiative mobilizes just a handful of supporters. The Congress of Intelligentsia that convened in the summer of 2015 for the purpose of judging Stalin, for example, brought together a mere twenty-six individuals, most of them in their sixties and seventies. The gathering failed to reach a consensus on how to go about judging Stalin and the Soviet Union. The participants felt demoralized by the lack of demand from below for their proposed initiative.[185] It was no different with a draft proposal submitted to the Federation Council a few months later. Outgoing senator Konstantin Dobrynin suggested treating the attempts to justify Stalin's crimes as extremism. Rebuking charges of genocide and crimes against humanity levelled against the Soviet leadership, however, would not be covered. By the same token, the proposed ban on commemoration of those complicit in mass crimes would only apply to toponomy.[186] Vaguely formulated, the draft proposal proved dead on arrival.

On top of that come legal hurdles. Not unlike the Constitutional Court's 1992 ruling on the legality of the Communist Party, Stalin's crimes will have been judged in accordance with the laws originally formulated in Soviet times.[187] Even if set in motion, again, the danger is that the prospective hearings would only generate limited attention. In practical terms, then, all that remains is the hope that the legal case may generate additional historical evidence. Out of all these futile efforts came one practical proposal, namely, focusing on the crimes against the peasantry, who had effectively paid for the industrialization, which in turn constitutes one of the achievements popularly attributed to Stalin (e.g., Stalin building effective defenses in the face of the subsequent fascist aggression).[188] The latest attempt to launch a criminal case against Stalin was made by Igor Stepanov, former prosecutor of the Russian Investigative Committee, in the spring of 2019. Although Stepanov knows full well he is bound to fail, he believes such a court case would help adjudicate Stalin's crimes.[189] There is no lack of sensible suggestions as to what should be done in order to counter the resurgence of Stalinism in Russia.[190] It is just that they cannot be realistically implemented in the present circumstances.

One may restate the question of de-Stalinization as follows: the efforts to block the glorification of Stalin have consistently failed. The most recent example is from St. Petersburg, where local deputies in March 2019 voted down the proposal to ban a political restoration of Stalin (e.g., by means of monuments and toponymy). The motion was tabled by the opposition party Yabloko, but was defeated by a coalition comprised of United Russia, the communists, and the nationalists.[191] Yabloko has been pushing for a law against the glorification of Stalin since at least 2017.[192]

A reminder about Stalin's victims makes mid-level officials feel uncomfortable. They react defensively, sometimes literally scrapping off the memory of repression. That is what an amateur artist from Borovsk has learned firsthand. Two dozen portraits of his fellow citizens who perished during the Great Terror he had painted on a wall were instantly vandalized. The artist believes it was done on purpose, while local bureaucrats declared such an impromptu means of commemoration potently wrong.[193]

State affiliates (in this particular case RVIO and the State Museum of Contemporary Russian History) dispute the claim that the memorialization of the victims of Stalin's terror is no longer on the state agenda. One counterexample they give is the recent reconstruction of the Katyn memorial, widely condemned in Poland and other countries as an attempt at historical relativism. As the argument goes, twice as many Soviet citizens were executed at Katyn in 1937–38 as Polish officers in 1940. By properly commemorating the former, justice has been served; everybody is equal in death.[194] Minister of Culture Medinskii supported the converting of the memorial to the slain Polish officers at Katyn into a site of joint suffering by arguing that "Russian people fell victim to repression alongside Poles. Ethnicity has nothing to do with that—such were the times."[195] For his role in the reconstruction of the memorial, RVIO's executive director Alexander Barkov subsequently received a personal commendation from Putin.[196]

The ambiguity surrounding Stalin and his crimes in contemporary Russia leaves the newly reopened Gulag History Museum in Moscow and its director in a tough spot. Reconstructed at a cost of 300 million rubles (USD 4.7 million), the museum is on the Moscow city budget. The director, Roman Romanov (b. 1982) is a professional museum administrator who looked up the best international examples in preparing the exhibition with the help of the newest in museology. Soft-spoken yet persistent, Romanov supervises a team of fifty plus some two hundred volunteers.[197] The rather minimalistic exhibition and the museum's public programs do, indeed, impress. Since its opening in the fall of 2015, the museum has become a gathering place for Gulag survivors and their descendants. However, there are certain red lines the Gulag museum cannot overstep. Along the official line, it puts emphasis on the *victims* of *political* repression and not the perpetrators. It does speak of the Gulag legacy in contemporary Russia but does not confront the issue of state criminality. Romanov sat on a panel that chose the winning design for the grand new monument in Moscow. It is Romanov, not his senior peers from Memorial and/or the Sakharov Center, who appear at various state-sponsored memorial events. The latter are respectful, yet cautious when speaking about the Gulag museum. After all is said and done, it is a state project that ultimately promotes the state agenda. As an indirect proof, in August 2018 Romanov received from Putin an award "for the services before the motherland." The same award was received at different times by RVIO's Miagkov and RAN's Chubarian.

Conclusion

It would be way too simplistic to paint the Russians as a "cruel" people shaped by "cruel history."[198] The notion that Russia and its people have become part of a death cult of sorts is also fallacious. Those who claim the Russians adore the dead should make a trip to a nearby cemetery with its many unkempt graves and few, mainly elderly, visitors. If the allegory of the underworld applies at all, it concerns disregard for human life, which the current regime has inherited from its communist predecessor. In other words, the government foments the (Second World) war hysteria as a subterfuge. Remarkably, when the initiative comes from below, like in the case of the Immortal Regiment, it makes death more humane. Outside of an ideological hold by the state, popular imagination instantly connects war with individual suffering. As soon as the government hijacked the Immortal Regiment, however, war became glorious again. By heading the annual Immortal Regiment in Moscow, Putin has sanctified not only the ritual and the myth that it stands for but also his hold on power. As someone once sarcastically remarked on social media, crushing Hitler's Germany is the only victory Putin got.[199]

Altogether, the Immortal Regiment is a textbook example of a grassroots initiative that the regime turned into a show of political support at home and a subversive operation abroad. By so doing, the state has corrupted people's memory of the war. Portraits of their relatives carried by millions of Russians participating in the Immortal Regiment should not be mistaken for a collective urge to draw a genealogical tree; personal history goes only as far back as June 22, 1941—as prescribed by unspoken rules. Thus, philosopher Mikhail Epstein does have a point in referring to the present regime as a "necrocracy"—a hybrid combining the Greek *nekros* and the French *bureaucratie*—but less so in speaking of "Russian Thanatos."[200] Svetlana Boym's discussion of nostalgia, and particularly its restorative form that feeds into a conspiracy of "falsified history," would have remained purely academic had not the Putin administration begun molding it into a state policy.[201]

Misappropriating popular history projects is part of a general state policy to assert control over public initiatives. Take, for example, such an innocuous thing as a bicycle ride. The Let's Bike project in Moscow was launched in 2012. Cooperation with the city authorities, though never smooth, had soured by 2018. In 2019, the city department of transportation launched a bike ride of its own.[202] In 2004, activists in Novosibirsk staged a "monstration," a creative way of expressing current concerns by displaying deliberately absurd placards in lieu of public demonstration. The event proved hugely popular among the youth and has since then spread to other Russian cities. On March 8, 2019, a pro-Kremlin youth organization, Molodaia gvardiia, staged a monstration of its own while denying it was a copycat.[203]

There is no denying that the collective perception of the Second World War in Russia and, say, in the United States is very different. A person visiting the National World War II Museum in New Orleans, for instance, would walk out of the permanent exhibition with the idea that the war was won single-handedly by the United States; the Soviet contribution to the defeat of Nazi Germany is scarcely mentioned. Americentrism on full display, it is still different from a conspiracy to erase Russia from history—as the Putin regime insists is the case. A private business association in London chose as it did by sponsoring back in 1995 a rather humorous statue of British prime minister Winston Churchill and US president Franklin D. Roosevelt, shown merrily chatting on a bench. The director of the Institute of Russian History of the Russian Academy of Sciences, Yuri Petrov, however, regards the statue as an example of the falsification of history. According to him, the sculptural composition called "Allies" should have also featured Stalin.[204]

The rapid ascent of Stalin in the Russian public sphere is comparable to the global spread of fake news. When the notion of *fake news* first emerged, most observers dismissed it as a marginal phenomenon. Very soon, however, fake news began drowning the actual news stemming from verified sources. The reaction on the part of world governments and the international media proved inadequate, not least because it came late. So deeply has Stalinism penetrated the state's foundational myth, that yet another de-Stalinization may be possible only under a democratic regime change in Russia, that is, in the unforeseeable future.[205]

4

Militant Patriotism

The 2018 Global Peace Index—prepared annually by an Australian think tank, the Institute for Economics and Peace—ranked Russia at 154, out of 163 countries surveyed. For a country that has not been under a direct military attack since the Second World War, this is a devastating result. Remarkably, the East European countries and, specifically, former Soviet republics, consistently projected by the Kremlin and its affiliates as hot spots of violent nationalism, are all ranked markedly higher than Russia on the Global Peace Index: Latvia at 31, Poland at 32, Estonia at 33, Lithuania at 36. Ukraine, at 152 is an exception—primarily on account of Russian aggression.[1] Indeed, the opposite of peacefulness assessed by the report, is aggressiveness.

Patriotism effectively denotes affinity for a particular place by members of a collectivity that claim it as their own. Scholars distinguish between passive and active patriotism, symbolic and unreflective patriotism. In the case of Russia, the civic patriotic education of the early Putin years gave way to a model built around militant patriotism. In effect, the current brand of patriotism promotes blind support for the statist ideology. That translates into manifest loyalty to the present authorities and cultivated intolerance toward perceived opponents. In the Russian context, patriotism serves as an umbrella concept uniting various government and pro-government agencies, including the military and the Orthodox Church, the United Russia Party and youth organizations. Underlining these efforts is a palpable nostalgia for the Soviet Union, which incorporates the fundamental principle of personal interests being subordinated to those of the state.[2] As journalist Alexander Nevzorov once caustically put it, the "Russian [type of] patriotism urges to protect not your own but somebody else's wellbeing and to die fighting not for your own rights but the lack of rights [*bespravie*]."[3]

Political scientist Valeria Kasamara at the Higher School of Economics has conducted a survey of values among the students at elite Russian universities. Her research shows that those young Russians who readily describe themselves as "patriots" are generally lacking in critical thinking as well as the basic knowledge of contemporary Russian history. The historical vectors typically mentioned are few and disjointed: the Russian Revolution, the Great Patriotic War, Gagarin's spaceflight, and Putin's ascent to power. The cultivated notion of patriotism has no space for collective shame. Simultaneously, it instills blind trust in the persona of the president. As Kasamara argues, the "young people want to live in a democratic country, but with Stalin as a ruler." In that sense, the Russian youth of today are not very different from their Soviet peers, she concludes.[4]

The perception of history is correlated with that of external threat. When Levada pollster for the first time, in 1989, asked if Russia had enemies, only 13 percent answered yes. (Back then, the "enemy list" included Islamists, communists, separatists, Democrats, and the CIA.) Nearly 50 percent of the respondents thought it was pointless identifying enemies when the problem lay with the Russians themselves and their history. Since then the negative sentiments have been growing exponentially, reaching the absolute maximum in the aftermath of Russia's aggression against Ukraine. As of October 2014, 84 percent of the Russians polled believed their country had enemies.[5] Meanwhile the conception of a heroic past has become dominant.

The Patriotic Education Program

The 14.5 million school students and 7 million kindergarten children presently in Russia are in one way or another involved in patriotic education. The Putin regime has successfully rebuilt a Soviet model of patriotic education in school. As Anna Sanina has argued, the success of the undertaking is largely due to the value system preserved by individual teachers and local school administration despite the collapse of the Soviet Union. Their invaluable input makes it all the more easy for the state to reestablish a formal framework for patriotic education. Furthermore, without the enthusiastic response from below, the state-sponsored patriotic program would have been dead on arrival. In spite of the myriad of new agencies and initiatives within the field of patriotic education, its core remains strikingly Soviet-like. Indeed, patriotism performed an important function also in the communist system.[6]

Sanina focuses on schoolteachers in her recent study of patriotic education in Russia. A large percentage of teachers, including history teachers, in provincial schools today are in their late fifties. They had completed their postsecondary education and begun their career in the former Soviet Union. Conversely, teachers, as a group, provide a steady support to the regime at the ballot box and beyond. The teachers interviewed by Sanina did not even bother reading programmatic documents on patriotic education they had been bombarded with, but, instead, drew directly from their professional experience in the 1980s Soviet Union. The fact that "patriotism" was a commodity for the state then and remains so now helps bridge a thirty-year gap. Most of what they know about patriotic education they had learned decades ago. Many an older-generation teacher sees it as either a revival or a natural regression. New elements injected into patriotic education do not contradict the basic Soviet model.[7]

No surprise, then, that teachers welcome various initiatives within patriotic education, including private ones. Thus, schoolchildren in Pskov got, in the academic year 2017/18, a new, optional course designed by Alexander Prokhanov and his Izborsk Club. The Izborsk Club is an archconservative think tank established in 2012. Among the club members are well-known Russian nationalists such as Alexander Dugin, Zakhar Prilepin, Nikolai Starikov, politicians such as Natalia Narochnitskaia, and clerics such as Bishop Tikhon; Minister of Culture Medinskii attended few of the meetings. Izborsk Club declares preserving the "sovereignty of Russian history, culture, and state" as one of its objectives. According to Prokhanov, the patriotic curriculum will tell kids about all things great in Russian history, including the conquest of Crimea and the Arctic. He hopes the new program would eventually be implemented across the Russian school and university system. Those among the Pskov educators interviewed by Radio Liberty for the most part take a positive view on the lesson in patriotism as offered by Prokhanov & Co.[8]

The legislative framework for patriotic education was put in place shortly after Putin's coming to power. Among the most important such acts is the five-year federal program on patriotic education (2001) and the Concept for Patriotic Education of the Russian Citizens (2003). The original five-year program, 2001–2005, was hastily conceived and poorly executed. Authorities doubled their efforts and tripled the budget of the subsequent five-year program to half a billion rubles (USD 18.2 million). Within the next ten years the total amount spent on patriotic education grew further, though only incrementally. The disproportionate weight attached to patriotic education in Putin's Russia can be illustrated by the number of manuals published on the subject. From two to three annually during the 1990s, the numbers grew exponentially in the following fifteen years, hitting eighty by 2015 (or twice the number of manuals during the peak Soviet years).[9]

The original focus on a military component in patriotic education (i.e., strengthening the country's defenses, military service) had shifted in 2006 toward civil education. Expected deliverables also got better defined. The third five-year program, 2011–2015, paid more attention to mass participation. The current program stresses the need for consolidation in the face of the perceived new geopolitical threats to Russia. As references to the Soviet practices in the present program, Sanina cites a link between military and law-enforcement agencies on the one hand and educational institutions on the other, and a system of patronage expected to strengthen it. In essence, it means more rigid ideological control. As regards the methodological aspect of the patriotic education program, it has remained as ill-defined as before.[10]

Patriotic education is one of the forty-four programs currently run by the government, consuming about 70 percent of the federal budget. In addition to the federal program on patriotic education, the government spends 450 million rubles, or USD 16.5 million annually on regional programs. The number of specific programs and their budget varies across Russia. According to Sanina, local bureaucrats are hardly sincere, or innovative for that matter, in their efforts to promote patriotism among the Russian youth. Some of the instances she cites point to corruption and/or incompetence. In other words, provincial administrations merely replicate the existing countrywide programs—and the pathos they contain—to get funds from Moscow. The only consistent theme in the federal and regional programs of patriotic education is the victory in the Great Patriotic War. Study trips and meetings with war veterans, memorial concerts and maintenance of war graves, exhibitions and sporting competitions—these and similar events primarily target schoolchildren. Taken as a whole, Sanina concludes, governmental programs on patriotic education serve a single goal: sustaining the loyalty of the population. One of her respondents, a provincial school director, explained the vicious circle by which authorities "give us money, which we pretend spending on patriotism, which they pretend to believe we do, and we [then vote for them]."[11]

As just mentioned, the patriotic education program gets reviewed every five years, beginning in 2005. Hence, the Russian youth is currently drawing wisdom from the program's fourth edition. For the purpose of this study, I decided to compare the last two programs, the one launched in 2010 under Medvedev and the other in 2015 under Putin. I am particularly interested in how history plays out in the conception of patriotic education. Fundamentally, the two programs are similar. Both identify patriotism as a unifying factor binding the nation together, and emphasize the central role of the state in framing it. A certain outlook on history is not among the program's specific objectives, while fostering a positive attitude toward military service is. As stated in the basic document, the ultimate goal of patriotic education is forestalling extremism, nurturing spirituality, strengthening political stability, and beefing up national security. When it comes to the federal agencies entrusted with the implementation, the Federal Agency on Youth Affairs (Rossmolodezh) in 2015 took over from the obscure Russian State Military History, and Cultural Center by the Russian Government.[12] The three other chief ministries remain the same: education, culture, and defense. The budget went up by over 100 percent, from 777 million rubles to 1,666 million.[13]

The 2016–2020 program is much more detailed as it is more ambitious. The list of auxiliary agencies now includes, among others, ministry of the interior, the foreign ministry, FSB, the Customs, and the RVIO, as well as the less obvious Russian State Space Corporation and the Russian State Nuclear Energy Corporation. In addition to central and local authorities, the latest program also refers to nongovernmental organizations and the family as core institutions. Private business is also expected to contribute. The ultimate goal is formulated more directly, too: to be ready both physically and psychologically to defend Russia's interests, specifically by military means, "in the trying conditions of an economic and geopolitical confrontation." The program is geared to showing practical results, if only statistically. In so doing, despite the assurances to the contrary, the Soviet-style formalism is making a comeback; figures come in lieu of a comprehensive assessment of the effectiveness of patriotic education. As of 2015, a total of 22,000 patriotic organizations and two thousand military/sports camps operated in Russia. This translates to 21.6 percent of the Russian youth presently being involved in some kind of patriotic activity. By 2020, the number of Russians aware of the program is expected to increase by 300 percent.[14]

Occasionally, the 2016–2020 program reads like emergency guidelines in the event of a major confrontation. It speaks of a "fluid situation," "further consolidation of the society for the purpose of safeguarding national security," "raising the prestige of military service and the service in law enforcement agencies . . . in times of peace and war." The program seeks to expand a volunteer movement and to more effectively engage young scholars and educators. The former should undergo standardization under the aegis of the central and local state agencies, while the latter should boost the expertise in "countering the falsification of history." History functions here as an appendix that props national unity under stress. The state policy on patriotic education aims to "strengthen the sense of belonging to the great history and culture of Russia, thus facilitating generational succession." The sense of ownership with respect to history is expected to help Russian citizens assume a proactive position in life. The keyword *great* determines the kind of history young Russians are supposed to embrace, namely the heroic past constructed around military victories and the state-building from ancient times onward. Furthermore, the program sanctifies it by evoking "reverence [*pochitanie*] for state symbols and respect for what is sacred in Russian history [*istoricheskie sviatyni*]."[15] Anything that does not contribute to forming a positive image of the country is not part of the program by default. In short, a history element in the 2016–2020 program on patriotic education is subservient to geopolitics ("reflects current challenges . . . facing the country"). To put it even more poignantly, history is a means of self-preservation for the Putin regime.

The content of the two subsequent programs is also similar. Anything and everything that can be utilized in pursuit of patriotism is being utilized: folk culture, sports, performing arts, music, and so on. What surprises one perhaps the most is not the specific programs per se, but the agencies charged with their implementation. For instance, college students are being encouraged to write their theses on particular episodes in Russia's "heroic past." In the long list of agencies overseeing this particular initiative one can find all sorts of ministries: agriculture, fisheries, health, energy, trade, customs, and extraordinary situations. The five agencies tasked with staging plays, making museum exhibits, and publishing on the subject of patriotism are the ministry of culture, the ministry of the interior, the ministry of defense, FSB, and DOSAAF (voluntary army assistance association). When it comes to the so-called falsification of history, the agency that calls more shots than the rest is the ministry of defense. It is also big on publishing within military history. The Academy of Sciences, at the same time, is way down the list. Some of the projects target narrowly defined groups, for instance, heads of memorial guards at the Second World War monuments. Crucially, among the target audiences are the young people pursuing higher education. Children with disabilities—typically neglected when it comes to primary care—are also drawn into the framework of patriotic education. Another novel aspect of the program(s) is the incorporation of veterans of the Afghanistan War into patriotic education and by extension into the new-old foundational myth of the Great Patriotic War. The Soviet war in Afghanistan has been recast as a "heroic deed" that serves the purpose of countering the "denial of historical facts." The 2010–2015 program attests to the state's intention to hijack and centralize the search movement. The militant form of patriotism draws, unsurprisingly, on military history. Outside of the Second World War and the Soviet war in Afghanistan, the list includes the Polish–Muscovite War, the Great Northern War, the Napoleonic Wars (i.e., Russia's victories in those wars). Any major triumph, say, lifting the siege of Leningrad in 1944, should not only instill pride in the Russian youth but also encourage them to join military service. The overall objective may be derived from a certain project description: "propaganda of heroism and courage of the immortal deed of the Soviet people in defense of independence of the Motherland."[16]

The 2016–2020 program keeps pushing the envelope on patriotism. The period up to 2020 may be regarded as a consolidation phase. College students writing their theses in "heroic" Russian history can now enter their works in a competition. Those engaged in historical reconstructions are invited to share their experiences in fellowship. Officials in the provinces in charge of the search movement can attend seminars on best practices. The search movement altogether did get a significant financial boost, possibly due to the runaway success of the Immortal Regiment. Recent initiatives such as the St. George's ribbon, the Patriot military theme park, and the just-mentioned Immortal Regiment get their own entries in the program. The centennial of Mikhail Kalashnikov, the AK-47 designer, in 2019 generated a string of commemorative events. (The ministry of education has supplemented it by recommending schools offering a thematic lesson on the gunsmith's anniversary, November 10.)[17] The latest program has also acquired an international aspect, for example, by attempting to attract foreign university students. The agency list got expanded on account of RVIO. The growing role of power ministries in what traditionally had been the domain of culture and education is illustrated by the novel practice of military bases patronizing educational organizations.

The post-Crimea conception of patriotism calls for a "revival of Russia's heroic past" derived from the Second World War and other military conflicts. The notion of "patriotically minded historical knowledge" effectively makes history into a propaganda weapon.[18] Notably, the 2016–2020 program, unlike its earlier editions, classifies the amount of funding that power ministries such as the FSB, the interior, and foreign affairs are allocated under the heading of patriotic education. Otherwise, all these agencies co-administer certain projects, including those related to history.

The Ministry of Defense Patronizing Children's Organizations

In the provinces, the school has traditionally been a gathering place for the community. From the perspective of patriotic education and its constituent part, memorialization, the school museum plays a central role. The museum exhibit is typically divided into two parts: memory of the Second World War and local history. The former segment is significantly larger and more elaborate than the latter. Most of the extracurricular activities evolve around commemoration of the war dead; school children have been coopted into the Victory Volunteers and the Russian Search Movement. There were also several attempts to revive the Soviet Pioneer organization, as a youth branch of the United Russia Party in 2004 and as a countrywide pioneer movement in 2012. Local children's groups organized at the teachers' initiative usually draw inspiration from Soviet pioneers, anyway.[19]

As with other aspects of Russian history politics, a qualitative leap had occurred in the wake of the annexation of Crimea. In late 2015, the federal agency for youth affairs established a nationwide Russian schoolchildren's movement, which saw its budget instantly doubling. According to its charter, the movement is a non-political, voluntary public association intended for children of age eight and above. At the same time, it is expected to promote the state policy of identity-building engrained in the uniquely Russian value system, which is suspiciously close to the wording of the 2015 Presidential decree, "On the National Security Strategy of the Russian Federation." Symbolically, Putin authorized the creation of the Russian schoolchildren's movement on October 29, 2015, ninety-seven years to the day the Young Communist League, Komsomol, came into existence. "Traditional Russian spiritual and moral values" had meanwhile become a staple of the Kremlin's propaganda. Government officials deemphasize the persistent rumor that they had been planning to take the Russian school youth "back to the USSR." What they do not deny, however, is that the government, by means of the Russian schoolchildren's movement, is seeking to superimpose its agenda on the larger strata of the population. Hastily produced manuals subsume the envisaged activities of the movement under "military-patriotic education." The public opinion was split on the virtue of the new-old body, with a majority welcoming it being modeled on the Soviet Pioneer organization. Individual school administrations—however ambiguous they might feel about the new type of organization for children—fell in line for the fear of being overlooked when it comes to distribution of resources.[20]

Few in the school administration had realized that by embracing the Russian schoolchildren's movement they were automatically signing up for the Youth Army (Iunarmiia)—a militaristic organization established simultaneously with the former and formally subordinated to it. Within the sphere of military-patriotic education, the Youth Army puts the emphasis on the former component. Under the patronage of Minister of Defense Sergei Shoigu, the Youth Army is directly tied to the Russian military and claims a section of its own in the Patriot military theme park near Moscow. It serves as an umbrella organization for over five thousand youth and military-patriotic groups. Originally, Youth Army branches were linked to military bases and military training institutions. Among its sponsors are the three biggest Russian banks, Sberbank, VTB, and Gazprombank. The organization currently has chapters in all eight-five regions of Russia. The sleek corporate identity of the Youth Army is surely to appeal to teenagers: sharp-looking paraphernalia and stylish uniforms resembling the desert military fatigues of the US Army, access to sports facilities, and newest weapons short of missile launchers. The army coopted a number of Russian athletes, including Winter Olympic gold medalist Dmitry Trunenkov, who promised to make the Youth Army the biggest and most effective such organization in Russia. Vice Admiral Nikolai Evmenov, who administered the oath to a group of Youth Army cadets on board Russia's only aircraft carrier in Severomorsk, felt emotional. "When I was accepted in the pioneer ranks, happiness made me speechless," reminisced a top navy official. "Today, when the kids were receiving their pins, I saw something similar. Their eyes were emitting absolute happiness as they responded: 'I'm in Russia's service.'" Once again, though ostensibly a volunteer organization, authorities make a projection that in a matter of a few years it will boast hundreds of thousands of members (241,000, or 1.6 percent of Russian schoolchildren, as of summer 2018).[21] What makes the Youth Army unprecedented in the context of both Russia and the Soviet Union is the defense ministry's sponsorship. In that respect, it differs markedly from any other pro-government youth organization.

Historically, the Youth Army builds upon the tradition of military training in Soviet schools and the annual paramilitary game "Zarnitsa" (dawn). Backed by school military-patriotic clubs and school museums of military glory, these remnants of the Soviet past survived throughout the tumultuous 1990s. The museum custodians, who had experienced the near death of their cherished institutions, welcomed the renewed attention from the Russian armed forces. In return, each school that joins the Russian schoolchildren's movement/Youth Army framework is expected to establish a dedicated room for cadets' study and recreation. The Youth Army's motto, "Nobody but us," is nearly identical to that of the former Komsomol and of the Russian Special Forces (Spetsnaz). Its insignia incorporates Soviet and Imperial Russian elements: a red star implanted on an eagle's head. The insignia translates into the slogan: "The eagle power has millions of eaglets, the pride of the country." The Youth Army's premises necessarily feature the portraits of President Putin and General Shoigu. Tellingly, Putin's "green men" who spearheaded the annexation of Crimea serve as a role model for the Youth Army. The figure of a soldier in a balaclava and no military insignia, holding a cat—immortalized in bronze in at least two cities—belongs to the organization's paraphernalia (see Chapter 5).[22] Indeed, the core purpose of the Youth Army is instilling the ethos of sacrifice, if not martyrdom, in the Russian schoolchildren.[23]

Along with military training, Youth Army members are encouraged to study the history of Russia, military history in particular. The study of local history incorporates learning about important personalities of "lesser" Russia. The oath includes a pledge to "cherish the memory of the heroes who fought for freedom and independence of our Motherland." The activities of the Youth Army since its inception in May 2016 indicate that by "freedom fighters" is meant almost exclusively the Soviet Army facing up to Nazi Germany. Thus, in early May 2017, members of the Youth Army in nine Russian cities quizzed kids on their knowledge of the Great Patriotic War. Those who answered correctly to the posed questions received bracelets in the colors of the St. George's ribbon and the emblazoned Youth Army logo. It is remarkable, though, that among the Youth Army's partner institutions is listed the Russian Geographical Society but not the Russian Military Historical Society (RVIO). Clearly, in the case of this particular organization, practical military training takes priority over expert knowledge of history.[24]

As an indirect proof, in late January 2019 a document circulated that obliged the children of the officers to join the Youth Army. Signed by deputy head of the western military district in charge of political education, the document laid down a 100 percent participation of children between 8 and 18.[25] The following month the military prescribed the establishment of Youth Army chapters at individual factories by the defense industries.[26] Most disturbing, however, is the linkage established between the Youth Army and foster homes (about fifty thousand children). Orphans, including children with disabilities, would be enrolled in the Youth Army automatically.[27] Already earlier, independent media had reported on individual cases in Kazan and Moscow region where entire school grades were inducted into the Youth Army, without prior consent from the parents.[28]

In a country as corrupt as Russia, it comes as no surprise that certain individuals close to the government have earned big on the new youth organization. Take, for example, uniforms, which children, or rather their parents, have to buy themselves. The full set of summer and winter uniforms includes ten pieces of clothes. Kids can also purchase additional items such as iPhones with the Youth Army logo. If everyone purchased two sets of uniforms, we are talking about 2.5 billion rubles. Suspiciously, all orders go through a single shop in St. Petersburg. As the Open Media was able to establish, the business—through various subsidiaries—is linked to Yevgeny Prigozhin, a close associate of Putin who made a fortune supplying meals, first to school children and government employees, and later to the Russian army. Recently, Prigozhin has been identified as the founder of an infamous "internet troll factory" in St. Petersburg and sponsor of Russian mercenaries (so-called Wagner men) who had fought in Syria and Libya, among other places. "Pioneers who also know how to shoot"—as a teacher at a Moscow school was trying to entice parents into enrolling their kids in the Youth Army—obviously do not know they are being exploited both politically and commercially.[29]

The Youth Army calls the Patriot military theme park at Kubinka a home. An hour's drive from Moscow, the enormous park was inaugurated by President Putin on June 16, 2015. Along with all things military, the ministry of defense is eager to put on display "traditional Christian values." The scale of the theme park is matched by the ministry's ambition to build the third-tallest Orthodox Church anywhere in the world on its territory. The cathedral in the works is a perfect illustration of the kind of history politics pursued by the Putin regime.

Meant as the main cathedral of the armed forces, it is, as the available blueprints show, a massive structure in a neo "Russo-Byzantine" style. Of the five altars envisioned, four are dedicated to the patron saints of various armed forces branches: Alexander Nevsky for the infantry, Apostle Andrew for the navy, Prophet Elias for the air force, and Martyr Barbara for the intercontinental ballistic missile program. The architect, Dmitry Smirnov, claims Bishop Tikhon as his patron. The influential cleric liked Smirnov's earlier work so much that he made the 33-year-old the artistic director of the "Russia: My History" multimedia exhibition. Announced in September 2018, the cathedral is expected to be completed in a record two years, through private donations. Pomposity obscures the basic fact that local parishioners are not nearly enough to fill its anticipated capacity of six thousand. Orthodoxy is altogether the only practical area of application so far for the military political department reestablished within the armed forces in July 2018.[30]

It took just a few months for the cathedral's original design to cheapen up and the idea of voluntary donations turn into a semi-enforced collect. As it appears on the official website, the building is a curious mix of a traditional Orthodox church, a greenhouse, and a train station. As regards financing, soldiers in certain military districts have reported a 500-ruble due imposed by the higher-ups, regardless of the faith of the "donor." One can only wonder if that is what the defense ministry meant by a "nationwide project."[31] To imbue his pet project with meaning, Shoigu came up with the idea of casting the cathedral's staircase with scrap iron from Nazi Germany. The problem is that each and every piece of Wehrmacht hardware is accounted for as a museum artefact.[32] Recycling is also the keyword in the case of a main icon. The icon, paid for personally by President Putin, is being painted on boards from a 1710 cannon gun carriage submerged in Neva River. The boards will be attached using parts of a 1944 rifle.[33] The Great Patriotic War will get formally sanctified through a series of bas-reliefs depicting major battles, including the disputed sacrifice by the Panfilov twenty-eight. Among other preselected episodes of military glory is the parade of German prisoners of war in Moscow in 1944 and Nazi Germany signing an unconditional surrender in 1945.[34]

Convergence has been complete: both pro-Putin biker Zaldostanov and Deputy Defense Minister Kartopolov speak in one voice of millions of Soviet soldiers who perished Christ-like on the battlefields of the Great Patriotic War and thus earned immortality. According to the latter, the Soviet victory over fascism is that spiritual bond that has prevented the collapse of the Slavic Orthodox civilization. The cathedral's décor features a mixture of religious and historical references (e.g., the cupola dedicated to the Holy Spirit containing 1,418 stars—the number of days the Great Patriotic War lasted). A sacred symbol, the cathedral is expected to also serve as the Immortal Regiment headquarters.[35] In the summer of 2019, the ministry of defense announced plans to open a film studio of its own at Patriot Park. As a challenge to RVIO and the ministry of culture, the military brass is planning to shoot historical movies as well as flicks about "heroes who fight against international terrorism."[36] The cathedral's opening ceremony on May 9, 2020 was postponed due to the coronavirus outbreak.

The Orthodox Church, and the so-called traditional values it stands for, neatly fit into the concept of military-patriotic education. Armed with spirituality, the clergy is increasingly drawn into various education projects aiming at both children and adults. Thus, in the run-on to the seventieth anniversary of the end of the Second World War, churchmen joined academics to teach the police rank and file about patriotism and spirituality. That was expected to increase the quality and effectiveness of this particular law-enforcement agency. In the Mari El Republic, a priest urged policemen to love their motherland and remember the veterans' heroism. As a Duma deputy has explained, brushing up on history could make the state security apparatus reconsider certain current issues. The policemen felt obliged, on pain of salary cut, to attend the practical training seminar with the participation of the clergy.[37]

Back to Shoigu: his passion for Russian history goes back at least ten years. As mentioned earlier, the minister of defense is one of the godfathers of the legislation against the so-called falsification of history. Creative ideas just keep coming from the army general and decorated Hero of the Russian Federation. In February 2019, for example, he commissioned RVIO to conduct a written test on the history of Russian arms for the military, in which a total of 122,000 servicemen participated.[38] Shoigu apparently believes that the best way of teaching history is by means of historical reconstructions. For all that, the guiding principle of military reenactment had changed from the early 1990s, when it was first introduced in Russia. Thus, "paths of past wars leading up to peace [*dorogami proshlykh voin k miru*]" gave way to "we may do it again [*mozhem povtorit*]."

Many a scholar has compared and contrasted coming to terms with history in Germany and Russia. The comparison comes in favor of Germany, hands down. An extra irritant, it frames the restrictive Russian legislation that prohibits a comparison between the Soviet Union and Nazi Germany, and by extension Stalin's and Hitler's crimes. As Nazi mass crimes dominate the conversation, it keeps spewing new, creative, and—I will allow myself to be frank—idiotic initiatives. One such initiative came, again, from Defense Minister Shoigu. In February of 2017, he announced that a replica of the German Reichstag was under construction in Patriot Park. Youth Army kids need to practice storming something, he reasoned, so they better participate in the reenactment of the 1945 siege of the Reichstag in Berlin. For whatever reason—possibly construction costs—the Reichstag's cupola looked more like Sir Norman Foster's design rather than an original piece.

Figure 10 History as replica. The Ministry of Defense has been playing an increasingly larger role in historymaking. The Soviet heroism in the Second World War is supposed to instill in young Russians pride in the Russian military might. Nowhere does this idea manifest itself better than in Patriot military theme park outside Moscow, which opened to the public in 2015. On April 24, 2017, the audience was treated to a recreation of the 1945 Battle of Berlin.

The storming of the Reichstag replica on April 23, 2017, did indeed showcase the newly established Youth Army. The organizers tried to keep close to the original, including a Hitler impersonator rallying his troops to hold on to the last. The audience at Kubinka burst into applause when make-believe Soviet soldiers hoisted the Soviet flag on the fake Reichstag. The Nazi flag that it had originally replaced, however, was not to be seen—so as not to inadvertently prompt criminal prosecution (Article 354.1 of the Russian Criminal Code, "glorification of Nazism"). The social media teemed with caustic jokes à la why should not the French reenact the 1812 burning of Moscow.[39]

Much like his counterpart in the ministry of culture Medisnkii, Shoigu has the unique capacity to deny what he is putting into practice. We are not engaged in the militarization of society, stated Shoigu two months after his brainchild, the Youth Army, had been formally registered.[40] Sometimes ridiculous, like the just-mentioned reenactment of the siege of the Reichstag, the militarization of youth is increasingly taking ominous forms. On July 17, 2014, pro-Russian separatists in Eastern Ukraine downed a passenger plane—as established in the course of several international investigations. All 298 people on board a Malaysian Airlines flight were killed. The plane was shot down by a Buk surface-to-air self-propelled launcher. Russia has consistently denied its hardware had been used in bringing down the plane. Two years later, a company in St. Petersburg presented a new item in its collection of children's beds. The camouflage-colored bed is crafted to look like the Buk missile launcher, complete with a red star and Russia's tricolor. Responding to criticism, the director of the company said they never intended to offend anyone with the new product. To avoid unfortunate associations, the bed's name has been changed to "Defender."[41] The bed is currently selling for 11,000 rubles. According to the description, this particular type of missile launcher has been "guarding the peaceful sky" since 1980.[42]

When observing current tendencies, political analysts have begun to speculate if the army is becoming a major institute in Russia. Indeed, after a series of reforms in the wake of the 2008 Russo-Georgian war, and particularly since the 2014 annexation of Crimea, the Russian army had enjoyed extraordinary popularity among ordinary Russians. The military literally underwent a rebranding, including registered trademarks "Army" and "Polite People" (e.g., Putin's "green men" in Crimea).[43] Historical references, as one could imagine, play an important role in making the army relevant again. Thus, speaking at the Army 2015 forum in Patriot Park—meant as both a military exhibition and a propaganda festival—a certain staff member of the military academy compared the cumulative effect of the "reunification" of Crimea to that of victory in the Second World War.[44] Leader of Night Wolves Zaldostanov, who was touring Patriot Park on the day it opened, said he liked the fact that the army is being romanticized. Among other merchandise, one can buy at Kubinka various pieces of clothes with either Putin's face or slogans extolling the victory in the Second World War. Also available are fridge magnets depicting, among others, Stalin and Beria.[45]

Unlike in Soviet times, history-based indoctrination in contemporary Russia reaches all the way to preschool age. The four manuals on how to teach patriotism to preschoolers from the period between 1970 and 1989 pale in comparison with the seventy-seven that have been produced since 2000 (or 10 percent of the total). Not all manuals focus on the military aspect of patriotic education, but those that do take it to extremes. Publications like *Having Taken an Oath, Never Retreat*, and *Pedagogical Sandbox: Teaching Patriotism to Preschoolers on the Example of the Armed Forces* go beyond specific commemorative dates in proposing military topics as a daily agenda for kids of age three and above. The latter manual, for example, suggests enacting battles showcasing the "glory of the Russian weapons" and identifies toy soldiers and fortification models as "symbols of socialization." Preschoolers should regard military service as an honorable duty, for the Russians only engage in wars of liberation, explains the manual. Children aged between four and six are urged to gain more hands-on experience, by learning how to plant toy mines in a sandbox, for example. May 9 celebration for preschoolers typically replicates the script designed for schoolchildren and includes singing military songs, listening to stories about wartime heroism, meeting with veterans, and doing war-themed crafts. The Second World War narrative conveyed to children as young as three years is nearly identical to the Soviet one. As the manuals have it, fascist Germany's attack on "our peaceful country" made everyone, including children, rise in defense of the motherland. Valiant Soviet soldiers drove the Nazis out all the way to Berlin, and since then every citizen of Russia as well as the people in other countries celebrate May 9 as the most important holiday. The manual goes on to explain the intended outcome: "The goal of such rituals, celebrations, and group activities is to make young children love the state, its symbols, and its past while the children are too young to contradict or protest. At that age, they will understand the military history of Russia as a history of victories, which creates the foundation for emotion-based education."[46] In short, the government is using Russian military history to cultivate blind support for the present regime from the earliest possible age.

All these recommendations have already been introduced in practice. On May 15, 2018, Stavropol's kindergarten number 17 held an annual "preschool army parade." Organized since 2013, the parade featured 430 children and was dedicated to the Soviet victory over Nazi Germany. Each kindergarten group stood for a particular military unit: marines, commandos, scouts, arctic warfare division, and so on. The director of the kindergarten performed the role of the supreme commander. Some of the 4–7-year-olds carried Immortal Regiment banners. According to a local newspaper, the kids rejoiced at the opportunity to explore actual armored military vehicles that had been brought for the occasion. All participants could browse through thematic family albums, "Remember that Life Goes on" and "A Doll in Military Uniform."[47] Select kindergartens in the Russian Far East have reportedly held a contest in which children perform tasks pertaining to various branches of the military.[48] Rostov-on-Don is yet another city that has held a children's military parade, at the initiative of the head of a military district; on average, some one and a half thousand children between 4 and 10 march in formations before a group of war veterans.[49] In 2019, the young participants clad in military uniforms "thanked their grandfathers for the victory" by riding scooters. Some of their mothers posted photographs on social media congratulating the compatriots on the "Great Patriotic War."[50] Similar parades have taken place in 2019 in Piatigorsk, Chekhov, Ivanov, and several other Russian cities.[51]

A military-patriotic club opened in 2017 in kindergarten number 115 in the industrial city of Cherepovets. The initiative came from a father who is active in a Spetsnaz veterans' organization. Small girls and boys in camouflage learn to march while singing: "Our young valiant Spetsnaz is always ready to serve!" Former commandos and kindergarten educators concur in the opinion that military training helps cultivate historical memory in children. Reportedly, the most popular inter-kindergarten event in Chrepovets right now is the annual song and marching contest, "Soldiers, the Brave Guys." Kindergarten number 33 had this message for the outside world: "The soldiers have weapons with which they'll crush just any enemy."[52]

Beside the ministry of defense and volunteer organizations, a plethora of state-sponsored agencies work to inculcate militant patriotism in the Russian youth. Governor of St. Petersburg Alexander Beglov once related a "touching" story of a particular artwork created by an eleven-year-old girl. As a submission to a young artist competition on the theme of the Great Patriotic War, she created a three-minute film, "War through a Child's Eyes." At the end of the film, the girl takes the clothes off her Barbie doll and dresses it in a military nurse's uniform.[53]

Military historical children's camps proliferate throughout Russia. By way of example, here is what the kids who were part of "I Salute" summer camp in Tambov have learned in order to become a new generation of "healthy patriots." The camp was co-organized in June 2018 by RVIO and Tambov Center for Social Assistance to Family and Children. The opening ceremony featured a joint parade by a local National Guard (Rossgvardiia) unit, the Flame military-patriotic youth group, the Phoenix sports club, and a Slav drummer band. The forty-odd boys—mainly from orphanages—were subsequently greeted by representatives of the Tambov social department, a regional Duma deputy, RVIO officials, and a priest. Workshops taught the kids marching songs, the ethos of Russian volunteers, the history of RVIO, and painting. The 7–10-year-olds attended the following master classes: "Self-Defense with no Weapon," "Assembling and Disassembling AK-47M," "Obstacle Course," and "Rope Town." Teams performed a Katusha dance, songs like "Soldier is always a Soldier" and "Because We are Pilots," and the poem "Heroic Russia." Particularly moving proved the play "A Ballade about Mother" and the dance "Angels of Good."[54]

The continuous political oppression, media censorship, cultivated militarism, and general aggression in the society—all these factors bear on how ordinary people assess Russian history and/or react to interpretations different from the official one. There are plenty of vigilantes out there who want to see the state agenda on patriotic education strictly implemented. Such popular reactions tend to be rigid, unwilling to engage in an informed dialog, and just plain unforgiving. Examples abound. In late May 2018, a video shot in Krasnoyarsk made rounds on social media. The video showed a young man jokingly picking up a few flowers left at a local Second World War memorial and handing them over to his girlfriend. The response to the incident was furious: five-year imprisonment, drowning, and/or denying college education and employment. The parents of the errant individual, online commentators proposed, should also be fined.[55] The general thrust of the commentaries was that this was, indeed, a criminal offense. The same month, a 52-year-old man in Volgograd was caught fraudulently misappropriating veterans' medals and other paraphernalia on the pretext of documenting their wartime exploits. Readers began competing with each other on the kinds of torture they would like to subject the swindler to: hanging him by the balls, boiling in oil, putting on a spear, and/or burning alive.[56] Despite the violent rhetoric, none of the ordinary online users would probably act out their threats. There are, however, a few nationalist groups that use violence programmatically.

With the myriad of nationalist entities operating in present-day Russia, one may trace the evolution of the Kremlin patriotism project by focusing on the major organizations. Among the first such organizations to be created by Putin's spin doctors was Molodaia gvardiia (Youth Guard) in the mid-2000s. As the youth wing of United Russia Party, it offered an easy career path. Almost simultaneously, in 2005, Kremlin ideologists created Nashi (Our Own). The influence of Vladislav Surkov, who has overseen Nashi's operations, is manifested in the organization's stated goal of helping advance "sovereign democracy." While its structure and agenda are similar to Molodaia gvardiia's, Nashi functions more like a shock unit, harassing pro-democracy activists and foreign diplomats. Its attempts to develop any sort of ideology beyond militant patriotism have failed; the Nashi Orthodox Corps did not take off. By 2014–15, Nashi had effectively run its course. To address political challenges in the wake of Russia's aggression against Ukraine, the Kremlin assembled an organization of a new kind. Ideologically driven, Sut vremeni (The Essence of Time) attracted a share of nationalist youth with a tinge of intellectualism. The idea of Soviet imperialism promoted by its leader, Sergei Kurginian, worked right in cofounding the Anti-Maidan movement on the one hand, and launching projects such as Stalinobus, on the other. An effective model of pocket, pseudo-intellectual opposition, Essence of Time features just too many ideological subcurrents to make it into a mass organization, though. Enter National Liberation Movement (NOD), a hybrid between Nashi and Essence of Time created in late 2012 with the specific purpose of keeping in check a liberal opposition. Spending no time on intellectual pursuits, NOD went after the so-called fifth columnists. As compared to Essence of Time, NOD boasts a larger membership and also employs more brutal methods. Both organizations joined forces under the Anti-Maidan umbrella, alongside patriotic bikers, Orthodox extremists, Nikolai Starikov followers, and others. Since the beginning of hostilities in Ukraine, the Anti-Maidan movement welcomed in its ranks various hit squads, the most infamous of which is the Russian Liberation Movement (SERB). Battle-hardened SERBs are there just to beat up people.[57] All these entities invoke history when playing out their conspiratorial vision of Russia surrounded by enemies.

History Textbooks Undergo Gleichschaltung

There are currently forty-eight thousand educational institutions in Russia.[58] Until recently, history teachers could decide which textbook to use. The government saw it as a problem. According to estimates, some two hundred different history textbooks had been printed in Russia by the time Putin reclaimed the presidency in 2012.[59] Sergei Chuev, deputy head of the Duma committee on education, cracked the numbers: taken in the aggregate, for each positive event in Russian history as presented in those textbooks there are three negative ones. If one takes the twentieth century, that ratio becomes 5 to 1. Keeping that in mind, in 2013 President Putin presented the idea of a unified textbook. What he meant was a streamlined concept of history teaching at school, with the prime goal of raising levels of patriotism among Russia's youth. The ministry of education at that point could not say anything sensible beyond "creating a unified cultural and historical space."[60]

The annexation of Crimea proved the single event that set the process in motion. The concept was elaborated by a working group led by Chubarian, head of the Institute of World History of the Academy of Sciences. Chuev does not mince words when explaining that the new textbook type interprets history in the way that would make young Russians proud of their country. On the contrary, accentuating dark pages of Russia's history, recounting past "mistakes," puts a break on raising good citizens. Those young people who feel ashamed of their own history do not accept "reality" and may flout social norms. When it comes to Stalin's terror, Chuev believes it should be taught only at a college level. That is a common practice, he insinuates, for example in the United States, where history textbooks fail to mention major facts concerning slavery.[61] One could not have said it more explicitly: basically, a unified history textbook would dissuade young Russians from rebelling against the present regime.[62]

The straight talk by the likes of Chuev did not prove as easy to implement in actual textbooks. Minister of education since August 2016, Olga Vasilieva sounded rather vague: Russian schools are getting new history textbooks that will use a "special approach" to contested issues. According to Vasilieva, all discussions surrounding unified textbook have been superseded by the imposition of a so-called cultural-historical standard. What that standard entails, however, she did not specify.[63] Shortly after her appointment, Vasilieva was sharing her views on history. In an interview to Interfax, the minister of education stated that myth and history belong together organically. Emphasizing the significance of heroism in history education, she naturally agrees with Medinskii's take on Panfilov's twenty-eight. "My teacher regards their heroism a historical fact," said Vasilieva, "and I do appreciate teachers." Like her fellow bureaucrat, Vasilieva is ambivalent about Stalin. While acknowledging that Stalin was a tyrant and that he bears direct responsibility for "political repressions," she simultaneously regards him a "statesman." That alone does not make her a "Stalinist," she insists: "Stalin, as a pragmatist, understood well that a horrific war was coming and that mobilization, also spiritual mobilization, was necessary. Hence the paintings, poems, and feature films about Alexander Nevsky and Ivan the Terrible."[64] Vasilieva maintains that the *Ogonek* magazine—a literary and political weekly that was among the first in the 1980s to steer a liberal course—had actively contributed to destroying the link between the Soviet and modern Russian history.[65]

Vasilieva evokes national security as the justification for a unified textbook. She shares in the nostalgia for the Soviet system of education, putting it in the category of "classical education." Vasilieva also wants to export this new-old system of education abroad. Launched in 2017, the long-term project Education for Export seeks to bring foreign students to Russia. She is outspoken about the ultimate goal of this project: using it as an element of soft power to extend Russia's influence internationally, while also earning some money.[66] Like other top bureaucrats, Vasilieva emphasizes "traditional Russian values" as the basis for a patriotic upbringing. The citizens who know Russian history and read Russian classical writers constitute the "state's main asset," Vasilieva declared in her 2016 address marking the Day of National Unity. As ever, invoked the minister of education, the Russian people should stand united against the enemy.[67] In 2017, the ministry of education and science, for the second time, held a countrywide competition for school teachers, "History in School: Traditions and Innovations." During the awards ceremony, Vasilieva spoke of "historical literacy." This "humble but essential goal" brought together the school, the family, and the society, she said.[68]

The unified textbook is essentially a series of textbooks for all school grades, covering history from ancient times onward. There are three such textbook series, produced by three preselected publishing houses. Once the first textbooks started to arrive in schools, it became easier to establish what the federal cultural-historical standard actually means. It effectively substitutes (select) facts for analysis. For example, one textbook includes the following statement: "The Soviet Union entered the Second World War on June 22, 1941," even though one could also date it by September 17, 1939. The 1940 Katyn massacre is presented as an uncomplicated sequence: Polish troops surrendered en masse; some of them ended up tragically; thousands of Polish officers were executed. Who put them to death and why falls by the wayside. Some teachers also note an excessive number of church personalities featured in the new textbooks—a nod to both the influence of the Orthodox Church and Vasilieva's own professional background. In conclusion, the unified textbook does not aim to foster critical thinking, while the "special approach" to complex issues of history constitutes an ideology in its own right.⁶⁹ As rendered by Naryshkin, who supervised the working group, the "difficult questions" all received "compromise formulations."⁷⁰ Naryshkin regards the textbook as one of the tools to counter "blatant anti-Russian statements by certain historians on the post-Soviet territory."⁷¹

The attempt to streamline history by means of a unified textbook did not help solve the inherent contradictions embedded in the state-approved narrative. Take, for example, the odd concept of defensive expansion. As stated in one of the textbooks, Russia had for three hundred years waged defensive wars and as a result expanded its territories from Kaliningrad in the east to Kuril Islands in the west.⁷² A "proper" history textbook cannot refer to a popular uprising in Ukraine as a "revolution." That single slip of the pen—described as "provocation" by the speaker of the Federation Council Matvienko—sent the textbook, *History of Russia in Early Nineteenth-Early Twenty-First Centuries*, to additional expertise. Notorious talk show host Dmitry Kisilev has falsely claimed that it was this particular textbook that inspired a student at an Novyi Urengoi school to allegedly twist the history of the Second World War (see Chapter 7).⁷³ The perceived link between history and national security has also been brought to bear on textbooks. For instance, in 2016 the Federal Agency for Nationality Affairs carried out an expert analysis of regional history textbooks on the matter of interpretations that might stimulate separatism.⁷⁴ In Perm, a teaching aid on how to present the history of Stalin's terror was subjected to a botched critique, which found it containing "information prompting antisocial behavior [*antiobshchestvennaia deiatelnost*]."⁷⁵

In spite of a fundamental flaw in the very concept of a unified textbook, a majority of history teachers had come out in favor of it. According to Chubarian, 85 percent of the teachers who had attended a symposium organized by the working group supported the idea.⁷⁶ While history teachers in the provinces receive a mere 13,000–20,000 rubles, or 200–310 US dollars, in monthly salary, Putin's cronies make excellent business on textbooks, not unlike that on the Youth Army uniforms.⁷⁷ Of the three publishing houses that originally got a state contract for printing the textbooks, only one is still in existence. The Soviet-era monopolist, Prosveshchenie (Enlightenment), saw its share of the market drop to 35 percent by the early 2010s. Things turned around after Putin's friend and billionaire Arkady Rotenberg came on board. Rotenberg purchased the company in 2011 and two years later became the head of the board of directors. Rotenberg has consistently occupied the top spot on the list of recipients of state contracts (e.g., Gazprom, Sochi Winter Olympics, bridges over the Volga and the Kerch Strait). By 2019, Rotenberg's Prosveshchenie controlled close to 95 percent of the Russian textbook market, worth some 25 billion rubles. Among particular state bureaucrats, Prosveshchenie has nurtured good relations with Minister of Education Vasilieva. The publishing house has participated in drafting the new educational standards, which oblige schools to purchase new textbooks more often.⁷⁸

History as Reconstruction

As the borderline between fact and fiction, politics and academia, becomes thinner, so does the distinction between historical artefacts and, well, a variation on the theme. Since the annexation of Crimea, history in Russia has undergone an aggressive populistic overhaul. As prime examples of that transformation feature Bishop Tikhon's "Russia: My History" multimedia exhibition, Defense Minister Shoigu's Patriot military theme park, and even biker Zaldostanov's annual show. Replicated throughout Russia, these unsophisticated, and therefore effective, displays remold historical evidence into a syncretic narrative of victory. A case in point is wartime hardware. Alexander "The Surgeon" Zaldostanov showed the way by procuring an actual T-34 tank for his 2015 biker show, "Forging the Victory." The tank, which constitutes a part of the Battle of Stalingrad memorial complex, travelled over one thousand kilometers from Volgograd to Sevastopol. In the occupied Crimea, the legendary tank had a star performance in the battle of Armageddon (i.e., the Soviet victory over Nazi Germany), as conceived by Putin's most trusted biker.[79] The same year, the remaining part of an engine that had been displayed in front of a railway club in Pskov was suddenly moved to the "Life Road" museum in Leningrad Region. The museum in Kobon village tells the story of a single supply route to the besieged Leningrad in 1941–44. The problem is that the production of this particular engine model began only in 1951, thus making it an odd addition to the museum collection. In July 2018, a Japanese tank was stolen from a museum on one of the disputed Kuril Islands. The tank was rumored to go on display at the newly opened Patriot military park in Vladivostok. After a while, however, it resurfaced eight time zones away, in Murmansk. Or take, for example, the recent proposal by Shoigu to repurpose the Wehrmacht armory in the construction of the Orthodox Cathedral at Kubinka. However ludicrous a proposition this might be, the defense ministry may have its way, for some military museums formally belong under the ministry.[80]

Much easier than moving around artefacts, historical reconstruction has become increasingly popular in Russia as a tool of patriotic-cum-political mass education. One may recall that the RVIO entry on the public stage was initially linked to historical reconstructions. In recent years, the passion for reenacting select battles of the Second World War, the First World War, and the Napoleonic Wars, has expanded to include historical events further afield. Other groups have joined in. One such project, "Rio Rita: The Joy of Victory," was launched in 2016 in St. Petersburg. "Rio Rita" is a famous song from the 1927 American musical, popularized by a movie with the same title two years later. The song was also frequently performed in the interwar Soviet Union. The idea was to capture the spirit of the May 9, 1945, street celebrations. Dressed up according to the fashion of the day—with many a man sporting a military uniform—couples gather in parks to dance to the 1920s–1940s music. To make the atmosphere appear even more authentic, the organizers serve Soviet-era ice cream, soft drinks, and sweets. As with other such impromptu initiatives from below, it was duly serialized and set under centralized supervision. As of 2018, "Rio Rita: The Joy of Victory" was held in eight different Russian cities and attracted an estimated eighty thousand participants. By 2020, the organizers intend to expand Rio Rita to all major Russian cities and the capitals of the former Allied countries. They refer to the defense industry moving its operations to other former Soviet republics in 1941–42 as sufficient grounds to hold Rio Rita in Baku, Azerbaijan and Tashkent, Uzbekistan, and in other cities and countries. Like earlier in the case of the Immortal Regiment, there is also an attempt to get the younger generation involved. Eventually, the "Joy of Victory," too, has undergone a militaristic makeover. Thus the 2018 edition of Rio Rita featured a street workshop for children where they could build a military truck, a plane, colored toy soldiers, and/or paint red stars. Regardless, both volunteer organizers and city authorities like thinking of the event as a "reconstruction of joy."[81] While the Immortal Regiment and Rio Rita are supposed to symbolize two sides of the 1945 victory—grief and joy—both have militaristic undertones, which refer back to the original source—the military parade on Red Square.

Historical reconstructions are typically billed as festivals. The amount of effort and money poured into those festivals has begun to pay off as they are becoming commercially viable by attracting private investments and stimulating local economy. According to RVIO, it supports over twenty-five historical festivals every year, bringing together some 3,000 club members and 600,000 onlookers. The three largest festivals at the moment are the Borodino Day (1812) near Moscow, the Siberian Fire (ninth to twentieth century) in Novosibirsk region, and the Battle of Gumbinnen (1914) in Kaliningrad region.[82]

In recent years historical reconstructions have been embraced on the city level, mainly in connection with the Second World War. More often than not, it exposes bad taste. For the anniversary of the liberation of Novgorod, in January of 2019, city authorities decided to run a column of "German POWs" alongside the replica of a bombed-out street. The organizers believe that a selfie with the actors dressed up as German prisoners and the Soviet liberators on the background is a better reminder of the war than the books and/or the old photographs.[83] The scale of the installation at Nizhniii Tagil later that year was much more modest, although it scored higher on account of grotesque. As part of the May 9 celebration, men dressed in Soviet wartime uniforms paraded another one, dressed as a Nazi. He was caged along with two dogs. The inscription on the cage invited throwing "fascism to the dustbin of history." The show was conceived by a circus director (no pun intended).[84] A Volgograd museum put on offer a reconstruction of the 1943 surrender of German Field Marshall Friedrich Paulus. The reenactment lasted about an hour and was included in the ticket price.[85] The catchall word *fascist*, not unlike in Soviet times, carries political connotations. By way of example, in late summer 2019 a military historical club in Altai region reenacted the 1943 Battle of the Dnepr. As part of the reconstruction, a Soviet execution squad carried out the death penalty of a Ukrainian "traitor to the Motherland."[86]

The overwrought subject of Soviet victory over Nazi Germany makes truly original projects hard to come by. Often, old Soviet clichés pass for creativity. Thus, the odd-sounding project "Vaccination against Fascism," which premiered in the spring of 2016 in Orel, turned out to be a compilation of wartime footage. The event poster featured a famous Kukryniksy cartoon of the wolf-like Hitler pierced by a red bayonet. One of the people behind the project wanted to "genetically pass on to the new generations our hatred of Nazism and fascism, so that the lessons of the Second World War could be learned by just anyone." The local governor backed this sentiment with a traditional reference to the evils of historical revisionism.[87] Typical for such projects, it has since then crisscrossed the country.

What distinguishes such projects is their scale and the extent of state support. To give just one example, since 2016 a youth affiliate of the Duma has administered an annual online quiz on the history of the Great Patriotic War. The quiz consists of thirty questions and is meant for Russians, citizens of Russia living abroad, and foreigners. Translated into six different languages, including Japanese and Chinese, the non-Russian version is dubbed "history test on the victory over fascism." The quiz expects to raise the levels of "historical literacy" about the "leading role of the Soviet people in the Second World War." As of summer 2018, an estimated 209,000 took the quiz; how many of them were foreign nationals is unknown. The quiz is part of the larger project, "Proud of Russia, Every Day."[88]

Coming soon to a movie theater near you: Medinskii is currently seeking state support for yet another film project of his, on the Nuremberg trial. According to him, that subject has been cinematically monopolized by the Americans, to the exclusion of the part played in the proceedings by the Soviet Union. For whatever reason (Putin's CV perhaps), the minister of culture wants to give a central part in the prospective movie to Soviet spies. Even more incongruously, he intends to solicit the participation of Western movie stars.[89] Medinskii's colleague from RVIO, Yuri Nikiforov, has formulated an ideal matrix for a war movie, which would depict the Soviet soldiers as "beautiful" people and ultimate warriors. It would be the right ideological move, he argued, or else "we have nothing to show to the Poles as regards the 1945 liberation."[90]

The Sacred in History: The Bolshevik Revolution, Tsar Nikolai II, and the Siege of Leningrad

All is clear with the Great Patriotic War, which is being celebrated on a grand scale each year and an even larger scale every five years. The last time the Bolshevik Revolution got such an honor was in 1987. As the centennial of the revolution drew nearer, speculations abounded on how the authorities would go about marking it.[91] The solution found was ingenious: near silence. There was no special programming on the Russian TV on November 7, 2017. Neither did Russia's foreign-language news outlets report on the subject.[92] Foreign Minister Lavrov had earlier warned the West to refrain from using the occasion to blame Russia for "pushing the European history into the abyss." In the opposite case, argued Lavrov, the Soviet regime would be seen as no different from the Nazi and hence co-responsible for the outbreak of the Second World War.[93] According to Chubarian, the major lesson of the Bolshevik Revolution is that violence can only be tolerated when directed against foreign intervention but not when used in a fraternal conflict.[94] This interpretation is effectively a variation on current policymaking, which seeks interethnic unity within the country only in the face of perceived encroachments by the West. Hence, the February Revolution and the Great October Revolution merged into a neutral Great Russian Revolution. The new designation extends to the subsequent civil war. The superimposed discourse declares all parties in the armed conflict—the Reds, the Whites, the Greens, and so on—as Russia's patriots and calls for a national reconciliation, without elaborating.[95] The emphasis has shifted from the causes of the revolution to the traumatic consequences of the state collapse, which automatically erases the question of responsibility.⁹⁶

This goes hand in hand with the pattern of desecralization of the Bolshevik Revolution, counter Soviet historiography. Consider the iconic *Aurora* cruiser in St. Petersburg, which in the run-on to the 2018 FIFA World Cup became a backdrop for a jovial video projection. The only exhibition in 2017 dedicated specifically to Vladimir Lenin was organized at the Russian State Archives in Moscow.⁹⁷ Still more popular proved Ilyich chocolates produced for the occasion by a St. Petersburg confectionery. A chocolate gift box features a tongue-in-cheek inscription, "revolutionary taste," while individual wrappers urge patrons, "Know the history of your country!"

The new, sanitized designation taps into the popular sentiment of the past two or so decades that rejects revolution as a phenomenon.⁹⁸ This also bodes well with the Orthodox Church, which proved to be one of the few players in the field of history politics that made use of the centennial—by advancing further the idea of martyrdom.⁹⁹ The city of Ulianovsk, the birthplace of Lenin, serves as a peculiar illustration of the legacy of the Bolshevik Revolution in Russia. Ulianovsk was the scene of a conflict between the adepts of Soviet and Imperial Russian history. The dispute was formulated as a question of whether or not Lenin Square should be given its original name, Cathedral Square. Those who sought a name change argued that Ulianovsk has one too many Lenins while Orthodoxy is a unified force in the society. The opponents pointed out that the cathedral that once graced the square had long been demolished while the Lenin monument and the former Communist Party headquarters are still standing. Besides, renaming the square would split the society. The regional governor attempted to cross religion with communism by reviving a Lenin prize and simultaneously agreeing to strike off Lenin's name. Communists staged acts of protest, during which they compared the governor to Hitler. Theirs, it seems, is a lost cause. To appease the communists, the city government performed an ultimate equilibristic act: to mark Lenin's centennial, yet another square in Ulianovsk would be renamed after Lenin.¹⁰⁰ Generally, however, communists in recent years have replaced Lenin with Stalin in the hierarchy of the greatest. Those communists who come to the Mausoleum on Red Square to mark the birthday of the Bolshevik leader typically leave the flowers they bring with them at Stalin's grave. A particular individual spotted on January 21, 2019 with a portrait of Lenin had another one depicting Stalin on his back.¹⁰¹

The messy situation at Ulianovsk illustrates well a split in the society concerning the Bolshevik Revolution. According to opinion polls, 48 percent of Russians regard it positively and 36 percent negatively. Most, however, simply do not care. When asked how many of them ever read Lenin's writings, none of the hundred students at the Higher School of Economics in St. Petersburg raised their hand.¹⁰²

Ironically enough, even the centennial of Komsomol, the communist youth organization, the following year was celebrated with greater pomp. Valentina Matvienko, Federation Council speaker and formerly Leningrad Komsomol boss, spearheaded the celebration in the Kremlin. In her address, Matvienko told former Komsomol members that their past experience is "priceless for the Russia thrusting into the future." In separatist-held Luhansk, the story of the celebration could have been painted by Samuel Beckett or Eugène Ionescu. Luhansk communists were eager to unearth the time capsule placed fifty years earlier by the local Komsomol organization. This they could not do, however, for the city government decided to read the note before select guests in a closed meeting. The communists, to their chagrin, did not even get the promised photocopy of the note.[103]

Here also belongs the never-ending discussion on whether Lenin's body should be buried. President Putin, in 2016, chose to err on the side of caution by coming out against it. Putin said he did not want to split the society on this sensitive issue. Chechen leader Kadyrov and Duma deputy Poklonskaia found themselves on the opposite side of the debate by politely suggesting that the people had had "enough staring at a corpse."[104] Think what you want of Putin's balancing act, it certainly does not translate into personal hatred for Lenin, which historian Nina Tumarkin ascribes to Putin due to Lenin's role in the destruction of the Russian Empire.[105]

Counterintuitively, it was not the centennial of the Bolshevik Revolution and the deposition of the last monarch that dominated Russian news in 2017. Rather, it was a controversy surrounding the feature film *Matilda*, based on a true story of the intimate relationship between Tsar Nikolai II and ballerina Mathilde Kschessinskaya in the 1890s. The official trailer of the film (featuring an erotic scene) that came out in late 2016 mobilized militant Orthodox groups in protest. The church and a few professed believers among politicians jumped into the fray. King's Cross, a virulently nationalistic, monarchist entity, deemed the movie an "anti-Russian and antireligious provocation" and turned for help to Natalia Poklonskaia.

A long-term official in the Ukrainian prosecutor general's office, Poklonskaia rose to fame due to her support of the Russian annexation of Crimea where she was shortly installed as Prosecutor General. In 2016 she was elected into the Duma on United Russia ticket. A telegenic, soft-spoken lawyer-cum-politician, Poklonskaia brandished her faith and admiration for the slain tsarist family. Along the way, she intimated that the film director, Alexei Uchitel, was doing somebody's bidding. Had he made a movie about the Holocaust or the Armenian genocide, Poklonskaia insinuated, it would have been a denialist feature. Alongside Uchitel, she also nailed Medinskii, who had earlier described attacks on the movie as undue pressure on the state. Among her potential supporters, the star politician listed President Putin, law-enforcement agencies, the human rights ombudsman, and all those who "love their Motherland and its great history."[106] Poklonskaia subsequently requested the prosecutor general's office to check the movie on the basis of Article 148 of the penal code law that proscribes "offending religious sentiments of the believers" and privacy laws more generally.[107] In this particular case, the Duma committee on culture came out on the side of artistic freedom, with no investigation based on Poklonskaia's allegations launched.[108]

Meanwhile, vigilantes took the matter into their own hands. In early 2017, a hitherto unknown organization, Christian State, Holy Russia, distributed leaflets to movie theaters, warning them against screening *Matilda*. Any act to the contrary would be regarded as an "intent to humiliate the Orthodox Church saints and a provocation leading up to 'Russian Maidan.'" The group's leader, born-again Christian Alexander Kalinin, intimated in an interview that potential viewers may interpret the film's message as a call for revolution.[109] That was also the underlining idea that informed a "prayer protest" co-organized by King's Cross and an organization with a similar ideology, Forty Forties, across Russia in the summer of 2017. Among the slogans carried by protestors were "Anathema to those who plot uprising and treason against Orthodox rulers" and "Against lies and the falsification of history."[110] Two autonomous republics, Dagestan and Chechnya, formally appealed to the ministry of culture to ban public screening of Matilda. The president of Chechnya Kadyrov decried the sacrilege and "desecration of centuries-long history of the peoples of Russia."[111] More curiously, during a football match between Spartak and Lokomotiv in Moscow, the fans from both teams unveiled the following banners: "In the name of Faith, Tsar, and Motherland: Uchitel, hands off Russian tsar!" That may as well be the first instance in history when football fans doubled as film critics.[112] Typically, none of the opponents actually watched the film or, like Poklonskaia, explicitly refused to do so.

From words, the religious extremists of Christian State, Holy Russia turned to action. On August 31, 2017, Uchitel's studio in St. Petersburg was firebombed. Days later, two cars were set ablaze outside his lawyer's office in Moscow. In an unrelated incident, a minivan loaded with gas cylinders rammed into an Ekaterinburg cinema hall set to show Matilda.[113] Car burning was carried out by Kalinin; the police discovered petrol canisters and leaflets that read "For Matilda—Burn!" when conducting a search. Kalinin had earlier defended his right to burn cinema halls and threatened to break Uchitel's legs or even impale him. Tellingly, Christian State, Holy Russia interlinked its religion-inspired activities and its support for Putin.[114] Under pressure, some movie theaters cancelled the film's screening. In other cases (e.g., in Novosibirsk) security was beefed up during the screening. The Orthodox Church, like it has done before in different contexts, was playing coy by distancing itself from some groups (Christian State, Holy Russia) but continuing to endorse others (Forty Forties). Some dioceses initiated a signature-gathering campaign against Matilda.[115] As if by coincidence, several weeks prior to the planned countrywide release of Matilda, a series of billboards under the heading "Nikolai and Alexandra Fedorovna: Words of Love" went up in Moscow. The billboards featured images of the tsar and his wife, interspersed with quotations celebrating the virtues of love, marriage, and family. The project was sponsored by the Orthodox Church.[116]

The controversy surrounding Matilda, the movie, is embedded in the idea of sacrilege. In a nutshell, the opponents have argued that any depiction of Nikolai II should build upon his status as a saint. While the commemoration of the Bolshevik Revolution has lost the character of a quasi-religious ritual, that of the Soviet victory over Hitler's Germany has effectively become a canon. What still brings these three historical episodes together in their public representation is the element of kitsch.

The rift between the collective emotion of sorrow and jubilation was on display in the run-on to the seventy-fifth anniversary of the lifting of the siege of Leningrad, on January 27, 2019. Public opinion was split on whether it should be marked by a solemn ceremony or by a victorious parade. Various opinion polls indicate that a majority of St. Petersburg's citizens wished for a more intimate commemoration of the victims of the German siege. In that, however, they were overrun by local politicians with Governor Beglov at the top, who staged a massive military parade and a "historical reconstruction." The Life Street (Italianskaia Street) in downtown St. Petersburg featured military trucks, Czech hedgehogs, sandbags, an old streetcar, and a few men dressed in wartime sheep coats. The banners showed this particular street as it was during the siege. What was conspicuously missing was the images of death and human suffering, including the disproportionately high number of Soviet soldiers who died in the final battle of Leningrad. The spirit ought to have been joyous. Overzealous bureaucrats, no doubt, prepared the parade in anticipation of President Putin, who was expected to preside over it. The native son of St. Petersburg, however, pulled out of the event at the last moment. Endowed with good intuition, he might have sensed that the heroic perspective on the siege of Leningrad was skewed.[117] High-level bureaucrats, however, have no such scruples. The Speaker of St. Petersburg legislature, for instance, advised the youth against participating in street protests by referring to some sort of "Leningrad siege code, the victor code."[118] Notably, the latest monument to the victims of the siege of Leningrad was scheduled to open not in Russia but in Israel, in May of 2019 in Jerusalem, in the presence of President Putin. For political reasons, Putin's scheduled visit to Israel was delayed, and so was the unveiling ceremony (see Chapter 6).[119]

Building History into National Holidays

Still, the easiest way to signpost history is by means of official commemoration. A look at the commemorative dates in the Russian calendar reveals the government's limited ability to implant a new historical narrative into the collective consciousness. The Unity Day is a good point to start. A minor confusion—though on account of the difference between the Gregorian and Julian calendar—was on display even in Soviet times when the country celebrated the Great October Socialist Revolution on November 7. In 1996, President Yeltsin renamed it as the Day of Unity and Reconciliation, without giving it any new substance. His successor, Putin, gave it yet another name in 2005, the Day of National Unity, and moved it to November 4. Formally, the date marks the dislodging of Polish troops from Moscow by Russian militias back in 1612. Yet the actual battle took place on November 1 (i.e., October 22, according to the Julian calendar). Even when reminded, a majority of Russians can hardly relate to the distant events and/or the mythologized figures associated with it. Hence, a good 43 percent of respondents neither remember nor know the name of the holiday celebrated on November 4. Besides, 40 percent of Russians do not even believe that such a thing as national unity exists in Russia.[120]

Consider another Yeltsin's initiative, the Constitution Day, marked since 1994 on December 12. During Putin's rule the very idea of constitutional rights became fancy. As an indication of sorts, in 2005 the holiday was denigrated to the status of a memorial date, that is, it is a normal working day now. There is also the Russia Day, June 12, marking the 1990 declaration of Russian sovereignty. That particular date, however, typically coincides with the City Day (*den goroda*) marked across Russia in pretty much the same fashion. Yet another relic from Yeltsin's time is the Flag Day, August 22, of which most people are simply unaware. Beginning in 2014, March 18 has been unevenly marked as the Day of Incorporation of Crimea. Still, it clearly remained a political event, with the authorities not daring to declare it a public holiday.[121] The regime found a way around it by instituting, in August 2018, a new memorial date, the Day of Incorporation of Crimea, Taman, and Kuban into the Russian Empire (1783). Signed by Putin, the amendment to the law on Days of Military Glory and Memorial Dates in Russia stipulates that the incorporation of Crimea in the eighteenth century occurred at the "request of its citizens worn off by wars" and that the so-called referendum in 2014 reaffirmed the continuity of Crimea's belonging to Russia. The new Memorial Day is set on April 19.[122] It is unlikely that ordinary Russians would be toasting to the strategic genius of Ekaterina II any time soon. It is even more unlikely that the feast would be held on the newly proposed Patriotism Day, August 6. Originally proposed in the fall of 2016, and semi-endorsed by such different entities as the ministry of culture and the Night Wolves biker club, it would mark the anniversary of food sanctions introduced against Russia by the West.[123]

Peculiar at most, the newly established Memorial Day serves as an invitation to consider an entire roster of such dates currently marked in Russia. At present, the calendar year contains seventeen Days of Military Glory and sixteen Memorial Dates.[124] The former block is in a way predictable, featuring military victories ingrained in the memory of every Soviet citizen such as Kulikovo, Borodino, Poltava, Stalingrad, and Ismail. The most unusual is perhaps November 7, which marks not the Bolshevik Revolution per se, but the 1941 military parade on Red Square "in commemoration of the twenty-fourth anniversary of the Great October Socialist Revolution." To make it even more confusing, November 7 is simultaneously a memorial date, this time as Day of the 1917 October Revolution. On a closer look, nearly half of all Memorial Dates are in one way or another linked to wars fought by Russia/Soviet Union in the short twentieth century. The utilitarian approach to history—as the Putin regime has demonstrated most recently in the case of the Day of Incorporation of Crimea, Taman, and Kuban into the Russian Empire—is played in reverse in the case of Day of Russian Parliamentarism (April 27), which actually marks the first ever Duma in 1906. Other Memorial Dates tiptoe around specific man-made disasters without naming them. Thus, Day in Honor of Internationalist Soldiers (February 15) is a gloss over the Soviet war in Afghanistan; Day of Remembrance of Victims of Radiation Accidents and Disasters (April 26) has obviously to do with the explosion at Chernobyl nuclear plant; and Day of Solidarity in the Fight against Terrorism (September 3) is a concealed reference to the Beslan hostage crisis. Just how hollow and easily manipulated those memorial days are can be illustrated by the following example. In the summer of 2019 Moscow was rocked by a series of protests against electoral fraud. In order to divert public attention, the authorities organized a series of free events such as rock concerts scheduled to take place on the days of protests. On August 24, the Moscow city government hastily organized a public gathering to mark 350 years of the Russian flag. The problem is that the anniversary falls on 2018, and was actually marked that year.[125] Regardless, only 50 percent of the Russians polled can put the flag's colors in the right order.[126]

In addition, the Russian calendar features a staggering number of professional holidays. In the case of the military, nearly every branch (thirty-eight in total) has one: divers and encoders, car drivers and signalers, interpreters and educational workers, scouts and radio electronic specialists. Nonmilitary dates worth remembering alternate between patriotism and mythology. Some of them are just plain bizarre: Birthday of Russian Vodka (January 31), Birthday of Ru.net (April 7), System Operator Day (July 25), Birthday of Father Frost (November 18). With so many things to commemorate, one date conventionally slips from the state's mind: Day of Remembrance of Victims of Political Repression, October 30. Introduced in the waning months of the Soviet Union, paying respect to the victims of Stalin's terror has increasingly become a private affair in Putin's Russia.[127] One is tempted to contrast October 30 with March 5, the anniversary of Stalin's death, which typically features a smallish crowd drowning Stalin's bust by the Kremlin wall in Moscow in a sea of red carnations.[128]

As far as Memorial Dates are concerned, local and federal authorities are walking a tightrope. Commemoration of ethnic deportations in Chechnya and Crimea is a case in point. The regional government in Russian-occupied Crimea is uncomfortable with the annual commemoration held on April 18. However, in view of the ongoing political repression against local Tatars, cancelling Day of Remembrance of Victims of Deportation would cause an outcry of a different kind and thus spell a PR disaster for the current administration. Consequently, the latter came up with a devious compromise whereby local bureaucrats hold a low-key official ceremony, while the Crimean Tatar activists are denied one.[129] Meanwhile, the Ukrainian online publication, Historical Truth, has been blocked in Crimea and the representative body, Mejlis of the Crimean Tatar People, outlawed in Russia as an "extremist organization." It might have been otherwise, had the leader of the Mejlis and one of the most respected Soviet-time dissidents, Mustafa Dzhemilev, agreed to endorse the Russian annexation of Crimea. Putin had courted Dzhemilev, promising the latter to shower the Crimean Tatar minority with money and facilitate the return of the remainder of the community still living in Central Asia to Crimea. Dzhemilev had publicly rejected Putin's offer and was subsequently blacklisted by Russian authorities.[130] Blacklisted was also the memory of Stalin's terror.

In spite of Putin's mantra that the victory over Nazi Germany is shared by all peoples of Russia, the contribution of certain ethnic groups—first and foremost, the Crimean Tatars—has consistently been denigrated. Sometimes even the veiled criticism of Russian history politics may be framed as an offense. Take, for example, the case of the Crimean Tatar poet, Alie Kenzhalieva. The prosecutor's office in Simferopol probed Kenzhalieva on account of her poems that had appeared in a local newspaper on May 9, 2018. The investigation claimed that the poet had "diminished the meaning of Victory, and thus exonerated Nazism." Kenzhalieva, for her part, insisted that she had just reflected on the mode of commemoration.

> They teach war.
> To forget the tragedy,
> To deny prayer to the unfortunate,
> To forsake this fragile world.
> They teach war,
> To feel good there was one.
> To wear military uniform,

To express one's pride in song and dance.
To hold a fest.

This particular poem was inspired by the Immortal Regiment parade in Simferopol the year earlier; alongside the portraits of their relatives killed in combat, participants carried that of Stalin, who had ultimately ordered a wholesale deportation of Crimean Tatars back in 1944. An Agora human rights lawyer representing Kenzhalieva, who otherwise works as a Russian literature and language teacher, believes that this and similar cases are used by the security agencies in Crimea to simply justify their existence.[131] As if to prove the existence of a conspiracy between the government and its proxies, on the night of May 9, 2019, near Sevastopol, vandals desecrated the recently erected monument to the Crimean Tatars who had fought against Nazi Germany.[132] Ten days later Ukraine renewed its call to the countries of the world to follow its bid and recognize the wholesale deportation of Crimean Tatars by Stalin in 1944 as genocide.[133]

Chechnya and its strongman, Kadyrov, constitute perhaps the most remarkable case. In spite of the unwavering loyalty Kadyrov has very publicly pledged to Russia and Putin, he is steadfast in his judgment of Stalin. In fact, no other high-ranking bureaucrat in Russia has condemned Stalin and his crimes as resolutely as has Kadyrov.[134] Still, it may not be just his ethnic origin that commands his moral imperative, but also his status as an irreplaceable leader. To put it differently, Kadyrov can afford to express himself freely on the tragic history of the Chechen people due to his absolute hold on power. Even the confessed Stalinists do not rush to attack Kadyrov, aware of his ruthless methods and his direct line to the Kremlin. While Sergei Aksenov may be sacked from his position as leader of Crimea at whim—as many other bureaucrats before him have been—Ramzan Kadyrov knows from experience that he is immune no matter what he says.

In spite of his condemnation of Stalin, Kadyrov is treading a common line when it comes to commemoration of Stalin's terror. In fact, he not just ignores it but also actively opposes it. The monument to the victims of the 1944 deportation—one of the symbols of Chechnya's aspirations for independence—has been under attack since the late 2000s. While the attempt at its demolition in 2008 failed due to public protest, two years later the memorial's territory was fenced off under the pretext of reconstruction. In 2013 Kadyrov effectively cancelled February 23 as the official day of commemoration and, in the shadow of the Sochi Olympics, ordered the monument to be dismantled. A local activist, Ruslan Kutaev, who organized an academic conference on the Chechen deportation that same year got a reprimand from Kadyrov. He was subsequently arrested, tortured, and sentenced on false charges.[135]

Conclusion

When measured against its own agenda, the government's patriotic education program has borne fruit. The authorities have succeeded in propping a sense of pride in Russian history among the population. Polled by Levada in November of 2015, 88 percent of Russians expressed that sentiment, up 8 percent since 2012 and 13 percent since 1996. The significance of history matches the popular pride in the Russian army and the country's (past) achievements in the field of literature, science, and sport.[136] Yet another tangible achievement of the program is ensuring mass participation. A break from the Soviet practices, the ministry of defense has assumed patronage over all Russian children's organizations. That alone brings a strong militaristic element into the patriotic education. The idea of "patriotic history," as understood by the defense ministry, is encapsulated in a volume it is preparing as part of the 2016–20 patriotic education program: *The Moral Spirit of the Red Army as the most important factor of the Great Victory*. Tellingly, in mid-2019 the government ordered military training centers to be established at colleges and universities. At the conclusion of the obligatory course, full-time students could join the military in the rank of an officer or reserve officer.[137]

Military discipline, coupled with a growing atmosphere of intolerance cultivated by the regime, create a fertile ground for vigilantes, who lash out against all those they regard as unpatriotic. Indeed, there is a dialectical link between streamlining the historical narrative and fending off "Russophobia." The government takes it seriously. In July of 2016 the ministry of culture announced a tender to investigate "De-Russification technologies" and propose effective countermeasures. As specified in the announcement, this research, including the assessment of the threat posed by the fifth column, is regarded as vital to national security.[138]

Seen from a long-term perspective, the archaic, top-down educational system adopted in Putin's Russia has since long been proven ineffective. According to Alexander Adamskii, head of an independent teacher training organization, the present concept of patriotic education draws not from the Soviet but the Imperial German practice.[139] A push for a generic history model—the so-called standard on history teaching—failed to solve the contradiction inherent in that very proposition. With the same measure of success, the Russian government might have commissioned to establish, once and for all, the historical truth. Where the world's most famous philosophers have failed, first Dmitry Livanov and later Olga Vasilieva were expected to succeed. The ministry of education has received a hopeless task defying logic: the new educational standard should incorporate no materials that falsify the history of Russia and/or pose a threat to interethnic relations within the country. Neither does it work the other way around, namely promoting the kind of scholarship "conducive to countering attempts to falsify history to the detriment of Russia's interests," despite the use of new primary sources from Russian and foreign archives. On the contrary, one is forced to conclude that certain falsifications *can* actually benefit Russia.

5

Monumental Mediocrity

A rush of monuments in recent years can tell much about the Russia the Putin regime wants to be and less about the Russia that was. That memorials project the past into the future is nothing new, of course, and it is true for just any country. Still, for a country that fits the category of *illiberal democracy*—whichever word one may choose to emphasize—the consistent reference to militarism and authoritarianism is quite remarkable. Unimaginative, pompous sculptures effectively draw on Leninist monumental propaganda, according to art historian Kirill Svetliakov. The Pantheon may be different, but a popular misconception that plastic art is something passed down from the top remains intact.[1]

As in all other aspects of life in Russia, the process of memorialization has since the late 2000s undergone Gleichschaltung. Generic memorials that pop up all over Russia aim to bind different parts of the country together through their common history. Simultaneously, building replicas discourages the emergence of individual sites of memory. As VIO's Pavel Gnilorybov has argued, multiplication of monuments contributes to standardization of history, to the detriment of local history.[2] According to Memorial, ten to fifteen new monuments appear in Russia every month. The decision to erect a monument is usually taken at the regional level. Sometimes local officials initiate the memorialization process.[3] Beside the ubiquitous Second World War memorials, monuments to Stalin have been most plentiful, as well as controversial, in the past fifteen years or so.

Golden Stalin

The Soviet-era term *Leniniana* stands for a composite representation of the Bolshevik leader, in books, cinema, the spoken word, figurative art, and so on. The Russian vocabulary has recently expanded to include a similar term, *Staliniana*.

As in the classical chicken or the egg dilemma, it is hard to tell what came first: newly erected monuments to Stalin or the public opinion in support of it. Whatever the answer, the number of Russians who approve of such monuments increased from 25 percent in 2007 to 40 percent ten years later. Reversely, the number of people who believe that Great Terror is the correct designation for the years 1937–38 dropped during the same period from 53 percent to 41 percent. The question of whether or not Stalin's Soviet Union can be compared to Hitler's Germany reveals a similar tendency:

the number of respondents who said "no" went up from 22 percent in 2009 to 37 percent in 2017. Lev Gudkov, director of the independent Levada pollster, sees "immunity against re-Stalinization" weakening in Russia. He blames it on state propaganda but also a personal desire to maintain status quo. Gudkov attributes the inability to render a political and moral judgment on Stalin to the absence of moral authority and the limited influence of the intellectuals in Russian society.[4]

Before Stalin began reappearing cast in plaster and bronze, he made his way underground. The renovation of Kurskaia Metro station in Moscow in 2009 faithfully restored a quotation from the 1936 Constitution: "Stalin has raised us to be faithful to the people, made us to commit heroic deeds." Despite the protests, the original inscription still remains.

How many monuments honoring Stalin are there in Russia today? This question is difficult to answer for the lack of credible data. One should also distinguish between the newly erected monuments, including replicas, and the few original busts of Stalin surviving from the Soviet times. According to my estimates, the number of brand new monuments to Stalin is approaching one hundred.

Geographically, close to one-half of all the monuments are situated in North Caucasus, with North Ossetia leading the way. The honor goes to Kazbek Taisaev, a high-ranking communist official and Ossetia native. For five years Taisaev had served as a member of the North Ossetia parliament and head of the Communist Party faction. In 2011 he was elected to the Duma and advanced to the position of Secretary of the Communist Party Central Committee. On Taisaev's initiative, the local party branch had installed thirty-seven busts of Stalin across North Ossetia and donated a further forty-four to party offices elsewhere in Russia.[5] The author of the original bust is a well-known Ossetian sculptor, Mikhail Dzboev (b. 1938). The monument to Stalin in Beslan is appropriately situated on Stalin Street. Another ten or so busts are scattered across Dagestan and Kabardino-Balkaria. A particular affinity for Stalin in North Caucasus (and in Georgia for that matter) is due to his ethnic origin; many in Ossetia regard him as a native son. The Generalissimo mass-produced by Ossetia communists typically sits atop a base (the height, material, and finishing depends on the zeal and fundraising prowess of the local party branch). Those who cannot afford bronze settle for plaster, usually painted gold.[6]

Due to the difficulties in acquiring an official permit, some monuments go up on private property, typically beyond the city center. Otherwise, Stalin can be found in the most unusual places: leaning against a traditional timber house, on the territory of mechanical works, in an outdoor café. Perhaps the most unusual location of Stalin sculpture is Tarkhankut Peninsula in Russian-annexed Crimea. Opened in 2006, Jason deCaires Taylor's underwater sculpture park on Grenada has been advertised as the first such attraction ever. This is factually incorrect. Back in 1992, a professional diver from Donetsk established what is now called the Alley of Rulers underwater museum off the Crimean coast. Currently, the museum boasts some fifty sculptures, including one of Stalin (added sometime before 2010). Twelve meters under the sea, Stalin shares space with Yuri Gagarin, Felix Dzerzhinsky, Vladimir Lenin, Leonid Brezhnev, Karl Marx, and others. The museum's founder intends to eventually add to his collection Napoleon, Mussolini, Mao Zedong, and Hitler (though Hitler may prove problematic due to Article 354.1 of the Russian penal code that proscribes the "glorification of Nazism"). Russian tourist operators advertise the Alley of Rulers as one of the most exciting adventures in Crimea.

Among other, less traditional monumental depictions of Stalin is the one in Tsey Gorge in North Ossetia. RuTraveller, which is comparable to Trip Adviser, puts the "portrait of Stalin on a big rock" in the category of "architecture and monuments." The fresco is described as follows: "Each side features portraits of two personalities, powerful and authoritative people who made history. One side of the polished rock features a portrait of Io. V. Stalin."[7] Sometimes, a newly erected monument of Stalin constitutes the only sightseeing, for example, in the village of Komgaron (population: 1,568), also in North Ossetia.

Irony is almost unavoidable in describing particular examples of monumental art devoted to Stalin. A case in point is the bust in Siberian Ishim. The plaster bust was hidden underground by the true believers during Khrushchev's campaign of de-Stalinization. Half a century later, local communists unearthed the sculpture and reinstalled it in the original location behind the local administration building. Time and nature, however, took its toll on the bust, which was literally crumbling. One day in 2009 the bust disappeared, only to be restored to its original shape by the city one month later. Not quite original, as anyone who has seen an image of Stalin can attest. The casting was done by a metal artist known mainly for his work on ornate lampposts in the nearby city of Tiumen. His Stalin became slimmer, with the nose and mustache larger, giving the Soviet leader the look of a drunkard. The result can be compared to a now famous botched restoration of the "ecco homo" fresco of Jesus in a village church in Spain.[8] As far as physical similarity/dissimilarity is concerned, another prominent example is the monument in Atkarsk, north of Saratov. The massive bust is the work of a stage painter in a local House of Culture. Counting Little Red Riding Hood among his previous commissions, back in 2001 he could not find any pictures of Stalin handy. All he could get his hands on was a magazine reproduction of Ilya Glazunov's monumental painting, which among a few hundred other characters also featured Stalin.[9] Hence the result. If it had not been for the mustache and the accompanying plaque, few would have recognized Stalin—the very picture of health.

The few monuments that had not been destroyed under Khrushchev, and that were restored after Putin came to power, all have a story to tell. Here is one from Tatarstan. A resident of Lashmanka village, a war veteran and inveterate communist, came across a full-size plaster statue of Stalin during one of his trips to Samara. The sculpture (probably from the early 1950s) was missing legs, hands, and certain facial parts. Brought to the village, Stalin got back the missing limbs, his other wounds were patched, and the body was repainted. The enthusiastic villager set up a metallic fence around the statue, installed light fixtures, and wrote an accompanying text in grammatically incorrect Russian as well as Tatar. The text reads:

Io. V. Stalin, great leader, Generalissimo.
   The Soviet Russian leadership with Stalin at the helm in 1924–1953 had declared the goal of achieving the ideal of social justice and creating a perfect society with no exploitation and based on equality.

> He [Stalin] had conscientiously, justly, and selflessly carried out the plans conceived by V. I. Lenin during the October Revolution and [the period of] building socialism. He called on toilers of all countries to fight for the liberation from slavery, and made great efforts [to that end] himself.
>
> Our great leader was born on December 21, 1879, in the capital of Georgia, not far from Tbilisi, in the town of Gori. He passed away on March 5, 1953 [sic], in the capital city of Moscow.
>
> We are thankful to him! He fought for peace in the Great Patriotic [War], and selflessly worked for the benefit of the motherland. He knew how to sustain patriotism, friendship, respect, and mutual assistance. We should not forget his bravery, optimism, his efforts to make our life better.
>
> The monument to Io. V. Stalin restored in conjunction with the 55th anniversary of Victory [2000].

The man who brought Stalin back to life had for a while corresponded with the dictator's grandson. Since then both have passed away; the ad hoc memorial is being taken care of by a Stalin aficionado's widow and son. As if to mark ownership, the Communist Party has planted its banner behind the statue.[10] From Novosibirsk comes yet another story. An excavator operator unearthed a bust of Stalin on the territory of an abandoned plant. He then painted Stalin's head gold and black and placed it on a chunk of concrete displaying the colors of the Russian flag. Exhibited next to his house, it had become a semi-shrine where elderly ladies occasionally place flowers.[11]

Individual efforts to restore statues of Stalin display elements of idiosyncrasy, which is not at all surprising given the current state policy on Russian history. Time and again, Stalin follows in the footsteps of Lenin, literally (e.g., in Takhankut, Vladimir). Russia is one of the few countries in the world that has committed to preserving monuments to Lenin. Those few statues of the Bolshevik leader that got felled during Perestroika started creeping back in the early-mid 2000s. The successor to Lenin, Stalin, is next in line, except that his original statues are a much rarer find. The deceased enthusiast from Lashmanka in Tatarstan originally intended to install a statue of Lenin next to that of Stalin. In Amga, Republic of Sakha (Yakutia), busts of Lenin and Stalin—and now also an Orthodox chapel—stand side by side. The head of the local administration and the project's driving force explained that he had spotted the uprooted busts in the shed of a school where he used to serve as director. The same shed contains yet another bust, that of the head of the Soviet government, Mikhail Kalinin. If the elderly inhabitants of the village would request it, he said, he would have no problem restoring Kalinin back to life as well. Why not![12] Sitting atop a high base, the monument to Sergo Ordzhonikidze in Kazan can be easily mistaken for that of Stalin. Gnilorybov has related heated discussions on this subject among the locals. An elderly lady who confessed her devotion to Stalin, put it as follows: "I don't care who this monument is dedicated to, Stalin or Ordzhonikidze, as they resemble each other. The most important for me is that such a monument exists in principle. This statue is from the time period I appreciate."[13]

Private individuals and organized groups do not always establish a consensus on the memorialization of Stalin. Sometimes the statue of Stalin becomes a subject of contestation, as in 2008 in Novocherkassk, the unofficial capital of the

Cossacks. Some seven years earlier, a local inhabitant had discovered a statue of Stalin broken into pieces, which the homeless had turned into a trash bin. He spent a good half-year fixing the statue, which he subsequently placed next to his garage and, coincidentally, a cemetery. Novocherkassk communists subsequently petitioned city authorities to move the statue to downtown and thus "restore the historical truth." The statue's caretaker, however, refused to relinquish it. He suggested the communists pay him, or else threatened to shoot the intruders. The Cossacks meanwhile ruled out formally erecting a monument to the tyrant. As of 2014, the statue was at the original spot.[14]

Recently, a small town in Cheliabinsk region made news. Shortly after Khrushchev's now famous 1956 Secret Speech, a group of Kusa dwellers, at night, took down the Stalin monument that had hitherto graced the town's only park, broke it into pieces, and tossed the pieces into a lake. The story has since become part of the local lore, coupled with the efforts to reclaim the statue. The opportunity arose sixty-two years later, in Putin's Russia. In August 2018 the water in the lake was partially drained in order to repair a dike. Among other things, there emerged from beneath the silt parts of Stalin's body. By the time the Kusa town museum—which sought to display the reconstructed monument on its premises—arrived on the scene, more prominent pieces of the statue had already gone. The trophy went to a local branch of the Essence of Time, a neoconservative pro-government organization run by Kurginian. The Essence of Time would agree to the rebuilding of the Stalin monument only in its original location, the decision allegedly backed by an opinion poll. The acrimony that followed displays all the elements of the idiosyncratic version of history passed down from the top. The activist called the museum director a "rabid anti-Stalinist" who would mock Stalin before children. Despite the fact that he counts Stalin's victims also in his immediate family, he absolves Stalin of responsibility for the mass terror. The director responded in a Kafkaesque manner, referring to the monument's demolition as a "terrible tragedy" that should not reoccur. As the town of Kusa suffered relatively less from Stalinist repression, she believes there are enough good people who would "treat the monument to Stalin with care and render volunteer help to the museum in its preservation." A local historian who has written two books on Stalin's terror, which directly affected his father, tends to agree with the museum director. Let us put the statue in front of the museum, he suggests. Some people may lay flowers, while others may spit on it, and that is fine. "We are not the ones to judge who's more to blame, those who persecuted or those who were persecuted. It may take another five to eight generations to objectively assess it."[15] As of this writing, the fate of the Stalin statue at Kusa remains unclear.

What happened at Kusa is, of course, not the first time when the memory of the tyrant came into conflict with the memory of its victims. Sometimes the "war of monuments" takes on a direct meaning. A case at hand is Surgut, an affluent city in Siberia built on oil. In September of 2016 the local Communist Party branch unilaterally erected a bust of Stalin on the Ob River embankment. Financed by crowdfunding, the bust featured a popular quote attributed to Stalin: "After my death a pile of rubbish will be heaped on my grave, but the wind of history will sweep it away." It is not just the quotation or a missing permit from city authorities that prompted a public outcry. A mere few meters away an initiative group had for many years planned to build a monument to the victims of Stalin's terror, namely those thirty thousand or so who had been forcibly exiled in the region. Confronted with that fact, the communists first argued that they had never heard of such plans. Next, one of the activists suggested the exiles should be grateful to Stalin to end up in the "rich" Surgut of all places. Finally, he stated the two monuments would be complementary to each other—one should know one's history! Typically, the communists referred to some sort of opinion poll, according to which 60 percent of the population of Surgut supported their efforts.[16] In a rare instance, the Surgut city government vowed to, and actually did, remove the monument a few weeks after it had been illegally erected.[17] Undeterred, the activists are currently looking for an alternative location for the bust.[18] An unauthorized Stalin bust also appeared in December 2019 in Magadan—the city in Kolyma region built by Gulag prisoners. The usual suspects, the communists, claim to have learned about the initiative from the media. Regardless, they see no reason why Stalin should not be revered in this part of Russia also. An even more cryptic ex post facto justification was provided by the deputy head of the local museum. If it had not been for Stalin, he rationalized, there would have been no prisoners in Magadan who had built everything from scratch. Hence, by paying respect to Stalin, descendants of the "settlers" reaffirm their own existence.[19]

A hard-core nationalist Prokhanov has proposed installing a statue of Stalin in each and every Russian city. In that case, countered former Duma deputy and opposition politician Vladimir Ryzhkov, next to it should be erected a monument to the victims of Stalin's terror. The Communist Party ridiculed Ryzhkov's argument by speculating that such a juxtaposition may apply to just any monument celebrating a historical figure, from Tsar Peter the Great to Prince Dmitry Pozharsky.[20] Prokhanov has long lobbied for the city of Volgograd (originally called Tsaritsyn) to receive its old name, Stalingrad. During the seventieth anniversary of the Stalingrad Battle, select share taxis in St. Petersburg, Chita, and Volgograd, featuring Stalin's image set among wartime photographs, called on the city dwellers to "return the victory its name."[21] (Vehicles so adorned are popularly known in Russia as "Stalinobus.") *Stalingrad* is altogether in the public domain by now. The 2010–15 patriotic education program, for example, had an international brass festival "The Stalingrad Cup" on its agenda for 2013. The subsequent program included a film festival "The Stalingrad Lilac."

Beside the familiar faces of public figures who have consistently pledged their love to Stalin, one of the most ubiquitous Stalinists who have emerged in post-Crimea Russia is Sergei Kurochkin (who coincidentally hails from Crimea). In August of 2015, in Sevastopol, communist Kurochkin grabbed the limelight by performing a song, "Bring Stalin Back!" The song he has composed calls upon listeners to "Remember, we're on alert. We don't tolerate fascists and, whenever necessary, will squash the bastards."[22] Kurochkin has performed the song on several occasions since then. Dressed up in a generalissimo-like military uniform and faking a Georgian accent, Kurochkin and his song served as a background to a young pioneer ceremony carried out by the Communist Party on December 16, 2017, in Sevastopol.[23]

While Kusa with its 17,000 inhabitants or Surgut with its 291,000 are still minor examples of the battles waged over Stalin's legacy, Novosibirsk—the third largest

Russian city—is not. The first attempt to erect a monument to Stalin in Novosibirsk dates by 1998. Back then, the city government instantly rejected the proposal by a pro-Stalin initiative group. The following decade saw a sea of change, so that when the group renewed its efforts in 2016, Novosibirsk had a communist mayor. Mayor Alexander Lokot, who holds a positive view of Stalin, has proposed placing the bust on the territory of the local Communist Party branch office that he heads. This, however, did not satisfy the activists, who sought maximum public visibility for their idol. The initiative group leader imbues the prospective monument with a broader meaning: "We demand the restoration of historical justice. Lifting Stalin to a pedestal in the downtown of one of the country's biggest metropolitan cities will put an end to a smear campaign against the memory of the leader and our entire glorious, heroic Soviet era." He further claimed an "aggressive" posture toward Stalin by the intelligentsia and minimized the number of Stalin's victims. What makes the city authorities' response problematic is the absence of a moral nadir. Every time the Stalinists received a negative reply, it was always on account of technicalities: a protected area, potential damage to a pipeline, and so on. Regarded as controversial, the city government nevertheless considered the idea of a public referendum on the possible location of a Stalin monument in Novosibirsk. A meeting of protest against the monument on October 30, 2018, gathered no more than thirty people in a city of 1.6 million. Nine days later the Novosibirsk culture board once again proposed the local Communist Party headquarters as a site.[24] The compromise solution smacked of hypocrisy. As the head of the board later explained, individuals who want to celebrate Stalin would now be able to do so, without offending those who regard him as a tyrant. The initiative group grudgingly agreed. Until the opening on May 9, 2019, the bust remained covered, in anticipation of vandalism. While unveiling the monument, Mayor Lokot described it as a "people's decision" and blasted the "liberals" who had opposed it. Putin's press secretary Peskov excused himself from commenting beyond the affirmation that Stalin belongs to the country's history.[25]

Erecting/restoring a monument to Stalin is a statement in and of itself. Commonly, it is an expression of nostalgia for the bygone days, a projection of an idiosyncratic view on history so common in present-day Russia. It may also serve as a form of criticism of the "weak" regimes past and present. Here Stalin emerges as the Red Tsar who did away with the conventional tsars, equally unmatched in his toughness by the current rulers. The bust of Stalin recently raised in Vladivostok is a case in point. According to an online poll, two-thirds of Vladivostok inhabitants supported the original idea from 2014 to build a monument to Stalin. The city authorities, claiming the lack of funds and a split public opinion, proposed that private business finance the project. A local businessman who responded to the call has announced he was doing it in opposition to the plans to erect a monument to Nikolai II in the city. The two busts opened three days apart in December 2016. The businessman condemned the last Russian tsar for having lost the war against Japan and the Great War and consequently provoking a revolution and civil war. Stalin, to the contrary, rebuilt the economy and guaranteed low prices, which he takes as proof of good governance. Along the way, he denies the high rates of incarceration in the Gulag and claims that people fared worse in the 1990s than during the 1937–38 Great Terror.[26]

It comes as no surprise that Stalin—a symbol of imperial power—found his abode in the Russian-separatist-held Donbass. One of the guerillas made the following statement at the unveiling of a Stalin bust in the occupied Luhansk on December 19, 2015: "Today, ideology and the symbol and personality of Stalin become important not just for the Luhansk region but for the entire world. Nazism is rearing its head, and to defeat it we need the firm, unwavering hand of a leader." The bust was made possible through yet another indefatigable individual, communist Kazbek Taisaev. Bearing Christmas (i.e., New Year) presents for the children of Donbass, Taisaev described the monument to Stalin as a "tribute to our great country, which we're going to inevitably build." The leaders of the separatists, Denis Pushilin and the late Alexander Zakharchenko, have joined Taisaev in the praise of the Soviet Union.[27] The top-ranking military commander, Eduard Basurin, has been spotted wearing a badge with Stalin on his uniform as recently as 2018. The capital of the so-called Donetsk People's Republic claims no Stalin monument of its own. Yet, the image of the Soviet dictator has long been incorporated into the city landscape, and, by extension, propaganda. Posters featuring a portrait of Stalin and his wartime quotation, "Our cause is just. Enemy will be routed. We will claim victory," for example hung in Donetsk for a good half-year in 2015.[28] Coincidentally, between 1924 and 1961 Donetsk was known as Stalino.

The communists scored yet another symbolic victory by unveiling a Stalin bust in Penza in December of 2015. The gold-painted Stalin (courtesy of Taisaev) flanks a center carrying his name—the first such institution anywhere in the world, as has been proudly advertised. Stalin Center aims to "promote those Stalinist practices that are still topical today."[29] As of now, the only regular activity associated with the center that remotely brings to mind its originally stated goal of "organizing roundtables and public discussions" is a flower-laying ceremony.[30] The inside features just newspaper stacks and Stalin photograph printouts. That does not humble local communist deputies to claim that Stalin Center should be state financed, on par with Yeltsin Center in Ekaterinburg, which had opened almost simultaneously.[31]

Among more recent additions is a full-size Stalin with his right hand raised in a salute, unveiled in September of 2015 in Sherlanger, Mari El Republic. Reportedly the tallest such statue anywhere in the world, the 5.5 meter (including the base) golden Stalin greets workers of a local meat-processing plant. The wall behind the statue sports a quotation by the director: "The success of the enterprise depends on each of you!" A conservative website that featured a story about the Sherlanger monument had this postscript by a contributing author: "Liberals, tremble, spit venom. The people remember the Man."[32] In May of 2019 a standard bust of Stalin was unveiled in Kirov region. The communists, at whose initiative it was erected, hope to eventually move it to a permanent location in downtown Kirov.[33] Another bust, painstakingly restored by a local sculptor, was installed in front of the Volgograd Communist Party headquarters on the occasion of Stalin's 140th birthday, on December 20, 2019.[34]

Out of the one hundred or so monuments to Stalin in Russia, two have been erected at the initiative of the Russian Military Historical Society (RVIO). One is situated where a Soviet defense line bearing his name once was, some twenty kilometers from the Latvian border. Curiously, the original bust was moved in November 2018 to the Military Historical Museum in Ostrov, and replaced with another, "dispatched from

Moscow."³⁵ Another marks the location of the Stalin house museum in Khoroshevo village near Rzhev. As the story goes, in August 1943 Stalin spent a night in that particular house and that is where he came up with the idea of a fireworks celebration in Moscow each time a new city had been recaptured from the Germans.³⁶ The exhibition diligently reflects Stalin's personality cult of seventy years ago: his contribution to military victory, his role in rebuilding industry, his efforts to revive the Orthodox Church, and so on.³⁷ The museum opened on July 3, 2015, in the presence of the minister of culture. That same day Medinskii published a piece in *Izvestia*, in which he proposed committing Stalin to history and stopping the unloading of "all our problems and differences" on the Soviet leader.³⁸

Medinskii and RVIO also stand behind a historical theme park, Alley of Rulers, in Moscow. The museum is situated next to the Military Uniform Museum, yet another one of RVIO's projects. The museum and the sculpture park opened within a three-month span, in February and May 2017, respectively. During the opening ceremony, Minister of Culture Medinskii used the catchphrase *historical succession* while Minister of Education Vasilieva declared the theme park a perfect place to hold a series of lectures on culture. The author of the busts (of which by 2018 forty-three had been installed)

Figure 11 Mediocrity rules. Unofficial court sculptor Zurab Tsereteli (left, b. 1934) easily finds a common language with the Soviet-type bureaucrats of history, former minister of education Olga Vasilieva (b. 1960) and former minister of culture Vladimir Medinskii (b. 1970). Here they have gathered in May of 2017 to open yet another pedestrian creation by Tsereteli, The Alley of Rulers in Moscow, sponsored by Medinskii's RVIO. Among the forty-plus busts of Russian and Soviet leaders on display is also Stalin.

is Zurab Tsereteli. Tsereteli has received heavy criticism on account of sloppiness and outright plagiarism in executing the sculptures. The style can be characterized as a nineteenth-century pastiche. The debate over the aesthetic value of Tsereteli's works, however, was overshadowed by the addition of two new busts later that year. On September 22, 2017, Medinskii inaugurated the first ever officially sponsored sculptures of Lenin and Stalin in post-Soviet Moscow. While Lenin prompted little to no public reaction, Stalin caused a stir.[39]

The concept of the "Alley of Rulers" containing Stalin is not quite new of course. It was pioneered in 2014 in Vladimir, by the boss of a local construction company. Displaying the busts of Soviet leaders, from Lenin to Gorbachev, in front of the company's main building, was his idea. All but the original bust of Lenin were made by a local sculptor, in concrete. The businessman said the money he spent on the project would be enough to buy a car, yet added "that's our history and we should respect it."[40] Hence Vladimir had acquired already its second Stalin. The original statue, not untypically, adores the local Communist Party headquarters.

Back in fashion are also the Stalin-era plaques that mark places the "great leader" once treaded. One in Makhachkala (originally installed in 1920, and reopened in 2005) announces that Stalin had passed through the local train station on his way to a congress. Another one, inside the Kutafin Moscow State Law University (1949, 2017), informs that back in 1924 Stalin spoke there on the issues facing the Communist Party.

No longer taboo, Stalin has acquired a market value. For as long as there are buyers, there will be sellers. Avito, a Russian classified advertisement website, features an impressive range of antique statues of Stalin for sale. One can get anything: from a standard concrete head (for an equivalent of USD 570) to a full-size sculpture, sans arms (USD 800) to a bust by a recognized sculptor (USD 13,000). As of fall 2017, the most expensive Stalin on the market was offered by an antiques dealer in Krasnodar region. The hefty price tag of 1.25 million rubles (USD 20,250) the dealer explained by rarity: "Someone is offering to buy the statue of Stalin from me as we speak, but for half the price. I'm not budging for I'm not in a rush. I also have a bust of Stalin for half a million and numerous busts of Lenin. The latter are much cheaper, for his cult of personality has never been denounced."[41]

Celebrating the New World Order Agreed at Yalta

The biggest statue of Stalin in the world had been personally negotiated by Putin. A monument commemorating the 1944 Allied meeting at Yalta was agreed upon in 2004 in conversation with the then president of Ukraine Leonid Kuchma. The monument is a work by Zurab Tsereteli, long-serving president of the Russian Academy of Arts who fits the definition of a court sculptor. Tsereteli made a name for himself as an adept of realism with a penchant for gigantism. The ten-ton bronze sculptural composition measures six meters in width and over three meters in height. Stalin is clearly a dominating figure, menacingly leaning toward Roosevelt in the middle, who has the appearance of a wise man. Indeed, Stalin is 10 centimeters taller than Roosevelt and Churchill, while in reality he was the shortest of the three.

The monument commemorating the sixtieth anniversary of the Yalta conference was meant as a "gift" to Crimea—Tsereteli's common practice. The sculptor intended installing two copies of the monument, one in Yalta and the other in Volgograd. The latter did not materialize, for the local authorities refused to bear the transportation and installation costs. As an alternative site, Mayor Yuri Luzhkov's office in Moscow proposed erecting the monument on Poklonnaia Hill, but this was overrun by public opinion.[42] Tserereli had proposed May 9, 2005, as the possible date for an unveiling ceremony at Yalta. However, public opinion in Crimea was split on the idea. Heated debates ensued in both the parliament of the Autonomous Republic of Crimea and the Supreme Rada in Kiev.[43] The monument was supported by local communists and the Crimean Union of Soviet Officers, but bitterly opposed by Crimean Tatars. Mustafa Dzhemilev, a Soviet-era dissident and veteran Crimean Tatar politician, said he did not mind Churchill and Roosevelt but was categorically against celebrating Stalin, who had committed crimes against the Tatar people and numerous other Soviet nationalities. A compromise solution to keep Stalin's chair empty was also rejected. Dzemilev pointedly noted that an "empty chair would sooner or later be occupied by Stalin," while the director of Livadia Museum claimed it would be wrong or even unethical for "those three great men who had decided the outcome of the war."[44] One way or another, the Orange Revolution in Ukraine put an end to the project.

While Tsereteli was contemplating what to do with his monument, the news arrived that a sculptural composition of Stalin, Churchill, and Roosevelt at Tehran by a different sculptor had opened in Sochi. The monument was unveiled in May 2008 in the territory of Krasmashevsky sanatorium. The question why there and then has more to do with shadowy business dealings than with history politics. Originally built in 1936 as Kirov sanatorium, it had served as a luxury vacation spot for members of the Central Committee of the Soviet Communist Party. In 2004 the control over the sanatorium was wrested by a Moscow businessman Victor Baturin. Baturin intended to raze the old buildings and build new ones. Historians sounded the alarm and the extensive reconstruction plans were put on ice. In order to get historians off his back, Baturin financed the monument and an exhibit on the Second World War through the Our Duty Foundation that he bankrolls.[45]

When reporting on the opening ceremony, the Russian media mistakenly spoke of the conference at Yalta—by far a more important reference point in Russia than the tripartite meetings at Tehran or Potsdam. Like Tsereteli, the Israeli Frank Meisler worked from photographs. Both executed in realistic style, neither monument is aesthetically pleasing. The heavy, intimidating Stalin of Tsereteli has transformed into the skinny, slightly disproportionate Stalin of Meisler. Meisler was obviously engaged in self-promotion, when he grandiloquently announced that a copy of the monument would be gifted to the leaders of the United States and the United Kingdom, which did not come to be. As of this writing, both the monument and the sanatorium are in a pitiful state. Only a plaque on the base, "dedicated to the collaboration between the Great Powers," reveals what lay inside a rotting crate in the boarded-off territory of the sanatorium.

Tsereteli's creation, meanwhile, received a second life following the annexation of Crimea. Within a year, the monument was installed in front of Livadia palace, as originally intended. The opening ceremony was attended by high-ranking Crimean politicians, Sergei Naryshkin, and Alexander Zaldostanov. A recorded voice introduced the Yalta conference as "one of the most important events in the twentieth century history . . . that bore on postwar geopolitics." The head of Yalta city council went even further in his speech by suggesting that the decisions made by the Big Three at Yalta "ensured the right of national self-determination, preserved national identity and culture." The keynote address was delivered by RIO's head Naryshkin. Naryshkin neatly weaved his former and current duties into a single narrative:

> The unveiling of the monument simultaneously functions as yet another warning to those politicians and history profiteers who are trying to shamelessly and cynically twist the history of the Second World War and the postwar world order. By so doing they betray the memory of millions of people who had perished in Nazi concentration camps and of millions more who died for our freedom, on the battlefields and the home front.

People in the audience—as available videos of the opening ceremony attest—at once started referring to the sculptural composition as a "monument to Stalin."[46]

The opening ceremony was preceded by an academic conference, "Yalta, 1945: Past, Present, and Future." The conference made a direct link between the establishment of the International Military Tribunal at Nuremberg and war crimes allegedly committed by Ukraine in Donbass.[47] President Putin appealed to the conference participants in a written address:

> Right here, in Livadia palace, took place the Allied meeting of the anti-Hitler coalition, which played a significant role in the ultimate defeat of Nazism. Most important, the Yalta conference laid the foundation for the postwar world order and the nature of international relations for years to come. . . . In the wake of the Yalta and Potsdam conferences and the Nuremberg trial it looked like as if the ideology and criminal nature of Nazism had been exposed and destroyed. However, recent events tell us otherwise. Right before our eyes, a campaign aiming to revisit the results of the Second World War is taking shape; the Red Army's contribution to the great victory is being diminished. . . . These circumstances cannot make us feel indifferent and/or impartial. We should firmly oppose any attempts at falsification of historical facts [and] defend the truth about the past war.[48]

The voices of protest from Crimean Tatars were promptly drowned by references to their collaboration with the Nazis during the Second World War.

The ambiguity surrounding the monument is manifested in its less than prominent location, deliberately so chosen in order to avoid "agitating minds . . . in difficult times," as the present director of Livadia Museum put it.[49] Although a popular path to the monument was quickly established, many a visitor ends up there by chance. Visitors report mixed feelings about Stalin and the artistic quality of the monument, yet typically regard it a poignant marker of an important historical event. Typical of grandiose statues such as this, a certain part of it had become a lucky charm of sorts, polished to a shine by numerous visitors' having touched it. In the case of the

Yalta monument, it is Stalin's pipe. Russian tourists who decide to take pictures by the monument, and have often to wait for their turn, mostly pose with Stalin. According to folklore, climbing onto Roosevelt's lap increases one's chances of getting a US visa. Churchill's ubiquitous cigar has meanwhile been stolen.[50]

Despite officials emphasizing that the Yalta monument commemorates a particular event rather than specific individuals, it is popularly understood as a homage to Stalin. In effect, it has spurred further memorialization. Already in March 2015, the Communist Party announced a campaign to commemorate Stalin by means of monuments, memorial plaques, and streets renamed in his honor. The presidential administration typically issues a disclaimer, taking no responsibility for the increased interest in Stalin's persona and delegating decision-making power regarding monuments to local authorities.[51] In Crimea, local communists, on May 8, 2015, unveiled a memorial plaque at the party's headquarters in Simferopol. The plaque relates that Stalin had passed through the city on his way to the Yalta conference. Twice in 2016, the bas-relief of Stalin was desecrated, with the word *henchman* scribbled next to it. The latter incident, speculated the then Prosecutor General of Crimea Poklonskaia, was a provocation carried out in conjunction with the Day of Commemoration of mass deportation of Crimean Tatars on May 18, 1944. The Communist Party, which anticipated such acts, appealed to the FSB and Prosecutor General's Office with the request to find and punish the "vandals who smear the patriotic history of our Motherland."[52]

As a postscript of sorts, yet another monument depicting Stalin, Churchill, and Roosevelt at Yalta opened in May 2017 in the capital of Mongolia. The initiative belonged to a Mongolian parliamentarian. A year later, the Russian Center for Science and Culture in Ulaanbaatar—as part of the series of academic events to "counter falsification of history"— hosted a temporary exhibition on the central events of the Second World War. The Yalta conference was described as one of the top three such events.[53]

With the media focusing on the monument dedicated to the 1945 tripartite meeting, few paid attention to another unveiling ceremony held in the city of Yalta, on April 22, 2017. The Russian-occupied Crimea was celebrating the thirty-second president of the United States! Created as far back as 1960, the bust of Franklin D. Roosevelt has since then been exhibited only indoors. Ten days after Donald Trump's inauguration as US president, however, the local administration announced plans to properly display the FDR bust on the street bearing his name, ostensibly on popular demand. At the opening ceremony, the mayor of Yalta hailed Roosevelt's contribution to preserving peace in the twentieth century. Duma deputy Ruslan Balbekov minced no words in explaining the current significance of the monument:

> Roosevelt is the example of a Western politician who, without impeding the interests of his own country, advanced cooperation with Russia. Although he didn't subscribe to Soviet ideology at the time, he understood that without Russia the world order was impossible [to establish]. Franklin Roosevelt sincerely helped the Soviet Union in the struggle against fascism. The current US president would be wise to learn from history and adopt the [effective] mode of cooperation with Russia.[54]

And that is what it actually was: an invitation to a dialogue, ideally a Trump–Putin summit like the one at Yalta seven decades earlier.[55]

Felix Dzerzhinsky as a Consensus Figure

In a sense, monuments to Felix Dzerzhinsky better capture the Zeitgeist in Russia than monuments to Stalin. The latter symbolizes breaking taboos, while the former, restoration. Even today, every new statue of Stalin is treated by the Russian media as a minor sensation, though markedly less than, say, in the early 2000s. The personality of Dzerzhinsky, in contrast, has long been normalized. Alternatively, the odium associated with his name did not stick. Although Dzerzhinsky, an Old Bolshevik, is a historical figure that stood at the creation of Soviet Russia—the period no one today has a personal memory of—semantically, he projects the continuity of the Soviet state better than does Stalin. Stalin's crimes are popularly known to a smallest detail while Dzerzhinsky's are known only in the abstract. The cult of Dzerzhinsky had been established, ironically, during Khrushchev's Thaw. The honorable "knight of the revolution" was contrasted with the "hangmen" Nikolai Ezhov and Lavrenty Beria, and the uncompromising but ultimately just Cheka with the corrupt NKVD. Since then, the "Iron Felix" has stood for someone who works incessantly to clear the rot, someone who speaks truth to power.

It was the colossal statue of Dzerzhinsky in Moscow that got debased in August 1991, accompanied by public cheers. Had there been Stalin monuments still around, they would, no doubt, have experienced the same fate. Yet there were none to be found. The dramatic moments of 1991 contrast with the matter-of-factness of today. Dzerzhinsky, the Chekist, appears an unambiguous character. Even if one were to disregard the consistent efforts to whitewash the reputation of the Russian security services, Putin's earlier career choice serves as a generational bridge. The Stalin in bronze and plaster is no Putin, who would have been the first to disavow the uncanny comparison. But Dzerzhinsky he may well imagine himself to be. When talking monuments, the tsars for Putin represent tradition and status. Dzerzhinsky, on the other hand, is a founding father with particular features of character worth emulating. That is also a likely projection made by those on whose initiative the Dzerzhinsky monuments are being erected. While the red flags flying at the unveiling ceremony of yet another Stalin bust leave no doubt who is behind it, the small crowd that gather around a new Dzerzhinsky monument tend to wear uniforms. The only citizen category that attends both are small in numbers war veterans.

The first new monument to Dzerzhinsky in post-Soviet Russia emerged, unsurprisingly perhaps, in the city of Dzerzhinsky. The old, plaster statue eventually crumbled down in 2003. Undaunted, the city authorities commissioned a grander, bronze monument resembling that on Lubyanka Square in neighboring Moscow. They were particular about the kind of uniform the Iron Felix would wear, though they were willing to compromise on the size (3.2 vs. 5.75 meter). The officials participating in the unveiling ceremony in September of 2004 did not have enough words of praise for the person who gave a name to their city. The head of the city administration brushed off potential criticism by saying everyone killed and/or gave killing orders during the revolution. The deputy head of the FSB for Moscow region emphasized Dzerzhinsky's "iron will and high professionalism, which had strengthened the nascent Russian state." Among the invited guests was also the grandson of the founder of the Cheka.

Felix Dzerzhinsky Jr. objected to his famous ancestor being called a "henchman."[56] The affinity for the author of the Red Terror can also be explained by the special status of Dzerzhinsky as one of those closed cities associated with the Soviet defense industry. A stone's throw from the Dzerzhinsky statue is a monument in the shape of a hammer and sickle, popularly known as the Soviet Legacy; a mere kilometer away lies a memorial complex (unveiled in December of 2004) celebrating the "creators of Russia's nuclear shield" and featuring a Topol ballistic missile, an M-1 Volna surface-to-air missile system, and a Grad multiple rocket launcher.

It took another eight years before the next, life-size statue of Dzerzhinsky was unveiled, this time in Tiumen, one of Russia's oil and gas hubs. Originally designed by a local police investigator–cum–sculptor, the monument has since the mid-1990s been languishing in a shed. It was the former members of the security agencies who had preserved it and lobbied for its reconstruction. A memorial plaque on the pedestal quotes Dzerzhinsky: "A chekist must have burning heart, cold head, and clear hands."[57] Tiumen is perhaps the only city in Russia that features not one but two monuments to Dzerzhinsky. The second statue is to be found in a sculpture park attached to a recently opened Pioneer House hotel complex a 20-minute drive from Tiumen. Where a communist party holiday home once was, local businessmen faithfully reconstructed a Soviet atmosphere, complete with a pioneer museum. A stocky Dzerzhinsky joined another fifteen or so mass-produced plaster statues of children and youth, the kind that once populated the Soviet Union's expanse.

What hitherto had been random attempts to memorialize Dzerzhinsky, in 2017 became a trend. In September of that year new monuments went up in Kirov and Kursk and the restored ones in Smolensk (bust), Kaluga, and Kamyziak, Astrakhan region. The date marks both the centennial of the Russian security services and the 140th anniversary of Dzerzhinsky. The initiative invariably came from the FSB veterans, who easily secure the support of the local administration and overcome the opposition of the victims of Soviet repression. A Dzerzhinsky monument typically finds its home in front of the local FSB headquarters. As before, size matters: Dzerzhinsky towers at 2.5 meters or higher.

In Magadan—closely associated with the history of the Gulag—officials apparently did not dare to challenge Ernst Neizvestny's famous Mask of Sorrow monument—one of the few cosponsored by the state.[58] So, instead of a statue, the local authorities approved of a memorial plaque. The plaque marks both the street named after Dzerzhinsky and the building that until 2011 housed, first, the KGB and, later, the FSB headquarters in Magadan. The bureaucrats only had good things to say about Dzerzhinsky: a great statesman, extraordinary politician, head of the predecessor of the heroic FSB entrusted with the most important task there is, national security. To balance out the system of police terror instituted by Dzerzhinsky—which typically gets glossed over through the use of Soviet-time euphemisms such as *counterrevolution* and *sabotage*—officials are particularly keen on emphasizing his work on behalf of orphans. The eulogy characteristically ended with the pious hope that history would eventually render its judgment on individuals such as Dzerzhinsky.[59]

The floodgates have been broken. The period of restoration is in effect. In Krasnodar and Saratov, the name of Dzerzhinsky was recently attached to a school and a college, respectively.[60] A new monument to Dzerzhinsky went up in May of 2018 in Ryazan, and in Belgorod, Amur region, authorities had in June of 2018 announced plans to rebuild a park honoring the man.

Moscow appears to be the last bastion in Dzerzhinsky's victorious path. Until now, the innumerable efforts to restore the Iron Felix to its original site on Lubianka Square have failed. For the Communist Party, which has been working to that end since 2010, the issue at stake is much more than just a monument. The communists sought to achieve their goal by means of a referendum. The system of a popular vote and the authoritarian form of government in Russia do not belong together. Conducting a referendum is nearly impossible, for the law sets a fifty percent participation threshold. The communists did not hide the fact that they wanted to create a precedent in order to raise further issues of significance to them, say, challenging the results of Yeltsin's privatization. By 2015 they had gathered 152,000 signatures in favor of the referendum, with bringing back the Dzerzhinsky statue as one of the three questions on the ballot. In a surprise move, the Moscow city government approved of the referendum, yet reduced it to a single question, that on Dzerzhinsky.[61] On July 21, 2015, the Communist Party killed their darling, citing the high costs associated with the referendum. Observers, however, proposed another, more plausible explanation: the communists had sensed that the referendum was bound to fail. Furthermore, Lubyanka Square suddenly appeared as the preferred site for the monument to Prince Vladimir that was originally planned for Sparrow Hills. Ironically, even Memorial supported this option, as the lesser of two evils.[62]

Still, the communists believe that time is on their side. In December of 2017, then Communist Party leader Gennady Ziuganov appealed to President Putin to reinstall the Dzerzhinsky monument in the center of Moscow. One of Putin's right-hand men, Naryshkin, did not seem to mind. Naryshkin, who proudly displays a Dzerzhinsky portrait in his office, said in an interview that he appreciates the role of Dzerzhinsky in laying the foundation of the Russian intelligence service. As regards Dzerzhinsky's role in carrying out mass repressions, it is all a part of history, stated the top Russian spy. Besides, Naryshkin hastened to add, the intelligence rank and file had also been a target during the Great Terror of 1937–38. As for the monument to Dzerzhinsky on Lubyanka Square, which Naryshkin said he personally likes a lot, he tends to see it exclusively as a work of art.[63] In other words, he is not opposed to the restoration of the monument as part of an architectural ensemble.

What is striking is the consensus on the personality of Dzerzhinsky that crosses a political divide and thus effectively serves the interests of the state. Like the high-ranking state bureaucrats, the communists skirt the issue of Red Terror, trivializing it in the process. In the Soviet mythology, Dzerzhinsky was perhaps the most heroic and romanticized figure after Lenin. As a popular symbol associated with the imposition of law and order, Dzerzhinsky is thus a consensus link to the Bolshevik Revolution—which the present regime had struggled to fit into the paradigm of continuum of Russian history. At the same time, the designation of a successful administrator (Russian: *khoziaistvennyi rukovoditel*) puts him on the same level with Stalin. Portrayed by the communists as an embodiment of honesty and self-sacrifice, Dzerzhinsky thus has the potential to "assist in formulating worthy moral guiding lines for our society."

In addition, by emphasizing the persona of Iron Felix the communists seek a symbolic revanche for the failed coup d'état of August 1991 and deliver a verdict on (imperfect) liberal democracy that followed. Last but not least, Dzerzhinsky's name is a free advertisement for the Communist Party, even though, according to party officials, issues related to history never make up more than 15 percent of its political platform.[64]

Popular perception of Dzerzhinsky is not significantly different from that of the communists. Consider, for example, how a travel website describes the monument to Dzerzhinsky in St. Petersburg. Dzerzhinsky, a brave revolutionary and prominent Bolshevik party leader, made a significant contribution to the foundation of the Soviet state and left a lasting impression on his contemporaries. The Dzerzhinsky monument is one of the most popular and recognizable sights in St. Petersburg.[65] This text may as well have been written in 1981 when the monument was unveiled.

All in all, Dzerzhinsky's name currently graces 1,342 squares, streets, avenues, and lanes in Russia. Take, for example, the great city of Russian military glory, Volgograd. Some foreign visitors who had attended Football World Cup games in Volgograd in June 2018 made a pilgrimage to the memorial complex commemorating the Battle of Stalingrad. Fewer of them, perhaps, visited the gigantic statue of Lenin—reportedly the largest such in the world—overlooking the Volga. Just a handful of them, however, might pay attention to subject-specific toponyms in the city celebrating the Soviet secret police. Indeed, Volgograd has Chekist Square and Chekist public garden, Dzerzhinsky Square, Dzerzhinsky Street, and Dzerzhinsky borough, not to mention NKVD Tenth Division Street.

Stalin is not in same league as far as toponymy is concerned, but he is getting there. According to the Yandex Maps web browser, there are currently over sixty streets and lanes in Russia named after Stalin. Most of them are situated in North Ossetia (fifteen) and Dagestan (seven). The city of Dagestanskie Ogni has bestowed on Stalin the highest toponymic honor by naming an avenue after him. Kaspiisk, in the same autonomous republic, is poised to become Russia's first city with not one but two streets honoring the maligned dictator. A popular initiative to rename one of the city's main arteries after Stalin had emerged in October 2014. Back then local deputies rejected it citing economic reasons; all but two persons who participated in public hearings in September 2018 approved of the motion.[66]

Still the record for the number of streets and lanes named after Stalin in a single locality belongs to a Slavianka hamlet near Novosibirsk. All there is in Slavianka—one street and twenty-five lanes with a total length of ten kilometers—bears the name of Generalissimo Josef Vissarinovich Stalin. Such an effort at toponymy is credited to a local elected leader; the contemporary legislation allots the decision-making power to local self-government. The inhabitants of Slavianka do not mind the name itself but grumble over the frequent spelling mistakes and own responsibility to display it in full.[67] Having a street in a metropolitan city named after Stalin has not worked so far. In St. Petersburg, communists organized an installation of sorts. In March of 2015 activists replaced a sign on the building on Tenth Communist Street where Stalin once lived. For a short while, Google Maps showed it as "Stalin Street." The communists refused to divulge the name of the person who performed that stunt, for fear that the "fifth column may attempt to assassinate him."[68]

Putin, the Shy Dictator

It may come as no surprise that the first ever full-size statue of Putin was built, in 2004, by Zurab Tsereteli, the ultimate self-promoter and chameleon of a sculptor.[69] Dressed in a judo uniform, Tsereteli's Putin strikes a victorious pose. The billionaire sculptor sounds modest by claiming he just loves watching the president in motion, that is to say, he was present at a martial arts competition in which Putin was participating. Thus, he says, it is not really about Russia's leader; the statue is called "A Healthy Mind in a Healthy Body." Tsereteli's ultimate wish to have his work installed in Moscow was thwarted by a formal requirement, according to which a monument to a person may be considered not earlier than five years after his/her death.[70] Hence, Putin the judoka ended up in Tsereteli's private gallery and occasionally traveled to other places in Russia. Putin himself, reportedly, was surprised at the sight of the statue, which did not prevent Tsereteli from insisting recently that its thirty-meter-high copy should eventually be erected in the president's native city of St. Petersburg.[71]

Otherwise, official monuments to Putin are conspicuous in their absence. Indeed, what other proof of his centrality to the project Russia does Putin need? With nearly total control over mass media, Putin populates the homes of ordinary Russians anyway. He is a cunning operator, not an African-type kleptocrat who seeks popular adulation. Hence, the presidential administration has issued a standard disclaimer, dissuading Putin's fans from rendering their idol in stone or metal. Ironically, that objection may also be read as a ban on the deity's depiction practiced in certain religions. Thus, the 3.5-meter-high statue of Putin was taken out a few days before the opening of a monument in his honor in Kurgan region. What remains of the monument—erected in May of 2018 on the initiative of a Duma deputy for the United Russia Party—is a map of Russia (sans Kuril Islands and Kaliningrad region), a rostrum with Russia's coat of arms and a book symbolizing the Constitution, and three flags (representing the Russian Empire, the Soviet Union, and present-day Russia). The overzealous politician, speaking at the opening ceremony, said that building monuments to Putin is not yet possible, for the president is a modest individual who eschews glory. He also claimed he did not want to inadvertently enter into a kind of cynical competition whereby citizen groups would strive to erect the biggest and boldest statue of the Russian leader. The time will come, and the Putin statue will take its rightful place, he promised the gathering.[72] For now, the bronze Putin swearing on the Constitution is languishing in a garage.

Whenever a private citizen or a group decides to commit Putin to posterity, however, freedom of expression is being safeguarded. The few known examples are comical in their stereotypy. A band of St. Petersburg Cossacks in May of 2015 sponsored a bronze-painted bust of Putin draped in a Roman tunica (reflecting on the idea of Moscow as the Third Rome, and Caesar as a guarantor of the state and God's representative on earth). The grand meaning invested in the bust contrasts with its physical environment—a private plot in the St. Petersburg suburbs. In this particular case, at least Putin's facial features were rendered correctly.[73] Almost simultaneously a plaster bust of a youngish Putin—executed in the spirit of Stalin-era mass-produced park sculpture—appeared near Novorossiysk. No publicity accompanied the unveiling of the bust, which praises the president for "restoring the ancient Russian lands [Crimea] to the Russian Federation."[74] An element of toadyism is unmistakable in a statue marking Putin's visit to Cheliabinsk in November of 2017. Slightly taller than his actual self, Putin is holding a pair of mountain skis with the name of the resort where the statue was unveiled. As a recurrent refrain, the president is credited with the promotion of a healthy lifestyle.[75]

That cannot be said about the creation by a certain Victor Kropachev in Astrakhan. The amateur sculptor worked just too hard trying to convey symbolism. A hideous two-meter tall creature—half beast, half Putin—is holding in his hand a fish. Reminiscent of works by Giacommetti, the smallish head of the Russian president sits on an oversize body with wings and disproportionately long hands. As the sculptor has explained, the bear signifies Russia, the eagle conveys that the president flouts external enemies, and the fish represents the Caspian Sea sturgeon. The sculpture got the name "Mind, Power, and Soul," which rhymes with that given by Tsereteli to his own statue of Putin. The sculptor was planning to send his creation as a gift to Putin.[76] It is doubtful the president would appreciate it. When the Congress of Russian Communities of Crimea in 2016 came up with the idea of erecting a monument to Putin in the regional capital Simferopol—preferably styled as a skipper steering a ship—the proposal received a gentle kick from the presidential administration.

Inasmuch as erecting Putin statues remains a semi-taboo, celebrating his strategic achievements is a safe bet. The greatest of them all is, of course, the 2014 annexation of Crimea. The creeping, almost benign, manner in which the takeover was carried out is associated with the eponymous image of a military man without insignia. Typically referred to as Putin's "green men," in Russia they got the name "polite people." A TASS photographer captured the "peaceful" character of the military occupation in a single shot of a soldier in camouflage handing over a cat to a boy. The image instantly became a meme. For his sixty-second birthday Putin received a score of gifts from the grateful citizens. An art collective painted graffiti on facades of seven buildings across Russia that came to spell the word *thank-you*. The first one, in Kaliningrad, reproduced the photograph taken half a year earlier in Simferopol.[77] It did not take long before local politicians started cashing in on the "Crimean Spring." The first monument to the "polite people," faithfully rendering the soldier in the photograph, opened in May of 2015 in Belgorsk, Amur region. For the occasion, a group of uniformed men carrying weapons formed the background.[78] Inevitably, Crimea paid the "liberating force" its due by installing a monument of its own, two as a matter of fact. The first one appeared in March of 2016 in Bakhchisarai. The name of the sculptor has never been revealed, for obvious reasons: the disproportionately shaped soldier—as if drawn by a child—appears to be torturing the cat.[79] By that time, the grand maître of capitalist realism, Salavat Shcherbakov, was already working on his version of the "polite people," to be installed in Simferopol. The original soldier in puffy fatigues turned under Shcherbakov's hand into a sleek cyborg with square chin; the boy in a spring jacket became a girl in a fancy coat; the cat—whose muzzle strangely resembles the sculptor's face—is rubbing against the soldier's boot while staring subserviently at him; the girl gets nothing from the soldier and still gives him a flower bouquet. While unveiling the monument in June 2016, head of the Crimea administration Sergei Aksenov pledged to further promote the "polite people brand."[80] Tula was next, in September of 2017.

By then, the cat symbolizing good intentions was gone, and instead of one cyborg there appeared three. With faces covered with ski masks, holding the newest models of automatic weapons, the trio is menacingly scouting the ground—an ultimate monument to militarism.[81] It was, in fact, the military that commissioned a monument to the "polite people"—even though it is only informally called that—in Rostov-on-Don. This time around, Shcherbakov's girl is depicted hugging the soldier.[82] Unveiled in May 2018, this is unlikely to be the last such monument to appear in Russia.

To dispel any doubts as to the message conveyed by the polite people brand, a miniature copy of the Simferopol monument was among the gifts presented in October 2018 to President Bashar Al-Assad of Syria by a visiting delegation from Crimea.[83] The monument itself meanwhile has been subjected to vandalism. On January 28, 2019, the police detained a man who allegedly doused the statue with paint. A local politician speculated that the offender had acted either in a state of intoxication or under the impact of "Ukrainian Nazism."[84]

Give the Tsar His Due

Russian tsars—some of them more odious than others—are another popular subject in contemporary monumental art. The last tsar, Nikolai II (1868–1918), who has been canonized by the Russian Orthodox Church as a martyr, has had the easiest lot. Several dozen Russian cities now have a standard bust of Nikolai II.[85] Less of a consensus is on display vis-à-vis Nikolai's father, Alexander III, whose grand monument President Putin opened in November of 2017 in Russia-annexed Crimea. The four-meter bronze Alexander shares with Stalin a park space near Livadia Palace in Yalta. Of all the Russian monarchs, Putin has developed a particular affinity for Alexander III (1845–94). On occasion, he has described Alexander III as one of the founders of the Russian state. As to the reason why, possibly because Alexander III is known for having pursued conservative, nationalist policies, or perhaps on account of a quote attributed to the emperor and prominently displayed on the monument base: "Russia has only two allies, its army and navy."[86] Portrayed as a wise ruler who pushed through counter-reforms—Ivan Kurilla has speculated—Alexander III fits the bill of a strongman successfully fending off Russia's enemies, both external and internal, without resorting to war and yet avoiding a revolution at home. One way or another, popular criticism focused not so much on the emperor himself as on his ostensible achievements depicted on a separate stela. As critics pointed out, few, if any, of those achievements took place during Alexander III's rule. The sculptor, Andrei Kovalchuk, refused point-blank to introduce any changes to the monument, which he says "conforms to the historical truth."[87] Needless to say, like most such monuments in Russia, the heavyweight Alexander III is hardly a masterpiece. Earlier, Alexander III had been put on a pedestal in Irkutsk (2003) and Novosibirsk (2012).

Although new and restored statues to Alexander II (1818–81) did appear in Russia, in waves in the early 2000s and since 2014, the authorities effectively sat out the emperor's bicentennial. The reason is pretty obvious, according to historian Andrei Zubov, namely major reforms associated with the name of that particular tsar.[88]

Among the historical figures who have been given a thumbs up by the authorities all the way since the late 1930s and one who is still riding high is Prince of Novgorod Alexander Nevsky (1221–63). Canonized by the Orthodox Church as early as the mid-sixteenth century and declared in 2008 by popular vote as the greatest Russian of all times, Alexander Nevsky has been steadily cast in bronze since the early 2000s. In 2018 alone, statues of St. Alexander appeared in Kaliningrad, Baltiisk, Ryazan region, and Russian-controlled Donetsk. The eulogies delivered on the occasion typically stress Alexander Nevsky's standing up against the enemies pressing from the west and pass in silence his subservient status vis-à-vis the Golden Horde in the east.

As compared to the serialized Alexanders, Ivan III (1440–1515) is a recent entry in the field of memorialization. In 2017 a competition of sorts ensued as to who would claim the honor of having Russia's first monument to Ivan the Great. The winner was a 4.5 meter bronze statue unveiled in June of that year on the territory of a monastery in Kaluga region. The solemn-looking monarch is blessing the Russian people with one hand and staving off the Mongol armies with the other. Since no actual images of Ivan III have been preserved, the sculptor incorporated facial features of his grandson, Ivan IV, in the work. Otherwise, the statue is an overblown copy of that appearing as part of the 1862 Millennium of Russia monument in Novgorod.[89] It took another five months before RVIO unveiled a statue of Ivan III of its own in Kaluga. Where once stood Lenin, now towers Ivan III. As a powerful reminder, the monument has the former headquarters of the Communist Party as the background, the building still sporting the Soviet coat of arms. The muscular, folksy Ivan commissioned by Medinskii & Co. thrusts forward while holding a staff with a nested eagle (a reference to the two-headed eagle that the tsar had introduced as Russia's symbol). Medinskii, who headlined the opening ceremony on November 12, 2017, was again wrong—as he has consistently been—by claiming that RVIO's statue of Ivan III was the only one in existence. Using superlatives in describing the reign of Ivan III, Medinskii then veered off to his favorite subject of continuity of Russian history. All subsequent victories originate in the Russia that Tsar Ivan had bequeathed us, thus Medinskii addressed the audience.[90] The local governor piously believes the eagle-bearing tsar is a masterpiece worthy of UNESCO's notice.

Continuing on the subject matter of tsars, the most controversial proved the monuments to Vladimir the Great (958–1015) in Moscow and Ivan the Terrible (1530–84) in Orel. The former statue raised the issue of timing and location, while the latter of personal traits of the ruler and moral judgment. All of these, naturally, underline Russian history politics. A design competition for the statue of Prince Vladimir was administered by RVIO, which proclaimed Salavat Scherbakov to be the winner. The twelve-meter-high Vladimir was promoted by the likes of Alexander Zaldostanov. The timing (2015) and the preferred location (Sparrow Hills overlooking the Moscow River) of the statue leave little doubt as to its ideological significance: the new Vladimir was supposed to overshadow the original one, erected in Kiev in 1833. While the Russian authorities have emphasized that Prince Vladimir united all the Slavs through the imposition of Christianity, in 988, their Ukrainian counterparts have reminded them that the entity in question was Kievan Rus.[91] After much debate and protest, the statue was moved next to the Kremlin, which in its turn alarmed the UNESCO. The monument was officially unveiled on November 4, 2016, in the presence of President Putin, minister Medinskii, and Patriarch Kirill.

In the case of the much maligned Ivan the Terrible, choosing a site for the prospective monument appeared like a minor problem. The word *grotesque* firmly belongs to the history of the Orel monument. For starters, the initiative belonged to the communist Vadim Potomskii, governor of Orel region. As a formal reason, in June of 2016 he referred to the forthcoming anniversary of the city, founded 450 years ago by Ivan IV. The governor holds unorthodox views on history. Thus, he regards Stalin, Ivan the Terrible, and Peter the Great as exceptional figures. As regards, specifically, Tsar Ivan, Potomskii believes he had been deviously slandered and turned into a devil. He does not believe the historical fact that Ivan the Terrible had killed his own son either. In fact, Potomskii argued at a press conference, Ivan simply failed to properly treat his sick child while traveling with him from Moscow to St. Petersburg (never mind that the latter city had only been founded a century later). Despite such a faux pas, city authorities went ahead with their plans.[92] Crucially, 56 percent of the Russians approved of the Orel monument, as established by the independent Levada pollster.[93]

The idea of placing the monument in front of a children's theater was eventually scrapped upon the latter's protest. Next, a site in front of the Orthodox Cathedral and Orel's oldest stone building came up for consideration. The Orthodox Church kept its distance from the project on the grounds that Ivan IV had not been proclaimed a saint, that the newly proposed plot did not belong to the church, and that erecting such a monument was the prerogative of the state. Patriarch Kirill, at the same time, reportedly said that Orel deserved a monument dedicated to its founder. Although Minister of Education Vasilieva and Minister of Culture Medinskii did not attend the opening ceremony on November 14, 2016, the latter sent his greetings to the participants. The VIP list included the notorious Russian/Soviet nationalists Sergei Kurginian, Alexander Prokhanov, and Alexander Zaldostanov.[94]

The present monument has effectively erased the centuries-old odium associated with the name of Ivan the Terrible; the tsar does not appear among the 129 figures on the Millennium of Russia monument in Novgorod, for example. The symbolism of Ivan the Terrible is hard to miss: he was the one who conquered new territories for Moscow in the East, and entered into the first major confrontation with the West. And so communist Potomskii was screaming in the microphone on the gloomy fall day: "We're having the greatest, most powerful president, who forced the entire world to respect Russia, as Ivan the Terrible had once done. God's with us!"

Shortly after the unveiling of the Orel monument, Vladimir Zhirinovsky proposed in the Duma to rename Lenin Avenue leading up to Moscow's Vnukovo airport into Ivan the Terrible avenue. In his argumentation, Lenin was the one who brought Russia to ruin, while Ivan the Terrible was a great statesman who had done much for his country. Along the way, the veteran nationalist politician proposed removing the famous painting *Ivan the Terrible and His Son Ivan* (1885) from the Tretyakov Art Gallery in Moscow, for the simple reason that the homicide never happened.[95] The story received an unexpected continuation. On May 25, 2018, a visitor to the Tretyakov Art Gallery committed an act of vandalism against the work by Ilya Repin. Under interrogation, the 37-year-old perpetrator stated that the tsar did not actually kill his

Figure 12 An unholy alliance (from left to right): Duma deputy Nikolai Zemtsov (b. 1967) who masterminded the government takeover of the Immortal Regiment; president of the "patriotic" Night Wolves biker club Alexander "The Surgeon" Zaldostanov (b. 1963); founder of a conservative think tank, Izborsk Club, Alexander Prokhanov (b. 1938); and leader of a nationalist organization, the Essence of Time, Sergei Kurginian (b. 1949). The occasion that brought these men together was the unveiling of a monument to Ivan the Terrible in Orel on October 3, 2016.

son. Consequently, the painting did not "conform to the historical truth" and should therefore be destroyed. He confessed he had been thinking of the "distorted" image of Ivan the Terrible for two years. "Even Putin said on the TV that what it depicts is not true. When I got to the Tretyakov I couldn't stop myself. Foreigners go there and look at it. What will they think about our Russian tsar or us? It's a provocation against the Russian people so that people would view us negatively."[96] Following the violent episode, a splinter group seeking the canonization of Ivan IV appealed to the ministry of culture with the request to remove the offending painting as it contained "slander against the Russian people, the Russian state, and the pious Russian tsars and tsarinas." Certain individuals, though they condemned the act of vandalism as such, labeled Repin the painter a "pathological Russophobe and hater of religious nationalism."[97] Since the Tretyakov Art Gallery incident, a new monument to Ivan the Terrible has been (re)opened in Alexandrov, Vladimir region. Among the VIPs who attended the opening ceremony on December 7, 2019 were the very same Prokhanov and Zaldostanov, as well as RVIO's Kononov representing the ministry of culture.[98]

The notorious Soviet doublespeak makes a comeback in various forms and contexts, including interpretations of history. As part of the commemoration of the 150th anniversary of the abolition of serfdom in Russia, on February 19, 2011 a series of billboards were supposed to go up. The billboards originally featured a quotation from Alexander II: "Serfdom must be abolished from the top before it gets abolished from the bottom." Extrapolating the tsar's dictum onto today's ruling elite, no advertisement agency agreed to display the quote, anticipating trouble if they did.[99]

Monuments to the Masses

As Gnilorybov has explained, to erect a monument in Russia today is relatively easy, and also cheap. A standard Stalin bust of the kind unveiled in Tambov, Lipetsk, or Surgut cost around 150,000 rubles (USD 2,500). That is to say, anyone can afford it. While the aesthetic standards have got lower, building replicas has become more generally acceptable.[100] Mass production of monuments requires know-how. If there is one company/initiative that has contributed most to proliferation of historical monuments in Russia, it is the Alley of Russian Glory. Based in Kropotkin, Krasnodar region, the company has put monumental art on a commercial footing. The company, which doubles as a foundation, has the following mission statement:

> The Alley of Russian Glory project was conceived with the single goal of reviving patriotic spirit of the Russian people. We believe that patriotic education is both the source and means of spiritual, political, and economic revival of the country, its wholesomeness and security. One hears a lot about patriotism nowadays, while our project has nothing fashionable about it. We do not inculcate pathos in our work, because we believe in the powerful Russia and Russians. By unveiling monuments and busts in various corners of Russia, we pay tribute to our great ancestors and countrymen.

Established in 2007, the company had produced over eight hundred monuments within seven years of its existence. As of this writing, the Alley of Russian Glory catalog contains 219 names, beginning with Alexander Nevsky and Ivan the Terrible and finishing with Russian military men killed by jihadists in Syria. The company's VKontakte webpage serves as a forum for all things memorial in Russia. Recent examples in monumental art are the subjects of lively discussions: anything from Tsar Pavel I to Donbass commando Alexei "Ghost" Mozgovoi.[101]

The lofty statement of purpose is followed by a detailed price list. So how much does "glory" sell for in Russia (in 2019 prices)? A "1941–1945" stele and "Warrior-Liberator" monument cost 250,000 rubles (USD 4,000) each; one is expected to pay 100,000 rubles more to commemorate "Russian Military Men who Participated in Local Conflicts" but 75,000 rubles less for "Workers of the Rear." Standard statues are priced at anywhere between 225,000 (concrete) and 1 million (bronze) rubles, and busts between 100,000 and 350,000 rubles. Personalized orders are more expensive, of course. The company offers a full package, including bases, plaques, flowerpots, and souvenir busts. To spread the word, the venture is committed to presenting "busts of citizens who brought glory to Russia" as free gifts to schools, military colleges, military bases, and Cossack units.[102] Simultaneously, it urges parents to take the initiative and express their gratitude to their kids' school in the form of a bust (for a set price). During the prospective opening ceremony, the patron is expected to cite the project leader, and within three days send the company some pictures.[103]

Inevitably with such production volumes and speed, quality takes a hit. Most common are inaccuracies in rendering military uniforms and decorations, but facial recognition is occasionally also an issue. Cosmonaut Yuri Gagarin appears unnaturally gloomy; an earlier version of Field Marshal Mikhail Kutuzov featured an odd bandage over his right eye.[104] Customers, however, do not seem to mind. Although a good half of the company's catalog features civilians—poets, writers, composers, artists, philosophers, scientists, sportsmen—and a collection called "Heroes of 1812," a great majority of busts unveiled in the period from 2014 to 2016 were military men, tsars, and saints (in that particular order). In comparison, among the first busts installed as part of the Alley of Russian Glory project, back in 2008, none was from the "Heroes of the Great Patriotic War" collection.[105] The shifting emphasis in Russian history politics dictate a bestseller list.

The Alley of Russian Glory is a constituent part of a broader patriotic project promoted by the government. It collaborates most closely with the Russian state Military History and Cultural Center (Rossvoentsentr). Established in 1997, the center works toward memorialization and consolidation of military veteran organizations (i.e., bringing together veterans of wars, former servicemen, and security apparatus officials). Most crucially, the center until 2015 was coordinating the five-year state program on patriotic education. The rear admiral currently heading the center has a historian as his deputy. Under the auspices of the center, the Alley of Russian Glory displayed in May 2012 a selection of its works on Red Square in Moscow.

As far as the politics of memorialization is concerned, no less instructive is the use of the word *alley*. On the one hand, it does not presuppose any standard: the alley can be short or long, wide or narrow, flanked by different types of trees and shrubs. On the other hand, alley has an element of familiarity, almost coziness to it; one imagines young mothers with buggies, children, retirees—all of them enjoying a leisurely stroll on a leafy promenade. While so doing, ordinary citizens can now also contemplate on the glorious pages of Russian history. Broadly defined, "glory" mainly applies to tsars and Second World War heroes.

Among the dozen or so sculptors who have received commissions from the Alley of Russian Glory is Salavat Shcherbakov. Shcherbakov (b. 1955) has by now eclipsed Tsereteli to become the face of the state-sponsored monumental art in Russia. He is the author of some 120 monuments across Russia, twenty of them in Moscow. The unveiling ceremonies featuring his works are often attended by the likes of President Putin and Patriarch Kirill. Shcherbakov is a member of RVIO, which has commissioned nine of his works.[106] In his interviews, Shcherbakov comes across as a staunch supporter of statism (*gossudarstvennost*), the key concept advanced by Putin. Monuments are erected by people, he says. The sculptor here serves as a mere conduit of an idea. Consequently, those who criticize his monuments are opposed to the idea that they represent. Shcherbakov associates himself with the traditionalist values promoted by the Orthodox Church and thus is in opposition to the "twisted" morale of the West. Serving the state is only natural, according to him. Hence, he has no scruples in admitting that the face of St. Michael piercing a dragon on the base of the monument to Mikhail Kalashnikov is sculpted after President Putin: "From our position, it's the struggle between good and evil. It's the [force of] good that hits the dragon. What else can he be, Santa Claus perhaps? It's us, it's Putin. It's an artistic take."[107] Like Tsereteli, Shcherbakov has been guilty of plagiarism.[108]

Ironically, mistakes that creep into historical monuments, commemorative banners, and so on have to do with the incessantly impressed Soviet–Nazi dichotomy. In spite of the present fascination with military hardware—exemplified by the Patriot military theme park—Nazi German weapons now and then end up being passed for Soviet. RVIO in the face of Shcherbakov has proved a recurrent offender. Among many others, RVIO had sponsored a statue Slavic Girl's Farewell, which was unveiled on May 8, 2014, in front of the Belorussian train station in Moscow. The ceremony was attended by the then head of the Russian Railways, Vladimir Yakunin, and minister of culture and head of RVIO, Vladimir Medinskii. The monument—which Medinskii in his speech described as a testament to "love, honor, and steadfast military oath"—depicts a soldier in a First World War uniform and a young girl saying goodbye to him. The problem was not with the statue itself but with the two accompanying decorative shields flanked by firearms from 1914 and 1941, respectively. The one from the Second World War period featured, as experts were quick to establish, a German Mauser rifle. The Russian Railways redirected the question to the ministry of culture, which put the onus on RVIO, which in turn pointed a finger at Shcherbakov, who then blamed the incident on an unidentified "history company" (The Alley of Russian Glory?). The offending rifle was sawed off five days later, to be replaced by an appropriate Soviet-made gun.[109]

No less embarrassing was Shcherbakov's monument to Kalashnikov (1919–2013), the man and the gun, which opened in September of 2017 in downtown Moscow. The monument was commissioned, once again, by RVIO, in anticipation of the celebration of Kalashnikov's centennial in 2019. Shcherbakov emerged the winner in a closed competition, by virtue of being the only sculptor invited to participate. The praise heaped on the AK-47 creator during the unveiling ceremony could be summed up as follows: the Russian devoted to his homeland, worth emulating by younger generations. Medinskii boldly declared the Kalashnikov assault rifle to be "Russia's cultural brand." The base features a quotation from Kalashnikov, who claimed to "have created a weapon for the defense of the Motherland."[110] (No mention was made of the doubts Kalashnikov expressed late in his life—like Robert Oppenheimer and Andrei Sakharov had done earlier—as to the destructive potential of the weapon he had designed.) Putting aside the artistic merits of the five-meter-tall statue of the gunsmith with his eponymous AK-47, military historians picked on automatic gun models incorporated in the monument's design. One of them, as it turned out, was the blueprint of a German Schmeisser, which had to subsequently be sawed off.[111] Shcherbakov casually explains away faux pas like these: "Anyone can make a mistake," "the internet has failed me," or "Some of my mistakes haven't yet been detected."[112] As journalist Matvei Ganapolskii has remarked, the regime does not care about details in its desire to make yet another "patriotic" statement.[113]

Brothers in arms or competitors, the Alley of Russian Glory and RVIO stand behind the largest number of monuments erected in Russia in recent years. By its own count,

Figure 13 Of tsars and tanks. Another exponent of Socialist Realism, Salavat Shcherbakov (b. 1955), has received a string of government commissions in recent years. Giant statues of saints, tsars, and military men serve to reinforce the notion of indelibility of state power. Here Scherbakov posing in early 2017 in front of a model of a monument to Mikhail Kalashnikov, the designer of the eponymous AK-47 assault rifle, to be installed in Moscow later that year.

RVIO has commissioned 235 monuments and 2,600 memorial plaques within six years of its existence, 2012–18. Replication does not apply only to monuments to strongmen. For instance, the ministry of culture in collaboration with RVIO has erected several dozen standard, boxy monuments called Borodino Bread (also known as "The Bread of Our Memory"). The monuments aptly link cultural and historical references from different time periods: the victory over Napoleon, the concept of a *patriotic war* that came to subsequently define the Soviet efforts in defeating Nazi Germany, and the beloved Soviet bread recipe.

The bigger the monument, the less appears to be the concern for the physical environment. Prince Vladimir in Moscow, for example, visually suppresses the so-called Pashkov House, a former visual dominant. The Kemerovo city government in December 2018 unanimously approved of a 25-meter-high statue of St. Barbara, along with a chapel and auxiliary buildings to be built on the riverbank. Before construction could commence, however, an entire pine forest had to be axed. The local authorities ruled out a popular vote on the monument, which they believe would bring tourists to the city.[114] Locally expressed enthusiasm to commit any given historical figure to memory does not always find the support of the authorities. To give just one example, a broad public consensus in Buryatia in favor of a monument to Genghis Khan—who was born there, according to legend—was not shared by local officials, who thought it might complicate relations with China.[115]

With literally thousands of monuments erected in Russia in the past ten years or so, the most Kafkaesque of them all is perhaps a sculpture dedicated to freedom. The rather smallish monument unveiled in November of 2017 in Kostroma has yet another name, "Authorities in the Service of the People." The odd combination of state power and individual freedoms is personified by a three-headed dragon of a classical Russian fairytale kind pulling a plough with no one behind. The three heads symbolize the executive, legislative, and judicial branches of the government—all working for the benefit of the Russian commoner. The man behind the monument, local Duma deputy and businessman Vladimir Mikhailov, has claimed it was the only one of its kind in the world. He said the idea came to him after he met scores of people who regard themselves as unfree. Instead of gathering once a year in front of a monument to the victims of political repression and reciting the names of those victims, Mikhailov suggested that all the people whose freedoms have been violated may report to sculpture sponsored by him. The dragon sculpture became an instant hit among the locals, eager to take selfies.[116]

Among the pro-government groups that tried their hand at monumental art is the Night Wolves (see Chapter 2). The leader of the biker club, Zaldostanov, feels sentimental about his first. Like many of his projects, the Children's Round Dance fountain in Volgograd ended up as kitsch. Featuring six children dancing around a crocodile with frogs around spewing water, the original statue is a reference to a beloved children's poem by Kornei Chukovsky's "Barmalei" whose main character is a repentant pirate. Such statues were mass-produced in the 1930s to be displayed in parks and playgrounds around the country.[117] The fountain was badly damaged during the Battle of Stalingrad and eventually demolished in 1951. For one, Zaldostanov proposed building two replicas simultaneously. City authorities enthusiastically supported the idea, promising a painstaking restoration. The result is anything but. The statue in front of the railway station is made of plastic instead of concrete and it is higher than the original, which was situated elsewhere in the city anyway. Nevertheless, in Zaldostanov's eyes, the replica fits its new physical environment perfectly, imbuing the space with the spirit of "Victory." He lets his imagination run wild in ascribing a supernatural meaning to the sculptural composition depicting a particular episode in Chukovsky's poem (children successfully pleading with the crocodile to disgorge a physician it had swallowed): "Russia is that round dance that keeps evil locked up. Thanks to Orthodoxy, our roots and our spirituality, we are the only ones who resist global Satanism in the direct meaning of the word."[118] Another replica, meanwhile, has been built in front of the iconic Gerhard's Mill, deliberately left in ruins after the war. The building is flanked by a diorama of the Battle of Stalingrad. In this case, the statue replicates the one in the famous 1942 photograph of the bombed-out city, complete with loose bricks scattered around. A local architect deemed the installation of the two replicas a stupid idea and fumed that the city architect's authority had been overridden. Both statues were unveiled on August 23, 2013, in the presence of President Putin, to coincide with the biker festival.[119]

In September 2014, in separatist-controlled Luhansk in Ukraine, the Night Wolves unveiled a monument symbolizing their vision of a new Russia. A free-standing granite stela features crude contours of the Soviet coat of arms with a double-headed eagle in the middle. The ribbon enveloping a stalk of wheat no longer carries the inscription "Proletariat of all countries, unite" written in the languages of the fifteen national republics. Instead, an accompanying plaque declares "Russia's destiny is to rise as a Eurasian giant." The leader of the club's Donbass chapter explained on camera that one president, Zaldostanov, has approached the other president, Putin, with the request to make the Night Wolves' design into Russia's new coat of arms.[120] Since then the Night Wolves have incorporated the new design into the Russian flag they regularly display and the man in the video received a medal for bravery from the self-proclaimed Luhansk People's Republic.[121]

Zaldostanov apparently has a special attachment to railway stations. On the eve of Day of Remembrance and Grief marking the German attack on the Soviet Union on June 22, 1941, he was in Ulianovsk, unveiling a monument to the citizens who had participated in the Second World War. This time around, Zaldostanov had settled for a more creative design—a segment of a two-dimensional freight car set inside a colonnade. The metallic stripes that follow up the contour of the car make it nearly vanish in the air. Whether the featured statistics are correct or not, one of the words in the text was spelled incorrectly, and had to be instantly fixed. The association of the freight car with Stalin's deportations obviously escaped Zaldostanov, who christened the new monument "The Roads of Great Victory." Evoking sacrifice and resilience in defending the motherland, he returned to his favorite theme of empire as Russia's future. He promised to be back in the city of Lenin's birth for the opening of the Museum of the USSR.[122]

The city traditionally associated with the name of Lenin, Ulianovsk has been trying to cash in on its red past, without much success though. Russia's overtures to China have led to, among other things, some peculiar historical encounters. Coinciding with Mao Zedong's 125th anniversary, a new exhibition celebrating his life and deeds opened in October of 2018 at the Lenin Memorial Center in Ulianovsk. The exhibition was organized by Mao Zedong House Museum in Hunan province, with its Russian counterpart having no say on the contents. The result is a bizarre panegyric to Mao not seen in Russia even in Stalin's times: the Chinese Communist leader as a wise man who loved children, liked to drink tea, appreciated calligraphy, and wrote poetry—as told on 120 panels. The Great Leap Forward and the Cultural Revolution, launched by Mao and estimated to cost over 70 million lives, barely find mention in the exhibition. It is hard to see what the memorial center, or the city of Ulianovsk or Russia for that matter, is going to gain by effectively letting Chinese communists run the show. The concept of "red tourism" catering to the Chinese tourists has so far yielded no tangible benefits, neither in Ulianovsk nor in the Baikal region where Mao had spent some time. That is to say, the numbers of Chinese visitors remain minuscule while Russian tourists find Mao's portrayal as the "most humane of all humans" puzzling. The lack of popular response is irrelevant, however, insofar as history geopolitics dictate the message that all things China is alright. In other words, criticizing China, past and present, is a no-no.[123]

Preservation of the Past at Its Worst and Its Best

Historicism may express itself in both benign and ominous forms. It comes across as just playful when Zenit St. Petersburg football club, in celebration of their fourth Russian Premier League title in 2015, posed dressed up as nineteenth-century

Russian aristocracy.[124] It is, however, a joke gone too far when during the City Day celebration in Moscow (Russian: *den goroda*) that same year visitors were treated, among other things, to a mock capital punishment of a "national traitor." Two men clad in nineteenth-century military uniforms dragged through the crowd yet another, while admonishing him for "staging a riot against our monarch." The bound-up victim was subsequently brought to an executioner's block where the executioner was waiting for him with an ax. Those who wished so could also be birched while being set in a pillory.[125] An enactment no doubt, it takes on a darker meaning in post-Crimea Russia.

The idea of high treason, one may argue, has permeated the history of Russia. Invariably, it also creeps into memorialization. A case in point is the two memorial plaques that were put up and shortly taken down in St. Petersburg within the span of one year. In a city that sports about 130 memorial plaques to Lenin alone, one in memory of Finnish military leader and statesman Karl Mannerheim, unveiled in June of 2016 by Medisnkii, made quite a splash. Prior to Finland's independence in 1918, Mannerheim had for over thirty years served in the Russian army. The plaque on the wall of St. Petersburg Military Academy appeared after a good ten years of debate. In the Russia hit by Western sanctions, however, the debates have given place to random acts of vandalism. In 1939–40 the Finnish troops under Mannerheim's command inflicted heavy casualties on the invading Red Army; the defense line that the Soviet forces stormed bore Mannerheim's name. Not only did Mannerheim manage to safeguard Finland's independence but he also went on to lead the Finnish Army in the subsequent occupation of Russian Karelia and, later, in the siege of Leningrad. Contemporary Russian nationalists expressed their indignation by repeatedly tagging the Mannerheim plaque, shooting at it, and eventually trying to hack it with an ax. A private citizen filed a legal case against the St. Petersburg administration while the Communist Party requested the prosecutor's office to investigate the fact of the memorial plaque as the "glorification of Nazism" in violation of Article 354.1 of the criminal code.[126] Head of the Historical Memory Foundation, Alexander Diukov, could not resist kicking RVIO. RVIO's glaring incompetence, he argued, unwittingly damaged the social cohesion that had emerged in Russia after the annexation of Crimea, to be malignantly exploited by "unfriendly countries."[127] On October 13, 2016, the memorial plaque vanished. According to RVIO, it will be exhibited in the First World War history museum at Tsarskoe Selo as a "symbol of historical debates in contemporary Russia."[128] In this particular case, the mythmaking underlying one war came into conflict with that of another and thus paralyzed decision-making.[129]

The plaque commemorating another military man, Admiral Alexander Kolchak, fared no better. Coincidentally, a leader of the White movement during the Russian Civil War received the honor one day before Mannerheim was scrapped of his. In the former case, popular dismay was expressed in a less violent form—as placards declaring Kolchak a war criminal, murderer, and Lord Voldemort himself. Eventually, Kolchak was demoted through a legal challenge by the pro-Kremlin organization the Essence of Time. In January of 2017 the court sided with the plaintiff, Sergei Kurginian, who argued that the city government had placed the Kolchak plaque illegally. The plaque was removed later that year.[130]

Certainly the most grotesque case to emerge from Russia in recent years is an act of vandalism against the famous Mephistopheles bas-relief. Perched on a 1911 Art-Deco building in St. Petersburg, it has given life to a moniker, House with Mephistopheles, in use throughout the Soviet period. In August of 2015, a man brutally destroyed the bas-relief with a crowbar. An organization called Cossacks of St. Petersburg took the responsibility for the act. The Orthodox Church sided with the vandal, pointing out the perpetrator's motivation to rid the city of symbols of evil. The clergy felt uncomfortable about the devil overlooking the construction of a new Orthodox church across the street.[131]

There are an estimated 142,000 listed buildings in Russia today. With all the talk about the "greatness" of Russian history, architectural legacy gets destroyed with alarming speed in Putin's country. The present elites appear to bring to completion what the Bolsheviks or the years of disrepair of the late Soviet and early Russian period did not accomplish. The glaring disregard for one's own legacy is due to a combination of corruption, ignorance, and flagrant indifference. Local bureaucrats rarely appreciate the significance of architecture, old and/or new, which makes it easy for greedy developers to replace dilapidated structures with standard high-rises. Sometimes it is not even obvious if full demolition is any worse than an attempted "modernization" by commercial owners. In the process, external walls get covered with cheap panels or plastered over, original wooden frames get replaced with plastic ones, traditional glass doors get shifted for plain metallic sheets, and plaster décor get altered beyond recognition. Ilya Varlamov has amassed an entire portfolio of such examples, which can only be described as vandalism.[132] One of the photo reportages from Vyshnii Volochek made even Minister of Culture Medinskii get involved. When Medinskii was confronted with the planned demolition of a number of historical buildings in Borovsk, Kaluga region, a year later, however, he simply washed off his hands. "Why everybody is always expecting the ministry of culture to intervene in such cases?" he wondered.[133] The collective nostalgia for the Soviet Union does not translate into public understanding of why to preserve, not to mention restore, at least some examples of Soviet architecture or its elements.[134] So far, the government's biggest contribution to the preservation of Russia's architectural legacy has come in the shape of a proposal that would prohibit installing air conditioners on landmark buildings.[135]

While new church buildings are going up all over Russia, an equal number of historical edifices are falling into disrepair, or undergoing so-called Euroremont. *Euroremont* is a Russian neologism meaning the repair of an interior according to European standards, supposedly. In reality, the purported restoration typically involves chiseling off "excessive" decorative elements and the use of cheap construction materials. Take, for example, the former abode of Bishop Tikhon—Sretensky Monastery in Moscow that goes back to the fourteenth century. During his tenure as dean (1993–2018), Tikhon installed plastic windows throughout. Bought on the cheap from Spain, the windows cost a mere fraction of what the restoration of the old, wooden frames would have cost.[136] Most recently, purported restoration works scarred another iconic structure, the Petropavlovsk fortress in St. Petersburg.[137]

The news spread as fast as the fire that consumed a church in Kondopoga, Karelia, in August of 2018. One of the few remaining, also tallest, examples of wooden church architecture in Russia, the late-eighteenth-century Church of the Assumption burned down completely within three hours. The church building was in a pitiful state and awaited (repeatedly delayed) restoration. The Orthodox Church took issue with the civil authorities, who were using the church building as a museum, while the latter put the blame on irresponsible "tourists." The following, official version appeared to everybody's liking: a teenage Satanist premeditatedly set the church alight. The blame game could not conceal the fact that, according to a local architect, *all* wooden landmarks in the region are on the way to being irrevocably lost.[138] The current Russian legislation concerning restoration of architectural landmarks serves the purpose poorly: commercial actors get preference over smaller companies dealing specifically with restoration while the cost of materials has skyrocketed. Regional governments lack the necessary expertise and funds. Consequently, they set unrealistic deadlines while the allocated money is typically just enough to take the remaining structure apart. That further reinforces the bureaucrats' idea that erecting a replica is better and certainly cheaper that restoring the original.[139]

While landmark buildings continue falling into disrepair, the state is eager to build a mythology around relatively well preserved architectural sites. One such site is Chersonesos near Sevastopol in Russia-occupied Crimea. Established by the Greeks in the fifth century BC, Chersonesos features one of the most expansive clusters of antique ruins north of the Black Sea. Now, Putin wants to turn it into a pilgrimage site, the "Russian Mecca," as he put it during his visit in the summer of 2017. Allegedly, Prince Vladimir was baptized in 988 at Chersonesos, which made Putin declare that the site was the "birthplace of Russian statehood." Historical records aside, building a visitor center (in accordance with the president's will) would inevitably disturb the rich cultural layer at Chersonesos.[140]

What amounts to architectural vandalism at the state level has sparked a popular counteraction in the form of volunteer restoration. Appalled with the pace of destruction of architectural legacy, several projects (e.g., Tom Sawyer Fest) have sprung up in Russia in recent years to restore individual historical buildings and thereby save them from potential demolition. Sure enough, limited funds, the lack of heavy machinery and sometimes prerequisite expertise typically limit the project to the restoration of a façade.[141] Even though the late nineteenth and early twentieth-century edifices rank lower in significance than, say, medieval church buildings, what is important here is the collective efforts to reverse the negative trend facilitated by the present regime. Although expressly apolitical as a group, individual participants in the restoration projects tend to be young, urban liberals. Sadly, a newly renovated building still offers a weak defense against greedy developers and corrupt bureaucrats, who occasionally find ways to raze it anyway, as it happened in 2018 in Kaluga, for example.[142]

Another welcome development is the emergence of private, ideology-neutral museums. One of the best such examples is the so-called House with a Lion, situated in the village of Popovka, Saratov region. The story goes back to 2010, when the owners of a traditional timber house decided to repurpose the logs for a sauna. The house, however, had a treasure inside: a rare example of oil-painted frescoes from the early twentieth century. An amateur painter had depicted fourteen different characters covering the inner walls and the ceiling. Among the characters are draft animals, Orthodox saints, and, well, a lion (deserved to have been painted by Henri Rousseau himself). Yulia Terekhova, an art historian from St. Petersburg, bought the house and converted it into a genuine feel-good museum. The house was in a precarious state; Terekhova organized volunteer camps, secured funds, and effectively preserved the house for future generations. If it had not been for the remote location, the number of people (around 3,000) who visit the museum annually would have been many more.[143] By 2019, the House with a Lion had been fully restored by one of the most recognized names in the business, Anton Maltsev, who had that same year received a prize for the restoration of the eighteenth-century wooden church in Vologodsk region.[144]

Much praise has also received the Museum of the Russian Icon in Moscow. Financed single-handedly by a businessman, the late Mikhail Abramov, the museum houses a well-curated collection of some 5,000 icons in a purpose-reconstructed building. Abramov's was the first private collection in Russia to become a part of the International Council of Museums (ICOM).[145] While the state media effectively ignored the centennial of the Russian Revolution, ingenious private initiatives filled in the void. For instance, Mikhail Zygar, former editor in chief of the independent Dozhd TV and the author of *All the Kremlin's Men: Inside the Court of Vladimir Putin*, has created an imitation Facebook page that chronicles 1917. Zygar and his team mainly used diaries of prominent Russians to create a snapshot of every day leading up to the Bolshevik Revolution.[146] Despite the limited exposure, the project generated many positive reviews. Needless to say, not all private initiatives have a solid academic foundation (e.g., the Grigory Rasputin house museum in St. Petersburg).[147] Perhaps the crassest example of an institution promoting outright pseudoscience is the New Chronology museum to be opened in Yaroslavl.[148]

Among state-sponsored, successful restoration projects are the Gulag History State Museum in Moscow and the Center for Contemporary Art on the territory of the Kremlin in Nizhnii Novgorod (2015). In both cases, the original building was repurposed using modern technologies while preserving the architectural authenticity. The Gulag museum has also been successfully using alternative media such as comics and street art to project the intended message.[149] Worth mentioning are also a few top-notch online exhibits developed by select state museums in the recent years. Whatever one may think of the overall message projected by Tula State Weapons Museum (or its hideous new building from 2012), its innovative, bilingual website featuring excellent graphics is truly impressive.[150] The reason why the ministry of culture decided to put money into this particular project has likely to do with its head, Medinskii, and his agenda. After all, museums for Medinskii, who doubles as the head of RVIO, are also a strategic asset. Or else RVIO would not have planned to create what they claim to be the northernmost museum in the world. Scheduled to open in 2020, the museum of Arctic exploration will be located on Franz Joseph Land, a few hundred kilometers east of Norwegian-administered Svalbard.[151] What is the point of establishing a museum on the archipelago inhabited only by military personnel? The answer is obvious: Russian military buildup in the Arctic region, including a newly built base on Franz Joseph Land.

The less ideology, the better is the museum, obviously. This constitutes a conundrum for Russian state museums. Take, for example, the Russian Railway Museum in St. Petersburg, which reopened in the fall of 2017 after extensive reconstruction. One of the biggest such museums in the world, it features a unique collection of engines and railway carriages—all lovingly restored and creatively displayed. The purpose-built pavilion houses an interactive exhibition on the history of the railway in Russia. The museum is a feast for children, some of whom walk out with the desire to become a railway worker. As always, there is a caveat. The gleaming new museum would not have been possible without Vladimir Yakunin, head of the state rail company in 2005–2015. A longtime associate of Putin, Yakunin had for years scooped lucrative state contracts, and along the way enriched himself. Eventually, allegations of corruption became too much to bear for the regime, which effectively forced Yakunin to resign. Neither does the Russian Railway Museum beat the retreat on state ideology; its mission statement includes "instilling patriotism."[152]

This does not come as a surprise. The 2010–2015 patriotic education program included an all-Russian competition for the best museum exhibit in "patriotic spirit." The 2016–2020 program put it straight: the state demand for museum exhibits for the purpose of military-patriotic youth education. The success of the "Russia: My History" theme park further alerted authorities to the potential of museums in historymaking. Typically, the signal comes from the very top. When opening the December 2018 meeting of the Victory organizing committee, President Putin projected the larger role of museums in preserving the memory of the Second World War. In particular, Putin was praising the volunteers' contribution, which he regards as an antidote to the attempted falsification of history. The state should systematically support military history museums in order to make the visitors "emotionally engage with the past events," Putin said.[153] The ministry of culture took the president's wish as a command, and in late January 2019 sent out a circular letter to regional governors with the request to bring museum displays in line with "state priorities." The document signed by Medinskii effectively makes historical exhibits serve the purpose of "patriotic education."[154] Vladislav Kononov, who curates museums within the ministry of culture, further explained that "patriotic education" should be implemented, for example, by means of exhibitions showcasing Russian history since 1991. However, the director of a provincial museum respectfully disagreed saying that this period is more fitting for political scientists rather than historians to handle.[155] Insofar as the state and church interests increasingly align in Russia, an off-the-wall proposal by Kaluga regional governor did not sound as outlandish either. In March of 2019 he suggested using relics in order to boost visitor numbers. While admiring the (fake) bones of saints, he speculated, museum patrons may as well look at other exhibits.[156]

With all the museums and exhibitions that have been created in Russia in the recent years, there are also a few that have never been, for example, a museum of the siege of Leningrad. In this particular case, the chasm between state interests and public expectations is just too wide to set the process in motion. To put it differently, the popular memory of the dying city does not let the regime mold the narrative into a stereotypical story of wartime heroism.

Conclusion

The phenomenon of serialized monuments goes back to the standardization practice in the nascent Soviet state. A penchant for uniformity commanded factory workshops in Stalin's Russia to manufacture archetypical farmers, workers, soldiers, and children in tens of thousands. The few remaining examples of that mass appeal art have now acquired the status of antiques, worth preserving and publicly displaying. Ingrained in the tradition of Socialist Realism, the dubious artistic quality of prefabricated statues is on display in the contemporary monumental art in Russia. Even the brutalism of the 1960s and 1970s does not have as significant an influence on modern craftsmen or sculptors, though the proclivity for gigantism persists.

The sheer scale of the monuments that have emerged in Putin's Russia in recent years reveals a penchant for historicism on the part of authorities, according to gallerist Marat Gelman. The regime has been trying to tweak history, among other means, by erecting humongous statues of tsars and military men. The generations to come will have difficulty changing that perspective for the simple reason that dismantling the kind of monuments to Prince Vladimir or the Yalta Conference would cost nearly as much as building them.[157] In a sense, all of these grand monuments can be seen as a reincarnation of Vladimir Putin: here he poses as Holy Vladimir, the guardian of the Orthodox faith, at other times as Piotr Stolypin, the reformer.[158]

The tendency in contemporary Russian monumental art builds on a popular sentiment for a "firm hand." Hence are the monuments to Stalin and Ivan the Terrible, Dzerzhinsky and Kalashnikov, Putin and his "green men." It also displays a commercial component—to attract tourists and funds. Nor should be overlooked the element of public relations, or *hype*—the word that has taken Russia by storm in recent years. Aggressive marketing does seem to be at play with marginal organizations and party branches in provinces when they propose erecting yet another Stalin bust, for example.

What sociologist Lev Gudkov has poignantly described as corrosion of immunity against de-Stalinization is apparent when it comes to Stalin monuments. The only remaining, consistent voices of protest come from Memorial and Free Historical Society (VIO). Whenever individual dissent arises from within the echelons of power, it is typically aired as an unwillingness to contribute to the "war of monuments," that is, unwillingness to rock the imaginary national-unity boat. Basing ultimate decision in each individual case on technical expertise takes historical judgment out of the equation. That, however, further reinforces the idea of subjective reality, and thus emboldens the growing army of Stalinists in Russia. As far as Stalin's legacy is concerned, the floodgates of the impermissible are about to be broken any time soon.

The open-ended question, "Why not?" aptly captures the popular sentiment in contemporary Russia. Just a handful of diehard communists and war veterans want statues of Stalin restored to their previous glory. The majority does not seem to mind, or at least is not actively opposed to it. This unreflective, holistic attitude is variously promoted by the state under the heading that all rulers are good rulers. Public acquiescence and the superimposed notion of Russian/Soviet history—to be appreciated in its entirety—mutually reinforce each other.

6

Hijacking the Holocaust

The Nazi mass murder of Jews was a nonsubject in the Soviet Union. Public commemoration of the Holocaust in Russia coincided with the revival of Jewish communal life in the late 1980s and 1990s. During that time, whatever educational and research programs there existed were linked to Israel. Vladimir Putin, early into his first presidential term, had recognized the significance of that link. Beginning in 2005, in the run-up to the celebration of the sixtieth anniversary of the victory over Nazi Germany, formal references to the Holocaust proliferated. Since then, the Putin regime has firmly incorporated the Holocaust into its foreign policy, making it essentially an instrument of soft power. The Holocaust is now a part of Russian history politics, coordinated at the highest governmental level.

Courting Israel's Jews, Building Historical Analogies

Like with any other developing discourse, it is difficult to pinpoint the exact point in time when the Putin regime added the Holocaust to its foreign political toolbox. The earliest indications are from 2003. Before Russia began exporting in earnest its interpretation of the Second World War, it tested it in Israel. This is a pretty obvious choice. Beyond the collective identity shaped in part by the experience of the Holocaust, Israel has a high percentage of former Soviet/Russian citizens, including several thousand war veterans.[1] Some of them exhibit nostalgia for the bygone Soviet days.[2]

Within an international setting, Putin referred to the Holocaust for the first time during the official visit of the Israeli prime minister Ariel Sharon to Russia in November 2003. Putin stressed the importance of building bridges to the Russian diaspora in Israel, and at once proposed organizing a Holocaust exhibition at the Victory Museum in Moscow. The war veterans in Israel would be pleased to know, he said, that such an exhibition would be opened in conjunction with the sixtieth anniversary of V-Day.[3] When meeting with a group of Russian war veterans two weeks later, Putin compared questioning the leading role of the Soviet Union in the defeat of Hitler's Germany to Holocaust denial.[4]

On January 27, 2005, Putin joined numerous other heads of state at the remembrance ceremony at former Auschwitz-Birkenau death camp. Putin chose a nonconfrontational tone in his address and even apologized, indirectly, for the occasional manifestations of antisemitism and xenophobia in Russia. Regardless, he issued a warning against any "attempts to rewrite history, by putting side by side victims and henchmen, liberators and occupiers." A historical discourse with a reference to the 600,000 Soviet troops who died liberating Poland and the total of 27 million lives lost by the Soviet Union in the Second World War was followed by a call to jointly fight against the new enemy—international terrorism. He described the present ceremony as the first in a series marking the sixtieth anniversary of the end of the Second World War, which would culminate on May 9 in Moscow.[5] Putin returned to the subject of antisemitism in the run-up to his historic visit to Israel in April 2005. This time around, in a TV interview, he redirected it to "certain states that have been traditionally regarded as Israel's strategic partners." In some post-Soviet countries, he stated without elaborating, Jews and Russians have the same (low) status. This is why Jewish organizations in those countries are among the first to react to the glorification of Nazis and the German Waffen SS.[6] Putin further impressed his views on both history and current affairs during his visit to Yad Vashem. Putin's guide was Aron Shneer, a Latvian-born Yad Vashem historian. Putin countered Shneer's assertion that the 1939 Molotov–Ribbentrop Pact paved the way to Nazi occupation of Poland with a reference to the 1938 Munich Agreement. When Shneer made mention of a different perspective on the Second World War in the Baltic States, the president brought up "attempts to legitimize the SS" in those same countries.[7]

Flanked by the Israeli president Moshe Katsav, Putin stated that the "Jewish people, like peoples of our country, incurred massive losses during the Second World War." The two presidents then unveiled a monument to the Holocaust—a gift from Russia to Israel.[8] The monument was hastily commissioned to Zurab Tsereteli, president of the Russian Academy of Arts, a billionaire, and unofficial court sculptor. During his long career Tsereteli has created numerous sculptures of Russian tsars and saints, and also writers, explorers, politicians, and so on. He is also the author of the Peoples' Tragedy monument at the Victory Museum grounds in Moscow (1996). Featuring a row of naked people turning into stones, the sculptural composition bears references to the Nazi gas chambers. Yet, the inscription just calls "to forever preserve their memory." The five human figures that comprise the Jerusalem monument were apparently culled out from the Moscow monument; as an indirect proof, Israeli newspaper *Maariv* pointed out that the male figures were uncircumcised.[9] To draw up a line under the official Russian evocations of the memory of the Holocaust up to that point: it appears to be a derivative of the traditional narrative of the Soviet victory in the Second World War with particular reference to the Baltic States (which became members of the European Union and NATO in the spring of 2004).

The pro-democracy protests of 2011–12 in Russia made the newly reelected president hike up levels of political repressions at home, and seek allies abroad. The doctrine on the history of the Second World War, and by extension the Holocaust, also became more stringent. Back in Israel, on June 25, 2012, Putin was opening the so-called Victory monument in Natanya. Designed by Salavat Schcherbakov and two other Russian sculptors, the monument to the victorious Soviet soldier was sponsored by Russian Jewish business. In his speech, Putin situated the Holocaust among other Nazi crimes and praised the Red Army for saving Jews "and many other peoples" from obliteration. Along the way, he called to preserve the "truth of the war and stand against attempts to whitewash Nazi accomplices." "Turning history inside out," continued Putin, "is a crime with respect to both the millions who sacrificed their life for Victory and the future generations who should know the true heroes of the Second World War, should be able to separate truth from cynical lies."[10]

Putin raised this issue nearly every time he met with the Israeli prime minister Benjamin Netanyahu. Both Russia and Israel are sensitive to a biased interpretation of history, he said at a joint press conference later that day. The people who had gone through the Holocaust—Putin put the words in his host's mouth—do not set in doubt the decisive role of the Soviet Union in the defeat of Nazism.[11] Netanyahu was happy to oblige, having on various occasions over the years emphasized that Israel and Russia see eye to eye on issues of history.

Back in Moscow, in November 2012, Putin was talking to the leaders of the Russian Jewry. There are currently about 156,000 Jews in Russia, or slightly over one percent of the total population. About half of some six hundred Russian Jewish organizations are religious, 218 of them ultra-Orthodox.[12] The Russian government has demonstrated a preference for interacting with, specifically, Orthodox Jewish leaders, which bestowed upon them even greater authority in the eyes of ordinary Jews. This is part of a general phenomenon—backed by the Russian Orthodox Church—of betting on so-called traditional values, including religion, as opposed to the "corrupt" values of the West. The two individuals who have repeatedly appeared by Putin's side are Rabbi Berl Lazar and Rabbi Alexander Boroda. The former is recognized by the government as Russia's chief rabbi. The Kremlin may not know how much their affiliation with the Chabad (Lubavich) movement is worth, but it is courting them on account of their international connections nevertheless, in the belief of the strength of the international Jewry.[13]

The conversation was held in conjunction with the opening of the Jewish Museum and Tolerance Center in Moscow. In the works since 2001, the museum was originally meant as an edutainment but later was put on a more solid foundation.[14] Putin has been a great supporter of the project; in 2007 he symbolically donated one month's salary toward the construction costs. The head of the FSB followed bid by handing over to the chief rabbi sixteen documents concerning the famed Swedish diplomat, Raoul Wallenberg. In fact, the Federation of Jewish Communities of Russia has a special department tasked with fostering cooperation with the ministry of defense and law-enforcement organs.[15] While Rabbi Lazar and Rabbi Boroda, who was dubbed as the president of the federation, stressed the tolerance aspect and the attempt to tell a comprehensive history of Russian Jews in the museum's exhibition, Putin advanced a rather different perspective. From the get-go, he suggested adding the word *Russian* in the name of the new institution: "It's located in Russia, right? And we made it happen together." Putin said he was impressed with the Yad Vashem Museum in Jerusalem and expected something similar in Moscow, with a caveat. There were many ethnicities in the Soviet Union who had suffered at the hands of the Nazis, stated Putin. The new museum would therefore serve as both a memorial to the murdered Jews of Russia and a reminder of the tragedy that had befallen other peoples. Putin saw the opening of the Moscow museum as reciprocal to the recent unveiling of the monument to the Red Army in Natanya. A bow to the Israeli leadership, he remarked, it is significant for the bilateral relations.[16] In an address read in his name during the opening ceremony,

Putin declared the Moscow museum to be the biggest such institution anywhere, and praised in particular the part of the exhibition honoring the "memory of victims of the Second World War."[17] The visiting president of Israel, Shimon Peres, echoed Putin in describing the Jewish Museum in Moscow as "unique," and the Red Army's contribution to victory over Nazi Germany an "unprecedented historical event." Peres confirmed in his address what Putin had sought all along: Israeli–Russian relations have strengthened further on account of history.[18] Although the name of the institution remained unchanged, the foreign ministry took Putin's suggestion to heart in referring to it as the Russian Jewish Tolerance Museum.

Russia's aggression against Ukraine in 2014 proved the first real test for the Russian Jewish communal leaders, the test they passed with dignity. Russian Jewish organizations managed to maintain their integrity by abstaining from directly commenting on the situation in Ukraine. At most, individual Russian Jews called upon their brethren in Ukraine to stay away from the Crimea issue for it had nothing directly to do with Jews.[19] No allusions to the Holocaust were made either. The Russian Chabad, however, ended up playing directly into Putin's hands when it received a group of Orthodox rabbis, which included senior figures in the Israeli religious establishment, in Moscow in July 2014. Among other things, the delegation declared its intention to attend a Holocaust commemoration ceremony at Sevastopol in the Russian-annexed Crimea. President Putin warmly welcomed the rabbis, praising them for what he called their assistance in Russia's fight against the revival of Nazism. Otherwise, Rabbi Lazar and Rabbi Boroda resisted recurrent attempts to make them reach out to, or worse, condemn their brethren in Ukraine. In particular, it concerned billionaire and Jewish community leader, Ihor Kolomoiskyi, who had declared his loyalty to the new Ukrainian government, shortly served as governor of Dnipropetrovsk (Dnipro) region, and bankrolled Ukrainian volunteer units in Donbass.[20]

Alongside Lazar and Boroda, Boris Shpigel, Ukrainian-born businessman and Federation Council member, has played a prominent role in promoting the official Russian discourse on the Second World War. Shpigel is primarily known as the chairman of World without Nazism, which is billed as an "international human rights NGO" and a kind of Moscow's answer to the Anti-Defamation League. Established in 2010 at the initiative of the World Congress of Russian Jews—also presided by Shpigel—World without Nazism is essentially a Kremlin front that helps advance its agenda on history internationally. The organization's stated objectives include consolidation of anti-fascist forces, mobilization of world public opinion in annunciating the significance of the Nuremberg judgment, promoting "denazification" of countries of Eastern and Central Europe, opposing the glorification of Nazism, safeguarding minority rights, and countering Holocaust denial. Back in 2008, in his capacity as president of the World Congress of Russian Jews, Shpigel indicted the Georgian military for "genocide" and "ethnic cleansing."[21] Three years later, Shpigel and World without Nazism proposed to the Council Europe preparing a single history textbook written, unsurprisingly, around the issues of interest to the organization.[22] In February 2014, a World without Nazism delegation with Shpigel at the helm met with the embattled president of Ukraine, Victor Yanukovich, in Kiev. Shpigel urged the latter to stand up against the forces of "extremism and neo-Nazism." In the heat of the fighting in Donbass, World without

Nazism deplored the absence of international outcry in the face of alleged Ukrainian mass crimes, which it said may bring about another Kristallnacht for ethnic minorities. Shpigel's "NGO" also endorsed the Russian annexation of Crimea. The likes of Efraim Zuroff, director of the Jerusalem office of the Simon Wiesenthal Center, and Rabbi Andrew Baker, OSCE personal representative on Combatting Antisemitism, have both expressed themselves on the pro-government bias of World without Nazism.[23]

In 2013 World without Nazism launched a new annual publication, *Belaia kniga natsizma* (White Book of Nazism). Based on a rather shaky methodology, the report gauges the extent of far-right extremism in the nineteen European countries, including Russia. Among the sixteen criteria used in the analysis is "glorification of German Nazism and Nazi German accomplices," which also incorporates Holocaust denial. The first edition of the White Book featured a whopping 1,126 pages of information. The final chart put Russia in the respectable eleventh place on the extremism index, way ahead of Estonia, Latvia, Ukraine, and Lithuania, in the second, third, fourth, and sixth places, respectively (Poland, for reasons unknown, was excluded from the analysis).[24] The 2014 edition proclaimed Latvia, along with Greece, to be the European country most imbued with radical nationalism. With reference to Ukraine, Duma deputy Tatiana Moskalkova designated the "White Book of Nazism" an essential tool in preventing the outbreak of the Third World War.[25] The yearbook launch subsequently took place in a number of European countries (e.g., Moldova, Greece, Latvia, Ukraine), and in the United States. The words *belaia kniga* struck a chord with the authorities, and so the following year the Russian Investigative Committee published a report of its own, "White Book of Crimes Committed in the Southeastern Ukraine" (read: by the Ukrainians in Donbass).

As far the Russian discourse on the Holocaust is concerned, Shpigel and World without Nazism should be credited for an important legislative initiative. In the spring of 2013 Shpigel introduced in the Duma two drafts of what eventually will have become the Law against the Glorification of Fascism. Although Shpigel's was neither the first nor the last draft of the law, it explicitly mentioned—for the first time ever in Russia— Holocaust denial as a form of propaganda of Nazism. In fact, the word *Holocaust* is used fifty-three times in the draft. Most likely, Shpigel referred to Holocaust denial tactically. According to Nikolay Koposov, the latter had been trying to make Russian memory laws resemble West European ones. When the Law against the Glorification of Nazism was eventually passed a year later, it no longer contained any reference to the genocide of the Jews. The reason why is simple. As Koposov has poignantly argued, the ultimate purpose of the law was "protecting the memory of the state against that of its victims."[26]

It would be way too easy to dismiss the discourse so far as Putin's personal opinion. In the undemocratic, top-down system of government instituted in Russia, the voice of the head of state gets passed down and amplified through multiple channels. Indeed, the new-old paradigm of Jews as a constituent of the "peaceful Soviet population" targeted for destruction by the Nazis is having an effect on patterns of memorialization locally. A case in point is a former Nazi mass execution site at Rostov-on-Don, honored by a massive memorial from 1975. In 2004, the Jewish community installed in Zmiiovsk Gorge a memorial plaque that read: "Here, on August 11–12, 1942, Nazis murdered over 27,000 Jews. This is the largest Holocaust memorial in Russia." In the course of its reconstruction seven years later, the original plaque was replaced with another: "Here, in Zmiioivsk Gorge, Hitlerite occupiers in August 1942 murdered over 27,000 peaceful citizens of Rostov-on-Don and Soviet prisoners of war. Among the victims were people of different ethnicities. Zmiiovsk Gorge is the largest in Russian Federation mass extermination site where fascist invaders destroyed Soviet citizens during the Great Patriotic War." Russian Jewish organizations were dismayed at the fact and took the local authorities to court. The latter purportedly based their decision on professional advice and argued that the old plaque had gone on display in the adjacent museum (which remained closed most of the time). The heated debates—punctuated by antisemitism peddled by certain Russian "patriotic" organizations—led to an uneasy compromise. In May 2014, Lazar and Boroda unveiled yet another memorial plaque. The new plaque reproduced the 2011 text, except that the words *Soviet citizens* were replaced with *Jews*.[27] In 2017, the local Jewish community tried but failed to secure permission to erect stelas with the names of the murdered Jews. The Rostov-on-Don administration set an impossible condition: the names of all the victims should be confirmed through archives, even though the cause of death had not been listed in obituaries issued in the immediate postwar years.[28]

Dmitry Medvedev, during his term as Russia's president generally used less militant rhetoric than his predecessor. When it comes to history politics, however, his utterances were not significantly different from Putin's. For instance, in August 2009 Medvedev and Shimon Peres issued a joint statement in which the "Presidents expressed their indignation at the attempts to deny the huge contribution of the USSR toward victory over Nazi Germany and to set in doubt the crime of Holocaust. Twisting real history to benefit one political scenario or another, as well as glorification of Nazism, is inadmissible, underscored D. Medvedev."[29]

Foreign Ministry Reworking the Holocaust into Its Talking Points

Taking cues from President Putin, the Russian foreign ministry began molding the subject of the Holocaust into its agenda beginning in 2004. As its first target, it chose Latvia. In March of that year, the foreign ministry published on its website a lengthy note, "On Participation of the Latvian Waffen SS Legion in War Crimes in 1941–1945 and the Attempts to Revisit the Nuremberg Tribunal Judgment in Latvia." Loosely following a Soviet historiographic thread, the note drew a direct line between the fascist groups in interwar Latvia, the mass murder of Jews, and Latvian military units, specifically the Waffen SS legion established by the Germans. The foreign ministry cited nebulous figures established by the Soviet Extraordinary Commission in the late 1940s, according to which 313,000 civilians and 330,000 Soviet prisoners of war perished in Latvia during the Nazi occupation. Having overwhelmed prospective readers with dates, figures, and proper names, the foreign ministry delivered its core message: alleged exoneration of war criminals in Latvia in the run-up to joining NATO and the European Union and the malicious intent underlining a comparison of mass crimes committed by the Nazi and Soviet regimes. The note linked past and present by insinuating that

> the concept of Latvian history in the Second World War superimposed on the society is regarded by the authorities as one of the chief factors in passing the naturalization exam, which is obviously unacceptable to a majority of Russians, Belorussians, Ukrainians, Jews, and other minorities. Such a position on problematic aspects of history is aggravating the split within the Latvian society.[30]

Within a month, the Latvian foreign ministry issued a rebuttal, prepared by well-known historians Inesis Feldmanis and Kārlis Kangeris. Not without rhetorical flourishes and logical inconsistencies, the Latvian note presented a more nuanced picture. Among the key points made by the Latvian historians was that the Waffen SS legion cannot *a priori* be considered a criminal organization, for an overwhelming majority of its rank and file were conscripts and that it engaged in combat operations mainly against the advancing Soviet troops. The word *volunteer* was deliberately used in the original designation of the unit by the Germans, while a substantial proportion of the recruits enthusiastically responded to a mobilization call in the hope of preventing the return of the hated Soviet power.[31] The response, three months later, is one of the most extensive historical treatises ever published by the Russian foreign ministry. The key issue remained whether individual Latvians joined the German Waffen SS as volunteers or if they were conscripted. If they had volunteered for the service (beginning in 1943), as the Russian foreign ministry insisted and the Latvians disproved, they automatically became members of a criminal organization, as proclaimed by the International Military Tribunal at Nuremberg. In support of its argument, it even quoted works by Raoul Hilberg and Robert White from the early 1990s—a sure sign that this was a new subject for the foreign ministry. The note made only a passing reference to the mass murder of Jews. In parallel, on April 16, Russia sponsored a resolution by the UN Commission on Human Rights that condemned the "glorification" of Waffen SS as an expression of racial intolerance and xenophobia, which contravened both the Nuremberg judgment and the UN Charter.[32] Later that month, Russia participated in the OSCE conference on antisemitism in Berlin. That time around, a Russian representative spoke of abstract "collaborators" and praised the initiative of the British Holocaust Educational Trust to identify sites of mass executions of Jews in the Baltic States.[33]

The same verbal sequence—glorification of Waffen SS, collaborators, antisemitism, revival of Nazism—was used by the Russian deputy foreign minister when the UN General Assembly came to discuss the memory of the Holocaust in its October 2005 session. He claimed, without giving any specifics, that "my country is religiously [*sviato*] preserving the memory of Nazi victims, including six million Jews, half of whom, that is, three million, were Soviet citizens." The same type of commemoration, he said, should be accorded to the soldiers (read: Red Army soldiers) who sacrificed their lives for rescuing Europe from fascism, saving Jews and other nations from sure destruction.[34] The Russian delegation took one step further during the UN debates on liquidation of racism and racial discrimination the following month. This time around, the Russian representative on the Third Committee (Social, Humanitarian & Cultural Issues) juxtaposed "glorification of Waffen SS" with "defiling memory of the countless victims of fascism and the Holocaust." It was also at New York, that Moscow, for the very first time, alerted world public opinion to the danger of "revisiting the results of the [Second World] War and rewriting history." Most significant, the UN General Assembly, on Russian initiative, on December 19 passed a resolution "Inadmissibility of Certain Practices that Contribute to Fueling Contemporary Forms of Racism, Racial Discrimination, Xenophobia and Related Intolerance," which effectively restated the earlier resolution adopted by the Human Rights Commission.[35] Resolution 61/147 reaffirmed that the Nuremberg statute and judgment in 1945–46 declared Waffen SS to be a criminal organization, and drew attention to the resurgence of neo-Nazism, neo-fascism, and violent nationalism. More specifically, it condemned the "glorification of the Nazi movement and former members of the Waffen SS organization, including by erecting monuments and memorials as well as holding public demonstrations." Such practices, according to the resolution, "do injustice to the memory of the countless victims of crimes against humanity committed in the Second World War, in particular those committed by the SS organization, and poison the minds of young people." The resolution placed the said offenses within the scope of the 1965 International Convention on the Elimination of All Forms of Racial Discrimination and declared that the freedom of speech and assembly, as provided in the 1948 Universal Declaration of Human Rights and the 1966 International Covenant on Civil and Political Rights, does not apply. Resolution 61/147 was passed by 107 votes, with the United States voting against and all EU countries abstaining.[36]

Although Resolution 61/147 did not mention any offending country by name— as Foreign Minister Lavrov had emphasized—Russia's permanent representative to the United Nations gladly filled in. Shortly before the document went to a vote in the General Assembly, *Rossiiskaia Gazeta* ran an interview with the late Vitaly Churkin. Did Russia have in mind the situation in the Baltic Republics when it had originally proposed that resolution, asked the newspaper. "Of course, it's no secret that all of this is of direct relevance to the processes going on in Latvia and Estonia," said Churkin, "We are concerned that officials in those countries join commemorative events in honor of the Waffen SS legionaries." Referring in passing to criminalization of Holocaust denial in select European countries, he further explained that the resolution makes it an international issue, going beyond bilateral, Russian–Baltic relations, as the United States and the EU would have liked it to stay.[37]

The Russian delegation in the United Nations invoked the language of the resolution in conjunction with yet another resolution, on Holocaust denial, sponsored by the United States and passed on January 26, 2007. According to a press release, it was symbolic that the United Nations had adopted a new resolution on the eve of International Holocaust Remembrance Day that marks the liberation of Auschwitz-Birkenau death camp by the Red Army.[38] Lavrov drew a connection between the latter and the "glorification of Waffen SS" in his address on the occasion of the Holocaust Remembrance Day.[39] A Russian representative on the UN Committee on Information several months later, however, chose to link the Holocaust and the removal of Soviet

Second World War memorials in Eastern Europe (i.e., in Tallinn, Estonia, on the night of April 27, 2007).⁴⁰

The foreign ministry has also displayed a certain creativity in pushing through its agenda. Thus, in 2007 it arranged for an organization of Soviet war veterans to be part of the Holocaust commemoration organized by the UN Committee on Information. The following year it sponsored a drawing exhibition, *Sketches in Memory of the Victims of the Holocaust and Their Liberators* by a member of the Russian Academy of Arts. The now usual reference to UN Resolution 61/147 and the call for a "correct, undistorted comprehension of the results of the Second World War," left no doubt as to Moscow's intention.⁴¹

The foreign ministry is one of many federal agencies represented in the Victory organizing committee, which was established in 2000 by President Putin mainly for the purpose of coordinating activities related to May 9 celebrations. Deputy Foreign Minister Alexander Yakovenko, who took part in the January 2009 committee meeting, referred to the Nazi mass murder of Jews just once in his address. His office was preparing a large-scale campaign to counter efforts by the West to redirect attention to the Molotov–Ribbentrop Pact and similar "ambiguous historical events," as well as Holocaust denial and glorification of Nazi collaborators, he said. From the foreign ministry's perspective, the international status of Russia can be further strengthened through an affirmation of the leading role of the Soviet Union in defeating Nazi Germany and liberating Europe.⁴² The attempted falsification of history was also the main subject of interest to the foreign ministry during a conversation with the visiting director of the US Holocaust Memorial Museum, Sara Bloomfield, in early 2010.⁴³

Since 2009, Russian Jewish organizations have been increasingly incorporated into Moscow's designs. On January 27, 2009, the foreign ministry, in collaboration with the UN Committee on Information, organized a panel, "Lessons of the Holocaust and Modernity" in New York. According to a Russian diplomat, the event featured "leading Russian and American nonprofit organizations," Moscow Human Rights Bureau, and the American branch of the World Congress of Russian Jews. In December 2009 in Berlin, the latter organization—in cooperation with unspecified Jewish and antifascist entities from Europe and CIS—held a conference with a modified title, "Lessons of the Second World War and the Holocaust."⁴⁴ Next, the foreign ministry deployed big guns, the government proxy World without Nazism. On February 10, 2011, at the UN Headquarters, the World Congress of Russian Jews and World without Nazism (both headed by Shpigel) put together a roundtable, "World without Nazism: The Global Goal of the Mankind Today and the Sixty-fifth Anniversary of the Nuremberg Trial." The roundtable proclaimed the Nuremberg judgment to be the ultimate truth, condemned the "glorification of Nazism," and decried an attempted falsification of history. To spread the truth about the Second World War, the roundtable participants proposed carrying out educational and "media propaganda" campaigns.⁴⁵

The foreign ministry classifies entities like World without Nazism and Historical Memory Foundation as "Russian NGOs with international exposure." Lavrov explicitly called for mobilization of such organizations, expected to "expose the fact and manifestations of glorification of Nazism," and subsequently communicate their findings to the UN Human Rights Council and the General Assembly. Poignantly, the Russian foreign minister made such a statement at a January 2012 conference in Moscow ostensibly dealing with the Holocaust.[46] A few months later, Lavrov specifically mentioned Jewish organizations—World Jewish Congress (of Russian Jews) and European Jewish Congress—as Russia's allies in the fight against historical revisionism, especially in the Baltic States. He regarded further cooperation with Israel in this field as particularly desirable: "The Holocaust constitutes holy memory for Israelis, and they very much appreciate the decisive contribution in the defeat of fascism and prevention of a global Holocaust that played the nations comprising the Soviet Union."[47]

Determined to keep up the heat on East Europeans, the Russian delegation in 2012 sponsored yet another condemnatory resolution in the United Nations. The General Assembly Resolution 67/154 arrived exactly six years after Resolution 61/147 and featured similar content, except that "glorification of Nazism" was now in the name of the document. Twice the size of the original document, the new resolution went into an all-important detail: Waffen SS members were now said to be collectively implicated in war crimes and crimes against humanity (read: standing up against the Red Army on the Eastern Front); anyone who fought against the anti-Hitler coalition (read: Soviet Union) could not be classified as belonging to a national liberation movement; desecration and/or demolition of monuments to those who stood up against Nazism in the Second World War (read: Soviet monuments) was deplorable. Vaguely worded, certain provisions of the resolution are hard to comprehend (e.g., nos. 8, 16): "attempts at commercial advertising aimed at exploiting the sufferings of the victims of war crimes and crimes against humanity committed during the Second World War by the Nazi regime"; "importance of history classes in teaching the dramatic events and human suffering which arose out of the adoption of ideologies such as Nazism and Fascism."[48] The Russian representative, Vasily Nebenzia, in explaining his country's position, cited the example of a monument honoring local members of the Waffen SS recently erected in Bauska, Latvia. "How come that in European countries, in some of which Holocaust denial is outlawed," he rhetorically asked, "one is allowed to erect monuments to exactly those who committed those crimes, those who perpetrated the Holocaust?"[49] The voting pattern was pretty much the same as six years ago, with the United States and Canada voting against the resolution, and EU countries abstaining. Both resolutions have since been reaffirmed on an annual basis on Russia's initiative. While the number of abstentions went down slightly over the years, Ukraine in 2014 joined the United States and Canada in the no vote. The foreign ministry instantly counteracted by weaving Ukraine into its spiel on the resurgence of Nazism—the very first time the words *Ukraine* and the *Holocaust* were mentioned within the span of a single statement: "Especially distressing and troubling is the position of Ukraine. It's hard to understand that the country whose people had fully experienced the horrors of Nazism and made a considerable contribution to the joint victory over it can vote against the document condemning glorification of Nazism."[50] In short, UN Resolution 67/154, to a larger extent than its antecedent, is a classic example of manipulation and obfuscation driven by the Putin regime.

In the spring of 2013 Shpigel was forced to resign from the Federation Council. The latest activities of World without Nazism, as reported by the Russian media, are from 2015; the organization's website is currently inaccessible. With no formal statement to that regard, it appears that Shpigel's outfit has outlived its usefulness for the authorities. As a hint, taking cues from the "White Book of Nazism," in 2015 the foreign ministry published a similar yearbook. The revamped report, "Neo-Nazism: A Dangerous Challenge to Human Rights, Democracy, and the Rule of Law," was presented in April 2015 by the foreign ministry's official in charge of human rights. As compared to the "White Book of Nazism," it was now available electronically, in both Russian and English; dramatically cut in size, it had dropped any subterfuge as to what it actually wanted to pin down—the falsification of the history of the Second World War as an element of current politics. The foreign ministry referred fleetingly to "denial of the Holocaust and crimes against humanity" to condemn the thesis equating Communism and Nazism and ascribing to the Soviet Union and Nazi Germany equal responsibility for the outbreak of the war. In addition to the EU countries, the report also surveyed the situation in Switzerland, Norway, Canada, the United States, and, "of course," Ukraine. While acts of vandalism against the Russian Orthodox Church buildings in Ukraine and Germany were promptly documented, Russia as a country was not part of the report.[51] Neither is Russia to be found among the thirty-one countries that make up the most recent report, published in May 2018. A close reading reveals a peculiar correlation between the reported extent of pro-Nazi sympathies and the degree of friendliness or hostility of any given country toward Russia. Thus, Hungary passes the test well (one page) while Latvia (five), Lithuania (eight), Estonia (eleven), Ukraine (five), and Poland (eight) do not.[52]

Even when the former Soviet Union was not part of an international conversation, the Putin regime never let the Holocaust be mentioned outside of the context of the Second World War. For example, the explosive remarks by the president of Iran, Mahmoud Ahmadinejad, in December 2005, in which he denied Israel the right to exist and denied the Holocaust ever occurred, was unequivocally rejected by Russia. Then and later, however, the Russian foreign ministry stated that the "historical facts in conjunction with the Second World War, including the Holocaust . . . cannot be subject to revision."[53] In other words, the foreign ministry implied certain mistruths about the Soviets and the war, while Iran's president was talking exclusively about the Jews and Israel.

From then onward, the Putin regime never failed to air any new episode in history politics playing out between Russia and its East European neighbors in connection with the Holocaust. For example, in May 2006, the Russian representative raised before the OSCE the case of vandalism carried out against the monument to the Soviet soldier in Tallinn. The "extremist incident" that had just occurred in Estonia, he said, goes against the grain of raising awareness about the tragedy of the Second World War and the Holocaust.[54]

As an interim conclusion, Russia's modus operandi is molding the Holocaust to fit any new twist in regional memory politics it regards as adversarial. Simultaneously, it came to increasingly use the UN forum in pursuit of its agenda, demonstrating good rhetorical skills and creativity in the process. Notably, Moscow's efforts to promote its particular take on the Holocaust never exceeds the confines of the UN Headquarters in the United States. Neither did Russian authorities attempt to sell—or apparently failed to, if they ever tried—their hastily assembled exhibitions highlighting the role of the Soviet Union in rescuing European Jews to Yad Vashem.

Unwanted at a Ceremony in Auschwitz, Putin Conceives of a Separate Agenda on the Holocaust, 2015

I date the beginning of a concerted propaganda campaign by the Russian government to influence the international discourse on the Holocaust by 2015. A year earlier, Russia had brazenly violated Ukraine's integrity by annexing Crimea and fueling unrest in Donbass. During and after the Maidan uprising in Kiev, Polish foreign minister Radosław Sikorski became one of the most recognizable faces among European politicians in Ukraine. For a short while, Poland had assumed the role of Ukraine's Big Brother. Even traditional historical acrimonies going back to the Second World War appeared to have been put to rest. Coincidentally, Sikorski is married to American journalist and author, Anne Applebaum, who authored such bestsellers as *Gulag: A History* (2003), *Iron Curtain: The Crushing of Eastern Europe, 1944–1956* (2012), and most recently, *Red Famine: Stalin's War on Ukraine* (2017).

As mentioned earlier, Putin participated in the 2005 ceremony commemorating the liberation of Auschwitz death camp by the Red Army. Ten years later, in his third term as Russia's president, Putin was conspicuously missing among the world leaders converging on Poland. Ostensibly, it was due to a glitch in diplomatic protocol. Unlike earlier, the Russian leader did not receive a personal invitation from the Polish government to attend. That was unintentional, insisted the Polish ambassador to Moscow. In order to avoid politicizing the event, the Polish foreign ministry delegated organizational issues to the State Museum of Auschwitz-Birkenau. The museum sent out bulk invitations to foreign diplomatic missions, leaving it to them to decide who specifically from each respective state would attend. That bureaucratic procedure, in its turn, was derided by Russia's foreign minister Lavrov. The Polish prime minister had personally invited President Petro Poroshenko of Ukraine to be part of the commemorative event during her official visit to Kiev earlier that January. Suddenly, it became an issue of status and prestige, but not only that.[55]

The Russian side promptly concluded that the diplomatic hand wrangling served a single goal—keeping Putin out in a time of heightened tensions between Russia and the West. It was also in Putin's own interests to avoid the type of vacuum that he had experienced only a few months earlier at the G20 meeting in Brisbane, Australia. Enter history politics. The non-invitation of Putin also served as a signal that the European leaders were to likely skip the forthcoming May 9 celebration in Moscow. Had Putin traveled to Poland nonetheless, he would likely have stressed that it was the Red Army that liberated the remaining Auschwitz prisoners.[56] A few days prior to the commemoration ceremony at Auschwitz, novice Polish foreign minister Grzegorz Shetyna added fuel to the fire by claiming in a radio interview that it was actually ethnic Ukrainians belonging to the First Ukrainian Front that had liberated the death camp. The Russian response was fast and furious. Russia's permanent representative to the United Nations, Vitaly Churkin, correctly pointed out that the Soviet units that entered the camp territory on January 27, 1945, were composed of dozens of different ethnicities. His boss, Lavrov, did not mince words when he called his Polish counterpart's statement a "blasphemy."[57]

Instead of Auschwitz, Putin, on January 27, 2015, visited the Jewish Museum and Tolerance Center in Moscow. Accompanied by Berl Lazar and Alexander Boroda, Putin toured the exhibition, *Human and the Holocaust*, that told the history of Nazi death camps. At the conclusion of the visit, Putin gave a long speech. Periodically returning to the theme of the Holocaust horrors, Putin effectively built his speech on juxtaposition and analogy. Thus, he spoke in one breath of antisemitism and Russophobia, nationalism and terrorism. Of the different ethnicities that fought within the Red Army ranks, Putin mentioned just two—Russians and Jews. In the opposite camp he put Bandera followers in Ukraine and Baltic Nazis. The former fought side by side to rescue the Jewish people from annihilation, while the latter collaborated in the Nazi mass murder. Putin craftily linked this "lessons of history" to the "coldblooded destruction of the peaceful population of Donbass." Any attempts to rewrite history, he stated, are unacceptable and immoral. Curiously, on this occasion he did not say a single word about Poland. The point Putin was making is hard to miss: bound by the tragic experience, Jews should join Russians in pushing back violent nationalism of the Ukrainian and Baltic kind, which is based on exactly the same ideology that made the Holocaust possible.[58]

The Putin regime proved wildly successful in building bridges to the world Jewry, and especially Israeli Jews. In May 2014, businessman and vice president of the Russian Jewish Congress German Zakhariev proposed expanding the Jewish religious calendar on account of 26 Iyar, Day of Deliverance and Liberation. Although Israel—in deference to its substantial Russian-speaking population—had traditionally celebrated the end of the Second World War on May 9 (as opposed to May 8, like in most countries in the world) it proved willing to walk an extra mile to accommodate the request in sync with the Kremlin's wishes. As Zakhariev put it, it was important to honor the "quarter million Jews who risked their lives during the war as part of the Allied armies and partisan units."[59] A reference to "partisan units" made it clear that he specifically meant the Soviets. His greater ambition is making 26 Iyar as significant as Passover and/or Yom Kippur—major Jewish holidays that symbolize victory over enemies and delivery from mortal danger. Beyond the religious connotations, 26 Iyar superimposes the now familiar Russian narrative: "So that Jews in the whole world could say no to attempts to exonerate fascism and their stooges, to attempts to rewrite history, to demonstrate to certain European nations an example of gratitude and good memory." Formally announced in both the Knesset and the UN Headquarters, the new date in the Hebrew calendar was for the first time marked in 2015.[60] If anyone may still be willing to give the new holiday the benefit of the doubt, President Putin made it straight in his address to Russian Jews and "all those who celebrate the Day of Deliverance and Liberation" in May 2016:

> Incorporation in the Hebrew calendar of 26 Iyar is a memorial tribute to the great heroism of the soldiers and officers of the Red Army who defeated Nazism, rescued from obliteration not only the Jews but also other nations of Europe and the world. Naturally, this is also the resolute response to all those who deny the Holocaust and attempt to revise the results of the Second World War.

I am certain, that the wide celebration of the Day of Deliverance and Liberation will help strengthening both spiritual and historical traditions of the Russian Jews and patriotic youth education, will become a major unifying event for the Jewish communities of our country and the foreign states.[61]

Minister of Education Olga Vasilieva expertly explained that "26 Iyar is a holiday when Jews [*iiudei*] prayed for the soldiers and officers of the Red Army who delivered the Jewish people from Nazism."[62] Vasilieva was given the honor of reading Putin's address at a semi-academic event on May 10, 2018, that aptly connected the Soviet role in the defeat of Nazi Germany and the establishment of the State of Israel. The gathering in Moscow was billed as an "international scientific conference 'The Victory in the Great Patriotic War as a Historical Event in the Life of the Jewish People.'"[63]

Back in January 2016, President Putin had a meeting with the leaders of the European Jewish Congress. He went straight to business by declaring the congress to be Russia's natural ally in fighting antisemitism, safeguarding the memory of the Second World War, and consistently standing up against "glorification of Nazism." Viacheslav Moshe Kantor, Russian-born billionaire and since 2007 president of the European Jewish Congress, paid in kind by designating Putin a "true friend of the Russian [Jewish] community" and supporting Russia's military operation in Syria. In the aftermath of the terrorist attacks in France, Kantor expressed concern about the rise of antisemitism in Europe. He believed that the situation of Jews was the best in Russia, among all European countries. Sure, agreed Putin, let Jews move to Russia: "[Jews] had emigrated from the Soviet Union—let them [now] come back."[64] The governor of the Jewish Autonomous Republic in Russia's Far East instantly backed Putin's proposal by extending a warm welcome to Jews fleeing Europe. The invitation, which arrived in the wake of a report of a racially motivated attack on a suburban train in Moscow, sparked little enthusiasm among European Jews. Population statistics pinpoint the opposite trend altogether: according to Israeli authorities, some five thousand Russian Jews immigrated to Israel in 2014—double the figure for any of the previous sixteen years.[65]

The Russian permanent representative at OSCE, Alexander Lukashevich, capitalized on Kantor's evocations to situate Holocaust denial within the attempted falsification of history. He contrasted the efforts to bury the information about Jewish massacres by "Baltic Nazis" and Bandera followers in Ukraine with the comprehensive Holocaust remembrance program in Russia: sites of mass murder being identified and marked (backed by an evangelical Christian organization); schools routinely holding Holocaust history lessons; a center for Holocaust and genocide studies established at the Russian State University for the Humanities, and so on. Along the way he incorporated a novel element into the official Russian discourse on the Holocaust and the civilizational mission performed by the Red Army in Europe. Jews not only counted among the victims of the war, but they also made a big contribution to the victory over Nazism by fighting within the Soviet Army ranks.[66] Lukashevich was on a roll when, a year later in the same setting, he extended this line of argumentation even further. He was now arguing that in some, unspecified, countries authorities have destroyed monuments to the Soviet soldiers "who had sacrificed their lives liberating concentration camp prisoners and putting an end to the Holocaust."[67] Ironically, now and then, the Russian diplomat resorted to what Moscow has been accusing neighboring countries of for decades, namely the falsification of history. Otherwise, no evidence came to light of Soviet soldiers killed en masse when overrunning the Nazi death camps.

When evoking, ad nauseam, "attempts to falsify history," Russian authorities fail to explain in detail how it relates specifically to the Holocaust—the new point of reference in the official lexicon. In the few cases when particular examples have been given, it does not take long to establish that those are actually the very same aspects of the Second World War Moscow has been hitting East European countries, especially former Soviet republics, with since the early 1990s. During his meeting with the representatives of the European Jewish Congress on October 10, 2007, President Putin specifically praised Jewish organizations for their work toward the "preservation of historical truth about the Holocaust, other Nazi crimes, and, of course, the heroism of the soldiers who died liberating Europe from 'brown plague.'" By historical revisionism in the new EU member states, Latvia and Estonia, Putin meant annual gatherings of former Waffen SS veterans held unopposed in those countries. Among more recent examples he cited the relocation of a monument to the Soviet soldier from central Tallinn. In the case of Ukraine, he mentioned "attempts by certain political forces" to whitewash the reputation of the Organization of Ukrainian Nationalists (OUN) and the Ukrainian Insurgent Army (UPA).[68]

When Russian diplomats do make a direct link between particular wartime organizations and the Holocaust, they invariably take it wrong. Hence, they do not differentiate between Himmler's SS and Waffen SS, and consequently state that the latter was proclaimed a criminal organization at Nuremberg (without mentioning the clause that accounts for post-1943 forced conscription). With some exceptions, the Waffen SS—or the former Baltic nationals among its ranks to be precise—did not take part in the Nazi mass murder of the Jews. Those who did, particularly in 1941–42, were paramilitary units/auxiliary police, local branches of the German Security Police, and police battalions. However, since that does not make the news in either the Baltic States or Russia, it is not reflected in the Russian history politics either and, consequently, is missing from formal statements. Hence are the references to abstract "collaborators who exterminated hundreds of thousands of peaceful citizens, prisoners or war, and camp inmates in the territory of Latvia, Lithuania, Estonia, Russia, Ukraine, Belorussia, Poland, and other countries."[69] Neither do Russian diplomats often have their facts right when they talk about the victims of the Holocaust. For instance, in January 2005, Foreign Minister Lavrov stated in a press conference that "millions of people who were imprisoned and murdered at [Auschwitz-Birkenau] camp had been deported [*ugnany*] from the Soviet Union." The Russian permanent representative at OSCE eleven years later modified that figure even further: millions of people murdered, including about one million Jews. While giving our dues to the victims of the Holocaust, he stated, we should also remember "some ten million Slavs . . . who perished in Nazi concentration camps."[70] All six Nazi death camps were situated in the occupied Polish territory, not in Germany, Czechoslovakia, or the Soviet Union—as the foreign ministry maintains (i.e., Theresienstadt was a ghetto, not a "death factory").[71]

This ignorance builds on Soviet precedents, that is to say, the Russian foreign ministry has dusted off the Cold War rhetoric, without much of a critical assessment. In part, this is a consequence of a consistent neglect of academic research on the Holocaust in Russia, which in its turn points to the government's lack of genuine interest in the history and lessons of the Holocaust. The Holocaust is typically evoked in just two cases: collaboration in the Nazi mass murder of Jews in Eastern Europe and/or Soviet contribution to putting an end to the Nazi genocide. Needless to say, this primitive juxtaposition of evil versus good does not account for the complexity of the phenomenon known as the Holocaust. The Holocaust is significant for the Putin regime only insofar as it helps advance its foreign political goals. In short, it makes good propaganda.

Osventsim, as Auschwitz has been traditionally referred to in Russian (Polish: Oświęcim), had been a permanent feature in the Soviet/Russian discourse on the Second World War. Soviet tourist groups in Poland had necessarily visited the Auschwitz Museum since the early 1970s. A zero-sum view on world politics, as exercised by the Putin regime, sees history as yet another battlefield. As RVIO described a temporary exhibition, *War and Myths*, that it opened in Bratislava, Slovakia, in May 2018: "our offense on the history front in Europe."[72] When seen from that perspective, the 2015 commemoration ceremony at Auschwitz proved a debacle for Russia. Five years on, it looks more like a strategic retreat. Back then, beside self-righteous rhetoric Russia could offer precious little in lieu of a response. No significant primary research has been done in Russia on the Auschwitz-Birkenau death camp. Due to its tragic destiny as the center of the Nazi Holocaust archipelago, the Auschwitz State Museum had always had a wide international academic network. That status alone makes it unassailable. Besides, in recent decades the museum has developed a unique expertise on conservation and statistical analysis. Not even the best among the Kremlin spin doctors could shake off that hard-won reputation. Naked criticism obviously would not do, but a different historical perspective might. Apparently, Russian authorities settled on a three-pronged strategy. One was to continue with the familiar rhetoric around Auschwitz, but link it to current issues and repackage it in formats that would appeal to audiences at home and abroad. Second was to foster Holocaust-related activities in Russia. And third, to choose a different former Nazi camp site that would make a specific Russian take on the Holocaust less controversial and thus more acceptable.

From 2015 onward, Russian diplomats started reaching out to further East European countries under the heading of Holocaust commemoration. In Romania, for example, they laid a wreath at a Holocaust memorial.[73] The Russian foreign ministry promptly, if indirectly, explained why the choice had fallen specifically on this country, and not any other. The commemoration of the Jews and Roma deported by the Antonsecu's regime during the war coincided with an exhibition on the postwar deportation of Transylvania Germans to the Soviet Union. The Bucharest exhibition, stated the foreign ministry spokesperson Maria Zakharova, had "clear anti-Soviet and anti-Russian overtones." She went on to remind that the Romanian Army had fought on the German side and referred to the over 300,000 Jews murdered in territory controlled by the regime, kicking the present German ambassador to Romania along the way.[74] The most extensive celebration of V-Day organized by a Russian embassy anywhere is held in the Republic of North Macedonia, which Moscow has been trying hard to talk out from joining NATO and the European Union. Among other institutions annually participating in the commemorative events is the Holocaust Memorial Center for the Jews of Macedonia in Skopje.⁷⁵ An even less obvious location to commemorate the Holocaust, with the participation of Russian diplomats, was Cuba, in July 2015. In fact, the word *Holocaust* (or *Jews*) was not even mentioned beyond the news item's title. A local artist in Matanzas, west of Havana, displayed a series of his works, "Auschwitz: Memory of Horror." The event was billed as part of the celebration of the seventieth anniversary of the Great Victory, and accompanied by the standard pledge to forestall the resurgence of Nazi ideology and whitewashing of Nazi war criminals and their accomplices.⁷⁶ Beginning in 2015, Moscow has also engaged the Commonwealth of Independent States—a rather symbolic alliance that had emerged from the rubble of the Soviet Union—to issue on an annual basis a solemn declaration, projecting the Russian take on the Second World War, with the prerequisite single reference to the Holocaust.

It was also in 2015 that the Norwegian Holocaust Center in Oslo for the first time received a direct communication from the Russian embassy. The center had received invitations for cooperation earlier, too, in December 2010 and August 2014, from the World without Nazism and the Russian State University for the Humanities, respectively. Yet, those are state affiliates while the invitation was likely on account of my own research on Estonian collaboration in the Holocaust.⁷⁷ This anecdote is worth telling in full. In September 2015 the center in Oslo opened a temporary exhibition, *Yiddish for All*, in which a group of Norwegian and Polish artists reflected on the past and future of the language that a majority of East European Jews had once held as their own. Among the invited guests were the embassies of the countries where Yiddish was once spoken, including Russia. Upon receiving the invitation, the Russian embassy in Oslo instantly contacted the center with a proposal for a joint event. The embassy proposed screening a TV documentary on the subject of the Holocaust that aired briefly on Russian Today (RT, generally known to be a propaganda outlet of the Russian government). "119 Lives Unlived" tells a story of betrayal and the eventual murder of a group of Jews from Amsterdam, with an unusual twist. Among other people, a reporter interviewed the leader of the far-right Dutch People's Union, whom she asked if he thought the memory of the Second World War was being "manipulated." On her visit to Auschwitz, she arranged to interview Rainer Höss, the grandson of the camp commander. To her question whether Nazism was rearing its ugly head in Europe and if the Holocaust could happen again, he said "absolutely" and singled out Muslims as the largest threat. The film ends with shots of a controversial annual March of the Living, whose participants go around the former campgrounds draped in Israeli flags. Jews are feeling threatened, the Holocaust may happen again, the Red Army liberated Auschwitz in 1944—impresses the documentary.⁷⁸

As it turned out, the film's narrator, Paula Slier, had earlier reported, among other places, from Donbass. That point was indirectly reinforced by the delegation from the Russian embassy that eventually came to visit the Holocaust Center. The first thing that the embassy's second secretary mentioned in the conversation was "fascists" running amok in the new Ukraine. The Norwegian Holocaust Center rejected the proposal. The way the Russian embassy handled this issue suggests that little thought had gone into it. I can imagine the embassy in Oslo asking the foreign ministry in Moscow if the latter could possibly propose, quickly, anything related to the Holocaust with the seal of state approval attached to it. Now, they have *Sobibor*.

Russian Motion Picture *Sobibor* as a Foreign Political Trojan Horse

In May 2018 a new Russian motion picture, *Sobibor*, hit movie theaters. Sobibor is one of the six death camps established by the Nazis in Europe, all of them in the occupied Polish territory. The movie titled *Sobibór*—spelled with diacritics, as if it were in Polish—is not just about the Holocaust, though.[79] The film trailer is built around the personal heroism of its main character, Alexander Pechersky, a Soviet prisoner of war who happened to be Jewish. Pechersky led an uprising at Sobibor, erroneously presented as the first successful Jewish rebellion in Nazi death camps. Homages to Pechersky that promptly went up in several Russian cities also emphasized the part that he played after 1945 by testifying at war crimes trials (e.g., the 1963 trial of eleven ethnic Ukrainian guards at Sobibor). Even though the film posters feature the Star of David, the tenet of the movie is different. The official trailer reminded one more of a blockbuster war epic. This was intentional. A year earlier, Minister of Culture Medinskii had presented *Sobibor* before Putin in the Kremlin as follows: "This is a movie about the first ever successful mass breakout from a death camp, led by our lieutenant Pechersky.... It's an international movie, a huge project with [the participation of] foreign stars." Medinskii placed *Sobibor* in the category of "military-patriotic films."[80]

Critics unanimously agree that the opening scene that shows a group of Jewish prisoners being gassed is also the movie's best. The movie as a whole, however, has a handful of problems. Written by several individuals, the scenario is a patchwork of characters and narrative lines that do not hang well together. The film's director, Konstantin Khabensky, who also plays the main character, allowed himself extensive artistic liberty. He did so by remaking specific individuals who participated in the uprising into composite characters. Many a dialogue is coated in sugary sentimentality and symbolism. The many languages spoken by the characters (i.e., German, Yiddish, Russian, Polish, and Dutch) do not always accurately reflect reality. For example, camp guards who were drafted from among ethnic Ukrainians and ethnic Germans from Ukraine, end up speaking in German with each other in the movie. The German SS meanwhile are all wearing black (instead of gray) uniforms, for additional effect. The subtitles do not do justice to the text. Worst of all, the movie is replete with historical inaccuracies (e.g., Pechersky was physically abused; most of the participants died during the actual uprising). The argument used by the film consultants in defense of making the story screen-friendly, namely that documentary evidence is scant, cannot be substantiated.[81] Scholarly literature on the Sobibor camp in general and the 1943 uprising in particular is, indeed, substantial, though in languages other than Russian.

Khabensky himself should not be judged too harshly perhaps, for *Sobibor* was his debut as a film director. (Medinskii was mentioned as the one who pitched the idea for the film and subsequently contributed to the script.) What matters is that Khabensky accepted the superimposed discourse on the Holocaust.[82] That discourse presents Jewish resistance as part of the fight against fascism. As if to reinforce this point, a temporary exhibition, *Alexander Pechersky as a Symbol of Resistance against Fascism*, opened at the Victory Museum in Moscow on May 11, 2018.[83] Thus the portrayal of the Holocaust in the Soviet historiography made a full circle. The only new element in the traditional depiction of Jews as one of many Soviet constituents victimized by Nazis is the attempt to integrate Soviet prisoners of war into the story. Indeed, imprisonment of Soviet soldiers and officers by the Germans had remained a stigma for the Soviet Union's duration. Even here, however, the hidden agenda comes to the fore: the heroic Pechersky is the antipode of the treacherous Vlasov, whose image of a quintessential traitor is cast in stone (as exemplified by the vicious campaign against Kirill Alexandrov's doctoral dissertation). Essentially, what counts most for the authorities is Pechersky's uniform: that of a lieutenant of the Red Army.

It is worth noting that the Russian *Sobibor* came out three decades after the British TV film *Escape from Sobibor* and sixteen years after Claude Lanzmann's documentary on the same subject. What is also left publicly untold is that Pechersky fell victim to Stalin's antisemitisim in the late 1940s and early 1950s, and that he was consistently prevented from testifying at war crimes trials abroad, including the Nuremberg Tribunal and the Eichmann trial. The Order of Merit of the Republic of Poland posthumously awarded to Pechersky in 2013 is much more significant than the Russian Order of Courage awarded by Putin's decree in 2016. A monument honoring Pechersky opened in Tel Aviv in 2012, and a memorial plaque and a monument in his native Rostov-on-Don only in 2017 and 2018, respectively. What is most significant, however, is not the personality of Pechersky or even the movie, but everything that was happening around it.

Insofar as the Second World War is painted in heroic colors in Russia, the Sobibor uprising fits the bill. Hence, the Alexander Pechersky Foundation made a connection between the "Battle of Sobibor" and the "main Victory."[84] The Alexander Pechersky Foundation was formally registered as a nonprofit organization in June 2017.[85] The foundation's website takes visitors directly to *Sobibor*'s promotional material. According to the mission statement, the foundation traces its origin to an international reference group convened in 2011 by Ilya Vasiliev for the purpose of committing Pechersky and his feat to memory. In addition, the foundation sets an overlapping goal of preserving the memory of the "heroism of Soviet prisoners or war," victims of the Holocaust, victims of Nazi camps, "heroes of antifascist resistance," and "millions of peaceful Soviet citizens" generally.[86] In contradiction to the official website, the media has reported that the foundation was established on the initiative of Pechersky's descendants (i.e., his granddaughter). Either way, the foundation's source of funding has not been revealed. Among its partner institutions the Pechersky Foundation lists RVIO and the ministry of culture.

The foundation has a director and a president, yet it is effectively run by Vasiliev in his capacity as head of the board of trustees. At first look, Vasiliev is an odd choice for the foundation's spokesman. Born in Russia, like many other Jews he has emigrated to Israel, where at one point he served as advisor to the Israeli minister of information. He is trained as a political scientist, with a doctoral dissertation on the factor of religion in Israeli politics. According to Vasiliev, it was he who first drew Putin's attention to Pechersky and his role in the Sobibor uprising during the former's official visit to Israel in 2012. In history diplomacy conducted by Russia vis-à-vis Israel, Vasiliev has been playing the role of a bad cop. Hence, Vasiliev has been pestering Yad Vashem for not doing enough in acknowledging Pechersky's centrality—an "outrageous devil-may-care attitude to the incredible story of the prisoner escape from Sobibor," to quote him. When Russian Defense Minister Shoigu visited Yad Vashem during his trip to Israel in October 2017, he inquired if the museum had an exhibition on Jews who served in the Red Army ranks. Vasiliev describes Yad Vashem's response as a lame excuse, not unlike the oblivion into which Pechersky and his deed were cast during the Soviet times. Subsequently, Vasiliev threatened to raise this issue with the American donors of the museum.[87]

Occasionally referred to in the Russian Jewish press as a "historian," Vasiliev came to embrace the self-promoted image of safe-keeper of Pechersky's memory. He even argued that *Sobibor* was based on "his" 2013 book, which is a mere reprint of Pechersky's 1945 memoirs, with the short introduction written by somebody else.[88] As Vasiliev kept appearing in various news programs in Russia and Israel, the nascent foundation he is heading was now said to have existed for six years. To keep up the heat, Vasiliev sharpened his rhetoric. He now argued that the Sobibor uprising was as significant as the Warsaw uprising, and that Yad Vashem was perpetuating a traditional Israeli stereotype, according to which "no Samson or Judas Maccabeus could ever be born in the Diaspora." School graduates in Israel, lamented Vasiliev, believe that the Second World War was won by Roosevelt and Churchill and know nothing about the one million Jews (actually half that number) who fought against the Nazis within the Red Army ranks.[89]

The annual Immortal Regiment parade in Moscow, which reportedly brought together a record one million participants in 2018, featured a group carrying placards with the heading "Sobibor" and the RVIO logo in the corner. A hundred or so people in the group—descendants of Sobibor prisoners who now live in different countries—were invited by the Alexander Pechersky Foundation.[90] The granddaughter of Alexander Pechersky appeared on the talk show Vremia pokazhet (time will show) on Channel One. When asked if she found the movie historically accurate, she vaguely replied that she knew it was a motion picture. The talk show host, Anatoly Kuzichev, used the expression "Polish death camps," immediately restating it as "German death camps in Poland." What he wanted to know most was the reaction of the people who had seen the movie. He emphasized that the film is noncommercial and simultaneously boasted how well it had done at the box office. The audience and the host spoke of a "war film"; the word *Jew* was not mentioned even once.[91]

So why a Russian film about the Holocaust and why now? Presented as a "military drama," the shooting of the film with a working title *Legenda o pobege* (a legendary escape) began in September 2016 in Lithuania, of all places. The film's sponsorship by the RVIO is strong enough an indicator that *Sobibor* has to do with history politics. *Sobibor*'s plot can be formulated as follows: the Russians came and taught the Jews how to fight for their freedom.[92] The larger issue at stake is confronting the consistent anti-Russian position taken by neighboring Poland and simultaneously nurturing Russian–Israeli relations.

In 2007 the Polish state memorial site Sobibor had established an international steering committee comprised of Poland, Slovakia, the Netherlands—the countries the Jewish prisoners mainly came from—plus Israel. Having failed to secure additional financial pledges from countries like Germany, by 2013 the museum could no longer operate. That same year, according to Russian officials, but disputed by Polish authorities, Russia received an invitation to serve on the steering committee and subsequently agreed to share the costs of building a new memorial complex on the former campgrounds. Minister of Culture Medinskii marked Holocaust Remembrance Day in 2016 with a visit to Sobibor. When concrete plans for a new museum were unveiled in late spring 2017, however, Russia was not mentioned as a steering committee member. To add insult to injury, on June 22 (the choice of the date was not coincidental), the Polish Parliament adopted an amendment to the law banning propaganda of totalitarianism. The amendment prescribed the removal of all Soviet-related monuments, including those to the Red Army. As regards the Sobibor memorial, Polish officials argued that the steering committee had been functioning successfully for ten years, that the decision had been taken unanimously by the committee members, that the museum was already under construction, and that the concept for the exhibition had been approved. Hence, there was no need for injecting further members. Otherwise, stated the Polish ministry of culture and national heritage, Russian representatives had been invited to be part of the ceremony marking the seventy-fifth anniversary of the Sobibor uprising.[93] The Russian foreign ministry issued a strong rebuttal, which stated:

> We see this decision as unethical in terms of the historical truth. It is hard to deny that Russia's involvement in building a new Sobibor memorial and museum is absolutely justified. There is no rational explanation for ignoring historic facts and this must not go unnoticed by the global community. The intention to prevent Russia from participating in the project is part of Warsaw's openly demonstrated anti-Russia sentiment and Poland's attempts to impose its own understanding of history by belittling the Soviet Union's and the Red Army's role as liberators during WWII.[94]

Earlier, the foreign ministry spokesperson, Zakharova, had lashed out at Israel, essentially accusing it of betrayal. The ambassadors of Israel, Slovakia, and the Netherlands were, in mid-August, summoned to explain the decision to continue work on the new museum without Russia's participation—"an outrageous fact of historical amnesia."[95] The reaction of Zakharova, who is typically poised when spitting venom, is remarkable in its own right. She appeared genuinely upset, like in a situation when one side in match-fixing does not communicate properly with the other. Vasiliev of the Pechersky Foundation further speculated that the Israeli member on the Sobibor museum steering committee did not actively vouch for Russia due to his role as chairman of the Yad Vashem board of directors. Israel found itself in hot water, for just the previous month President Putin had announced that Russia would start paying lifelong pensions to the veterans of the Great Patriotic War residing in Israel (i.e., an estimated four thousand former Soviet/Russian citizens). Rather symbolic, monthly allowances of up to 1,000 rubles (USD 16) would be paid out to war veterans beginning in January 2018; former Nazi camp prisoners are entitled to only half that allowance, that is, USD 8.[96] This initiative belongs under Putin's plan to provide "geopolitical and political assistance to the veterans of the Great Patriotic War in Russia and abroad."[97] Prime Minister Netanyahu, who was meeting Putin at Sochi on August 23, 2017, hastily reaffirmed Israel's support for Russia's membership. Both the Israeli Parliament and he personally, said Netanyahu, will always remember the important role that Russia and the Soviet Army played in the defeat of Nazism.[98]

Meanwhile, the Russian authorities kept arguing about trifles. They expressed general concern that the information in the new exhibition might not be presented accurately. Another issue was the language. As in other Polish museums, the exhibition text would be available in Polish and English. This, the Polish side explained away by practical considerations: there are barely any Russian tourists visiting the site; there are still more tourists coming from Germany and yet no information in German is available, unfortunately. Yulia Markova, director of the Alexander Pechersky Foundation in Russia, begged to differ: the entrance to the Sobibor memorial complex until recently featured bronze plaques with inscriptions in eight different languages, none of them Russian. She claimed this was a deliberate omission on the part of the Polish authorities. The plaques, countered the spokesperson for the State Museum at Majdanek, had been taken down already in 2014 and would not be part of the new museum. Baruch Gorin, the spokesperson for the Federation of Jewish Communities of Russia, backed up Zakharova and the foreign ministry by stating that the exclusion of Russia from the decision-making process on the new Sobibor museum was an "example of the war on memory."[99]

The Russian ambassador in Tel Aviv promptly commented that Israel and Russia have the "responsibility . . . to join and strengthen the efforts on an international arena in the fight against the growing attempts to falsify history" and that he is convinced *Sobibor* is "bound to be a potent antifascist statement."[100] Netanyahu was the only foreign leader, besides select leaders of the Soviet rump states and Serbian President Aleksandar Vučić, who participated in the May 9, 2018, festivities in Moscow. *Sobibor*, the film and the museum, might, or might not, have been mentioned in informal conversations Netanyahu held in Russia. The controversial Holocaust legislation passed in Poland on February 6, 2018, caused an uproar around the world, and particularly in Israel. Among other things, the amendment criminalizes claims that Poland is co-responsible for the crimes committed by the Nazis (e.g., references to "Polish death camps"). The main reason for Netanyahu's visit to Moscow was rather different, though, namely securing Russia's pledge of noninterference in the event of air strikes by Israel against Iranian targets in Syria. That Netanyahu apparently received, as Israeli jets carried out a series of bomb raids the very next day, destroying, among others, a number of Russian-built missile launchers.

The efforts by the Russian state to cash in on *Sobibor* politically are all too obvious. Most fascinating, perhaps, is the attempt to inject the state-commissioned movie— the fact that reflects on the way the story is told—into international Holocaust commemoration. The first screening of *Sobibor* took place on January 27, 2018, in the Jewish Museum and Tolerance Center in Moscow in the presence of Putin and Netanyahu. That particular date, reminded Putin, marks two important events—the liberation of Auschwitz and the lifting of the German siege of Leningrad—whose victims he put on the same plane as far as their suffering is concerned. As he had done numerous times before, Putin did not fail to mention that several hundred thousand among the murdered European Jews were Soviet citizens and that Pechersky was a Soviet prisoner of war in the rank of lieutenant. In a circumspect way, Putin likened the present manifestations of antisemitism and Russophobia to the Nazi theory of racial superiority. Israel and Russia work hand in hand to counter the revision of history of the Second World War, against Holocaust denial and belittling the role of the Soviet Union in the victory over Nazi Germany, Putin said. Netanyahu, responded in kind, mentioning the Natanya memorial and the institution of the 26 Iyar holiday among other reverential history-based acts of Israel vis-vis Russia. Though, predictably, the prime minister of Israel spent most of the time talking about the significance of countering antisemitism.[101] To mark the occasion, Rossiia One reported that a street in Moscow (actually a stretch of the highway going out of Moscow) will be named in honor of Pechersky.[102]

During the exclusive screening of *Sobibor* in the Duma on April 10, Vasiliev personally thanked President Putin for taking the memorialization efforts to a qualitatively new level, both inside Russia and internationally. He proposed approaching the parliaments of Poland, Slovakia, the Czech Republic, France, and the Netherlands with the request to bestow on Pechersky their respective national honors posthumously. On top of that, he suggested pushing for a Europe-wide resolution designating October 14 as the day

Figure 14 The Holocaust as a story of Soviet heroism. Russian president Vladimir Putin and Israel prime minister Benjamin Netanyahu (not seen in the photo) watching a preview of the Russian blockbuster, *Sobibor*, at the recently built Jewish Museum and Tolerance Center in Moscow, January 29, 2018. Konstantin Khabensky, center on the screen, is playing the role of Alexander Pechersky in the movie.

marking the victory of good over evil.[103] The idea fell on fertile ground, and so the following month such a request was made during the film screening in Bratislava.[104]

The following day, the film was screened as part of a Russia–Israel satellite linkup between the Knesset and the Duma. The date, April 11, was deliberately chosen as it marks the eve of Yom Hashoah (Holocaust Memorial Day) in Israel. In Moscow, the tone of the conversation was set up by the chairperson of the Federation Council, Valentina Matvienko. In her introductory speech she mentioned the initiative of the Federation Council, which had requested the United Nations to proclaim the victory over Nazism a part of world heritage. The discussion then swiftly turned to falsification of history and the refusal to inject Russia in the steering committee of the Sobibor memorial. Israeli participants, in fluent Russian, let their counterparts know that Jerusalem and Moscow were in full agreement on these and similar issues. Subsequently, Matvienko proposed establishing a joint Russian–Israeli commission to monitor instances of falsification of history. Specifically mentioned—mainly within the context of demolition of Soviet war monuments—were Poland, Ukraine, and the Baltic States. Konstantin Kosachev, chairman of the Federation Council's Foreign Affairs Committee, speculated that, had a monument to Pechersky been erected in socialist Poland, it would probably have been razed by now.[105]

Next, Russian embassies around the world apparently received a command from Moscow to arrange a screening of *Sobibor* locally. Among the institutions contacted, within a week after Duma members got to see the movie, was the Norwegian Holocaust Center in Oslo. The center declined the offer on the grounds that it normally does not screen movies as part of its public programs. No information is available if any other similar institution in Europe agreed to screen *Sobibor*. Subsequently, the foreign ministry took Khabensky and his artistic creation on a world tour. Whenever the movie traveled, the question lingered as to whether it was a part of the Russian history politics. The answer, implicitly given, is "yes." The world premiere of the movie took place on April 23 in Warsaw. On the occasion, the defense ministry's TV channel, Zvezda, presented the Sobibor uprising as "one of the most dramatic episodes of the Great Patriotic War."[106] A week later, the movie was screened in a closed event at the Russian embassy in Washington, DC. Among the invited guests in Washington were State Department and USHMM officials, whom the Russian ambassador urged to protect the memory of the Second World War, including by means of movies. Khabensky expressed the belief that the American audiences would "get" his motion picture.[107] On May 4 *Sobibor* premiered at the UN Headquarters in New York. The international audience of the movie was rather modest: diplomats from China, Israel, Belarus, Uzbekistan, and Tunis.[108] To double down, an exhibition in conjunction with the end of the Second World War opened in the building's lobby on May 9. The exhibition featured panels by nine CIS states. The one by Russia was prepared by RVIO and contained information on the Sobibor death camp and the famous revolt. UN Secretary General António Gutteres did not realize he was unwittingly playing along with the Russians when he stated during the opening that "the Soviet Union made the biggest military contribution to the defeat of Nazism . . . [and that] the memory of those who defeated Nazism in 1945 will help defeat any manifestations of Neo Nazism today." The original exhibit on Sobibor had been displayed by RVIO several months earlier at the Kazan train station in Moscow and inside a Moscow–Rostov-on-Don train.[109]

Khabensky, sporting the St. George's ribbon, was also present at the screening of *Sobibor* in Berlin on May 9. In two hours' time, when the movie will be over, victory fireworks will go off in Moscow he announced.[110] At the press conference that followed, he insisted that *Sobibor* had no political underpinning. The Russian ambassador to Berlin, with whom he shared the podium, however, contradicted Khabensky. A movie ingrained in history (*s serioznym istoricheskim podtekstom*) such as *Sobibor* cannot not have a political component, argued Sergei Nechaev. This movie is not anti-German, though, but anti-fascist and anti-Nazi.[111] Among other places and countries, the movie was also shown in the Council of Europe in Strasbourg and at the Cannes Film Festival. General Director of the Federal Agency on Culture and Cinematography (Roskino), Ekaterina Mtsituridze, made the underlining idea of *Sobibor* clear: "Those who saw the film got it. Everyone understands that we're talking not about the past war but about the current situation. Russia comes with peace, and that's very important."[112] Sergei Medvedev of Rossotrudnichestvo—a federal agency tasked with "spreading objective information about Russia abroad"—went into further detail. He found the movie very topical and volunteered an example: the shots of Jews being led to a gas chamber reminded him of those of pro-Russian activists who died in the fire in Odessa on May 2, 2014. Both instances have the same roots, he contended, and watching the movie may help explain why we should prevent another Odessa and acts of terrorism. He compared the interest shown by international distributors to *Sobibor* to the growing number of foreign editions of the Immortal Regiment.[113]

Of all the individuals mentioned in this chapter, Khabensky owes the state the least in terms of a successful career. After all is said and done, he tried his best as both film director and actor to convey the horrors of the Holocaust. The problem is that, in the absence of a nonpartisan, professionally executed and comprehensively implemented Holocaust education program in Russia, his personal efforts ran into the sand. Khabensky was visibly upset by the question from a female St. Petersburg reporter, who inquired how the younger, unprepared audience might react to *Sobibor*. "Do you think people are stupid?" he snapped.[114] Unfortunately, Khabensky has been proven wrong. To begin with, the movie did not do as well as expected at the box office. In the worst Soviet tradition, schoolchildren were coerced to collectively watch *Sobibor*. Middle and high school students from cities across Russia—Perm, Sarapul, Nizhnevartovsk, Marks, and others—reported on obligatory group trips to movie theaters ordered by the school administration, and typically paid for by the students themselves. In Nevinnomyssk, schools bought out entire shows in the city's only movie theater. Individual teachers vaguely explained the mandatory screening of *Sobibor* by the need to "remember and respect . . . those who sacrificed their lives for you." The punishment for no-show varied from reprimand to bad grades to denial of sitting for final exams. Exposing Russian youth to "patriotic" films around May 9 has become a tradition; in 2018 "patriotism" became infused with the Holocaust, though only implicitly. When asked by students why they had to watch this particular movie, a teacher in Perm replied, "It's Russian and it's about the war."[115]

The politicized representation of the Holocaust simply does not fit in the historical picture internalized by ordinary Russians. Generally, whenever the Nazi mass murder of the Jews is alluded to publicly, it comes across as awkward. For example, on May 9, 2015, in Syktyvkar, the Holocaust became a part of a theatrical performance staged right after the parade on the city's main square. A group of teenagers dressed up in striped pajamas moved zombie-like across the square. As a way of explanation, the performers carried boards with the names of Nazi death camps. A peculiar way, indeed, to commemorate the six million lives lost.[116]

Pechersky and his surviving descendants are nothing but pawns in the Kremlin's grand game. As Vasiliev has explained, the goal is to make the "Soviet war hero Pechersky . . . into a universal symbol." The host of the televised roundtable in which Vasiliev had taken part reformulated it as an open-ended question: Would people in the West stop razing monuments to the Soviet soldier after they had watched *Sobibor*?[117] The Sobibor uprising is commemorated on a postage stamp and is now part of the school curriculum. In conjunction with the film release, RVIO published an edited volume, *Sobibor: Khronika vostaniia v lagere smerti* (Sobibor: a chronicle of the uprising in a death camp). A coeditor and head of the History of Motherland Foundation, Konstantin Mogilevskii, was not apologetic about exploiting the interest generated by the film (the book features a screenshot from the film on the front cover). In a video interview given to RIA news agency, Mogilevskii stressed that the camp guard was composed of ethnic Ukrainians and that those Jewish prisoners who had decided to hide in Poland in the aftermath of the successful escape were subsequently betrayed by the Poles. In conjunction with the recent Polish legislation on the Holocaust and the removal of Soviet war memorials, it all leads to falsification of the memory of the Second World War, he said. Mogilevskii ultimately blamed the ruling Polish government and "propagandists" for corrupting the notion of good and evil, for equating the crimes of the Nazis and the Soviets. Mogilevskii did not use the word *Holocaust* (or *Katastrofa*, commonly used in Russia) during the interview; according to him, the Sobibor uprising belongs to the "popular memory of the Great Patriotic War."[118]

In the fall of 2018 Russian lawmakers were considering promulgation of an official date commemorating the Sobibor uprising.[119] The Russian authorities, flanked by the chairman of the Alexander Pechersky Foundation, were also lobbying with the Council of Europe to declare October 14 a pan-European date honoring the "heroic deed of the Soviet officer, Alexander Pechersky." The appeal was accompanied by the now standard evocation against the resurgence of Nazism and the importance of remembering the "lessons of the Second World War for a peaceful development of Europe."[120] In short, the movie *Sobibor* is part and parcel of the Russian propaganda campaign fought by means of history. Pushing an agenda through a movie about the Holocaust (without qualifying it as such) is as devious an act as sending a physically disabled female singer (who happened to support the Russian annexation of Crimea) to the 2017 Eurovision song contest held in Kiev, Ukraine. Any negative reaction would, and did, provoke righteous anger from Russia, putting potential critics in a fix.

The brazenness with which the Russian government pushes its agenda on the Holocaust borders on ignorance. There is a series of questions that the unprecedented promotion of *Sobibor* prompts. Why the shift of focus from the Soviet liberation of Auschwitz on January 27, 1945, to the Pechersky-led uprising at Sobibor on October 14, 1943? After all, it is January 27 that the United Nations designated in 2005 as International Holocaust Remembrance Day. That alone makes a recent call on the Council of Europe to establish an official date commemorating the 1943 event superfluous. The Russian state media and its foreign-language services make it sound as if between the British (*a priori* imperfect) 1987 TV film *Escape from Sobibor* and the Russian 2018 motion picture *Sobibor* nothing has happened within the genre of Holocaust movies. As far as the cinematic quality is concerned, Khabensky's *Sobibor* is no match for Spielberg's 1992 *Schindler's List*, Nemes's 2015 *Son of Saul*, Polanski's 2002 *Pianist*, or even Benigni's 1997 *Life is Beautiful*. A masterpiece, it certainly is not. Instead, *Sobibor* features numerous cinematic borrowings from Hollywood, including what have now become clichés (e.g., the arrival of a train with prisoners). Khabensky serves a dose of horror interspersed with heroism, with little nuance or variation. When it comes to historical accuracy, none of the Russian court historians who were involved in the film production and/or promotion have the relevant expertise. Medinskii's doctoral thesis examined how foreigners in the sixteenth and seventeenth century misinterpreted Russia's realities, Mogilevskii's analyzed Stolypin's reforms in the late Tsarist Empire, and Vasiliev's studied the aspect of religion in Israeli politics. No surprise, then, that Mogilevskii believes the Soviet Extraordinary Commission records is a "new" and ultimate source on the history of the Sobibor camp while Vasiliev tries to teach Yad Vashem how to present that history. In short, all of these individuals are uniquely unqualified in their self-imposed role. By way of example, a study of the Auschwitz death camp featuring an illustration from *Schindler's List* would automatically put it in the category of popular history; that is what the publication jointly released by RVIO and the History of Motherland Foundation have done with respect to Sobibor.

The hype around *Sobibor* in the Russian media obscures other, earlier efforts at artistic representation of the Holocaust in Russia. Here I mean specifically Konstantin Fam's short film trilogy *Witnesses*, the last installment of which was released in the summer of 2017. Although Fam did receive his share of criticism for using too much symbolism in his work, the three shorts—especially the first, *Shoes*, from 2012—got much praise internationally. One can only speculate as to why Khabensky and *Sobibor* but not Fam and *Witnesses*. Is it because Fam was born and spent his childhood in Ukraine while Khabensky entirely in Russia? Is it the fact that the first two shorts, *Shoes* and *Brutus*, were joint productions with countries like Poland and Ukraine, respectively? Or perhaps because Fam's shorts fit the category of art film while Khabensky's is a blockbuster? Khabensky, a famous actor, versus Fam, a little-known independent film director? Still, the main reason is likely this: Khabensky effectively received a state commission while Fam came to the subject of the film through a personal journey. Consequently, *Sobibor* pushes all the right buttons of Russian history politics while *Witnesses* do what the film title suggests.

In September 2018, as widely expected, the Russian Oscar committee nominated *Sobibor* in the category of best foreign-language film.[121] By then, it had been distributed in fifty countries. When the American Film Academy announced the contenders three months later, *Sobibor* was not among the nine movies shortlisted for this particular category. Was an Oscar the *Sobibor*'s ultimate raison d'être? Whatever the answer, in the aftermath of the announcement, the movie, its main actor, and the very Holocaust theme slipped from the headlines. The only time it came up again, briefly, was in March 2019, when the ministry of defense bestowed on Khabensky and the *Sobibor* film crew an arts and culture award (another laureate that year was Vasily Lanovoi for his work on promoting the Immortal Regiment).[122]

Memory of the Holocaust as a Weapon

By now the Kremlin has grown accustomed to blending the Holocaust into current politics. To give a recent example, on Yom Hashoah, 2018, Netanyahu spoke with Putin over the phone. Putin did mind the recent Israeli airstrike in Homs province and called for safeguarding Syria's sovereignty. Netanyahu tried to sweeten the bitter pill by saying that Israel was going, for the first time ever, to officially mark the Victory Day, that is, 26 Iyar, on May 9. Both leaders agreed on the need to counter the attempts to falsify history.[123] Russia has assumed the same air of moral superiority with respect to the Holocaust that it has long assumed with regard to the Second World War generally. In 2005, the Russian Federation supported Israel's UN resolution honoring the victims of the Holocaust, the resolution that led to the establishment of International Holocaust Remembrance Day on January 27.[124] Contemporary Russian media reports, however, sometimes give the honor exclusively to Russia.

On May 22, 2019, the Russian deputy foreign minister presented a temporary exhibition, *The Holocaust: Annihilation, Liberation, Rescue*, in the Argentine National Assembly. Taking Sobibor and Auschwitz as the point of departure, the exhibition tells the story of the liberation of Nazi camps by the Red Army. The exhibition advances a twofold thesis, namely that 45 percent of Holocaust victims had perished on Soviet soil (without mentioning that the bulk of the murdered Jews came from the territories annexed by the Soviet Union in 1940–41) and that Soviet soldiers sacrificed their lives for saving Jews (extrapolating from the example of the 350 military men who died in the battle of City of Auschwitz).[125] After a month-long engagement in the Holocaust Museum of Buenos Aires, the exhibition traveled to Uruguay. The exhibition was organized by the Russian Center for Holocaust and Genocide History (established in 2016) headed by Ilya Altman, in cooperation with the Russian Jewish Congress. During the opening of the exhibition, a top Russian diplomat described it as "our yet another contribution to the massive efforts aimed at safeguarding the truth about and tragic pages of the war" and referred to the Holocaust as "one of the most heinous crimes against humanity." Once again, one may wonder why the Russians decided to bring the exhibition all the way to South America. The deputy foreign minister has indirectly answered this question by praising Argentina's support for the Russian-sponsored UN Resolution 67/154, "Glorification of Nazism."[126] Besides, Argentina boasts the largest Jewish and Russian communities in South America.[127] Dispatching to Argentina a temporary exhibition documenting the role of the Soviet Army in the liberation of

Nazi death camps pursues the same objective as giving a loan to Venezuela. That goal is extending Russia's influence abroad and, on the sidelines, sticking it to the West.

That exhibition is the result of a research project, "Liberators" carried out by the Altman-run center at the Russian State University for the Humanities in Moscow. The project encourages students and professionals to examine the fate of individual Red Army servicemen who entered the Auschwitz campgrounds on January 27, 1945. Featuring some seventy original photographs, documents, and drawings, the exhibition was unveiled on January 20, 2017, in Moscow. Since then it has traveled to the United Nations in New York, the Parliaments of Austria, Slovakia, and the Czech Republic, the Israel Knesset, and Queen Mary University of London. Following a short tour of South America, the exhibition headed to Europe, with stopovers in the Council of Europe in Strasbourg and UNESCO in Paris. According to Altman, it was the Russian ambassador in Argentina, who in May 2016 suggested that the "Liberators" project—which until then was confined to Russia—take on an international dimension.[128] Foreign Minister Lavrov, who gave a speech at the opening ceremony in Moscow, used the Holocaust as the backdrop to his main thesis. Taking cues from the Soviet propaganda toolkit, Lavrov linked the Nazi genocide to an "ideology of misanthropy." He commented approvingly on teaching the history of the Holocaust in school, which should make the Russian youth respect both the Nazi victims and the "heroic deeds of those who stamped out that horrible phenomenon."

> Unfortunately, we have to admit that in many countries today, including those calling themselves developed democracies, essentially is going on exoneration of Nazism, celebration of Hitlerites and their stooges, rewriting history for narrow expedience reasons. Particularly troubling is the dirty war on monuments, in the course of which a number of European Union countries are destroying and defiling monuments to the Red Army soldiers who sacrificed their life in the name of liberation of concentration camp prisoners, in the name of saving Europe from "brown plague."
>
> All this is not only deeply immoral but also in violation of the UN Charter and other international documents. Let me remind you that the last year we marked 70 years of the Nuremberg Tribunal which, for the first time in history, sentenced for war crimes and crimes against humanity those who were responsible for unleashing the Second World War. The Tribunal judgement clearly and unequivocally established who stood on the side of good and who on the side of evil. Russia will continue resisting the efforts to revisit that judgment.

At the end of his speech, Lavrov reported on his earlier conversations with the Russian Jewish Congress on the matter of showing the exhibition abroad, including in the UN Headquarters. That would help preserve the historical memory of both the war horrors and the Soviet contribution to rescuing the Jews of Europe. In pursuit of that goal, Lavrov promised, the foreign ministry was ready to cooperate with Jewish organizations in Russia and abroad.[129]

At the moment there are just a handful of organizations and/or research units in Russia that work specifically on the Holocaust, all of them in Moscow. The honor goes to the just-mentioned Ilya Altman, the pioneer of Holocaust studies in Russia. Due to the peculiarities of Soviet and post-Soviet Jewish history, Holocaust research, education, and commemoration in Russia had traditionally been linked to major international Jewish organizations. Consequently, the way the Holocaust is being taught and presented at Yad Vashem in Jerusalem has become a golden standard of sorts. Back in 1992 Altman cofounded the Russian Holocaust Center, and twenty years later he published a major overview of the Holocaust in the German-occupied Soviet territories (in Russian). Altman served as the editor of an unabridged version of the famous *Black Book* (1993) and the encyclopedia of the Holocaust in the Soviet Union (2009). Since 2009 Altman has been teaching at the Russian State University for the Humanities where he established a Program in Holocaust and Genocide History, the first and only such in Russia.

Altman and his fellow Holocaust historians in Russia are forced to perform a balancing act that ultimately puts their professional integrity on the line. On the one hand, governmental grants supporting research on lesser known aspects of the Holocaust such as camp liberation is a welcome sign. Making use of state assistance in the dissemination of research both nationally and internationally is also a boon, in ideal circumstances, that is. No historian, or any other professional for that matter, in Russia can plead ignorance that the state is using the results of their work for political purposes.[130] Altman knows it firsthand. After all, his Holocaust Center along with Shpigel's World without Nazism stood behind the establishment of the Historical Memory Foundation in Moscow in 2008.

Furthermore, the state support does not go beyond a select few entities such as the Museum of Tolerance or Altman's center. In the eyes of the mid-level bureaucrats, the study of the Holocaust is "unpatriotic." That is what a historian from Briansk, Ekaterina Derevianko, was told point-blank. For the past ten years or so, Derevianko has been doing research on local collaboration in the Nazi mass murder of Jews (thanks to her efforts, a local history museum now features a section on the Holocaust). According to certain Briansk officials, what she describes on the basis of archival documents does not "meet the challenges facing the contemporary Russian society in need of a heroic history." Notably, some commentators reject the very fact of individual Russian complicity in Nazi genocide on the dubious logic that it was the Soviet Union that liberated death camps and ultimately saved the world from fascism.[131]

Due to the peculiarity of the Russian memory laws, books on the Nazi mass murder of the Jews withdrawn from circulation include both denialist and antisemitic treatises and Holocaust literature classics. Thus, the Extremist Materials list run by the ministry of justice contains the Russian translations of Ivor Benson's *The Zionist Factor: The Jewish Impact on Twentieth-Century History* and Jürgen Graf's *The Myth of the Holocaust: The Truth About the Fate of the Jews in the Second World War* (as a supplement to the right-wing *Russkii Vestnik*). Simultaneously, authorities in 2015 confiscated copies of an international bestseller, Art Spiegelman's *Maus: A Survivor's Tale*—due to a swastika featured on the front cover.

Whenever the exhibition created by Altman and his team has traveled, the accompanying message has been something other than documenting the final phase of the Holocaust. In the Czech Republic, where the exhibition went on display on April 17, 2018, the emphasis was on the "indissoluble link between the liberation of the Nazi 'death factories' Auschwitz and Therezin (Theresienstadt) and the heroism of the Soviet soldiers-liberators of the First Ukrainian Army under the command of Marshall of the Soviet Union I. S. Konev, whose monument had been erected in Prague."[132] The level of detail alludes to the fate of the repeatedly vandalized Konev statue, which was eventually removed, in April 2020. The Nazi mass murder of Jews had not been part of these debates, until Russian officials brought it up, that is.

Proving that Russia has been evoking the Holocaust vis-à-vis its neighbors instrumentally is relatively easy. Nearly all references in conjunction with the Holocaust through 2014 had been to Latvia and Estonia. One may wonder why the Russian government would not mention in the same breath also Lithuania. After all, nearly three times as many Jews were murdered in Lithuania (195,000) than in Latvia (70,000) and twenty-two times more than in Estonia (8,614). Proportionally, more Jews perished in Lithuania than in Latvia, while the general levels of antisemitism were also higher in the former. More significant, brutalities committed by ethnic Lithuanians against local Jews in the summer of 1941 (e.g., the notorious Lietūkis garage massacre in Kaunas on June 27) have been meticulously documented. If the Russian state genuinely wanted to draw attention to local collaboration in the Nazi mass murder of the Jews in the Baltic, it ought to have brought up Lithuania. The key factor, once again, is Waffen SS. Attempts by the Nazis in 1943 to raise a Waffen SS division among Lithuanians—whom they trusted politically and regarded racially much less than they did Estonian and Latvians—fell miserably.[133] Consequently, there were no major Lithuanian-staffed military units facing up to the Soviets on the Eastern Front. It is the efforts to undo the consequences of the Molotov–Ribbentrop Pact—militarily in 1943–44, and politically, legally, and psychologically since 1991—that the Putin regime had held against the Baltic States, now also with reference to the Holocaust.

Consider yet another obvious inconsistency. While sparring with Poland over the substance and representation of the Holocaust, Russia has kept mum about the controversial amendment passed in January 2018, popularly known as the "Polish Holocaust law." The foreign ministry spokesperson refused to comment on the new Polish law.[134] When Zakharova got a similar question from the press, she engaged in a long-winding tirade that dwelled on revision of the results of the Second World War, the Nuremberg trial, the removal of monuments to the Soviet soldier—anything but the Holocaust and the ill-founded law.[135] Given the pattern of rhetoric emanating from the Kremlin, one would expect the Russian authorities to jump upon this opportunity to further stick it to the Poles. Yet they did not. This may have to do with the part of the amendment less frequently discussed in the media. Article 2a condemns crimes committed by Ukrainian nationalists and members of the Ukrainian units within the German Army and the police against Jews and ethnic Poles in Volhynia and Lesser Poland. As stated, the Ukrainians carried out genocide against the Poles. In effect, the new Polish amendment takes specific aim at Ukraine, which cannot but be appreciated in Moscow. Hence, in this particular case, the Putin regime apparently concluded that a historical reference to atrocities committed by Ukrainian nationalists against the Poles and the Jews was worth its silence on the issue of the Holocaust in occupied Poland.

Equally remarkable is Russia's position, or rather the lack thereof, vis-à-vis International Holocaust Remembrance Alliance (IHRA). That organization, under a different name, came into existence in the wake of the 2000 Stockholm Declaration on the Holocaust. Tasked with fostering international cooperation on Holocaust education, remembrance, and research, the organization currently boasts forty-two member states, including eleven in the rank of observer and liaison countries. The Russian foreign ministry made mention of the international forum at Stockholm and Swedish Prime Minister Göran Persson on whose initiative it had been convened as early as 2004.[136] Although IHRA is an intergovernmental organization with national delegations coordinated through the respective foreign ministries, Moscow chose to denigrate it to the level of an NGO.[137] I asked the Russian ambassador in Oslo during his courtesy visit to the Norwegian Holocaust Center in February 2018 why Russia has not joined IHRA until now. The ambassador expressed his amazement at the question, for he said he had never heard of such an international body. In view of the disproportionate attention paid to the Holocaust in recent years in the official quarters, the only plausible explanation as to Russia's unwillingness to seek membership in IHRA is that Moscow does not regard it an ideal conduit for its long-term strategy within history politics. This, too, is a continuation of the time-honored Soviet policy of advancing the state's agenda through various front organizations over which it can exercise direct control.[138]

Yad Vashem has been running a database of the Righteous among the Nations—individuals who had rescued Jews during the Holocaust. Out of 27,362 individuals on the list, 209 are from Russia. For Eastern Europe, the largest number of rescuers is registered for Poland (6,992), Ukraine (2,634), Lithuania (906), and Hungary (867).[139] Politicians in those and other countries are usually eager to participate in the award ceremonies held under the aegis of the Israel embassy—an easy way to show a commitment to the cause of preserving the memory of the Holocaust. President Putin, during his twenty years in power, has not been reported meeting individual Jewish survivors and/or their (few in number) rescuers outside of the context of the Soviet victory over Nazi Germany. Neither have lower-ranking government officials been spotted attending to Holocaust victims, unless so directed from the top. Whenever they appear at local commemorative events, it is usually in their individual rather than official capacities. In that respect, it has been no different from the conspicuous absence of state representatives in comparable ceremonies commemorating the victims of Stalin's terror. The regime takes notice of Jews—necessarily as a group—only when and where it fits its agenda.

Holocaust denial is typically rhymed in Russia with "belittling the decisive contribution of our country to the victory over fascism," which is a fallacy in its own right. If one can still make that logical connection, an extension to "falsification of substantive events in conjunction with the famine of 1932–1934 in the Soviet Union," is inexplicable, especially in the context of Russian–Israeli bilateral relations.[140] What Moscow actually means by that was spelled out by Foreign Minister Lavrov, who invited his Israeli counterpart, Avigdor Lieberman, to help Russia counter persistent claims by Ukraine that the 1932–33 famine—which affected most severely that particular Soviet republic—is an instance of genocide. The Holocaust, thus, is just a ruse.

Conclusion

The present Russian discourse on the Holocaust is surprisingly similar to the late Soviet one. The Holocaust is being instrumentalized, that is to say, references to the mass murder of Jews serve purposes other than an accurate historical representation or genuine commemoration. As historian Pavel Polian has sarcastically remarked: six million Jews, by the fact of having been murdered by fascists, became Russia's allies in the fight against neo-fascism.[141] Anti-methodology such as decontextualization and the use of inflated victim numbers is making a comeback. As a consequence, Jews are once again primarily identified by their nationality rather than their ethnicity and/or religion.[142] This evokes the generic designation of "peaceful Soviet citizens murdered by the fascists," which serves well the official narrative on Soviet victory in the Second World War. The portrayal of the Holocaust on the screen and in the exhibition hall is typically based on secondary sources, with no comprehensive primary research involved. To illustrate, it was not the Russian, but the French, scholars who had carried out comprehensive research in Russian archives, which resulted in an excellent exhibition, *Filming the War: The Soviets and the Holocaust, 1941–1946*, which went on display in Mémorial de la Shoah in Paris in 2015.[143] When it comes to the sources mined, the scope and depth of analysis, no comparable project has ever been attempted in Russia. Indeed, the professionalization of Holocaust research never came to be. Most of the scholars doing research on the Holocaust in Russia come from within the Jewish community. They have produced quality overviews, which nevertheless do not exceed national boundaries. In other words, no breakthrough has occurred that would amount to a significant contribution to Holocaust studies internationally. To put it still differently, Russian historians and their scholarship did not become integrated in Holocaust studies, not to mention the broader field of Holocaust and genocide studies.

Perhaps the most troubling aspect is the concerted effort by the Russian government to promote its take on the Holocaust internationally. Until recently, the focus on local collaboration in the Nazi genocide of the Jews served mainly to ruffle East Europeans' feathers. An element of the Holocaust currently emphasized by the Putin regime, namely the decisive role of the Red Army in the liberation of surviving Jewish prisoners, has a global appeal. Both local collaboration in the Holocaust and the liberation of Jewish camp inmates have been duly acknowledged as well as researched. It is true, though, that the sheer number of academic studies dealing with the former subject is significantly larger than that examining the latter. On that account alone, Russian authorities do have a point in giving the Red Army its due. The problem is that they are doing it in an un-nuanced manner, to the detriment of other aspects of the Holocaust specific to the German-occupied Soviet territories, and in pursuance of goals other than academic.

Individuals mentioned in this chapter—Kantor, Lazar, Boroda, Shpigel, Khabensky, Vasiliev, Tsereteli, Shcherbakov—who have been instrumental in projecting the official Russian position on the Holocaust abroad have all in one way or another benefited from state largesse (e.g., subsidies, grants, commissions, worldwide promotion). Wittingly or unwittingly, they have become a part of the patron-client system of governance instituted by Putin in Russia. Designated as NGOs, World without Nazism, the

Alexander Pechersky Foundation, RVIO, and similar outfits are actually GONGOs—government nongovernmental organizations, to use international affairs jargon. Their role is promoting the state agenda by means of manipulating public opinion. As journalist and author James Kirchick has pointedly argued with respect to a specific front organization: "By perverting and politicizing the memory of the Shoah—digging into the Stalinist playbook and labeling anyone and everyone who disagrees with them a "fascist" or a "Nazi"—World without Nazism has in fact contributed to the very problem it was purportedly founded to combat: it has trivialized the Holocaust."[144]

When it comes to engaging with the Russian Holocaust narrative, Israel, of all countries, finds itself in the trickiest situation. Overrepresented among other segments of the Israeli population, Russian-speaking Jews, and the nostalgia that some of them may feel for their country of origin, that is, the Soviet Union, make them less critical vis-à-vis Russia's overtures. It is a truism to state that Israel finds itself in a tough neighborhood. In the wake of the Syrian crisis, and especially after Putin's decision to support Bashar al-Assad militarily, Israel needs to maintain good working relations with Russia more than ever. Although playing along with the official Russian discourse on the Second World War and the Holocaust may seem like a small price to pay, in the long term it may drag Israel even closer in Russia's orbit. Unless, of course, Israeli historians and politicians alike start taking history politics as advanced by the Russian government more seriously. Otherwise, the cultivation of Jewish support by the Putin regime is purely instrumental, which shows up in occasional slips of the tongue. In March 2018, for example, Putin received universal condemnation when he dismissed the accusations of Russian interference in the 2016 US Presidential elections by suggesting it might be just anyone, say, Jews.[145]

The student of Soviet history may discover a striking number of similarities between the present Russian and the former Soviet discourse on the history of the Second World War. Insofar as the Holocaust representation is concerned, the hybrid history of Russia promoted by the Putin regime has produced grotesque formulations that may feature, side by side, "Nazis" and "Hitlerite invaders," "Jews" and "people of different ethnicities." In an extended interview with Vladimir Soloviev—the dean of Kremlin's propagandists—in the spring of 2018 Putin went as far as to claim that what the Russian people had experienced at the hands of the Nazis was not unlike the Holocaust.[146] Much like during the Soviet times, Auschwitz-Birkenau is frequently described in today's Russia as a concentration camp, Jews presented as one of many victim groups, and the Red Army given the ultimate honor of a rescuer. The genocide is said to have been committed not only against the Jews but also against the Slavic peoples. Russian diplomatic lexicon is replete with Soviet clichés such as "brown plague," primacy of the Nuremberg judgment, Nazism as "absolute evil" or a "virus," "altar of Victory," "alarm bell of Oświęcim," and last but not least "historical revanchism." Indeed, statements by Russian UN officials draw heavily on Soviet Cold War rhetoric pioneered in 1947–48. Remove references to current affairs, and Foreign Minister Lavrov and his junior colleagues sound almost identical to Soviet representatives in the United Nations who advanced Moscow's agenda on human rights and genocide back in the late 1940s. Notably, the Russian officials, like the Soviets before them, shy away from referring to the Holocaust as genocide.[147] Instead, they prefer using the term *crimes against humanities*—a pattern that can be traced as far back as the late 1940s.[148] *Genocide* they reserve for more contemporary instances, for example, the alleged Ukrainian atrocities in Donbass.[149] By the same token, Russian officials routinely refer to the Nuremberg trial and the International Convention on the Elimination of All Forms of Racial Discrimination—but rarely to the Genocide Convention (beginning in 2015)—as the documents that came about as a consequence of the victory over Nazi Germany. That is what the Kremlin is currently trying to sell to the West. The deliberate confusion thus sowed has the same function as the rest of Russia's policy, namely to split democratic opinion abroad and cement authoritarian rule at home.

The Holocaust for the Russian state becomes significant only where and when it fits the narrative of a heroic Red Army bringing salvation to the Nazi-savaged Europe. The liberation of Auschwitz-Birkenau camp is one such instance, entering the Budapest Jewish ghetto the same month in 1945 is another.[150] Predictably, similar cases involving the Allied armies warrant no comparable statements by the Russian foreign ministry. As we know from the Holocaust scholarship, the Soviet forces that overran the death camps in occupied Poland in 1944–45 were shocked with what they discovered and did take good care of the few surviving inmates, including Jews. The Soviet wartime propaganda, however—with a few notable exceptions—paid little heed to the ethnic identity of the victims. In the face of an imminent Soviet takeover, the Nazis evacuated the majority of Jewish prisoners by the brutal method of "death marches" and attempted to destroy the most damning evidence of their atrocities. As a result, the overwhelming majority of Jewish survivors ended up in the part of Europe liberated by the Americans and the British, and consequently this reinforced the common perception that the Jews were primarily liberated by the Western Allies.[151] It is important to pinpoint, however, that neither the Anglo-Americans nor the Soviets had incorporated rescue of Jews in their military planning. Up until now, Russian officials have not presented any evidence as to a specific camp liberation mission inbuilt in the Soviet military strategy. There was none: the Soviet Army entered the Nazi death camps as it rolled over Poland in pursuit of the ultimate goal, conquest of Berlin. Stalin was in a rush to carve as much territory in Europe as he could to later claim suzerainty over it.

The Russian efforts to fashion the (Soviet) victory over Hitler's Germany as a central event in world history is a carbon copy of the discourse developed by the Soviets right after the end of the Second World War. Only references changed, while substance remained the same. Back in 1948, Stalin's government linked genocide to fascism and "similar racial ideologies," while the Putin regime today has become reconciled to using a universally accepted term *Nazism*. In the 1940s the Soviets intended to get at the United States and the colonial powers like Britain by means of the Genocide Convention; since the mid-2000s the Russians have been evoking the UN resolution condemning glorification of Nazism to nail select East European countries, specifically the Baltic States. In either case, for Moscow the Holocaust functions as a mere background and/or a convenient tool. The sanctification of the Nuremberg judgment—impressed through Article 354.1, "Rehabilitation of Nazism," of the Russian penal code (May 2014)—is yet another example of marrying history and politics. Needless to say, Russian authorities never evoke recent academic research that exposes the extent of manipulation of the 1945–46 trial by Stalin's regime or make reference to the subsequent twelve Nuremberg trials administered by the Americans, including those that address specifically the Holocaust.[152]

Marked similarities between the Holocaust narrative advanced in today's Russia and that in the former Soviet Union undermine the moralistic tone assumed by the Kremlin. To illustrate, here is how Karen Khachaturov, a Soviet official with a PhD in history, perceived the representation of the Holocaust during his January 1985 trip to Israel. Khachaturov did not make it to Yad Vashem but visited, instead, Ghetto Fighters' House near Haifa, the first Holocaust museum ever built. A visitor from Moscow found numerous lacunae in the museum exhibition: the plight of nations other than Jewish; the Soviet contribution to both the liberation of the camps and the decisive victory over Nazi Germany; the words *Nazi* and *Nazism* used in lieu of *fascism* and *Hitlerite*, and so on. Khachaturov also lashed out against a documentary on the Sobibor uprising that was briefly aired on Israel TV. He fumed that the documentary failed to mention that the uprising was organized in collaboration with Soviet prisoners of war and led by a Soviet officer. Referring to an Israeli communist and member of the Israel–Soviet Friendship Association, he decried the "imperialist slander" regarding the Molotov–Ribbentrop Pact. According to him, the 1939 pact gave the Soviet Union the much-needed respite and eventually saved the lives of hundreds of thousands of Jews fleeing the Nazis. The article in *Izvestiia* was characteristically titled "Thieves of Common Sense" and was divided under the subheadings "Poisonous Shoots of Fascism," "Zionist Intoxication," and "Patented Liars."[153] By reading the 1985 article vis-a-vis the present Russian discourse on the Holocaust, one might inevitably arrive at the following conclusions: (a) Israel and its historians have consistently rejected the ideologically driven Soviet narrative, and (b) the Kremlin's core narrative on the Nazi mass murder of the Jews goes back to the Cold War period. Indeed, Russian propaganda failed to develop its own, unique take on the history of the Second World War. Thirty-five years on, it resorts to the canon and language that at one time appeared to have been discarded for good.

References to Holocaust denial are universally interspersed with those to falsification of history. A close look at what Moscow regards as examples of "falsification of history" reveals no new, specific links to the Nazi mass murder of Jews. Those are essentially the same historical issues in the countries of Eastern Europe that Russia has had problems with since the outset (e.g., fighting within the ranks of German Waffen SS, OUN/UPA, etc.). The Putin regime has been exploiting the subject of the Holocaust primarily to condemn those East European nationals who fought against the Soviet Union on the side of Nazi Germany. That goes back to the division of Eastern Europe between Hitler and Stalin in August 1939. The Molotov–Ribbentrop Pact and its consequences have been a hot-button historical and political issue for the Soviet Union, and now Russia, ever since.[154] The Holocaust is thus just a means to help reinforce the traditional view on the history of the Second World War. In effect, the Putin regime is making use of the universally recognized, and condemned, phenomenon of the Holocaust to serve old wine in new bottles. To do so, it is using the entire propaganda machinery of the state, and not without success.

In the recent years the Russian foreign ministry has displayed a certain finesse it had until now lacked in presenting its perspective on the Holocaust. This goes hand in hand with the potential of soft power rediscovered by Moscow since the 2011–12 democratic protests in Russia and particularly in the aftermath of a military aggression against Ukraine in 2014. Since 2015 Russia has been building an alternative, popular Holocaust narrative, complete with own commemoration dates, NGOs, motion pictures, and exhibitions. So, in addition to International Holocaust Remembrance Day, January 27, it has pushed for 26 Iyar, Day of Deliverance and Liberation, May 9, and most recently for a yet unnamed date marking the 1943 uprising at Sobibor, October 14. The United Nations has proved to be an important, and malleable, conduit for Russian history politics. Under the guise of a tribute to the victims of the Holocaust, the foreign ministry has been able to take its pitchfork battles with East European neighbors to an international level. Formal Russian statements outwardly honoring the Jewish victims of the Nazis is an affront to the memory of the Holocaust. Like with other aspects of Russian hybrid warfare, their goal is to subvert and obfuscate.

On the one hand, the chances of Russia succeeding in changing the global perspective on the Holocaust are close to zero. Research on the Nazi genocide of the Jews in Russia, in Russian, added little to the fundamental knowledge of the Holocaust, regretfully. Few dedicated scholars and the public at large are aware of Moscow's concerted efforts to shift the focus from the victims and perpetrators of the Holocaust to the rescuers, those wearing Soviet military uniforms, that is.[155] Few may register Moscow raising the issue of the Holocaust where and when it wants to stick it to its former East European vassals. Mobile exhibitions and talks sponsored by the Russian delegation to the United Nations are seen and heard only by random diplomats passing through the UN building in New York. UN Resolution 67/154, "Glorification of Nazism," is one among the 120 adopted by the General Assembly in December 2012. Not many people take notice, and here lies the danger. After all is said and done, Russia's objective is not to radically change the conversation—which it has been unable to accomplish anyway—but to muddle it. With a document backlog at the United Nations, convoluted Russian formulations that could be understood only by those with experience in Soviet doublespeak easily escape critical attention. The Putin regime seeks to divert the conversation, to sow confusion, which effectively amounts to a divide-and-rule policy. And the Russian agenda on the Holocaust *is a policy*, coordinated at the highest governmental level. It is part and parcel of a hybrid warfare strategy adopted by the Kremlin.[156]

In the standard Russian interpretation, Holocaust victims appear in connection with either the (unjustly forgotten) Soviet soldiers, who had brought them salvation, or the (now celebrated) East European collaborators, who had brought them to perdition. This one-dimensional, black-and-white picture makes the Holocaust a mere background for a civilizational battle between good and evil. Remarkably, this ideologically driven conception unwittingly refers back to both a Jewish religious interpretation that prefigured empirical study of the Holocaust and the Soviet account of German fascism from the late 1940s. Lost in their own rhetoric, Russian diplomats do not see a contradiction when claiming they regard the Holocaust an event of universal significance, because immediately after they refer to the Nuremberg trial, Waffen SS, removal of Soviet war memorials in East Europe, historical revisionism, and so on.[157] In my previous research, I came to calling this phenomenon "ideological self-righteousness." It is encapsulated in Putin's warning against "using historical speculations in the geopolitical games, provoking political phobias, setting nations against each other."[158]

In spite of a massive investment in history politics, the Russian state displays a fundamental misunderstanding of how the knowledge of the past may, or may not, influence current politics. Here I refer specifically to the mythical "lessons of history," which Russian authorities appear to believe in. It can only be described as deeply naïve of the foreign ministry to posit that emphasizing the leading role of the Soviet Union in the victory over Nazi Germany can strengthen Russia's international status today—as expressed by Lavrov's deputy at a January 2009 intergovernmental meeting in the Kremlin, for example. The deepest irony of them all is that the alleged conspiracy to rewrite the history of the Second World War and to whitewash Nazi crimes exists only in the Kremlin rulers' minds. All of these is due to a single cause—first, the inability and, later, the unwillingness to turn the page on the Soviet past.[159] In the final analysis, Russia participates in the commemoration of the Holocaust internationally only when it helps reinforce the foundational myth of the Soviet victory over Nazi Germany and/or counter the evocation of communist crimes. It is purely instrumental and, therefore, never sincere. History of the Holocaust, or history in general, is a mere commodity used by the Putin regime in pursuit of its nefarious goals.

From the regime's perspective, seating the Russian delegation in the first row at the annual commemoration ceremony in the former Auschwitz death camp is no different from reasserting Russia's role in the world. Indeed, a member of the Presidential Human Rights Council was complaining that she and her colleagues got seats in the very last row at the 2019 event. Besides, not a single word of Russian was spoken at the commemoration ceremony, despite the fact that it was "our grandparents and great-grandparents who stopped the advance of the brown plague in Europe."[160]

Working through different channels, the Russian government scored a major victory the following year. President Putin was among the major invited guests at the fifth World Holocaust Forum, held on January 23, 2020, in Israel. The forum, which focused on the issue of antisemitism that year, is the brainchild of Viacheslav Moshe Kantor, president of the European Jewish Congress. The US Treasury Department identifies Kantor as one of the ninety-six Russian oligarchs with ties to the Kremlin. According to Emil Shleimovich, Israeli journalist and political scientist, Russian oligarchs are expected to promote certain causes in exchange for the concessions they receive from the government. One of the oligarch clusters is tasked with advancing all things Jewish. Among specific examples of the "humanitarian" work by Putin's cronies are the 2012 Victory monument in Natanya and the 2020 Memorial Candle monument in Jerusalem.[161] As regards Putin's personal take, at Jerusalem he declared the Holocaust and the siege of Leningrad as two interlinked tragedies like no other and stressed that 40 percent of all Holocaust victims were Soviet citizens—one of the central theses of the traveling exhibition created by the Altman's center.[162] Using the opportunity, Putin proposed holding a summit of the five permanent members of the UN Security Council and participants in the wartime anti-Hitler coalition. From the subject of global fight against antisemitism he swiftly turned to the mission of the Great Powers to "preserve civilization." According to Putin, the countries that jointly fought against Nazism should reaffirm the "spirit of cooperation [*soiuznichestvo*] and historical memory."[163] In short, Putin is pushing for a Yalta 2.0 on historymaking.

7

Injustice of Historic Proportion

Invoking disregard for the rule of law in Russia has become commonplace. In an ominous twist, in December of 2015, President Putin signed a law that enabled the Russian Constitutional Court to ignore any ruling of the European Court of Human Rights deemed as contravening the constitution. Five years on, Putin sought to enshrine it in the letter of the constitution. By so doing Putin effectively invalidated an independent judiciary. In this context, evoking the constitution is nothing but a mockery of justice, for the very notion of constitutional rights sounds hollow in Russia. Only half of the Russians believe that the constitution guarantees them any rights at all. According to an independent opinion poll conducted in November of 2016, 41 percent of Russians have never read the constitution, another 48 percent have read it but cannot elaborate on it, and only 11 percent know its contents well. To the question if Russian authorities pay heed to the constitution, 12 percent responded "no" and another 37 percent said "in part."[1] In early 2020, President Putin proposed revisiting the constitution. A working group has considered a whooping 500 amendments. Putin personally suggested a number of amendments, among others, declaring Russia the state with one-thousand-year history and successor to the Soviet Union, defending the historical truth and preventing the defamation of "defenders of the Motherland." The most significant amendment, however, was rushed in at the last minute: the draft constitution provides for Putin serving another two presidential terms, through 2036, if he chooses so. Indeed, the mass abuse of justice in Russia incorporates history.

Hostile Takeover of Perm 36

The state takeover of Perm 36, a Soviet prison camp turned Gulag museum, underlines the link that the authorities are making between political dissent and certain views on history. The camp operated between 1946 and 1987. Originally meant as a forced labor camp, in 1972 it was converted into a penal colony for political prisoners, primarily from Ukraine and the Baltic states, sentenced on charges of anti-Soviet propaganda. In 1994, a group of enthusiasts affiliated with Memorial began a long-term restoration project on what was clearly the best preserved Gulag campsite anywhere in Russia. For a good decade, the Perm regional government has covered roughly one-half of the museum's operating costs. The rest came from private businesses and foundations in Russia and abroad. Counting in outreach and educational programs, Perm 36 drew some forty thousand visitors annually. At one point, the campsite was considered for inclusion on the UNESCO World Heritage List, and in 2011 the Russian Government designated Perm 36 as part of its "program for memorialization of victims of political repression," alongside two other museums. Registered as an NGO, the museum for nearly twenty years was run by historian Victor Shmyrov. Shmyrov and his associates regarded free exchange of ideas as important as the preservation of the memory of the Gulag. Consequently, in 2005 they introduced a hugely successful, annual civic forum. Conceptually, the forum did not limit itself to issues related to history but engaged with current politics, especially human rights. In their attacks on the museum, its critics have gone particularly hard against the civic forum with its focus on contemporary Russia.[2]

The pro-democracy protests of the winter of 2011–12 caught the regime unprepared. Everyone and everything that was seen as having fomented the "color revolutions" came under fire. In the spring of 2012 a newly appointed regional governor cut the museum's funding, followed by a new draconian law, which required any NGO receiving foreign funds and engaging in political activities to register as a "foreign agent." The authorities drew support from a motley group comprising former Perm 36 guards, communists, and members of Kurginian's Essence of Time in launching in the summer of 2012 a smear campaign against the museum. Collectively, they argued that the Perm 36 inmates were common criminals and not some sort of political prisoners, that the conditions in the camp were humane, and that the museum exemplified the foreign-funded fifth column. The shortage of funding made the museum cancel the civic forum beginning in 2013.[3]

Russia's aggression against Ukraine made things worse for the museum. By early 2014, employees stopped receiving salaries, while the museum's water and electricity was cut off. In May of that year the museum director was sacked. Simultaneously, rumors began to circulate that the authorities intended to convert Perm 36 into a museum of repression generally, stretching all the way to the times of Ivan the Terrible. Another possibility mentioned was a permanent exhibition on the destiny of the last tsar and his family.[4] In June of 2014, state-controlled NTV aired a vicious commentary on Perm 36. Among other things, the documentary insinuated that the museum was teaching schoolchildren that the Ukrainian "fascists" were not as bad as (Russian) history books portrayed them, while the latter's grandchildren were carrying out "genocide" in Eastern Ukraine.[5]

Historian Steven A. Barnes has speculated that the appearance of the "Fifth Column" episode on national television signaled the government's ultimate wish to destroy the museum. The state seized control not only of the facilities but also of all the materials Perm 36 had collected over twenty years. Shmyrov accused the new museum administration of erasing all references to Stalin and refocusing the exhibition on the perpetrators instead of the victims (i.e., the camp guards vs. the political prisoners).[6] Even though the fears appear to have been overblown, and the museum itself ultimately survived, its contents and the broader mission have, indeed, been gutted. Facing the prospect of forcible registration as a "foreign agent," in March of 2015 the NGO chose to disband.[7] Subsequently, ticket sales dropped by two-thirds. Shmyrov believes it was premeditated, whereby the government could claim irrelevance of the Perm 36

Museum, and by extension of the Gulag history.⁸ The museum keeps hanging in the balance. The new governor revealed in 2017 his intention to turn Perm 36 into an open-air museum, which can mean just anything.⁹

A great majority of Russians have probably never heard of Shmyrov. If there is one historian in Russia who does enjoy name recognition—for all the wrong reasons—it ought to be Andrei Zubov. One of the most respected in the profession, known for his liberal views as well as his deep religiosity, Zubov published, on March 1, 2014, an article in *Vedomosti* in which he compared Russia's annexation of Crimea to Nazi Germany's annexation of Austria and parts of Czechoslovakia. All hell broke loose. On the wave of public condemnation, MGIMO where Zubov had taught since 2001 sacked him. Although that decision was shortly revoked, Zubov eventually lost his job anyway, (his contract was not renewed). Harassment has continued in various forms. For example, the second volume of a fundamental study *History of Russia in Twentieth Century* that he had edited, was effectively removed from circulation. An observant Christian from the age of twenty-five, Zubov had for many years taught at Moscow Theological Academy and sat on the board of a number of Orthodox Church bodies. Not only was he forced to step down from all those bodies, but even his own parish showed him to the door. The only legal employment Zubov has been able to secure is that of a commentator in *Novaia Gazeta*, supplemented with occasional grants.¹⁰

Seeking Justice at Sandarmokh

Sandarmokh is one the most recent, and crassest, examples of historical revisionism attempted by the state. The story began in 1997, when a Memorial search party discovered a former NKVD mass execution site at Sandarmokh in Karelia—one of the largest in this part of Russia. During the Great Terror, the NKVD executed and hastily buried nearly ten thousand people of sixty different ethnicities there. Records from the FSB Archives helped to establish the names of 6,431 victims. The honor of the discovery belongs to historian Yuri Dmitriev, head of the Karelia branch of Memorial and a leading expert on the history of the White Sea Canal. The site was properly marked and commemorated in an annual ceremony on August 5.

From the outset, Dmitriev made an effort to reach out to ethnic communities inside and outside Russia whose members had perished at Sandarmokh. He urged the Poles, Ukrainians, Georgians, Estonians, and others to erect separate monuments at the memorial site.¹¹ The Polish ambassador in Russia awarded Dmitriev a medal for his memorial work and his services before the Polish people. In a short while, the Sandarmokh memorial turned into a kind of open-air museum that featured tours steeped in the history of the Gulag. The entrance to the memorial complex features a poignant message by Dmitriev: "People, do not kill each other!"¹² It is not only the international aspect of the commemoration that distinguishes Sandarmokh from similar Stalin-era killing fields. Death at a remote Karelian site was anything but anonymous, for the victims and perpetrators are all known by name.¹³

The first signs that the authorities had begun viewing a memorial pilgrimage to Sandarmokh with displeasure appeared in 2014. Russia's aggression against Ukraine that year did not prevent foreign delegations—Polish and Ukrainian to be specific—from participating in the commemoration ceremony. Official statements read by the foreign visitors differed markedly from the position adopted by the Russian state. Dmitriev had a gut feeling his mission to commit Stalin's victims to memory was causing annoyance in certain quarters. He received telephone threats while tires on his car were slashed; he began carrying a knife for self-defense. He just did not know who exactly stood behind it. The likely source was the FSB.[14]

In 2016, for the first time ever, no state representatives from the regional capital of Petrozavodsk attended the commemorative ceremony (or, rather, were ordered from the top not to attend). In December of that year Dmitriev was arrested on bogus charges of child pornography. By that time he had nearly finished composing a memorial book, which contained the names of 64,000 "special settlers" who wound up in Karelia in the 1930s (these and other records have been confiscated). The sixty-two-year-old historian spent one full year in prison awaiting a sentence. The state prosecutor demanded a nine-year sentence, but in part due to public outrage, the local court in April 2018 acquitted Dmitriev. Beyond the particularities of the case, this was an extraordinary ruling in its own right: only 0.2 percent of all criminal cases end up

Figure 15 A martyr of history. Yuri Dmitriev (b. 1956), a historian and member of Memorial, is a caretaker of the memorial cemetery of victims of Stalin's terror at Sandarmokh in Karelia. In the crass attempt to rewrite history, authorities in December of 2016 opened a criminal case against Dmitriev. As a consequence of a botched, politically motivated investigation, Dmitriev has languished in jail ever since, depicted here in a Petrozavodsk courtroom on June 28, 2018.

in acquittal in Russia (2017), less, perhaps, than in any other developed country.[15] The liberal intelligentsia celebrated the not guilty verdict as a victory for the entire Russian civil society. Some, however, adopted a cautionary tone.[16] Indeed, the authorities could not reconcile to losing face and, two months later, the Supreme Court of Karelia ordered a retrial. Dmitriev himself took the news with remarkable stoicism: "What's confronting us, let's call them mighty agencies. Clearly, they're not used to losing."[17] As requested by the prosecution, Dmitriev remained in custody through June 2020. He is indicted on five counts of child sexual abuse and the illegal possession of weapons, which carry a maximum penalty of twenty years.

Meanwhile, the state machinery made a foray into alternative history. Shortly before Dmitriev's arrest, two historians at the Petrozavodsk State University came up with a hypothesis, according to which alongside Stalin's victims the mass execution site at Sandarmokh might contain the remains of Soviet prisoners of war who had died in Finnish captivity. The defense ministry's TV channel Zvezda hastily prepared a reportage, "Another Truth of the Sandarmokh Concentration Camp: How the Finns Tortured Thousands of Our Soldiers." As evidence, the channel published on its website select documents from the FSB Archives, declassified for the occasion. Memorial popped up in the developing narrative as an organization with no interest in the fate of the deceased Soviet soldiers. Rossiia 24 doubled down by airing, three weeks after Dmitriev's arrest, an extensive feature on Memorial. Among other things, the documentary said that the organization had employed people of dubious character such as Dmitriev.[18] (Memorial, for its part, has declared Dmitriev a political prisoner.) At the heart of those efforts is historical and moral relativism: a plurality of victims and executions that would make Russian citizens capitulate in the face of their own (complex) history and eventually make them malleable. Had there appeared a monument to the slain Soviet POWs at Sandarmokh, Stalin's injustice vis-à-vis own people would no longer appear exceptional.

Since the original hypothesis had been aired, and accepted *a priori* by the Russian state agencies, no additional evidence has resurfaced that it was exactly at Sandarmokh where the Finns buried Soviet POWs en masse. Rather, a number of Finnish and Russian historians—some of the latter on the condition of anonymity—regard that proposition ill-founded and/or politically motivated.[19] Regardless, out of the blue, in late August of 2018 Russian Military Historical Society (RVIO) began excavations at Sandarmokh, without procuring a proper permit. Within three days, RVIO's search party dug out human remains of three men, who they were quick to establish were executed by bullets fired from a foreign-made guns and were wearing the type of clothes distributed by Finnish occupation authorities. In short, the exhumed bodies were those of Soviet prisoners of war who had died at the hands of the Finns. This rushed conclusion teems with contradictions. The search party claimed they were digging outside the perimeter of the memorial, while actually they did so within the site. Despite claims to the contrary, it was the ministry of culture and not the local museum (which administers the Sandarmokh memorial) that had requested to establish the outer limits of the mass execution site anew.[20] The historians at Petrozavodsk State University who had come up with the original hypothesis did not participate in the exhumation; nor did they get a chance to review its findings. The press conference hastily organized by the RVIO ended up discussing anything but the details of the test dig. The Finnish archival authorities reminded that all documents concerning Soviet prisoners of war had been declassified and were available at both Helsinki and Moscow; no Finnish historian was invited to take part in the press conference on September 7. Furthermore, the question remains as to why the RVIO decided to dig exactly at Sandarmokh, while Karelia abounds with burial sites of Soviet prisoners of war—all confirmed by Finnish authorities.[21]

In June 2019 the Russian Investigative Committee rendered its judgment, which went both ways. The expertise neither confirmed nor disproved that the remains unearthed a year earlier were those of Soviet prisoners of war who died in Finnish captivity.[22] That proved enough for the authorities to continue tampering with evidence at Sandarmokh. The following month the Karelian ministry of culture requested RVIO to carry out further excavations at the burial site to back up the shaky new hypothesis. This document serves as a perfect illustration of the goals and means of Russian history politics:

> The idea that "Sandarmokh" contains burials of victims of political repression has been exploited by a number of countries in pursuit of a destructive propaganda within the sphere of historical consciousness.... Speculations around [what exactly had happened at; *sobytiia*] Sandarmokh not only harm Russia's international image, reinforce in the public perception an unwarranted sense of guilt before the so-called repressed representatives of the foreign countries, facilitate groundless [financial] claims against our state, but also serve as a consolidating factor for the antigovernment forces within Russia.[23]

Like the year earlier, the random excavations were carried out with all sorts of violations. In essence, RVIO, with the backing of the ministry of defense, had carried out an act of vandalism, punishable under Articles 243 and 244 of the criminal code ("destruction or damage to sites of cultural heritage"; "destruction, damage, or desecration of burial sites").[24]

Had anyone thought authorities reached rock bottom in their attempts to rewrite history and to destroy the lives of those who resist those efforts—they took it wrong. On October 2, 2018, director of Medvezhiegorsk museum, Sergei Koltyrin, was arrested on pedophilia charges. Koltyrin did not participate in the RVIO excavations, yet in his capacity as the museum director he had been supervising the Sandarmokh memorial. Koltyrin regarded himself as Sandarmokh's guardian—the most important job in his life. State TV channels left no doubt as to the true cause of his detention when they described Koltyrin as Dmitriev's associate and a Memorial "propagandist," which he hardly was.[25] Koltyrin had seen the writing on the wall when local authorities had forbidden him from attending the commemoration ceremony at Sandarmokh earlier that year. In February of 2018 Koltyrin publicly questioned the hypothesis that the memorial grounds might contain bodies of Soviet POWs executed by the Finns. In private, Koltyrin confided that he was afraid he might suffer the same fate as Dmitriev. People of Medvezhiegorsk who knew Koltyrin did not believe even for a moment the criminal charges filed against him. Koltyrin breathed new life into the museum, which he had headed since 1991. This had earned him popular respect and the status of an honorable citizen of Medvezhiegorsk.[26]

In the Russian officials' eyes, however, by means of their personal engagement with one of Stalin's mass execution sites, Dmitriev and Koltyrin had somehow been engaged in anti-government politics. The punishment for the nonexistent offense was severe: in May 2019 Koltyrin was sentenced to nine years of penal labor. With both historians taken out, the future of the memorial can no longer be assured.[27] The attack on Dmitriev and Sandarmokh can also be regarded as part of the onslaught against Memorial and other independent NGOs. Indeed, Memorial was assigned the status of a "foreign agent" in November 2015, and its affiliate, International Memorial, in October of the following year.

The state misappropriation of the Sandarmokh in 2018 had followed that of the Katyn in 2007 (2018) and the Perm 36 in 2012. In the case of Katyn, we are dealing with the quintessential episode of memory politics that stretches back to 1945, while Perm 36 features a strong element of current politics (i.e., the civic forum).[28] In all three cases, the state had brazenly tried to whitewash Soviet mass terror by engaging in historical relativism. By means of false comparisons (e.g., the plight of Russian POWs in Polish captivity) and shifted focus (e.g., from the mistreatment of prisoners to the travails of the guard on duty) the authorities had introduced extraneous historical layers whose goal is to confuse the public. With regard to the Perm 36 Museum, the dismissal of Shmyrov from the position of director constituted the most blatant state intervention. What makes Sandarmokh stand out is the willingness of the regime to use criminal justice to twist the historical narrative. What in 2014 was just a statement of intent—criminal prosecution involving certain interpretations and presentations of history—by 2020 had become a nearly routine application. To a certain extent, obfuscating the history of mass violence in the Soviet Union falls in the same category as the desire to pass in silence the man-made disasters that had occurred under the present government's watch, beginning with the sinking of the Kursk submarine in 2000 and finishing with the fire in a Kemerovo shopping center in 2018.

Fait Accompli at Yoshkar-Ola

While the demise of Perm 36 and Sandarmokh received considerable media attention, also internationally, the recent closure of a Gulag history museum in Yoshkar-Ola has gone largely unnoticed. Both the fact of closure and the apparent lack of public interest is unfortunate, for the People's Memorial House Museum of Gulag History is/was perhaps one of the most remarkable such institutions in Russia. In many respects, the professional and personal journey of the museum's founder, Nikolai Arakcheev, is the exact opposite of Yuri Alexeev in Pskov (see Chapter 1). Arakcheev holds advanced degrees from a history department and a police academy. He has seen the collapse of the Soviet Union and independent Russia's first two decades through a professional lenses. Thus he has overseen the closure of the Mari El Communist Party, headed the local anti-corruption office, and investigated common crimes. During his last five years on the job, Arakcheev got to work with top secret documents. All of these not only earned Arakcheev respect from his peers in law enforcement agencies but also taught him to navigate the power structures. Outside his career, for a good thirty-five years, Arakcheev has been dealing with the history of Stalin's terror. That history runs through his own family: his paternal grandfather died performing forced labor in mines while on his mother's side nearly all men perished. To dig deeper into the tragic history of his family and the country, Aarkcheev joined Memorial.[29]

His quest culminated in a Gulag history museum, which officially opened in the capital of Mari El Republic on May 9, 2011. What made the museum unique is the location—a nineteenth-century mansion that housed, consecutively, Cheka, GPU, and NKVD local headquarters. The building contained offices, and interrogation and detention cells; those condemned to death were executed in an adjacent prison. Anecdotally, Leon Trotsky and Nikolai Ezhov had passed through the building. When clearing the attic and the basement of rubbish, Arakcheev and his associates found a great many artefacts of NKVD provenance, which constitutes the core of the permanent exhibition. In effect, that building was the centerpiece of Stalin's terror in modern-day Mari El.[30]

The Gulag museum has firmly established itself as part of the Mari El tourist landscape, that is to say, it proved a major actor. Some 40,000 visitors from a total of twenty-eight countries have gone through the museum, and filled sixteen guest books with their comments, in the seven years of its existence. Among others who came to visit were "history connoisseurs"—as Arakcheev chose to call them—from the FSB and the police force, the prosecutor general's office and the defense ministry. At least once a month a busload full of tourists from other parts of the republic came to visit; during the annual Night of Museums, it held the longest opening hours for any museum in Yoshkar-Ola. The museum co-organized funerals of the deceased Gulag victims, took care of a memorial cemetery, and ran tours to nearby sites associated with the history of Stalin's terror. All of these it could achieve only through the work of volunteers, usually descendants of the Gulag victims.[31]

According to director Arakcheev, by investigating the tragic period in Soviet history, the museum "compels everyone to remember and grieve, and some to repent." That mission statement is apparently not to everybody's liking. The authorities neither actively supported nor obstructed the museum's work. Local officials attended the annual commemoration on October 30 and did not seem to mind the museum searching for mass execution sites. The most recent finding was made in May 2018. The law prescribes human remains to be reburied and, in the case of Stalin's terror, commemorated. This is unlikely to happen this time around, however. One month later the museum was closed, on the formal grounds that its rental agreement was up and that the building was in need of urgent repairs. Remarkably, no other tenant was forced out, while the building itself had until then not been declared to be in danger of collapse. This did not come entirely as a surprise, as the museum had been overloaded with paperwork and threatened with fines for at least a year. Meanwhile, Arakcheev was no longer on traditional guest lists nor had he got the opportunity to publicly address the situation surrounding the museum. Given the specificity of the building, he ruled out moving somewhere else.[32]

Where Arakcheev's professional past shows through is in his argumentation in favor of keeping the museum alive. Hence, he emphasizes the history of cooperation with both the local administration and the Orthodox Church, and the absence of advance warning from the lawenforcement agencies. The local Memorial, he says, never applied for or received foreign grants. At times, Arakcheev appears lost in trying to comprehend the rationale of those in power. The museum does not aim to deliberately discredit anyone: "In fact, it's grist to the authorities' mill." He wonders why the communists and security officials today refuse to acknowledge that a significant number of their peers had been purged under Stalin, too. Arakcheev refutes the claim that the present government seeks to erase Stalin's terror from the collective memory. As counter examples he cites Putin's unveiling of the central memorial to the victims of political repression in Moscow, the opening of a new Gulag history museum, also in the capital city, and the comprehensive program on memorialization signed in 2015 by Prime Minister Medvedev. The attack on the museum and its director has taken the form of a denunciation. On occasion, the building got plastered with anonymous posters urging the museum to alternately "tell the truth" and stop "telling lies." Never intimidated or disheartened, Arakcheev nevertheless does not plan to appeal against the decision to close the museum in court and/or organize public protests. He believes in reasoning and negotiations, he says.[33]

There are striking parallels between the history and, possibly, fate of the Gulag history museum in Yoshkar-Ola and the NKVD investigative prison in Tomsk. The museum of history of political repression opened in Tomsk way back in 1989. The building that housed, first, the OGPU and, then, the NKVD also served as an execution site. The museum is on the basement level and features the reconstructed prison cell and the investigator's office. In 2017, the last year on record, the museum had 26,000 visitors. A prime real-estate property in downtown Tomsk, the building is owned by a local businessman, who is planning to sell it. The businessman has asked the city to take over the building, but the negotiations have stalled. At a time when the extent of Stalin's terror is being downplayed in Russia, Tomsk authorities have good reasons to remain undecided.[34] As of this writing (summer 2019), there is a chance that the part of the building containing the museum may be bought out by a foundation that works to commit the Gulag victims to memory.[35]

Criminal and Administrative Cases: Censoring History to Crush Dissent

There are three articles in the Russian penal code and one in the administrative code that cover a majority of legal cases involving historical interpretations: Article 354.1, "glorification of Nazism and desecration of symbols of Russian military glory"; Article 282, "incitement of ethnic, racial, and/or religious hatred"; Article 244, "desecration of dead bodies and burial sites" (specifically in the context of the Second World War); and Article 20.3, "display and dissemination of Nazi symbols."[36] Looking for consistency in the application of those articles by local courts is futile. In effect, the Russian judiciary has received yet another tool to clamp down on (the vestiges of) political dissent. Notably, the Soviet penal code contained no specific laws regulating pronouncements about the past. The so-called falsification of history could only be addressed under Article 70 (anti-Soviet propaganda) or Article 71 (propaganda of war).[37]

Of the four, Article 354.1 has received the most attention. Signed by Putin in May of 2014, the Law against the Glorification of Nazism had been in the making for a period of time. The legislation, sponsored by the likes of Irina Yarovaia and Vladimir Medinskii, was originally introduced in Duma five years earlier. However, the newly created commission against the falsification of history rendered the initiative obsolete. The draft bill received a boost, and a new meaning, in the aftermath of Russia's aggression against Ukraine. According to Nikolay Koposov, the new law served to rally the population behind the regime on the one hand and legitimize the violation of Ukrainian sovereignty as a symbolic continuation of the Great Patriotic War on the other. Specifically, Article 354.1 proscribes

> the denial of facts established by the Judgment of the International Military Tribunal for the trial and punishment of major war criminals of European countries of the Axis, the justification of crimes established by the above-mentioned Judgment, as well as dissemination of knowingly false information on the activities of the USSR during the Second World War, when expressed publicly, are punishable by a fine of up to three hundred thousand roubles [. . .] or by deprivation of liberty for up to three years.[38]

A comprehensive report published in the spring of 2018 by Agora human rights group reviewed criminal and administrative cases related to interpretation of history that have been processed by the Russian judiciary since 2007. Among the hundred or so known cases, seventeen are criminal and eighteen are administrative. An additional forty-one cases include book and online publication censorship, as well as refusal to grant access to archives. The authors of the report have identified as a risk group individuals active in the political opposition. The harsher the language used by the defendant, the easier it becomes for an outside expertise—which is required in all of those cases—to clear the path for prosecution. In terms of taboo subjects, there is actually just one: the Soviet Union in the Second World War. Insofar as censoring history is part and parcel of the growing assault on freedom of expression in Russia, a criticism of the Soviet leadership may appear as a veiled criticism of the present Russian authorities. By that logic, all those who express dislike for the Soviet Union must also hate all things Russian and, thus, are extremists. By comparison, condemning the Bolshevik Revolution or claiming that the Soviet space program was not worth it, is fairly safe for Russian citizens. Even though no imprisonment on the basis of Article 354.1 has been ordered so far, it is just a matter of time, speculates Damir Gainutdinov. The Agora lawyer points out that the very fact of sentencing has grave, long-term consequences for a defendant.[39]

Cases involving interpretation of history, especially the Soviet role in the Second World War, are increasingly winding up in court. Given that non-guilty verdicts have traditionally been rare in the Soviet Union and now Russia, history books fare no better. Local courts typically invoke Article 354.1. The scientific expertise ordered by the court in such cases rarely lives up to its name. In the case of the book by Polish author Jan Nowak-Jeziorański, for example, expertise was performed by an individual with a PhD in "Scientific Communism." A judge of appeal stated, without elaborating, that the abovementioned book contains viewpoints "prohibited on the territory of the Russian Federation." St. Petersburg historian Daniil Kotsiubinskii reads this and similar cases as preparations for a show trial of historians sometime in the future.[40]

The chronic incompetence of academic expertise ordered by the authorities came to the fore in the fall of 2018 in the case of Alexander Panchenko. The well-respected professor of anthropology at Smolny College of St. Petersburg State University was sacked (i.e., his contract was not renewed) on account of his expertise, which the Antiterrorism Center did not find to its liking. Panchenko, an authority on Pentecost Church, failed to support the predetermined conclusion that the sermons of William M. Branham (1909–65) were of an extremist nature. Having rubbed shoulders with so-called experts, Panchenko attests to their low professional qualifications, substandard even to those acceptable in the former Soviet Union. According to him, the entire system of expertise is corrupt, meant to endorse retributive acts already in effect. The kind of questions the prosecutor's office poses before an expert hints at the answers it wants to receive. In that particular case, it had to do with persecution of religious minorities in contemporary Russia. By pushing Panchenko out, the university administration got rid of a faculty member regarded as insufficiently loyal.[41] Ironically, the court did not find any element of extremism in the American preacher's sermons.[42]

Unlike foreign nationals, Russian citizens cannot simply shrug off accusations of attempted rehabilitation of Nazism as nonsensical. The 2014 Russian memory law has had immediate consequences for those who habitually share their opinions online on historical issues. The first person ever to be convicted on the basis of Article 354.1, in June 2016, was Vladimir Luzgin. A car mechanic from Perm, Luzgin did not actively participate in politics, yet consistently criticized Russian foreign policy on his webpage. In particular, he came out against Moscow's intervention in Ukraine. In September 2016, the Russian Supreme Court upheld the local court's decision to fine Luzgin 200,000 rubles for an article reposted by the defendant on social media. The article addressed the 1939 Soviet–Nazi conspiracy to dismember Poland. The original court ruling stated that Luzgin, as someone sufficiently well versed in history, would have known that the said article might cause harm to the general public, including children. The court interpreted as harm advancing "persistent beliefs about the USSR's negative actions" during the Second World War.[43] Prominent defense lawyer, Henry Reznik, had slammed the verdict as nonsensical, for conspiracy in a criminal act (i.e., the division of Poland) serves as an aggravating, not a mitigating, circumstance.[44] Luzgin pleaded not guilty, refused to pay the fine, and eventually requested political asylum in the Czech Republic. Simultaneously, he filed a case with the European Court of Human Rights. In May 2018 the Czech authorities rejected his asylum application on the grounds that no action taken against Luzgin in Russia can be classified as persecution.[45]

Biologist and journalist Igor Dorogoi was, in March 2017, indicted for "expressing disrespect to the Russian society" and specifically Victory Day celebration. The court in Magadan declared select images that Dorogoi had posted on his webpage as "defaming symbols of Russia's military glory." The outspoken scientist was found "guilty" of criticizing the extensive use of the St. George's ribbon as well as "historical personalities closely related to the Great Patriotic War, and identified by the peoples of Russia with the V-Day." Dorogoi supposedly condoned the Nazi crimes established by the Nuremberg Military Tribunal and thus committed a "premeditated crime against the peace and security of mankind."[46] A similar case, in Ulan-Ude in Siberia, rendered a 300-hour communal service sentence. The court declared that the defendant "despised May 9" and "endorsed Nazism by pitching St. George's ribbon against the Nazi German flag."[47] The indictment, which essentially censors personal views on history, unwittingly falls back on the Soviet legal doctrine: since the late 1940s, the Soviet Union had fought for incorporating the Nuremberg judgment into both the definition of aggressive war and the Code of Offenses against the Peace and Security on Mankind.[48]

A political calculus makes even the most innocuous cases appear sinister. When opening a field office in Barnaul in March of 2017, Navalny was doused with brilliant green (an antiseptic commonly used in the former Soviet Union)—not for the last time, as it turned out. In an act of defiance, his supporters around the country posted selfies with their faces painted green. Alexei Volkov, head of Navalny's presidential campaign in Volgograd, did a variation on the theme by circulating a photoshopped image of the famous Motherland Calls statue with a green face. Reported in the local press, the "offense" brought out scores of protestors among members of Molodaia gvardiia, who provoked a clash during the opening of Navalny's field office in Volgograd later that month. Subsequently, the police carried out a search at both Volkov's home and the office. The head of the local chapter of the Russian Search Movement (a state-sponsored organization engaged in identifying and reburying the remains of the fallen Soviet soldiers) requested the prosecutor's office to open a criminal case against Volkov on charges of vandalizing a war monument. As a framework for the criminal investigation, authorities used Article 354.1 and subsequently Article 244. Volkov and his defense lawyer have failed in their appeal to common sense: the alleged desecration of the memorial occurred in a virtual space while the green color per se is no more offensive than any other. Obviously, the real target was Navalny's challenging the Putin regime.[49] The fact that the case was personally supervised by head of the Investigative Committee, Alexander Bastyrkin, guaranteed a guilty verdict. To add to the absurdity, one of the plaintiffs who claimed moral damage turned out to be a ninety-year-old blind war veteran, who literally could not see the "offensive" image. Furthermore, an investigator made a trip to the actual monument to collect evidence of the crime. In March 2019 the court fined Volkov 200,000 rubles under Article 354.1.[50] By January 2020, the legal interpretation of "glorification of Nazism" has got expanded further on account of a fiction. A young author from Kaliningrad is facing criminal charges for a satirical story he has published online. In the story, Hitler and Stalin rise from hell to comment on mass rapes by Soviet soldiers in 1945 Germany. Not coincidentally, the defendant has expressed criticism of various government policies.[51]

Since 2017, authorities have been increasingly evoking Article 20.3 of the Russian administrative code against individuals known for their dissenting political views. Originally enacted in 2002, the article proscribes "displaying and popularizing fascist symbols." The November 2014 amendment provided for an ambiguous interpretation, according to which displaying Nazi symbols alone constitutes an offense. No less significant, individuals found in violation of Article 20.3 cannot run for office for one full year.[52] In January 2018 Article 20.3 was used against two volunteers in Alexei Navalny's presidential campaign. Yet another volunteer, in Pskov, was charged three months later with posting a historical photograph of a Russian Orthodox priest standing next to German soldiers with a swastika on the background. Another Navalny supporter, seventeen-year-old Daniil Smetanskii, has erred by posting (four years earlier) a photograph of Putin and Hitler side by side along with an ironic inscription. Preventively, in the run-on to Navalny's May 2018 "He's No Czar" protest, authorities tested students in select St. Petersburg schools for patriotism. The questionnaire (sporting a few grammatical mistakes) implied the existence of a singular "correct" ideology and inversely implicated those among the respondents who provided injudicious answers. In the case of fifty-nine-year old Mikhail Listov, incriminating evidence was found in a world-famous photograph of Soviet soldiers lowering captured Nazi banners during the 1945 Victory parade on the Red Square. The judge declared that the photograph—which is also featured, coincidentally, on the cover of the Russian history textbook for eleventh grade—may cause "anguish to the people whose relatives had perished during the Great Patriotic War."[53] In a rare instance, Listov has been eventually cleared of wrongdoing. Polina Danilevich from Smolensk, however, was not; she could not fathom how a photograph of her house during the Nazi occupation could serve as evidence of the purported crime.[54]

Traditional disregard for law goes hand in hand with its arbitrary application in contemporary Russia. When law encroaches on history, in the attempt to safeguard a dogmatic interpretation adopted by the state, it borders on travesty. The post-Crimea Russia has supplied numerous cases, which in other times and under different circumstances would be considered plain absurd. In April 2015 a teenager and two other women in their twenties were incarcerated for fifteen and ten days, respectively, for performing an "obscene" dance in front of a war memorial in the southern Russian city of Novorossiysk. The offenders, who filmed the video to promote dancehall classes for a local school, reportedly violated a criminal statute against "desecrating dead bodies and burial sites." Those in Russia who came out in defense of the unfortunate three claimed double standards by posting photographs of locals sunbathing and drinking alcohol on the beach next to the monument. The notorious St. Petersburg lawmaker Vitaly Milonov, who spearheaded the 2013 antigay legislation, however, suggested that the women should do forced labor—to teach them a lesson.[55] Quite a few administrative cases involve the desecration of the eternal flame. Typically, such cases end with a fine for both the underage perpetrators and their parents. The only reported instance in which sentencing was expected took place in late 2018 in Cheliabinsk region: a fourteen-year-old girl used the eternal flame to light up a cigarette. She could get up to one year of forced labor or a three-month detention for her misdeed.[56]

The media keep reporting cases one more grotesque than the other. In Krasnodar region, the police was investigating a high school student who spit into an eternal flame commemorating Soviet losses in the Second World War. Another student, this time in Khabarovsk region, was slapped with the label of an extremist for posting a photo of

Joseph Goebbels. The investigator forced the teenager to write a note of explanation and threatened him with a house search. A prisoner in a penal colony in Chuvashia was ordered by the court to remove the swastika tattoos from his body (rendered as "confiscation of the subject of administrative offense").[57] A designer from Omsk got a fine for reposting a screenshot from a comedy show that had aired ten years ago on the Russian TV. It just so happened that the actor in the video wore an armband with a swastika on it. The defendant's argument that, as a Jewish person whose relatives perished in the Holocaust, he rejects Nazism in any form did not convince the investigator, who claimed that the war veterans may find the sight of swastika offensive. (The judgment was subsequently overturned by the district court.)[58]

Liberal commentators have pointed out that Article 20.3, in its present interpretation, can be extended ad absurdum. In effect, just any historical display—a Soviet-era cartoon or a reproduced photograph featuring Nazi symbols—can be deemed an offense, which carries a fine of up to 50,000 rubles for juridical persons and 2,000 rubles or a fifteen-day detention for individuals. The Museum of Great Patriotic War, the Central Armed Forces Museum, or even the "Russia: My History" theme park—these and similar conduits of Russian history politics are in clear violation of Article 20.3.[59] Not to mention the dilemma faced by antique dealers, journalists, and bookstore owners. For instance, in April of 2015, an antique dealer in Sochi was fined for having on sale a German Navy uniform.[60] In September 2018 came the turn of a documentary, "Hitler vs. Picasso and Others," which tells the story of Nazi-looted art. The ministry of culture refused to issue it a screen license, ostensibly because the film displayed Nazi symbols.[61] It should probably be pointed out that all things fascist is not the only taboo that can be upheld with the help of Article 20.3. The amended Article 20.3.1 has claimed its first victim already in March 2019, and the afflicted individual was Ivan the Terrible. A Tatar youth activist was detained for three days for steering ethnic hatred against Russians. All that he did was condemning the Russian takeover of Kazan in 1552. The defendant pleaded not guilty on the grounds that he was merely citing a historical fact.[62] Like many others among his countrymen, he obviously could not comprehend how a particular angle on history may be regarded a criminal offense in contemporary Russia.

Article 282 of the criminal code, which falls under the antiextremist legislation, has generated an even stream of absurdities, too. One of the earlier cases is from April 2015, when authorities raided a scale-model shop and the largest toyshop in Moscow. From the former were confiscated model kits with Nazi symbols, and from the latter, sets of toy soldiers sporting the Wehrmacht uniform. Toy companies found themselves in a fix when searching for relevant pieces of legislation administering the sale and display of military-themed toys. As an unspoken rule, swastikas have been erased in spite of historical accuracy. What about a Great Patriotic War-themed board game featuring Soviet and German troops? Would the model maker who included in a box a sticker (in the shape of a square, for example) that can be modified into a swastika be liable for prosecution? None of these questions have been adequately answered while the Moscow prosecutor's office has launched legal action, formally to restore the dignity of the Soviet war veterans.[63] To avoid trouble, authorities in Samara preemptively removed the swastika from a Second World War monument during the reconstruction. Erected in 1975, the original monument featured a sword cleaving the swastika.[64]

Both Article 282 and Article 354.1 served as the basis for sentencing three teenagers in Krasnoyarsk. The sentence—sixty to hundred hours of communal service—from August 2015 adjudicated an episode that had occurred eight months earlier in which the defendants had scribbled a swastika on a Second World War memorial.[65] If the Krasnoyarsk Three was the first ever legal case under Article 354.1, the one from May 2015 involving an Astrakhan teenager set a different kind of precedent. As prime facie evidence, prosecution used a photograph of German soldiers in the Second World War posted by the young man on social media. By so doing, he allegedly approved of the Nazi invasion of Poland on September 1, 1939.[66] The Republic of Tuva on the Chinese border went one step further by launching in April of 2018 an online competition, "Stop Extremism." Local authorities urged the population to report fascist symbols as well as calls for public disorder and civic resistance found on the internet.[67] Ivan Liubshin from Kaluga holds an informal record of having been sentenced under Articles 354.1, 282, and 205.2 ("justification of terrorism"), though acquitted under Article 242 ("distribution of pornography").[68]

Sometimes anti-extremism and anti-Nazism legislation is being used as a form of blackmail. The threat to evoke articles 282 and 354.1 against historians non-gratae is documented, for example, in Kaliningrad region. What can be formulated as an anti-Germanization campaign started off in the Russian enclave around 2016. The local media began airing reportages about "creeping Germanization," which targeted anything and everything from memorial plaques to beer ("Königsberg"). As experts, the "patriotic" journalists enlisted war veterans and a local history professor, who claimed that the enemy was seeking to "weaken Russia's Western outpost." As its first victim it claimed Anzhelika Shpileva, the director of Sovetsk City Museum. A mistake in a translation and a photo of a German antifascist in the Waffen SS uniform proved enough for the local administration to seek Shpileva's resignation, which she refused to submit. The museum director was subsequently threatened with criminal procedure and reprimanded for "falsification of history." Studying and showcasing the region's German past suddenly became "separatism." In December 2018, after twenty-six years of service, Shpileva was eventually sacked. The museum itself, she fears, will shortly be "reformatted."[69] In an unrelated incident that same year, an Aeroflot flight attendant was also fired. She was punished thus for announcing that a flight bound for Kaliningrad was to land shortly in "Königsberg."[70] Kaliningrad served as one of the eleven sites that hosted the 2018 FIFA World Cup. The German national team, known for its stellar performances, was not at its best that year and crashed out at the group stage. The governor of Lipetsk region volunteered an explanation as to Germany's defeat: "Just because it unleashed two world wars and the souls of tens of millions of its victims are having their revenge. HISTORY and TIME has intervened."[71] A short distance northwest, in St. Petersburg, writer Elena Chizhova has angered the nationalists by proposing in a Swiss newspaper that Hitler and Stalin bear equal responsibility for mass death in the besieged Leningrad. In response, political scientist Natalia Eliseeva urged the Investigative Committee to open a criminal case against Chizhova under Article 354.1.[72]

In the fall of 2018 Article 282 was hanging like a dark cloud over the head of film director Alexei Krasovskii. Krasovskii had dared to challenge the heroic-cum-tragic narrative of Leningrad under siege by making a comedy set in the besieged city. Taking place on the New Year's Eve 1941, *Celebration* tells the story of a well-to-do family of a scientist who have food on their table in spite of the ravaging mass starvation. The pro-Kremlin media and politicians lambasted the film in the making as "blasphemy" and "mockery of people's history." Minister Medinskii—who did not see the actual movie and who insists he endorses artistic license—said the film director had spat on Russia's history and defiled the memory of the dead.[73] The infamous TV anchor and head of RT, Dmitry Kisilev, compared it to "Goebbels's propaganda." Despite the fact that Krasovskii self-produced the film, he was accused of corruption. The prosecutor's office demanded the screenplay and film outtakes for the purpose of investigation. Under no illusion that *Celebration* would ever get a distribution certificate, Krasovskii was considering posting his film on YouTube. That is exactly what the state proxies—who expressed their righteous indignation over a film they had not seen—did by breaking in the computer and stealing the raw copy of *Celebration*.[74] Subsequently, nationalists from SERB tried to disrupt free screenings of the movie attempted by the creators.[75]

The grotesque does not stop here. On occasion, even pro-Kremlin historians end up fighting off Article 354.1 thrown at them. In March of 2015, Stalin's grandson, Yevgeny Dzhugashvili, appealed to the Investigative Committee to check if a certain professor had violated the letter of Article 354.1. The latter had denounced the mass execution of Polish officers at Katyn in the spring of 1940 as a crime committed by the NKVD. The head of Historical Memory Foundation, Alexander Diukov, who stands by this judgment, called Dzhugashvili an "idiot" on his Facebook account and challenged the 79-year-old Dzhugashvili to indict him, Diukov, too, for the "glorification of Nazism." And so the late Dzhugashvili did.[76]

The sense of arbitrary justice empowers lynching mobs, who occasionally take on the function of legislative organs. In November 2017, a high school student from Novyi Urengoi became the subject of a harassment campaign on social media. Nikolai Desiatnichenko was part of the delegation that attended an annual ceremony in the German Bundestag commemorating the victims of war and tyranny. In his speech, Desiatnichenko suggested that some among the perished German soldiers had joined the war against their will. "Patriotic" online users, taking his words out of context, trampled the seventeen-year-old into dirt. Among the epithets used were "idiot," "traitor," "evil seed," "reptile," and so on. A concerned citizen instantly alerted the prosecutor's office, while certain Duma deputies demanded that the quote be checked against the letter of Article 354.1. The director of the school where Desiatnichenko was studying got a reprimand, while the boy himself has lost seven kilograms in weight within a month.[77] Even though not directly involved, the state has effectively issued a license to all those who poured their righteous anger on the student from Siberia.

It would be wrong to suggest that only members of the liberal opposition become a target of prosecution revolving around history. Sometimes the nationalists get caught up in regime's nets as well. Thus, in July of 2018 the police in Tula detained some twenty members of a neo-Stalinist movement, The Partisan Truth of the Partisans. The authorities regarded the outfit as a paramilitary group, while its leader claimed they only wanted to build a private museum of the Great Patriotic War. The cult of

Stalin and, just in case, of Putin, preached by the movement apparently also extended to Hitler; alongside other banned literature recovered during the search at the band leader's house, the police found a copy of *Mein Kampf*.[78] Whatever views defendants may hold—what is essential is that the Russian government is using history, among other tools, to squash dissent.

The articles of the Russian penal and administrative code discussed earlier essentially fall in the category of blasphemy laws. The Duma in June of 2013 amended Article 148 by extending it to "public acts demonstrating obvious disrespect toward the society and committed with the purpose of offending religious sentiments of the believers." The offense carries a maximum penalty of 500,000 rubles or a three-year imprisonment.[79] When proposing the amendment, Russian lawmakers referred to a similar legislation in a number of European countries. Even though the comparable legislation does, indeed, exist in countries such as Poland, Spain, Italy, and Greece, many more countries—Denmark, Iceland, Norway, the Netherlands, and most recently Ireland—have come to repeal blasphemy laws in the past few years.[80] As of May 2019, a total of twenty-seven individuals—fewer than might have been expected—have been sentenced in Russia under Article 148.[81]

In the case of both Orthodox believers and war veterans, the regime purports to speak on behalf of an afflicted constituency. Indeed, there is a definite religious element in the very attempt to codify specific historical events such as the Second World War. The loosely defined *dolus specialis* opens up for a possibly wide interpretation and, consequently, an ever-broader offender category. Consider the outcry over a viewer poll run by an independent TV channel Dozhd. On January 27, 2014, the anniversary of the lifting of the German siege of Leningrad, the channel posed the question whether surrendering Leningrad to the Nazis could have saved lives. The St. Petersburg prosecutor's office instantly launched a probe on whether Dozhd has "exceeded acceptable limits," while local lawmakers proposed shutting down the channel altogether. Leading Russian cable and internet providers subsequently removed Dozhd from TV channel packages, inflicting a blow from which it has never been able to recover. In addition, Dozhd was slammed a 200,000 ruble fine in favor of two St. Petersburg retirees, who claimed moral damage caused by the evocation of the Leningrad Blockade.[82]

While political activists are being silenced, among other means, on account of historical comparison, state officialdom has no problem doing exactly that. Thus, Patriarch Kirill claimed popular indignation over gay marriage—the same way the civilized world treated discriminatory Nazi laws. A school teacher in Khabarovsk berated a student for wearing a lapel pin with a Navalny campaign logo. She compared it to advertising Nazi concentration camps.[83] Andrei Khvyli-Olinter, a former state security official turned Orthodox priest, spoke at an international forum, "Russophobia and the Information War against Russia," which was held in September 2015 in Moscow. During his presentation, he displayed two maps that purportedly showed the countries supporting Nazi Germany in 1940–45 and those that imposed sanctions against Russia in 2014. The overlap was not coincidental, claimed the newly born Christian.[84]

Meanwhile, legislative initiatives just keep coming, from various quarters. While the efforts to introduce, at the federal level, a generic law proscribing the "deliberate falsification of truth about the Great Patriotic War" have consistently failed, the hope lives on at the local level. In February 2018 such a law was proposed by President Kadyrov of Chechnya. Unanimously approved by the Chechen parliament, the proposal would subsequently be sent to Duma for further consideration.[85]

Since late 2018, the Russian customs have begun checking books ordered through foreign online shops such as Amazon on the matter of "propaganda of certain views." Books found contravening the country's political interests are being confiscated.[86] Even though history books have not been specifically mentioned, the arbitrary application of justice makes it possible to extend the definition of national interests indefinitely. It is just a matter of time before select history books published abroad, including those by Russian authors, start appearing on the Justice Department's Extremist Materials list.

In March of 2019 a new article was introduced in the administrative code. The controversial Article 20.1 censors online information that shows "obvious disrespect toward the society, the state, symbols of state power, and state agencies." Most of the cases so far have involved individuals who dared to criticize President Putin. It took barely three months, however, before the first derelict with historical connotations was reviewed by the court. A professional dancer got the minimum fine of 30,000 rubles for performing in front of the Second World War memorial in downtown Briansk. Although the actual monument does not even appear in the video, the female dancer was forced to admit her guilt; she said she did not mean to offend the memory of the fallen.[87]

The ministry of defense, in June of 2019, proposed a new article of the penal code, "Destruction or Damage to the Symbols of Russian Military Glory." The offenders would face a three-million fine or three years in jail. The element of conspiracy motivated by hatred would hike the punishment to five million or five years behind bars. Prospective Article 243.4 would also extend to Soviet monuments abroad; individuals implicated in the crime would be banned from entering Russia.[88]

The Last Line of Defense

An unprecedented onslaught against individual and collective freedoms, including historians' professional integrity, has left just a handful of independent institutions in Russia still standing. The latest casualty is the Alexander Yakovlev Democracy Foundation, which in the spring of 2018 was forced to shut down due to the lack of funds. The potential label of a "foreign agent" made the foundation decide not to seek funding abroad. Established in 1993, the Yakovlev Foundation had made a major contribution by publishing nearly forty volumes of documents on Soviet history.[89]

Not counting local initiatives in the provinces, there are currently just three large institutions that exercise a degree of academic freedom: Memorial and the Sakharov Center in Moscow, and the Yeltsin Center in Ekaterinburg.[90] Memorial, which stood at the beginning of both the historical and moral reckoning with Stalinism in the late Soviet Union, has been fighting for survival ever since the passing of the so-called Foreign Agent law in 2012.[91]

The notion of *foreign agent* was introduced by the Duma in July of 2012 as an amendment to the law on nonprofit organizations. According to the amended law, the ministry of justice can designate as foreign agent any Russian organization that deals in politics and receives funding from abroad. Vaguely formulated on purpose, the notion of *political activity* can, and has been, interpreted at whim by the authorities. In practical terms, it means constant state audits, massive paperwork, and eventually fines. Worse still, local partners (e.g., schools) stop cooperating with a "foreign agent," being spooked by the label.[92] With time, the law has become even more stringent, ostensibly to block the constant inflow of foreign money. In November of 2018 authorities declared as "foreign agents" the media outlets dependent on Western financial support (e.g., Radio Liberty). Half a year later, Russia's prosecutor general proposed expanding the list on account of NGOs bankrolled by Russian entities, even those with a single foreign founder.[93] Finally, in November of 2019, the Duma passed an amendment that allows slapping the damaging status also onto individuals who distribute news items by media outlets that have earlier been declared as "foreign agents."[94] Under pressure, NGOs are typically forced to curtail their activities. Although technically possible, getting one's organization off the foreign agent list is a daunting task. Insofar as the decision is taken by the ministry of justice, it is regarded by courts as legally binding. In early 2015 Russian lawmakers inaugurated yet another, more stringent notion of *undesirable organization*. Defined as such are those organizations that "pose a threat to the constitution, defensive capabilities, and security of Russia." To that list, Putin's press secretary Dmitry Peskov added "Russia's national interests." The designating authority in this case is the prosecutor general's office, in coordination with the foreign ministry. The status of an undesirable organization triggers a ban on activities on the Russian territory.[95]

The Memorial's heroic efforts not only to stay afloat but also to continue sharing its perspective on Soviet history have been well documented. Memorial, a human rights center, was the fourth organization to receive the status of a "foreign agency," in July of 2014. Within the following two years, one by one, the justice ministry had put on the list Memorial's branch offices in Ekaterinburg and Syktyvkar, St. Petersburg and Ryazan. Finally, in October of 2016 came the turn of International Memorial. According to a standard note, the organization in question aims to influence state policies and challenge specific decisions by the state apparatus.[96] More specifically, Memorial stands accused of "forming a negative public opinion on state policies and expressing disagreement with the decisions and acts by the authorities."[97] Kafkaesque no doubt, the ministry of justice gave the following two examples of political activities by Memorial: arguing against the Foreign Agent law and criticizing the police investigation of the Boris Nemtsov assassination.[98] For starters, Memorial incurred a 600,000 ruble fine.[99] A legal challenge filed by the organization failed to scrap the pejorative status. Memorial, the academic and educational center in Moscow, has until now avoided the label. More recently, in January of 2019, the ministry of justice initiated yet another verification based on allegations that Memorial had engaged in activities that would warrant the foreign agent status.[100] This time around the authorities spared Memorial's Moscow office, concluding that the archival research it has been pursuing cannot be qualified as a political activity.[101] Consider it a minor setback for the authorities, for in 2019 alone Memorial was slapped thirty fines amounting to 3.9 million rubles for having failed to add to its electronic publications a "foreign agent" label.[102] As of this writing, seventy-five NGOs—mainly human rights organizations—appear on the "foreign agent" list. A few major human rights organizations that had publicly declared they would no longer seek and receive foreign grants had for a number of years continued to exist thanks to presidential grants. Beginning in the fall of 2018, those grants dried out, too, effectively putting an end to such venerable organizations as Lev Ponomarev's For Human Rights movement and the late Liudmila Alexeeva's Moscow Helsinki Group.[103]

There is a strong sense that Yeltsin Center, which opened its doors in November of 2015, may repeat the fate of Perm 36. This premonition is amplified by the presence of such high-profile personalities as Nikita Mikhalkov among its opponents. Mikhalkov, a famed film director and ardent Putin supporter, did not rejoice at the news that the Yeltsin Center had received an award as one of the best European museums—the first Russian institution to receive the honor. Instead, he compared it to the Iron Cross bestowed by the Nazi German Army.[104] The particular ire of the patriots has caused the museum's introductory animation video on Russia's history. First out was that same Mikhalkov, who spoke metaphorically about the "daily injection causing the destruction of national consciousness among children" before the Federation Council. In the case of war, he preached, young Russians would find nothing in the country's history worth defending. Framing it as an issue of state security, Mikhalkov proposed a government intervention by means of shifting the focus of the exhibition rather than closing the center entirely. Minister of Culture Medinskii backed him up, detecting in the video more ideology than in the Stalinist *Brief History of the Soviet Communist Party*.[105]

As Medinskii perceives it, the thousand years of Russian history at Ekaterinburg has been presented as one uninterrupted abomination sequence. Calling the Brezhnev period "stagnation" and Gorbachev's period a "breakthrough into the civilized world" is incorrect, according to him. What about all the numerous achievements that came in between? Every negative fact can be counterbalanced with a positive one— Medinskii reiterated his core argument. For support, he turned to President Putin and his doctrine of Russia's information security. Among other things, Putin in early December 2016 spoke of boosting defenses and neutralizing the efforts to "undermine the historical foundations and patriotic traditions."[106] In response to the discourse developed by two high-profile figures, insofar as Yeltsin Center is indeed "destroying the Russian statehood," a leader of the North Caucasian Muslims proposed to blow it up.[107] Although, fortunately, that remained an empty threat, Mikhalkov has continued his crusade against Yeltsin Center, most recently in the summer of 2018.[108]

While the independent institutions under attack keep on fighting back, they are struggling to protect what really matters—the younger generations and their perception of history. Deviously, the Kremlin has unleashed state proxies to strike where it hurts most, the schoolchildren. For over twenty years now, Memorial has organized a competition for high school students, "People in History: Russia, XX Century." The idea of the competition is to encourage children and youth to collect evidence and critically reflect on the history of Russia through the prism of family. Memorial makes an extra effort to engage school students in the provinces. Out of the around two thousand texts submitted, the forty best get nominated at an annual ceremony in Moscow. Up until now, some fifty thousand children from all over Russia have taken part in Memorial's competition. In the past few years, the award ceremony was brazenly sabotaged by the pro-Kremlin National Liberation Movement (NOD) and the Russian Liberation Movement (SERB), with the connivance of the police.

On April 28, 2016, a few dozen members of NOD—mainly males in their late teens, sporting May 9 paraphernalia—hurled abuses and eggs at the people arriving for the award ceremony. Several of them, including writer Liudmila Ulitskaia, had brilliant green thrown in their faces. "Liberal bastards," "you came here for money," "we don't need alternative history"—shouted the assailants, while the police stood by without intervening. Simultaneously, one of the state-owned TV channels aired a segment that accused Memorial of exploiting the school youth in order to twist history. The Memorial officials tried to put on a brave face, while the schoolchildren were visibly shaken by the ugly incident.[109] The following year NOD used more refined methods in their attempt to disrupt the event. Breaking into the Memorial electronic system, they stole the names and addresses of the winners. Subsequently, they made calls to the respective school administrations and, in the name of the ministry of education, demanded that the students cancel their trip to Moscow. The organizers were also forced at short notice to change the venue of the award ceremony.[110] Yet newer techniques were used to derail the twentieth edition of the competition in 2019. A barrage of online posts labelled Memorial's initiative "unpatriotic" and insinuated that it revisited the history of the Great Patriotic War to score political points. SERB and NOD came in force, sporting the slogans "Memorial is making Vlasovites [traitors] out of our children" and "Memorial is rewriting history for the fascists' benefit."[111] A story aired on Rossiia 24 claimed that Memorial—labelled "Judas" for the occasion—was using German money to brainwash Russian children.[112] In the meantime, participating history teachers, and some of their students, received calls from the local administration and the FSB, who pressured them to discontinue collaboration with Memorial.[113]

Beside the direct pressure exercised by the authorities, a different kind of problem is that the few remaining independent institutions do not necessarily see eye to eye on certain issues of history. One such issue is specific to communist regimes and the successor states, namely how, if at all, to commemorate perpetrators who at one point became victims.[114] There were three major execution and burial sites in and around Moscow during the Great Terror. One of them, known as Kommunarka, contains the identified remains of 6,609 people. After years of debates, in October of 2018, a memorial featuring the names of all the victims opened at the former execution site. The thing is that among those executed in 1937–41 at Kommunarka, an estimated 254 had previously served in the NKVD. The leader of Memorial, Ian Rachinskii, defended the decision while acknowledging the dilemma. He argued that the criteria for unambiguously establishing individual guilt was missing. In that he was attacked by the likes of Andrei Zubov and Yuri Samodurov. Having failed to differentiate between victims and perpetrators, contended the former head of the Sakharov Center, "Memorial is unwittingly assisting the Kremlin and the FSB in concealing the names of individuals who carried out political repression in the Soviet Union." Rachinskii dismissed this claim as conspiratorial, for the state did not participate in the creation of the monument, he said. Subsequently, another critic, Andrei Shalev, who runs

Immortal Barracks website, posted a list of eighty-eight most odious names among those listed on the memorial wall.[115]

An Act of Resistance

Examples of popular resistance to outrages involving history, and mass protests generally, are few and far between in Russia.[116] So successful has been the regime at stamping out dissent, that only few citizens can think of staging protests over an issue as ephemeral as history. In November of 2018 in St. Petersburg, a group of parents vowed to boycott what they considered an inappropriate home exercise their children had been assigned at school. The kids were asked to write a letter to an imaginary father fighting in the Second World War. The parents found it both creepy and unwarranted.[117] Even such innocuous means as a single picket makes the authorities overreact. Thus, history professor Alexei Mosin was briefly detained by the police for demanding a memorial plaque commemorating Stalin's victims be installed on an Ekaterinburg building that had once housed the NKVD. Not untypical for such institutions, the building currently serves as the regional police headquarters. Mosin vowed to continue with the individual protest until his demand was met.[118]

Among the brightest spots in recent years is the establishment of a Free Historical Society (VIO), in February of 2014. To an extent, VIO has both augmented and superseded Memorial, which until recently had been the face of history opposition so to speak. Memorial has a strong identity rooted in Gorbachev's Perestroika—now a distant memory for many. Historians who came to form VIO, however, speak the same academic language as their peers abroad, say, in the United States. Despite obstacles such as the Foreign Agent law, individual historians find ways to present and exchange their ideas both inside and outside Russia. VIO also symbolizes a generational shift. Whether it will be able to expand and thrive depends mainly on two things: open channels of communication within Russia and support from the Western academia. Authorities, it seems, have left VIO be, at least for now. One probable reason is that the society poses no tangible threat to the historical establishment. VIO has offered comprehensive, poignant criticism of RVIO, which never bothered to acknowledge the former's existence.

The problem with VIO, as I see it, is that it still entertains the fundamental belief that history in Russia—like anywhere else in the world—is a professionals' abode. For their comprehensive 2016 report, VIO collaborated with professional historians and students of local lore, textbook authors and museum workers, school teachers and history buffs. In normal circumstances, that would, indeed, be the kinds of people who preserve and channel historical memory. However, it is no longer the case in Russia. The one, central, category that VIO did not engage, for understandable reasons, is Kremlin's spin doctors. Their impact has been so profound that it has generated a new term "political technology" within the Russian context. Working closely with power ministries, it is they who make history in Russia today.

VIO emphasizes the existence of two layers of memory, one superimposed from above and another advanced from below. One may well speak of a resurgence of popular memory in today's Russia. In that sense, Russia is moving in the same direction as the rest of the world. The crucial question, however, is how the *state* goes about this second tier of memory. Until now, one could argue that the medium of internet—which non-state history and historians call home—will remain a free arena for informed debate in the foreseeable future, as it is impossible to fully control. For each grassroots history project hijacked by the state there will be another popular initiative. Some in VIO—certainly the authors of the 2016 report—express confidence that the two forms of historical memory will continue to coexist side by side, despite the state's abhorrence of any form of grassroots organization.[119] Yet the series of recent legislative acts passed by the Duma point in the opposite direction, namely the consistent efforts to implement internet censorship à la the Great Firewall of China.[120] Once that window is closed, the state stranglehold on history in Russia would be complete.

The regime can tolerate just one, preapproved form of historical memory. Alternative interpretations are still possible, but only in the following two instances: (1) they pass both risk and cost-effectiveness assessment, that is, it is considered safe by the authorities and (2) they come from agencies under effective government control. In a country where history and politics have collapsed into one, entities such as RVIO may stand for so-called systemic opposition and VIO for opposition in its traditional meaning. For as long as this political setup exists, VIO has as few chances as Navalny in rallying popular support.[121] Conversely, a dynamic relationship between different forms of memory will come to be if there is a momentous political shift in Russia. That, however, does not appear likely to happen any time soon. In short, there will be no coming to terms with the past in Russia for as long as the future is clouded.

Among other prominent volunteer academic associations in Russia is Dissernet. Despite its rather rowdy self-description as a "free internet association of experts, researchers, and reporters that strive to unmask crooks, falsifiers, and liars," Dissernet takes upon itself the important task of oversight of PhD theses produced in Russia. Specifically, it assesses the scholarly quality of individual research and monitors the process of doctoral defense. Since it came into existence in January 2013, the association had assembled a massive dissertation database and had petitioned the ministry of education with the request to repeal the doctoral degrees of over one hundred individuals. The most high-profile individual that got into Dissernet's crosshairs so far is the former minister of culture Medinskii.[122] In the fall of 2019, several concerned citizens, including historian Sergei Prudovskii, established a volunteer association called Archives Watch. As the name suggests, the association will work to ensure unrestricted access to Russian archives, as provided by law.[123]

Coming back to Memorial, it had powerfully enunciated the human cost of Stalin's terror through such initiatives as "Restoring the Names" and "The Last Address." Beginning in 2007, Memorial has organized a public reading of names of the victims. Lasting ten hours, the central event takes place by the so-called Solovetsky stone on Lubyanka Square in Moscow. In spite of the conspicuous absence of top officials and the presence of occasional provocateurs, thousands of people across Russia find it the best way to mark the Day of Remembrance of Victims of Political Repression, October 30.[124] In 2013 Memorial conceived of yet another memorial project, "The Last Address." Activists attach a simple metallic plaque with the name of an individual victim on the building where he/she last lived. As of 2018, some eight hundred such plaques had been installed in Russia and several other countries. Notably, Memorial receives requests not only from the relatives of the victims but also from concerned citizens generally.[125] The Last Address concept brings to mind that of *Stolperstein* (German: stumbling block) in Germany and now across Europe commemorating individual victims of the Nazis, primarily Jews.

Yet Memorial appears to be struggling to connect with the younger generations. Its decades-long efforts to educate the public about Stalin's crimes suddenly appeared outdated after the release of Yuri Dud's documentary, *Kolyma: The Cradle of Our Fear* in the spring of 2019. On the surface of it, the creator does not say anything new in his special feature. In a nutshell, Dud and his crew travel across Siberia visiting former places of incarceration and talking to people. The documentary is nearly primitive in treating Stalinism as a tabula rasa, and that is where its strength lies. Dud, a popular talk show host of 32, talks to his peers in the language they understand. The documentary hit thirteen million views on YouTube in a span of weeks. Most important, it got the young people talking about Stalin and his deadly legacy.[126]

Beating the Putin Regime at Its Own Game

One may reasonably ask if there is any way at all of challenging the official Russian historical discourse from within. To reformulate the question: Is there anything that can make the Kremlin pause in its pursuit of history politics? Unexpectedly, perhaps, it is legal action. In a country where an independent judiciary has effectively ceased to exist, a rare lawsuit by a private individual claiming a false historical interpretation by the state catches authorities off guard. No matter how the state reacts, legal proceedings generate enough publicity to cause embarrassment. It adds yet another level of complexity (from the perspective of the state) if the claimant possesses insider knowledge about how the judiciary operates. In late 2018, a former member of the Russian Investigative Committee, Igor Stepanov, filed a lawsuit against *Rossiiskaia Gazeta* and the FSB head Alexander Bortnikov. Stepanov argued that Bortnikov, in his infamous newspaper interview a year earlier, had justified Stalin's violence by explaining it away as overzealousness on the part of the NKVD. Stepanov's indignation was caused in part by the fact that twenty of his relatives had fallen victim to Stalin's terror. Stepanov had earlier filed separate lawsuits (involving matters other than history) against the FSB, the mayor of Moscow Sobianin, and Prime Minister Medvedev. Although Stepanov is uncomfortable with the designation *civil activism*, that is what he is essentially pursuing. For him, it is a matter of dignity and self-respect. It can also be very dangerous, though, he admits. Stepanov is prepared for any sort of provocation and therefore does not recommend replicating his chosen method.[127] The court in Moscow had declined to hear the case. Undeterred, Stepanov filed yet another lawsuit in the summer of 2019 against Bortnikov and *Rossiiskaia Gazeta*.[128]

Denis Karagodin (b. 1982), who began his quest for justice in 2012, is using a slightly different method. Karagodin seeks to identify and incriminate those responsible for the judicial murder of his great-grandfather in 1937. In so doing, he is also tracing the chain of command all the way from the Kremlin to the man who pulled the trigger.

By now Karagodin has collected documentary evidence implicating thirty-three such individuals. His is essentially a criminal investigation building up for a court case. In legal terms, he is dealing with conspiracy to murder.[129] Such an individual approach to historical injustice may, indeed, be more effective than seeking redress through a Nuremberg-like legal procedure, which had been a subject of an ongoing public conversation, inconsequentially. Furthermore, Karagodin's quest for justice has sparked a public discussion; just as Gulag victims were once writing to Solzhenitsyn, they are now sharing their stories with Karagodin.[130] One of the letters, and an apology, came from the granddaughter of an NKVD executioner on Karagodin's list. Six of his correspondents are planning to conduct a similar investigation on behalf of their own relatives murdered by Stalin regime.[131]

Karagodin is determined to bring his criminal investigation to a logical end. Lawyer Alexander Busarov, who knows the Russian legal system from within, is not so sure such a straightforward approach has a chance to succeed. This is why, simultaneously with but independently of Karagodin's, he launched a project of his own. Busarov did so in secret, which is the reason why his findings became public knowledge only recently. His modus operandi is truly fascinating. A great grandson of an NKVD officer who had been arrested and executed in 1939, Busarov grasped with the question as to what turned his relative and thousands like him into seasoned killers. He also wanted the present regime to acknowledge the criminality of the NKVD, and by extension of its successor agencies. To do so, he engaged in an elaborate roleplay. Posing as a hard-core Stalinist, he appealed to the Military prosecutor general's office with the request to absolve certain NKVD executioners who had been sentenced. Busarov thought that the authorities would argue that such individuals cannot be exonerated on principle and thus indirectly admit that the Soviet security police was a criminal organization. To his amazement, he got a reply that many of the NKVD officers on his list had been formally exonerated in 2012 and 2013. Busarov then doubled down, requesting that the military ranks and whatever decorations those men had received while on active duty also be restored to them. Busarov's ingenious method worked: the system began breaking down. Next he was informed that the letters of acquittal had been revoked; officials who made the decision back in 2012 are no longer to be found on the employee list. Meanwhile Busarov kept receiving documents labeled as secret from the Supreme Court and the prosecutor general's office. When the number of files in his collection reached two hundred and the danger grew that the authorities would eventually discover his true intention, Busarov packed up his treasured archives and went abroad.[132]

The next page in Busarov's captivating legal adventure is yet to be written. He is effectively a saboteur who brought the state machinery to a halt by throwing a spanner in the works. The overall conclusion is rather distressing, though: the Putin regime cannot be convinced or forced, but only cheated out, to modify a historical narrative. This is probably why one of the most powerful commentaries on Russian history politics has been delivered not by a historian or lawyer but by a performance artist. On November 9, 2015, Piotr Pavlenskii (b. 1984) set alight the entrance door to the FSB headquarters in Moscow. The artist framed his act as a challenge to a terrorist organization. Although Pavlenskii was not indicted on charges of terrorism—as he hoped to—he was found guilty of vandalism "motivated by political hatred" (Article 214 of the penal code). Corpus delicti was eventually requalified as "destroying or inflicting damage to objects of cultural legacy or cultural value" (Article 243). The prosecution saw no pun in declaring the NKVD/KGB building a part of cultural heritage, for in the 1930s a "number of prominent state, public, and cultural figures had been incarcerated there."[133]

Conclusion

Yuri Dmitriev (b. 1956), Victor Shmyrov (b. 1966), Sergei Arakcheev (b. 1956)—the three members of Memorial who saw their life's work being destroyed before their own eyes—are all very different in the way they handled their ordeal. Dmitriev is a stoic. The way he describes his imprisonment renders an image of the "zek" immortalized by the likes of Dostoyevsky and Solzhenitsyn. Dmitriev is a martyr, surviving through the strength of his faith. He is the kind of individual who does not break under torture. But neither does he have any illusions as to the regime's deadly resolve to impose its will. Dmitriev was poised upon receiving the news of a retrial: the dragon does not unclench its teeth. During his four-year ordeal, Dmitriev has received continual public support.[134] As compared to the leader of Karelia Memorial, Shmyrov is a very modern man. He had fought for several years to keep Perm 36, his brainchild, true to its original concept. Shmyrov enjoys a wide professional network of support within Russia and abroad, and he is aware of the media's importance in waging his battle. No matter what, Shmyrov will keep on fighting. Thus, he resolved to rebuild Perm 36, this time as an online project, organized limited editions of the legendary civic forum elsewhere in Russia, and arranged summer schools for historians abroad. Sure enough, unlike Dmitriev, Shmyrov never faced criminal charges (even though he was effectively accused of embezzlement). Arakcheev is the least typical of Memorial historians. As someone who comes from within the security apparatus, Arakcheev never expressed the will to challenge the system. If he blames anyone, it is particular individuals, who he believes hold a grudge against him and his museum. Yet he is genuine in his disbelief as to the extent the state is willing to go in censoring history, and he cannot fathom why. Sad and incomprehensible as it is, he saw no choice but to let the staff go; the biggest challenge would be finding a home for the two trucks full of artefacts amassed during the museum's existence. Still, Arakcheev's faith in the system appears to be under stress. As of May 2018 he still believed he could retain the exhibition by merely "updating" it in consultation with the ministry of culture. A few months later the very same ministry slapped a fine on Arakcheev for unearthing the remains of the victims of Stalin's terror.[135] The short five years that have passed between the beginning of the assault on Perm 36 and the closing of the museum in Yoshkar-Ola have seen a sea change in Russia, all for the worse. The former was able to survive, albeit in an altered form, thanks largely to the intervention of the presidential human rights council, which could do nothing but express its concern about the imminent demise of the latter. As for the human rights council itself, by late 2019 it had been effectively eviscerated.

The hostile takeover of Perm 36 proved to be a sign of things to come. Not only did the authorities demonstrate a commitment to root out the perceived historical dissent but they also colluded with ostensibly independent nationalist groups in making a case for gutting the museum. State auxiliaries play an important role in the legal crackdown on the political opposition by the state. It is typically nationalist vigilantes who denounce individuals in purported violations of law. The corrupt regime has no scruples in manufacturing a number of new, and amending existing, articles of the Russian penal and administrative code to enable prosecution involving interpretations of history. Like with other aspects of Russian historymaking, this process was triggered by the 2011–12 pro-democracy protests and accelerated in the wake of the military incursion in Ukraine two years later.

Stigmatizing certain views on history by legal means is bordering on the absurd, which is of little help to the defendants whose numbers are growing and whose sentences are becoming harsher. The perusal of cases leaves no doubt that the individuals under investigation have been critical of the Putin regime. As far as the Kremlin is concerned, history is, indeed, politics. The Russian human rights lawyer, Mark Feigin, has spelled doom on the prospects of winning political cases in Russia with Putin in his fourth presidential term and counting. Speaking in November of 2018 at the Atlantic Council, he stated that legal defense as such is utterly corrupt, and therefore ineffectual, in today's Russia. According to Feigin, the authoritarian system of rule is undergoing an ultimate transformation into dictatorship. The growing repression may be interpreted as a defensive function of the regime preoccupied with legitimizing Putin's hold on power.[136]

There is very little that stands in the way of the regime's juggernaut. Pinned down by the 2012 Foreign Agent law and harassed by government proxies, nongovernmental organizations such as Memorial have limited possibilities at public outreach. While some of its initiatives such as "Restoring the Names" and "the Last Address" have attracted significant attention, there is a question mark on whether Memorial is capable of capturing younger generations exposed to Putin's "patriotic education." Free Historical Society (VIO), an independent professional association, stepped in where Memorial has struggled. Yet VIO has only few means at its disposal to influence the government policy on history. So far, the history establishment has effectively ignored open letters and online debates initiated by VIO.

The prospects of making the regime change its ways on history are dim. At best, it can be tricked into indirectly admitting the absurdity of its conception of history. Even then, it does not go beyond frustration expressed by certain members of the elite.

Conclusion

The notion that the present history framework in Russia has gradually emerged as a result of confluent social and cultural trends cannot be substantiated. Stopgap initiatives in support of an official interpretation of history, the Soviet period in particular, roughly follow political developments within Russia. The trajectory of state involvement in history politics can be traced back to the early years of Putin's presidency. While the Kremlin's core attitude toward history has remained constant since the early 2000s, the strategic use of history became more devious beginning in 2012.

Domestic and foreign politics in combination determined how and when the regime would recalibrate its position on history. In that respect, pro-democracy protests that had erupted in late 2011 in response to Putin's intention to reclaim the presidency was a much stronger catalyst than Russia's aggression against Ukraine in 2014. The framework for the present Russian history politics was effectively put in place in 2012. Everything that followed is essentially a modification to the 2012 policy. The government has by now achieved high levels of coordination within historymaking, working tirelessly toward that goal. There is plenty of evidence—never explicitly denied by the state—that the contents and methods of historymaking have been preapproved at the very top, by Putin himself.

Politicization of history in Russia has reached unprecedented proportions, to the extent that the chief actors no longer feel the need to hide it. I am not aware of any other country where a conservative body such as a historical society would be headed by a spymaster (Sergei Naryshkin), historical mythmaking be endorsed by state ministers with advanced degrees in history (Vladimir Medinskii, Olga Vasilieva), an official historical narrative be shaped by church authorities (Bishop Tikhon), and youth history education be promoted by a biker (Alexander "The Surgeon" Zaldostanov).

Personalities mentioned in this book—Bishop Tikhon, Patriarch Kirill, biker Zaldostanov, intelligence officer Naryshkin, minister Medinskii, bureaucrat Vasilieva, speaker Matvienko, academician Chubarian, sculptor Tsereteli, President Putin, and others—are the collective product of the Soviet system, and history. All of them were once young pioneers, then members of the communist youth, only to later serve the cause of the new-old post-Soviet Russia. The transition they made from "matured socialism" to neoconservative nationalism did not see any fundamental change to their worldview. They appear at the same events, channel funds from one agency to another, sit on each other's boards of trustees, praise and award each other medals. Curiously, some of the adepts of Russian history politics such as Medinskii or Matvienko were born in what is nowadays Ukraine.

The intricate link between the individuals who collectively advance the state agenda on history has been indirectly underscored by the Russian Academy of Sciences, of all institutions. Speaking in January of 2015 in the Duma, Patriarch Kirill proposed that universities start awarding a PhD in theology. That was promptly done, and in June of 2017 an Orthodox priest received the first ever doctoral degree in theology in independent Russia—over strenuous objections from the academics.[1] The Academy of Sciences has gone even further in acknowledging Kirill's efforts at "popularization of science" by awarding him, and Federation Council speaker Matvienko, an honorary professorship. The academy spokesperson substantiated the nomination by a nonexisting quotation from Albert Einstein, taken from a series currently running on Russian television. True, shortly after the news of the nomination spread, in January 2019, the academy indefinitely postponed it and subsequently withdrew its initiative altogether. It did not really dent the rock-solid reputation of the leader of the Russian Orthodox Church as a man of science; Patriarch Kirill already holds an honorary degree from a few dozen institutions of higher learning.[2] Select churchmen and politicians thus receive a validation of their nonexistent expertise in outlining the contours of Russian history.

Insofar as one may consider Putin's Russia a mafia state, it is safe to speak of a Russian history establishment. While the word *establishment* can be imbued with various meanings, in the Russian context it is fairly distinct. The Russian history establishment incorporates major "nongovernmental" organizations such as Russian Historical Society (RIO) and Russian Military Historical Society (RVIO), traditional yet hollowed-out entities such as the Academy of Sciences, influential individuals close to the government such as Tsereteli and Shcherbakov, and core officials within the supervising agencies such as Medinskii in the ministry of culture, Naryshkin in the intelligence service, and Sergei Shoigu in the ministry of defense. In effect, it is a superstructure created by, and controlled from, the Kremlin. The collective portrait of a Russian history bureaucrat renders an archaic men's club comprising members in their fifties and older. Their imagination level is capped by their Soviet upbringing, which even the newest in media technology cannot help reformat. The few fresh faces such as Konstantin Mogilevskii (b. 1982) of the History of Motherland Foundation, Konstantin Pakhaliuk (b. 1991) of RVIO, or Sergei Belov (b. 1991?) of the Victory Museum have not so far distinguished themselves, even though they may in the future. Backed by the mighty state propaganda, the historical establishment carries a larger segment of the Russian population but has virtually no impact on foreign audiences.

The present book attests to the existence of a centralized state policy on history in Putin's Russia. Conversely, there is no significant discord in historical interpretations as advanced by various participating agencies. Whatever small differences there might be, they are levelled out by a common desire to benefit from state largesse.[3] For that reason alone, the discourse on history is remarkably homogeneous across the board. It is true that the state, in the attempt to dampen social conflict, sometimes finds itself managing a pluralistic debate on the meaning of Russian history.[4] However, that does not mean that a master narrative is lacking.

The unified front on history in Russia is due to three overlapping factors. First, the message hammered out by the government machinery is so straightforward and unsophisticated, if not primitive, that it does not require further mediation. Russia has a long, great, heroic past exemplified by the Soviet victory over Nazi Germany. Any attempt to complicate that picture purportedly serves to undermine national unity and harm Russia's position internationally. Applicable to Putin's Russia, the following two analytical threads come from within the field of Holocaust studies. "Working toward the Führer" relates to Nazi officials who had progressively raised the stakes in trying to outbid each other in anticipation of Hitler's will. Since this concept had emerged in the early 1990s, historians have successfully applied it to Stalin during the Great Terror. In fact, "working toward the leader" is an essential element of just about any authoritarian regime. The paternalistic, corporate system of governance established by Putin in Russia entails subordinates vying for privileges in exchange for loyalty. That loyalty can take on different forms, including politically correct interpretations of history.[5] Opaque as he can be, Putin made himself understood on issues related to history, the Soviet period in particular.

In equal measure, the Russian case validates the notion of *cumulative radicalization*. While fighting for the scarce resources and benefits, multiple actors are eager to demonstrate their zeal before the higher-ups. In the process, they propose increasingly more radical solutions to perceived problems. This is certainly true in the case of the legislative branch and the so-called memorial laws, but also in the case of nationalist organizations. The latter act in the belief that they have received carte blanche from the government to attack the opposition, now also under the pretext of an "unpatriotic" perspective on Russian history. This is the system that works on autopilot, that is, for as long as Putin is in the driver's seat. President Putin has no need to publicly endorse or even acknowledge that system. All that matters is that he does not contradict or make any efforts to dismantle it.

All the actors in the field of history politics are eager to preserve and nourish their link to the state. That, however, is fraught with danger: stand too close and you can get a fourth degree burn. The Orthodox Church, by nature of its entanglement with the Kremlin, is perhaps taking the biggest risk. The church fathers are advised to learn from twentieth-century Russian history, which saw a warm embrace by the state eventually strangling the Orthodox Church to death. Furthermore, as theologian Andrei Kuraev has reasoned, too cozy a relationship with the regime impairs the church's normal missionary work and eventually causes rot.[6]

Insofar as independent history-writing and history-telling belong under freedom of expression, the Putin regime has succeeded at stamping it out. Looking at Putin's period of rule as a whole, one may draw a direct line from the hostile takeover of the independent TV channel NTV in 2001 to the proposed institute of history politics to be established sometime soon. Tellingly, the Russian institute of history politics in the making bears no reference to "national/people's memory" in its title—unlike comparable entities in East Central Europe (i.e., Poland, Ukraine, Estonia, etc.). Obviously, the government machinery has no use for subtleties. The cold pursuit of realpolitik is also evident in the fundamental shift away from the grand old institutions of higher learning such as the Academy of Sciences and Moscow State University to schools that approach history through the prism of politics and/or patriotic education, for instance Moscow State University of International Relations or Moscow State

Pedagogical University. Meanwhile the new breed of state affiliates such as RVIO and RIO function as self-regulating bodies. Consider that it was not someone in the government who had proposed FSB's Sergei Ivanov as prospective new head of RVIO's board of trustees. The initiative had come from within the organization. The government agenda on history has little use for professional historians, preferring, instead, propagandists and political scientists. History in contemporary Russia is on the way to being subsumed under so-called political technology.

Members of the establishment advance a syncretic view on history, which they cannot but maintain in order to stay afloat as loyal state officials. What the officialdom with Putin at the top regard as an interrupted course of Russian history is nothing more than an exercise at decontextualization. Literary scholar Sergei Toymentsev chose calling it "post-traumatic reduction ad absurdum." "Insofar as the Soviet regime had never been pronounced 'criminal,'" he contends, "Russia's future is bound to remain its violent, medieval past."[7] Liberal politician Boris Vishnevskii has chosen a less academic language in calling the same phenomenon "political schizophrenia."[8] The word *schizophrenia* does, indeed, come to mind insofar as history politics in Putin's Russia is concerned. For a rational observer, historymaking à la russe functions to methodically undermine the mental capacities of the majority population. It begins to make sense, however, if one takes into account the Kremlin's covert goal—the destruction of a civil society that could otherwise pose a challenge to the regime.

One cannot avoid the impression that the Russian state policy aims at creating a fictitious history in which replica comes in lieu of the original. This is being done with the single purpose of convincing the populace of the inevitability of the present, authoritarian rule in Russia. The staff at Tiumen art museum were both heartbroken and indignant at the sight of ancient Orthodox icons hastily packed in plastic and dumped in the museum's basement in the winter of 2017. This disgrace came to pass because the authorities had decided that the museum building should host the massive "Russia: My History" multimedia exhibition. Instead of original sacral paintings, the visitors would get to see their video projections, courtesy of Bishop Tikhon and the Russian Orthodox Church. The historical novel *The Wall* was penned by the omnipotent, former minister of culture Medinskii. In the play based on Medinskii's book there is a scene in which an icon begins to shed real tears during a collective prayer in the besieged Smolensk. In the following act, spectators learn that a cleric "made it happen" in order to inspire the population to continue resisting the enemy. A fake is a fake is a fake.

Selling to the population this kind of synthetic history is only possible by first intentionally impairing their mental capacity. And that is what the Putin regime has been effectively doing by suppressing the freedom of opinion. Conversely, the collective self-identification with state power bears on the ability and/or will to render a moral judgment on the Soviet past, including Stalin's crimes.[9] The Putin regime has committed a crime against humanity by leaving behind nothing but scorched earth, in people's minds as well. The popular, vulgar Russian slogan "We can do it again" rings as true as ever.

The system of state funding and accreditation keeps independent voices at bay. The law on foreign agents meanwhile prevents the injection of funds from, and the free exchange of ideas with, other countries. The Russian academia has consistently been strangled, for it cannot exist in a vacuum. The tendency toward isolationism is growing by the day. It reached a crescendo in the summer of 2019 when academic institutions received a circular from the ministry of education regulating contacts between Russian and foreign scholars. The conspiratorial way of thinking, the kind that had produced the quintessential myth of Jewish world domination, has effectively taken Russian history and Russian historians hostage. Just to be able to work in the profession involves endorsing historical myths promoted at the highest governmental level. This spells a disaster in the making. We are in the presence of a systematic deprofessionalization of history. If this tendency persists—and there is nothing to suggest otherwise—in a short while the institutional framework for the study of history in Russia will be in tatters.

Much like Putin does not let power slip from his hands, so does he keep history close by his side. That makes the outlook for both Russia and the humanities in Russia dim. Even getting to pre-Putin levels of academic freedom appears unattainable at this point. Neither can one imagine the West—maligned and alienated by the Putin regime, in its precarious current state—attempting anything like a new Marshall Plan to return Russia to normality. Even less willing is the West to engage with the aggrandized idea of Russia's place in history. History is politics in Russia. For many outside of Russia, this realization has not yet sunk in. Tellingly, the Czech Republic in May 2018 rejected the asylum application of Vladimir Luzgin, one of the first Russian citizens sentenced under the notorious Article 354.1 ("glorification of Nazism"). The Czech authorities found no fact of persecution in his case.

* * *

Like any other scholar, I strive for objectivity. I have thus tried to avoid typical historians' fallacies as well as emotional language and uncanny comparisons in my analysis. Still, having reread what I have written, I cannot shake off a profound sense of disbelief. Efforts at the militarization of Russian society, steeped in past historical experience, are unprecedented in the post–Cold War world.

No less disturbing is the brazenness with which the state is driving history-based patriotic propaganda. The amazing part is that nearly all the sources I have used in the book are in the public domain. The five-year patriotic education programs are available online; the RVIO website features a section "Monumental Propaganda." It is not dissimilar to Bellingcat having been able to piece together the circumstance of the 2014 downing of a Malaysia Airlines plane over Ukraine almost exclusively on the basis of electronic sources.[10]

The book is replete with anecdotes. In fact, I am just scratching the surface. Out of an estimated 22,000 "patriotic" organizations in Russia, I have looked closely at barely a dozen. Out of the thousands of historical monuments that have been erected in Russia in the past decade I have had space to mention only a few. For each Medinskii, there are tens of thousands of school teachers and bureaucrats who implement his ideological vision of history. For each Kirill Alexandrov, there are (fewer and fewer in numbers) professional historians who risk their career by upholding high academic standards and refusing to conform. Whether it is history or patriotism, broadly defined, it is invariably featured in conjunction with the word *military*. The military aspect dominates just any historical narrative as told to the public. "That's what kids like," as one bureaucrat once blurted.

The annexation of Crimea in 2014 is a watershed event that underscores the kind of militant patriotism cultivated by the Russian state. The conquest of Crimea entered the pantheon of major Russian victories (real or mythologized), as peddled by nationalists: over fascism in 1945, Khazaria in 965, and China in 5508 AD.[11] The so-called reunification of Crimea with Russia serves as both the apotheosis and catalyst of historical revisionism. The reverse side of historical revisionism sees the state legitimizing, directly or indirectly, specific acts of aggression by the Soviet Union such as the division of Poland in 1939, the annexation of the Baltic States in 1940, the invasion of Czechoslovakia in 1968, and/or the war in Afghanistan in 1979-89.[12]

Among the most contested issues remain the secret protocols to the 1939 Molotov–Ribbentrop Pact. This particular historical event effectively ushered (Soviet) historymaking. Eighty years on, it still ruffles elites' feathers. The tenor has changed, though. Medinskii is now presenting the division of Eastern Europe between Hitler and Stalin as a "triumph of Soviet diplomacy."[13] Echoing the 1948 publication "Falsifiers of History," RIO's Naryshkin in August 2019 presented a new document collection, *The USSR–Germany, 1932–1941*. According to the director of the intelligence service, the initiative for a nonaggression agreement came from Germany. The Soviet Union signed the pact reluctantly, anticipating that only some of its provisions would ever be implemented.[14] The facsimile of the Soviet copy of the secret protocols was published online, for the first time ever in Russia, earlier that summer by the Historical Memory Foundation. Simultaneously, the pro-Kremlin Institute of Foreign Political Studies and Initiatives prepared a collection of essays on the same subject. The introduction was penned by the head of the institute, Veronika Krasheninnikova—a career diplomat with a PhD in history, top official in the United Russia Party, advisor to the director of Russian Today (RT) Margarita Simonian, and coauthor of the 2012 Foreign Agent law.[15] Meanwhile, the State Historical Museum later in October cancelled the planned roundtable discussion of the Molotov–Ribbentrop Pact organized by *Diletant*, describing it as "unethical," and a major bookseller in Moscow withdrew the issue of the magazine on the same subject.[16]

The official state policy goads revision of history—by violent means if necessary—or else does not allow for historical complexity. There is no doubt that the 2000 sanctification of Nikolai II by the Russian Orthodox Church and the tsar's ongoing memorialization have strengthened the hand of religious extremists who sabotaged the screening of *Matilda* in 2017. The May 2018 act of vandalism vis-à-vis the painting depicting Ivan the Terrible killing his son refers back to the unveiling of the monument to Ivan the Terrible one and half years earlier and the nationalist rhetoric that accompanied it. With the colossal resources invested in the glorification of the Soviet victory over Nazi Germany, the emergency of nationalist vigilantes keen on censoring alternative narratives was also to be expected. These and similar instances project the sense of impunity, the moral license given by the state to all those who seek to avenge what is portrayed as the injured dignity of the afflicted population groups such as war veterans, Orthodox believers, and others.

The Soviet victory in the Second World War has become a one-stop shop that can stimulate all sorts of emotional responses in the population. According to the head of the social department within the St. Petersburg administration, the Rio Rita happening (held on an annual basis since 2016) enjoys the latter's support for it causes a sensation of joy in the people, which they so clearly miss in their everyday life.[17] That can be interpreted as if May 9 eliminates the need for the state to invest in the general well-being of its population through comprehensive social programs, job creation, crime prevention, and so on. One day in history seems to solve all the Russians' problems, once a year.

The syncretic approach to history, as promoted in Putin's Russia, has an obvious side effect. When the truth is no longer possible to ascertain, even the official storyline gets blurred in the popular mind. Hence all the numerous faux pas: German weaponry gets mixed up with the Soviet ammunition and American soldiers pass for Russian, military decorations get conflated and historical dates travel back and forth in time. Typically brushed off as inconsequential, these kinds of mishaps are undermining the very fabric of history—a concept, a discipline, and a profession. This, however, does not seem to bother the present regime, which has since long, and definitively since 2012, seen history as a political tool.

Among the recent victims in the war on history waged by the Putin regime, with fierce determination since 2014, are Perm 36 Museum (2012–2015), the Sandarmokh memorial (2016–2018), the Alexander Yakovlev Foundation (2018), and the Gulag museum in Yoshkar-Ola (2018). It does not take long to establish that the wrath of the establishment is directed against the history of Stalin's mass terror. Given the prominence accorded to the gleaming new Gulag museum in Moscow, the authorities have an issue with the perpetrators, not the victims. In accordance with the superimposed idea of the continuum of Russian history, Stalin deserves a place in the pantheon of rulers. The conventional role of security agencies in ensuing stability within the country—as has been consistently emphasized by state officials—highlights the FSB's origins as an organization born into the post-revolutionary Red Terror. The unwillingness of the regime to face up to Soviet mass crimes creates a situation in which mobilizing state resources for the purpose of massaging history appears a lesser evil. The present rulers have inherited from the Soviet Union the irresistible appeal of self-righteousness. "Falsification of history," evoked ad nauseam by the Putin regime, is exactly what it has been guilty of. Moscow practices what it preaches—looking at a mirror image of the world concocted in the Kremlin's corridors.

With every passing year, the regime is raising the stakes as to the lengths it is willing to go in suppressing dissent and massaging history. The public display of Stalin's image came as a shock in 2005, appeared a provocation in 2010, and became commonplace by 2015. In 2016, Free Historical Society (VIO) argued that the "creeping rehabilitation of dark pages and figures in Russian history enables political reactionaries to promote the kinds of ideas that *decency and residual respect for Constitution have until now prevented them from doing* [emphasis added]." Vladislav Surkov's manifesto of February 2019, in which he presented Putin as the new Atatürk and Putinism as a historical inevitability, proved just that.[18] Gloves are off and everything is possible after the unveiling of plans for an institute of history politics in 2018. Nothing is shocking anymore. Things do, indeed, move fast in contemporary Russia. Back in 2004, five years into Putin's rule, Tsereteli was unable to publicly display his statue of Russia's leader, as proscribed by the law governing monuments to still living people. Fifteen years later, that same law does not seem to apply, as monuments to Putin keep popping up across Russia, with Tsereteli pushing for a 30-meter-high copy of his original statue to be erected in St. Petersburg.

History—as it has been understood, studied, and narrated since the time of ancient Greece—is under existential threat in Russia Anno Domini 2020. Yet another anniversary of the end of the Second World War and the anticipated unveiling of an institute of history politics are certain to hike up the levels of militant rhetoric. Meanwhile, the few remaining channels through which the dwindling body of independent, nongovernment historians are able to share their vision of history with the masses are on the verge of closure. One of the most Orwellian legislative initiatives to ever emerge in Russia is also the most recent. In December of 2018 a group of Duma deputies proposed to simultaneously ban dissemination—by both private citizens and the media—of fake news and disparaging information about the state, its symbols, and institutions. The proposal defines neither "fake news" nor "socially important information," leaving internet users in the dark as to which of their posts may potentially be regarded as an administrative offense punishable by fine. The authors of the initiative justify it as an international effort to stamp out "online disinformation." As one of the lawmakers has explained, fake news may pose a threat to private life, cause mass unrest, and undermine security.[19] On March 6, 2019, Duma passed the bill. Even though the new law does not come under antiextremist legislation, the agency that will be investigating individual cases is the Antiterrorism Center, which deals specifically with extremism (formally) and protest movement (informally).[20] What is so hypocritical about the proposal is, of course, the fact that Russia and the Russian Government *are* the prime generators of fake news in the world, now also in the field of history. Another bill, on "sovereign internet," which came into force in late 2019, effectively superimposes government control over online discussions. Meanwhile, Putin—by means of his January 15, 2020, proposal to change the constitution—has indicated that he is going to have a hold on Russian politics indefinitely. Neither tsars nor deities, the president and a few of his retainers were recently proclaimed by a local court as a "social group" and as such protected against criticism.[21]

A political change in Putin's Russia does not mean a change in policy. A sudden cabinet reshuffle in January of 2020 ostensibly brought fresh faces into the government. Sergei Kravtsov came to replace Vasilieva as the minister of enlightenment, and Olga Liubimova replaced Medinskii as the minister of culture. It makes little difference that Kravtsov is fifteen years Vasilieva's junior. A teachers' college graduate, Kravtsov made his career entirely within the ministry of education. For the past seven years, he had served as head of Rosobrnadzor (the inspectorate), known for withdrawing accreditation from European University at St. Petersburg and Moscow School of Social and Economic Sciences, on the one hand, and clearing Medinskii of charges of academic plagiarism, on the other. The Kravstov-led department had reviewed history textbooks on the matter of the "accurate" representation of the past. Although ten years younger than her predecessor, Liubimova speaks the same folksy language. Trained as a journalist, she has been working closely with the Russian Orthodox Church. In her latest position as head of the cinematography department in the ministry of culture—endowed with importance by her ex-boss—Liubimova, among other things, judged *The Death of Stalin* to be offensive. Reportedly, Liubimova got the job thanks to the lobbying done by Nikita Mikhalkov. As regards Medinskii, he has gotten even closer to the seat of power now, as President Putin's aide on issues of culture. His final act as the outgoing minister of culture was to delay the scheduled release of Hollywood movies in the run-up to the May 9 celebration—expected to be the grandest ever (due to the coronavirus outbreak, the military parade was moved to June 24).

Like eugenics, history politics in Putin's Russia can be divided into positive and negative. Positive historymaking aims to fashion a linear, heroic narrative for the purpose of rallying the population behind the regime. Meant for domestic consumption, it is a large undertaking supported at all levels of state bureaucracy. Negative historymaking, on the other hand, is confined to a select few think tanks and individual academics associated with them. Their objective is to put up effective defenses against the perceived, concerted attack on Russian history from abroad. The false inference makes negative historymaking highly ineffectual, as opposed to positive historymaking.

Even though specific historical complexes may be put on both a positive and a negative spin, the government's agenda makes all the difference. For example, the core argument in the newly advanced discourse on the Holocaust is that the Soviet Army had saved the remaining European Jews from annihilation. Ultimately, however, that narrative serves to berate West Europeans for not appreciating enough the Soviet victory over Hitler's Germany and simultaneously blaming the East Europeans for collaborating in the Nazi genocide of the Jews. Installing mass-produced statues of Orthodox saints, Russian tsars, and Soviet military commanders across the country projects the exact opposite dynamics. The hero pantheon is expected to boost patriotism and fundamentally support the Putin regime among the Russian population.

Positive or negative, all elements of Russian historymaking eventually become "unified"—school textbooks, the principles guiding historical research, entities that speak in the name of historians, and so on. One of the functions of the recently proposed charter of the historian is to regulate historical discourse internationally. Think of it as an academic Yalta Agreement, which presupposes the existence of anti-Russian historians as a category. The world is in midst of a new cold war, argue self-styled patriotic historians, and history is a weapon.[22] RVIO and RIO have been created on that very premise. As RVIO's former executive director Vladislav Kononov has stated, "history is politics collapsed [*oprokinutaia*] in the past."[23]

The authoritarian and thus utilitarian mindset of the Russian officialdom make them imagine the West operating according to the geopolitical principles they take as given. The foreign ministry in particular believes that the West—as a composite and immutable body politic—consistently works to undermine Russia's interests, including my means of history. The history discipline is considered in Russia a constituent element of soft power. The Russian authorities explicitly, if only internally, state their intention to influence historymaking in order to strengthen Moscow's position internationally. Hence, the study of history for the establishment is just a means to an end. For instance, it is rather unnatural for RVIO research director Mikhail Miagkov to make a public statement on the United States pulling out from a nuclear arms treaty with Russia.[24] Works deemed to be falsifying history sometimes end up on the extremist materials list administered by the ministry of justice. Among such works, for instance, are a handful of academic books and articles that define the 1932–33 famine in Ukraine as genocide.[25] Had the justice ministry ever decided to list the present book as extremist, that fact alone would have endorsed the book's thesis.

In the context of Russia, history politics is not an allegory, a concept, or an intellectual framework. From the perspective of Putin's government, history is a matter of foreign politics. That is what top officials say verbatim. In the run-up to the May 9 celebration in 2015, chief of the presidential administration and currently head of RVIO's board of directors, Sergei Ivanov, declared the "battle for history and the historical truth to be among principal issues [*vyidet na pervyi plan*] of foreign policy."[26] President Putin is not far behind in defining the "falsification of the past, including belittling the decisive role of our country in the destruction of Nazism" as one of the most important aspects in the foreign ministry's work. It is, indeed, a priority for the foreign ministry, echoes Sergei Lavrov.[27] That makes Kirill Alexandrov's research on the Russian collaborationist forces in the Second World War, or an abstract American PhD student working on a subject such as mass rape of German women by Soviet soldiers in 1945, a direct challenge to Russia's international status and as such warrants a political response.

History for the regime is not just politics but an existential battle as well. As RVIO's Miagkov was arguing in the spring of 2019: "Today's Russia is subject to a total information war. . . . Major strikes target culture, as the foundation of national security of our country, and the historical memory of our people."[28] His boss, Medinskii, contends that European countries and the United States have been trying to superimpose their perspective on history, encapsulated in the notion of *post-truth* incorporated in the Western propaganda.[29] Yet another prominent RVIO member, Yuri Nikiforov, claims that the West is working to undermine the Russians' trust in their own state by besmirching the history of Russia. The ultimate goal, according to Nikiforov, is mobilizing potential collaborators in the event of an armed conflict with Russia.[30] Needless to say, these types of allegations is prima facie conspiracy theory. Now and again, the authorities attest that history is geopolitics, whether it is a new museum being proposed in the vicinity of a freshly built military base in the Arctic or a sudden interest in the joint Russian–Chinese study of history.

Cognitive dissonance defines not only the social contract between the Russian state and its people but also state policies, including that on history. To give just one example, a joint meeting in the Kremlin in April of 2017 declared as a goal extending the official Russian conception of history abroad. Yet the resolution, one of many that came out of an hour-long discussion, called for "depoliticization of history discipline and historical debates."[31] It is not Russia's consistent efforts to superimpose its perspective on history, but a "methodical, premeditated pseudo-historical propaganda against Russia that makes the contemporary youth doubt the horrors of Nazism and, by extension, the decisive role of our people in the Great Victory."[32]

While Russia is not the only country in the world pursuing "patriotic education" and/or militarization of the society, with respect to historymaking it essentially has no rivals. Perhaps the only comparable case would be Turkey. Emerging from within the Turkish government, the term *deep state* can be matched against (now less frequently used) *sovereign democracy* introduced by the Kremlin spin doctors. As Nikolay Koposov has observed, the 2014 Law against the Glorification of Nazism comes the closest to Article 301 of the Turkish penal code. The authoritarian form of governance and the suppression of dissent invite further parallels. Still, Turkey is reactive, insofar as its official policy of denial of the Armenian genocide is concerned, while Russia has taken a proactive approach to the professed falsification of history.

The prognosis is bleak. Although interpretations of history fall under creative license and thus freedom of expression, it has become a part of the ongoing suppression of political dissent. To put it differently, professional historians—or just about anyone who dares to publicly comment on issues related to history—suddenly find themselves in uncharted territory. The German model of coming to terms with the past is considered unacceptable in contemporary Russia, because it might involve an unsavory comparison between the Soviet and Nazi regimes.[33] It does not help that the history discipline is considered a science in Russia. Ironically, it does not extend to the rules of evidence, applied at whim by the state and its affiliates. What we are witnessing is essentially the emergence of state monopoly on history-telling, much like on foreign policy or defense or education. Not surprisingly, then, all these vital functions of the state have been aligned, beginning in 2012, in pursuit of an official policy on history. Falsification of history is one of the means by which the Putin regime has been waging the war on truth.

By 2019 the regime has run out of ideas. The fierce determination with which the authorities crushed political protests in Moscow that summer and continued imposing restrictive legislation bodes ill for historymaking. While the regime succeeded at streamlining a historical narrative at home, it gained no ground whatsoever internationally. The lack of a mechanism of checks and balances prevents the Russian government from assessing the effectiveness of its long-term policy on history. Kremlin spin doctors may want to ask themselves if the decades of pitchfork battles with the East Europeans around such issues as participation in the war within the German Waffen SS ranks or the significance of the Molotov–Ribbentrop pact have made a dent in the collective perception in those countries. The answer is, of course, no. The postulate of the Red Army bringing freedom to Europe in 1945 is so crudely constructed that it cannot find any takers outside of Russia by default. After my institution at Oslo was approached by the Russian embassy four times in a row on the matter of displaying a traveling Holocaust exhibition with a veiled ideological message, the path to cooperation have shut down. The Putin regime has been pushing just too hard, including on issues relevant to history, to the opposite effect. An authoritarian regime referring to a liberal democracy as its only ally in the field of history politics is no complement to the latter. For Israel, the praise coming from Moscow is a liability. It is painful to watch President Putin—backed up by the stone-faced Lavrov, Volodin, and the rest of the coterie—delivering tirades on the lessons of the Second World War. The old man does not get history.

Notes

(Full notes can be downloaded at
Bloomsbury.com/Weiss-Wendt-Putins-Russia-and-the-Falsification-of-History)

Introduction

1 Anton Weiss-Wendt, *The Soviet Union and the Gutting of the UN Genocide Convention* (Madison, WI: University of Wisconsin Press, 2017), 61–62.
2 Geoffrey Roberts, "Stalin, the Pact with Nazi Germany, and the Origins of Postwar Soviet Diplomatic Historiography," *Journal of Cold War Studies* 4, no. 4 (Fall 2002): 96–100, 103.
3 *Falsifiers of History (Historical Survey)* (Moscow: Foreign Language Publishing House, 1948), passim.
4 Ibid.
5 Cf. https://varjag-2007.livejournal.com/2712681.html#/2712681.html; Nikolai Starikov, *Falsifikatory istorii: Pravda i lozh o Velikoi voine* (St. Petersburg: Piter, 2015).
6 Masha Gessen, *The Future is History: How Totalitarianism Reclaimed Russia* (New York: Riverhead Books, 2017).
7 Radio Svoboda, January 29, 2017.
8 Radio Svoboda, October 10, 2016.
9 Cf. Nikolay Koposov, *Memory Laws, Memory Wars: The Politics of the Past in Europe and Russia* (Cambridge: Cambridge University Press, 2018), 214, 243–44.
10 See *Novaia Gazeta*, August 29, 2015.
11 Cf. Catherine Merridale, *Night of Stone: Death and Memory in Twentieth-Century Russia* (London and New York: Viking, 2000); Svetlana Boym, *The Future of Nostalgia* (New York: Basic Books, 2001); Dina Khapaeva, *Nightmare: From Literary Experiments to Cultural Project* (Leiden: Brill, 2012); Alexander Etkind, *Warped Mourning: Stories of the Undead from the Land of the Unburied* (Stanford, CA: Stanford University Press, 2013).
12 Cf. Lev Gudkov, "1917 god v strukture legitimnosti rossiiskoi vlasti," *Neprikosnovennyi zapas* 6 (2017): n.p.
13 Cf. Timothy Garton Ash, *History of the Present: Essays, Sketches, and Dispatches from Europe in the 1990s* (New York: Random House, 1999).

Chapter 1

1 Michael McFaul, *From Cold War to Hot Peace: An American Ambassador in Putin's Russia* (Boston: Houghton Mifflin Harcourt, 2018), 122–23.
2 *Nezavisimaia Gazeta*, February 11, 2019.
3 BBC Russian, February 11, 2019.
4 Radio Svoboda, July 10, 2018.

5 Konstantin Pakhaliuk, "Istoricheskoe proshloe kak osnovanie rossiiskoi politiki: Na primere vystuplenii Vladimira Putina v 2012–2018 gg.," *Politiia* 4 (2018): 7, 10–11, 13.
6 For details see Chapter 7.
7 Nikita Sokolov et al., "Kakoe proshloe nuzhno budushchemu Rossii" (Moscow: VIO, 2017), 1–15, 18, 23–25, 45, 47–48.
8 Radio Svoboda, January 23, 2017.
9 See the text of the May 2005 resolution at http://sbornik-zakonov.ru/101977.html.
10 Pravo, February 24, 2009.
11 Pravo, May 6, 2009.
12 Cf. Koposov, *Memory Laws, Memory Wars*, 259–70.
13 See the text of the May 2009 decree and related documents at http://archives.ru/documents/decree/ukaz549.shtml.
14 Radio Svoboda, July 4, 2009.
15 Gazeta, May 31, 2009.
16 Cf. RVIO, April 25, 2018.
17 Russian Federation Council, *O protivodeistvii popytkam falsifikatsii istorii narodov v ushcherb interesam Rossii, sbornik materialov* (March 2013), 36, 49. Cf. Ekho Moskvy, June 14, 2016.
18 *Vedomosti*, January 14, 2010.
19 Russian Federation Council, *O protivodeistvii popytkam falsifikatsii istorii*, 1–4, 52.
20 Ibid., 41–43.
21 Ibid., 43.
22 Ibid., 44–46.
23 Ibid., 47.
24 Ibid., 6–11.
25 Ibid., 11–14.
26 Ibid., 17–19.
27 Ibid., 19–21.
28 Ibid., 27.
29 Ibid., 22–23.
30 Ibid., 24–25.
31 Ibid., 28–30.
32 Ibid., 25–27.
33 Ibid., 31–32.
34 Ibid., 32–33.
35 Ibid., 34–36.
36 Ibid., 36–37.
37 Ibid., 37–39.
38 Ibid., 39–40.
39 Ibid., 50.
40 RVIO, June 1, 2018.
41 Pavel Polian, "Istoriomor: Strukturizatsiia pamiati i infrastruktura bespamiatstva," *Neprikosnovennyi zapas* 3 (2015): n.p.
42 Cf. Koposov, *Memory Laws, Memory Wars*, 245.
43 Cf. TV roundtable, "Sobibor as an Apogee of Jewish Resistance to Fascism," RIA, April 10, 2018.
44 *Kommersant*, October 31, 2016.
45 See interview with Igor Permiakov on Rossiia 24, April 28, 2016.
46 Russian Federation Council, *O protivodeistvii popytkam falsifikatsii istorii*, 30–31.

47 See the text of the Ukrainian Law no. 376V, adopted on November 26, 2006.
48 Vladimir Kozlov, Preface, *Golod v SSSR, 1930–1934 gg./Famine in the USSR, 1930–1934* (Moscow: Federal Archival Agency of the Russian Federation, 2009), 7.
49 Anton Weiss-Wendt, *A Rhetorical Crime: Genocide in the Geopolitical Discourse of the Cold War* (New Brunswick, NJ: Rutgers University Press, 2018), 171.
50 Ekho Moskvy, June 22, 2017; Radio Svoboda, July 7, 2018.
51 "Osvobozhdenie Polshi: Tsena pobedy," http://poland1944.mil.ru/, June 18, 2017. Cf. RIO, January 18, 2019.
52 Radio Svoboda, March 31, 2015. See also Radio Svoboda, November 27, 2017; Radio Svoboda, September 8, 2018.
53 Information received on the promise of anonymity from USHMM, January 2, 2018.
54 Radio Svoboda, November 23, 2018.
55 Meduza, July 22, 2015; Radio Svoboda, November 18, 2017; *Kommersant*, March 14, 2019.
56 Cf. the text of the March 12, 2014, decision by the Intergovernmental Commission and a public initiative to revoke it (March 2018). See also Memorial, October 28, 2014; *Moskovskii Komsomolets*, December 19, 2017.
57 Fontanka, March 2, 2010; Radio Svoboda, October 30, 2018; Realnoe Vremia, June 13, 2018.
58 NGS, March 14, 2019.
59 *Kommersant*, March 21, 2019.
60 Radio Svoboda, July 5, 2019. See also Meduza, July 6, 2019.
61 Radio Svoboda, October 23, 2019.
62 With few exceptions, investigation files of the Gulag survivors had been routinely destroyed beginning in the 1950s. What remained was a personal card, which documented the person's movement from one camp to another up until their eventual release. Even though the cards themselves remained off-limits, victims' relatives could upon request receive a summary of the record.
63 *Kommersant*, June 8, 2018; Radio Svoboda, June 8, 2018.
64 Radio Svoboda, June 13, 2018.
65 Radio Svoboda, December 9, 2017.
66 Article 275 speaks vaguely of rendering assistance to a foreign state, an international or foreign organization of their representatives. According to official statistics, Russian courts review fifteen to twenty cases dealing with high treason per year; only one case, from 2000, ended up in acquittal.
67 Radio Svoboda, April 15, 2017.
68 Cf. Minutes of the annual staff meeting of the Defense Ministry Archives, February 12, 2019.
69 Radio Svoboda, July 15, 2019.
70 Radio Svoboda, June 3, 2019.
71 Cf. project's website (September 2018), https://pamyat-naroda.ru/about/. See also, Russkii Mir, March 4, 2018.
72 RIA, January 18, 2020.
73 Personal communication with Yuri Alexeev, April 25, 2010.
74 Yuri Alexeev, *Moglinskii lager: Istoriia odnoi malenkoi fabriki smerti* (Moscow: Historical Memory Foundation, 2011). See also *Pskovskie Novosti*, March 22, 2011.
75 Pskovkaia Guberniia online, November 1, 2016.
76 Radio Svoboda, April 15, 2017.
77 Lynne Viola, *Stalinist Perpetrators on Trial: Scenes from the Great Terror in Soviet Ukraine* (Oxford: Oxford University Press, 2017).

78 Radio Svoboda, April 5, 2018. Cf. Diskurs, May 17, 2016.
79 See committee's website (July 2018), http://www.cish.org/index.php/en/.
80 On the history of ASEEES see David C. Engerman, *Know Your Enemy: The Rise and Fall of America's Soviet Experts* (New York: Oxford University Press, 2009), 69, 72, 77–79.
81 *Izvestia*, May 30, 2016.
82 Cf. Radio Svoboda, December 19, 2019; Gover Furr's webpage, https://msuweb.montclair.edu/~furrg/.
83 Cf. *The Chronicle of Higher Education*, November 15, 2017.
84 *Moskovskii Komsomolets*, June 3, 2016.
85 *Izvestia*, May 30, 2016.
86 Kremlin, June 22, 2016.
87 RVIO, August 24, 2018; RVIO, July 10, 2019; *Izvestiia*, July 12, 2019. Cf. *Die Welt*, July 9, 2019.
88 RVIO, August 21, 2018.
89 Radio Svoboda, May 9, 2019.
90 Meduza, August 26, 2015. Cf. *Rossiiskaia Gazeta*, August 26, 2015.
91 7×7, January 13, 2016; BBC Russian, January 14, 2016.
92 Radio Svoboda, July 1, 2019.
93 7×7, July 28, 2018. Cf. Radio Svoboda, January 13, 2016; Meduza, May 7, 2018; Radio Svoboda, May 7, 2018.
94 *Kommersant*, October 31, 2016. Cf. Open Democracy, April 13, 2015.
95 RBK, October 12, 2015.
96 Ministry of Defense, November 11, 2018.
97 *Kommersant*, October 31, 2016.
98 *Nezavisimaia Gazeta*, February 21, 2018.
99 Sputnik, April 28, 2018.
100 RVIO, May 16, 2018. Cf. RVIO, March 6, 2019; Radio Svoboda, June 26, 2019.
101 RVIO, May 17, 2018.
102 Ibid.
103 Civic Chamber of the Russian Federation, October 30, 2018.
104 Cf. European Parliament resolution 2019/2819(RSP), September 18, 2019.
105 BBC Russian, December 30, 2019.
106 *Russia in Global Affairs*, December 31, 2019. See also Bloomberg, January 10, 2020.
107 Duma, January 14, 2020; *Tverskie Vedomosti*, January 14, 2020. See also First Channel (Georgia), January 11, 2020.
108 Sputnik, January 15, 2019.
109 Radio Svoboda, January 23, 2020.
110 Sokolov et al., "Kakaia istoriia nuzhna budushchemu Rossii," 35.
111 Cf. Kremlin, July 22, 2011.
112 Cf. BBC Russian, December 12, 2016; Radio Svoboda, December 14, 2016.
113 *New York Times*, December 11, 2017.
114 Cf. Radio Svoboda, June 25, 2018; Meduza, July 23, 2018.
115 Cf. Polit, July 3, 2009.
116 Conversation with historian Tatiana Borisova of the St. Petersburg School of Economics, September 16, 2017.
117 Radio Svoboda, November 2, 2016.
118 Ekho Moskvy, April 29, 2016.
119 Meduza, August 14, 2019; *Kommersant*, August 15, 2019.

120 Radio Svoboda, December 19, 2018.
121 Radio Svoboda, August 22, 2018. Cf. BBC Russian, June 18, 2015.
122 Fontanka, March 2, 2010.
123 Kirill Alexandrov, "Generalitet i ofitserskie kadry vooruzhennykh formirovanii Komiteta osvobozhdeniia narodov Rossii, 1943–194." (PhD Thesis, St. Petersburg Institute of History of the Russian Academy of Sciences, 2015), 9, 841–44, 856.
124 *Fontanka*, March 2, 2016.
125 PhD v Rossii, no date.
126 Russkaia narodnaia linia, April 6, 2016.
127 Radio Svoboda, April 6, 2016.
128 PhD v Rossii, no date.
129 *Novaia Gazeta*, September 12, 2014.
130 Radio Svoboda, November 3, 2017.
131 See St. Petersburg court decision no. 33-13964/2017, December 14, 2017.
132 Cf. *Novaia Gazeta*, January 12, 2018.
133 Cf. Francine Hirsch, "The Soviets at Nuremberg: International Law, Propaganda, and the Making of the Postwar Order," *American Historical Review* 113, no. 3 (2008): 701–30.
134 Radio Svoboda, April 19, 2018.
135 Radio Svoboda, August 17, 2018.

Chapter 2

1 VTsIOM, December 27, 2018.
2 Cf. video interview with Narochnitskaia, Tsargrad TV, February 1, 2018.
3 Cf. foundation's website (March 2019), http://www.fiip.ru/.
4 Cf. institute's website (March 2019), http://www.idc-europe.org/en/The-Institute-of-Democracy-and-Cooperation.
5 Cf. institute's website, https://ipn.gov.pl/en/; Dariusz Stola, "Poland's Institute of National Remembrance: A Ministry of Memory?" in *The Convolutions of Historical Politics*, ed. Alexei Miller and Maria Lipman (Budapest: CEU Press, 2012), 45–58.
6 Cf. institute's website, http://www.memory.gov.ua/; Georgiy Kasianov, "The 'Nationalization' of History in Ukraine," in *The Convolutions of Historical Politics*, 150.
7 112.ua, December 5, 2019.
8 Alexei Miller, "The Turns of Russian Historical Politics, from Perestroika to 2011," in *The Convolutions of Historical Politics*, 256, 262–63.
9 See http://www.historyfoundation.ru/index.php.
10 Information shared by Olesia Orlenko, March 5, 2012.
11 Alexander Diukov, blog entry, March 11, 2016.
12 BBC Russian, March 11, 2016.
13 Radio Svoboda, January 29, 2019.
14 Cf. IGSP's website, http://igcp.eu/en/; Alexander Diukov, blog entry, January 15, 2016.
15 Vladimir Medinskii, *Rossiia nikogda ne sdavalas: Mify voiny i mira* (Moscow: Knizhnyi mir, 2016), 3.

16 Vladimir Medinskii, *Skelety iz shkafa russkoi istorii* (Moscow: Abris-Olma, 2017), 5–7.
17 Cf. Reader reviews posted on the publisher's website (June 2018), https://www.labirint.ru/reviews/goods/249895/.
18 Vladimir Medinskii, *Osobennosti natsionalnogo piara: Pravdivaia istoria Rusi ot Riurika do Petra* (Moscow: Abris-Olma, 2011), 611.
19 Cf. Reader reviews posted on the publisher's website (June 2018), https://www.labirint.ru/reviews/goods/322084/.
20 Meduza, May 11, 2018.
21 Cf. photos (November 4, 2015), https://gdb.rferl.org/A04724D2-B634-4195-BE59-417BE96FAC08_x974_n_s.jpg, https://gdb.rferl.org/2418365E-2E9C-42C9-BFD8-5B84BF4403DE_w974_n_s.jpg.
22 RVIO, May 15, 2018.
23 Cf. BBC Russian, November 9, 2015.
24 *Novaia Gazeta*, December 16, 2016.
25 Ibid.
26 Cf. Weiss-Wendt, *The Soviet Union and the Gutting of the UN Genocide Convention*, 11–13.
27 *Kommersant*, April 20, 2015. See also Radio Svoboda, November 25, 2016.
28 Lenta, July 30, 2015.
29 *Rossiiskaia Gazeta*, August 26, 2015; BBC Russian, November 26, 2016.
30 *Novaia Gazeta*, December 16, 2016.
31 Radio Svoboda, November 27, 2016.
32 Radio Svoboda, July 4, 2009.
33 Radio Svoboda, September 4, 2015.
34 Snob, July 6, 2017.
35 Vladimir Medinskii, "Problemy obiektivnosti v osveshchenii Rossiiskoi istorii vtoroi poloviny XV–XVII vv.," abstract (Moscow State Social University, 2011), 4, 7, 9–11, 16, 27–39.
36 BBC Russian, July 7, 2017.
37 *Rossiiskaia Gazeta*, July 7, 2017. See also *Argumenty i fakty*, November 28, 2018; Radio Svoboda, December 4, 2018.
38 VIO, July 6, 2017.
39 Meduza, October 2, 2017.
40 *Novaia Gazeta*, October 3, 2017.
41 *Novaia Gazeta*, October 18, 2017.
42 RBK, October 20, 2017.
43 Ministry of Education, October 4, 2017.
44 Ministry of Education, October 5, 2016.
45 Besogon TV, episode no. 120 (May 3, 2018).
46 Medinskii, "Problemy obiektivnosti v osveshchenii Rossiiskoi istorii," 6, 10, 40–45.
47 Kremlin, July 22, 2011.
48 Kremlin, June 20, 2012.
49 Novosti.rs, October 21, 2019. See also Radio Svoboda, October 22, 2019.
50 See full text of the decree at https://rvio.histrf.ru/officially/ukaz-1710.
51 Radio Svoboda, December 5, 2016.
52 RVIO, June 3, 2019.
53 Gazeta, November 9, 2019.
54 RVIO, June 5, 2018.

55   RBK, July 13, 2015.
56   Radio Svoboda, November 18, 2015.
57   In late 2018 the exhibition found a permanent home at Tambov. By that time, a total of two million people had reportedly seen it.
58   Cf. exhibition's website (June 2019), http://xn--80adtacueg4dwd.xn--p1ai/.
59   Quoted in Manezh press release, "Voina i mify: Vystavka priurochena v 75-letiiu Bitvy za Moskvu," November 2016, http://moscowmanege.ru/vojna-i-mify/.
60   Radio Svoboda, December 5, 2016.
61   RVIO, April 25, 2018.
62   Cf. *Rossiiskaia Gazeta*, August 26, 2015; text of Putin's decree no. 1710 (December 29, 2012).
63   RVIO, March 26, 2019; RVIO, April 15, 2019.
64   See video at RVIO, November 15, 2018.
65   RT, February 14, 2018.
66   Cf. TV roundtable, "Sobibor as an Apogee of Jewish Resistance to Fascism."
67   Cf. institute's website, http://inmrf.ru/.
68   See foundation's website, https://fond.historyrussia.org/fond/struktura-fonda.html.
69   Cf. Press conference of History of Motherland Foundation, TASS, February 15, 2017.
70   Memorial, January 13, 2012.
71   Cf. the contents of the exhibition at the Dagestan, St. Petersburg, Kaliningrad, Novgorod, Nizhnii Novgorod, and Kurgan region police museums.
72   RVIO, February 25, 2019. See also, RVIO, November 8, 2018.
73   RVIO, February 23, 2019.
74   RVIO, February 21, 2019.
75   *Rossiiskaia Gazeta*, December 19, 2017. Cf. Ekho Moskvy, December 22, 2015.
76   Radio Svoboda, May 7, 2019.
77   Radio Svoboda, August 31, 2018.
78   Radio Svoboda, May 27, 2019.
79   Katia Dianina, "Vozvrashchennoe nasledie: Nikolai II kak novodel," *Novoe Literaturnoe Obozrenie* 1 (2018): n.p.
80   BBC Russian, January 4, 2018.
81   Ekho Moskvy, June 26, 2017.
82   Radio Svoboda, March 15, 2019.
83   Radio Svoboda, November 1, 2018.
84   Cf. text of the amended Article 148, http://ukodeksrf.ru/ch-2/rzd-7/gl-19/st-148-uk-rf.
85   Radio Svoboda, March 12, 2018.
86   Kathy Rousselet, "The Church in the Service of the Fatherland," *Europe-Asia Studies* 67, no. 1 (2015): 51.
87   Ekho Moskvy, December 30, 2018.
88   Radio Svoboda, December 24, 2018.
89   BBC Russian, November 27, 2018; Ilya Varlamov, blog entry, November 27, 2018.
90   Radio Svoboda, December 3, 2018.
91   Radio Svoboda, November 30, 2018.
92   Ekho Moskvy, November 28, 2018.
93   Cf. exhibition's website, http://xn--80adtacueg4dwd.xn--p1ai/zaly/#zal2.
94   RVIO, April 21, 2019.
95   RVIO, June 20, 2019.
96   Gazeta, June 25, 2019.

97 RBK, August 19, 2016.
98 *Vzgliad*, August 19, 2016.
99 RIA Novosti, August 19, 2016.
100 Radio Svoboda, October 1, 2017.
101 "Confessor," documentary by Sergei Erzhenkov and Vladislav Pushkarev aired on TV Dozhd on November 15, 2017.
102 Moscow Municipality, December 29, 2015.
103 Pravoslavie, December 29, 2015.
104 This is remarkable in its own right, given that just a handful of purpose-built museum buildings had been erected in Russia since 1991. As of October 2019, twenty "Russia: My History" theme parks have been built.
105 Radio Svoboda, February 16, 2017.
106 Bloomberg, November 16, 2017.
107 Radio Svoboda, October 7, 2019.
108 Cf. visitor reviews posted, for example, on Trip Advisor (barely 0.5 percent by foreigners).
109 Ibid.
110 VIO, December 7, 2017; BBC Russian, January 4, 2018; Radio Svoboda, January 6, 2018; Ivan Kurilla et al., "Russia, My History: History as an Ideological Tool," PONARS Eurasia, August 5, 2018.
111 *Sobesednik*, December 14, 2017.
112 *Moskovskii Komsomolets*, December 18, 2007.
113 Radio Svoboda, October 7, 2019. See also, Ekaterina Klimenko, "Building the Nation, Legitimizing the State—My History and Memory of the Russian Revolutions in Contemporary Russia," *Nationalities Papers*, https://doi.org/10.1017/nps.2019.105.
114 Meduza, January 8, 2019.
115 Radio Svoboda, November 4, 2015.
116 Radio Svoboda, April 18, 2018.
117 Radio Svoboda, January 6, 2018.
118 BBC Russian, May 14, 2018.
119 Radio Svoboda, November 28, 2017; Ekho Moskvy, November 28, 2017.
120 Radio Svoboda, November 28, 2017.
121 BBC Russian, November 28, 2017.
122 Radio Svoboda, November 28, 2017.
123 BBC Russian, January 4, 2018.
124 BBC Russian, May 14, 2018; Radio Svoboda, May 15, 2018.
125 *Moscow Times*, January 11, 2014.
126 Ekho Moskvy, September 21, 2015.
127 Radio Svoboda, July 11, 2018.
128 BBC Russian, May 29, 2015.
129 Ridus, June 17, 2015.
130 Radio Svoboda, October 30, 2017.
131 For a representative history of the Solovetsky Monastery see Roy R. Robson, *Solovki: The Story of Russia Told through Its Most Remarkable Islands* (New Haven: Yale University Press, 2004).
132 Radio Svoboda, February 6, 2018.
133 Russkaia narodnaia linia, June 23, 2017.
134 Cf. David Satter, *It Was a Long Time Ago, and It Never Happened Anyway: Russia and the Communist Past* (New Haven: Yale University Press, 2012), 132.

135 Russian Orthodox Church, January 7, 2018.
136 Radio Svoboda, March 5, 2018.
137 Radio Svoboda, March 9, 2018.
138 Radio Svoboda, February 19, 2018.
139 BBC Russian, May 18, 2015.
140 *Moscow Times*, May 19, 2015.
141 Head of the Russian Government, August 29, 2011.
142 *Segodnia*, July 1, 2011.
143 Cf. *Acteurs*, January 22, 2018.
144 That was the slogan sported by the Night Wolves, for example, at the National Unity Day march in Moscow on November 4, 2015, http://nightwolves.ru/nw/gallery/2300/.
145 Simon Shuster, "Russia Ups the Ante in Crimea by Sending in the 'Night Wolves,'" *Time Magazine*, February 28, 2014.
146 *Sobesednik*, June 30, 2014.
147 Politnavigator, October 1, 2015.
148 Lenta, August 23, 2015.
149 Radio Svoboda, May 5, 2017; Radio Svoboda, May 9, 2018; Radio Svoboda, May 8, 2018.
150 RVIO, April 28, 2018.
151 BBC Russian, June 17, 2015.
152 Anna Sanina, *Patriotic Education in Contemporary Russia: Sociological Studies in the Making of the Post-Soviet Citizen* (Stuttgart: Ibidem, 2017), 164–66.
153 *Komsomolskaia Pravda*, June 1, 2018.
154 Cf. http://nightwolves.ru/nw/news/.
155 Night Wolves, August 17, 2017.
156 *Acteurs*, January 22, 2018.
157 *Komsomolskaia Pravda*, January 7, 2018.
158 *Sobesednik*, June 30, 2014.
159 See the video at https://www.youtube.com/watch?v=3NofhC8mORc (August 10, 2014).
160 See the video at https://www.youtube.com/watch?v=z2WfiaZzwKQ (August 22, 2015). See also Radio Svoboda, August 31, 2015.
161 NSN, July 22, 2015.
162 See the video at https://www.youtube.com/watch?v=_fRiRiQQcQ0 (August 17, 2016).
163 Documentary on the making of the 2016 edition of the Night Wolves biker show aired on Zvezda, the Defense Ministry TV channel.
164 See a documentary about the making of the 2015 edition of the Night Wolves biker show at https://www.youtube.com/watch?v=43rr-MR4iFk.
165 Night Wolves, September 1, 2017.
166 See the video at http://nightwolves.ru/nw/news/4374/ (August 19, 2017).
167 Ibid.
168 See the video at https://www.youtube.com/watch?v=Gp686L0wmQg (August 17, 2018).
169 See the video at https://www.youtube.com/watch?v=IcrpNQtAQqc&feature=youtu.be (August 10, 2019).
170 Night Wolves, August 19, 2019.
171 Kremlin, August 10, 2019.

172 RBK, February 3, 2017. See also *The Times*, May 15, 2015.
173 Radio Svoboda, January 30, 2018.
174 Radio Svoboda, August 18, 2015. See also ForPost, February 9, 2014.
175 Cf. David Hackett Fischer, *Historians' Fallacies: Toward a Logic of Historical Thought* (New York: Harper Perennial, 1970).
176 Letter to Putin posted on RVIO's VKontakte account, May 21, 2018.
177 Radio Svoboda, May 21, 2018.
178 Cf. RVIO's website, https://rvio.histrf.ru/activities/news.
179 Cf. Miller, "The Turns of Russian Historical Politics," 268, 275.

Chapter 3

1 BBC Russian, January 17, 2019.
2 Ekho Moskvy, September 2, 2015. See also Reuters, February 26, 2015.
3 Cf. BBC English, March 27, 2015.
4 McFaul, *From Cold War to Hot Peace*, 259, 319, 335–36, 361.
5 Olga Malinova, "Tema proshlogo v ritorike prezidentov Rossii," *Pro et Contra* 3–4 (May–August 2011): 106–22.
6 Kremlin, November 5, 2014.
7 Radio Svoboda, August 17, 2019.
8 Ibid.
9 Ibid.
10 Kremlin, October 1, 2014.
11 Kremlin, November 5, 2014.
12 Radio Svoboda, August 17, 2019.
13 Ibid; Radio Svoboda, December 24, 2019. Cf. RVIO, September 27, 2018.
14 Hillary R. Clinton, *Hard Choices* (London: Simon & Schuster, 2014), 243.
15 Kremlin, July 22, 2011. Cf. Kremlin, November 14, 2008.
16 RVIO, April 4, 2019.
17 Pakhaliuk, "Istoricheskoe proshloe kak osnovanie rossiiskoi politiki," 16–23.
18 Kremlin, January 16, 2014.
19 Kremlin, June 22, 2016.
20 Cf. *Nezavisimaia Gazeta*, February 11, 2019; Sergei Lavrov, "Russia's Foreign Policy in a Historical Perspective," *Russia in Global Affairs*, March 30, 2016.
21 Cf. Kremlin, February 10, 2007.
22 Lavrov, "Russia's Foreign Policy in a Historical Perspective."
23 Ibid.
24 Kremlin, June 22, 2016.
25 Ibid.
26 Radio Svoboda, May 4, 2016. See also Radio Svoboda, June 22, 2017; Radio Svoboda, June 22, 2018.
27 Koposov, *Memory Laws, Memory Wars*, 247–50.
28 McFaul, *From Cold War to Hot Peace*, 68, 125–26, 295–96. See also *Washington Post*, May 4, 2015.
29 Ekho Moskvy, March 1, 2017.
30 See, for example, Vladimir Pozner's interview with Yuri Petrov, head of the RAN Institute of Russian History, Channel One, May 22, 2017.

31 Kremlin, March 17, 2015.
32 Radio Svoboda, May 10, 2017.
33 Kremlin, December 12, 2018.
34 Kremlin, April 20, 2017.
35 Government of Russia, April 28, 2015.
36 *Fontanka*, May 20, 2016.
37 Ekho Moskvy, April 26, 2018.
38 *Novaia Gazeta*, February 3, 2018.
39 Kremlin, June 22, 2016.
40 Cf. Radio Svoboda, May 10, 2018.
41 RVIO, May 3, 2018.
42 Cf. BBC English, May 8, 2015.
43 BBC Russian, May 3, 2017; Radio Svoboda, May 11, 2017.
44 Radio Svoboda, May 8, 2017.
45 Kremlin, March 17, 2015.
46 Kremlin, April 5, 2016.
47 Kremlin, May 9, 2019.
48 Kremlin, March 17, 2015.
49 Ibid.
50 Kremlin, April 5, 2016.
51 Ibid.
52 Kremlin, March 17, 2015.
53 Cf. RT's dedicated webpage, https://9may.rt.com/.
54 Kremlin, September 7, 2016.
55 RVIO, March 18, 2019.
56 RIO, June 19, 2019.
57 Kremlin, April 20, 2017.
58 Ibid.
59 Kremlin, May 4, 2017.
60 RVIO, May 8, 2018.
61 Cf. http://www.historyworldwar2.net/.
62 Cf. State Military Historical Museum, Prokhorovo Pole, January 18, 2016.
63 Alexandrina Vanke, "Landshafty pamiati: Park Pobedy na Poklonnoi gore v Moskve," *Neprikosnovennyi zapas* 3 (2015): n.p.
64 Kremlin, April 20, 2017.
65 RIO, January 18, 2019.
66 Meduza, September 4, 2019.
67 Cf. Radio Svoboda, August 15, 2016.
68 Kremlin, March 17, 2015.
69 Kremlin, April 22, 2015.
70 Kremlin, March 17, 2015. Cf. Ia-Kapitalist, April 12, 2019.
71 *Rossiiskaia Gazeta*, April 9, 2019.
72 Radio Svoboda, January 14, 2020.
73 Radio Svoboda, May 9, 2017.
74 Ekho Moskvy, October 6, 2016.
75 Russian Realty, May 13, 2014.
76 Radio Svoboda, May 11, 2018.
77 Radio Svoboda, April 30, 2019.
78 Meduza, December 10, 2019.

79 Radio Svoboda, March 7, 2017.
80 Radio Svoboda, November 17, 2017.
81 Radio Svoboda, March 24, 2017.
82 Cf. Kremlin, July 22, 2011.
83 Etymologically, *Iskander* comes in lieu of defender of mankind or a ruler who built a protective wall against evil forces, usually associated with Alexander the Great.
84 BBC Russian, June 17, 2015.
85 Lenta, August 16, 2015.
86 See video at http://victorymuseum.ru/?part=13&id_single=4780 (May 1, 2018).
87 The song celebrates a Soviet tank counterattack during the Japanese incursion at Lake Khasan in the summer of 1938.
88 Bumaga, May 1, 2018.
89 Fontanka, April 30, 2018.
90 Cf. http://podarki.ru/kupit/Tapki-T-34-2967455; http://www.ehmapodarki.ru/voilochnie-tapochki-22/; http://svetelka.rosbizinfo.ru/products/1.html.
91 Novosti NGS, November 3, 2016.
92 Meduza, April 23, 2018.
93 Meduza, December 26, 2018.
94 Ekho Moskvy, January 16, 2019; Meduza, December 14, 2019.
95 TASS, January 18, 2019.
96 Meduza, January 9, 2019.
97 Radio Svoboda, January 29, 2017.
98 Radio Svoboda, June 1, 2018; Radio Svoboda, May 9, 2017.
99 *Moscow Times*, May 6, 2016.
100 Radio Svoboda, May 9, 2017.
101 Kremlin, March 17, 2015.
102 Kremlin, December 12, 2018.
103 Cf. Immortal Regiment Russia website (November 2018), https://polkrf.ru/about/.
104 Radio Svoboda, June 1, 2018.
105 Cf. Immortal Regiment Tomsk website (November 2018), http://www.moypolk.ru/letopis-polka. See also Radio Svoboda, May 8, 2018.
106 Radio Svoboda, May 9, 2017.
107 Immortal Regiment Tomsk, May 1, 2019.
108 Radio Svoboda, May 9, 2017; Ekho Moskvy, May 3, 2017.
109 Kremlin, April 5, 2016.
110 Ekho Moskvy, May 9, 2019.
111 Radio Svoboda, May 26, 2018.
112 Radio Svoboda, May 10, 2018. Cf. Ilya Varlamov, blog entry, May 9, 2018.
113 Ilya Varlamov, blog entry, May 9, 2018. Cf. Ekho Moskvy, May 9, 2019.
114 Radio Svoboda, May 4, 2016.
115 Radio Svoboda, May 17, 2018.
116 Ekho Moskvy, May 7, 2017.
117 Radio Svoboda, April 22, 2018.
118 Radio Svoboda, May 10, 2018.
119 Radio Svoboda, May 9, 2017.
120 Ekho Moskvy, May 9, 2017.
121 Radio Svoboda, June 1, 2018.
122 Radio Svoboda, May 12, 2019.
123 Radio Svoboda, May 9, 2017.

124 Kremlin, April 20, 2017.
125 Radio Svoboda, June 1, 2018.
126 Radio Svoboda, May 7, 2018.
127 Sputnik, May 6, 2018.
128 Cf. Kremlin, June 22, 2016. See also BBC Russian, May 9, 2017.
129 Radio Svoboda, May 10, 2018. Cf. BBC Russian, May 23, 2018.
130 Ekho Moskvy, May 9, 2017.
131 BBC Russian, May 5, 2019.
132 Ekho Moskvy, May 9, 2019.
133 Koposov, *Memory Laws, Memory Wars*, 210–13, 238–41, 246–47.
134 Ekho Moskvy, December 11, 2017.
135 *Newsweek*, June 26, 2017; Radio Svoboda, June 26, 2017.
136 Radio Svoboda, May 7, 2019; Ekho Moskvy, November 10, 2015; Levada, March 31, 2015; RIA, September 6, 2019.
137 Radio Liberty, December 24, 2019.
138 Ilya Varlamov, blog entry, December 15, 2019.
139 Sokolov et al., "Kakoe proshloe nuzhno budushchemu Rossii," 17.
140 Cf. Radio Svoboda, February 16, 2017.
141 Ivan Kurilla, "The 'Return of Stalin': Understanding the Surge of Historical Politics in Russia," PONARS Eurasia 429 (May 2016): 4–5.
142 BBC Russian, October 30, 2014. See also Kremlin, May 7, 2010.
143 TASS, October 1, 2015. See also Kremlin, June 22, 2016.
144 Ilya Varlamov, blog entry, January 23, 2019.
145 Cf. Ilya Varlamov, blog entry, October 29, 2015.
146 Ekho Moskvy, December 11, 2018.
147 Radio Svoboda, January 10, 2018.
148 See, for example, *Rolling Stone*, June 16, 2017.
149 Cf. Oliver Stone's *The Putin Interviews* (Showtime Networks, 2017).
150 Cf. Vesti, March 24, 2019.
151 Meduza, February 12, 2016.
152 BBC Russian, December 13, 2016; Radio Svoboda, July 20, 2017, Radio Svoboda, November 5, 2019.
153 Ekho Moskvy, November 11, 2018.
154 Ilya Varlamov, blog entry, August 24, 2016.
155 *Financial Times*, October 31, 2017.
156 Ekho Moskvy, August 18, 2016.
157 Radio Svoboda, September 1, 2017.
158 *Novaia Gazeta*, December 22, 2019.
159 Meduza, October 7, 2015.
160 Radio Svoboda, May 25, 2016.
161 BBC Russian, September 10, 2015. See also Ilya Varlamov, blog entry, December 12, 2018; Ekho Moskvy, December 13, 2018.
162 Radio Svoboda, August 16, 2017. See also Ekho Moskvy, February 25, 2016.
163 Ekho Moskvy, December 1, 2016.
164 Cf. Radio Svoboda, August 27, 2017; Radio Svoboda, October 29, 2018.
165 Meduza, January 24, 2018.
166 Meduza, January 23, 2018.
167 BBC Russian, January 23, 2018.
168 Ilya Varlamov, blog entry, January 23, 2018; Radio Svoboda, January 23, 2018.

169 Radio Svoboda, January 24, 2018.
170 Meduza, January 23, 2018.
171 Ekho Moskvy, January 31, 2018.
172 BBC Russian, February 28, 2018.
173 Radio Svoboda, June 29, 2018.
174 Meduza, April 16, 2019.
175 Government of Russia, August 15, 2015.
176 Kurilla, "The 'Return of Stalin,'" 1, 5.
177 BBC Russian, February 12, 2015; BBC Russian, March 20, 2015.
178 *Novaia Gazeta*, October 30, 2017.
179 Ekho Moskvy, March 9, 2018. Cf. Radio Svoboda, June 22, 2018.
180 BBC Russian, August 20, 2015.
181 Realnoe Vremia, June 13, 2018.
182 Interfax, May 23, 2017; BBC Russian, October 2, 2017.
183 Radio Svoboda, October 30, 2018.
184 Radio Svoboda, May 11, 2016.
185 BBC Russian, June 24, 2015; BBC Russian, September 3, 2015; *Novaia Gazeta*, November 10, 2015.
186 BBC Russian, September 21, 2015.
187 Cf. Sergey Toymentsev, "Legal but Criminal: The Failure of the 'Russian Nuremberg' and the Paradoxes of Post-Soviet Memory," *Comparative Literature Studies* 48, no. 3 (2011): 296–319.
188 Radio Svoboda, September 4, 2015.
189 Radio Svoboda, August 9, 2019.
190 Cf. Ekho Moskvy, November 10, 2015.
191 Ekho Moskvy, March 6, 2019.
192 Radio Svoboda, September 27, 2017.
193 BBC Russian, August 25, 2016; Radio Svoboda, September 14, 2019.
194 RVIO, November 15, 2018.
195 Kremlin, April 20, 2017.
196 RVIO, October 9, 2018.
197 *Moscow Times*, November 5, 2015. See also *Novaia Gazeta*, February 1, 2013; *Kommersant*, April 18, 2016.
198 Cf. Ekho Moskvy, July 20, 2017.
199 Radio Svoboda, January 30, 2019.
200 Cf. Radio Svoboda, December 16, 2016; Snob, May 22, 2016.
201 Cf. Boym, *The Future of Nostalgia*, passim.
202 Meduza, November 7, 2018.
203 BBC Russian, March 15, 2019.
204 Vladimir Pozner's interview with Yuri Petrov on Channel One, May 22, 2017.
205 Cf. Ekho Moskvy, June 27, 2017.

Chapter 4

1 Cf. Global Peace Index 2018.
2 Sanina, *Patriotic Education in Contemporary Russia*, 21–23, 36–37, 95, 142–43. Cf. BBC Russian, December 5, 2016.

3 Ekho Moskvy, March 27, 2019.
4 Radio Svoboda, October 28, 2015.
5 Radio Svoboda, October 23, 2014.
6 Sanina, *Patriotic Education in Contemporary Russia*, 25–32, 37, 65, 83–84.
7 Ibid., 84–93.
8 Radio Svoboda, June 11, 2017.
9 Sanina, *Patriotic Education in Contemporary Russia*, 66.
10 Ibid., 38–46.
11 Ibid., 49–61, quotation at 62.
12 Cf. Memorial, February 22, 2011.
13 Cf. Government of Russia, October 5, 2010; Government of Russia, December 30, 2015.
14 Government of Russia, December 30, 2015.
15 Ibid.
16 Government of Russia, October 5, 2010.
17 Meduza, October 29, 2019.
18 Cf. Radio Svoboda, January 5, 2016.
19 Sanina, *Patriotic Education in Contemporary Russia*, 97–105.
20 Ibid., 97–109; Meduza, December 2, 2015.
21 Open Russia, August 12, 2016. Cf. the Youth Army's official website, https://yunarmy.ru/.
22 Sanina, *Patriotic Education in Contemporary Russia*, 109–15.
23 Cf. Ksenia Okhapkina's documentary *Bessmertnyj* (Vesilind, 2019). See also Radio Svoboda, November 9, 2019.
24 Cf. https://yunarmy.ru/about; Youth Army, May 3, 2017.
25 Ekho Moskvy, February 6, 2019.
26 Radio Svoboda, March 12, 2019.
27 *Novaia Gazeta*, March 15, 2019.
28 Meduza, October 6, 2017.
29 Open Media, May 30, 2018. See also Radio Svoboda, May 9, 2017.
30 Radio Svoboda, September 11, 2018; Radio Svoboda, September 17, 2018.
31 Ilya Varlamov, blog entry, December 18, 2018. Cf. the cathedral's official website, https://hram.mil.ru/.
32 Radio Svoboda, December 27, 2018.
33 *Krasnaia Zvezda*, March 13, 2019.
34 BBC Russian, May 31, 2019.
35 Cf. the 2015 edition of the biker festival, "Forging Victory," at Sevastopol (https://www.youtube.com/watch?v=z2WfiaZzwKQ) and the opening statement by Kartopolov at the presentation of the cathedral in St. Petersburg on November 15, 2018 (https://rvio.histrf.ru/activities/news/item-5607).
36 Meduza, June 30, 2019.
37 *Nezavisimaia Gazeta*, March 6, 2015.
38 RVIO, February 21, 2019.
39 Radio Svoboda, April 24, 2017.
40 Interfax, February 22, 2017.
41 Reuters, October 13, 2016.
42 Cf. company's website (March 2019), http://carobus.net/catalog/detskaya-krovat-tank-buk-m-1/.
43 Cf. Radio Svoboda, May 9, 2017.

44 BBC Russian, June 25, 2015.
45 *The Guardian*, June 16, 2015.
46 Sanina, *Patriotic Education in Contemporary Russia*, 137–41.
47 Stavropol-Poisk, May 17, 2018.
48 Russkii Puls, November 2, 2018.
49 Ekho Moskvy, May 14, 2015.
50 Radio Svoboda, May 7, 2019.
51 Radio Svoboda, May 8, 2019.
52 Radio Svoboda, April 7, 2017.
53 Kremlin, March 17, 2015.
54 RVIO, June 5, 2018.
55 Alexander Pechersky Foundation, May 23, 2018.
56 Ibid., May 24, 2018.
57 Radio Svoboda, April 26, 2018.
58 Kremlin, March 17, 2015.
59 On the earlier attempts to produce a standard history textbook (Alexander Philippov and Alexander Danilin's *Russian History, 1945–2007*), see Miller, "The Turns of Russian Historical Politics," 258–61.
60 Government of Russia, July 2, 2013.
61 *Izvestiia*, June 20, 2018.
62 Cf. Tatyana Tsyrlina-Spady and Alan Stoskopf, "Russian History Textbooks in the Putin Era: Heroic Leaders Demand Loyal Citizens," in *Globalisation and Historiography of National Leaders: Symbolic Representations in School Textbooks*, ed. Joseph Zajda et al. (Dordrecht: Springer, 2017), 15–33.
63 Ekho Moskvy, August 23, 2016.
64 Meduza, November 7, 2016.
65 The Insider, August 19, 2016.
66 Ministry of Education, September 27, 2017.
67 Ministry of Education, November 4, 2016.
68 Ministry of Education, October 5, 2017.
69 Ekho Moskvy, August 23, 2016.
70 Kremlin, January 16, 2014.
71 RIO, June 30, 2017.
72 Quoted in Sokolov et al., "Kakaia istoriia nuzhna budushchemu Rossii," 28.
73 Meduza, January 11, 2018.
74 Pakhaliuk, "Istoricheskoe proshloe kak osnovanie rossiiskoi politiki," 11.
75 Radio Svoboda, July 25, 2017.
76 Kremlin, January 16, 2014. Cf. Radio Svoboda, January 7, 2016.
77 Cf. Ekho Moskvy, August 23, 2016; Radio Svoboda, June 15, 2019. The average teacher's salary in Russia is currently 38,000 rubles or 590 US dollars.
78 Meduza, October 21, 2019.
79 Radio Svoboda, August 31, 2015.
80 Radio Svoboda, December 27, 2018.
81 Nevskie Novosti, May 3, 2018.
82 RVIO, June 10, 2018.
83 Radio Svoboda, November 18, 2018.
84 *Novaia Gazeta*, May 9, 2019.
85 RVIO, January 29, 2019.
86 Radio Svoboda, August 25, 2019.

87 Channel One, Armeiskii magazine (February 2016).
88 Cf. project's website (July 2018), http://xn--c1abr0a.xn--p1ai/.
89 Kremlin, December 12, 2018.
90 RVIO, April 25, 2018.
91 Radio Svoboda, November 7, 2016.
92 *New York Times*, March 10, 2017; Transitions Online, November 7, 2017; Ivan Kurilla, "History and Memory in Russia during the 100th Anniversary of the Great Revolution," PONARS Eurasia 503 (January 2018).
93 Lavrov, "Russia's Foreign Policy in a Historical Perspective."
94 *Izvestiia*, June 20, 2018.
95 Radio Svoboda, January 19, 2017.
96 Gudkov, "1917 god."
97 Radio Svoboda, November 17, 2017.
98 Gudkov, "1917 god."
99 Radio Svoboda, November 7, 2017.
100 Radio Svoboda, May 17, 2018.
101 Radio Svoboda, November 30, 2019.
102 Transitions Online, November 7, 2017.
103 Radio Svoboda, October 29, 2018.
104 Radio Svoboda, November 2, 2017.
105 Radio Svoboda, November 30, 2019.
106 BBC Russian, September 13, 2017; RBK, November 2, 2016; Ekho Moskvy, November 29, 2017.
107 BBC Russian, November 2, 2016; Ekho Moskvy, April 17, 2017.
108 BBC Russian, September 14, 2017.
109 Radio Svoboda, February 1, 2017.
110 Radio Svoboda, August 7, 2017.
111 Ekho Moskvy, August 9, 2017. Cf. Radio Svoboda, August 9, 2017.
112 Radio Svoboda, July 17, 2017.
113 BBC English, September 11, 2017.
114 Radio Svoboda, September 20, 2017; Radio Svoboda, October 1, 2017.
115 Ekho Moskvy, June 29, 2017.
116 Ekho Moskvy, September 27, 2017.
117 Radio Svoboda, January 29, 2019; Radio Svoboda, January 29, 2019. See also *Süddeutsche Zeitung*, January 24, 2019.
118 Radio Svoboda, August 27, 2019.
119 *Times of Israel*, July 29, 2019.
120 Cf. *Kommersant*, November 3, 2017.
121 Cf. Ilya Varlamov, blog entry, November 1, 2018.
122 RBK, August 3, 2018.
123 As of summer 2019, there has been no new development on Patriotism Day.
124 The Memorial Day list may soon be expanded on account of the Great Confrontation on Ugra River in 1480. Endorsed by President Putin, but opposed by Tatarstan authorities, that date ostensibly marks the beginning of the end of the Tatar Mongol rule over Russian lands.
125 Meduza, August 21, 2019.
126 *Kommersant*, August 22, 2019.
127 Tellingly, none of the Memorial Day lists available on the internet include Day of Remembrance of Victims of Political Repression.

128 The popular initiative, "Two Carnations to Comrade Stalin," was launched in 2001.
129 Radio Svoboda, May 18, 2016; Radio Svoboda, May 18, 2017. See also Ekho Moskvy, May 20, 2016.
130 Radio Svoboda, January 24, 2017; *Aftenposten*, May 19, 2019.
131 Radio Svoboda, August 17, 2018.
132 Radio Svoboda, May 9, 2019.
133 Latvia did just that on May 10, 2019.
134 Ekho Moskvy, February 23, 2017. See also Ekho Moskvy, January 11, 2017; Radio Svoboda, November 21, 2017; Ekho Moskvy, February 23, 2018.
135 Cf. BBC Russian, February 21, 2014; Radio Svoboda, February 24, 2017; Radio Svoboda, February 23, 2018.
136 Cf. Levada, December 7, 2015.
137 Radio Svoboda, July 8, 2019.
138 Meduza, July 1, 2016.
139 Radio Svoboda, January 7, 2016.

Chapter 5

1 Radio Svoboda, August 17, 2018.
2 Pavel Gnilorybov, "Kto i zachem stavit pamiatniki Stalinu v sovremennoi Rossii?" lecture delivered at Yeltsin Center in Ekaterinburg, July 28, 2017.
3 Memorial, August 31, 2012.
4 BBC Russian, September 7, 2017.
5 X-Time.Info, March 5, 2015.
6 For examples, see "Stalin in Your City" thread on skyscrapercity.com.
7 Cf. https://rutraveller.ru/place/63956.
8 Cf. *Tiumenskie Izvestiia*, October 22, 2009; *New York Times*, August 23, 2012.
9 *Komsomolskaia Pravda*, June 19, 2001.
10 LiveJournal, July 24, 2013.
11 Gnilorybov, "Kto i zachem stavit pamiatniki Stalinu."
12 Life, November 27, 2009.
13 Gnilorybov, "Kto i zachem stavit pamiatniki Stalinu."
14 *Rossiiskaia Gazeta*, January 17, 2008; Bloknot-Novocherkassk, May 1, 2014.
15 Radio Svoboda, August 17, 2018; *Wall Street Journal*, October 22, 2018. See also the Essence of Time's website, https://eot.su/.
16 Radio Svoboda, September 16, 2016.
17 Radio Svoboda, October 6, 2016.
18 Radio Svoboda, May 27, 2019.
19 Baikal 24, December 20, 2019.
20 Russian Communist Party, March 19, 2018.
21 Ekho Moskvy, February 2, 2013.
22 Federal News Agency, August 29, 2015.
23 Ilya Varlamov, blog entry, December 17, 2017.
24 Radio Svoboda, November 28, 2017; Radio Svoboda, November 3, 2018; Radio Svoboda, November 18, 2018.
25 Radio Svoboda, May 9, 2019. See also Ilya Varlamov, blog entry, June 9, 2019.
26 Vl, January 14, 2017.

27 Panoptikon, December 22, 2015.
28 *The Telegraph*, October 19, 2015.
29 Penza branch of the Russian Communist Party, December 21, 2015.
30 Gnilorybov, "Kto i zachem stavit pamiatniki Stalinu."
31 Meduza, February 25, 2016.
32 Cont, September 10, 2015.
33 Radio Svoboda, May 25, 2019.
34 *Novaia Gazeta*, December 20, 2019.
35 PLN-Pskov, November 16, 2018.
36 See information about the museum, along with visitor reviews at https://autotravel.ru/otklik.php/9561.
37 Radio Svoboda, March 15, 2015.
38 *Izvestia*, July 3, 2015.
39 Radio Svoboda, September 22, 2017.
40 Smartnews, January 4, 2014.
41 Moika78, November 7, 2017.
42 *Kommersant*, February 6, 2015.
43 BBC Russian, February 5, 2015.
44 *The Telegraph*, February 5, 2005; Online812, February 10, 2015.
45 PrivetSochi, May 21, 2011.
46 See, for example, https://www.youtube.com/watch?v=a08gdzCJD8E (February 5, 2015).
47 *Kommersant*, February 6, 2015.
48 *Pravda*, February 4, 2015.
49 Online812, February 10, 2015.
50 See user reviews on TripAdvisor, https://www.tripadvisor.ru/Attraction_Review-g3442087-d8604498-Reviews-Monument_Yaltinskoi_Troike-Livadiya.html#photos;aggregationId=101&albumid=101&filter=7&ff=219784368.
51 *Kommersant*, March 19, 2015.
52 Lenta, May 8, 2015; ORT, Russian Public Television, March 7, 2016; Lenta, May 18, 2016.
53 Presidential Library, April 24, 2018.
54 RIA, April 22, 2017.
55 Cf. *Novaia Gazeta*, September 21, 2015.
56 NTV, September 9, 2004.
57 Trudovaia Rossiia, September 2012.
58 Out of the three such monuments originally planned two have been built so far, in Magadan in 1996 and in Ekaterinburg in 2017; the third at Vorkuta is in limbo.
59 Vesma, September 12, 2017.
60 Krasnodar school no. 32 has FSB as a sponsor and features a history museum, The Generation Link, which mainly tells the story of Cheka-KGB-FSB. The RossGuard (*Rossgvardiia*) college in Saratov has been restored to its original name, The Dzerzhinsky Institute of the Order of the Red Banner.
61 BBC Russian, June 26, 2015.
62 *Nezavisimaia Gazeta*, July 22, 2015.
63 *Moskovskii Komsomolets*, December 19, 2017.
64 BBC Russian, June 26, 2015; Meduza, December 4, 2017.
65 KudaPiter, December 2018.
66 Ekho Moskvy, September 6, 2019.

67 Radio Svoboda, April 10, 2019.
68 Meduza, February 25, 2016.
69 Cf. *Die Welt*, October 10, 2012; *The Guardian*, June 19, 2016.
70 *Sobesednik*, October 28, 2016.
71 Rambler, December 29, 2018.
72 Radio Svoboda, May 29, 2018; Meduza, May 29, 2018.
73 Lenta, May 17, 2015.
74 Segodnia, June 8, 2016.
75 Ural Information Buro, November 9, 2017.
76 Radio Svoboda, November 17, 2017.
77 Ridus, October 7, 2014.
78 Lenta, May 6, 2015.
79 Sevas, March 19, 2016.
80 Lenta, June 11, 2016; RIA, June 14, 2016. See also Open Russia, November 14, 2015.
81 Myslo, September 25, 2017.
82 Vechernii Rostov, May 4, 2018.
83 RIA, October 16, 2018.
84 RIA, January 28, 2019.
85 On the cult of Tsar Nikolai II in contemporary Russia see Dianina, "Vozvrashchennoe nasledie: Nikolai II kak novodel."
86 Radio Svoboda, November 18, 2017. See also Ekho Moskvy, June 16, 2016.
87 Radio Svoboda, November 20, 2017.
88 Radio Svoboda, April 26, 2018.
89 Regnum, June 13, 2017.
90 *Rossiiskaia Gazeta*, November 12, 2017.
91 Ekho Moskvy, September 9, 2015; Ekho Moskvy, November 3, 2015.
92 BBC Russian, October 14, 2016.
93 BBC Russian, November 1, 2016.
94 BBC Russian, October 14, 2016.
95 Ekho Moskvy, November 2, 2016.
96 Reuters, May 29, 2018.
97 Radio Svoboda, May 28, 2018.
98 ProVladimir, December 9, 2019.
99 Sokolov et al., "Kakoe proshloe nuzhno budushchemu Rossii," 12–13.
100 Gnilorybov, "Kto i zachem stavit pamiatniki Stalinu." Cf. Sakha Press, May 8, 2013.
101 Cf. http://www.alroslav.ru/; https://www.youtube.com/watch?v=dGiVHK2IF5Y (November 2013); https://vk.com/alrosslav; interview with Mikhail Serdiukov on TV Krym, September 11, 2014, https://www.youtube.com/watch?v=PLbj2rph28s.
102 Cf. http://www.alroslav.ru/zakaz/price; https://www.youtube.com/watch?v=dGi VHK2IF5Y (November 2013).
103 Memorial, April 20, 2011.
104 Ibid.
105 Cf. http://www.alroslav.ru/otkritiya1.
106 See *Izvestiia*, May 21, 2015.
107 *Novaia Gazeta*, February 9, 2018.
108 LiveJournal, blog entry, March 2, 2014.
109 RBK, May 13, 2014; Moskva24, May 27, 2014.
110 RBK, September 19, 2017.
111 Radio Svoboda, September 22, 2017.

112 *Novaia Gazeta*, February 9, 2018.
113 Ekho Moskvy, September 25, 2017.
114 Radio Svoboda, December 11, 2018.
115 Memorial, January 10, 2012.
116 Kostroma Today, November 16, 2017.
117 Cf. Galina Yankovskaia, "Triumfalnoe vozvrashchenie? Iskusstvo epokhi stalinizma v muzeinykh i gorodskikh praktikakh 2010-kh godov," *Neprikosnovennyi zapas* 2 (2017), n.p.
118 Ulgrad, June 21, 2018.
119 V1, July 5, 2013.
120 See video at http://nightwolves.ru/nw/gallery/2300/ (December 6, 2016).
121 See Night Wolves, November 4, 2015; Night Wolves, February 21, 2018.
122 Ulgrad, June 22, 2018.
123 Radio Svoboda, January 29, 2019.
124 CNN, June 2, 2015.
125 Radio Svoboda, September 7, 2015.
126 Inosmi, September 20, 2016.
127 Alexander Diukov, blog entry, June 23, 2016.
128 BBC Russian, October 13, 2016.
129 Sokolov et al., "Kakoe proshloe nuzhno budushchemu Rossii," 12.
130 Radio Svoboda, February 18, 2017; Radio Svoboda, July 5, 2017.
131 BBC Russian, August 27, 2015.
132 Cf. Ilya Varlamov, blog entries, December 27, 2018; November 13, 2018; October 31, 2018; October 28, 2018; September 23, 2018; August 3, 2018; August 23, 2018.
133 Ilya Varlamov, blog entries, July 23, 2017; October 18, 2018; October 24, 2018. See also Interfax, October 23, 2018.
134 Cf. Ilya Varlamov, blog entry, January 18, 2019.
135 Meduza, August 23, 2019.
136 Radio Svoboda, May 21, 2018.
137 Ilya Varlamov, blog entry, November 2, 2019.
138 Radio Svoboda, August 19, 2018.
139 Radio Svoboda, September 12, 2019; Radio Svoboda, January 10, 2020.
140 Radio Svoboda, August 21, 2017.
141 For examples see Ilya Varlamov, blog entries, January 3, 2019; July 18, 2018.
142 Cf. Ilya Varlamov, blog entry, October 14, 2018.
143 Ilya Varlamov, blog entry, August 11, 2018.
144 Radio Svoboda, January 10, 2020.
145 See museum's website at http://new.russikona.ru/.
146 See project's website at https://project1917.ru/.
147 Radio Svoboda, April 1, 2019.
148 Radio Svoboda, November 19, 2019.
149 Cf. Radio Svoboda, March 3, 2019; Radio Svoboda, March 31, 2019; Radio Svoboda, May 26, 2019. Cf. Ekho Moskvy, September 4, 2019.
150 Cf. museum's website (June 2019), http://heroes-arms.ru/en/.
151 RVIO, April 4, 2019. Cf. *Barents Observer*, September 3, 2018.
152 Cf. museum's website, https://rzd-museum.ru/en/museum/about-us. See also *New York Times*, August 21, 2015; Ilya Varlamov, blog entry, November 24, 2017.
153 Kremlin, December 12, 2018.
154 Radio Svoboda, February 27, 2019.

155 Radio Svoboda, March 14, 2019.
156 SOVA, March 22, 2019.
157 BBC Russian, September 19, 2017.
158 Radio Svoboda, January 23, 2017.

Chapter 6

1 Kremlin, April 20, 2005.
2 To give just one example, the festival of Russian bard music has become increasingly popular in Israel over the years.
3 Kremlin, November 3, 2003.
4 Kremlin, November 18, 2003.
5 Kremlin, January 27, 2005.
6 Kremlin, April 20, 2005.
7 Kremlin, April 28, 2005; Kremlin, May 7, 2005; Kremlin, June 22, 2016.
8 Kremlin, April 28, 2005.
9 *Komsomolskaia Pravda*, May 16, 2005.
10 Kremlin, June 25, 2012.
11 Ibid.
12 Figures from Olena Bagno-Moldavsky, "The Jewish Diaspora and the Russo-Ukrainian Crisis," report published by the Institute of National Security Studies, Tel Aviv University (March 2015): 13.
13 Kirill Feferman, "The Crisis in Ukraine: Attitudes of the Russian and Ukrainian Jewish Communities," *Israel Journal of Foreign Affairs* 9, no. 2 (2015): 228–30.
14 Cf. museum's website (June 2018), https://www.jewish-museum.ru/about-the-museum/museum-history/.
15 Interfax-Religion, December 25, 2007. Cf. *Segodnia*, July 27, 2017; Radio Svoboda, July 13, 2019.
16 Kremlin, November 7, 2012.
17 MID, November 8, 2012.
18 Kremlin, November 8, 2012.
19 Bagno-Moldavsky, "The Jewish Diaspora and the Russo-Ukrainian Crisis," 13.
20 Feferman, "The Crisis in Ukraine," 230–32.
21 *Tablet Magazine*, September 20, 2010.
22 *Rossiiskaia Gazeta*, October 14, 2011.
23 *Daily Beast*, August 2, 2015.
24 *Belaia kniga natsizma*, ed. Valery Engel et al. (Moscow: Terra, 2013), 3–13, 1107.
25 Nakanune, September 10, 2014.
26 Koposov, *Memory Laws, Memory Wars*, 281–87, 293–95.
27 Cf. *Novaia Gazeta*, May 29, 2012; Memorial, May 31, 2012; Revizionizm Holokosta, December 12, 2012; Holocaust.su, June 5, 2014.
28 Radio Svoboda, August 11, 2019.
29 Kremlin, August 18, 2009. Cf. Kremlin, January 27, 2010.
30 MID, February 13, 2004.
31 Latvian Foreign Ministry, March 16, 2004.
32 MID, July 30, 2004.
33 MID, April 30, 2004.

34 MID, November 2, 2005.
35 MID, November 9, 2005.
36 Cf. text of Resolution 61/147 at https://www.un.org/en/ga/search/view_doc.asp?symbol=A/RES/61/147&Lang=E.
37 Cf. MID, November 21, 2006; MID, September 1, 2012.
38 MID, January 27, 2007.
39 MID, January 29, 2007.
40 MID, May 1, 2007. For details of the 2007 events in Tallinn see, for example, Martin Ehala, "The Bronze Soldier: Identity Threat and Maintenance in Estonia," *Journal of Baltic Studies* 40, no. 1 (2009): 139–58.
41 MID, February 21, 2008.
42 MID, January 28, 2009.
43 MID, February 1, 2010.
44 MID, February 18, 2010.
45 MID, February 11, 2011.
46 MID, March 14, 2012.
47 MID, December 10, 2012.
48 See text of Resolution 67/154 at https://www.un.org/en/ga/search/view_doc.asp?symbol=A/RES/67/154&Lang=E.
49 MID, November 27, 2012.
50 MID, November 22, 2014.
51 Cf. MID, April 23, 2015; BBC Russian, April 24, 2015.
52 The 2018 report is available at http://www.mid.ru/diverse/-/asset_publisher/zwI2FuDbhJx9/content/neonacizm-opasnyj-vyzov-pravam-celoveka-demokratii-i-verhovenstvu-prava.
53 Cf. MID, December 12, 2005; MID, December 15, 2005; MID, December 13, 2006.
54 MID, May 26, 2006.
55 BBC Russian, January 27, 2015.
56 Ibid.
57 BBC Russian, January 22, 2015.
58 Kremlin, January 27, 2015.
59 *The Jerusalem Post*, May 13, 2014. See also Kremlin, August 18, 2009.
60 Ridus, May 22, 2017.
61 Kremlin, June 3, 2016.
62 Ministry of Education, May 10, 2018.
63 Ministry of Education, May 10, 2018 [different news item].
64 Kremlin, January 19, 2016.
65 Radio Svoboda (English), January 20, 2016. See also Meduza, September 19, 2019.
66 MID, January 22, 2016.
67 MID, January 27, 2017.
68 Kremlin, October 10, 2007.
69 Cf. MID, April 30, 2004; MID, June 9, 2005; MID, November 2, 2005.
70 Cf. MID, January 19, 2005; MID, January 22, 2016.
71 MID, April 18, 2018.
72 Cf. RVIO, May 22, 2018.
73 MID, October 12, 2015.
74 Ibid.; MID, February 4, 2016.
75 MID, May 10, 2016; MID, May 23, 2017; MID, May 9, 2018.
76 MID, July 20, 2015.

77 Cf. Anton Weiss-Wendt, *Murder without Hatred: Estonians and the Holocaust* (Syracuse, NY: Syracuse University Press, 2009).
78 Cf. "119 Lives Unlived," documentary by Paula Slier, RT, May 20, 2015.
79 The Polish spelling is *Sobibór*.
80 Kremlin, April 20, 2017. Cf. Kremlin, May 4, 2017.
81 Radio Svoboda, May 13, 2018; Radio Svoboda, May 28, 2018.
82 See Khabensky's TV interview with Vladimir Pozner on Channel One, April 23, 2018.
83 See news item posted on RVIO's VKontakte account (May 11, 2018).
84 Cf. news item posted on the Alexander Pechersky Foundation Facebook account (May 10, 2018).
85 Cf. https://zachestnyibiznes.ru/company/ul/1177700009827_7733321713_FOND-ALEKSANDRA-PEChERSKOGO.
86 Cf. Alexander Pechersky Foundation's website at http://pechersky.org/.
87 Detali.co.il, January 2018, http://detaly.co.il/nenuzhnyj-geroj/.
88 Cf. *Alexander Pechersky: Proryv v bessmertie*, ed. Ilya Vasiliev (Moscow: Vremia, 2013); Vasiliev's interview to Israel's Channel Plus, August 14, 2017.
89 Isrageo, October 17, 2017.
90 See video posted on RVIO's VKontakte account, May 14, 2018.
91 Channel One, May 10, 2018.
92 Cf. RVIO, April 25, 2018.
93 MID, January 22, 2016; *Times of Israel*, April 11, 2018.
94 MID, July 31, 2017.
95 Sputnik, August 17, 2017.
96 Interfax, July 9, 2017; *Moskovskii Komsomolets*, July 11, 2017. Cf. Pensiia i Lgoty (May 2018).
97 Inosmi, April 11, 2016.
98 TASS, August 23, 2017.
99 *Times of Israel*, April 11, 2018.
100 TASS, April 11, 2018.
101 Kremlin, January 29, 2018. Cf. MID, July 13, 2017.
102 Rossiia One, January 29, 2018.
103 Duma, April 10, 2018.
104 RIA, May 8, 2018.
105 See Russia–Israel satellite linkup (April 11, 2018) at https://www.youtube.com/watch?v=-UYnDpz0ljI.
106 Zvezda TV, April 24, 2018.
107 MID, May 10, 2018.
108 St. Petersburg TV Channel, May 4, 2018.
109 RVIO, May 10, 2018.
110 See video of the Berlin premiere on May 9, 2018 at https://www.youtube.com/watch?v=JS72Ptiew7k.
111 See the press conference in Berlin on May 9, 2018 at https://www.youtube.com/watch?v=Zog09VkZn6M.
112 Channel One, May 11, 2018.
113 Cf. TV roundtable, "Sobibor as an Apogee of Jewish Resistance to Fascism."
114 *Moskovskii Komsomolets*, May 6, 2018.
115 TJournal, May 23, 2018.
116 ProGorod, May 10, 2015.

117 Cf. TV roundtable, "Sobibor as an Apogee of Jewish Resistance to Fascism."
118 See interview with Mogilevskii about the book, May 20, 2018.
119 TASS, April 11, 2018; *Times of Israel*, April 11, 2018.
120 TASS, May 4, 2018.
121 Film director Sergei Dvortsov was informed ahead of time that Russia would nominate *Sobibor* for the Academy Awards. Cf. Meduza, January 19, 2020.
122 RVIO, March 28, 2019.
123 Kremlin, April 11, 2018.
124 Kremlin, September 15, 2005.
125 Cf. exhibition pamphlet, "The Holocaust: Annihilation, Liberation, Rescue," 2019.
126 TASS, May 22, 2018.
127 Bringing the exhibition to Argentina may have had something to do with a scandal that involved stacks of cocaine discovered in December 2016 in the Russian diplomatic compound in Buenos Aires, ready to be shipped to Moscow. Cf. Meduza, February 28, 2018.
128 Sputnik Español, May 19, 2018.
129 MID, January 20, 2017.
130 Altman must have been aware of Sputnik's reputation as a Russian state propaganda outlet when he was interviewed by its Spanish-language service in Montevideo in May 2018.
131 Gorod TV, April 30, 2019.
132 MID, April 18, 2018.
133 Cf. Weiss-Wendt, *Murder without Hatred*, passim; Weiss-Wendt and Uğur Ümit Üngör, "Collaboration in Genocide: The Ottoman Empire 1915, the German-Occupied Baltic 1941–1944, and Rwanda 1994," *Holocaust and Genocide Studies* 25, no. 3 (2011): 418–21.
134 MID, February 15, 2018.
135 MID, January 31, 2018.
136 MID, April 30, 2004.
137 MID, December 9, 2016.
138 Consider, for example, the Soviet peace offensive of the early 1950s. Cf. Weiss-Wendt, *The Soviet Union and the Gutting of the UN Genocide Convention*, 246–60.
139 Cf. Yad Vashem's statistics as of January 2020 at http://www.yadvashem.org/right eous/statistics.html.
140 MID, June 3, 2009.
141 Polian, "Istoriomor: Strukturizatsiia pamiati i infrastruktura bespamiatstva."
142 Consider, for example, the memorial plaques honoring individual participants in the Sobibor uprising that were installed in several Russian cities in 2018 and 2019. The one in Ryazan identifies the person as a "veteran of the Great Patriotic War" and the other in Samara as "hero of antifascist resistance," without mentioning that both were Jewish.
143 Cf. exhibition's website, http://filmer-la-guerre.memorialdelashoah.org/index.html.
144 *Daily Beast*, August 2, 2015.
145 *Washington Post*, March 11, 2018.
146 Tsargrad TV, March 7, 2018.
147 One of the reasons may be that the Nuremberg judgment, so often invoked by Russia, does not incorporate charges of genocide. Cf. Hilary Earl, "Prosecuting Genocide before the Genocide Convention: Raphael Lemkin and the Nuremberg Trials, 1945-1949," *Journal of Genocide Research* 15, no. 3 (2013): 317–37.

148 Cf. Weiss-Wendt, *A Rhetorical Crime*, 146–48.
149 See Douglas Irvin-Erickson, "Genocide Discourses: American and Russian Strategic Narratives of Conflict in Iraq and Ukraine," *Politics and Government* 5, no. 3 (2017): 130–45.
150 Cf. MID, January 18, 2005.
151 See, for example, Dan Stone, *The Liberation of the Camps: The End of the Holocaust and Its Aftermath* (New Haven, CO: Yale University Press, 2015), 29–64.
152 See, in particular, research by Francine Hirsch.
153 Cf. *Izvestiia*, January 13, 1985.
154 Cf. MID, September 3, 2009.
155 Cf. TV roundtable, "Sobibor as an Apogee of Jewish Resistance to Fascism."
156 On the subject of hybrid warfare carried out by Russia see, for example, Mark Galeotti, *Russian Political War: Moving beyond the Hybrid* (Abingdon: Routledge, 2019).
157 Cf. MID, November 11, 2008.
158 Quoted on page 5 of foreign ministry's report, "Neonatsizm – opasnyi vyzov pravam cheloveka, demokratii i verkhovenstvu prava," April 2015.
159 As a recent example, consider the disparaging comments on the interview by Vakhtang Kikabidze to Deutsche Welle, in which the famous Georgian film actor said, among other things, that he had rejoiced at the collapse of the Soviet Union. Cf. St. Petersburg TV Channel, June 21, 2018.
160 Radio Svoboda, January 29, 2019.
161 Radio Liberty, January 23, 2020.
162 *Times of Israel*, January 23, 2020.
163 RBK, January 23, 2020.

Chapter 7

1 Cf. Levada, December 8, 2016. See also Radio Svoboda, September 6, 2016.
2 For details see Steven A. Barnes, "Keeping the Past in the Past: The Attack on the Perm 36 Gulag Museum and Russian Historical Memory of Soviet Repression," in *The Future of the Soviet Past: The Politics of History in Putin's Russia*, ed. Anton Weiss-Wendt and Nanci Adler (Bloomington, IN: Indiana University Press, 2021), in print.
3 Ibid.
4 Radio Svoboda, August 18, 2016.
5 See documentary feature, "Pro Perm-36. Professiia reporter: Piataia kolonna," NTV, July 7, 2014.
6 BBC English, March 3, 2015; *The Telegraph*, May 6, 2015.
7 Barnes, "Keeping the Past in the Past."
8 Radio Svoboda, February 16, 2016.
9 Radio Svoboda, June 24, 2018.
10 BBC Russian, January 29, 2016.
11 BBC Russian, April 5, 2018.
12 Radio Svoboda, April 18, 2017.
13 Meduza, August 16, 2019.
14 Meduza, October 2, 2018.
15 Cf. Meduza, March 1, 2019.
16 Radio Svoboda, April 6, 2018.

17 Radio Svoboda, June 15, 2018.
18 7×7, December 17, 2017; cf. *Izvestia*, July 15, 2016; Zvezda TV, August 4, 2016.
19 7×7, December 17, 2017.
20 Radio Svoboda, August 29, 2018; *Novaia Gazeta*, September 3, 2018. For an official version see RVIO, September 7, 2018.
21 *Novaia Gazeta*, September 8, 2018.
22 7×7, June 10, 2019.
23 Ministry of culture of Karelia to RVIO, July 15, 2019, posted on a dedicated Facebook page covering the legal case against Yuri Dmitriev.
24 Radio Svoboda, August 15, 2019; Meduza, August 16, 2019.
25 Meduza, October 2, 2018.
26 Meduza, October 4, 2018.
27 Meduza, May 27, 2019. About to be released on health grounds, Koltyrin died in prison hospital in late March 2020.
28 Cf. Radio Svoboda, April 10, 2017.
29 Realnoe Vremia, June 13, 2018.
30 Radio Svoboda, May 20, 2017.
31 Realnoe Vremia, June 13, 2018.
32 Ibid. See also RFI, June 11, 2018.
33 Ibid.
34 Radio Svoboda, March 15, 2018. See also museum's website, http://nkvd.tomsk.ru/.
35 Cf. RIA Tomsk, March 13, 2019.
36 On Article 282, see BBC Russian, March 6, 2019.
37 Koposov, *Memory Laws, Memory Wars*, 221.
38 Ibid., 207, 261–75, 281–99. See also Ivan Kurilla, "The Implications of Russia's Law against the 'Rehabilitation of Nazism,'" PONARS Eurasia 331 (August 2014).
39 Radio Svoboda, May 8, 2018; Radio Svoboda, May 13, 2018.
40 Radio Svoboda, January 16, 2018.
41 Radio Svoboda, December 4, 2018.
42 Radio Svoboda, December 28, 2018.
43 Cf. Meduza, July 7, 2016; Radio Svoboda, December 24, 2016.
44 Ekho Moskvy, September 5, 2016. See also Radio Svoboda, September 8, 2016.
45 Radio Svoboda, May 15, 2018.
46 Radio Svoboda, February 19, 2018.
47 Report by Agora human rights group, "Russia against History: Revision Prosecuted," May 2018.
48 Cf. Christi Scott Bartman, *Lawfare: Use of the Definition of Aggressive War by the Soviet and Russian Federation Governments* (Newcastle: Cambridge Scholars Publishing, 2010); Weiss-Wendt, *The Soviet Union and the Gutting of the UN Genocide Convention*, Ch. 5, 13.
49 Ekho Moskvy, May 12, 2017; Radio Svoboda, June 23, 2018.
50 Radio Svoboda, March 15, 2019.
51 Radio Svoboda, January 14, 2020.
52 Ekho Moskvy, August 24, 2017.
53 Ekho Moskvy, February 6, 2018; Radio Svoboda, April 3, 2018; Radio Svoboda, January 9, 2018; Radio Svoboda, April 29, 2018.
54 Report by Agora human rights group, "Russia against History: Revision Prosecuted," May 2018.
55 *Guardian*, April 25, 2015.

56 Gazeta, March 29, 2019.
57 Meduza, January 29, 2018; Radio Svoboda, April 26, 2018; Meduza, February 20, 2018.
58 Radio Svoboda, June 16, 2019.
59 Cf. Ilya Varlamov, blog entry, August 10, 2018.
60 Report by Agora human rights group, "Russia against History: Revision Prosecuted," May 2018 (case list).
61 BBC Russian, September 5, 2018.
62 Lenta, March 6, 2019.
63 BBC Russian, April 4, 2015; BBC Russian, April 9, 2015.
64 Radio Svoboda, December 3, 2019.
65 SOVA, August 15, 2015.
66 BBC Russian, May 12, 2015.
67 Ilya Varlamov, blog entry, May 16, 2018.
68 Meduza, October 17, 2019.
69 Radio Svoboda, December 10, 2018.
70 Meduza, April 29, 2018.
71 Radio Svoboda, June 29, 2018.
72 Radio Svoboda, May 9, 2019.
73 See Medinskii's interview on NTV, November 5, 2018. See also RVIO, October 15, 2018.
74 Radio Svoboda, January 4, 2019.
75 Radio Svoboda, February 24, 2019.
76 Historical Memory Foundation, April 7, 2015.
77 Radio Svoboda, November 21, 2017; Radio Svoboda, December 12, 2017; Ekho Moskvy, December 20, 2017.
78 Meduza, July 18, 2018.
79 See full text of Article 148 at http://ukodeksrf.ru/ch-2/rzd-7/gl-19/st-148-uk-rf. See also Radio Svoboda, May 15, 2019.
80 Radio Svoboda, September 11, 2017; Meduza, June 17, 2018.
81 Cf. report by Agora human rights group, "Liberalization à la russe," May 2019. See also Radio Svoboda, May 5, 2019.
82 Cf. report by Agora human rights group, "Russia against History: Revision Prosecuted," May 2018.
83 BBC Russian, May 29, 2017; Meduza, December 4, 2018.
84 BBC Russian, September 25, 2015.
85 *Novaia Gazeta*, February 15, 2018.
86 *Novaia Gazeta*, November 22, 2018.
87 Meduza, June 27, 2019.
88 Meduza, June 19, 2019.
89 *Kommersant*, May 15, 2018. Cf. the Alexander Yakovlev Foundation website, http://www.alexanderyakovlev.org/fond.
90 On Yeltsin Center see Ekaterina Boltunova, "Prostranstvo (ushedshego) geroia: obraz lidera, istoricheskaia pamiat i memorialnaia traditsiia v Rossii (na primere Yeltsin-tsentra)," *Novoe Literaturnoe Obozrenie* 2 (2017).
91 For an early history of Memorial, see Nanci Adler, *Victims of Soviet Terror: The Story of the Memorial Movement* (Santa Barbara, CA: Praeger, 1993). Cf. Memorial's website, https://www.memo.ru/ru-ru/.
92 Radio Svoboda, September 7, 2016.
93 Radio Svoboda, May 29, 2019.

94 Meduza, November 19, 2019.
95 BBC Russian, May 26, 2015.
96 Cf. the list of NGOs proclaimed "foreign agents" by the Russian justice ministry (January 2019), http://unro.minjust.ru/NKOForeignAgent.aspx (the list can no longer be retrieved).
97 BBC Russian, November 10, 2015.
98 BBC Russian, December 16, 2016.
99 RIA Novosti, September 4, 2015.
100 Meduza, January 14, 2019.
101 Radio Svoboda, February 12, 2019.
102 Radio Svoboda, December 31, 2019. See also Ekho Moskvy, October 23, 2019; Radio Svoboda, January 9, 2020.
103 BBC Russian, November 12, 2019.
104 Yeltsin Center, May 7, 2017.
105 *Rossiiskaia Gazeta*, July 7, 2017. Cf. Yeltsin Center, December 18, 2016.
106 RVIO, December 13, 2016.
107 Radio Svoboda, December 14, 2016.
108 Cf. Besogon TV, episode no. 123 (July 17, 2018). See also Radio Svoboda, May 8, 2017.
109 Radio Svoboda, April 28, 2016.
110 Ekho Moskvy, April 26, 2017.
111 Ekho Moskvy, May 24, 2019.
112 Cf. Rossiia 24, April 23, 2019.
113 Meduza, June 5, 2019.
114 This dilemma has also been acknowledged by VIO. Cf. Sokolov et al., "Kakoe proshloe nuzhno budushchemu Rossii," 41–42.
115 Radio Svoboda, December 27, 2018. Cf. Memorial, November 2, 2018; Ekho Moskvy, November 6, 2018; Bessmertnyi Barak, November 10, 2018.
116 For a comprehensive overview, see Mischa Gabowitsch, *Protest in Putin's Russia* (Cambridge and Malden, MA: Polity, 2016). Cf. *Novaia Gazeta*, August 29, 2015; Meduza, June 4, 2019.
117 Meduza, November 27, 2018; Radio Svoboda, December 2, 2018.
118 Radio Svoboda, November 23, 2018.
119 Radio Svoboda, January 23, 2017.
120 Cf. Radio Svoboda, March 16, 2019.
121 Cf. Radio Svoboda, April 18, 2018.
122 Cf. association's website (March 2019), https://www.dissernet.org/. Cf. Meduza, May 28, 2019; Radio Svoboda, May 31, 2019.
123 Radio Svoboda, August 30, 2019.
124 Cf. *Novaia Gazeta*, October 22, 2018. See also Ekho Moskvy, August 10, 2017.
125 BBC Russian, February 23, 2016; Radio Svoboda, November 25, 2018.
126 Radio Svoboda, May 19, 2019.
127 Radio Svoboda, December 2, 2018.
128 *Kommersant*, June 20, 2019.
129 Radio Svoboda, November 19, 2016. Cf. project's website, https://karagodin.org/.
130 Radio Svoboda, November 26, 2016.
131 Radio Svoboda, December 25, 2016.
132 Radio Svoboda, May 11, 2019.
133 Radio Svoboda, May 8, 2018.

134 Radio Svoboda, October 28, 2019; Meduza, December 18, 2019.
135 Cf. Realnoe Vremia, June 13, 2018; Nikolai Arakcheev, blog entry, September 22, 2018.
136 Radio Svoboda, November 17, 2018.

Conclusion

1 Meduza, October 12, 2015; Meduza, June 2, 2017.
2 BBC Russian, January 18, 2019; Radio Svoboda, January 21, 2019; Meduza, May 17, 2019.
3 For a different opinion, see Pakhaliuk, "Istoricheskoe proshloe kak osnovanie rossiiskoi politiki," 12.
4 Cf. Transitions Online, November 7, 2017.
5 Cf. Pakhaliuk, "Istoricheskoe proshloe kak osnovanie rossiiskoi politiki," 27.
6 Radio Svoboda, November 28, 2017.
7 Toymentsev, "Legal but Criminal," 315.
8 Cf. *Novaia Gazeta*, November 10, 2015.
9 Cf. Gudkov, "1917 god"; Radio Svoboda, February 16, 2017.
10 BBC Russian, December 12, 2019.
11 Victor Shnirelman, "Kniaz Sviatoslav i politika pamiati," *Neprikosnovennyi zapas* 2 (2017): n.p.
12 Cf. Radio Svoboda, June 7, 2016; Radio Svoboda, November 21, 2018; RVIO, March 15, 2019; RVIO, February 16, 2019; RVIO, February 15, 2019; RIO, June 19, 2019.
13 RIA, August 23, 2019.
14 *Izvestiia*, August 14, 2019.
15 Historical Memory Foundation, June 3, 2019.
16 Radio Svoboda, October 28, 2019.
17 Nevskie Novosti, May 3, 2018.
18 Cf. Sokolov et al., "Kakoe proshloe nuzhno budushchemu Rossii," passim; *Nezavisimaia Gazeta*, February 11, 2019.
19 Meduza, December 12, 2018.
20 Meduza, March 18, 2019.
21 Radio Svoboda, January 13, 2020. At St. Petersburg international airport one can buy, for 79,000 rubles, what looks like a Putin icon.
22 Cf. RVIO, May 17, 2018.
23 RVIO, May 9, 2018.
24 RVIO, October 25, 2018.
25 Cf. Federalnyi spisok ekstremistskikh materialov (July 2018), http://minjust.ru/ru/node/243787.
26 Kremlin, February 17, 2015.
27 Kremlin, April 5, 2016.
28 Quoted in RVIO, May 29, 2019.
29 RVIO, April 5, 2019.
30 RVIO, April 25, 2018.
31 Cf. Kremlin, April 20, 2017; Kremlin, May 4, 2017.
32 Quoted in Kremlin, December 12, 2018.
33 Cf. RVIO, April 25, 2018.

Bibliography

Russian Government Agencies

Civic Chamber of the Russian Federation (oprf.ru)
Duma (duma.gov.ru)
Federal Archival Agency (archives.ru)
Federation Council (council.gov.ru)
Government of Russia (government.ru)
Head of the Russian Government (premier.gov.ru)
Ministry of Defense of the Russian Federation (mil.ru)
Ministry of Enlightenment of the Russian Federation (formerly Ministry of Education and Science of the Russian Federation) (edu.gov.ru)
Ministry of Foreign Affairs of the Russian Federation (mid.ru; facebook.com/MIDRussia)
Ministry of Justice of the Russian Federation (minjust.ru)
Moscow Municipality (mos.ru)
Kremlin (kremlin.ru)
Presidential Library (prlib.ru)
Russian State Military Archives (rgarchive.ru)

Russian Pro-Government Agencies, News Outlets, Nationalist Organizations, and Online Publications

Alexander Pechersky Foundation
    (pechersky.org; facebook.com/AlexanderPecherskyFoundation)
Alley of Russian Glory (alroslav.ru; vk.com/alrosslav)
Baikal 24
Besogon TV
Bloknot-Novocherkassk.ru
Bumaga (paperpaper.ru)
Channel One
Channel One, Army Magazine (1tvam.ru)
Communist Party of Russia, Penza branch office (kprfpenza.ru)
The Essence of Time (eot.su)
Evpatoria city government (my-evp.ru)
Expert Institute of Social Studies (eisr.ru)
Federal News Agency (riafan.ru)
ForPost (sevastopol.su)
Gazeta.ru
Gorod TV (gorod-tv.com)
Historical Memory Foundation (historyfoundation.ru)

I'm a Capitalist (yakapitalist.ru)
Immortal Regiment Russia (polkrf.ru)
Imperial Orthodox Palestine Society (ippo.ru/)
Inosmi.ru
Institute of Foreign Political Studies and Initiatives (invissin.ru)
Institute of National Memory (inmrf.ru)
Interfax
Kostroma Today
KudaPiter.ru
Lenta.ru
Life.ru
Moika78.ru
Moskva24 (m24.ru)
Myslo.ru
Nakanune.ru
Nevskie Novosti (nevnov.ru)
NGS.ru (news.ngs.ru)
Night Wolves (nightwolves.ru)
NSN, National News Service (nsn.fm)
NTV
Online812.ru
ORT, Russian Public Television
Pln-pskov.ru
Politnavigator (politnavigator.net)
Pravoslavie.ru
PrivetSochi.ru
ProGorod (pg11.ru)
Pskovskaia Gubernia Online (gibernia.prskovregion.org)
Pskovskie Novosti (nwpskov.ru)
Rambler.ru
Realnoe Vremia (realnoevremya.ru)
Regnum
RIA, Russian Information Agency
Rossiia 24
Rossiia One
Russian Communist Party (kprf.ru)
Russia in Global Affairs
Russia Today, RT
Russian Military Historical Society, RVIO (rvio.histrf.ru; vk.com/rvio_ru)
Russian Historical Society, RIO (historyrussia.org/)
Russian Orthodox Church (patriarchia.ru)
Russian Realty
Russkaia Narodnaia Linia (ruskline.ru)
Russkii Mir (russkiymir.ru)
Russkii Puls (russianpulse.ru)
Sakha Press
Sevas.com
Smartnews.ru
Sputnik (sputniknews.com)

Stavropol-Poisk (stavropol-poisk.ru)
St. Petersburg TV Channel (topspb.tv)
TASS
TJournal.ru
Trudovaiia Rossiia (tr.rkrp-rpk.ru)
Tsargrad TV (tsargrad.tv)
Ulgrad.ru
UralInformBiuro (uralinform.ru)
Vechernii Rostov (vechrost.ru)
Vesti.ru
Vl.ru
VTsIOM (wciom.ru)
X-Time.Info (archive.li)
Youth Army (yunarmy.ru)
Zvezda TV (tvzvezda.ru)

Independent Organizations, News Agencies, and Online Projects

Agora International Human Rights Group
The Alexander Yakovlev Democracy Foundation (alexanderyakovlev.org)
BBC Russian Service
Bessmertnyi Barak (bessmertnybarak.ru)
Bloomberg
CNN
Daily Beast
Detali (detail.co.il)
Diskurs (discours.io)
Dissernet (dissernet.org)
Dozhd TV (tvrain.ru)
Ekho Moskvy
First Channel (1tv.ge)
Free Historical Society, VIO (volistob.ru)
History of Propaganda (propagandahistory.ru)
Immortal Regiment Tomsk (moypolk.ru)
The Insider (theins.ru)
Isrageo
Levada
Meduza
Memorial (memo.ru; urokiistorii.ru)
Open Democracy (opendemocracy.net)
Open Media (openmedia.io)
Open Russia (openrussia.org)
Panoptikon (panoptikon.org)
PhD in Russia (phdru.com)
Politnavigator (politnavigator.net)
PONARS Eurasia

Radio Liberty
RAPSI, Russian Agency for Legal and Judicial Information
Reuters
RFI
Ridus (ridus.ru)
Segodnia (segodnya.ua)
7×7 (7×7-journal.ru)
Snob (snob.ru)
SOVA, Center for Information and Analysis
Transitions Online (tol.org)
Varlamov, Ilya, blog (varlamov.ru)
Yeltsin Center (yeltsin.ru)

Newspapers and Journals

Aftenposten
American Historical Review
Argumenty i fakty
The Barents Observer
The Chronicle of Higher Education
Comparative Literature Studies
Europe-Asia Studies
Financial Times
Fontanka
The Guardian
Israel Journal of Foreign Affairs
Izvestiia
The Jerusalem Post
Journal of Cold War Studies
The Journal of Power Institutions in Post-Soviet Societies
Kommersant
Komsomolskaia Pravda
Krasnaia Zvezda
Moskovskii Komsomolets
Neprikosnovennyi zapas
Newsweek
The New York Times
Nezavisimaia Gazeta
Novaia Gazeta
Novoe Literaturnoe Obozrenie
Novosti (Serbia)
Politics and Government
Politiia
Pro et Contra
RBK
Rolling Stone
Rossiiskaia Gazeta

Sobesednik
Süddeutsche Zeitung
Tablet Magazine
The Telegraph
Time Magazine
The Times
The Times of Israel
Tiumenskie Izvsetiia
Tverskie Vedomosti
Vesma
Vzgliad
The Wall Street Journal
The Washington Post
Die Welt

Secondary Sources

Adler, Nanci, *Victims of Soviet Terror: The Story of the Memorial Movement* (Santa Barbara, CA: Praeger, 1993).
Alexander Pechersky: Proryv v bessmertie, edited by Ilya Vasiliev (Moscow: Vremia, 2013).
Alexandrov, Kirill, "Generalitet i ofitserskie kadry vooruzhennykh formirovanii Komiteta osvobozhdeniia narodov Rossii, 1943–1944 gg." (PhD Thesis, St. Petersburg Institute of History of the Russian Academy of Sciences, 2015).
Barnes, Steven A., "Keeping the Past in the Past: The Attack on the Perm 36 Gulag Museum and Russian Historical Memory of Soviet Repression," in *The Future of the Soviet Past: The Politics of History in Putin's Russia*, edited by Anton Weiss-Wendt and Nanci Adler (Bloomington, IN: Indiana University Press, 2021), in print.
Bartman, Christi, *Lawfare: Use of the Definition of Aggressive War by the Soviet and Russian Federation Governments* (Newcastle: Cambridge Scholars Publishing, 2010).
Belaia kniga natsizma, edited by Valery Engel (Moscow: Terra, 2013).
Boltunova, Ekaterina, "Prostranstvo (ushedshego) geroia: Obraz lidera, istoricheskaia pamiat i memorialnaia traditsiia v Rossii (na primere Yeltsin-tsentra)," *Novoe Literaturnoe Obozrenie* 2 (2017): n.p., http://magazines.russ.ru/nlo/2017/2/prostranstvo-ushedshego-geroya.html.
Boym, Svetlana, *The Future of Nostalgia* (New York: Basic Books, 2001).
Clinton, Hillary R., *Hard Choices* (London: Simon & Schuster, 2014).
Dianina, Katia, "Vozvrashchennoe nasledie: Nikolai II kak novodel," *Novoe Literaturnoe Obozrenie* 1 (2018): n.p., http://magazines.russ.ru/nlo/2018/1/vozvrashennoe-nasledie.html.
Ehala, Martin, "The Bronze Soldier: Identity Threat and Maintenance in Estonia," *Journal of Baltic Studies* 40, no. 1 (2009): 139–58.
Engerman, David C., *Know Your Enemy: The Rise and Fall of America's Soviet Experts* (New York: Oxford University Press, 2009).
Falsifiers of History (Historical Survey) (Moscow: Foreign Language Publishing House, 1948).
Feferman, Kiril, "The Crisis in Ukraine: Attitudes of the Russian and Ukrainian Jewish Communities," *Israel Journal of Foreign Affairs* 9, no. 2 (2015): 227–36.

Gabowitsch, Mischa, *Protest in Putin's Russia* (Cambridge and Malden, MA: Polity, 2016).
Golod v SSSR, 1930–1934 gg./Famine in the USSR, 1930–1934, edited by Vladimir Kozlov (Moscow: Federal Archival Agency of the Russian Federation, 2009).
Gudkov, Lev, "1917 god v structure legitimnosti rossiiskoi vlasti," *Neprikosnovennyi zapas* 6 (2017): 154–72, http://magazines.russ.ru/nz/2017/6/1917-god-v-strukture-legitimnosti-rossijskoj-vlasti.html.
Hirsch, Francine, "The Soviets at Nuremberg: International Law, Propaganda, and the Making of the Postwar Order," *American Historical Review* 113, no. 3 (2008): 701–30.
Irvin-Erickson, Douglas, "Genocide Discourses: American and Russian Strategic Narratives of Conflict in Iraq and Ukraine," *Politics and Government* 5, no. 3 (2017): 130–45.
Kasianov, Georgiy, "The 'Nationalization' of History in Ukraine," in *The Convolutions of Historical Politics*, edited by Alexei Miller and Maria Lipman (Budapest: CEU Press, 2012), 141–74.
Klimenko, Ekaterina, "Building the Nation, Legitimizing the State—My History and Memory of the Russian Revolutions in Contemporary Russia," *Nationalities Papers*, https://doi.org/10.1017/nps.2019.105.
Koposov, Nikolay, *Memory Laws, Memory Wars: The Politics of the Past in Europe and Russia* (Cambridge: Cambridge University Press, 2018).
Malinova, Olga, "Tema proshlogo v ritorike prezidentov Rossii," *Pro et Contra* 3-4 (May–August 2011): 106–22.
McFaul, Michael, *From Cold War to Hot Peace: An American Ambassador in Putin's Russia* (Boston: Houghton Mifflin Harcourt, 2018).
Medinskii, Vladimir, "Problemy obiektivnosti v osveshchenii Rossiiskoi istorii vtoroi poloviny XV–XVII vv." (PhD Thesis, Moscow State Social University, 2011).
Miller, Alexei, "The Turns of Russian Historical Politics, from Perestroika to 2011," in *The Convolutions of Historical Politics*, edited by Alexei Miller and Maria Lipman (Budapest: CEU Press, 2012), 253–78.
Montefiore, Simon Sebag, *Romanovs, 1613–1918* (London: Weidenfeld & Nicolson, 2017).
Naimark, Norman M., *Fires of Hatred: Ethnic Cleansing in Twentieth-Century Europe* (Cambridge, MA: Harvard University Press, 2001).
Norris, Stephen M., "War, Cinema, and the Politics of Memory in Putin 2.0 Culture," in *The Future of the Soviet Past: The Politics of History in Putin's Russia*, edited by Anton Weiss-Wendt and Nanci Adler (Bloomington, IN: Indiana University Press, 2021), in print.
Pakhaliuk, Konstantin, "Istoricheskoe proshloe kak osnovanie rossiiskoi politiki: Na primere vystuplenii Vladimira Putina v 2012–2018 gg.," *Politiia* 4 (2018): 6–31.
Polian, "Istoriomor: Strukturizatsiia pamiati i infrastruktura bespamiatstva," *Neprikosnovennyi zapas* 3 (2015): n.p., http://magazines.russ.ru/nz/2015/3/16pp.html.
Roberts, Geoffrey, "Stalin, the Pact with Nazi Germany, and the Origins of Postwar Soviet Diplomatic Historiography," *Journal of Cold War Studies* 4, no. 4 (Fall 2002): 93–103.
Rousselet, Kathy, "The Church in the Service of the Fatherland," *Europe-Asia Studies* 67, no. 1 (2015): 49–67.
Russian Federation Council, *O protivodeistvii popytkam falsifikatsii istorii narodov v ushcherb interesam Rossii, sbornik materialov* (March 2013).
Sanina, Anna, *Patriotic Education in Contemporary Russia: Sociological Studies in the Making of the Post-Soviet Citizen* (Stuttgart: Ibidem, 2017).
Satter, David, *It Was a Long Time Ago, and It Never Happened Anyway: Russia and the Communist Past* (New Haven: Yale University Press, 2012).

Sieca-Kozlowski, Elisabeth, and Vanessa Voisin, "Interview with Olesya Orlenko, in Charge of the International Relations Department at the Historical Memory Foundation in Moscow, conducted in February and October 2011 in Paris," *The Journal of Power Institutions in Post-Soviet Societies* 12 (2011), https://journals.openedition.org/pipss/3895.

Sokolov, Nikita, Grigory Iudin, and Alexander Rubtsov, *Kakoe proshloe nuzhno budushchemu Rossii* (Moscow: VIO, 2017).

Stola, Dariusz, "Poland's Institute of National Remembrance: A Ministry of Memory?" in *The Convolutions of Historical Politics*, edited by Alexei Miller and Maria Lipman (Budapest: CEU Press, 2012), 45–58.

Stone, Dan, *The Liberation of the Camps: The End of the Holocaust and Its Aftermath* (New Haven, CO: Yale University Press, 2015).

Toymentsev, Sergey, "Legal but Criminal: The Failure of the 'Russian Nuremberg' and the Paradoxes of Post-Soviet Memory," *Comparative Literature Studies* 48, no. 3 (2011): 296–319.

Tsyrlina-Spady, Tatyana, and Alan Stoskopf, "Russian History Textbooks in the Putin Era: Heroic Leaders Demand Loyal Citizens," in *Globalisation and Historiography of National Leaders: Symbolic Representations in School Textbooks*, edited by Joseph Zajda et al. (Dordrecht: Springer, 2017), 15–33.

Vanke, Alexandrina, "Landshafty pamiati: Park Pobedy na Poklonnoi gore v Moskve," *Neprikosnovennyi zapas* 3 (2015): n.p., http://magazines.russ.ru/nz/2015/3/15va-pr.html.

Weiss-Wendt, Anton, *A Rhetorical Crime: Genocide in the Geopolitical Discourse of the Cold War* (New Brunswick, NJ: Rutgers University Press, 2018).

Weiss-Wendt, Anton, *The Soviet Union and the Gutting of the UN Genocide Convention* (Madison, WI: University of Wisconsin Press, 2017).

Weiss-Wendt, Anton, and Uğur Ümit Üngör, "Collaboration in Genocide: The Ottoman Empire 1915, the German Occupied Baltic 1941–1944, and Rwanda 1994," *Holocaust and Genocide Studies* 25, no. 3 (2011): 404–37.

Yankovskaia, Galina, "Triumfalnoe vozvrashchenie? Iskusstvo epokhi stalinizma v muzeinykh i gorodskikh praktikakh 2010-kh godov," *Neprikosnovennyi zapas* 2 (2017): 51–66, http://magazines.russ.ru/nz/2017/2/triumfalnoe-vozvrashenie.html.

Index

Ab Imperio journal 61
Abkhazia 75
Abramov, Mikhail 181
academic freedom 4, 23, 34–40, 240, 255
Academy Awards 6, 211–12. *See also Sobibor* movie
Adamskii, Alexander 148
Adventists 91
Aeroflot 98, 237
Afghanistan 23, 125, 145, 256. *See also* Soviet war in Afghanistan
Agora human rights group 147, 232
Ahmadinejad, Mahmoud 195
AK-47, 100, 112, 126, 134, 174–5
Aksenov, Sergei 57, 78, 147, 167
Alexander II 72, 168, 172
Alexander III 65, 168
Alexander Pechersky Foundation 203–4, 206, 210, 218. *See also* Pechersky, Alexander
Alexander Yakovlev Democracy Foundation 46, 240, 257
Alexandrov 171
Alexandrov, Kirill 36–8, 40, 46, 203, 255, 260
Alexeev, Yuri 25, 229
Alexeieva, Liudmila 110, 242
Alexy II, Patriarch 72
Alley of Rulers sculpture park 150–1, 157–8
Alley of Russian Glory company 172–4
Allies, wartime 1, 10–11, 86, 95, 97, 107, 138, 158–60, 194, 197, 199, 219, 222
Altai region 139
Altman, Ilya 40, 212–14, 222
American independence 89
Americans 1, 108, 140, 204, 219–20
Amsterdam 201
Amur region 164, 167
Ananchenko, Alexei 31–2
Andreev, Konstantin 116

Andrei Rublev Museum of Ancient Russian Culture and Art 62
Andrew, Apostle 129
Ankara 108
the Antarctic 108
Anti-Defamation League 188
Anti-Maidan movement 71, 74, 79, 134–5
antisemitism 32–3, 69–70, 185, 190–1, 197–8, 203, 207, 215, 222
Antiterrorism Center 233, 258
Antonescu, Ion 200
Applebaum, Anne 196
Arakcheev, Alexander 21, 166, 229–31, 248
archeology 27–8, 85
architectural heritage 179–81. *See also* heritage buildings
archives 4, 11, 18–26, 37–9, 59, 114, 116, 148, 190, 217, 225, 227–8, 241, 245, 246–7. *See also names of individual archives*
Archives of the Russian Academy of Sciences 24. *See also* Russian Academy of Sciences
Archives Watch 245
Arctic 123, 181, 260
Argentina 212–13
Arkhangelsk 107, 110, 112
Arkhangelsk Pomor University 36
Arkhipova, Alexandra 106
Armenian genocide 13, 41, 142, 261
Armenians 41
Armistice Day (November 11) 93
Artizov, Andrei 38
Asia 39
Al-Assad, Bashar 168, 218
Association for Slavic, East European, and Eurasian Studies (ASEEES) 26
Association for the Study of Nationalities (ASN) 26

Association of the Institutes of History of CIS Countries   14
Astana   15
Astrakhan   163, 167, 237
Atatürk   7, 257
Atkarsk   151
Atlantic Council   249
Aurora cruiser   141
Auschwitz-Birkenau death camp   6, 185, 192, 196, 199, 201, 206, 211–13, 215, 218–19, 222. *See also* the Holocaust; Nazi death camps
Auschwitz-Birkenau State Museum   97, 185, 196–7, 200–1, 222
Australia   40, 121, 196
Austria   27, 213, 225
Austrians   27
Axis Powers   57, 232
Azerbaijan   138
Azov Battalion   81

Babitskii, Ivan   80
Bagdasarian, Vardan   31
Baikal region   177
Baker, Andrew   189
Bakhchisarai   167
Baku   138
Balakhna   112
Balbekov, Ruslan   161
ballistic missiles   100, 129, 163. *See also* Iskander
Baltic Federal University   31, 63
Baltic Germans   46
Baltic Navy   64
Baltic States   4, 9, 11, 13–14, 16, 27, 186, 191–2, 194, 197–9, 208, 215, 219, 223, 256. *See also names of individual countries*
Baltiisk   169
Bandera, Stepan, alleged followers of   37–8, 73, 197–8
Bandidos biker club   79
banks   66, 112, 127. *See also names of individual banks*
Baptists   91
Barbara, Martyr   129
Barcelona   108
Barkov, Alexander   118
Barnaul   99, 106–7, 234

Barnes, A. Steven   224
Bastyrkin, Alexander   69, 234
Basurin, Eduard   156
Battle of Stalingrad Museum   101, 138. *See also* Stalingrad, Battle of
Baturin, Victor   159
Bauska   194
Beckett, Samuel   141
Beevor, Antony   29
Beglov, Alexander   133, 143
Beijing   96
Beirut   108
Belarus   101, 199, 208
Belgorod   64, 71
Belgorod State University   52–3
Belgorsk   164, 167
Belgrade   108
Belkovskii, Stanislav   83
Bellingcat investigative journalism website   255
Belorussia. *See* Belarus
Belorussians   191
Belov, Sergei   252
Benigni, Roberto   211
Benson, Ivar   214
Beria, Lavrenty   61, 73, 109, 112, 132, 162
Berkut security detachment, Ukrainian   105
Berlin   57, 74, 76–7, 98–9, 108, 130, 132, 191, 193, 209, 219
Berlin, Battle of (1945)   98–9, 101, 130–1
Berlin Wall   49
Beslan   150
Beslan school hostage drama (2004)   68, 145
Besogon TV   54. *See also* Mikhalkov, Nikita
Bezborodov, Alexander   68
biker festivals   5, 73, 75–8, 81, 101, 138. *See also* Night Wolves biker club; Zaldostanov, Alexander
Bishops' Council   69. *See also* Russian Orthodox Church
Bismarck, Otto von   67
Black Sea   180
blasphemy laws   239
blood libel   69–70. *See also* antisemitism
Bloomfield, Sara   193

Bolshevik Revolution   5, 8, 30, 67, 77, 86, 121, 140-1, 143-5, 152, 164, 181, 232
Bolsheviks   3, 67, 93, 162, 165, 179
Bolshevism   65
Bonaparte, Napoleon   14, 150, 175
Boroda, Alexander   69, 187-8, 190, 197, 217
Borodino, Battle of (1812)   139, 145
Borodino Bread sculpture (2012)   175
Borovsk   117, 179
Bortnikov, Alexander   60-1, 246
Boym, Svetlana   3, 119
Branham, William M.   233
Bratislava   200, 208
Brazil   96
Brest, defense of (1941)   48, 86
Brexit   96
Brezhnev, Leonid   78, 89, 150, 242
Briansk   214, 240
BRIC countries   95
Brisbane   196
Britain. See United Kingdom
British   107-8, 219
British Commonwealth   93
British Holocaust Educational Trust   191
Brodsky, Yuri   72
Bucharest   200
Budapest   34
Budapest ghetto   219. See also the Holocaust
Buddhists   91
Buenos Aires   212
Buk missile launcher   131-2
Bulgaria   72, 97
Bundestag   238
Buryatia   175
Busarov, Alexander   247
Bush, George W.   90
Butovo mass execution site   71. See also Stalin's crimes
Byzantine Empire   88

Calgary   108
Canada   74, 108, 194-5
Cannes Film Festival   209
Carley, Michael Jabara   27
Caspian Sea   167
the Caucasus   15. See also North Caucasus

Celebration movie (2018)   238
censorship   1, 22, 35, 134, 232, 245
Central Archives of the Russian Defense Ministry   19, 23-4, 30
Central Armed Forces Museum   236
Central Asia   15, 146
Central Border-Guard Museum of the FSB   60
Central Election Commission   112
Central Europe   188, 253, 259
Central European University   34
Central Museum of the Great Patriotic War   64, 74, 87, 96-7, 101, 185-6, 202, 236, 252
Chabad   187-8
Chaika, Yuri   10
Channel One   98, 103, 204
Chapaeva, Diana   3
Charter of the Russian Historian, proposed   31-2, 259
Chechens   58, 147
Chechen Wars   25
Chechnya   15, 23, 74-5, 143, 146-7, 240
Cheka   60, 162, 165, 230. See also Dzerzhinsky, Felix; FSB; KGB; NKVD; OGPU
Chekhov   133
Cheliabinsk   61, 153, 167, 235
Cherepovets   133
Chernobyl nuclear disaster (1986)   145
Chersonesos   86, 180
Children's Round Dance fountain   73, 78, 176
children with disabilities   125, 128
China   26, 33, 95-6, 140, 175, 177, 208, 245, 256, 260
Chita   154
Chizhova, Elena   237
Christianity   56, 64, 69, 85-6, 169, 180
Christians   52, 72
Christian State, Holy Russia fundamentalist organization   142-3
Christ the Savior Cathedral   75
Chubarian, Alexander   10, 13-14, 26-8, 30, 40, 59, 81, 118, 135, 137, 140, 251
Chuev, Sergei   135
Chukovsky, Kornei   176

Churchill, Winston   74, 119, 158–9, 161, 204
Church Slavonic language   52
Churkin, Vitaly   192, 196
Chuvashia   236
CIA   122
Civic Chamber by the Russian President   32
civic religion   5, 89–93. *See also* May 9 celebration; Second World War
Civil Platform Party   112
Clinton, Bill   67
Clinton, Hillary   86
Code of Offenses against the Peace and Security on Mankind   234
Cohen, Stephen F.   27
Cold War   1–2, 27, 37, 74, 88, 100, 199, 218, 220, 255, 259
colonialism   14–15, 30. *See also* decolonization
"color revolutions"   8, 20, 68, 137, 224. *See also* Maidan uprsing
Commission to Counteract Attempts to Harm Russia's Interests by Falsifying History (2009–12)   4, 10–12, 14, 17, 27, 34, 39, 43, 56, 79, 87, 232
Commonwealth of Independent States (CIS)   14–15, 18, 32, 36, 193, 201, 208
Communism   81, 111, 195, 222
Communist Party   37–8, 46, 65, 95, 103, 109, 111–13, 141, 150, 152–6, 158–9, 161, 164–5, 178, 229
communists   6, 103, 109, 117, 122, 141–2, 150–6, 161, 164–5, 169, 177, 224, 231
computer games   31, 101
Concept for Patriotic Education of the Russian Citizens (2003)   123
Concert of Europe (1814–1914)   88
Congress of Intelligentsia (2015)   116–17
Congress of Russian Communities of Crimea   167
Constitution   34, 144, 150, 166, 223, 257
Constitutional Court   117, 223
Coronavirus outbreak (2020)   130, 259
Cossacks   29, 105, 153, 166, 172, 179

Council of Europe   14, 18, 33, 95, 188, 209–11, 213. *See also* European Court of Human Rights; European Parliament; European Union
courts   38, 43, 117, 190, 226–7, 231–6, 240, 246–7
Crimea   3, 5–6, 35, 50, 57, 63, 73–6, 78, 83–4, 86, 101, 104, 110, 123, 126, 128, 132, 135, 138, 142, 144–7, 150–1, 154, 158–61, 167–8, 178, 180, 188–9, 196, 210, 225, 235, 256
Crimean Tatars   146–7, 159–61
Crimean Union of Soviet Officers   159
crimes against humanity   194–5, 212, 218–19, 254
criminal prosecution   6, 147, 225–9, 231–40, 247–9. *See also* political dissent, suppression of; Russian Penal Code
Cuba   201
Cultural Revolution   177. *See also* Mao Zedong
Customs   124–5, 240
Czechoslovakia   30, 86, 199, 225, 256
Czech Republic   207, 213–14, 233, 255

Dagestan   143, 150, 165
Dagestanskie Ogni   165
Danilevich, Polina   235
Daudov, Magomed   74
Day of Deliverance and Liberation, Israel (May 9)   197–8, 207, 212, 221
The Death of Stalin movie (2017)   113, 259
decolonization   88. *See also* colonialism
deep people, concept of   7, 111. *See also* Surkov, Vladislav
deep state, concept of   7, 261
Dekabrists   67
Denikin, Anton   86
Denmark   52, 239
deportations   15, 36, 58, 73, 114, 146–7, 177. *See also* Stalin's crimes
Derevianko, Ekaterina   214
Desiatnichenko, Nikolai   238
de-Stalinization   71, 117, 119, 151, 183. *See also* Stalinism

Die Welt 28
Diletant magazine 256
Diplomatic Academy of the Russian Foreign Ministry 64
Disney 59, 78
Dissernet 80, 245
Diukov, Alexander 4, 25, 45–6, 79, 178, 238
Dmitriev, Igor 103–4
Dmitriev, Yuri 23, 225–9, 248
Dnepr, Battle of (1943) 139
Dnepropetrovsk. *See* Dnipro
Dnipro 188
Dobrynin, Konstantin 117
Dolgov, Konstantin 16
Donbass 46, 63, 73, 102, 104–5, 156, 160, 172, 177, 188–9, 196–7, 201, 219
Donetsk 108, 150, 156, 169
Donetsk People's Republic 75, 156
Dorogoi, Igor 72–3, 233–4
DOSAAF 125
Dostoyevsky, Feodor 248
Dozhd TV channel 62, 181, 239
Dresden 83
Druon, Maurice 85
Dud, Yuri 246
Dugin, Alexander 71, 122
Duma 9, 13, 31–3, 37, 43, 45–7, 62–3, 74–5, 103, 130, 140, 142, 145, 150, 154, 161, 166, 170, 176, 189, 207–8, 232, 238–40, 245, 252, 258. *See also* Federation Council
Duma Culture Committee 142
Duma Education Committee 135
Duma Foreign Relations Committee 43
Duma Legal Committee 10
Dutch People's Union 201
Dzboev, Mikhail 150
Dzerzhinsky (city) 162
Dzerzhinsky, Felix 6, 50, 150, 162–5, 183
Dzerzhinsky, Felix, Jr. 162–3
Dzhemilev, Mustafa 146, 159
Dzhugashvili, Yevgeny 152, 238

Eastern Front 194, 215
East Europe 9, 12, 14, 16–17, 19, 27, 44–5, 58, 74, 83, 97, 108, 121, 186, 188, 193–5, 199–201, 216–17, 219, 221, 253, 256, 259, 261
East Germany 30
Efremenko, Dmitry 33
Eichmann trial (1961) 203
Eidman, Igor 108
Einstein, Albert 252
Ekaterina II 145
Ekaterinburg 69, 92, 143, 156, 240–2, 244
Elias, Prophet 129
Eliseeva, Natalia 237
Elizabeth 63
Engels, Friedrich 24
Epstein, Mikhail 119
Escape from Sobibor movie (1987) 203, 211
Essence of Time nationalist organization 134–5, 153, 171, 178, 224. *See also* Kurginian, Sergei
Estonia 108, 121, 189, 192–3, 195, 199, 201, 215, 253
Estonian Institute of Historical Memory 30–1
Estonians 25, 46, 225
eternal flame memorial 100, 235
Etkind, Alexander 3
Europe 1, 9, 14, 25, 33, 44, 56, 59, 61, 67, 74, 88, 97, 140, 189, 191–4, 196–202, 207–8, 210, 213, 219, 222, 239, 242, 246, 259–61
European Court of Human Rights 16, 223, 233
European Institute for Democracy and Cooperation 44
European Jewish Congress 194, 198–9, 222
European Parliament 32. *See also* Council of Europe; European Union
Europeans 48, 67
European Union 33, 97, 186, 191–2, 194–5, 199–200, 213
European University at St. Petersburg 33–4, 258
Eurovision 108, 210
Evmenov, Nikolai 127

exhibitions   56–61, 64–8, 70, 96, 111, 114, 118, 123, 125–6, 132, 177, 181–2, 185, 187, 193, 195, 197, 200–2, 204–6, 208–9, 212–14, 217, 221–4, 230, 236, 242, 248, 261
Expert Institute of Social Research (EISR)   30–1
Extraordinary State Commission for the Investigation of Crimes Committed by the German-Fascist Invaders and Their Accomplices in the Occupied Territories of the Soviet Union (1942–46)   190, 211
Extremist Materials list   20, 214, 240, 260. See also Ministry of Justice
Ezhov, Nikolai   162, 230

"Falsifiers of History" pamphlet (1948)   1–2, 256
Fam, Konstantin   211
family history   100
famine of 1932–33   15, 20, 114, 216, 260. See also Stalin's crimes
Far East   33, 40, 95, 101, 133, 198
fascism   9, 17, 33, 38, 49, 57, 73, 79, 83, 89, 130, 139–40, 154, 161, 191–2, 194, 201–2, 214, 216–21, 224, 236, 243, 256
February Revolution   77, 140
Federal Agency for Nationalities Affairs   137
Federal Agency for the CIS Affairs, Compatriots Living Abroad, and International Humanitarian Cooperation (Rossotrudnichestvo)   96, 209
Federal Agency for Youth Affairs (Rossmolodezh)   104, 124, 126
Federal Agency on Culture and Cinematography (Roskino)   209
Federal Archival Agency (Rossarkhiv)   10, 12, 15, 19–21, 25
Federation Council   11–19, 24, 33–4, 39, 54, 117, 137, 141, 188, 194, 208, 242, 252. See also Duma

Federation Council Analytical Department   13
Federation Council Foreign Affairs Committee   97, 208
Federation Council Legal Department   13
Federation of Jewish Communities of Russia   69, 187, 206
Feigin, Mark   249
Feldmanis, Inesis   191
FIFA 2018 World Cup   141, 165, 237
fifth column   37, 79, 93, 108, 148, 165, 224
financial claims against Russia   11–12, 14, 16, 25, 41, 228
Finland   72, 227
Finnish occupation of Karelia (1941–44)   178, 227–8
Finns   227–8
First World War   57, 85–6, 88, 100, 138, 155, 174, 178
Foreign Agent law (2012)   6, 29, 35, 79, 224, 229, 240–2, 244, 249, 254, 256. See also lawmaking; political dissent, suppression of; Russian Penal Code
Foreign Literature Library   29
Foreign Ministry. See Ministry of Foreign Affairs
Foreign Policy Archives of the Russian Foreign Ministry (AVP MID)   23–4
For Human Rights movement   242
Forty Forties fundamentalist organization   143
Foster, Norman   130
France   7, 32, 97, 198, 207
Franz Joseph Land   181, 260
Free Historical Society (VIO)   6, 8–9, 34, 53, 67–8, 80, 110, 149, 183, 244–5, 249, 257
French   107, 131, 217
FSB   6, 13, 21–3, 25, 35–6, 43, 58–61, 63, 65, 70, 75, 81, 106, 116, 124–6, 147, 161–3, 173, 187, 225–6, 230, 239, 243, 246–8, 254, 257
FSB Archives   22–3, 225, 227
Fukuyama, Francis   89
Furr, Grover   27

Gagarin, Yuri   62, 121, 150, 173. *See also* Yuri Gagarin Memorial Museum
Gaida, Feodor   33
Gainutdinov, Damir   232
Galeotti, Mark   73
Ganapolskii, Matvei   174
Gandlevskii, Sergei   112
Garkusha, Irina   19–20
de Gaulle, Charles   7
Gazprom   66, 127, 137
Gazprombank   127
Gelman, Marat   183
Geneva   108
Genghis Khan   175. *See also* Golden Horde
genocide   33, 40, 46, 72, 147, 188–9, 200, 213–16, 218–19, 224, 259–61. *See also* UN Genocide Convention
geopolitics   3–5, 7–41, 44, 56, 65, 70, 86, 93–4, 97, 102, 123–4, 177, 259–60. *See also* political technology
Georgia   15, 68, 88, 150, 152, 154, 188
Georgians   38, 225
Gerasimov, Alexander   111
Germans   14, 28, 63, 73, 97, 102, 157, 191, 200, 202–3
Germany   27, 36, 74, 86, 130, 148, 195, 205–6, 237–8, 243, 246, 261
Gessen, Masha   2
Ghetto Fighters' House   220. *See also* Yad Vashem Museum
Giacometti, Alberto   167
Girkin, Igor. *See* Strelkov, Igor
Glazunov, Ilya   151
Global Peace Index   121
"Glorification of Nazism". *See* Russian Penal Code: Article 354.1
Gnilorybov, Pavel   149, 152, 172
Goebbels, Joseph   58, 236, 238
Golden Horde   66, 88, 169. *See also* Genghis Khan
Golos election monitor   35
Gorbachev, Mikhail   8, 242, 244
Gori   152
Gorin, Baruch   206
Goskonsert   29

Gozman, Leonid   58
Grad multiple rocket launcher   163
Graf, Jürgen   214
the Great Leap Forward   177. *See also* Mao Zedong
Great Northern War (1700–21)   125
Great Patriotic War. *See* Second World War
the Great Terror   21–2, 32, 36, 60–1, 71, 117, 149, 155, 164, 225, 230, 243, 246–7, 253. *See also* Stalin's crimes
Greece   33, 70, 189, 239, 258
Greeks   180
Grenada   150
Grigory Rasputin House Museum   181. *See also* Rasputin, Grigory
G20 meetings   196
Gudkov, Lev   89, 105, 150, 183
Gulag   6, 38, 71–3, 112, 114, 116, 118, 155, 223–31. *See also* Stalin's crimes
Gulag History State Museum   116, 118, 181, 231, 257
Gulag victims   21–2, 37, 61, 71, 112–17, 153–5, 163, 176, 216, 223–8, 230–1, 243–7, 257
Gumbinnen, Battle of (1914)   139
Gundiaev, Vladimir. *See* Kirill, Patriarch
Gutteres, António   208

Haifa   220
Harley Davidson motorcycle   74
Havana   201
Hellboy movie (2019)   113
Hells Angels biker club   73–5, 79
Helsinki   228
heritage buildings   179–81. *See also* architectural heritage
Hermitage museum   23, 81
Herzen, Alexander   2
Higher School of Economics   33, 35, 68, 121, 141
high treason   36–8, 63–4, 178, 203
Hilberg, Raoul   191
Himmler, Heinrich   199
Historical Memory Foundation   4, 25, 45–6, 61, 79, 178, 193, 214, 238, 256. *See also* Diukov, Alexander

Historical Perspective Foundation   4, 10, 43–4, 58, 79. *See also* Narochnitskaia, Natalia
historical reenactments   5, 56, 125, 130, 138–9, 143–4
History of Motherland Foundation   56, 59–60, 210–11, 252. *See also* Mogilevskii, Konstantin
history textbooks   5, 15–18, 29, 59, 64, 86–8, 95–6, 135–7, 188, 224, 235, 244, 258–9. *See also* patriotic education program; schoolchildren; schools; school teachers
Hitler, Adolf   1, 14, 32, 58, 85–6, 113, 116, 130–1, 139, 141, 150–1, 220, 234–7, 239, 253, 256
Hollywood   59, 113, 211, 259
the Holocaust   6, 14, 21, 32–3, 40, 45, 142, 185–222, 246, 259, 261
The Holocaust: Annihilation, Liberation, Rescue traveling exhibition   212–13
Holocaust denial   9, 13, 27, 38, 185, 188–9, 192–5, 197–8, 207, 216
Holocaust Remembrance Day, International (January 27)   97, 192, 205, 211–12, 221
Holocaust studies   214, 217, 253
the Holodomor. *See* the famine of 1932–33
Homs province   212
Höss, Rainer   201
House with a Lion museum   180–1
human rights   14, 16, 21, 110, 142, 218, 224, 242
Hunan province   177
Hungarian uprising (1956)   30
Hungary   195, 216
hybrid warfare   9, 30, 108, 221

Iceland   239
icons   66, 71, 129, 254
Ilyin, Ivan   65
Immortal Barracks online project   116, 244
Immortal Regiment parade   5, 60, 72–3, 91–2, 95–6, 98–9, 103–9, 116, 118–19, 126, 130, 133, 138–9, 146–7, 171, 204, 209, 212

Immortal Stalin Regiment parade   109
Imperial Orthodox Palestine Society   70
Information Group on Crimes against the Person (IGSP)   46. *See also* Diukov, Alexander; Historical Memory Foundation
Institute of Foreign Political Studies   256
Institute of Social, Economic, and Political Studies   61
intelligence services   21, 62–3, 65, 67, 97, 164, 251–2, 256
Interfax news agency   136
Intergovernmental Commission on the Protection of State Secrecy   21. *See also* archives
International Association of World War II Museums   96
International Commission for the Advancement of Objective Approaches to Evaluation of Historical Facts (2016)   27
International Committee for the History of the Second World War   96
International Committee of Historical Sciences   26
International Convention on the Elimination of All Forms of Racial Discrimination (1965)   192, 219
International Council of Museums (ICOM)   181
International Covenant on Civil and Political Rights (1966)   192
International Holocaust Remembrance Alliance (IHRA)   216
"internet troll factory"   129
Ionescu, Eugène   141
Iran   195
Iraq   37
Ireland   239
Irkutsk   168
Irkutsk State University   35
Ishim   151
Iskander mobile ballistic missile system   100. *See also* ballistic missiles
Islamic State jihadist organization   27
Islamists. *See* jihadists
Ismail, Battle of (1790)   145

Israel   6, 33, 69, 108, 144, 185–7, 194–5, 197–8, 201, 203–8, 211–13, 216, 218, 220, 222, 261
Israelis   6, 159, 194, 208, 222
Istorik journal   61
Italy   75, 239
Ivan III. *See* Ivan the Great
Ivan IV. *See* Ivan the Terrible
Ivanov   133
Ivanov, Sergei   58–9, 81, 94, 104, 254, 260
Ivan the Great   169
Ivan the Terrible   48, 50, 67–8, 136, 169–72, 183, 224, 236, 256
Ivan the Terrible and His Son Ivan painting   170–1, 256
Izborsk Club   71, 122, 171. *See also* Prokhanov, Alexander
Izvestia   157, 220

Japan   33, 95, 99–101, 138, 140, 155
Jehovah's Witnesses   91
Jerusalem   33, 144, 186–7, 189, 214, 222
Jewish Autonomous Republic   198
Jewish Museum and Tolerance Center   187–8, 197, 206–7, 214
Jewish organizations, Russian   186–7, 190, 193–4, 197–9, 206, 212–3. *See also names of individual organizations*
Jews   33, 45, 69–70, 91, 185–222, 236, 246, 255, 259
jihadists   122, 172

Kabardino-Balkaria   150
Kadyrov, Ramzan   74, 142–3, 147, 240
Kalashnikov, Mikhail   126, 174–5, 183
Kalashnikov assault rifle. *See* AK-47
Kalinin, Alexander   142–3
Kalinin, Mikhail   152
Kaliningrad   31, 63–4, 74–5, 100, 112, 137, 139, 166–7, 169, 234, 237
Kaluga   163, 169, 179–80, 182, 237
Kangeris, Kārlis   191
Kant, Immanuel   63–4
Kantor, Iulia   28–9
Kantor, Viacheslav Moshe   198, 217, 222
Karagodin, Denis   22, 246–7
Karelia   6, 178–9, 225–9, 248
Kartopolov, Andrei   59, 129–30

Kasamara, Valeria   121
Kaspiisk   165
Katsav, Moshe   186
Katyn, mass execution of Polish officers at (1940)   15–16, 46, 117–18, 136, 229, 238
Kaunas, massacre of Jews at (1941)   215. *See also* the Holocaust
Kazakhstan   15
Kazan   66, 128, 152, 236
Keegan, John   29
Kemerovo   104, 175
Kemerovo shopping center disaster (2018)   229
Kennedy, John   7–8
Kenzhalieva, Alie   146–7
Kerch Strait   137
KGB   10, 21, 25, 56, 58–60, 63, 67, 72–3, 80, 83, 115, 163, 248. *See also* Cheka; FSB; NKVD; OGPU
Khabarovsk   235, 239
Khabensky, Konstantin   202, 207–9, 211–12, 217
Khachaturov, Karen   220
Khaibakh massacre (1944)   58
Khanty-Mansi region   91
Khazaria, victory over (965)   256
Khodorkovskii, Mikhail   105
Khoroshevo village   157
Khrushchev, Nikita   151, 153, 162
Khvyli-Olinter, Andrei   239
Kiev   20, 25, 57, 74, 76, 108, 159, 169, 188, 196, 210
Kievan Rus   73–4, 85–6, 169. *See also* Moscovite Rus
kindergartens   92, 101, 106, 122, 132–3. *See also* patriotic education program; preschool education
King's Cross nationalist organization   142–3
Kirchik, James   218
Kirill, Patriarch   62–6, 68–72, 75, 81, 115, 170, 173, 239, 251–2
Kirillova, Ksenia   109
Kirov   156, 163
Kisilev, Dmitry   111, 137, 238
Klimenko, Ekaterina   68
the Knesset   197, 208, 213
Knowledge Foundation   30–1

Kolchak, Alexander   22, 178
Kolomoiskyi, Ihor   188
Kolotovkin, Sergei   103
Koltyrin, Sergei   228–9
Kolyma region   154
Kolyma: The Cradle of Our Fear
    documentary (2019)   246. *See
    also* Dud, Yuri
Komi Republic   29
Kommersant   30, 48
Kommunarka mass execution site   243.
    See also Stalin's crimes
Komsomol   46, 126, 128, 141–2, 251
Komsomolskaia Pravda   113
Kondopoga   179
Konev, Ivan   215
Königsberg. *See* Kaliningrad
Konkova, Alexandra. *See* Sergia, Mother
Kononov, Vladislav   57, 59, 92, 171, 182,
    259
Koposov, Nikolay   19, 90, 109, 189, 232
Korolev   105
Kosachev, Konstantin   97, 208
Kosmodemianskaia, Zoia   51
Kostroma   176
Kotsiubinskii, Daniil   68, 233
Kovalchuk, Andrei   168
Kozlov, Vladimir   10, 20
Krasheninnikova, Veronika   256
Krasnodar   112, 158, 163, 172, 235
Krasnoyarsk   134, 237
Krasovskii, Alexei   237–8
Kravtsov, Sergei   258
the Kremlin   3–5, 8, 26, 32, 40, 43–4, 46,
    81, 83, 88–90, 94, 108, 110–11,
    113, 121, 126, 134, 141, 146–7,
    169, 181, 187–8, 197, 200, 202,
    210, 215, 218–22, 242–3, 246,
    249, 251–4, 257, 260–1
Kropachev, Victor   167
Kropotkin   172
Kschessinskaya, Mathilde   142
Kubinka   129, 131–2, 138. *See also*
    Patriot military theme park
Kuchma, Leonid   158
Kukryniksy   139
Kulikovo, Battle of (1380)   145
Kuraev, Andrei   253
Kurgan region   166

Kurginian, Sergei   134–5, 153, 170–1,
    178, 224
Kuril Islands   137–8, 166
Kurilla, Ivan   80, 110, 114, 168
Kurochkin, Sergei   154
Kursk   163
Kursk, Battle of (1943)   28, 101
Kursk submarine disaster
    (2000)   68, 229
Kusa   153–4
Kutaev, Ruslan   147
Kutafin Moscow State Law
    University   158
Kutuzov, Mikhail   173
Kuzenkov, Pavel   66
Kuzichev, Anatoly   204

Lanovoi, Vasily   103, 212
Lanzmann, Claude   203
Laos   102
Lapenkov, Sergei   103–4, 108
The Last Address project   112, 245–6,
    249. *See also* Memorial
Latvia   9, 14, 45, 63, 121, 156, 186,
    189–92, 194–5, 199, 215
Latvians   46, 191
Lavrov, Sergei   28, 59, 81, 88–9, 95, 97,
    140, 192–4, 196, 199, 213, 216,
    218, 222, 260–1
lawmaking   9–11, 13–14, 16–17, 20, 31,
    35, 55, 62, 117, 130, 145, 189,
    205–6, 210, 214–15, 231–42,
    249, 253–4, 258, 261. *See also*
    criminal prosecution; political
    dissent, suppression of
law on Archival Matters
    (2004)   21, 36
law on Countering Extremist Activity
    (2002)   16
law on Days of Military Glory and
    Memorial Dates (1995)   145
law on Protection of Personal Data
    (2006)   21
Lazar, Berl   187–8, 190, 197, 217
League of Nations   26
Lemkin, Raphael   20
Lenin, Vladimir   8, 24, 47, 61, 63, 71,
    108, 141–2, 149–50, 152, 158,
    164–5, 169–70, 177

Leningrad, the siege of   5, 29, 33, 45, 48, 86, 98, 125, 138, 143–4, 182, 206, 222, 237–9. *See also* St. Petersburg
Leningrad region   138
Lenin Memorial Center at Ulianovsk   177
Let's Bike project   199
Levada pollster   21–2, 83, 107, 109, 121, 147, 150, 170. *See also* opinion polls
Libya   37, 129
Lieberman, Avigdor   216
Liege   108
Life is Beautiful movie (1997)   211
Lipetsk   172, 237
Lisbon   108
Lisovoi, Nikolai   70
Listov, Mikhail   235
Lithuania   16, 25, 36, 41, 72, 121, 189, 195, 199, 204, 215–16
Lithuanians   38, 46, 215
Liubavich. *See* Chabad
Liubertsy   107
Liubimova, Olga   258–9
Liubshin, Ivan   237
Livadia Museum   159–60, 168
Livanov, Dmitry   148
Ljubljana   97
local history   126, 128, 149, 214
Lokomotiv football club   143
Lokot, Alexander   155
Lomanov, Alexander   33
London   108, 119
Lubkov, Alexei   68
Lubyanka Square   50, 65, 114, 162, 164, 245
Luhansk   73, 141–2, 156, 176
Luhansk People's Republic   104, 177
Lukashevich, Alexander   198
Luxembourg   96
Luzgin, Vladimir   233, 255
Luzhkov, Yuri   159

Maariv   186
Macedonia. *See* Republic of North Macedonia
McFaul, Michael   84, 90
Machinskii, Sergei   92

Madrid   108
Magadan   22, 112, 154, 163, 234
Maidan uprising (2013–14)   19–20, 159, 196
Main Cathedral of the Russian Defense Forces   129–30, 138. *See also* Patriot military theme park
Majdanek State Museum   206
Makarov, Nikolai   27–8
Makhachkala   66, 158
Malaysian Airlines Flight 17, downing of (2014)   131, 255
Maltsev, Anton   181
Manchester   108
Manchuria   33
Manezh exhibition hall   57, 65, 68
Mannerheim, Karl   178
Mao Zedong   150, 177
Mao Zedong House Museum   177
March of the Living   201. *See also* the Holocaust; Israel
Mari El Republic   130, 156, 229
Markova, Yulia   206
Marks   209
Marx, Karl   7, 24, 150
Marxism   7, 50, 88
Mask of Sorrow monument (1996)   163
Matanzas   201
Matilda movie (2017)   69, 113, 142–3, 256
Matvienko, Valentina   15, 54, 137, 141, 208, 251–2
Maus: A Survivor's Tale (1991)   214
May 9 celebration   5, 34, 61, 77, 89–109, 132, 138–9, 146, 185, 186, 193, 196–7, 200–1, 206, 209–10, 233–5, 257, 259–60
Medinskii, Vladimir   4–5, 19, 26, 40, 46–60, 64–5, 69, 80–1, 88, 92, 97, 102, 111, 113, 118, 122, 131, 136, 140, 142, 157–8, 169–70, 174, 178–9, 181–2, 202, 205, 211, 232, 238, 242, 245, 251–2, 254–6, 258–9
Medvedev, Dmitry   10–13, 55, 81, 85–7, 91, 110, 113, 124, 190, 231, 246
Medvedev, Sergei   209
Medvezhiegorsk   228–9
Mein Kampf   239. *See also* Hitler, Adolf

Meisler, Frank   159
Mejlis of the Crimean Tatar People   146.
    See also Dzhemilev, Mustafa
Memorial   6, 25, 71, 110, 113–14, 118, 149, 164, 183, 223, 225–31, 240–6, 248–9
Memorial Candle monument (2020)   33, 144, 222
memorial days. *See also* state holidays
    Constitution Day (December 12)   144
    Day in Honor of Internationalist Soldiers (February 15)   145
    Day of Incorporation of Crimea (March 18)   144–5
    Day of Incorporation of Crimea, Taman, and Kuban into the Russian Empire (April 19)   145
    Day of the 1917 October Revolution (November 7)   145
    Day of Remembrance and Grief (June 22)   116, 177
    Day of Remembrance of Victims of Deportation, Crimea (April 18)   146, 161
    Day of Remembrance of Victims of Political Repression (October 30)   146, 245
    Day of Remembrance of Victims of Radiation Accidents and Disasters (April 26)   145
    Day of Russian Parliamentarism (April 27)   145
    Day of St. Peter and Fevronia (July 8)   75
    Day of Solidarity in the Fight against Terrorism (September 3)   145
    Day of the Security Service Official (December 20)   60, 63
    Patriotism Day, proposed (August 6)   145
Mémorial de la Shoah   217
Memorialization of the Victims of Soviet Political Repression policy framework (2015)   213–14, 224, 231
Mephistopheles bas-relief   179
Merkel, Angela   95
Merridale, Catherine   3

Miagkov, Mikhail   28, 53–4, 58–9, 64, 89, 118, 260
Miasnikov, Alexander   66
Middle East   70, 72
Mikhailov, Vladimir   176
Mikhalkov, Nikita   54–5, 242, 259
Military Prosecutor General's Office   247
Military Uniform Museum   157
Millennium of Russia monument (1862)   169–70
Miller, Alexei   33, 81
Milonov, Vitaly   37, 235
Ministry of Agriculture   125
ministry of culture   4, 18, 23, 26, 29, 51, 57, 59, 80–1, 113, 124–5, 130–1, 145, 157, 171, 174–5, 179, 182, 203, 227–8, 236, 248, 252, 258–9. *See also* Medinskii, Vladimir
ministry of defense   5, 18–20, 22–4, 30, 39, 59, 64, 75–6, 81, 91, 124–33, 138, 148, 187, 212, 227–8, 230, 240, 252. *See also* Shoigu, Sergei
ministry of education and science   15–17, 26–7, 35, 38, 52, 54, 59, 64, 67–8, 81, 98, 124, 126, 135–6, 148, 157, 243, 255, 258. *See also* Vasilieva, Olga
Ministry of Emergency Situations   9, 125
Ministry of Energy   125
Ministry of Enlightenment. *See* Ministry of Education and Science
Ministry of Fisheries   125
Ministry of Foreign Affairs   4, 9, 12, 15–16, 18, 23, 39–41, 58, 64, 74, 81, 88–9, 95, 97, 108, 124, 126, 190–5, 199–200, 205–6, 212–13, 216, 218–19, 221–2, 241, 259–60. *See also* Lavrov, Sergei
Ministry of Health   125
Ministry of Justice   20, 22, 70, 214, 240–1, 260
Ministry of the Interior   22, 36, 70, 124–6, 230
Ministry of Trade   125
Mironenko, Sergei   25–6, 38, 50–1, 54
Mogilevskii, Konstantin   59–60, 210–11, 252
Moldova   189

Molodaia gvardiia nationalist youth organization   119, 134, 234
Molotov, Vyacheslav   28
Molotov–Ribbentrop Pact (1939)   1, 10, 30, 32–3, 86, 186, 193, 215, 220, 233, 256, 261
Mongolia   108, 161
"monstration" happening   119
Montclair State University   27
Montreal   108
Montreal University   27
monuments
  Alexander II   168
  Alexander III   168
  Alley of Russian Glory   172–4
  Authorities in the Service of the People   176
  Borodino Bread   175
  Brezhnev, Leonid   150
  Children's Round Dance fountain in Volgograd   73, 78, 176
  Churchill and Roosevelt in London   199
  commissioned by RVIO   173–5
  Dzerzhinsky, Felix   50, 150, 162–5, 183
  First World War   57
  Gagarin, Yuri   150, 173
  Genghis Khan   175
  Gorbachev, Mikhail   158
  the Holocaust   186, 189–90, 200, 203, 208
  Ivan the Great   169
  Ivan the Terrible   169–72, 183, 256
  Kalashnikov, Mikhail   174–5, 183
  Kalinin, Mikhail   152
  Kant, Immanuel   63–4
  at Katyn   117–18
  Kolchak, Alexander   178
  Konev, Ivan   215
  Kutuzov, Mikhail   173
  Lenin, Vladimir   71, 141, 150, 152, 158, 165, 169, 178
  Mannerheim, Karl   178
  Marx, Karl   150
  Millennium of Russia   169–70
  Mozgovoi "Ghost" Alexei   172
  Nevsky, Prince Alexander   169, 172
  and Night Wolves biker club   176–7
  Nikolai II   155, 168, 256, 259
  Ordzhonikidze, Sergo   152
  Panfilov's twenty-eight   50
  Pavel I   172
  Peter the Great   154
  Pozharsky, Prince Dmitry   154
  Putin, Vladimir   166–8
  Putin's "green men"   128, 167–8, 183
  St. Barbara   175
  saints   259
  Second World War   9, 14, 20, 32, 56, 74, 77, 90, 96–7, 100, 102, 125, 134, 147, 165, 172, 177, 186–7, 193–5, 198–9, 207–8, 210, 213, 215, 221–2, 234–7, 240
  security services   60
  siege of Leningrad   144, 222
  Slavic Girl's Farewell   174
  Solzhenitsyn, Alexander   112
  Soviet Legacy   163
  Stalin, Josef   6, 45, 71, 74, 112, 117, 119, 146, 149–62, 168, 172, 183
  victims of Stalin   6, 15, 71, 112–15, 147, 154, 176, 225, 229, 243–5
  Vladimir, Prince   169–70, 175, 183
  Waffen SS   192
  Yalta Conference   74, 158–61, 183
Mordovia   107
Morozov, Alexander   7–8
Moscovite Rus   7, 88. *See also* Kievan Rus
Moscow   5–7, 23–5, 27–9, 44–6, 50, 57, 60, 62, 65–6, 71, 74–6, 79, 83–4, 90, 93, 96, 100–1, 103–4, 107–9, 111–16, 118–19, 128–9, 131, 139, 141, 143–6, 150, 152, 157–9, 162, 164, 166, 169–70, 173–5, 178–9, 181, 186–8, 194, 196, 198, 200–2, 204, 206–9, 213–15, 220, 228, 231, 236, 239–40, 242–3, 246–7, 256–7, 261
Moscow Helsinki Group   242
Moscow Human Rights Bureau   193
Moscow Patriarchate   62–3, 66, 69–70. *See also* Russian Orthodox Church
Moscow Patriarchate Cultural Council and Humanitarian Project Foundation   66. *See also* Tikhon, Bishop

Moscow Pedagogical State
    University   31–2, 43, 68, 253–4
Moscow Region State University   31
Moscow River   169
Moscow School of Social and Economic
    Sciences   34, 258
Moscow State University (MGU)   12, 15,
    30–1, 33, 52, 66, 253
Moscow State University of International
    Relations (MGIMO)   35, 46,
    225, 253
Moscow theater hostage crisis
    (2002)   68
Moscow Theological Academy   225
Mosin, Alexei   244
Moskalkova, Tatiana   189
Motherland Calls statue (1967)   234
"Motorola". *See* Pavlov, Arseny
movies, historical   18, 26, 50–1, 59–60,
    113, 130, 136, 140, 142–3,
    202–12, 217, 221. *See also names
    of individual movies*
Mozgovoi "Ghost" Alexei   172
Mtsituridze, Ekaterina   209
Munich Agreement (1938)   1, 86, 186
Murmansk   138
Museum of Arctic Exploration   181, 260
Museum of History of the Military
    Commandant's Office   60
Museum of the Russian Icon   181
Museum of the USSR, proposed   177
museums   57, 60, 62, 64–8, 71–2, 74, 87,
    96–7, 111, 114, 116, 118–19,
    125–8, 138–9, 150–1, 153–4,
    156–7, 159, 176–8, 180–2,
    186–7, 190, 195–7, 200, 202–6,
    214, 220, 223–31, 236–8, 240–4,
    248–9, 254, 256, 260. *See also
    names of individual museums*
Muslims   91, 201, 242
Mussolini, Benito   150

Napoleonic Wars (1803–15)   89, 125,
    138, 173
Narian-Mar   91
Narochnitskaia, Natalia   4, 10, 43–4, 58,
    79, 122
Narodnyi sobor   37
Narusova, Liudmila   54

Narva   108
Naryshkin, Sergei   10–11, 21, 56–9, 80–1,
    95–7, 137, 160, 164, 251–2, 256
Nashi nationalist youth organization   7,
    134–5
Natanya   186–7, 207, 222
National Alliance of Russian Solidarists
    (NTS)   36
National Guard (Rossgvardiia)   133
National Liberation Movement (NOD)
    nationalist organization   135,
    243
national security program   8, 114, 126
National World War II Museum   119
NATO   27, 37, 56, 88, 97, 186, 190, 200
Navalny, Alexei   75, 81, 234–5, 239, 245
Nazi death camps   6, 98, 185, 192, 196–7,
    199–200, 202–6, 208–15, 217,
    219–21. *See also names of
    individual camps*
Nazi Germany   1, 5, 9–11, 14, 17, 56–8,
    70, 73, 76–7, 84–6, 90–2, 94, 97–
    8, 100, 102, 116, 119, 129–30,
    132–3, 138, 140, 143, 149–50,
    174, 185, 188–95, 198–9, 207,
    213, 216, 219–21, 225, 233–4,
    236–9, 242, 253, 256–7, 259, 261
Nazi mass murder of Jews. *See the
    Holocaust*
Nazis   4, 9, 14, 37, 75, 103, 108, 132, 139,
    160, 186–7, 189, 198, 202–4,
    206–7, 210, 215, 218–21, 239,
    246, 253
Nazism   10, 14, 16–18, 25, 32, 55, 58,
    83, 94, 96–7, 139, 146, 156, 160,
    168, 187–91, 193–5, 197–8, 201,
    206, 208, 210, 213, 219–20, 222,
    231, 233–4, 236, 238, 255, 260
*Nazi-Soviet Relations from 1939 to
    1941* document collection
    (1948)   1–2
Nebenzia, Vasily   194
Nechaev, Sergei   209
Neizvestnyi, Ernst   112
Nemes, László   211
Nemtsov, Boris, assassination of
    (2015)   241
neo-Nazism   14, 57, 192, 195, 208, 217
Netanyahu, Benjamin   187, 206–7, 212

the Netherlands   128, 204–5, 207, 239
Neva River   129
Nevinnomyssk   209
Nevsky, Prince Alexander   47, 129, 136, 172
Nevzorov, Alexander   121
New Chronology museum, proposed   181
New Orleans   119
New York City   43, 192–3, 213, 221
New York Times   95
Nezavisimaia Gazeta   7
Night Wolves biker club   5, 72–9, 81, 101, 132, 135, 145, 171, 176–7. *See also* biker festivals; Zaldostanov, Alexander
Nikiforov, Yuri   58, 140, 260
Nikolai II   69, 77, 85–6, 100, 142–3, 155, 168, 224, 256
Nizhnevartovsk   209
Nizhnii Novgorod   112, 181
Nizhnii Tagil   139
NKVD   21–2, 46, 58, 60–1, 73, 102, 107, 109, 112–13, 162, 165, 225, 230–1, 238, 243–4, 246–8. *See also* Cheka; FSB; KGB; OGPU
NOD. *See* National Liberation Movement
nongovernment organizations   4–6, 35, 43, 217–18, 249. *See also names of individual organizations*
Norman theory   85
North America   26
North Caucasus   6, 66, 150, 242. *See also* Caucasus
North Ossetia   150–1, 165
Norway   181, 195, 239
Norwegian Holocaust Center   201, 208, 216, 261
Novaia Gazeta   38, 49, 54, 225
November 7 parade, Soviet   105, 145
Novgorod   139, 169–70
Novocherkassk   152–3
Novodevichii Convent   80–1
Novorossia. *See* Donbass
Novorossiysk   73, 166–7, 235
Novosibirsk   22, 63, 102, 112, 119, 139, 143, 152, 154–5, 165, 168
Novosti   56
Novosti news agency   93

Novyi Urengoi   137, 238
Nowak-Jeziorański, Jan   233
NTV channel   224, 253
Nuremberg judgement (1946)   10–11, 13, 18, 38, 188, 190–3, 213, 218–19, 232, 234
Nuremberg trial (1945–46)   15, 17, 38–9, 95, 140, 160, 191, 193, 199, 203, 213, 215, 219–21, 232, 234, 247

Obama, Barack   90
Obninsk   105
Ob River   153
Odessa, fire at (2014)   209
Ogonek magazine   136
OGPU   60, 230–1. *See also* Cheka; FSB; KGB; NKVD
oligarchs   32, 48, 137, 222. *See also names of individual oligarchs*
Olma Media Group   48
Olympic Games. *See* Sochi Winter Olympic Games
Omsk   100, 236
"On Attempts at Falsification of History" statement (2005)   9
Open Media   128
opinion polls   10, 21–2, 43, 61, 83, 100, 107, 109–10, 116, 121, 141, 143–5, 147–50, 154–5, 169–70, 223
Oppenheimer, Robert   174
Orange Revolution. *See* Maidan uprising
Orbán, Viktor   34
Ordzhonikidze, Sergo   152
Orekh, Anton   110
Orel   100, 139, 169–71
Orenburg   62
Organization for Security and Cooperation in Europe. *See* OSCE
Organization of Ukrainian Nationalists/Ukrainian Insurgent Army. *See* OUN/UPA
Orthodox churches and chapels   5, 61–2, 70–1, 75, 129–30, 138, 152, 170, 179–81, 195, 225
Orthodox clergy   64, 71, 74–5, 91, 107, 114, 130, 235, 239, 252
Orwell, George   53

Oscars nominations. *See* Academy Awards
OSCE   33, 95, 189, 191, 195, 198–9
Oslo   201, 208, 216, 261
Ostrov   156
Otstavnykh, Valery   62
Ottawa   108
Ottoman Empire   72
OUN/UPA   15, 19, 45, 199, 220
Our Duty Foundation   159

Pacific Ocean   100
Pakhaliuk, Konstantin   252
Pale of Jewish Settlement   67
Palmyra   27
Panchenko, Alexander   233
Panfilov, Ivan   50
Panfilov's twenty-eight   26, 50–1, 57–8, 129, 136
Panfilov's 28 movie (2016)   51, 57, 102
Paris   44, 86, 213, 217
partisans. *See* Soviet partisans
Passover   197
patriotic education   5, 44, 48, 58, 60, 65, 81, 93, 100, 114, 121–7, 130, 132, 134–5, 147–8, 172–3, 182, 198, 209, 249, 251, 253, 255–6, 261
patriotic education program   122–6, 147–8, 173, 182, 255
Patriot military theme park   5, 101, 126, 129–32, 138, 174
Paulus, Friedrich, surrender of (1943)   139
Pavel I   40, 172
Pavlenskii, Piotr   247–8
Pavlov "Motorola" Arseny   108
Pavlovskii, Gleb   84
Pechersky, Alexander   6, 202, 207–8, 210–1. *See also* Alexander Pechersky Foundation
Pentecost Church   233
Penza   156
People's Memorial House Museum of Gulag History   229–31, 248, 257
People's Memory online project (2015)   24. *See also* Ministry of Defense
Peoples' Tragedy monument (1996)   186

Peres, Shimon   188, 190
Perestroika   8, 31, 50, 73, 110, 152, 244
Perm   112, 137, 209, 223, 233
Perm 36 Gulag Museum   6, 28, 223–5, 229, 242, 248–9, 257
Permiakov, Igor   19
Persson, Göran   216
Peskov, Dmitry   113, 155, 241
Peter the Great   154, 170
Petropavlovsk fortress   179
Petrov, Alexei   35
Petrov, Nikita   21, 25
Petrov, Yuri   68, 119
Petrozavodsk   226
Petrozavodsk State University   227
PhD theses   36–8, 40, 46, 51–5, 64, 68, 80, 203, 211, 233, 245, 252, 258
Philippov, Alexander   33
Pianist movie (2002)   211
Piatigorsk   133
Pikhoia, Rudolf   21
Pink Floyd   49
Piotrovsky, Mikhail   23
Pivovar, Efim   40
plagiarism, academic   34, 52–5, 158, 174, 258
Pobeda low-cost airline   98
Pobeda TV channel   98
pobedobesie   98–9, 101–2, 118
Podolsk   19
Poklonnaia Hill   97, 103, 159
Poklonskaia, Natalia   113, 142–3, 161
Poland   9, 12, 16, 20, 24–7, 32–3, 41, 44, 72, 74, 86, 97, 117, 121, 186, 189, 195–7, 199–208, 210–11, 215–16, 219, 225–6, 229, 233, 237, 239, 253, 256
Polanski, Roman   211
Poles   15, 20, 45–6, 97, 117–18, 136, 140, 144, 210, 215, 225, 233
Polian, Pavel   19, 217
Polish Academy of Sciences   44
"Polish Holocaust law" (2018)   215
Polish Institute of National Remembrance   12, 30–1, 44–5
Polish–Moscovite War (1609–18)   47–9, 125
Polish Parliament   20, 33, 205
"polite people". *See* Putin's "green men"

political dissent, suppression of   6, 88,
    145, 232, 258, 261. *See also*
    criminal prosecution; Russian
    Penal Code
political technology   2–3, 244, 254. *See
    also* geopolitics
Polivanova, Alexandra   110
Poltava, Battle of (1709)   145
Ponomarev, Lev   242
Ponomarev, Mikhail   14
Popov, Gavriil   58
Poroshenko, Petro   108, 196
Portugal   108
Potomskii, Vadim   170
Potsdam Conference (1945)   56, 159–60
Pozharsky, Prince Dmitry   154
Prague   215
preschool education   122, 132–3. *See also*
    kindergartens
Presidential Administration   6, 10, 56,
    59, 80, 94, 104, 161, 166, 260
Presidential Human Rights Council   51,
    110, 222, 248
Prigozhin, Yevgeny   128–9
Prilepin, Zakhar   122
Princeton University   27
prisoners of war   33, 36–7, 46, 97, 129,
    139, 190, 199, 202–3, 207, 220,
    227–9
pro-democracy protests of 2011-12, 4, 8,
    39, 55, 62, 68, 186, 220–1, 224,
    249, 251. *See also* public protests
Prokhanov, Alexander   71, 77, 122–3,
    154, 170–1
Prokhorov, Mikhail   112
pro-Kremlin organizations   4–5, 7, 10,
    13–14, 29–30, 37–8, 43–6, 55–
    61, 70, 72–81, 98, 119, 134–5,
    173, 178, 188–90, 193–4, 197–9,
    201, 203–4, 206, 210, 212–13,
    217–18, 221–2, 224, 227–8, 234,
    238, 242–4, 249, 252–3, 255–6,
    259. *See also names of individual
    organizations*
Prosecutor General's Office   10, 12, 22,
    39, 111, 113, 142, 161, 230, 241
prosecutor's office   35–7, 146, 178, 233–9
Prosveshchenie publishing house   137.
    See also Rotenberg, Arkady

Prudovskii, Sergei   21–2, 245
Pskov   25, 63, 65, 69, 122–3, 138, 229,
    235
Pskov-Pechory Monastery of the
    Caves   65
public protests   100, 145. *See also* pro-
    democracy protests of 2011–12
Pushilin, Denis   156
Pushkin State Art Museum   23
Pussy Riot   62
putsch of August 1991   165
Putin, Vladimir
    and Alexander III   65, 168
    an antisemitic remark by   218
    and archives   19, 24–6, 59
    and Article 354.1 (glorification of
        Nazism)   232
    and Bishop Tikhon   63, 65
    and the Bolshevik Revolution   86
    and Clinton, Hillary   86
    compared to Hitler   235
    and the Constitution   223, 258
    and Crimean Tatars   146
    criticism of proscribed   240, 258
    cronies of   44, 54, 69, 103, 137, 182,
        222, 242, 258–9
    and the cult of the Second World
        War   5, 24, 30, 32–3, 85–7,
        89–97, 100, 119, 140, 182, 261
    and Dzerzhinsky, Felix   6, 162, 164
    and the European University at St.
        Petersburg   34
    and the Holocaust   6, 45, 144, 185–8,
        196–7, 202–3, 205–7, 212,
        216–18, 222
    and ideology   2–4, 7–8, 47, 72, 86,
        110, 173
    and Immortal Regiment   96, 104–5,
        118
    and the information security
        doctrine   242
    in Israel   144
    and Ivan the Terrible   171
    joins Yeltsin's administration   65
    and Kadyrov, Ramzan   147
    and Katyn memorial   118
    as a KGB officer   83–4, 140, 162
    and Lenin, Vladimir   142
    and *Matilda* movie   142–3

and memorial days   145
Munich speech by   88–9
and museums   182
neologisms by   48–9
and Night Wolves biker club   73, 75, 77–9, 81, 138, 176–7
and *Panfilov's 28*   51
parents of   86
and Patriarch Kirill   68, 71
and patriotic education   121, 123–6, 128, 249
and Patriot military theme park   129, 132
as president   7, 9, 11, 36, 39, 69, 75, 80, 84, 109, 121, 135, 151, 170, 185–6, 196, 223, 239, 249, 251, 253, 257
and Prigozhin, Yevgeny   128
and Prince Vladimir   170, 180
proclaimed the Year of Memory and Glory in Russia   97
promotes Chersonesos   86, 180
and "Russia: My History" theme park   65–6
and the Russian Orthodox Church   61, 69
and Shcherbakov, Salavat   173–4
and the siege of Leningrad   86, 144
and Stalin, Josef   5, 68, 85, 87, 109–11, 115, 121, 132, 158, 162
and Stalin's crimes   87, 110, 114–15, 118, 231
and state holidays   144
statues of   6, 166–8, 183, 258
and Strelkov, Igor   63
and a system of governance instituted by   39, 56, 58–9, 80, 217, 252–5, 257–8
and a unified textbook   135
and Victory organizing committee   93–5, 193
views on history by   3–5, 14, 16, 28, 33, 41, 69–70, 83–9, 96, 221, 242, 251, 253–5, 260
and war veterans   24–5, 98, 205–6
on Yalta Conference   74, 158, 160–1
and Youth Army   128
Putinism   7, 89, 257

Putin's "green men"   73, 101, 128, 132, 167–8, 183

Queen Mary University of London   213

rabbis   187–9
Rachinskii, Ian   243
racism   9, 14, 191–2, 219
Rada   159
Radev, Rumen   72
Radio Liberty   109, 113, 123, 241
Rasputin, Grigory   40, 77, 181. *See also* Grigory Rasputin House Museum
Red Army   6, 20, 24–5, 36–7, 84, 92, 128, 160, 178, 186–8, 191–2, 194, 196–8, 201, 203–6, 212–14, 217–19, 259, 261. *See also* soldiers, Soviet
Red Cross   36
Red Square   24, 95, 97, 101–2, 139, 141, 145, 173, 235
Red Terror (1918–22)   60, 162–4, 257
Reichstag building, storming of a replica at Patriot military theme park (2017)   130–1
relics   75, 182. *See also* saints
REN TV   101
Repin, Ilya   170
Republic of North Macedonia   200–1
Republic of Sakha   71, 152
Republika Srpska   75
Restoring the Names ceremony   71, 245, 249. *See also* Memorial
Reznik, Henry   233
RIA news agency   210
Righteous among the Nations database   216. *See also* Yad Vashem Museum
RIO. *See* Russian Historical Society
"Rio Rita: The Joy of Victory" happening   138–9, 257
Rogozin, Dmitry   94, 112
Roma people   200
Romania   200
Romanov, Roman   118
Rome   108
Roosevelt, D. Franklin   74, 119, 158–9, 161, 204

Roskino. *See* Federal Agency on Culture and Cinematography
Rossgvardiia. *See* National Guard
Rossiia One TV channel   111, 207
Rossiia 24 TV channel   54, 227, 243
Rossiiskaia Gazeta   52, 58, 60, 192, 246
Rossotrudnichestvo. *See* Federal Agency for the CIS Affairs, Compatriots Living Abroad, and International Humanitarian Cooperation
Rossvoentsentr. *See* Russian State Military History and Cultural Center
Rostov-on-Don   133, 168, 189–90, 203, 209
Rotenberg, Arkady   48, 137
Rotterdam, bombing of (1940)   97
Rousseau, Henri   181
RT. *See* Russia Today
Russia in Global Affairs   32–3
"Russia: My History" theme park   5, 65–8, 70, 81, 129, 138, 182, 236, 254
Russian Academy of Education   15
Russian Academy of Arts   158, 186, 193
Russian Academy of Sciences   4, 10, 12–13, 15, 18, 27–8, 32–4, 36–8, 66, 68, 81, 84–5, 91, 118–19, 125, 135, 252–3. *See also* Chubarian, Alexander
Russian Administrative Code. *See also* criminal prosecution; political dissent, suppression of; Russian Penal Code; Soviet Penal Code
  Article 20.1 (disrespect toward the society and the state)   240
  Article 20.3 (display of Nazi symbols)   231, 234–6
Russian Army   95–7, 100–1, 132, 145–6, 148, 173, 181. *See also* Red Army
Russian Association of History Teachers   17
Russian Center for Holocaust and Genocide History   198, 212–14, 222. *See also* Altman, Ilya
Russian Central State Museum of Contemporary History   61, 117

Russian Civil War (1918–22)   77, 86, 93, 100, 140, 178
Russian Criminal Code. *See* Russian Penal Code
Russian Empire   3, 7, 15, 20, 30, 55, 62, 65, 72, 76, 86, 88, 128, 141–2, 166, 211
Russian Geographical Society   128
Russian Government   3–4, 6, 16, 25–6, 28, 39, 73, 80–1, 84, 90, 98, 118, 123, 135, 147–8, 173, 176, 187, 196, 200, 210, 215, 218, 222–4, 239, 251–5, 258–61. *See also* Duma; Federation Council. *See also names of individual ministries*
Russian Historical Society (RIO)   5, 13–15, 17–18, 21, 26–7, 30, 32, 46, 55–6, 59, 79–80, 84–5, 95, 160, 251–2, 254, 259. *See also* Naryshkin, Sergei
Russian Imperial Historical Society   79
Russian Institute of History Politics, proposed   4, 29–31, 253, 257–8
Russian Institute of National Remembrance   59
Russian Investigative Committee   69, 117, 189, 228, 234, 237–8, 246
Russian Jewish Congress   197, 212–13
Russian Liberation Army   15. *See also* Vlasov, Andrei
Russian Liberation Movement (SERB) nationalist organization   135, 238, 243
Russian Military Historical Society (RVIO)   5, 27–8, 31–2, 46, 51, 53, 55–61, 64, 74, 80–1, 84, 89, 92, 95, 97, 111, 117–18, 126, 128, 130, 133–4, 138–40, 156–7, 169, 171, 173–5, 178, 181, 200, 203–4, 208–11, 218, 227–8, 244, 252, 254–6, 259–60. *See also* Medinskii, Vladimir
Russian Orthodox Church   2, 5, 23, 43–4, 61–75, 81, 90–1, 105, 115, 121, 129–30, 136, 141–3, 157, 168–70, 173, 176, 179–82, 187, 225, 231, 239, 251–4, 256, 259. *See also* Kirill, Patriarch;

Moscow Patriarchate; Orthodox churches; Orthodox priests; "Russia: My History" theme park; Tikhon, Bishop
Russian Orthodox University   66
Russian Penal Code. *See also* criminal prosecution; political dissent, suppression of; Russian Administrative Code; Soviet Penal Code
   Article 148 (offending religious sentiments of the believers)   62, 142, 239
   Article 205.2 (justification of terrorism)   237
   Article 214 (vandalism)   247–8
   Article 242 (distribution of pornography)   237
   Article 243 (destruction of cultural heritage)   228, 240
   Article 244 (desecration of burial sites)   228, 231, 234
   Article 275 (high treason)   23
   Article 282 (incitement of ethnic hatred)   6, 231, 236–8
   Article 354.1 (glorification of Nazism)   6, 37–8, 72–3, 131, 150–1, 178, 189, 219, 231–4, 235, 238, 255, 261
Russian Political Scientists Society   30
Russian Railway Museum   182
Russian Railways   56, 93, 174, 182
Russians   2, 7, 14, 18, 30, 33, 48, 51, 58–9, 62, 65, 68, 77, 83–90, 94, 100, 102, 105–13, 116, 118–19, 121–5, 131–2, 135–6, 140–1, 144–5, 147–9, 152, 166, 169, 171–2, 174, 177, 181, 185–6, 191, 197, 204, 208–10, 212, 218, 225, 236, 242, 257, 259–60
Russian Schoolchildren's Movement   126–7
Russian Search Movement   64, 95, 100, 125–6, 234
Russian State Archives (GARF)   21, 25, 38, 50–1, 54, 141
Russian State Archives of Literature and Arts (RGALI)   24

Russian State Archives of Social and Political History (RGASPI)   24
Russian State Historical Museum   23, 111, 256
Russian State Library   54
Russian State Military Historical Archives (RGVIA)   19–20
Russian State Military History and Cultural Center (Rossvoentsentr)   124, 173
Russian State Nuclear Energy Corporation   124
Russian State Social University (RGSU)   46
Russian State Space Corporation   124
Russian State University for the Humanities (RGGU)   29, 66, 68, 198, 201, 213–14
Russian Supreme Court   22, 233, 247
Russian World, concept of   44, 78
Russian Writers Union   48
"Russia's Foreign Policy in a Historical Perspective" opinion piece (2016)   88. *See also* Lavrov, Sergei
Russia Today (RT)   8, 59, 95, 201, 238, 256. *See also* Simonian, Margarita
Russkaia narodnaia liniia nationalist organization   37
Russkii lad nationalist organization   38
Russkii Vestnik   214
Russo-Georgian War (2008)   68, 88, 132, 188
Russophobia, allegations of   27, 38, 112, 148, 171, 197, 207, 239
RVIO. *See* Russian Military Historical Society
Ryazan   29, 164, 169, 241
Ryzhkov, Vladimir   154
Rzhev   157

St. Barbara statue, proposed   175
St. George   75, 78, 101, 104
St. George's Cross   93
St. George's ribbon   93, 95, 98, 108, 128, 234. *See also* May 9 celebration
St. Isaak's Cathedral   23
St. Matrona of Moscow   71

St. Michael   174
St. Nicholas   75
St. Peter's Basilica   75
St. Petersburg   23–4, 28, 33, 35–8, 49, 66, 68, 71, 75, 81, 93, 100–2, 117, 128–9, 131, 133, 138, 141, 143–4, 154, 165–6, 170, 177–9, 181–2, 209, 233, 235, 237, 239, 241, 244, 257–8. *See also* Leningrad, the siege of
St. Petersburg Military Academy   178
St. Petersburg State University   31, 38, 233
saints   6, 62, 71, 143, 168–9, 173, 175, 181–2, 186, 256, 259. *See also* relics
Sakha Republic   71, 152
Sakharov, Andrei (historian)   10
Sakharov, Andrei (scientist and human rights activist)   174
Sakharov Center   6, 115, 118, 240, 243
Samara   151, 236
Samodurov, Yuri   115–16, 243
Samoilova, Yulia   108, 210
Sandarmokh memorial cemetery   6, 225–9, 257. *See also* Dmitriev, Yuri
Sanina, Anna   122–3
Sarapul   209
Saratov   79, 100, 151, 163, 180
Saratov State University   35
Satanism   79, 176, 180
Savenkov, Alexander   14
Sberbank   127
Scandinavia   52
Scandinavians   85
Schindler's List movie (1992)   211
schoolchildren   17–18, 67, 105, 108–9, 116, 122–3, 126–31, 133–5, 148, 173, 204, 209–10, 235–8, 242–4. *See also* history textbooks; patriotic education program; Youth Army children's organization
schools   5, 17–18, 67, 75, 85, 88, 92, 104–5, 107, 122–3, 126–7, 135, 172–3, 198, 209–10, 213, 235, 238, 241–4
school teachers   17, 67, 122, 126, 135–7, 147–8, 209, 239, 243–4, 255
Schwarzenegger, Arnold   112
Scopus citation database   31. *See also* Web of Science
Second World War   1–2, 4–5, 9, 11–12, 14–15, 18, 24, 30–4, 36–9, 41, 45–6, 50–1, 56–9, 64, 67, 73–6, 83–109, 112, 115–16, 118–19, 121, 123, 125–6, 128–32, 134, 136–40, 149, 152, 156, 159–61, 172–4, 176–8, 182, 185–201, 203–5, 207–8, 210, 212–13, 215, 217, 219–20, 222, 227–8, 232–40, 243–4, 253, 257–8, 260
Secret Speech by Khrushchev (1956)   153. *See also* de-Stalinization; Khrushchev, Nikita
Security Council, Russian   30, 59
security services. *See* FSB
Selin, Adrian   68
Semenov, Vitaly   35
Seoul   108
SERB. *See* Russian Liberation Movement
Serbia   37, 56, 93, 97, 206
serfdom, abolition of   171–2
Sergia, Mother   63
Sevastopol   73–6, 78–9, 86, 101, 104–5, 133, 138, 147, 154, 180, 188
Severomorsk   127
Shablinskii, Ilya   51
Shalev, Andrei   243–4
Shapovalov, Vladimir   32
Sharon, Ariel   185
Shcherbakov, Salavat   167–9, 173–5, 186, 217, 252
Sheremetyevo airport   79
Sherlanger   156
Shetyna, Grzegorz   196
Shevkunov, Georgy. *See* Tikhon, Bishop
Shies, proposed landfill at   110
Shkolnik, Alexander   96–7
Shleimovich, Emil   222
Shmyrov, Victor   224–5, 229, 248
Shneer, Aron   186
Shoigu, Sergei   5, 9–11, 81, 102, 127–31, 138, 204, 252

Shpigel, Boris   4, 45, 79, 188–9, 193–5, 214, 217
Shpileva, Anzhelika   237
Shtyrev, Viacheslav   16–17
Shutov, Andrei   30, 32
Siberia   66, 104, 139, 151, 153, 234, 238, 246
Sikorski, Radosław   196
Sillamäe   108
Simferopol   73, 146–7, 161, 167–8
Simindei, Vladimir   45
Simonian, Margarita   95, 256
Simon Wiesenthal Center   189
Skopje   108, 200–1
Skripal, Sergei, attempted assassination of (2018)   40
slavery   135
Slaviansk   63
Slavic Girl's Farewell statue (2014)   174
Slavs   33, 67, 75, 130, 169, 199, 218
Slier, Paula   201
Slovakia   200, 204–5, 207, 213
Slovaks   78
Slovenia   97
Smetanskii, Daniil   235
Smirnov, Dmitry   129
Smolensk   47–8, 163, 235, 254
Smolny College   233
Sobchak, Ksenia   55
Sobianin, Sergei   11, 65, 246
Sobibor death camp   6, 32, 202–5, 208, 211–12, 220–1. *See also* the Holocaust; Nazi death camps
Sobibor memorial   204–6, 208
Sobibor movie (2018)   6, 60, 201–12
Sochi   96, 110, 112, 159, 206, 236
Sochi Winter Olympic Games   3, 76, 94, 98, 127, 137, 147
Social Science Library of the Russian Academy of Sciences   24
Sofia   72, 108
Sofrino   70
Sokolov, Nikita   9
Sokolov, Oleg   57
soldiers, Soviet   6, 14, 18, 24, 64, 75, 84, 97–8, 100, 128–32, 140, 144, 186, 191, 198–9, 203, 210, 212, 220–1, 227–8, 234–5, 260. *See also* Red Army
Solonin, Mark   58
Solovetsky Islands   71–2
Solovetsky Monastery   71–2
Solovetsky stone memorial (1990)   71, 114, 245
Soloviev, Vladimir   218
Solzhenitsyn, Alexander   112, 247–8
Son of Saul movie (2015)   211
Soros Foundation   29
South America   212–13
South Europe   33
South Ossetia   75
sovereign democracy, concept of   7, 134, 261. *See also* Surkov, Vladislav
Sovetsk   237
Soviet Army. *See* Red Army
Soviet Extraordinary Commission. *See* Extraordinary State Commission for the Investigation of Crimes Committed by the German-Fascist Invaders and Their Accomplices in the Occupied Territories of the Soviet Union
"Soviet Genocide in Ukraine" article (1953)   20
Soviet Information Bureau   1
Sovietization of Eastern Europe   58, 74, 97
Sovietology   15, 26, 39
Soviet partisans   13, 197
Soviet Penal Code. *See also* Russian Penal Code
    Article 70 (anti-Soviet propaganda)   232
    Article 71 (propaganda of war)   232
Soviet people   1–2, 37, 50, 58, 76, 88, 94, 111, 113, 117, 140, 145, 185, 189–91, 203, 207, 217, 222
Soviet Pioneer organization   126–7, 251
Soviet Union   1–3, 7–12, 14–15, 17–18, 23–7, 30–9, 45–6, 49, 57–61, 65, 70–2, 74–8, 81, 83–110, 113–19, 121–3, 127–30, 132, 136, 138, 140, 143–6, 148–51, 155–6, 161–6, 174–7, 179, 183, 185–7, 190–1, 193–4, 198–201, 203–5, 207–8, 210, 212–23, 229–30, 232–4, 236, 240, 243, 251–4, 256–7, 259–61

Soviet war in Afghanistan   23, 125, 145, 256
Soviet war memorials   7, 14, 20, 32, 96–7, 100, 125, 134, 193–5, 198–9, 207–8, 210, 213, 215, 221, 234–7, 240. *See also* monuments
space program   83, 112, 232. *See also* Gagarin, Yuri; Rogozin, Dmitry
Spain   33, 151, 179, 239
Sparrow Hills   164, 169
Spartak football club   143
Spaso-Andronnikov Monastery   62
Spetsnaz, Russian special forces   128, 133
Spiegelman, Art   214
Spielberg, Steven   211
Sputnik   95
Sretensky Monastery   63–5, 179
Sretensky theological seminary   64, 66
Stalin, Josef   1–2, 5–6, 15, 32–3, 37, 45, 50–1, 57, 61, 68, 70–1, 73–4, 76–8, 85–6, 89–90, 92, 102–3, 105, 108–19, 121, 130, 132, 134, 136, 141, 146–7, 149–62, 164–6, 168, 170, 177, 183, 203, 219–20, 224, 234, 237–9, 242, 246, 253, 256–7
Stalingrad. *See* Volgograd
Stalingrad, Battle of (1942–43)   28, 30, 48, 76, 92, 138, 145, 154, 165, 176
Stalin house museum   157
Stalinism   6, 8, 14, 17, 21, 31, 37, 55, 70, 81, 110, 112–13, 116–17, 119, 150, 218, 240, 246, 257. *See also* de-Stalinization
Stalinists   90, 109, 111–12, 136, 147, 153–4, 183, 238, 247
Stalino. *See* Donetsk
Stalin's crimes   4, 6, 9, 14, 21–2, 25, 27, 31–2, 36, 45–6, 58, 60–1, 67–8, 71–3, 81, 87–9, 109–18, 135–7, 146–7, 149, 153–5, 162, 164, 176–7, 222–31, 243–8, 254, 257, 260. *See also* Butovo mass execution site; deportations; the famine of 1932–33; Great Terror; Gulag; Khaibakh massacre; Kommunarka mass execution site; NKVD; Perm 36; Red Terror; Sandarmokh memorial cemetery
Stalin's victims. *See* Gulag victims
Starikov, Nikolai   2, 71, 122, 135
State Academic Malyi Theater   48
state holidays. *See also* memorial days
  Day of the Defender of Motherland (February 23)   102
  Flag Day (August 22)   144
  National Unity Day (November 4)   49, 136, 144
  Russia Day (June 12)   144
  Victory Day (May 9)   102
State Museum of Contemporary Russian History   57, 61, 117
Stavropol   133
Stepanov, Igor   117, 246
Stepashin, Sergei   59, 70
Stockholm Declaration on the Holocaust (2000)   216
Stolypin, Piotr   183, 211
Stone, Oliver   110
Strasbourg   209, 213
Strelkov, Igor   62–3
Subetto, Alexander   37
Supreme Attestation Board (VAK)   38, 52–4
Suprun, Mikhail   36
Surgut   153–4, 172
Surkov, Vladislav   7, 88–9, 111, 134, 257
Sut vremeni. *See* the Essence of Time
Suvorov, Victor   18
Svalbard   181
Svanidze, Nikolai   51
Sverdlovsk region   29
Svetliakov, Kirill   149
Sviridov, Georgy   76
swastikas   214, 235–7
Swedes   187
Switzerland   195, 237
Syktyvkar   210, 241
Syria   27, 37, 60, 72, 75, 88, 90, 100, 129, 168, 172, 198, 206, 212, 218

Taisaev, Kazbek   150, 156
Takhankut   152
Tallinn   108, 193, 195, 199
Tambov   133–4, 172
tanks   100–2, 104, 138. *See also* T-34 tank

Tanks movie (2018)   102
Tarasov, Vladimir   15
Tashkent   138
TASS news agency   45, 167
Tatarstan   63, 66, 151–2, 236
Taylor deCaires, Jason   150
Tbilisi   152
Tehran   159
Tehran Conference (1943)   159
Tel Aviv   203, 206
Tepliakov, Dmitry   25
Terekhova, Yulia   181
Terminator movie (1984)   112
terrorism   130, 145, 186, 197, 209, 237, 247–8
Thatcher, Margaret   67
the Thaw   162. *See also* Khrushchev, Nikita
theology   65
Theresienstadt ghetto   199, 215. *See also* the Holocaust
Thomas theorem   86
"Three Tank Drivers, Three Jolly Friends" song (1939)   101
Tikhon, Bishop   5, 44, 59, 63–72, 81, 85, 122, 129, 138, 179, 251, 254
Tishkov, Valery   10, 55, 59
Titov, Vladimir   59
Tiumen   66, 104, 112, 151, 163, 254
Tobolsk   112
Tokyo   74
Tomb of the Unknown Soldier in Moscow   90
Tom Sawyer Fest volunteer club   180
Tomsk   103–5, 108, 116, 231
Tomsk Memorial Museum "NKVD Investigative Prison"   231
toponymy   150, 165, 207
Toymentsev, Sergei   254
Transneft   56
Transnistria   75
Transylvania   200
Treptower Park   74, 77
Tretyakov Art Gallery   170–1
Troitsky, Artemy   73
Trotsky, Leon   230
True History Foundation   25
Trump, Donald   96–7, 161
Trunenkov, Dmitry   127

Tsarist Empire. *See* Russian Empire
Tsaritsyn. *See* Volgograd
tsars   3, 6, 15, 40, 52, 65, 68–70, 77, 88, 100, 110, 142–3, 145, 155, 168–73, 175, 178, 183, 186, 224, 256, 258–9. *See also* names of individual tsars
Tsarskoe Selo   178
Tsereteli, Zurab   157–60, 166, 173–4, 186, 217, 251–2, 258
TsSKA football club   98–9
T-34 movie (2018)   102
T-34 tank   100–2, 138
Tula   62, 167–8, 238
Tula State Weapon Museum   181
Tumarkin, Nina   142
TU-95 "Bear" strategic bomber   100
Tunis   208
Turkey   7, 41, 261
Turks   72
Tuva, Republic of   237
Tvardovsky, Alexander   2
TV2 channel   103

Uchitel, Alexei   142–3
Ukraine   4, 6, 12, 15, 19–20, 25, 37–8, 46, 52, 57, 62–3, 73–4, 76, 79, 81, 83, 88, 90, 105, 108, 121–2, 131, 134–5, 137, 142, 146–7, 158–60, 168–9, 176–7, 188–9, 194–9, 201, 208, 210–11, 215–16, 219, 221, 223–4, 226, 232–3, 249, 251, 253, 255, 260
Ukrainian Institute of National Remembrance   12, 30–1, 45
Ukrainian Museum of National History   45
Ukrainians   45–6, 102, 139, 189, 191, 196, 202, 210, 215, 225
Ukrainian Secret Services Archives   25
Ulaanbaatar   108, 161
Ulan-Ude   100, 234
Ulianovsk   141, 177
Ulitskaia, Liudmila   243
UN Charter   191, 213
UN Commission on Human Rights. *See* UN Human Rights Council
UN Committee on Information   192–3
UNESCO   169, 213, 224

UN General Assembly 74, 191–3, 221
UN Genocide Convention (1948) 192, 219. *See also* genocide
UN Human Rights Council 9, 191–3
United Kingdom 1, 18, 32, 40, 97, 108, 159, 219
United Nations 43, 192–7, 208, 211, 213, 218, 221
United Russia Party 10, 46, 50, 56–7, 65, 79, 103–4, 117, 121, 126, 134, 142, 166, 256
United States of America 1–3, 7, 16, 27, 33, 36–40, 47, 73–4, 79, 83, 88, 90, 96–7, 108, 119, 135, 159, 161, 189, 192, 194–5, 218–19, 244, 260
Universal Declaration of Human Rights (1948) 192
universities 12, 15, 27–40, 43, 52–5, 63–4, 66, 68, 84, 96, 104–5, 121, 123, 135–6, 148, 158, 198, 213, 225, 233, 252. *See also names of individual universities*
university students 18, 27, 35, 55, 63, 67, 84, 106–8, 121, 125–6, 136, 141, 148, 213
UN Resolution 60/7 ("on the Holocaust Remembrance") 211–12
UN Resolution 61/147 ("countering racism and xenophobia") 9, 192–4
UN Resolution 67/154 ("glorification of Nazism") 95, 194, 212, 219, 221
UN Secretary General 208
UN Security Council 58, 222
UN Third Committee 191–2
Urals Federal University 52
Uruguay 212
US Army 37, 99–100, 127, 257
US Department of State 1, 86, 105, 208
US Department of the Treasury 222
US Holocaust Memorial Museum (USHMM) 21, 193, 208
Uzbekistan 138, 208

Vaino, Anton 97
Valentine's Day 75
vandalism, acts of 63–4, 117, 147, 155, 161, 168, 170–1, 178–9, 195, 215, 228, 234, 248, 256
Varlamov, Ilya 105, 179
Vasiliev, Ilya 203–5, 207, 210–11, 217
Vasilieva, Olga 4, 26–7, 40, 54, 59, 64–5, 80–1, 98, 135–7, 148, 157, 170, 198, 251, 258
Vatican 75
VDNKh exhibition grounds 65
Vedomosti 225
Venezuela 213
veterans of war 24, 30, 37, 58, 80, 94, 98–9, 105, 107–9, 116, 123, 125, 130, 134, 151, 162, 173, 183, 185, 193, 199, 206, 234, 236–7, 239, 256
Viatrovich, Volodymyr 45
Victory Day. *See* May 9 celebration
Victory Museum. *See* Central Museum of the Great Patriotic War
Victory organizing committee 24, 90–1, 93–8, 103–4, 107–8, 182, 192
Victory Volunteers 84, 93, 98, 126
Vienna 108
vigilantes 134, 142–3, 148, 249, 256. *See also* pro-Kremlin organizations
Viking movie (2016) 69
VIO. *See* Free Historical Society
Vishnevskii, Boris 93, 254
Vladimir 86–7, 152, 158, 171
Vladimir, Prince 69, 86, 164, 169–70, 175, 180, 183
Vladimir I. *See* Vladimir, Prince
Vladivostok 112, 138, 155
Vlasov, Alexei 15–16
Vlasov, Andrei 15, 36, 203, 243. *See also* Russian Liberation Army
Vnukovo airport 170
Volchek, Dmitry 23
Volga River 137, 165
Volgograd 30, 73, 78, 92, 101, 112, 134, 138–9, 154, 156, 159, 165, 176, 234
Volhynia 216
Volkov, Alexei 234
Volodin, Viacheslav 33, 261
Vologodsk region 181
Volokolamsk, Battle of (1941) 51

Vorkuta   29
Voronezh   57
VTB bank   112, 127
VTsIOM pollster   10, 43. *See also* opinion polls
Vučić, Aleksandar   206
Vyshinskii, Andrei   50
Vyshnii Volochek   179

Waffen SS, German   9, 186, 190–2, 194, 199, 215, 220–1, 237, 261
Wagner mercenaries   105, 129. *See also* Prigozhin, Yevgeny
Wallenberg, Raoul   187
The Wall historical novel (2012)   48–9, 254. *See also* Medinskii, Vladimir
"The Wall" music album (1979)   49
Wall of Grief monument (2017)   71, 114–15, 118, 231
war crimes   190–1, 194
Warsaw   44, 208
Warsaw ghetto uprising (1943)   204. *See also* the Holocaust
war veterans. *See* veterans of war
Washington, DC   21, 40, 102, 108, 208
Web of Science   31. *See also* Scopus
Wehrmacht   100, 129, 138, 236. *See also* Nazi Germany; Waffen SS, German
welfare state   88
Western sanctions   27, 53, 85, 100, 145, 178, 239
West Europe   9, 16, 189, 259
West Germany   73
White, Robert   191
White Sea Canal   225
Wikipedia   68
World Congress of Russian Jews   188, 193–4
World Holocaust Forum, fifth (2020)   222
The World of Tanks videogame   101
World War I. *See* First World War
World War II. *See* Second World War
World without Nazism   4, 45, 79, 188–9, 193–5, 201, 214, 217–8. *See also* Shpigel, Boris

World Youth and Student Festival   96

xenophobia   185, 191–2
Xi Jinping   33, 97

Yabloko Party   117
Yad Vashem Museum   186–7, 195, 203–4, 211, 214, 216, 220
Yakovenko, Alexander   193
Yakunin, Vladimir   174, 182
Yakutia. *See* Sakha Republic
Yakutsk   66
Yalta   6, 74, 158–61, 168
Yalta Conference (1945)   56, 90, 158–61, 183, 222, 259
Yamburg, Yevgeny   15
Yanukovich, Victor   188
Yaroslav, Prince   85
Yaroslavl   181
Yarovaia, Irina   75, 232
Year of Memory and Glory (2020)   97
Year of Russian History (2012)   12–13, 39, 55
Yeltsin, Boris   2, 8, 21, 65, 144, 164
Yeltsin Center   156, 240, 242
Yemen   37
Yom Hashoah   208, 212
Yom Kippur   197
Yoshkar-Ola   6, 21, 116, 229–31, 248, 257
Youth Army children's organization   5, 99, 127–31, 137, 148
Yugoslavia   52, 56
Yuri Gagarin Memorial Museum   62. *See also* Gagarin, Yuri

Zadornov, Mikhail   2
Zakharchenko, Alexander   156
Zakhariev, German   197
Zakharova, Maria   40, 200, 205–6, 215
Zaldostanov "The Surgeon," Alexander   5, 73–9, 81, 129–30, 132, 138, 160, 169–71, 176–7, 251
Zaliuzhnyi, Alexander   16
"Zarnitsa" paramilitary game, Soviet   127
Zemtsov, Nikolai   103, 108, 171
Zenit football club   177

Zhirinovsky, Vladimir   75, 170
Zhivaia istoriia journal   61
Zhukov, Andrei   23, 35
Zhuravsky, Alexander   15
*Zhurnal rossiiskikh i vostochno-
      evropeiskikh istoricheskikh
      issledovanii*   61
Ziuganov, Gennady   164

Zmiiovsk Gorge monument (1975,
      2011)   189. *See also* the
      Holocaust
Zubov, Andrei   35-6, 46, 58, 168, 225, 243
Zurich   108
Zuroff, Efraim   189
Zvezda TV channel   208, 227
Zygar, Mikhail   181

www.ingramcontent.com/pod-product-compliance
Lightning Source LLC
Chambersburg PA
CBHW072121290426
44111CB00012B/1735